Praise for *Kanban Maturity Model: A Map Organizational Agility, Resilience, and Reinve*

"Without a doubt, this book is perfect for those who are interested in both introducing and delving more deeply into the Kanban Method, offering you the tools to streamline workflow and change the organization through introducing Agile culture.

By using practical examples with clear and comprehensive language, it helps to develop this type of working culture and helps teams to adapt to this methodology in the most natural way."

Cedric Escoriza Redón
Service Delivery Manager, Silk Aplicaciones S.L.U.

"The KMM book is the management book of the decade. In the post-Agile world, this is what managers and executives need to understand why their agile transformations didn't give the results they were expecting. For the businesses interested in pragmatic approaches to achieve consistent and repeatable results, the KMM provides guidance and plenty of actionable patterns to get there. Brilliant!"

Amanda Varella
AKT, AKC, Development Team Lead at Envato

"Let us start with a warning—this book is not an easy read that you can finish in a few hours and then add to your trophy cabinet of 'I also read it.' Instead, it is a must-have reference guide for any Kanban practitioner that you will consult regularly.

The KMM can be compared to a topographical map for a cross-country hiker. With it you can determine your current position, but you can also use it to agree on an (interim) destination and then navigate toward it along a set of key waypoints.

But this book is so much more than just a map, as it does not just describe the model and its practices in detail, but it also ventures into the sociology of driving evolutionary change, provides guidance on implementing evolutionary change in an organisation throughout the different Maturity Levels, and it lastly also provides a deep dive into the mathematical models behind some of the concepts used.

Well done to the authors for creating a masterpiece! We will definitely keep a copy close by when coaching clients."

Mathias Tölken & Mark Geschke
Co-founders and Principal Business Agility Coaches, Xuviate

"Our experience is completely positive. Our results generate trust with our customers and our NPS has increased. The KMM is easy to apply in any business unit."

José Manuel Garcia Valdivia
Operations Director of Employee Benefits, Nationale Nederlanden

"This new release of the *Kanban Maturity Model* fulfils the essence of Kanban: continuous improvement through evolutionary change. The context changes and the model help organizations to adapt and even anticipate changes. The cohesion between practices, cultural values, and business benefits are the basis of management, and in the book the authors involve these ingredients in a dance which grabs you and encourages you to try it."

Juan J. Gil Bilbao
Agile Coach, BBVA Spain

"The words that describe this book are: solid, useful, and deep. This is not only a guide to understand the journey of organizations towards Kanban, it is also an endless number of clues and tips for the challenge of deploy the method into organizations. It is an approach where culture and values take a fundamental role, helping making sense of the set of Kanban practices."

J. Andrés Guerrero
IT Architect, Silk Aplicaciones S.L.U.

"David and Teodora put decades of expertise in delivering customer value at scale smoothly, efficiently, and predictably into a single text. They break down difficult concepts into consumable practices and help your organization measurably evolve from madhouse to market domination."

Eric Brechner
author of *Agile Project Management with Kanban*

"We coach and teach the KMM as part of our consulting and training business and it has been a game-changer for our clients. This new edition is very timely and is sure to help many build upon the success they've already had with the first edition."

Martiz Aziz
Consultant, Squirrel North

"When you first start to learn about KMM it is very hard to put all the pieces together to make sense. You have to trust, start to follow it, apply it, and, most importantly, learn from the process. After some time it will become clear, and you will see that you have already started improving even if you didn't realize it."

Daniel Escudero Romero
Europe Regional Processes Head at CEMEX

"A great source of inspiration for your Kanban journey."

Javier Ferrer
Programme & Change Manager, Nationale Nederlanden Group

Kanban Maturity Model
A Map to Organizational Agility,
Resilience, and Reinvention
Second Edition

David J Anderson

Teodora Bozheva

Kanban University PRESS
Seattle, WA

Kanban Maturity Model: A Map to Organizational Agility, Resilience, and Reinvention, 2nd Ed.
Copyright © 2020 Kanban University Press

ISBN: 978-1-7328212-4-8
Second Print Edition, October 2020

All rights reserved under International and Pan-American Copyright Conventions. Published by Kanban University Press, Seattle, WA. This publication is protected by copyright, and permission must be obtained from the publisher prior to any reproduction, storage in a retrieval system, or transmission in any form or by any means, electronic, mechanical, photocopying, recording, or likewise.

CMMI and Capability Maturity Model are registered in the US Patent and Trademark Office by ISACA®.

Email contact@kanbanbooks.com for rights requests, customized editions, and bulk orders. Additional print copies of this and other Kanban publications can be purchased via https://shop.kanbanbooks.com.

Library of Congress Cataloging-in-Publication Data
Applied for

Cover design by Armando Bayer Zabala
Interior design by Vicki Rowland

For Nastya —DJA

For Bela —TB

Contents

Preface   xi

Acknowledgments   xix

Part I Outcomes and Benefits

1 Understanding Maturity Levels 0 through 2   3
  The Three Pillars of the KMM: Culture, Practices, and Outcomes   3
  Maturity Level 0 – Oblivious   5
  Maturity Level 1 – Team-Focused   8
  Maturity Level 2 – Customer-Driven   12

2 Understanding Maturity Levels 3 through 6   17
  Maturity Level 3 – Fit-for-Purpose   17
  Maturity Level 4 – Risk-Hedged   22
  Maturity Level 5 – Market Leader   26
  Maturity Level 6 – Built for Survival   29

3 Benefits of the KMM   33
  Developing Organizational Agility and Adaptability   33
  Better Business Outcomes   36

4 Case Study: BBVA Finance Division (Spain)   39
  From Team-Focused to Fit-for-Purpose in One Year   39
  Getting Started with Kanban in the Finance Area   40
  Conclusions   50
  Fifteen Months Later   51

Part II Culture

5 Culture in Low-Maturity Organizations   55
   Maturity Level 0 – Oblivious   56
   Maturity Level 1 – Team-Focused   57
   Maturity Level 2 – Customer-Driven   63

6 Culture in Fit-for-Purpose Organizations   71
   Maturity Level 3 – Fit-for-Purpose   72
   Maturity Level 4 – Risk-Hedged   77

7 Culture in High-Maturity Organizations   83
   Maturity Level 5 – Market Leader   84
   Maturity Level 6 – Built for Survival   88

8 Culture Hacking   93
   Three Social Dimensions of Culture   94
   Decision Filters   103
   Tribal Culture and Motivating Change   105
   Making the Culture Stick   108

Part III Practices

9 KMM Architecture   111
   Organizational Maturity Levels   111
   Kanban Maturity Model Architecture   112

10 Visualize   117
   Goals of the General Practice   117
   Benefits from Applying the General Practice   118
   Specific Practices Summary   118
   Specific Practices Descriptions   120

11 Limit Work-in-Progress   163
   Goals of the General Practice   163
   Benefits from Applying the General Practice   164
   Specific Practices Summary   165
   Specific Practices Descriptions   165

12 Manage Flow   175
   Goal of the General Practice   175
   Benefits from Applying the General Practice   175
   Specific Practices Summary   176
   Specific Practices Descriptions   177

13 Make Policies Explicit   229
   Goal of the General Practice   229
   Benefits from Applying the General Practice   229
   Specific Practices Summary   230
   Specific Practices Descriptions   230

14 Implement Feedback Loops   249
   Goal of the General Practice   249
   Benefits from Applying the General Practice   249
   Overview   250
   Specific Practices Summary   251
   Specific Practices Descriptions   252

15 Improve Collaboratively, Evolve Experimentally   271
   Goal of the General Practice   271
   Benefits from Applying the General Practice   272
   Specific Practices Summary   272
   Specific Practices Descriptions   273

Part IV   Managed Evolution & the Pursuit of Organizational Agility

16 Why Pursue Evolutionary Change?   295
   Evolutionary Relics   301
   The J-Curve Effect   303

17 Evolutionary Change Model   311
   Insert a Punctuation Point as a Last Resort, Not as a Starting Point   313
   Leading Change in Periods of Equilibrium   315
   The Evolutionary Change Model   317
   Escalating Motivation for Change   321

18 Why Do People Resist Change?   323
   The Human Condition   323
   Resistance to Practice Adoption   326
   Escalating Motivation for Change   328

19 Barriers to Adoption   339
   Generally Observed Barriers to Adoption   339
   Barriers to Maturity Level 2   344
   Barriers to Maturity Level 3   347
   Barriers to Maturity Level 4   354

20 Building Resilience   361
   Four Principles of Resilience   361
   Coping with Crisis   364
   The House of Resilience   368

Appendices

A The Kanban Method 371
Kanban's Three Agendas 371
Service Delivery Principles 371
Kanban Scaling Principles 372
Change Management Principles 373
Kanban General Practices 373
STATIK 373

B Integration with Other Models and Methods 375
Integration with Lean/TPS 375
Integration with the Real World Risk Model 376
Integration with Agendashift 378
Integration with Mission Command 379
Integration with Capability Maturity Model Integration® (CMMI) v2.0 379

C Understanding Lead Time 383
Definition 383
Nature of Lead Time 384
Mathematical Properties of Lead Time Curves 389

D Triage 403
Deciding on Now, Later—and If So, When—or Not at All 403
The Four Dimensions of Priority 417

E Cost of Delay 419
Prerequisite 419
Calculating Delivery Delay Cost 420
Calculating the Probable Cost of Delay in Starting (PCoDS) 425
Shelf-Life Ratio 431
Triage Table Configuration 432
Adjusting the Class of Service Based on Start Date 433

F Dependency Management 435
Reservation Systems 436
Classes of Dependency Management 438

G The KMM in a Nutshell 447
The KMM Architecture 447
The KMM Cultural Values 448
The KMM Outcomes and Benefits 449
The KMM Evolutionary Change Model 450
The KMM Practices 451

References 457

Index 459

About the Authors 479

Preface

Purpose, Influences, Intent, & Benefits of the Kanban Maturity Model

The Kanban Maturity Model (KMM) emerged from the need to democratize adoption of the Kanban Method so that others may reap the benefits that using it has brought to companies large and small around the world over the past decade. We have codified patterns of successful adoption in a manner that enables consultants, coaches, and managers to employ the methods used by others with a high probability of success. The model classifies more than 150 practices into seven levels of organizational maturity and provides clear guidance on how to catalyze and lead improvement using the Kanban Method. The Kanban Maturity Model emerges as the result of more than fourteen years of experience training and coaching in various organizations, all the while capturing data, writing and publishing case studies, and collecting experience reports given at more than fifty worldwide conferences between 2009 and 2019. The Kanban Maturity Model provides pragmatic, actionable, evidence-based guidance and shows how to achieve true enterprise agility. It shows how to successfully deploy the Kanban Method to greatly improve the economic performance of your business. It provides a playbook and a roadmap to transform your enterprise. We believe that you will find the KMM immediately useful and extremely powerful.

Purpose

The purpose of the Kanban Maturity Model is to support the development of the following organizational benefits:

- Relief from overburdening
- Workforce cohesion and employee fulfillment
- Meeting customer expectations
- Delivering satisfaction to customers
- Defining and managing organizational identity and purpose
- Resilience to setbacks and market turbulence
- Predictable, sustainable economic performance and financial robustness
- Organizational agility
- Congruence of decision making from top to bottom
- Long-term survival
- Meaningful, institutionalized change that sticks

We developed the Kanban Maturity Model because reaching these outcomes is observed to be challenging for many organizations. The model responds to the need for help in coping with resistance to change and properly introducing the practices needed to make an entire organization resilient, robust, and ultimately, adaptable to stresses from changing external technological, business, economic, and governmental environments.

Our goal has been to deliver a method that produces meaningful change that institutionalizes and sticks around even as personnel and managers change over time. We believe that new ways of working stick when they are truly internalized by individuals as part of who they are as people and as part of the wider social groups in the organization—their team, their service delivery unit, their business unit, and so forth. We believe that we have developed and codified an approach that makes this repeatable, using the KMM as a playbook.

With more than fourteen years of Kanban implementation experience around the world and a year of validating the KMM beta release, it is now possible to categorize why resistance happens and to provide pragmatic guidance on actions that can help build unity around common goals, improve business outcomes, and strengthen cultural values, including appropriateness of specific practices in the context of existing organizational maturity. The model contains this codification and defines proven steps for correct practice implementation. In addition, it draws a roadmap to broader and deeper adoption over time. In particular, it clearly specifies which practices can be introduced next with little resistance, or which, by design, produce just enough stress to cause the organization to react in an antifragile[1] manner, resulting in improvement.

---

1. This is a concept that Nassim N. Taleb captured in the word—and book of the same name—antifragile.

Two Failure Modes with the Kanban Method

With more than a decade of observations and experience from around the world and across a broad spectrum of industries, two patterns of failure, or failure modes, have emerged with the implementation of the Kanban Method: the false summit plateau and overreaching. A predecessor of the KMM was known as the Depth of Kanban Assessment Framework. Its purpose was to assess the appropriateness of Kanban practice adoption mapped to organizational readiness. There was a general recognition that each of the six General Practices of the Kanban Method could be implemented with differing degrees of fidelity. When failures of adoption occurred, these were generally because inappropriate practices had been chosen—either too simplistic, failing to push the organization to a higher level of performance, or too challenging, resulting in failure to adopt. The coaching or consulting skill required was that of a sports coach: knowing the playbook of practices and being able to map them to the existing skill level and capability. The goal was to stress the organization just enough to provoke it to a higher level of performance, but not stretch it so much as to break it, causing a regression to a lower level of performance. The KMM represents a considerable advance over its predecessor—it provides extensive guidance on appropriate practice adoption, but it goes much further in terms of understanding organizational readiness with a much more thorough map of organizational culture and observable outcomes.

False Summit Plateau

The false summit plateau comes from the arrogance of believing that since an organization has adopted Kanban already, they've already experienced all of its benefits. Typically, we hear a reaction of "We've done Kanban! It helped us […]." Usually from a shop-floor, bottom-up initiative, they list some or all of these practices and benefits that map to Maturity Level 1:

- Relief from overburdening and stressful, abusive environment
- Improved transparency
- Improved collaboration
- "Gave us what we needed."

In part, the Kanban Maturity Model exists to show that these shallow adoptions have left a lot of additional benefits on the table, and that the organization can take Kanban a lot further.

Overreaching

Overreaching usually results in aborted adoption. The problem is rooted in an overly ambitious transition plan, often to a design intended to achieve Maturity Level 4 or even 5 in an organization currently at Maturity Level 0 or 1. The problem often manifests because of "the smartest guy in the room." This person is a consultant or a coach who feels psychological or social pressure to show off their knowledge and expertise or is simply too optimistic and overly ambitious.

When the practices are too advanced for novices or organizations with immature culture, existing behaviors, or supporting practices, the result is that the new practices simply don't stick. Often, the people are incapable of understanding the benefit. For example, if every work item is a task, what would be the point of risk hedging using capacity allocation of WIP limits across work items of different types? In a world where everything is homogeneous, the concept of hedging risk is incomprehensible.

The Kanban Maturity Model also exists, in part, to provide a roadmap and a means to interpret and appraise organizational maturity and readiness for any specific Kanban practice. A competent coach can use the model as a guide to suggest the right next steps and avoid overreaching.

Avoiding Structural Tension

There is a concept in psychology known as structural tension. It exists for an individual when they cannot see how to get from where they are now to a future destination. For example, imagine a young girl watching champion gymnasts on television as they compete in the Olympic Games. She likes gymnastics; in fact, she attends a gymnastics club twice a week. However, as she watches the champions on television, their skills seem like magic to her. Their level of achievement and performance is incomprehensible to her.

If this young girl were to receive a directive from, say, an overly ambitious parent who demands that she raise her performance to the level of the Olympians, she will suffer structural tension—the stress and anxiety that comes from not knowing how to get from where she is now to where she needs to be in the future.

Structural tension represents the opposite of overreaching. In this case, rather than overly ambitious striving, there is resistance, inertia, even fear at attempting to progress further. Structural tension is overcome in sports coaching through the use of an extensive playbook, a developmental guide to evolve athletes from novices to experts. The Kanban Maturity Model is that playbook for organizational maturity and business resilience, and it is achieved by implementing the Kanban Method. Kanban Coaching Professionals become "sports coaches" for your organization. The Kanban Maturity Model is their playbook. The Kanban Maturity Model removes structural tension. If an executive sponsor describes a business outcome that matches closely to Maturity Level 4, the KMM provides a map to take your organization from where it is now to those desired Maturity Level 4 outcomes.

Influences and Integrations

The Kanban Maturity Model is influenced by several management models that have preceded it. The KMM introduces a number of innovations, most notably a focus on business outcomes: fitness-for-purpose in the eyes of the customer and other stakeholders. The model describes management practices and actionable guidance that develop an organization's capability to continually satisfy customer expectations in a sustainable manner as well as anticipate market changes and take advantage of the opportunities these present.

The model also provides a proven map between cultural values and management practices; together, they enable the achievement of business outcomes as well as develop the capabilities of an organization to adapt to changing customer expectations and to successfully overcome turbulence or crisis situations.

In addition, the model provides a number of mappings and integration points with existing models such as the Lean/Toyota Production System (TPS), the Capability Maturity Model Integration (CMMI™),[2] the Real World Risk Institute model Agendashift, and Mission Command/*Auftragstaktik*. Its seven maturity levels have been influenced by concepts from Jerry Weinberg and the CMMI and the many similar models that preceded it in other fields and other industries.

Intended Users and Needs Addressed

Kanban coaches[3]

- Understand maturity-level behaviors.
- Get useful guidelines for leading their customers' initiatives.
- Appraise the depth and breadth of a Kanban implementation.
- Determine appropriateness of certain practices.
- Define an approach for taking an organization to the next level; in particular, define what to do next and how to stress the organization enough to provoke it to go to the next level.
- Explain to organizations what they can get from the KMM, what happens when they are under stress, and from that, determine what the appropriate maturity level for the organization is.
- Enhance professional credibility—avoid appearing overly ambitious or lacking sufficient ambition.

Improvement Initiative Leaders and Executives

- Develop a realistic roadmap for driving the initiative, aligned with the organization's business objectives.
- Clearly communicate the improvement initiative's objectives, defined roadmap, concrete actions, and expected benefits to other managers and staff.

---

2. CMMI and Capability Maturity Model are registered in the US Patent and Trademark Office by ISACA®.
3. Kanban Coaching Professionals, Accredited Kanban Consultants

- Develop an organizational culture and management practices that enable achieving better business outcomes while avoiding resistance and evolving steadily.
- Understand and measure the progress of the improvement initiative.
- Lead change initiatives with confidence.

Agile Practitioners and Coaches

- Understand how Kanban practices can help to satisfy customers' expectations.
- Define a roadmap to develop further the organization's agility.
- Educate customers so they understand that Kanban is a lot more than a visual board; communicate the breadth and depth of Kanban and the benefits of using the method.
- Meet all the needs defined above.

Product and Service Managers

- Introduce appropriate practices that provide insight into and reveal information about the real state of their products and services and enable better coordination of their teams' work.
- Improve service predictability.
- Apply effective practices that facilitate meeting customer expectations.
- Effectively manage shared resources.
- Effectively manage capacity to respond to changing service demand.

Benefits of the Kanban Maturity Model

- Helps managers and teams understand the system they manage and avoid making poor decisions that lead to negative effects on projects, services, workers, customers, and the business
- Describes the characteristics of an organizational culture that facilitates understanding real-world situations and defining an appropriate approach to improving them effectively
- Describes a set of practices for use at enterprise scale; avoids focusing on compliance to a framework; does not define processes or a methodology
- Guides organizations toward fit-for-purpose products and services with appropriate exposure to risk and reasonable economic returns
- Allows objective assessment of the current state of an organization to see where challenges and opportunities lie on the path to greater business and organizational agility
- Provides guidelines on the improvement actions to take, creating just enough stress to catalyze improvement without overreaching and risking failure of adoption
- Helps benchmark organizational agility and fitness-for-purpose
- Improves positioning in the market by appropriately developing capabilities to satisfy and exceed customer expectations

- Aligns stakeholders and team members around a common understanding of the purpose of an improvement initiative and how to approach it
- Complements other models and methods, such as CMMI and PMBoK,[4] with a systems thinking approach that incorporates an understanding of the psychology and sociology of the workforce

Organization of This Book

We've organized this book into four parts: Outcomes and Benefits, Culture, Using the Model, and Managed Evolution & the Pursuit of Organizational Agility. We also included appendices defining The Kanban Method, and describing in detail the understanding of cost of delay and the techniques for mapping it to classes of service, together with the solution for dependency management. These are included as necessary techniques to achieve Maturity Level 4. Since they have not been published elsewhere in an easily consumable form, we felt it necessary to include them here.

Part I describes the three pillars of the Kanban Maturity Model: Culture, Practices, and Outcomes, managed through Evolutionary Change. It goes on to provide a detailed explanation of the seven maturity levels and the observable culture, practices, and outcomes at each level. This is followed by a description of the benefits of using the KMM to facilitate implementing the Kanban Method. It concludes with a case study based on more than two years of using the KMM to drive the adoption of Kanban at the second-largest Spanish bank, BBVA. This ongoing implementation continues to deliver impressive results, enabling more improvements than BBVA achieved using Agile methods, including a 28 percent reduction in management overhead.

Part II addresses organizational culture, with detailed descriptions of the cultural values at all maturity levels (low, ML0–ML2; mid-levels, ML3 and 4; and deeper levels, ML5 and 6). The section concludes with a chapter describing how to hack the culture—to lead with values adoption, introducing new values by guiding behavior through the use of decision filters. Culture is defined by the sociology of the organization and its three dimensions of social innovation, social capital, and social cohesion. The chapter provides an overview of the elements that contribute to each social dimension and gives you a set of tools, techniques, and levers with which to influence and move organizational culture.

Part III provides a reference catalog for the 150+ specific practices observed in the Kanban Method mapped against the seven levels of organizational maturity and the six general Kanban practices. Part III is a reference section, intended to be used to look up specific practices. The descriptions of the practices are given in varied levels of detail. In general, where a practice is well-documented and easily accessible in broader Kanban literature, we have not dedicated much space to it here. With practices that are less

---

4. Project Management Institute's *Project Management Body of Knowledge*

well-known, or poorly documented elsewhere, we've explored them in greater depth so that you have sufficient information to attempt to implement them.

Part IV describes the evolutionary approach to change and the use of the KMM Evolutionary Change Model (ECM) to drive a guided and managed approach to evolution in your organization. This section explores the psychological benefits of evolutionary change over traditional designed and managed change initiatives. It describes in detail how to use the ECM, mapping it to the KMM architecture, which includes the use of transition and consolidation sub-level practices.

The section continues with an exploration of why humans resist change, and what you can do about it. We have catalogued a number of commonly recurring types of resistance against the organizational maturity levels as "barriers to adoption" at each level. This gives you a map of the obstacles to expect and guidance on what to do about them.

Part IV and the main text conclude with a chapter describing why and how evolutionary change, implemented with Kanban and the KMM, provides the core elements of business resilience, together with the observation that organizational maturity is analogous to organizational resilience.

The book concludes with an extensive collection of appendices.

Appendix A provides a summary of the Kanban Method for your convenience and to obviate the need to consult another text.

Appendix B provides a summary of mappings to other well-known methods of organizational improvement or risk management. This material previously appeared as part of Chapter 3 in the first edition of this book. It has been extensively updated and expanded for this edition.

Appendices C, D, E, and F provide early access to chapters from a future book on Enterprise Services Planning. Specifically, these appendices provide the insights and mathematical evidence behind the use of classes of service, classes of dependency management, and classes of booking in a dynamic reservation system, as well as a comprehensive explanation of the mathematics behind the concept of cost of delay and how cost of delay relates to classes to service and classes of dependency management. This material is provided here because, at the time of going to press, it is not available in any other publication. Because using classes of service, using triage, and managing dependencies effectively are all necessary capabilities to enable successfully achieving Maturity Level 4, we felt it essential to include this material in this volume. However, we have placed it in the appendices to indicate that we consider this work part of Enterprise Services Planning and not core to the Kanban Maturity Model or the Kanban Method.

Acknowledgments

Creating a pragmatic model to guide the integral development of organizations toward resilience, trust, and reinvention could hardly happen without the collection and analysis of evidence-based experience in a variety of real-world cases.

We defined the beta release of the KMM using proven experience with Kanban over more than ten years. We were motivated to develop coaching guidance for organizations seeking successful evolutionary change.

Although the background experience was authentic, the model itself was not yet validated. Therefore, in 2018 and 2019 we ran a beta program to check whether the KMM was fulfilling its intended use in real-world businesses contexts.

We are thankful to Susanne Bartel, Steve McGee, Frank Vega, Minton Brooks, Brad Hughes, Ivaylo Gueorguiev, Kaveh Kalantar, Pavel Klimenko, Amit Kaulagekar, Ivan Font, and Kirill Klimov for their active participation in the beta program. They all are professional Kanban coaches and consultants who volunteered to use the model for guiding the change initiatives in the organizations they were working with. They are living and working in different countries: Germany, USA, Bulgaria, Czech Republic, Mexico, Ukraine, India, and Spain. Their clients were large, medium-sized, and small businesses in a variety of sectors: banking, IT, pharmaceutical, construction, travel agency, fintech. The methodological backgrounds of these organizations were very different as well.

During our weekly meetings, we discussed the characteristics of the maturity levels based on observing the companies we were working with, the practice definitions, and the improvements in cultural values, behaviors, and business outcomes that were achieved.

All this collected feedback was valuable input for developing a deeper understanding of the organizations and how they evolve in terms of culture, practices, and outcomes. This led to the definition of the four pillars of KMM.

We appreciate Steve McGee's visit to Bilbao in June 2018 and his participation in deepening the understanding and descriptions of the cultural values as well as uncovering new values that characterize each level of organizational maturity. David and Steve continue working together on the Leadership extension for the model and on new training courses on organizational change management and leadership development.

Minton Brooks and Pavel Klimenko contributed to developing our understanding of how KMM integrates with Agendashift, a well-known change management approach. We believe that this information is valuable to coaches who use Agendashift.

We are grateful to the Finance area of BBVA Spain, which pioneered the usage of KMM in the banking sector. Developing agility of a strongly regulated business that operates in a highly interconnected and fast-changing environment is a particular challenge. Beatriz Aguiriano, Head of Strategy, Solution Development, and Business Execution; Javier Marco-Gardoqui, Head of Business Execution; and Juan José Gil Bilbao, corporate Agile coach and Kanban Coaching Professional lead the adoption of the Kanban practices and values in the business area with the objective to improve the BAU (Business as Usual) services. Nagore Bilbao, Discipline Manager of Core Data, led her team to Maturity Level 3, Fit-for-Purpose, and is actively contributing to extending the high-purpose culture in the organization. We learned a lot along this two-and-a-half-year journey and used the acquired experience to codify better guidance for similar organizations seeking business agility. In addition, BBVA documented and published their case study, which is a valuable contribution to the KMM society.

David Hughes wrote a great case study about the experience of Vanguard with Kanban and retrospectively mapped Vanguard's evolution to the Kanban Maturity Model. The case study is also published on the KMM website and we use it in the KMM training classes. Therefore, we thank David as well.

We recognize the early research work of Troy Magennis and his discovery that lead time data could be modeled with the Weibull function. Alexei Zheglov's extensive analysis on thin and fat tails, number of data points needed to safely model, or forecast using models, and the risk trade-offs at and around the exponential function, form the foundation of the guidance in Appendix C.

We also acknowledge early work by Andy Carmichael modeling delivery delay cost, his discovery that most of the models produced a concave asymptotic function, and that the probable cost of delay in starting generally followed an S-curve. Without Andy's initial contribution, David would not have gone on to further the analysis and produce a general solution for cost of delay. Don Reinertsen first suggested the notion of a shelf-life taxonomy to David in 2012. Erik Jan-Kaak, perhaps accidentally, suggested the initial ratios for shelf-life as relative to lead time. The idea for Triage Tables was suggested by Dragos Dumitriu, inspired by SCUBA dive tables.

We acknowledge Andreas Bartel's contribution to developing the Kanban Cadences art. He was also responsible for digging up the original research on social psychology, and the material in Chapters 16 and 18 is significantly improved by his contribution.

Andreas Bartel, Craeg Strong, and Joey Spooner reviewed an early version of the manuscript and provided comments and feedback, which we appreciate.

Part I | Outcomes and Benefits

1 | Understanding Maturity Levels 0 through 2

The Kanban Maturity Model (KMM) is a roadmap for improving an organization through managed evolution. We begin with the three pillars.

The Three Pillars of the KMM: Culture, Practices, and Outcomes

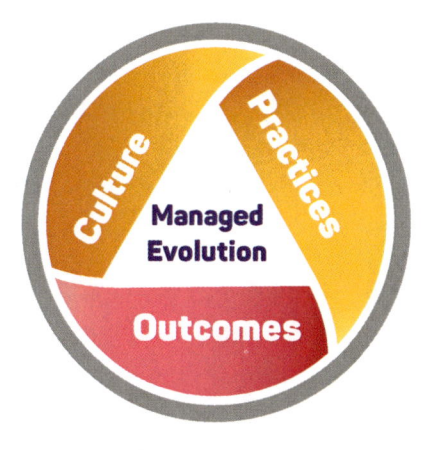

Figure 1.1 The three pillars of the KMM

The roundel shown in Figure 1.1 presents the three pillars of the Kanban Maturity Model: Culture, Practices, and Outcomes. They are developed in organizations following a Managed Evolution approach. We present pragmatic, actionable, and evidence-based guidance for each pillar in detail later. We start by explaining the three pillars and the seven levels of organizational maturity, illustrated using roundels (Figure 1.2).

Culture describes "how we live" as well as "who we are" and "what we stand for." Culture defines what people value—also referred to as principles, or norms, whether explicitly defined and written down or not. The accepted cultural norms are used to justify behaviors and actions, or to enable a system of justice to evaluate the virtue of specific behaviors or actions.

- Things people value and refer to as principles or norms (written or unwritten) that justify behaviors and practices

  "how we live"

- Routine activities
- Observable patterns of interactions
- Settled, regular Kanban practices
- Habits

  "how we do things"

- Meeting customer expectations
- Achieving business goals
- Resilience and reinvention

  "what we achieve and the capabilities we acquire"

Figure 1.2 The KMM roundel explained

Practices are regular activities, observable patterns of interactions, measures and metrics, decision frameworks, and routines, habits, or rituals. Practices are "how we do things around here."

Outcomes are observable results and describe "what our business looks like" to customers, users, and stakeholders. Outcomes demonstrate whether our business is fit-for-purpose and, if it is, in which contexts. Outcomes also indicate whether our business is sustainable, robust, and likely to survive over the long term. Outcomes illustrate our resilience and demonstrate our ability to recover from setbacks and unexpected events.

Culture and outcomes are changed through the adoption of practices guided by the Evolutionary Change Model, an approach designed and intended to create "pull" from the participants—the employees and managers of the organization—such that the changes institutionalize and stick. Evolutionary change drives sustainable, robust improvement.

The following pages describe each of the first three levels of organizational maturity as they relate to these pillars.

Maturity Level 0 – Oblivious

The characteristics of Maturity Level 0 are shown in Figure 1.3.

- Work is not managed (more likely, people are).
- The organization is oblivious to the need for polices, processes, or governance.
- Individuals heroically cope with high workload.
- People are focused on time management ("Getting Things Done").

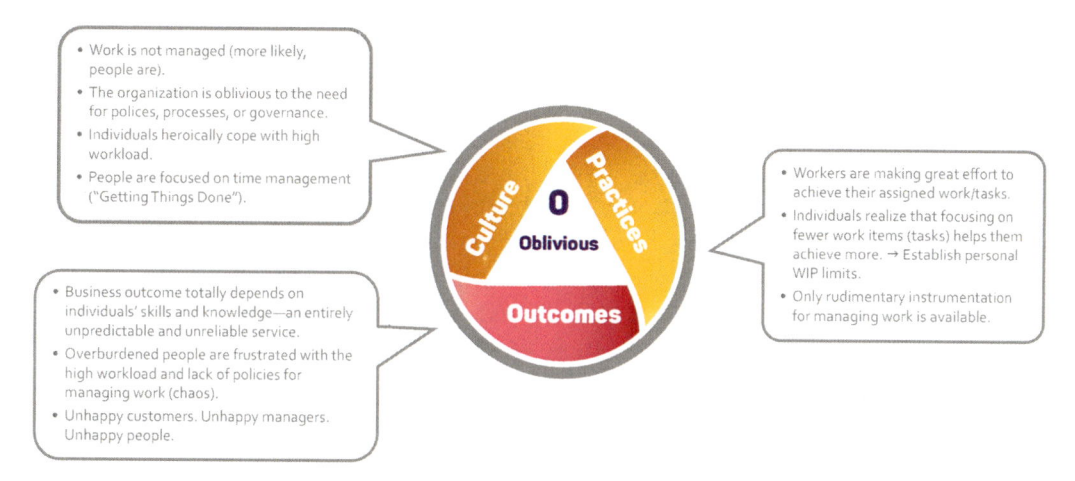

- Workers are making great effort to achieve their assigned work/tasks.
- Individuals realize that focusing on fewer work items (tasks) helps them achieve more. → Establish personal WIP limits.
- Only rudimentary instrumentation for managing work is available.

- Business outcome totally depends on individuals' skills and knowledge—an entirely unpredictable and unreliable service.
- Overburdened people are frustrated with the high workload and lack of policies for managing work (chaos).
- Unhappy customers. Unhappy managers. Unhappy people.

Figure 1.3 The KMM Maturity Level 0 roundel

Overview

At Maturity Level 0, individuals are responsible for handling their own tasks. Frequently, the person who performs the work is the user of its outcome as well; that is, the work consists of self-generated tasks rather than customer-requested work orders. The organization is oblivious to the need to follow a process. Workers are ambivalent about the value of management of organizational processes or policies.

Culture

This is a loosely affiliated group of individuals. There is no collaborative working. Every customer has their "pet" worker, their go-to person. We have observed two forms of Maturity Level 0: the stoic, with serfs and victims; and the anarchistic, comprised of neo-communists and liberals.

In the first type, we find stoicism and coping with a heavy workload. A sense of inevitability. Despondency. We have observed this type in large public-sector organizations—civil servants working in specialist areas in inherently low-trust organizations. We also see it in private companies with very traditional management styles dating to the 19th or early 20th Centuries. Organized into functional units through similar skillsets and similarity of work, each person works individually with no need to collaborate.

In the second type, we find a disregard for the need for any social organization, formal processes, or governance rules. Potentially a true and honest belief in anarchy in its primal form: a belief that humans will always self-organize to produce the desired outcome and that no governance structure or management is required. While idealistic, we have observed this pattern when a particularly liberal group of individuals organize themselves into a business: no one wants to assume a position of power, authority over others, or be perceived to have status that exceeds that of anyone else—communism in its purest form. We have seen this form only in idealistic, small-scale startup companies, and for only a short period of time, as the evidence suggests that it isn't sustainable.

Practices

Individuals are focused on completing their own tasks—"getting things done"—a time- and resources-focused approach to managing the workload and completing tasks. If there has been any Kanban intervention, we see the use of individual kanban boards. The fidelity of the individual kanban board depends on the individual, and they range from a simple visualization of tasks to a sophisticated system with WIP limits, *Next* columns, identifying separate types of work, and risk categories for allocating capacity to different types of risks to create a balance in life and outcomes for the specific individual. There is no instrumentation, as there is no defined process to instrument. Metrics and measures are not used. Decision making tends to be reactive, emotional, spontaneous, and sometimes difficult to explain.

Kanban Patterns

The focus is completely on handling personal tasks. Therefore, the observed kanban patterns include three basic types of individual kanban boards, used primarily to visualize tasks (see Figure 1.4). The designs observed reflect a growing level of individual maturity and capability at self-management. There is an intention to achieve a level of self-improvement through reflection, and often a cadence emerges as the use of the individual kanban system becomes habitual.

A *trivial* individual kanban visualizes invisible work, relieving the user of the burden of carrying the list of open tasks in their head. A *simple* individual kanban introduces work-in-progress (WIP) limits and recognizes a limit to human capacity, a desire for relief from overburdening, and a belief that multitasking causes individual tasks to take longer and their completion to be unpredictable. This second level could be described as a result of the epiphany that it is better to "stop starting and start finishing." The consequence is a feeling of personal achievement. The *true* individual kanban emerges when individuals realize that there is an existential overhead to a large backlog of unstarted tasks. This third, more mature design includes the act of personal commitment to items to do next, while there is recognition that backlog items are actually uncommitted, remain optional, and may be discarded. There is often a cadence to the personal reflection needed to select what will come next. A individual triage capability develops to decide what will be done: now; later, and if later, roughly when, based on a sense of urgency of the task; or not at all.

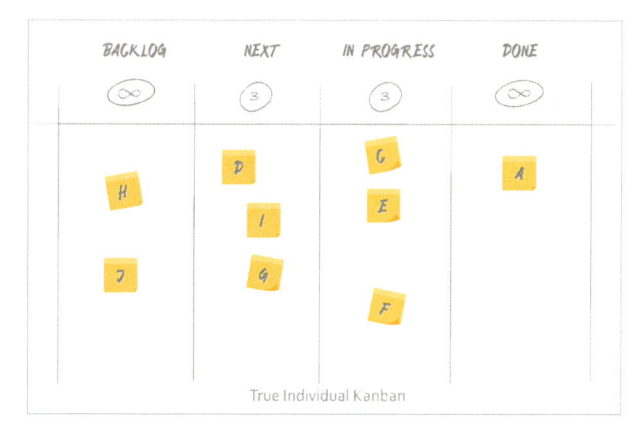

Figure 1.4 Maturity Level 0 kanban patterns

From an organizational maturity perspective, this third style of board is still a Maturity Level 0 (ML0) pattern; however, it reflects the thinking and actions of a more mature individual likely to want to participate in a more mature organization.

Outcomes

The quality and consistency of work done or services performed is entirely associated with individuals and their capabilities, skills, experience, and judgment. The customer experience depends entirely on which staff member performs the work. The organization, and its performance, is extremely fragile to changes in personnel.

Example

We are operating a takeout pizza restaurant, and we have a staff of individuals who know how to make pizza. Staff members compete to take a customer's order, then compete for resources such as countertop space, ingredients, and access to the ovens so they can fulfill the order. The customer experience depends entirely on who is serving them, and customers often develop a preference for a specific team member, effectively choosing them as their pet pizza producer. Customers wait to place their order with their pet chef, as they have no trust in the restaurant's systems.

Maturity Level 1 – Team-Focused

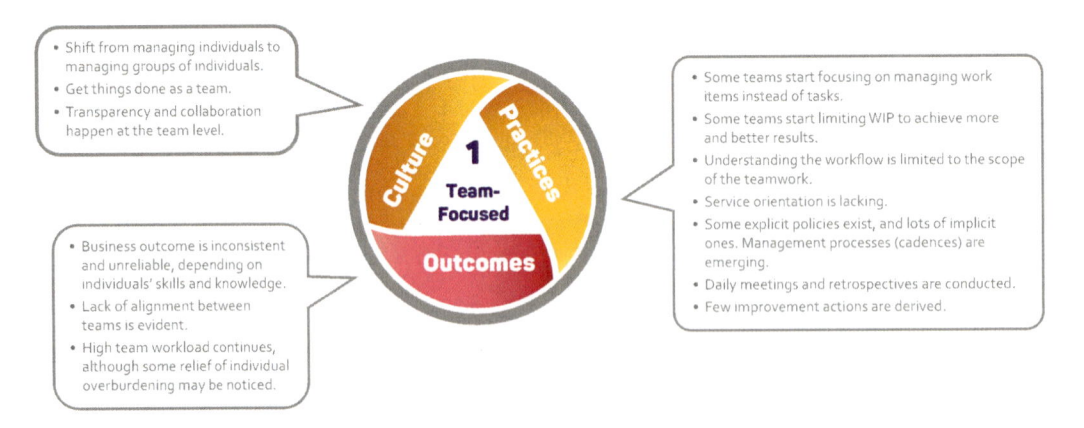

- Shift from managing individuals to managing groups of individuals.
- Get things done as a team.
- Transparency and collaboration happen at the team level.

- Business outcome is inconsistent and unreliable, depending on individuals' skills and knowledge.
- Lack of alignment between teams is evident.
- High team workload continues, although some relief of individual overburdening may be noticed.

- Some teams start focusing on managing work items instead of tasks.
- Some teams start limiting WIP to achieve more and better results.
- Understanding the workflow is limited to the scope of the teamwork.
- Service orientation is lacking.
- Some explicit policies exist, and lots of implicit ones. Management processes (cadences) are emerging.
- Daily meetings and retrospectives are conducted.
- Few improvement actions are derived.

Figure 1.5 The KMM Maturity Level 1 roundel

Overview

Maturity Level 1, illustrated in Figure 1.5, may be characterized as "never the same way twice." Processes and ways of doing things are poorly understood and emergent, or undefined, with poor repeatability. Teams of workers may be oblivious to a wider context. There is an understanding of what the work is, but perhaps not how it should be done, what the finished product should look like, or what the customers expect of service delivery. There is little understanding of who the customer is or why they have requested the work. There is constant pressure to find new customers because former customers, reacting to the unreliable service, fail to return.

The organization remains oblivious to the need for processes, policies, and governance beyond the team level. Consequently, there is an observable lack of alignment among teams. This affects the consistency of product design and implementation as well as service delivery. Work is pushed into the process. Priority is set based on superstition, or political leverage, or is purely ad hoc and random. The process, system, or value stream is overloaded. Individuals are often overburdened, and heroics are routinely required. There is no concept of the system's capability or capacity. Hence, it is impossible to try to balance demand against capability. There is an expectation that everything that is requested will be done. There is no triage capability nor opportunity to refuse work.

The workplace is stressful because of the inconsistency and poor quality, and there is a significant amount of rework. It is highly likely that loss of discipline occurs when workers are under stress and handling exceptional circumstances. When stressed, the organizational maturity is likely to slip back to Level 0, and then the organization relies entirely on individual heroics to pull out of a crisis.

Culture

Groups of individuals now identify as teams. Two forms exist: (1) a group of individuals who sit together, feel an affinity and a shared identity, but work separately on similar tasks; and (2) a true team of individuals who work collaboratively on a single task toward a shared goal—they share an identity and a purpose. The culture is tribal and focused on the identity of the team and status within the team. Trust exists within the team, but there is little comprehension of the world beyond the team and little cooperation with other teams. There may be a general sense of inevitability and a victim mentality. The team might feel that they are overburdened and abused, that their work is irrefutable, and they are overwhelmed. A sense of shared victimhood may strengthen team cohesion. Many team rituals might reinforce their self-image as victims while offering therapy and security in support of fellow team members. There is a focus on recruiting heroes, and heroics are an expected, rewarded, and celebrated part of the culture.

Practices

There is no consistency of process, policy usage, or decision frameworks. Teams may work in isolation without appreciating their contribution within the context of a customer request. There is little or no cooperation across teams nor any broader collaboration.

Teams use kanban boards, so there is transparency within the team. The teams hold daily Kanban Meetings and regular Team Retrospectives. They use vanity, or "feel good," metrics. Metrics tend to focus on individuals rather than on instrumenting still emerging and inconsistently followed processes. They tend to collect data and report on that which is easy to measure, with little thought as to whether the measure is useful or actionable. Some local activity measurements may serve as general health indicators, though many may be of little actionable value and are essentially vanity metrics—they make a team or its individual members feel good, feel as though they are making progress, but they serve no meaningful purpose in improving business outcomes. Decision making is emotionally driven and superstitious in nature.

Kanban Patterns

At the transition to Maturity Level 1, several individuals work on a common function, but assignments are separated. There may be specialization of tasks to individuals with specific skills. Everyone is responsible for organizing and performing their own tasks, or tasks are assigned and dispatched by a supervisor.

An aggregated individual kanban board (Figure 1.6) is used to visualize all the tasks and their status for a department or a function, typically using one lane per person. Hence, each lane is essentially a individual kanban board, and displayed together they are aggregated. This design often facilitates the supervisor as a dispatcher who assigns tasks to individuals. However, having awareness of what the other people do, and with which work they may require assistance, fosters collaboration. It is the first step to creating a real team and developing the understanding that working jointly produces better results more efficiently than working in isolation with limited comprehension of how one's work affects others'.

When consolidating to Maturity Level 1, collaboration happens habitually in a small team performing work with a shared goal or shared responsibility and accountability. Pools of people with different specializations may exist. Each team member is still responsible for handling their own tasks; however, the team has an emerging comprehension of the overall development process, in particular, how it begins and ends. This lays the foundation for Maturity Level 2, at which teams start seeing their jobs as a service conducted in response to a customer request or as part of a larger workflow. Therefore, Maturity Level 1 is fundamental for making Kanban Service Delivery principles one and two work:

1. Understand and focus on your customer's needs and expectations.
2. Manage the work, let people organize around it.

The team visualizes its work and meets daily to check its status. However, the process is not consistent yet, and under stress it is likely to lose discipline and consistency. Performance depends almost totally on the availability and individual efforts of certain team members and varies as widely as the spread in individual capabilities across the team.

Outcomes

Maturity Level 1 is described as "never the same way twice" because there is little to no cooperation amongst teams, and service delivery workflows are at best emergent. There is no consistency in a desired outcome. Work is not seen as a combination of services, and customers perceive service delivery as unreliable. There is considerable luck attached to whether a product or service is "fit-for-purpose." Customers with sufficient transparency show a preference for or demand the involvement of specific individuals on their work

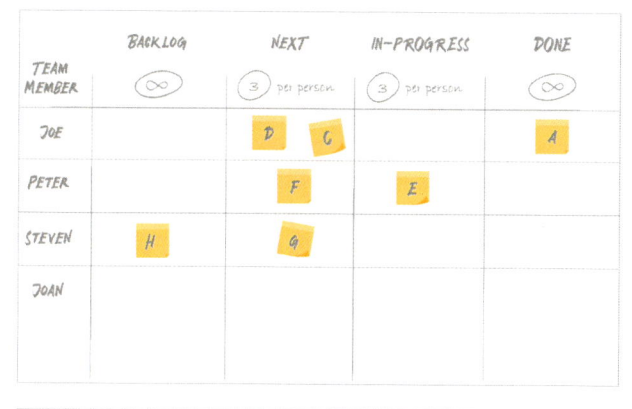

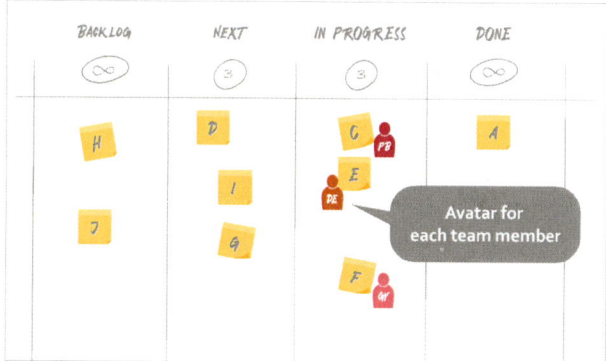

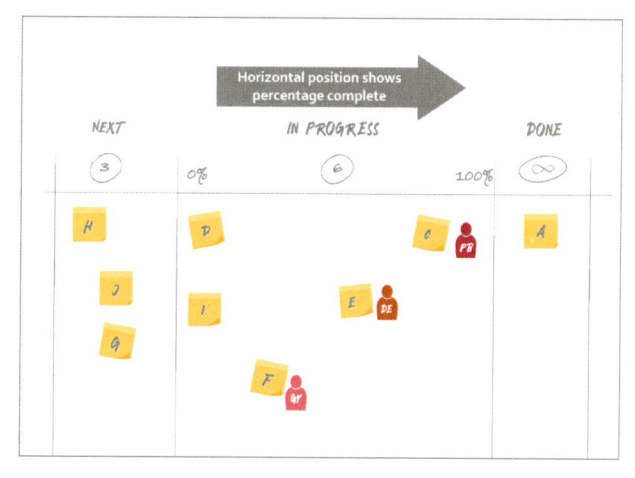

Figure 1.6 Maturity Level 1 kanban patterns

requests as a means to mitigate risks of inconsistent, poor performance and resulting disappointment. Customers have their favorite superhero. Like Maturity Level 0, customer trust is held with individuals, not in the organization or its systems and processes.

Observable outcomes depend on who is working on this shift, project, or product increment. The customer experience is incredibly variable. If the customer is satisfied, it is usually the result of individual heroics. You know you are dealing with a Maturity Level 1 organization when you see a recruitment advertisement with the headline, "Ninja developer required for dynamic environment," which we translate as, "We need a hero for our emergent workflow that produces extremely unpredictable outcomes."

Example

We are in the pizza delivery business. The method of preparing, baking, and delivering pizza, the accuracy of order fulfillment, and the quality and taste of the pizza depends highly on the individual making it. The process is emerging but is still inconsistent. Often, the pizza is the wrong type, is missing ingredients, or is of poor quality upon delivery, or the delivery time depends dramatically on the person who delivers it. The customers' experience leads them to conclude that the vendor is extremely unreliable.

Maturity Level 2 – Customer-Driven

- Focus to understand customer perspective and needs.
- Focus on creating end-to-end-flow.
- Evolve in small steps.
- Cooperation is key.

- Transition from managing tasks to managing work from a customer perspective.
- Start seeing and managing work as a service.
- Consistent process and basic policies are defined for managing product development and/or service delivery.
- Introduce the role of Flow Manager.
- Basic management of end-to-end flow, blockers, rework, and dependencies exist among teams. Some flow-related metrics are in place (capacity, demand, blockers, rework, work aging).
- Problematic policies are periodically revised.

- Initial understanding of customer expectations, demand, and capacity develops.
- Improved service quality and delivery is evident, but it's not fully reliable and consistent.
- Coordination between teams is insufficient.

Figure 1.7   The KMM Maturity Level 2 roundel

Overview

Characterized as "never the same result twice," Maturity Level 2 organizations exhibit consistency of process (see Figure 1.7), but not necessarily consistency of outcomes. Processes, workflows, policies, and decision frameworks are understood, defined, and are repeatable. New staff members are trained in "how we do things around here." Work is done consistently regardless of who is doing it. There is an understanding of what the work is, and both how it should be done and what the finished product should look like, including the service delivery expectations. However, there may not be a full understanding of who the customer is or why they have requested the work.

This is most often true for shared and internal services that lack visibility to the end customer as well as the motivation or purpose behind a work request or the risks associated with that work or its delivery. Consequently, there may be an observable lack of alignment among teams and interdependent service workflows. This affects how the customer views the consistency of service delivery. The workplace is notably less stressful because of both the consistency of process and that there are defined roles and responsibilities. Workers know what is expected of them and what they can expect of their colleagues. Poor quality is still an issue, though less so than at Level 1, and there is still some rework. Some pressure to find new customers remains because some existing customers fail to return as a reaction to the unreliable service. Additionally, there is some tendency to lose discipline when under stress and handling exceptional circumstances. When stressed, the organizational maturity tends to slip back to Level 1.

At ML2, there is less reliance on individual heroics than at previous levels; however, because the processes do not produce consistent outcomes, the organization relies on heroic managers to expedite important customer requests. Customers come to learn that they can trust certain managers and may insist that they manage their projects or ensure expedient, effective delivery. Customers do not yet trust the organization or its systems.

Culture

Trust and cooperation amongst teams and across the wider organization begins to emerge. Recognition of a shared purpose drives cooperation in the service of customers. Transparency broadens to the service delivery workflow. At the team level, the focus switches to the flow of work rather than merely completing tasks. It is no longer about getting things done; rather, the goal becomes making things flow. Maturity Level 2 is a world of managerial heroes cajoling work through the value chain, a world where customers have their own pet manager. If customers request certain project or delivery managers because they trust them, it shows that they don't trust the processes. The belief that successful outcomes are tied to the involvement of specific managers is a sure-fire indicator of a Maturity Level 2 organization.

Practices

The main shift at Maturity Level 2 is a transition from managing tasks to managing customer-valued and customer-requested deliverables. The organization starts to view its work as a service. Practices and the workflow process are now consistent, and it is possible to visualize a step-by-step workflow. The kanban board now supports multiple teams that cooperate across a shared workflow with the shared purpose of delivering customer-requested work. Nevertheless, work tends to be pushed into the process because policies are neither strong enough nor sufficiently internalized to prevent it. There is little observable capability to prioritize work. Priority, if it exists, may be superstitious (based on historical patterns or old habits: "we've always done it this way," or "in this sequence" or "it is bad luck not to do it in this order"), political, or simplistic—such as first-in-first-out (FIFO). The process, system, or value stream is often overburdened because of a tendency to say yes to everything (or to too many things) and an inability to balance demand against capability. Metrics appear to report the customer-valued work flowing through the service delivery workflow. Metrics have matured from vanity, or "feel good," team-level metrics to health indicators and improvement drivers for the entire workflow. A Flow Review develops as the main reflection mechanism driving improvement. We see improvement suggestions from this meeting implemented, resulting in improvements in flow.

Kanban Patterns

The main characteristic of the transition from the Team-Focused to the Customer-Driven Maturity Level is that the kanban board now has per-person WIP limits (the bottom board in Figure 1.8). Here, instead of a generic *In Progress* column, a sequence of the main workflow phases is visualized on the team kanban board. The types of work are identified and visualized by different colors (in this example) or by different lanes across the board. The team begins to understand that their performance depends on the amount of work-in-progress (WIP); that is, the more WIP, the longer work takes and the less predictable its completion is. They recognize that work left unfinished in a waiting state is not helpful and can lead to much higher defect rates and increased rework. Nevertheless, teams using delivery kanban boards with per-person WIP limits deliver better quality results and feel relief from overburdening.

Although the workflow is still basic and the overall process is not consistent at the transition stage, customer focus emerges—an understanding that work flows through a series of steps toward completion of something a customer values. Workers realize that a smooth flow of work is a desirable state for relief from unevenness. Uneven arrival of work creates temporary periods of overburdening. Uneven flow makes predictable delivery challenging and directly affects customer satisfaction. Properly coordinating the team's work (mainly among different specializations) appears to avoid peaks and troughs in workload. There is growing appreciation and awareness of more of the Kanban Method's values, but values such as Customer Focus and Balance are not yet fully embraced, and the cultural focus remains inward—"who we are" and "what's in it for us." Improvements are justified on selfish grounds at the team level. There isn't yet an outward-looking altruism or a focus on contributing for the benefit of customers and other stakeholders.

At the core stage of Maturity Level 2, organizations are better able to coordinate activities with different audiences and decouple the cadences of planning, committing, or selecting work from the cadence of delivery. This reduces the effect of losing rhythm due to concentrating team effort on packaging and handing over completed work and then restarting development. In addition, developing a tolerance for work to be in progress while a delivery is being made requires strengthening other technical capabilities, such as configuration management. Hence, decoupling the rhythm of planning, committing, doing, and delivering creates positive stress for improving specific enabling practices such as configuration management.

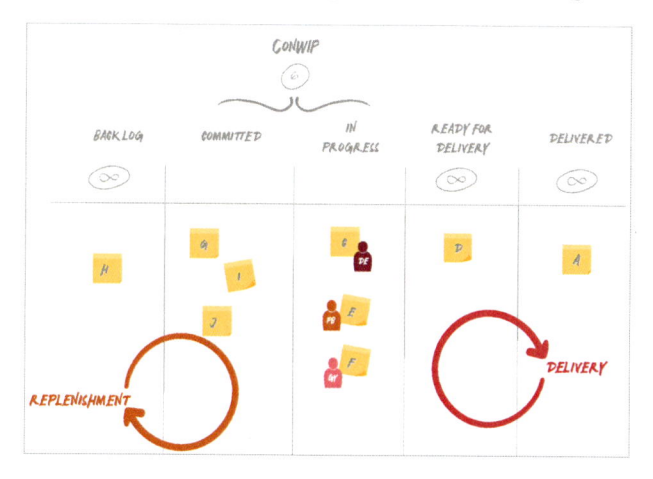

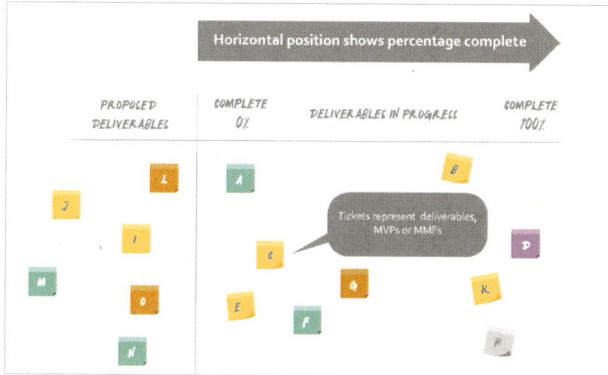

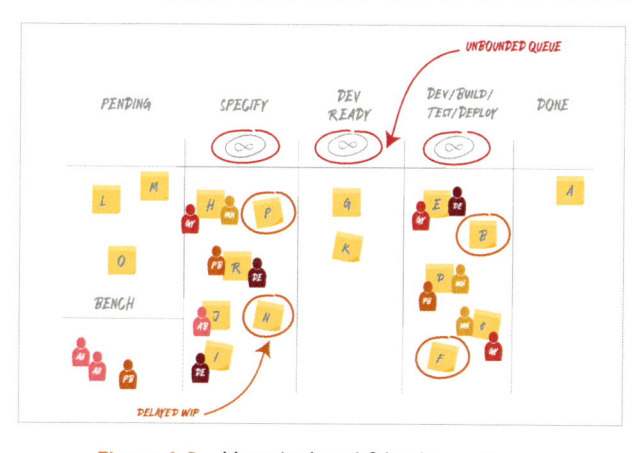

Figure 1.8   Maturity Level 2 kanban patterns

At this level, some teams recognize the need to control the workflow and do it by using a delivery kanban board with a defined commitment point and constant WIP (CONWIP), which is a true pull system, but without a defined workflow (the top board in Figure 1.8). Basic policies for prioritizing and committing work and visualizing work status are established. Parameters like *% Complete* are introduced and are used to provide additional information about project status and track its conformance to plan. Portfolio kanban boards are used for visualizing the status of multiple projects to enable making relevant decisions.

Nevertheless, the workflow management responsibility is not explicitly defined. Even in organizations with established project management processes, project managers' duties include planning, monitoring, and controlling project activities against plan, but not managing the workflow. There is no one playing the Service Delivery Manager (SDM) role. In some organizations, we've observed the emergence of a Flow Manager role at Maturity Level 2. This role tends to have an internal focus, actively managing flow for its benefit of relieving temporary overburdening due to unevenness.

At this level, established policies and workflow controls do not enable managing unforeseen events because the feedback from the system is insufficient. Behavior is entirely reactionary. Consequently, unforeseen events caused by the occurrence of specific risks, or more complex situations for which there is no specific guidance on how to handle them, can render a project or a service out of control. The result is failure to meet expectations and, often, a regression in observed maturity level to a more individualistic, heroic culture.

Outcome

Maturity Level 2 is characterized as "never the same result twice." We now have stable, defined practices and workflow, but the results fail to meet customer expectations consistently.

Example

We are in the pizza delivery business. The method of preparing, baking, and delivering pizza is consistent, and the defined procedures are now followed consistently. However, the pizza delivered depends highly on either the main cook or the manager being involved in the process. If she or he is not there, the pizza delivered might be the wrong type, might be missing some ingredients, or be slightly burnt. Therefore, the customer's perception is that vendor's reliability depends on the supervisor on duty.

LEVEL 2 CUSTOMER–DRIVEN

2 | Understanding Maturity Levels 3 through 6

Operating at Maturity Levels 0 through 2 of the Kanban Maturity Model can bring an organization only so far. Here, we describe the next four levels of the model: Fit-for-Purpose, Risk-Hedged, Market Leader, and Built for Survival.

Maturity Level 3 – Fit-for-Purpose

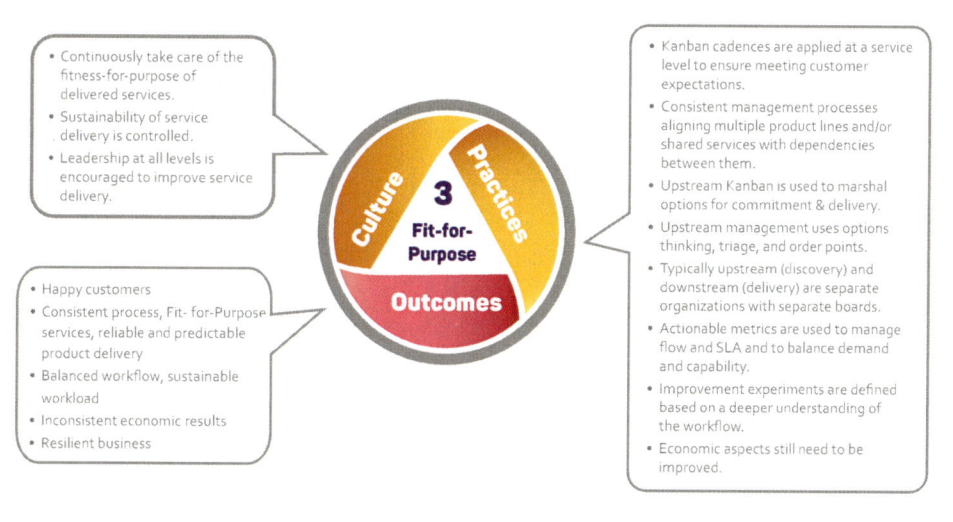

- Continuously take care of the fitness-for-purpose of delivered services.
- Sustainability of service delivery is controlled.
- Leadership at all levels is encouraged to improve service delivery.

- Happy customers
- Consistent process, Fit-for-Purpose services, reliable and predictable product delivery
- Balanced workflow, sustainable workload
- Inconsistent economic results
- Resilient business

- Kanban cadences are applied at a service level to ensure meeting customer expectations.
- Consistent management processes aligning multiple product lines and/or shared services with dependencies between them.
- Upstream Kanban is used to marshal options for commitment & delivery.
- Upstream management uses options thinking, triage, and order points.
- Typically upstream (discovery) and downstream (delivery) are separate organizations with separate boards.
- Actionable metrics are used to manage flow and SLA and to balance demand and capability.
- Improvement experiments are defined based on a deeper understanding of the workflow.
- Economic aspects still need to be improved.

Figure 2.1   The KMM Maturity Level 3 roundel

Overview

Maturity Level 3 (Figure 2.1) can be characterized by a line from a famous Stranglers song: "No more heroes anymore." The organization now has consistent processes, policy usage, and decision frameworks as well as desired outcomes. Product design, quality, and service delivery are all within customer expectations and tolerance levels. The organization is considered trustworthy. Its customers are satisfied.

At Level 3, the organization understands what the work is—both how it should be done and what the finished product should look like—as well as what the service delivery expectations are. There is a strong sense of unity and purpose along the value stream or across the workflow, a sense of a larger team collaborating to deliver a piece of work. The teams fully understand who the customer is and why they have requested the work, so there is a strong sense of fulfilment amongst the workers when delivering finished work.

The workplace runs very smoothly under both normal and exceptional circumstances, with little tendency to panic under stress. There is a strong sense of process, roles, and responsibilities, and workers know how to react to unusual or exceptional circumstances. There is little urgency to find new customers because existing customers provide steady demand.

The product or service is now completely "fit-for-purpose," which is achieved without heroics. Instead, people rely on defined methods, processes, and decision frameworks.

Organizational capability and performance are now resilient. Customers now trust that work is done consistently, and they no longer request specific individuals or managers to handle their work.

People are now thinking explicitly about services from an external, customer-facing perspective. The notion that the organization consists of a network of interdependent services is starting to emerge, along with some recognition of the power and efficiency of effective shared services.

There is a clear metrics and reporting strategy with fitness criteria, improvement drivers, and general health indicators being used appropriately. The process is instrumented to collect and report customer fitness criteria metrics. Improvement-driver metrics may also be actively used. Metrics and measures tend to be end to end, with only specific improvement drivers focused on local activities or value-adding steps. The presence of vanity metrics is unusual but may exist for cultural reasons or may be explained as evolutionary relics to which there is an emotional attachment, and the conditions needed to successfully remove them have not yet materialized.

Despite the considerable instrumentation and availability of metrics, decision making remains mostly qualitative or emotionally driven.

Culture

At ML3, the culture of heroes and individualism is gone, and there is now appreciation for defined practices and workflows, explicit policies, and feedback mechanisms to review practices, workflows, and policies regularly. The culture values the system in operation, and this way of working, in part, defines who they are. When things don't go as planned, the organization takes action to revise methods and procedures rather than blame individuals.

There is now extensive transparency, trust, and collaboration along the entire customer service workflow. The teams performing functions along that workflow are now collaborating as one much larger team—with a shared purpose and a shared goal. There has been a shift from mere customer awareness to a shared belief in customer service, an awareness that customer satisfaction is rooted in fitness-for-purpose, and understanding why a customer requested something becomes important.

Practices

At ML3, kanban boards not only map the workflow but have end-to-end WIP limits. Metrics now track customer fitness criteria against threshold levels such as an SLA on lead time. Metrics reflect fitness criteria, improvement drivers, and health indicators. There is a Service Delivery Review to reflect on how effectively the organization is meeting customer expectations. There has been a shift to symmetrical and synchronous commitment through fully functioning Replenishment Meetings; there is a clearly defined commitment point, and risk is now better shared by the upstream business organization and the downstream delivery organization. An effective triage process is in place to prioritize work into three categories: (1) do it now; (2) leave it until later, comprehending when is ideal; or (3) discard, reject, do not do it. Demand can be refuted or scheduled later. There is now balance between demand and capability, relieving the system of over-burdening. Only expedite requests are "pushed."

Replenishment Meetings, Service Delivery Reviews, and Delivery Planning Meetings all include the customer.

Kanban Patterns

A key characteristic of a Maturity Level 3 transition organization is that the kanban systems visualize a service-oriented, customer-focused workflow. An aggregated team kanban board visualizes workflow across different teams, which is shown on the top board in Figure 2.2.

Pull criteria, work item dependencies, defects/rework, and blocked work items are consistently visualized. This facilitates a deeper understanding of the system that performs the work. Initial actions for stabilizing the workflow are in place, in particular, establishing WIP limits for different states and for the entire system, as well as through plotting and interpreting the cumulative flow diagram.

Replenishment Meetings are held to move work items over the commitment point to control the workload and avoid destabilizing the entire system, although a customer might still tend to push starting a work item despite the pull criteria defined by the team.

The processes are repeatable, and the teams follow their routines, although they might still abandon them in crisis.

2 | Understanding Maturity Levels 3 through 6

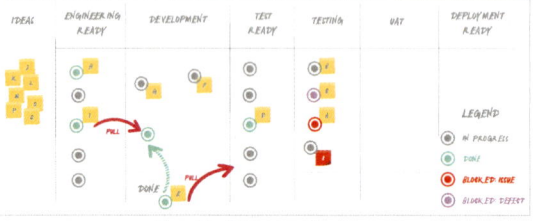

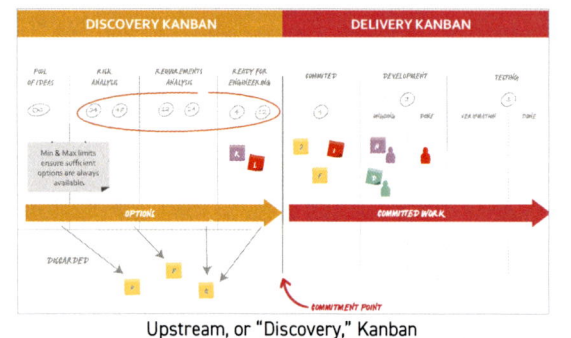

Figure 2.2 ML3 Kanban patterns

- Aggregated Team Kanban
- Physical Slot Kanban
- Movable Tokens as Kanban
- Virtual Kanban Board
- Upstream, or "Discovery," Kanban

At the consolidation stage of ML3, managers and teams have developed a good understanding of the workflow based on experience, collected historical data, and established feedback mechanisms (Delivery Planning, Service Delivery, and Risk Reviews). They make decisions using recent information about what is actually happening. In addition, they are able to flexibly manage work to effectively deliver expected results. Policies and processes are respected by managers and teams and are followed even in crisis.

The deeper understanding of the workflow allows managing larger and riskier product developments and services with a greater degree of success. Multiple product and service managers are in place, and dependencies between products and services are taken into account. Initial Operations Reviews are conducted to understand and address service dependencies.

Higher-level management is convinced of the benefits reaped by properly managing work. The roles of Service Request Manager and Service Delivery Manager are introduced to ensure sound management both up- and downstream.

Workflow data is collected and plotted on charts. Although data quality is not very good yet, and the entire process is not stable enough to produce meaningful measurements, the available data provide information that enables comparing the actual and desired service states and defining relevant actions.

Analyzing data facilitates an understanding of the processes and starts developing a culture of making decisions based on quantitative information.

Delivery Planning Meetings are held to schedule deliveries to customers and to make specific delivery date commitments. The act of committing to do something is separated from the act of committing to a specific date for delivery. In doing so, customer expectations are better managed and service delivery effectiveness improves. Service Delivery Reviews are conducted to monitor and improve service effectiveness. Risk Reviews are conducted to understand and respond to the risks that impede effective delivery of services.

Outcomes

The customers' expectations are met regularly and sufficiently well that customers are satisfied with the level of service. There is consistency of process and consistency of outcome. The organization has developed the capability to respond quickly to changing customer expectation. However, Level 3 might not be sustainable in the long run. Although customers' needs are met, other stakeholders' needs may yet be lacking. The organization follows the changes in their customers' needs, but does not anticipate them. Level 3 could be martyrdom—the organization may satisfy the customers but lose money on every transaction.

Example

We are in the pizza delivery business. The method of preparing, baking, and delivering pizza is consistent, and defined procedures are followed consistently, regardless of which night of the week it is, who is working that evening, or whether the manager is there. Consistently, the pizza delivered matches the order, is of high quality, and is within service delivery expectations. The customer's perception is that the vendor is reliable and trustworthy. Because the process and the outcomes are consistent, we have time to think about growing our business—open restaurants in other locations, or offer pizzas for people with dietary restrictions, or develop special menus that differentiate us from our competitors.

However, although our Maturity Level 3 organization can fulfill orders within expectations, we aren't yet good at understanding why customers choose us or what additional expectations they might have. We sell a lot of basic Margherita pizzas for delivery to business premises after 5 p.m. on Thursday evenings, but no one has bothered to think about it, or to ask why. We haven't yet achieved customer intimacy, and our ability to anticipate demand and expectations hasn't yet evolved.

Maturity Level 4 – Risk-Hedged

- Keep close relationships with customers.
- Meet regulatory requirements.
- Fairness is evident.
- Use the deep understanding of the workflow to develop competitive advantages for the business.

- Good quantitative understanding of the workflow is used for optimizing service delivery.
- Predictive models are used to improve forecasting of business outcomes.
- Focus is on risk identification and hedging.
- Capability to manage shared resources and fluctuating demand is well developed.
- Kanban cadences are scaled across the entire network of interdependent services at a business unit level.

- Services are fit-for-purpose from customers' and stakeholders' perspectives.
- Consistent portfolio management is key.
- Consistent economic outcomes are achieved.
- Anticipate risks.
- Business is robust.

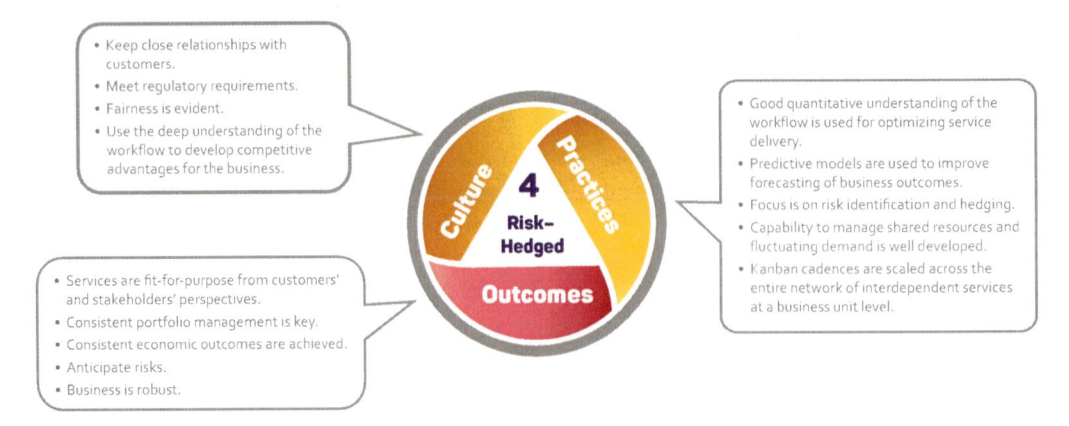

Figure 2.3 The KMM Maturity Level 4 roundel

Overview

At Maturity Level 4 (Figure 2.3), design, implementation, and service delivery are routinely fit-for-purpose. Consistency of both process and outcome relieves a lot of stress, and the organization shifts its focus to economic outcomes as well as to developing robustness against unforeseen events and exceptional circumstances. The organization now pays attention to quantitative risk management and economics. The question is now whether it can achieve consistency of delivery within economic expectations of cost or margin, and whether performance can be robust to unforeseen circumstances through appropriate risk hedging. Quantitative analysis of metrics and measures becomes more important. The goal is to be ever fitter-for-purpose from the perspectives of a variety of stakeholders.

In addition to all of the Maturity Level 3 behaviors, a Maturity Level 4 organization has a consistent economic performance, such as steadily meeting particular cost targets and margins. The concept of everything in balance now applies across customers, types of demand, risk categories, and a variety of stakeholders. While Maturity Level 3 introduced balance between demand and capability to supply, Level 4 extends that to ensure fairness and appropriate risk hedging. At Level 4, an organization seeks a risk-balanced, predictable economic performance.

Work is now classified by customer risks, and a variety of classes of service is offered. Demand shaping or capacity limitations by work type and class of risk are present. Triage is now driven by risk assessment, and class of service is directly linked to risk. Scheduling is influenced by cost of delay and a quantitative understanding of service delivery risks such as the probability distribution of lead time.

Under stress, the organization follows emergency or exception procedures and takes mitigation and remedial action to reduce the likelihood and/or impact of such an occurrence, or to completely prevent a recurrence.

Organizational capability and performance are now robust. Risk hedging is effective against the occurrence of unforeseen, though not unforeseeable, events. Customers now trust that work is done consistently, and there are no customer requests for specific workers or managers. Managers, shareholders, and other stakeholders, such as regulatory authorities, now trust that work is conducted within defined constraints and that economic outcomes are within a defined range of expectations.

The organization now extensively uses holistic thinking and has a service orientation. Organizational units are now forming around defined services with known and understood dependencies. Shared services are recognized as a highly effective and efficient approach and therefore are desirable economically. It is understood that they provide an advantage to organizational agility—the ability to reconfigure quickly to changing market, regulatory, or political conditions.

There is a notable shift to quantitative decision making, and a cultural norm is established that decisions must be underpinned with solid data, with risks assessed and adequately hedged prior to action.

Culture

At ML4, there is a deeper appreciation that everything must be kept in balance—that sustainability comes from meeting the expectations of all stakeholders. There is a drive for fairness—fair treatment of all stakeholders' concerns.

There is now a focus on customer intimacy. It isn't enough to know who the customers are, what they ask for, and what their expectations are. In addition, it's important to know why they have these expectations and why they ask for what they do when they do. From this, an organization learns how to best serve its customers and to anticipate their needs.

The culture has become much more anticipatory and less reactionary. Maturity Level 4 can be characterized as "no more surprises." A marked shift has taken place such that the expense of risk management—reduction, mitigation, and contingency—is seen as insurance against unforeseen events. When unexpected events do occur and require a nimble response, the organization reacts by learning, in an effort to anticipate such events in the future. At this level, the organization values competition and the way it drives improvement. It aspires to be fitter-for-purpose, to be better than the competition. Quantitative data and data-driven decision making emerge. The use of frameworks for decision making and risk assessment enable a move toward institutional knowledge and capabilities rather than relying on individuals' skills and capabilities. There is a repeatable system for recruitment and a commitment to employee and leadership development. Rather than recruiting for what it needs in the open market, the organization develops what it needs internally.

Transparency, trust, and collaboration now exist at a large scale, such as a business unit of 450 to 600 people.

2 | Understanding Maturity Levels 3 through 6

Practices

At Maturity Level 4, risk is managed by using a risk-assessment framework and risk-hedging techniques such as capacity allocation to create balance, fairness, robustness, and sustainable outcomes. The Fit-for-Purpose Framework helps an organization achieve customer intimacy. Classes of service are aligned with customer fitness criteria. Dependencies are managed using dynamic reservation systems, classes of booking, and classes of dependency management based on the work item's class of service and related customer expectations. The dominant feedback loop for driving improvement becomes the Operations Review. The Risk Review becomes more sophisticated and quantitative in nature.

Kanban Patterns

Maturity Level 4 is realized more through using metrics and feedback loops than through specific practices. It is characterized more by adopting the Kanban Cadences and the Fit-For-Purpose Framework than by specific kanban board designs. However, an organization that is solidly at ML4 visualizes and successfully manages different services and classes of services using shared resources. Capacity is allocated to each service so as to respond to a particular organization's goal or strategy (Figures 2.4a and b). In addition, capacity allocation is used flexibly as a risk-hedging mechanism against a fluctuating or unpredictable arrival of unplanned work.

Outcomes

Maturity Level 4, as previously noted, is characterized as having no more surprises and everything in balance. ML4 is a long-term, sustainable version of Level 3. All stakeholders' needs are now met in a sustainable fashion.

Figure 2.4a Maturity Level 4 kanban patterns: Capacity allocation across classes of service

Maturity Level 4 – Risk-Hedged

Figure 2.4b Maturity Level 4 kanban patterns: Capacity allocation across several services

Example

We are in the pizza delivery business. We are running an economically successful business offering several different classes of service, such as an express delivery menu. We successfully cope with ebb and flow in demand and understand the cyclical nature of our business. We are optimally staffed most of the time and our costs are tightly controlled without affecting our delivery capability or impacting customer satisfaction. We have a well-respected brand, and solidly predictable profitability.

We sell a lot of basic Margherita pizzas for delivery to business premises after 5 p.m. on Thursday evenings, and we know why. Thursday is the night that colleagues hang out together after work. On Fridays, people have plans for the weekend, but on Thursday nights they can afford to stay late for an hour or two. A Margherita pizza is the perfect accompaniment for a glass of beer or soda, just enough to take the edge off hunger at the end of a day's work. Because we know why our customers order, we can anticipate this demand—it's not luck! We also can anticipate when the demand will ease off, drop completely, or shift to a different evening of the week. If we have to introduce a new type of cheese because the one used so far is no longer produced, we study our customers' preferences, offering them pizzas with several alternative types of cheese to find out which they like best.

At Maturity Level 4, customer satisfaction is invisible—it is always there. Customers learn simply to take it for granted.

Maturity Level 5 – Market Leader

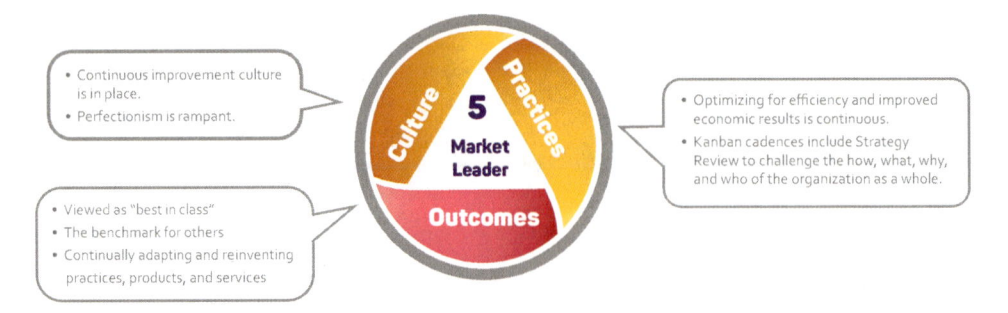

Figure 2.5 The KMM Maturity Level 5 roundel

Overview

At Maturity Level 5 (Figure 2.5), not only have design, implementation, and service delivery become routinely fit-for-purpose, the business is now entirely fit-for-purpose from a shareholder's perspective. The focus is now on optimizing for efficiency and improved economic outcomes, increasing productivity without sacrificing quality, increasing margins, extracting premium prices for premium classes of service or quality, minimizing costs, and optimizing the value of work done through a superior prioritization and triage capability. The goal at ML5 is to be fittest-for-purpose. A strong culture of continuous improvement has emerged, and acts of leadership at all levels contribute to improved performance. The workforce feels empowered to suggest and implement changes. Workers have a sense of ownership over their own processes and a sense of pride in their capabilities and outcomes. There is a culture of seeking forgiveness rather than asking permission, and consequently the organization is able to act and move quickly. Individual units can act with autonomy while remaining aligned with strategy, goals, and objectives. The organization has agility through a service-oriented organizational design. It is readily reconfigured to offer new services and/or classes of service by orchestrating and tailoring existing services using a customer-facing service delivery kanban system. The business is now solidly robust to changing customer expectations and other externalities.

There is extensive process instrumentation. Improvement opportunities are aligned with customer fitness criteria metrics. Improvement driver metrics are formally established. Improvement drivers have achievable targets. Improvement initiatives are predictive, model-driven, and there is a known causation between improvement action and forecast outcome. Significant job satisfaction is now derived from delivering improvements, as delivering customer-requested work within expectations and to the customer's satisfaction is now routine and is taken for granted.

Economic performance is improving consistently. Process improvement is used as a competitive weapon and an enabler of new services, new classes of service, new markets, and new market segments. Competitors are being outmaneuvered by superior organizational agility, enabling new and better products and services faster than ever.

Culture

Maturity Level 5 is characterized by a "relentless pursuit of perfection." This is the world of marginal gains, where the organization tries to squeeze the last ounce of efficiency out of its working practices to be the fittest-for-purpose. It aspires to be the best and to maintain that market-leading position. Only unforeseeable events rock the ship. Under stress, everyone maintains their discipline. Stressful circumstances always result in improvement. There is no complacency or arrogance. It is inherently understood that success comes from humility and respect.

Practices

At ML5, all of the Kanban Cadences, including Strategy Review, are fully used. Quantitative data is analyzed extensively. Kanban boards are full-featured and include mechanisms to maximize the liquidity in the system and maintain optimal flow. Improvement suggestions are model driven, backed by quantitative data, and changes are deployed as experiments with instrumentation in place to determine whether a change produces the anticipated improvement. At this level, the organization uses the Fit-for-Purpose Framework and Enterprise Services Planning practices extensively.

Kanban Patterns

Maturity Level 5 is largely characterized by behavior: the organization uses models and quantitative analysis, and it uses feedback mechanisms extensively—with most or all of the Kanban Cadences—perhaps augmented by additional feedback mechanisms for product management and integration of other evolutionary change methods such as Lean Startup, A3 Thinking, Toyota Kata, or Theory of Constraints. Innovative visualization at ML5 tends to focus on advanced risk-management techniques, using simple kanban boards to visualize and manage improvement initiatives, or using additional work item types and capacity allocation for improvement opportunities (sometimes called *kaizen* events).

Across a set of aggregated services, it is possible to visualize fixed or permanently allocated personnel or teams versus floating personnel who can be quickly assigned to assist on any service.

As shown in Figure 2.6, names of permanently assigned, fixed team members are displayed on rows of the board allocated for specific services. At the same time, more generalist, cross-trained personnel are visualized using avatars with their initials. The avatars can be moved from row to row to help where their skills are most needed at any given time.

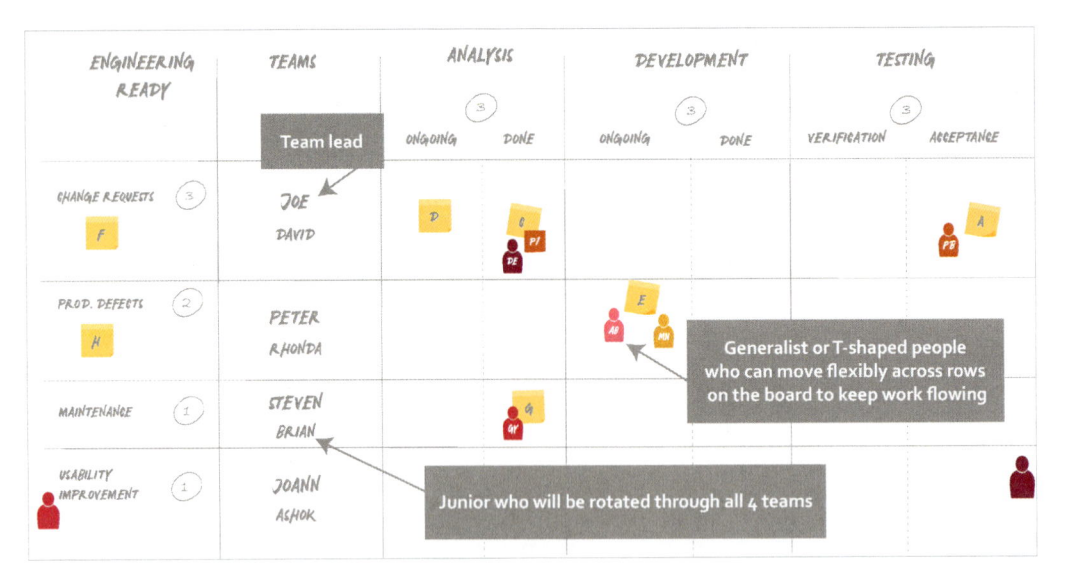

Figure 2.6 Staff liquidity visualization

Outcomes

At ML5, the organization challenges what it does and how it does it and is willing to replace old methods with new ones in a controlled and experimental fashion. Customers and other stakeholders are continually satisfied. The business shakes off unexpected events; only a completely unforeseeable event can rock it from its market-leading position.

Example

Our pizza delivery business is widely viewed as the best in the city, like Zak's, the fictitious gourmet pizza restaurant in downtown Toronto described in David's book, with Alexei Zheglov, *Fit for Purpose*. Residents boast about us to visitors, for whom experiencing our dine-in or home-delivered gourmet pizza is a necessary rite of passage. Our pizzas excel in design—we have the best menu; implementation—our dough and crust are legendary and always baked to perfection; and our delivery service is second to none—effective, with polite, well-trained, uniformed riders who ensure our pizza arrives in perfect condition every time.

Maturity Level 6 – Built for Survival

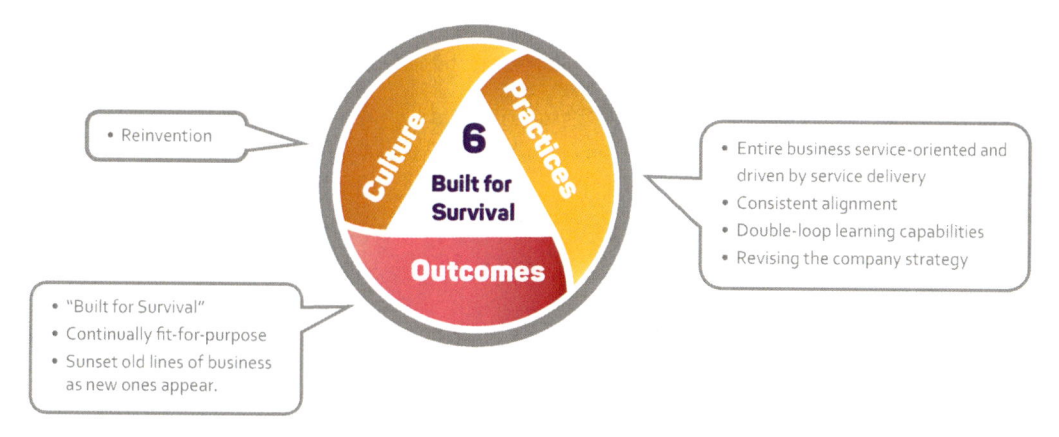

Figure 2.7 The KMM Maturity Level 6 roundel

Overview

At Maturity Level 6 (described in Figure 2.7), a business can claim that it is truly built for survival. At Level 6, it practices several double-loop learning exercises. The business is capable of asking the following questions:

- Is the way we do things still competitive? Are new technologies, processes, methods, or means becoming available that we should be investigating or adopting?
- Do we offer the right products and services? And if not, how should we change?
- Are we serving the right markets? And are we capable of serving our chosen markets adequately?
- Who are we as an organization? Is our current identity relevant and appropriate, or do we need to reinvent ourselves?

These are correctly characterized as strategic concerns, and answering these questions is a key part of strategic planning. Although the ability to challenge some of these four areas (using double-loop learning) may occur at shallower maturity levels, a Level 6 organization can challenge all four—how, what, why, and who. A Level 6 organization not only is capable of doing this strategic planning work, but it also exhibits alignment of capability and service provision with that strategy. When the strategy needs to change, the organization quickly reconfigures to align with the changes. This concept of strategy being continually aligned to operational capabilities is referred to as congruent action. Congruent action is leadership that everyone can believe in. A congruent organization is set up for success. Such an organization is extremely robust and adaptable to changing externalities, including disruptive, discontinuous innovation, and hence not only exhibits longevity but absorbs dramatic changes to its strategy relatively easily without significant impact to economic performance.

A Maturity Level 6 organization exhibits all the behaviors associated with Level 5. In addition, it has a strong strategic planning capability and uses Strategy Reviews to question current market segmentation and its product and service mix, to compare observed capability with strategy, and to define a strategy against which the organization is capable of successfully delivering.

At this level, extensive market instrumentation provides feedback on whether the firm's products and services are viewed as fit-for-purpose. Market segments are oriented around customer purpose. The entire business is service oriented and driven by service delivery. It assesses design, implementation, and service delivery capabilities against expectations in each market segment. The organization is capable of transparently reporting its fitness-for-purpose in each segment. Improvement actions are driven by a desire to amplify a segment or switch it off.

There is a strong sense of identity and an institutionalized understanding of who we are as an organization and how that affects decision making. However, although identity is well understood, the organization is not dogmatically, blindly attached to it. There is a recognized willingness to evolve and move with the times. Senior leaders understand their role as social engineers in defining and managing the identity of the business and its workforce as a social group. Defining and actively managing the culture of the firm is recognized as the main task of senior leaders. Identity management is an organizational capability. Tangible actions to manage the identity of the business and the sociology of the workforce are observable.

Culture

At ML6, there is an almost paranoid awareness that the organization and its business can be disrupted by discontinuous innovation, new technology, new business models, or political or regulatory changes. There is an understanding that the organization must not cling too tightly to a single purpose or to a narrowly defined sense of identity. Leaders move to expand the sense of identity to promote a culture of "strong convictions, loosely held." Survival is the most valued attribute, and it guides decision making.

Practices

The practices at Maturity Level 6 are defined in the Enterprise Services Planning Framework for Digital Transformation and in the Fit-for-Purpose Framework. Most notably, strategy and leadership focus on purpose and identity, and senior leaders focus their attention specifically on culture hacking and defining and communicating the enterprise's purpose.

Outcomes

At this level, lines of business are dropped, and new ones begun. There is innovation and experimentation with new lines of business, and often, a transition from one dominant line of business to another. The history of IBM is particularly illustrative, moving from time-recording machines to mainframe computers, and then later reinventing itself as a professional services company. Today we see IBM feeling its way toward becoming an artificial-intelligence platform company with its Watson technology. The name Watson, a hat tip to its founder, is a clear indication that its leaders see AI as not only the future of the company but as its next core business.

Example

Zak's Gourmet Pie & Crust restaurants have been closed due to the Covid-19 pandemic. Consequently, facing an extinction-level event, owner Zak thinks deeply about the identity and purpose of the business and the core motivation for starting it. He concludes that Zak's exists to deliver exotic gourmet pizzas with the highest quality fresh, local, organic ingredients atop the finest pie with crust thrown from fresh, live fermenting dough. However, he realizes that the delivery model can change.

As many other restaurants around the greater Toronto metropolitan area reinvent themselves as gourmet markets and delicatessens, Zak decides that he simply cannot follow their lead. However, perhaps they provide him with a new distribution channel. Perhaps he can partner with them to distribute pizza? Zak's reinvents itself, making gourmet pizza kits. Each kit contains the fresh dough and ingredients for a lovely, tasty, home-baked gourmet pizza experience. It isn't "Zak's to go!" rather, it is "Zak's at home!" Zak's switches to supplying his take-home pizza kits to these new markets. They shoot video of the sous chef demonstrating how to throw the dough to make the crust, how to spread the ingredients, and how to set the oven to bake the pizza to perfection. Zak's highly perishable, totally fresh-ingredient pizza kits aren't to be stored; they're to be used within two days of purchase.

With a solid understanding of who they are, why they exist, and what makes them happy and delivers satisfaction from doing business, Zak's Gourmet Pie & Crust successfully pivots and reinvents itself as Canada's favorite premium brand of gourmet, bake-at-home pizza.

3 | Benefits of the KMM

The KMM exists to drive the development of organizational culture and management practices that enable improving customer satisfaction, business resilience, and reinvention. The KMM provides a validated playbook for predictable, successful implementation across a wide range of industries. First and foremost, its main benefit is to ensure effective evolution of enterprises toward resilient and adaptable organizations with the Kanban Method.

The KMM also provides the foundation for appraising organizational maturity to ensure appropriate implementation of the Kanban Method at the current level of maturity. Effectively, this provides a catalog of patterns for that implementation at each level. Each of these, in turn, delivers business, cultural, organizational, psychological, and sociological benefits.

Developing Organizational Agility and Adaptability

Relief from Overburdening

Implementing Kanban at Maturity Levels 0 through 2 provides differing levels of relief from overburdening. At Level 0, the focus is entirely on the individual. A individual kanban board enables individuals to place limits on their current work and provides a way to get relief from too much work-in-progress. This results in happier individuals who take pride in their work and focus on finishing, with high quality, tasks that they have started. Tasks are completed faster, with greater predictability, and rework is reduced. There is little to no concept of service delivery, however, and the customer experience is that service delivery is unfit-for-purpose.

At Level 1, the scale of Kanban implementation grows to a team level, which affords a team the opportunity for relief from too much work-in-progress. This results in happier teams taking pride in collaborative work and focusing on finishing, with high quality, tasks that they have started. Tasks are completed faster, with greater predictability, and rework is reduced. As with Level 0, the customer experience is that service delivery is unfit-for-purpose.

At Level 2, an understanding of a service delivery workflow, or value stream, emerges. Each team or individual in the workflow is locally relieved of overburdening, but the whole system may still be overwhelmed with work, and queues or buffers between value-adding functions may be extensive. Queuing discipline is often ad hoc or non-deterministic and, as a consequence, although individuals and teams produce more work faster, with both higher quality and less rework, the entire system fails to exhibit predictability. From an external perspective, Maturity Level 2 offers few additional benefits over Level 1. From an internal perspective, though, more teams are happier, completing more work with greater pride of workmanship and motivation to improve further.

At Maturity Levels 0 through 2, local cycle times may be reduced, but the customer's experience of lead time and predictability is that things take too long, and lead time is too variable; in short, service delivery is unpredictable and remains unfit-for-purpose some or most of the time—although less so at ML2 than at ML1 or ML0. The customer might show sympathy toward an improving level of service delivery, but overall, service levels remain unsatisfactory.

Predictability and Faster, Smoother Flow

At Maturity Level 3, an end-to-end workflow, value stream, or system is now relieved of overburdening. Queues or buffers between value-adding steps are greatly reduced in size, and queuing discipline, defined by classes of service, is emerging. Consequently, lead times are reduced dramatically, as is the variation, or tail, in the lead time distribution function. The customer experience is faster service with greater predictability. At Level3, customers are likely to start reporting that service delivery is fit-for-purpose.

Service Delivery

The KMM makes the role of the customer explicit, first introducing it at Maturity Level 2, and defining Maturity Level 3 by the outcome that customer expectations are met satisfactorily. The Kanban Method exists in its original form to provide better customer service and to achieve it through incremental, evolutionary change. Whether a change represents an improvement is defined through the eyes of the customer. This concept is formalized in the Fit-for-Purpose Framework, with the notion that customer fitness criteria drive the design, implementation, and service delivery (or experience of consumption) of a product or service. These concepts and practices are captured in the model at Maturity Levels 3 and 4.

Pursuing and achieving Maturity Level 3 using the KMM provides the direct business benefit that customer expectations are regularly met, that customers are satisfied, and that the business is strongly driven by a sense of purpose—to serve the customer and fulfill their needs and expectations.

Organizational-Level Agility and Resilience

From Maturity Level 1 on up, the KMM introduces various feedback mechanisms (visualization, metrics, Kanban Cadences, cultural values) and decision-making frameworks (metrics, policies, leadership actions) that develop the enterprise's abilities to adapt quickly to changes in customer expectations, market conditions, and business context.

At Maturity Level 4, the organization has a firm grasp of systems thinking and views itself as a network of interdependent services—a system of systems. Each service may have implemented a kanban system.

The effect is that work with complex dependencies can be delivered efficiently, with little delay, as a result of interdependent work orders across the network. There is a high level of predictability, even for work with complex dependencies. The customer experience is that, even for large, complex work requests, the service delivery is fit-for-purpose.

Adopting the service-oriented organizational (SOO) paradigm and developing the skills to quickly rearrange the services to construct new ones without adversely affecting those already in place allow for faster recovery from exceptional, emergent circumstances, which is fundamental to business resilience and adaptability. Developing a culture of empowered people, customer focus, aligned action around a shared purpose, and leadership at all levels is the foundation and the key success factor for building a resilient and adaptable business.

Risk Management and Improved Economic Performance

At Maturity Level 4, the business's economic performance improves dramatically. Both better governance and appropriate risk hedging improve revenues, margins, and cost control. Demand shaping, capacity allocation, advanced forms of classes of service, risk-assessment techniques, and a strong triage capability that separates work into three categories—do it now; leave it until later, but with a specific schedule; or choose not to do it at all—all contribute to highly predictable outcomes and superior economic results.

At Maturity Level 5, a continuous improvement culture and the use of quantitative analysis of system capability metrics contribute to ever-improving economic results without the loss of customer satisfaction or fitness-for-purpose.

Reinvention and Long-Term Survivability

Maturity Levels 1 through 5 provide various scales of single-loop learning—the organization is getting better at what it does and how it does it. Maturity Level 6 sees the emergence of two forms of double-loop learning: the business's ability to question how

and what it makes, as well as why it exists and what it is—and whether that identity and/or purpose remains relevant. This manifests as leadership's capability to question:
- Is our strategy correct? Are we offering the right products and services to the right markets? Should we redefine our market segmentation and change the products and services we offer?
- If people are not buying what we are selling, is it because we aren't fit-for-purpose or is it because the market has moved on and changed its needs and desires?
- Is our purpose for existing still relevant? Has our purpose been overtaken by events, or obviated by new technologies or societal or social changes?
- Do we as a business have the right identity for the current business, political, economic, and technological environments in which we compete?

A Level 6 organization is capable of both questioning its own identity and reinventing itself in a new image, with a new identity.

Although some elements of double-loop learning that manifest in Kanban implementations, such as Strategy Review, may emerge at lower levels, their effectiveness is diminished because of lower maturity across the rest of the organization. For example, what is the point of defining new markets and new services to offer if the organization is not capable of reconfiguring itself to offer them in a timely and effective manner? What is the point of targeting new market segments if the organization is not capable of meeting the product specification, quality, or service delivery expectations of customers in that segment? What is the point of targeting new markets with new products if the organization cannot guarantee to exploit them profitably? Put simply, implementing Level 6 practices in a Level 2 organization is likely to be ineffective, and it might result in disappointment, finger-pointing, and assigning blame for failure. The difference between identity and/or purpose change—a so-called pivot—at Maturity Level 2 is that luck and/or heroic effort from individuals or managers is likely necessary to achieve it, while at Maturity Level 6, an identity and/or purpose change is a controlled and managed strategic activity—heroes are not mandatory.

Maturity Level 6 organizations are robust to rapidly changing external environments. They can react quickly and effectively to disruptive, discontinuous technological innovation; or to changes in the regulatory environment, the political or economic climate, or customer tastes; or to raised customer expectations.

Better Business Outcomes

The culture of an organization has a direct relationship to its ability to achieve a given level of maturity and maintain it consistently. To effectively reach high levels of maturity, senior leaders must view part of their role as culture hackers or, using more traditional language, as social engineers. If a leader desires the benefits of higher maturity levels, then it is their job to lead and steer the culture such that higher maturity is achievable.

People in lower-maturity organizations at Levels 0 through 2 tend to have an individualistic focus on their identity or their culture: Who am I? and What's in it for me? Or at a team level, Who are we? and What's in it for us? There can be selfishness in low-maturity organizations, or in the workers and their teams. Individuals, teams, or the whole organization may cast themselves as victims, with a culture of shared affinity in victimhood, powerless to affect their circumstances or break free from an abusive environment. Alternatively, lower-maturity organizations are nascent, emerging, and perhaps working in nascent or emergent markets. They are still finding themselves, defining who they are and why they exist. With enough time and leadership, they might mature to Level 3 or beyond.

Low-maturity organizations are often highly socially cohesive, and conformance to social norms and established tribal behaviors tends to drive decision making and outcomes. Consequently, there is considerable inertia against change. In highly socially cohesive cultures, change must come from the top. Leaders must signal changes and give permission for them to happen. They must communicate a change in "how we see ourselves"—the self-image and identity of the organization—and perhaps a change in "what we value"—the organizational values. Dependence on a single strong leader implies fragility.

At Maturity Level 3, an organization has a strong sense of "who we are" and is very comfortable with its identity. As such, it can focus energy and attention on the more important topic of "why we exist." A Level 3 organization has a strong sense of purpose, defined and communicated by its leaders. Pursuit of that purpose is considered culturally more important than "who we are," the collective identity and self-image of the organization. As such, the organization is more flexible, more tolerant, more trusting, and, consequently, more agile through the cultural importance of "why we exist" rather than obsessing over "who we are." Level 3 organizations have *Einheit*—unity and alignment behind a sense of purpose. Level 3 organizations can act with greater autonomy and exhibit greater agility because of this shared sense of purpose.

At Maturity Level 4, the organization understands very well "why we exist" and "who we are." The focus now changes to "what we do" so that we deliver on "why we exist." Selecting the right things to do to produce the best results is culturally important to a Level 4 organization. They don't just know why they exist; they are good at delivering against that purpose because they select the right products or product features and the right services to best deliver on their goals, and they have a strong and justifiable sense of pride in who they are.

At Maturity Level 5, the organization and its people have a strong sense of who they are, are comfortable in their skin, know why they exist, believe in their purpose, and make good choices to deliver against that purpose effectively in a manner that customers love. This enables them to focus on "how we do it," with a goal of being the best at what they do through superior processes and capabilities.

At Maturity Level 6, an organization is capable of questioning and changing all of the above. It questions how, what, why, and who. Although it has a strong sense of how, what, why, and who, these ideas are loosely held. It has cohesion, unity, agreement, and pride in its collective mastery, but also a strong culture of challenging established norms and finding better ways. It values challenging established conventions, norms, and behaviors. It values innovation and embraces change. This is driven from an overarching value: the desire for longevity, the desire to survive for generations. A Level 6 organization recognizes that stubbornness, and a refusal to change its how, or its what, or its why, or even its identity—its self-image, its "who"—may lead to its extinction.

4 | Case Study: BBVA Finance Division (Spain)

From Team-Focused to Fit-for-Purpose in One Year

BBVA is one of the world's largest international banks and a pioneer in introducing Agile methods in the global banking sector. Running services and projects that require a high level of domain knowledge and must meet strict deadlines needs fast decision making and flexible management, so in 2014, the bank initiated the adoption of Agile work methods to satisfy better the expectations of their customers. Now, in 2020, more than 30,000 employees use Agile practices on a daily basis. The entire bank is immersed in a journey of continuous learning and has evolved to enable rapid adaptation to market conditions

The Management Information Systems (MIS) Discipline of the Finance area is the pioneer in adopting Agile work methods at BBVA. By the end of 2017, more than thirty project teams from five programs were introduced to Agile. Business as Usual (BAU), which occupied the largest part of the area's capacity, was relegated to a secondary position. However, it was affecting the execution of a number of projects. The Discipline Leader and the Program Managers requested effective practices for managing both projects and BAU, as well as the dependencies among the teams.

Within one year, five MIS programs evolved to achieve systematic, customer-driven management of projects together with BAU. Furthermore, the Rentability program introduced portfolio management of their projects and started planning new work based on a better understanding of their capability and work in progress. The Core Data program reached a quantitative understanding of their demand and capability and defined service levels. In addition, they developed concrete improvement initiatives and now track them consistently using appropriate indicators.

The Kanban Method and the Kanban Maturity Model are being used as guidelines for driving this evolution.

4 | Case Study: BBVA Finance Division (Spain)

Getting Started with Kanban in the Finance Area

The Finance area of BBVA was one of the first non-IT areas to initiate their Agile transformation. Five Programs were initially involved in the endeavor.

Each one of these Programs runs in parallel two types of activities:

- Business as Usual (BAU) services to other business units within the bank, the largest part of their business
- Projects for internal or external customers

Both BAU and projects require deep domain knowledge. Therefore, as often happens in knowledge work, some activities depend heavily on individuals with specific expertise.

Moreover, particularly in the Finance area, all services and projects must comply with regulatory requirements, meet strict deadlines, and deliver high-quality results.

The need to increase the success rate of their projects and develop higher flexibility in managing their BAU services caused Luis Garín, Director of Management Information Systems, to introduce Agile methods in the in the beginning of 2017.

For approximately a year, fifteen project teams (out of more than thirty) adopted Scrum practices and started working in a relatively autonomous manner. One program only, Core Data, started using a simple kanban board for visualizing their work (see Figure 4.1).

Project teams were demonstrating good results and in general were positive about the new work practices.

Nevertheless, the Program Managers had some concerns related to the transformation of the area as a whole. The projects were a small proportion of all the work that was carried out, and it was not clear to them how BAU should be managed in parallel with projects, especially where there were strong dependencies on individuals with certain expertise. Therefore, the overall perception was that although Scrum was appropriate for project teams, more practices would have to change if they were to become a true Agile organization. And the approach to meeting this goal was not yet clear.

Figure 4.1 Initial kanban board of Core Data

Challenges

Building an Agile organization entails a lot more than having project teams apply Agile practices. It requires connecting all the teams delivering products and services into a fully synchronized entity that meets customer expectations in a predictable and sustainable manner. From this perspective, transforming the MIS programs into an Agile organization presented several challenges, described as follows.

Effective Management of BAU

About eighty percent of the business is BAU. This comprises multiple types of services (information requests, incidents, recurring reporting, audits, and so on), the demand for which comes from a variety of sources in a planned or unplanned fashion. However, very little was done to improve the management of BAU because the focus was on selected projects, leaving the majority of the work unaffected by the new Agile practices. Only the Core Data program started with Kanban because they were involved in the project work of all programs. Nagore Bilbao, the program manager for Core Data, thought that more needed to be done to improve process management, that the adoption of Agile practices was too focused on projects.

Overburdening

Many people had been involved in both projects and BAU for years and possessed valuable domain knowledge. Accelerating project development while maintaining the same BAU workload led to a significant overburdening of knowledgeable people, resulting in unforeseen delays of affected projects or services.

Managing Dependencies

Agile was taught as practices for teams. Managing dependences between teams, between project teams and BAU, and between operational and strategic levels continued to be done in an ad hoc manner. Therefore, waiting on others often produced long delays. In addition, priorities often changed during the two-week time boxes known as sprints.

From a systemic point of view, the project teams were bettering their performance while the other parts of the system were functioning as before, and there was very little visibility on the underlying dependencies. Viewed at a holistic level, little improvement was evident. The need to avoid local optimization and bring a balanced and sustainable approach to carrying out all work was growing. Dependencies needed to be resolved quickly to produce observable global improvements in performance.

Dedicated Flow-Management Tool

Having plenty of white boards with sticky notes and a collection of tools that some teams were experimenting with was not enough for the effective and coordinated management of the multiple projects and services that the area was delivering. They needed a proper tool that enabled faster and better feedback about the actual status of the ongoing work, making decisions supported by data, and identifying further opportunities for improvements to processes.

Initial Appraisal of the Situation Based on the Kanban Maturity Model

At this point, Teodora Bozheva joined the teams of coaches facilitating the Agile transformation of the area. At the time, she was working with David J Anderson on defining the Kanban Maturity Model. She used that knowledge and experience to help extend BBVA's methodology so that the Finance area could evolve further toward organizational agility. Juan José Gil, Agile Ambassador for the Finance area, delved deep into the model to see how well it addressed the needs of the area and ensure that its intent was fully aligned with the bank's global initiative goal, namely developing into an Agile organization.

In a services business where meeting deadlines and regulatory requirements is crucial, Kanban outlines the practices and principles that allow you to manage changing demand effectively and ensure predictable delivery of customer value in a sustainable manner. Teodora did an appraisal of the current situation in the area using KMM. It revealed characteristics typical of a team-focused organization (Maturity Level 1), summarized as follows.

Visualize

- Partial visibility on the work to be carried out

Visual boards were used in the projects that were applying Scrum. However, service work (BAU) was visualized only in the Core Data program. The rest of the programs were not visualizing service work. This significantly reduced the shared understanding of what the real workload and work situation were.

Limit WIP

- Work-in-progress (WIP) limits not established for any team

The systems managed by the teams were congested. Little or no focus was placed on finishing work and limiting WIP to enable flow.

Manage Flow

- Lack of understanding of the end-to-end workflow
- Frequent interruptions and priority changes
- Blockers and rework not registered and managed systematically
- Lack of quantitative understanding of demand and capability of the teams

- Predictability of the projects dependent on external teams very low; often, deadlines for projects and services met as a consequence of unsustainable extra effort from a few dedicated individuals

Make Policies Explicit
- Agile practices and ceremonies introduced to project teams but policies for managing work (e.g., based on their type or impact of delay) not defined

Individuals were focused on managing tasks, not really on deliverable work items.

Feedback Loops
- The following meetings were held: Daily, Sprint planning, Demo, Retrospective, and Backlog refinement.

Improve Collaboratively, Evolve Experimentally
- Retrospective meetings were used for discussing problems in the processes. Nevertheless, few improvements had been identified, and very little process experimentation had taken place.

Culture
- **Achievement** Everyone was doing their best to accomplish the work and meet expectations.
- **Transparency** It existed in teams using visual boards. People participated openly in daily meetings.
- **Collaboration** People were collaborating to the extent that was possible—within local teams. Because a lot of knowledge was concentrated in several people, strong dependencies on these individuals were created. Under the pressure of the high volume of work, jobs were typically assigned to individuals with appropriate qualifications and conducted without collaboration.
- **Flow** Blockers were managed in an ad hoc manner. Few people were applying the principle of "Stop starting, start finishing." Little attention was paid to a work item's age.
- **Customer and Service Orientation** There were no key performance indicators (KPIs) defined. Rather, managers were focused on optimizing resource utilization instead of improving service delivery.

Figure 4.2 on the next page summarizes the situation at the end of 2017.

BAU services must meet strict regulatory requirements and fixed deadlines. Therefore, project team members who were also working on BAU were suffering from overburdening and/or causing delays in their projects.

4 | Case Study: BBVA Finance Division (Spain)

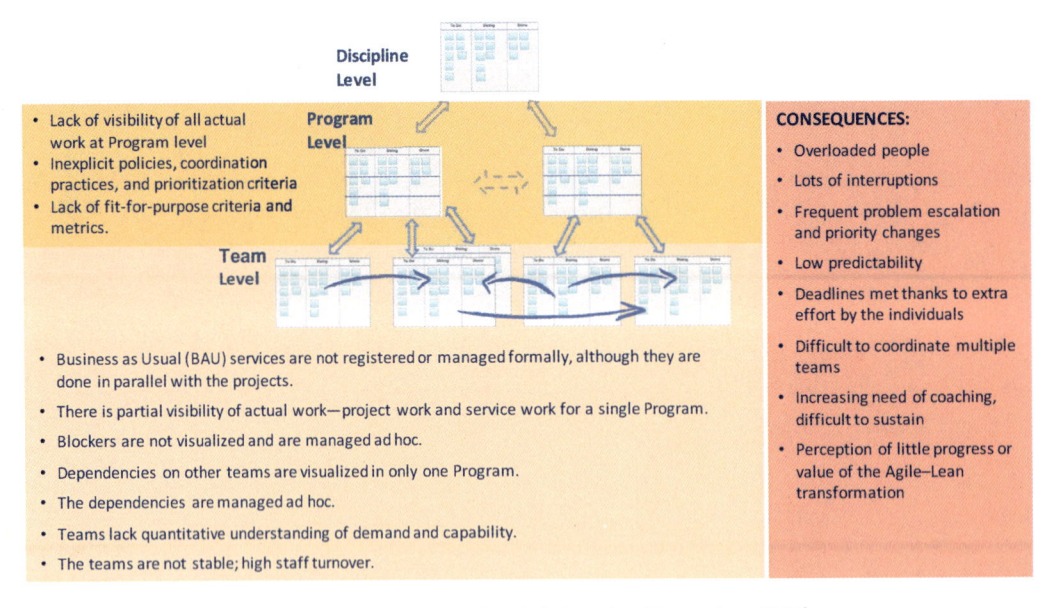

- Lack of visibility of all actual work at Program level
- Inexplicit policies, coordination practices, and prioritization criteria
- Lack of fit-for-purpose criteria and metrics.

- Business as Usual (BAU) services are not registered or managed formally, although they are done in parallel with the projects.
- There is partial visibility of actual work—project work and service work for a single Program.
- Blockers are not visualized and are managed ad hoc.
- Dependencies on other teams are visualized in only one Program.
- The dependencies are managed ad hoc.
- Teams lack quantitative understanding of demand and capability.
- The teams are not stable; high staff turnover.

CONSEQUENCES:
- Overloaded people
- Lots of interruptions
- Frequent problem escalation and priority changes
- Low predictability
- Deadlines met thanks to extra effort by the individuals
- Difficult to coordinate multiple teams
- Increasing need of coaching, difficult to sustain
- Perception of little progress or value of the Agile–Lean transformation

Figure 4.2 Summary of initial situation (December 2017)

Objective

The objective of the Agile transformation of the bank included the following three aspects:

- Time-to-Market: On-time delivery of value to customer
- Adaptation to change: Ability to adjust to changing demand by means of frequent feedback
- Transparency, collaboration, and continuous communication within business areas and between them

In terms of the Kanban Maturity Model, we had a ML1 Team-Focused organization with the goal of becoming a ML3 Fit-for Purpose organization (see Figure 4.3).

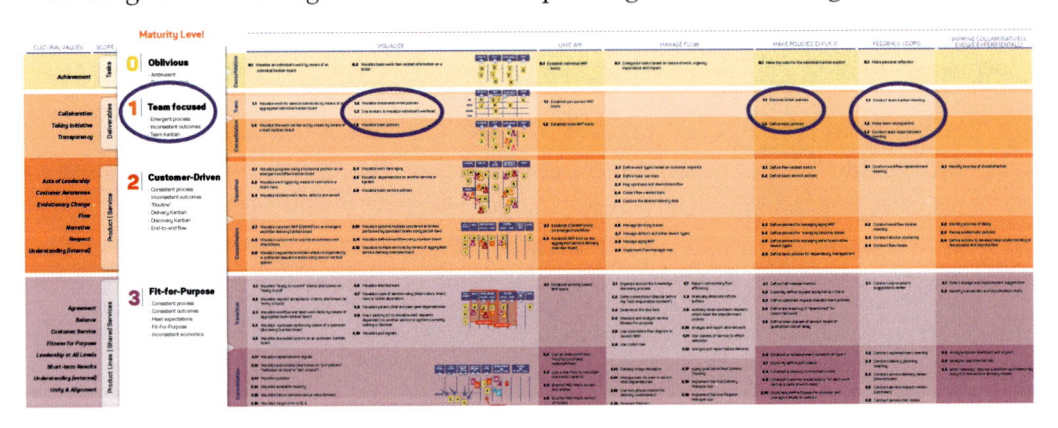

Figure 4.3 Initial situation

Toward a Fit-for-Purpose Organization

Two main challenges were associated with accomplishing the bank's objective:

- The purpose for the Agile transformation of the bank was defined rather generally, and making it more concrete required obtaining a deeper understanding of the demand and capability of the service teams.
- The service orientation and the concepts of managing flow had not been introduced as part of the Agile training; therefore, time was needed to introduce and incorporate them into the routines of the teams and program managers.

The first step was providing workshops for the Program Managers and the teams to introduce the basic Kanban practices from Maturity Level 2: focus on flow, managing blockers, re-work, lead time per work type, and dependencies between teams. After that, periodic working sessions with the Program Managers focused on their particular programs. Monthly joint meetings of the five Program Managers were held as well.

Service-Oriented Management at Core Data

The Core Data program, led by Nagore Bilbao, is a cornerstone for most of the bank's projects and services. All their clients expect predictability as well as fast, on-time delivery. Ensuring this requires a good understanding of the services they provide, the patterns of the demand, and the team's capability.

The types of work they are developing are as follows:

- Information requests
- Incident resolution
- Business as Usual (recurring requests)
- Project work (involvement in projects)
- Change requests

They updated their kanban board to reflect the work types and the corresponding workflow phases (see Figure 4.4).

The concept of flow, the benefits of limiting WIP, and of finishing work before starting something else were new for these teams. These concepts had to be frequently explained, rehearsed, and reiterated. Still, the big challenge was collecting data about their demand and capability. People interpreted this

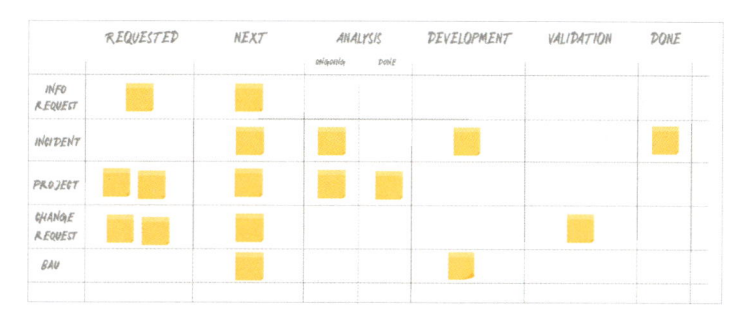

Figure 4.4   Core Data kanban board

data collection as a new means of control, one not aligned with Agile values. Instead, people saw it as a harsh intervention that threatened their autonomy.

In several meetings with the teams, Nagore promised that all collected data would be used only to obtain a better understanding of their processes so as to improve the services they provide. She kept her promises.

Gaining the trust of the workforce was a key factor in the success of this initiative.

They started collecting the following data in a document that came to be known as "Nagore's Excel":

- Type of work
- Customer who requested it (area of the bank that initiated the request)
- Date and time of receiving a work item
- Date and time of starting work on the work item
- Date and time of delivering the work item
- Amount of time the work item is being processed by another department
- Person who works on the work item (in case a further analysis is necessary)

While it may seem a trivial task, collecting good quality data takes time and effort. Three months into collecting the data, Nagore and Teodora did the first data analysis.

One discovery was that part of the demand was in fact false demand, that is, work they should not do. That led to the first update of the policies—namely, clarifying what services they as a business unit were meant to provide and who their customers were.

The data also revealed that delivery times were long because work items were blocked for extended periods. So, "blocked time and causation" became the next data point to be collected.

Since then, Nagore and Alberto Blanco, in his role of Process Owner, analyze the data monthly and then present the results to everyone in the Program, including those from supplier companies. These meetings have brought several positive effects:

- Gaining trust that all collected data is used for improving the service
- Strengthening the understanding of the process (demand, effects of WIP, and benefits of focusing on finishing work before starting new work), service orientation, and using data for improving the flow
- Obtaining feedback from people directly involved in doing the work and creating unity around the goal of the initiative

Nagore was pleased that they had developed the capability to manage based on data, not on perceptions, which helps them foresee future needs and resolve blockages due to dependencies on other teams in a fast and simple manner.

In mid-2018, the physical boards and the Excel spreadsheet were exchanged for an electronic tool. This transition required some adaptations of work practices but introduced some benefits related to automatic data collection.

By this point, there was a good understanding of the key aspects of the demand and capability of the program:

- Who the customers were
- What they requested
- Patterns of arrival and distribution of demand per type and period of time
- Distribution of the delivered work items per type and period of time
- Distribution of the delivery time (lead time) per type of work or service
- Blockage time distribution

This understanding of their work processes allowed them to define their first improvement initiatives, namely:

- Establish acceptable and reachable service levels
- Reduce the time spent in Agile ceremonies
- Reduce delivery time, starting with reducing blocked time and trimming the tail of the delivery time distribution

Alberto was tracking these objectives biweekly. Service levels were defined, and time spent in ceremonies reached an acceptable level (see Figure 4.5).

Reducing delivery time is an ongoing process, but it has improved. The Core Data teams made great progress in 2018. They evolved from workers who believed that data

Service Levels Baseline

Type of work	Demand (per week)	Capability (per week)	Lead time (days)
Information requests	5–20	2–19	0–2
Incidents	2–12	1–10	1–15
Change requests	1–11	5–13	1–13

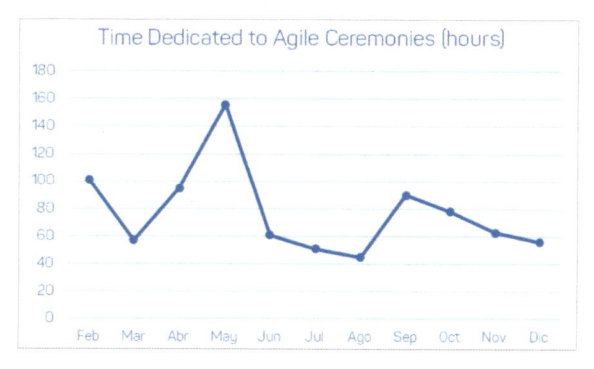

Intervals with 80% of confidence

Figure 4.5 Service Levels baseline and time dedicated to Agile ceremonies

collection was a means of corporate control to workers who understand what services they provide and what workflows produce them; additionally, they've become workers who take an active role in improving the process. In the autumn of 2018, Nagore's teams were proud to share their experience with other BAU teams within their own and other business areas.

Service Orientation in Product Development

A common misconception is that Kanban is appropriate for services but not for product development. Nowadays, however, product development is rather embedded in complementary services. Think about buying a product from an online or physical store, going to a pizza restaurant, obtaining a report from public agency, and so on. Do you buy the product or the service? Can you get the product without the service?

Service orientation in product development is about applying the same thinking as in service delivery to the product development process. Some parts of the process are without a doubt services, for example, revision, approval, and validation. Others are services that deliver a part of the product, for example, customer requirement specifications, implemented features, and user documentation.

Therefore, a product development process can be seen as a sequence of services provided by groups of individuals with necessary qualifications. Delivering a valuable product in a predictable, timely, and sustainable manner depends on the proper coordination of related services, hence the policies for managing these services. This is summarized in the Kanban Service Delivery Principles, as shown in the sidebar on the facing page.

In the second quarter of 2018, Elixabet Osa, Program Manager of the Rentability Program, started using a simple portfolio kanban board for managing the projects in her program (see Figure 4.6). As a Program Manager accountable for the results of three projects, she needed to see the essential information about her projects' status in a single

Figure 4.6 Simple portfolio kanban board for the Rentability program

place. Moreover, she wanted to align the overall view of work in the program to enable product owners to make better prioritization decisions. She wanted to see the entire program functioning as a well-synchronized entity.

Some of the teams providing service to the development of these projects were in Madrid, so the portfolio kanban board was located there. The synchronization meetings were held biweekly in Madrid or via Webex, exchanging photos of the portfolio board. For the first time in their practice, the Product Owners were exposing the status of their projects and were openly discussing the impediments they were experiencing and ideas for possible resolutions. The Sponsor of the projects, Patricia Bueno, was participating in many of these meetings too.

> **Kanban Service Delivery Principles**
>
> Your organization is a network of interdependent services with policies that determine its behavior. Therefore:
> - Understand and focus on the customer's needs and expectations.
> - Manage the work; let workers self-organize around it.
> - Regularly review the network and its policies to improve outcomes.

Running biweekly meetings involving three levels of management (Sponsor, Program Manager, and Product Owners) was a new experience, and initially it was quite time consuming, lasting about three hours. However, they were committed to reaching a shared, deeper understanding of the development process and the dependencies between the projects; their goal was to achieve a steady flow of value and aligned prioritization of features in all the projects. Lorena Caaveiro's support as an internal coach and facilitator of this initiative in Madrid was essential to meeting that goal.

A few months into the process, the group realized that these tough-in-the-beginning meetings created a real sense of belonging to a team at the Program level, which was helping them to progress further, resolve blocking issues and dependencies faster, allow joint planning of projects, and come to consensus on common objectives for the program.

They also started collecting work-related metrics, such as the number of features of a certain size (S, M, or L) that were developed in a two-week period. This facilitated better planning of projects as well as of upstream work prior to delivery commitment. This information allowed them to focus on preparing just enough feature specifications to feed the next two-week period.

By the end of 2018, the portfolio management of the Rentability program transitioned to an electronic tool. This change had its own challenges, but in general, it facilitated the visualization and management of dependencies between the portfolio board and the project teams' boards, as well as efficient portfolio meetings. The synchronization meetings now take only about an hour.

The other three programs started applying the same practices for managing their BAU and projects. The experience gained in the Core Data and Rentability programs facilitated successful implementation of Kanban practices in each one of the contexts.

In December 2018, the first actions for integrated management of projects across three programs—Core Data, Rentability, and Reporting Network—took place.

Conclusions

In only one year, two programs of the Finance area of BBVA have evolved from team-focused management to service-oriented entities with deep understanding of their real capability and the types of services they are delivering to their customers.

Quantitative Understanding of Demand and Capability and Related Further Improvements

Core Data has gained a quantitative understanding of their demand, the patterns of its arrival, and the ranges of delivery times they can commit to, by type of service provided. Furthermore, they reached a more profound comprehension of the causes of blockages in their workflows and their management routines. This knowledge allowed them to carry out four initiatives to improve their fitness for purpose.

Flow-Oriented Project Portfolio Management

The Rentability program is managing successfully the project portfolio for the area using shared policies and prioritization criteria. They also plan multiple projects based on a quantitative understanding of their capability to deliver product features.

Flexibility in Managing Projects and BAU

Both programs report higher flexibility in managing their BAU and multiple projects as well as stronger unity and commitment by the team members.

Three more programs, which started after Core Data and Rentability, have evolved from team-focused to flow-oriented management of their BAU and projects. The approach taken using the Kanban Maturity Model has proven to be repeatable.

Managing Flow across Programs

For the first time at BBVA, an initiative has been started to manage wider, end-to-end workflows involving teams across different programs. The Kanban Method and the Kanban Maturity Model have been used for guiding this evolution with full compliance within the Agile Transformation initiative of the bank. Referring to the model, this progress can be described as advancing from ML1: Team-Focused to entering ML3: Fit-for-Purpose organization (although it is not yet completely stable).

Leadership

The leadership and dedication of several people has been an additional key factor in achieving the result. Juan José Gil, Agile Ambassador for the area, looked for pragmatic guidance to boost and facilitate the adoption of Agile in the Programs. He followed closely all activities of the program managers, contributing his valuable understanding of their organizational context and thus smoothing the progress of the entire initiative.

Nagore Bilbao and Elixabet Osa introduced the customer-driven, service-oriented approach to managing work in their programs. Gaining individuals' trust and overcoming team members' perceptions that the new practices were intended to tighten control and their fears that the collected data might be used against them was a serious challenge. Both Nagore and Elixabet worked closely and transparently with their teams, involving them in reaching understanding of the problems in the workflow and making decisions based on the collected data.

In mid-2018 Nagore and her teams developed four improvement initiatives based on analyzing the data from their services. They are currently working on them.

The entire initiative has been actively supported by the Discipline Leader, Luís Garín. He aspires to see MIS as an organization that consistently and sustainably delivers high-quality results on time. In early 2019, he introduced an operations review for the five Programs, at which they review issues and risks in the wider flow, beyond the team level.

The overall experience has demonstrated that introducing service orientation and flow thinking is key for increasing Agility at the program level and for allowing an organization to pursue aims such as bettering time-to-market, adaptability to changes in demand, transparency, collaboration, and continuous communication between business areas.

Fifteen Months Later

By the end of 2018 the Core Data team had a consistent process and improved significantly the reliability and quality of their service. However, as is typical for BAU in the banking sector, there were many other teams delivering highly specialized services. In addition, all the services are deeply interrelated, and they must respond to a large number of customer requests, delivering precise information within a very short time, as well as meeting regulatory deadlines.

The maturity of the entire organization needed to be improved. Therefore, in the beginning of 2019, the head of Strategy, Solution Development, and Business Execution of the Finance area requested that all thirty-three BAU teams be introduced to Kanban and gradually improve the efficiency of their processes.

Resuming our coaching role, the next months were dedicated to delivering hands-on training to all teams, coaching them on adapting and adopting appropriate practices for managing work at a team level, working transparently and collaboratively, introducing flow metrics, and developing a proper data analysis tool, as well as helping teams analyze data and make decisions about how to improve their workflow.

Soon it became clear that working at a team level was not enough, because a number of processes required effective and on-time coordination between different service teams that belonged to different disciplines (area units). Under the leadership of the head of Business Execution (BEx), the first end-to-end service, composed of three teams from three different disciplines, started to operate. They visualize the end-to-end workflow on a common kanban board, they defined and now use explicit policies for managing their joint work, conduct weekly coordination meetings (Workflow Kanban Meeting), and recently started analyzing their end-to-end flow data. Defining the policies for coordinating the end-to-end process is key at this point in the evolution of the entire area. These policies guide them to manage effectively the dependencies among the teams across the borders of the disciplines they belong to. This increases their agility and improves their capability to deliver higher quality services faster, without affecting the organization's structure, and hence, avoids resistance. Strengthening the relationships among the teams has also increased the level of trust in the organization, creating a resilient network of services capable of responding quickly to customers' varying expectations.

Initially, the head of BEx was acting in the role of Flow Manager. Later, this team of teams decided that the Process Owner of the dominating process in the end-to-end service should take this responsibility. This decision was another step further in the development of an Agile organization that stimulates the professional growth of the Process Owner role without creating resistence to the suggested change.

An additional objective for this end-to-end service team was to define the operational model to be used by other similar processes in the area. In the beginning of 2020, despite complications due to the start of the coronavirus crisis in Spain, the second end-to-end process was launched.

In May of 2020, the Core Data team reported the following data about the improvements they were conducting in 2019:

- 28 percent reduction in management costs (time dedicated to Agile ceremonies)
- 25 percent reduction in lead time of information requests
- 17 percent reduction in lead time of incident resolution

From a KMM perspective, the organization as a whole is currently working on consolidating Maturity Level 2, with a clear objective to continue optimizing their workflow and introducing defined KPIs for the delivered services.

The journey continues. . . .

Part II | Culture

5 Culture in Low-Maturity Organizations

SCOPE	LEVEL	CULTURAL FOCUS
Task	0 Oblivious	Individualism
Deliverable	1 Team-Focused	Individual Heroics
Product/Service	2 Customer-Driven	Managerial Heroics
Product lines/Shared services	3 Fit-for-Purpose	(Customer) Purpose
Product lines/Services Portfolio	4 Risk-Hedged	Unity & Alignment
Business Lines Portfolio	5 Market Leader	Pursuit of Perfection
Business Lines Portfolio	6 Built for Survival	Reinvention

Figure 5.1 Cultural focus by maturity level

The seven levels of the Kanban Maturity Model are shown in Figure 5.1. For each level, we have identified a set of cultural values that are necessary to enable improvement and achievement of the organizational capabilities described in Chapter 1. This chapter describes the values necessary to enable the lower Maturity Levels 0 through 2. At low maturity, the culture focus is on employees—relieving them of overburdening, removing unnecessary stress from their environment, and giving meaning and purpose to their work.

These are core enablers of deeper maturity later. The Kanban Maturity Model focuses on employees first. The premise is that happy employees, appropriately led and motivated, will work to make customers happy. The corollary—that it is impossible to sustain adequate customer satisfaction without happy and well-motivated employees—is assumed to be equally true.[1]

Maturity Level 0 – Oblivious

At Maturity Level 0 there is no social cohesion; the organization is simply a loosely affiliated group of individuals who work on their own and largely seek to fulfill only their own goals, perform their own tasks, and have personal responsibility for their own performance, fulfillment, happiness, and development. The organization is said to be oblivious to the need for more formal organization and cooperation. The key cultural characteristic, as shown in Figure 2, is a focus on "self" and a distinct lack of cooperation, collaboration, or altruism. Individuals spend time pondering, "Who am I?" They are satisfied and comfortable in their position if their job description and the function they perform closely match their internal self-image—their own concept of who they are. They do not need or seek to ask, "Who are *we*?" The larger organization is of little concern to them other than as a source of economic support through their regular salary.

Although it sounds implausible that real businesses might be organized in this fashion, we have observed several in our case study literature and in anecdotal reports from our global community and our training clients from around the world.

In such an organization, there are no working standards or defined methods and procedures. Each individual has their own way of doing things. There are no real governance policies or processes for requesting and authorizing work. When a customer wants something, for example, a few new web pages for the company's public website, they simply lift the phone and call their favorite IT worker and ask them to take care of it. In a Maturity Level 0 organization, every customer has their "pet."

At Maturity Level 0, there is essentially no social capital: there is little or no trust between the individuals with respect to the work they do, and they do not collaborate. The development of organizational trust, or social capital, is essential to achieving organizational maturity and the superior economic results that go with it. Social capital begins to develop at Maturity Level 1 with individuals organized socially into small teams.

As shown in Figure 5.2, the important cultural value at Maturity Level 0 is achievement. A value is not unique to just one level; rather, we anticipate for it to continue and to be embraced more thoroughly at deeper levels.

---

1. Some readers will recognize this position of "employees come first" as a core mantra of successful billionaire Richard Branson and his leadership of the Virgin Group empire. We believe that Richard Branson is truly a Maturity Level 6 leader and that the right thing often comes naturally to him. The Virgin Group is therefore an archetype for a large-scale, high-maturity business built for long-term survival.

Achievement

A sense of achievement is important for an individual's happiness and fulfillment. We would expect that an organization that embraces achievement as a value would recognize it and celebrate it. We might expect to see evidence signaling achievement such as awards, certificates, trophies, and their like on display. However, on a simple day-to-day basis, some visual indicator showing work recently completed, for example, a metaphorical trophy cabinet—a collection of tickets off to the right-hand side of a individual kanban board—would be evidence that the individual recognizes achievement and the importance of acknowledging it for their own wellbeing and effectiveness.

At Maturity Level 0, there may be little public display or recognition for achievement: a individual kanban board may be hidden in the privacy of a cubicle or an office; it need not be on public display. Individuals do not necessarily seek social status or social reward or publicly take pride in their achievements. The overt display of achievement, recognition and reward for achievement, and taking pride in achievement should emerge at:

Maturity Level 1 – Team-Focused

At Maturity Level 1, small social groups—of two to perhaps twelve as an upper limit—exist to work collaboratively on the same tasks or similar work. They can be perceived as offering a service, even if only in a very narrow sense.

With a sense of identity as a team—an understanding of "who we are"—social capital begins to develop. See Figure 5.3 on the next page for a mapping of focus, trust, and leadership attributes to each maturity level. Managing identity and helping an organization to understand "who we are" is a crucial building block to greater success. Identity is a foundational enabler of the development of wider organizational trust. In his book *Identity*, Francis Fukuyama describes its importance succinctly, although the text addresses geopolitical and national concerns rather than those of businesses, non-profits, or

Organizational Maturity		VALUES
0	Oblivious	· Achievement
1	Team-Focused	· Collaboration · Taking Initiative · Transparency
2	Customer-Driven	· Acts of Leadership · Customer Awareness · Evolutionary Change · Flow · Narrative · Respect · Understanding (internal)
3	Fit-for-Purpose	· Agreement · Balance · Customer Service · Fitness for Purpose · Leadership at All Levels · Short-term Results · Understanding (external) · Unity & Alignment
4	Risk-Hedged	· Business Focus · Competition · Customer Intimacy · Data-driven Decision Making · Deeper Balance · Fairness · Leadership Development · Regulatory Compliance
5	Market Leader	· Equality of Opportunity · Experimentation · Perfectionism · Social Mobility
6	Built for Survival	· Congruence · Long-term Survival · Tolerance & Diversity

Figure 5.2   Values attributed to each maturity level

civil-service organizations. We have edited the following passage to remove the political context, for clarity.

> "A ... function of ... identity is to promote a wide radius of trust. Trust acts like a lubricant that facilitates ... economic exchange. ... Trust is based on what has been called social capital, that is, the ability to cooperate with other people based on informal norms and shared values."[2]

When one individual does something trustworthy for another, they feel a sense of achievement and a sense of accomplishment through the release of dopamine within their brain. The neurotransmitter for trust is oxytocin.[3] The other individual, who observed and perhaps received the benefit of a trustworthy act—for example, a task completed with high quality as promised—experiences the release of oxytocin, and they both feel good as a result (this is discussed in more detail in Chapter 18, Why Do People Resist Change?).

With teams, we can now anticipate that individuals seek status and recognition and, in time, a sense of personal pride emerges. We can also anticipate that the team seeks recognition for its efforts within the wider organization and a sense of pride in the team—the team is a social entity in and of itself. Individuals feel peer pressure not to let the team down, and the team develops its own set of values and expected behaviors. Maturity Level 1 is the land of individual heroics. Individuals make heroic effort in order to win recognition for the team and status within the team as reward for their own efforts.

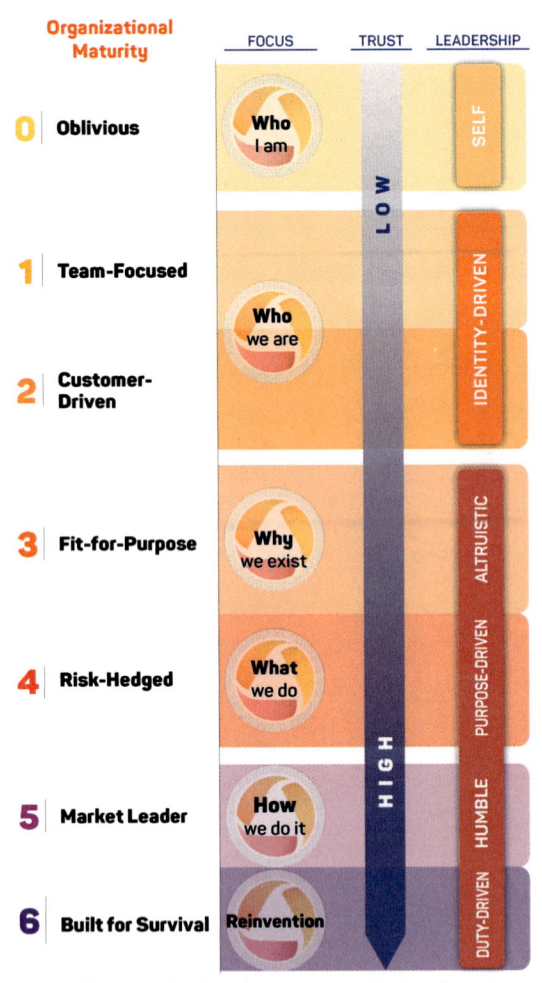

Figure 5.3 Focus, trust, and leadership attributes of each maturity level

---

2. Francis Fukuyama, *Identity: The Demand for Dignity and the Politics of Resentment* (New York: Farrar, Straus and Giroux, 2018).
3. https://www.scientificamerican.com/article/the-neurobiology-of-trust/

The dominant cultural behavior at Maturity Level 1 is that of the heroic individual contributor. In his book, *Quality Software Management* (volume 1), Jerry Weinberg labeled Maturity Level 1 as the "hero programmer" level. You know that you are in a Maturity Level 1 organization when your business openly advertises for a Ninja Javascript developer and describes the workplace as a dynamic environment.

At Maturity Level 1, any processes, procedures, or methods are at best emergent; there is that dynamic environment from the job advertisement, and there is little cooperation between teams. Teams work, and are measured and rewarded, in isolation. Sociologically, the behavior is tribal—each team is its own tribe. Tribal identities may emerge with teams taking on names, artifacts, and rituals unique to their own team. They may decorate their area of the building to mark their territory and define a tribal homeland. Although there may be affiliation or adherence to a wider organizational creed or process framework, for example, Scrum, each team has its own unique identity and markers.

Starting at Maturity Level 1, we might expect to see celebrations and rituals as a part of meetings, where individual or team achievements and those attributed to larger-scale organizational units are recognized.

Several new values are needed to enable Maturity Level 1: collaboration (within the team), taking (individual) initiative, and transparency (within the team and to some limited degree outside of the team).

Collaboration

Collaboration implies that individuals work together as a team to achieve a common goal. In fact, the definitions of collaboration and team are effectively mutually dependent: to be a team requires collaboration and to collaborate effectively requires a team. Generally, collaboration is seen as a deeper form of cooperation—a more worthy form of cooperation. Cooperation implies that humans work on their own but in a manner that is compatible with the work of others and may enable a shared outcome or a common goal. A value stream in which each function in a chain is performed separately can be viewed as a cooperative chain; there isn't collaboration—one function does not assist another—they merely do their own part and pass the work on for the next function to do its part. Strangely, our observation is that collaboration appears at the team level before effective cooperation appears between teams to deliver a product or service. There could be several reasons for this: the scale involving more people makes it more complicated to achieve cooperation at a wider level than collaboration at a team level; the greater leadership required at a higher level to drive collaboration at a larger scale and effectively form a much larger team; or the metrics and incentives used focus too heavily on the individual or small, easily identified and contained groups of individuals, namely a team. We don't see the emergence of cooperation across teams until Maturity Level 2. The degree of difficulty is higher, and it takes greater leadership and more developed managerial skills.

An organization must encourage and value collaboration to foster resilient and robust teams capable of producing a variety of work with consistent quality. To do this, it must encourage sharing and altruistic behavior from individuals to other team members. Collaboration is what truly separates Maturity Level 1 from Maturity Level 0. When a small group has an identity but they consistently work alone as individuals, even if the work is of a similar nature, they are not truly a team. The Maturity Level 1 sub-level Transition captures this concept. We have seen it in case studies and believe it is a necessary transitional step. A small group of individuals with a shared identity are most likely being managed by focusing on people and resource efficiency or utilization rather than embracing the Kanban service delivery principle of "manage the work and let the workers self-organize around it." In Kanban, we want you to measure flow efficiency and customer-valued items such as work-in-progress, lead time, and delivery rate. In a service-oriented organization, it's important to care more about the where and when of the customer-requested work and less about the where and when of the workers.

We must encourage managers and team leaders to see themselves as serving the delivery of products or services to the customer. Often, we find that department managers and team leads believe their role is to best match tasks with available workers, optimizing for efficiency based on the skills and experience of the individual. As a truly service-oriented approach, the Kanban Method discourages this. Instead, we need managers to manage work and to encourage a broad range of skills to be developed and shared by most or all team members. We require that individuals collaborate by sharing their skills and developing those skills in others.

In general, a business needs to shift away from an inward, individual focus and encourage altruistic behavior. Initially, this is altruism toward fellow team members, and as it progresses to higher, deeper levels of maturity, this altruism must grow in scope and scale.

Collaboration builds trust. The act of collaborating with someone—getting to know them closely, understanding their skills and competencies, and seeing them act altruistically to help you—releases oxytocin and strengthens trust between team members. Collaboration is key to enabling trust, and greater trust encourages greater collaboration—a virtuous cycle, where one reinforces the other and so forth.

Evidence for collaboration can exist in both the positive sense—demonstrating collaborative behavior—and in the negative sense—demonstrating failure to make the shift to service-oriented and altruistic behavior. Positive evidence might include personal goals and incentives to share knowledge and pass on skills to other team members. Negative evidence would include individual utilization and resource-efficiency metrics or stack-ranking staff in annual reviews. If perverse incentives exist to hoard information or selfishly protect skills, the organization clearly fails to embrace collaboration as a value.

Taking Initiative

For some readers, it may seem strange that we have included taking initiative as an explicit value, and you may wonder how anything ever gets done without it. However, others may recognize that they've grown up in a culture in which people wait to be told what to do, an "ask permission" culture in which there are long delays while permission is sought before action occurs. Instead, we want to foster an action-oriented culture in the name of better service delivery. "If you see something, do something about it!" If an individual sees an opportunity to take action that they know will help the team, and they know that they have the skills and experience to accomplish it, they should take the initiative and "just do it!"

Taking initiative is a degenerate form of "leadership by example," which appears later, at higher maturity levels. For example, a mother, tired of her messy teenagers, takes initiative and cleans up after them. We all recognize that this isn't the ideal behavior; the teenagers, already naturally lazy, may now take it for granted that their mother will clean up after them. However, there may be times when the tactical choice just to do something about it is preferred over the more strategic and long-term fix of changing the teenagers' behavior to keep their bedrooms and the living room tidy.

It is common in fast-food restaurants or cafés to see a sign reminding staff to "clean as you go." This recognizes that it is almost always easier and faster to clean equipment immediately after use than to do it later; and equally, it is important to realize that no one else is there to clean up—every staff member must be responsible for the cleanliness of the working environment.

Evidence for taking initiative can exist in the negative sense as a lack of direction and requesting permission, as well as in the positive sense—acting with empowerment, seeking forgiveness for actions taken with the best intentions, and a general lack of the accumulation of unpleasant or boring tasks. We may also see explicit evidence that employees take on tasks in the name of good customer service even though it isn't their explicit role or within their job description to do so. We may also see evidence that taking initiative is recognized and rewarded, and more extreme examples may have become part of the narrative and identity of the organization, such as stories shared with new employees as part of the onboarding process.

Transparency

Valuing transparency means valuing information availability over information hiding. At a team level, transparency means that everyone on the team knows what others are working on. This transparency may extend to the manager and to people external to the team, potentially including customers. The control of information and its flow is a source of power in organizations and social groups, so valuing transparency explicitly undermines this source of power. Consequently, transparency can meet with resistance if individuals, usually managers, find that transparency has undermined their source of power and therefore undermined their self-esteem and their sense of self. We have seen anecdotes of, for example, the vice president of a project-management organization (PMO) at a Southern California–based internet company ripping a portfolio kanban board from a wall early one morning and trashing it. Why would a VP of a PMO not want such a board on a wall? Why would he feel motivated to destroy it? Because transparency eliminates his ability to control information and to control the narrative. He cannot lie to his superiors about progress on projects if the information is freely available.

Hence, valuing transparency embraces the idea that the organization must face up to its reality, however ugly that picture may be. Transparency is about pragmatism and action orientation rather than wishful thinking and deferring action in the hope that problems magically fix themselves or simply go away altogether. Transparency and action orientation go hand in hand.

Transparency increases social capital. You no longer need to trust that someone is working on something if the information is freely available. You no longer need to trust that someone is capable of making good decisions if the decision framework they use, and information about their actual decisions, are transparently available. Transparency removes uncertainty from the environment and improves the trustworthiness of that environment. Social capital measures the trustworthiness of a social group or a social entity such as a business.

The ability to value transparency requires leadership development coupled with the development of management skills and competence. No one need fear transparency when they have the skills, competence, and confidence to "do something about it!"

What we aren't saying here is that all information should be available to everyone. Such a rule could overwhelm people with data and render them paralyzed if they are swamped and unable to interpret what they are seeing. Equally, some information should be hidden for regulatory and compliance reasons or hidden in order to maintain confidence and security. Recognize also that some information may be seen as humiliating and affect the dignity of individuals or teams and consequently their ability to function effectively. Leaders need to choose carefully when ritual (and potentially public) humiliation may be necessary, either to rebuild trust or as the correct motivator for change. So, our directive that your organization embrace transparency as a core value isn't a blanket demand to make all information available to everyone; rather, it is a request to share as much information as possible to enable an ever more trustworthy organization capable of taking action faster and more effectively.

Evidence of valuing transparency is easy to find and easy to measure—information is either available or it is hidden. Policies are either explicit or they aren't. Values are either explicit or they aren't. Decision frameworks and information about how decisions are made—the reasoning behind them and the trade-offs they require—are either explicit or they aren't. People are either recognized and rewarded for being transparent—such as honestly reporting progress on a task or the existence of an impediment or blocker, or admitting that they lack the skills or experience to complete a piece of work—or they aren't.

Maturity Level 2 - Customer-Driven

At Maturity Level 2, teams begin to cooperate with other teams on a shared goal of delivering a requested product or service to a customer. In Kanban literature this cooperation amongst teams on customer-requested, and hence, customer-valued, work is referred to as a workflow. In other business and process-improvement literature it may be referred to as a value stream or value chain. The main cultural change that emerges at Maturity Level 2 is the recognition that there is a customer, that the customer has requested something they value, and that serving that customer requires cooperation across teams or within an organizational unit potentially significantly larger than just one team.

This understanding develops a shift in the management's thinking from "my team has done their job" (defensive behavior) to "what can my team do so that our team-of-teams can deliver the job to the customer as soon as possible?" (cooperative behavior).

The dominant cultural behavior at Maturity Level 2 is that of the heroic manager who whips and cajoles work to flow through the chain of teams and ensures that an important customer gets what they requested within their expectations. You know that you are in a Maturity Level 2 organization when customers request and trust specific managers to take care of their needs. When customers have their pet manager, the business is unlikely to be higher than Maturity Level 2.

For Maturity Level 2 to function effectively and for there to be a possibility of reaching Maturity Level 3, there must now be trust between teams, not merely within a team. The behavior may be one of cooperation rather than deeper collaboration, and there isn't necessarily any expectation that one team offers altruistic help to other teams. Such assistance may be impractical when the skills required are quite distinct.

Francis Fukuyama helps us to understand the role of identity and the need for a wider group identity at the service delivery or product unit level in order to build the trust needed to encourage team cooperation to enable flow and successful customer delivery. Continuing from the previous quote,[4] and without edits:

> "Identity groups promote trust among their members, but social capital often remains limited to the narrow in-group. Indeed, strong identities often decrease trust between in- and out-group members. Societies thrive on trust, but they need the widest possible radius of trust to do well."

---

4. Francis Fukuyama, *Identity: The Demand for Dignity and the Politics of Resentment* (New York: Farrar, Straus and Giroux, 2018).

This helps us to understand the role of leaders and how they must foster strong, superordinate identities at various layers within an organization. Individuals need to be able to feel part of a team and to know their place and their role within the team, but they must also feel part of a service delivery or product organization, and part of a wider business unit, and perhaps that they are members of an entire corporate tribe, and that all of these contribute in part to their sense of self and their professional identity and are not in any way conflicting.

Several new values are needed to enable Maturity Level 2: acts of leadership, customer awareness, evolutionary change, flow, narrative, respect, and understanding. We examine each of these in turn.

Acts of Leadership

It might seem strange to value acts of leadership. However, we contend that if you don't value leadership, and explicitly encourage it, you'll see very little of it. Leadership is a core ingredient of evolutionary change. As we explain later,[5] there are three elements needed to drive evolutionary change: a stressor, a reflection mechanism, and an act of leadership.

The now-famous cartoon from the front cover of *Kanban: Successful Evolutionary Change for Your Technology Business* (Figure 5.4) contains all three elements. It is clear from the tickets on the board and the comments by the first three characters that there is some stress in their environment—things are not running smoothly. The Kanban Meeting taking place acts as the reflection mechanism. The fourth character observes the situation and states, "Let's do something about it!" This is an act of leadership.

Figure 5.4 Cartoon from the original cover of *Kanban: Successful Evolutionary Change for Your Technology Business*

---

5. See Chapter 17, Evolutionary Change Model, for more on this.

Note that this goes beyond taking initiative as seen in Maturity Level 1. Here, this character calls the others to action to discuss and implement changes. Taking initiative can manifest as individual heroics or martyrdom; an act of leadership catalyzes action from a group.

An act of leadership always entails some personal risk. It is less risky simply to say and do nothing. In the cartoon, if the fourth character said nothing, the collective group might shrug their shoulders and grumble, "Oh well, back to work then." Nothing ever gets better; they are condemned to a life as victims, overburdened and unsupported. Leadership can be expressed several ways: by signaling, by inspiration, by example, and by command. The personal risk to the individual rises with each type.

Leadership by signaling can mean doing and saying nothing when you see some failure; for example, an auto manufacturer has developed an algorithm to cheat at an emissions test. You observe this and know it to be unethical and potentially illegal. You do nothing. This signals agreement or, at least, acquiescence. Signaling carries little risk to the individual. Signaling is the most passive leadership type, and its effects are likely to take the longest to appear.

Leadership by inspiration requires a leader to say or do something evocative; the goal is to engage people emotionally and motivate them to aspire to a higher level of achievement or to undertake things they don't believe they can do. The uncertainty for individuals in the group rises, and consequently the risk that they will fail to follow—or worse, proactively try to derail—the initiative increases. The risk to the leader's status and power is therefore greater than that of merely signaling. Leadership by inspiration produces results more quickly than signaling does. Although the personal risk to the leader is higher, the payoff is likely to be greater in situations where the cost of delay is higher.

Leadership by example requires a leader to assume more personal risk by taking direct action themself in the hope that others will follow. What if they don't? The leader's status and power will be dramatically undermined. Leadership by example is most useful and necessary when there is great urgency and some action is needed immediately. The leader needs to show initiative and personal "skin in the game" by taking action themself. In doing so, they compel others to follow and copy that action. Leadership by example sets a standard for the group. It defines the group's values through action. It creates direct emotional pressure on group members to conform by copying the leader's behavior.

Finally, leadership by command carries the greatest risk. Military officers are taught to use command sparingly and generally only at times when the cost of delay may result in serious consequences such as the death or endangerment of troops or civilians under their care. Leadership by command using authority vested through positional power, rank, or experience is powerful and fast acting. However, what happens if the group defies the leader? What happens if the group were to mutiny rather than follow the command? The loss of status and power would be immediate and drastic.

Great leadership starts with signaling, motivates through inspiration, escalates by direct example, and resorts to command only when there is no time to use the first three. We should be able to find evidence of all four styles: signals and signaling, symbols and symbolic actions (discussed in Chapter 8, Culture Hacking); narratives of motivation and inspiration; taking initiative, with others following the example and establishing new behavior norms; and explicitly, by command with specific records of memos or orders directing action.

Because acts of leadership carry personal risk for the individual, we need to signal that psychological safety exists and encourage risk taking by making acts of leadership an explicit value. It should not only be okay to suggest that we "do something about it"; rather, it should be unacceptable that we simply shrug our shoulders, moan and grumble, and play the victim of circumstance.

Customer Awareness

Maturity Level 1 is a world of siloed teams who work in isolation and have little regard for who comes before or after them in a service delivery workflow. To advance to Maturity Level 2, an organization needs to break down this siloed behavior and encourage cooperation across teams in the workflow. To do this, it must give each team a purpose greater than serving their own productivity. It must help them to understand that their work contributes to a greater goal—serving a customer and serving them with a specific product or service. Ideally, team members need to understand not only who the customer is and what they've requested, but also why they've requested it and what business risks they are managing. The latter is important for understanding the motivation for the customer's expectations. These are all elements addressed in the demand analysis step of the systems thinking approach to introducing Kanban (STATIK), discussed in Appendix A, The Kanban Method.

Being able to identify the customer, their request, and their needs and motivation for the request takes time and energy. Communicating the context for team-level and individual tasks as part of the broader customer context also takes time and energy. As such, raising customer awareness carries a cost. However, it also enables a huge benefit: it motivates cooperation in the name of good customer service. It gives a wider group of people a higher purpose. A business must value the impact of customer awareness so that it commits to the cost—and takes the time and makes the effort—for everyone to comprehend the greater value of their individual and team's work.

Evidence that an enterprise values customer awareness should be easy to find. At Maturity Level 2, the work item types should reflect customer requests. At this level, anyone in the workflow should be able to describe the customer-valued work items. This information should be designed into Kanban boards or the tickets on the board. At Maturity Level 3, the customer should be transparent, and some expectations such as a lead time expectation should be explicit. At Maturity Level 4, there should be intimate understanding of the customer's context, and fitness criteria should be explicit as part of a class of service for that customer or work type.

Evolutionary Change

With the Kanban Method, we explicitly embrace evolutionary change rather than a traditional approach with a defined or designed process or workflow definition. The Kanban Method's change principles require you to "start with what you do now." We value and respect what you do now. Some aspects of what you do now are good and should be honored and preserved. At the same time, the organization recognizes that it has room for improvement and that some aspects of its methods of working and decision making need to change.

Equally, we recognize that evolving in an experimental fashion—identifying opportunities for improvement and trying new ways of working based on models—is likely to produce a uniquely tailored solution that is highly resilient in your environment. We believe that your situation is unique and that no prescription from a textbook can adequately account for your circumstances. Equally, we believe that no process expert is smart enough to play the grand designer and imagine every circumstance and outcome that may occur in your environment as you go forward. Grand designs are inherently brittle and fail to cope when external circumstances change.

We believe that fit-for-purpose processes emerge as the consequence of evolutionary forces in an environment. An organizational design will be emergent and will adapt to changing circumstances, but only if the organization has been wired with inherent adaptive capability. An enterprise invests in the Kanban Method and uses the Kanban Maturity Model to guide that adoption because it believes that its resilience, robustness, and long-term survival as an organization depend upon such an evolutionary change capability.

Evidence that an organization values evolutionary change is in its definition of basic policies for coordinating the work of different service teams, conducting Flow Reviews, and taking actions to understand the process and improve flow. At higher maturity levels, it is that there is clear support for core elements of the Kanban Method such as Service Delivery Review, Operations Review, and Risk Review. Additionally, we think about change and improvement through the lens of creating stress through the deliberate introduction of stressors, but we never condone consciously introducing a stressor without enabling a suitable reflection mechanism via one of the Kanban Cadences. Finally, we have clear evidence of acts of leadership and emergent changes occurring as a consequence of stress reported during a reflection meeting, such as Operations Review, and someone making an intervention as a consequence.

Flow

Flow may also seem like a strange thing to value as an organization. However, embracing the Kanban service delivery principle to "manage the work and let the people self-organize around it," then the pursuit of an efficient flow of work becomes natural. When an organization recognizes that lead time and timely and/or predictable delivery are almost always customer fitness criteria, then it recognizes that it improves the optionality in its processes by improving flow. High flow efficiency enables it to manage risk better and produce superior economic results.

Delay is often the largest contributor to customer dissatisfaction. Impediments to flow result in failure to be fit-for-purpose. Flow is key to improving the management of knowledge work and professional services. If work is delayed, waiting for any reason, then it isn't flowing. Valuing flow means valuing removing delay.

Beyond the basic removal of delay, the organization also values smoothness. A smooth, steady arrival of work is respectful to the people doing the work, and a major contributor in providing relief from overburdening. Smoothness also produces more predictable outcomes and is therefore attractive to customers. Smoothness also reduces the need for contingent staffing and slack resources, improving economic results without affecting customer satisfaction.

The Toyota Way identified three main types of problems in workflows: *muri*, or overburdening; *mura*, unevenness; and *muda*, non–value adding activity, or waste. Valuing flow directly addresses *mura* through the pursuit of smoothness and acknowledges its contribution to *muri*, relieving overburdening through an even flow that can be managed effectively with a simple WIP limit.

Evidence that an enterprise values flow can be seen through the adoption of many Kanban practices described in the Kanban Maturity Model, such as the use of WIP limits, visualization of blockers and WIP aging, blocker clustering and Risk Review, dependency management, and the use of policies for "definition of ready" and local "definitions of done," showing that work is available to pull to the next step. Greater collaboration between teams, going beyond mere cooperation to include providing assistance when needed, is also an indicator that flow is valued.

Narrative

To value narrative, businesspeople want more than just the facts; they want the story that provides context and history. Narrative helps to create an emotional connection and hence it is important for social cohesion and trust; it also provides vital information that puts work in context and enables greater empathy and understanding of customer needs and expectations.

Narratives help define identity, and they give context to meaning and purpose. Narratives tell us who we are and why we exist. Ultimately, narrative helps with the who, why, what, and how. Narrative is a core enabler at every level of maturity.

Starting at ML2, narratives also help to develop a better understanding of the context in which processes are performed, which, combined with the quantitative information about demand and capability, enables making appropriate decisions for improving flow.

Collecting and sharing narratives is costly. It takes time and needs attention. However, like the oral history tradition of Iceland—the passing down of the sagas of ancient times to the next generation—our organizations must value narrative and find ways to capture it and share it. Is someone taking a lot of photographs as your Kanban implementation grows and deepens? Do you have a visual history or a diary of events? Perhaps you have the presentations from a year of Operations Reviews. Consider whether the final review of the year should be extended by an hour to feature a retrospective on the full year. Is the story of your organization on display? Do you use the history of your company as an integral part of new-hire orientation? Are you taking explicit steps to reinforce identity and recognize that identity evolves and matures as history progresses? Metaphorically speaking, every organization needs to gather around the campfire and tell its stories. If people are to spend time and energy on it, you need to signal that you value it.

Respect

Respect here does not mean "courtesy" or "politeness," although these are both important aspects of a culture and the social norms in an organization. In this usage, respect means recognition of capability, circumstances, or context. In Kanban, we respect people, systems, customers, regulators, sponsors, owners, taxpayers, and other stakeholders and benefactors.

We respect people by providing them with an organization and a system in which to work that sets them up for success. They should have the training, resources, skills, equipment, time, and space in which to do great work. They should be trusted and empowered through the use of explicit policies. They should understand why they are there, how they can contribute, and what a desirable outcome looks like. They should be respected such that they have autonomy, can achieve mastery of their work, and have a deep sense of purpose and the value they provide. In doing so, individuals should feel fulfilled. This is what we mean by "respect."

We respect circumstances, context, and capability by understanding it, seeing it as a result of transparency onto work and workflow, analyzing it, and modeling it such that outcomes can be predicted based on a realistic comprehension of how things currently work. There is no wishful thinking in Kanban! If you find yourself sighing and saying, "If only ... then our strategy would have worked." Fill in the blank—if only our people worked harder, we had better people, we had more time, we had more money, we were better at execution, we were better at delivery, and so on, and so on—then you failed to respect the current operating reality of your circumstances and capability.

Respect is about recognizing your current circumstances and capability for what they are and making plans accordingly. If your current capabilities don't match your needs, expectations, or desires, you need to invest in improving them before you set stretch goals. Respect means that you live in a pragmatic world, rooted in a solid understanding of reality. There is no wishful thinking in Kanban!

Understanding (Internal)

In the context of the Kanban Method and the Kanban Maturity Model, understanding means that we seek to understand the nature of our environment. We seek to understand the world around us and what drives it.

A Maturity Level 2, and progressing to Maturity Level 3, we want organizations to understand how, what, why, and who through study, observation, collection of evidence, use of models, and experimentation. At Maturity Level 2, our focus is on understanding our internal environment and the forces that shape it—what we do, how we do it, and the variability, risk, and uncertainty that relate to the work and our ability to deliver it within expectations.

We want people to gain an understanding of the work that they are asked to do and how to perform it with consistency and deliver it with quality; the services that they provide, their workflows, and the collaboration involved in providing those services; and the impact their policies have on their capability and performance. Basic understanding focuses on the pragmatism of accepting their own environment and their current capabilities for what they are. There is no wishful thinking in Kanban.

6 Culture in Fit-for-Purpose Organizations

For convenience, the seven levels of the Kanban Maturity Model are repeated in Figure 6.1. In this chapter we describe the values necessary to develop an organization that produces fit-for-purpose results, exhibiting Maturity Level 3 or 4. At Maturity Level 3, the consumer experience is fit-for-purpose—employees and customers are happy. At Maturity Level 4, the organization is fit-for-purpose, satisfying all stakeholders. Employees, customers, owners, regulatory authorities, and any other relevant stakeholders' needs are met.

SCOPE	LEVEL	CULTURAL FOCUS
Task	0 Oblivious	Individualism
Deliverable	1 Team-Focused	Individual Heroics
Product/Service	2 Customer-Driven	Managerial Heroics
Product lines/Shared services	3 Fit-for-Purpose	(Customer) Purpose
Product lines/Services Portfolio	4 Risk-Hedged	Unity & Alignment
Business Lines Portfolio	5 Market Leader	Pursuit of Perfection
Business Lines Portfolio	6 Built for Survival	Reinvention

Figure 6.1　Attributes of the Culture pillar

Maturity Level 3 – Fit-for-Purpose

At Maturity Level 3, customers report that the product or service they requested is fit-for-purpose and that they are satisfied with the service they've received. They'll be happy to make more requests and will trust that the product and service delivery will meet their standards. At Maturity Level 3, social capital now extends out beyond the service delivery workflow, beyond the chain of teams cooperating to produce something of customer value, to the customers themselves. Overall, the level of social capital is rising. In order to achieve this, each team subordinates their own local, immediate, and arguably selfish needs to the greater good, the just cause of serving the customer. They understand that they must subordinate their own desires because they have a greater purpose than merely serving their own needs and egos—they have a customer to satisfy, and they believe that delivering good work and making customers happy provides benefits for everyone: the customer benefits, and perhaps how they consume the product provides a wider community or society benefit; the business wins because happy customers will lead to repeat business and growth; and teams and individuals win because they can take pride in their work and achievements. This is enabled by valuing customer service and appreciating the customer's needs and their purpose for choosing to do business with the organization. Fulfilling customer needs and understanding that a "good job" is only defined by a satisfied customer becomes a unifying force. It binds previously loosely coupled teams into a much larger team collaborating to achieve a shared goal. Teams start collaborating at ML2. However, at ML2 they are focused on creating the flow of outcomes, while at ML3 they develop the understanding of their customers' expectations and put delivering customer fitness-for-purpose at the center of their management decisions.

The culture at Maturity Level 3 is best characterized as "no heroes anymore!" Leadership has moved its focus away from defining shared identity and is now focused on shared purpose. Employees are happier because they can see that their work has meaning. They can be proud to be part of an organization that has mastery over its work. They have mastery over the design, implementation, and service delivery of their product or service. They are sufficiently skilled and experienced in all aspects of what they do that customers are happy, and everyone's work has meaning because everyone is professional, no one lets the organization down, and a satisfactory product or service is delivered to the customer.

A second cultural shift appears at Maturity Level 3, toward absolute rather than relative measurements. At this level, our customer is either happy or not. This is an absolute measurement. It isn't sufficient to say, "Our customers are happier than our competitors' customers," therefore, we are somehow better than our competitors in relative terms. At Maturity Level 2, leaders can get distracted taking actions that aim to hinder competition so as to make their own performance look better by comparison. At Maturity Level 3, that behavior has disappeared; we value customer service more than we value our rank and social status in a peer group of other suppliers.

The third significant culture shift is that our collective behavior is now inherently altruistic. We believe that if we do the right thing for the customer, then the customer will do the right thing by us. If we trust our customers, then they will reciprocate and trust us. This shows that not only do we believe in the positive side of human nature, but we believe that humans are wired to reciprocate trust. This enables us to start thinking of customers as collaborators, as partners. We often hear businesses refer to their customers as "partners," but unless they clearly exhibit altruism and trust in their customers, it is merely a platitude and not a deeply held belief.

The last cultural change that begins at Maturity Level 3, but isn't fully consolidated until Maturity Level 4, is that of becoming anticipatory rather than reactionary. Greater levels of understanding enable anticipatory behavior, but the willingness to invest in risk management, risk reduction, mitigation, and contingency may not yet exist. Consequently, Maturity Level 3 remains fragile to extreme or unforeseen events, lack of foresight, and inadequate planning. Under stress, a business at Maturity Level 3 can regress to a lower level.

Maturity Level 3 organizations can also suffer from a form of martyrdom; for example, although every customer transaction results in a happy customer, the business might be losing money each time. The ability to sustain this pattern depends on available capital. As we don't have infinite capital, good customer service must eventually suffer. When the business comes under financial pressure and responds by cutting costs, customer service will decline and the business will lose its fit-for-purpose customer rating. It will have regressed to Maturity Level 2.

Although reaching Maturity Level 3 is a significant achievement, we must recognize that it isn't sustainable and carries inherent fragility. It is therefore necessary for leaders to continue to push and aspire to Maturity Level 4.

Achieving Maturity Level 3 requires that we imbue our culture with yet more values, namely agreement, balance, customer service, fitness-for-purpose, leadership at all levels, short-term results, an understanding of how our product or service workflow fits into the wider ecosystem of interdependent services and its relationship with the outside world, our customers and our market dynamics, and unity and alignment with shared purpose and common goals.

Agreement

Valuing agreement means that we wish to move forward with consensus and shared understanding. In a Kanban implementation where we want to achieve "pull," we agree on system capacity and we respect that capacity, and we agree on what to pull next and when to pull. Policies are made by agreement. We strive for shared understanding as much as possible. As a general rule, we do not allow or encourage bullying behavior, but we recognize that exceptions are necessary, and we push when we must.

Although we value agreement, we recognize that there are times when full consensus and broad agreement are unrealistic. There is no wishful thinking in Kanban. Hence, there might be times when delaying for consensus is not in our best interest, and therefore we will trade our value of agreement for strong, decisive leadership.

Balance

Balance plays a key role in respect and avoiding overburdening people, teams, value streams, service delivery workflows, and entire business units. Balance shows that we value sustainability both at the personal level and at the organizational level. If we are to have consistent customer service, to maintain fitness-for-purpose, we must have balance.

At Maturity Level 3, balance implies that we strive to avoid overburdening individuals and service delivery workflows (systems). We want to balance demand against capability to deliver, and we want to limit work-in-progress to the capacity of individuals and the workflow within which they work. WIP limits are used to avoid overburdening people and workflows, while capacity allocation, demand-shaping, and triage are used to keep demand in balance with capability to deliver.

Customer Service

Valuing customer service shows that we recognize that a core purpose of our organization and the services we provide is to serve our customers adequately and meet their expectations of us. We measure our success, our self-esteem, and our capability relative to our ability to meet customer expectations. When we can meet customer expectations consistently, then we can say that each of our services is fit-for-purpose. To be fit-for-purpose is our guiding principle, our true north, our ongoing ambition.

Fitness-for-Purpose

From studying and understanding numerous patterns of Kanban adoption over the past decade, we recognized that many were shallower and incomplete compared to the method described in *Kanban: Successful Evolutionary Change for your Technology Business*.[1] It was important to ask why this was happening and why these shallow implementations were failing to mature to the deeper, richer, fuller practices that matched more closely the archetypal implementation at Corbis in 2007, from which the canonical Kanban Method was derived. Our conclusion was that outward-facing examples—in which there was a recognition of a customer with needs and expectations and a desire to serve that customer and meet those needs—produced deeper, fuller implementations. When this awareness and desire to serve the customer was not present, the implementations were shallower. Shallow implementations were inward-facing, self-centered, and mostly focused on relief from overburdening; perhaps also was the sense of achievement that comes from a job well done, with higher quality, enabled through that relief from overburdening. We

---

1. David Anderson (Seattle: Blue Hole Press, 2010).

concluded that to enable deep Kanban implementations, it was key that there was a sense of altruism, a devotion to customer service.

In the Mission Command body of knowledge, also known as *Auftragstaktik*, or Mission Orders, the concept of *Einheit*, meaning unity and alignment, is key to moving with agility and enabling autonomy of action. To create such unity and alignment there is a need to communicate the purpose of any action—to explain why we are undertaking this action.

Purpose creates unity and encourages broader collaboration. Purpose enables alignment and autonomous action. Purpose improves trust and social capital across the whole system. Understanding purpose helps us move effectively with agility.

We choose to define that purpose as achieving good customer service and happy customers. To do that, we need to understand the customer's purpose in requesting work from us. We need to understand how to define customer satisfaction and measure how well we are performing against expectations. To do this, we must value the idea that our work is fit for the customer's purpose. We must want to satisfy our customers with products and services that meet their needs and fulfill their expectations.

Leadership at All Levels

At Maturity Level 3, we need to extend our view of leadership. At Maturity Level 1, we valued taking initiative. At Maturity Level 2, this deepened to valuing acts of leadership and acknowledging that leadership entails personal risk. Maturity Level 3 is better enabled with an understanding that leadership only from the top causes delay, and that leaders at the top are not best placed to know what is needed or to see the need for action at the bottom. For an organization to move with agility, leadership is needed at all levels. Acts of leadership should be encouraged and expected at all levels, and more senior leaders must seek to provide the confidence, safety, and failure tolerance required to encourage risk taking. Leadership at all levels doesn't happen magically; it happens because more senior leaders hack the culture to enable it. Mature leaders are not threatened by leadership from below; rather, they are empowered by it. Leadership at all levels frees senior leaders to focus on strategic concerns and organizational culture while mid- and lower-level people focus on operational and tactical concerns. It should become a cultural norm for anyone, regardless of their rank or station in the organization, to "do something about it!"

Short-Term Results

Sometimes you need quick wins to build trust. Aspiring to Maturity Level 3, we recognize that we need to build trust in order to have sufficient social capital to adopt many of the practices that enable consistent, trustworthy, predictable service delivery. Hence, at Maturity Level 2 or below, we must focus on building trust and, to do so, we must focus on short-term results. We must make promises we can keep, and we must start to deliver within expectations—and do it regularly and consistently. Building trust is so important that we must, for now, sacrifice longer-term objectives or goals on cost or efficiency. Once we have achieved Maturity Level 3, or even better, Level 4, then we can switch our focus to longer-term business objectives.

When there is no trust, you must first build trust. We recognize that to do so, we must focus on short-term results, which can mean that we have to adapt to our environment, adopting tactical choices rather than pursuing longer-term system fixes. Making promises we can keep may mean a focus on delivery dates and agreed scope rather than on reducing failure demand and rework. Adopting the use of practices such as classes of service may provide a tactical advantage, necessary to build trust. Some of these practices can be discarded later, once the process operates effectively and consistently and trust has been established.

External Understanding

At Maturity Level 2 and progressing to Maturity Level 3, we wanted to understand how, what, why, and who through study, observation, collection of evidence, use of models, and experimentation. For deeper understanding at Maturity Levels 3 and 4 and beyond, we need additional insights about the customers we serve and the context of, and business risks associated with, the work they request. We want to understand our customer's purpose—why they have chosen us. And we want to understand the customer's context and the risks, uncertainties, or demands they face in their own environment. We seek as much context and to achieve as much empathy with our customer as possible. Deeper understanding is about understanding the context beyond our own organization, about empathizing with the external environment and our customer's circumstances.

We value an external understanding because it helps us make better decisions and, as a consequence, drive better customer satisfaction.

Unity and Alignment

Maturity Level 3 requires that multiple teams of people cooperate and collaborate with a shared purpose on shared goals and objectives, such as creating and delivering customer-requested work. As such, ML3 requires us to move away from autonomous action based on local objectives, designed to achieve narrow measures and metrics, and instead see our contribution as part of a bigger system within which we cooperate with others to achieve an objective that we could not achieve on our own.

Maturity Level 3 requires that multiple teams of people cooperate and collaborate with a shared purpose on shared goals and objectives, such as creating and delivering customer-requested work. As such, ML3 requires us to move away from autonomous action based on local objectives, designed to achieve narrow measures and metrics, and instead see our contribution as part of a bigger system within which we cooperate with others to achieve an objective that we could not achieve on our own.

To value unity and alignment is to suggest that we do not act entirely autonomously. While we may make local decisions, we do so in a manner that we believe aligns with the actions of others in the pursuit of the common goal. Doing so should enable a large organization—a network of services, consisting of chains of interdependent teams—to move in unison. No decision should be made without consideration of the wider objectives and organizational goals; no action should be taken without consideration of how it aligns with those of others in pursuit of the immediate objectives and achieving the desired (organizational) results.

Valuing unity and alignment means that we make time to consider the bigger picture, to communicate externally, and to provide transparency on our own actions and decisions such that others may align with us.

Maturity Level 4 – Risk-Hedged

Maturity Level 4 is best characterized as "no more surprises." Everything is now in balance—all stakeholder needs are met, not only the needs of the customer. The organization can do business in a sustainable fashion and it is robust to uncertainty. We might have chosen to name this level Risk-Managed, as there is a strong argument that what we have observed and describe is an organization that does so much more than just hedge risk. However, we felt that had we named this level Risk-Managed, many organizations would have responded with, "We already manage risk and therefore we must be at least at Maturity Level 4." This would almost certainly be an incorrect assumption. So, we specifically chose the name Risk-Hedged because this causes people to pause and think before they comment. "What do you mean by risk-hedged?" is usually an indicator that the organization isn't risk hedged. Or it invokes a defensive response, such as, "We don't have time to be adequately risk hedged" or "We don't have the resources and capital to be adequately risk hedged." Whereas this may be true, it is also an indicator that the organization has not reached Maturity Level 4.

At Maturity Level 4, an organization is capable of keeping everything in balance: happy employees, happy customers, happy shareholders, happy regulatory authorities; and these things are not seen as being in conflict with each other. There is a culture of fairness. Everything gets its fair share.

At Maturity Level 4, social capital has increased significantly across a network. Employees trust managers and managers trust their employees. The regulatory authority trusts the work of the organization and the organization respects the value of regulation. Customers trust that they will receive products or services that consistently meet with their expectations.

The culture has now shifted to one of anticipation and any need for reactionary behavior is analyzed so that future issues may be anticipated. Surprises are undesirable and unacceptable. Thinking now happens at the system level, questioning, "What was it about our system and procedures that meant we didn't see this coming?" Surprises stress the organization in a manner such that it responds by changing its processes and procedures, it rules and policies.

The most notable cultural shift at Maturity Level 4 is a move to use quantitative data and a more scientific approach to experimentation. The organization now values data, and science, and causal analysis. Superstitious behavior and emotional, or gut-feeling, decision making are now frowned upon.

Achieving Maturity Level 4 requires that our culture exhibit yet more values: deeper balance, business focus, competition, customer intimacy, data-driven decision making, fairness, being fitter-for-purpose, leadership development, and regulatory compliance.

Deeper Balance

At Maturity Level 3, balance was about avoiding overburdening the system. Demand and capability to supply must be kept in balance. We must be pragmatic and realistic about what we can achieve and what can be delivered within customer expectations.

However, at Maturity Level 4 we must take balance further. Balance is now about fairness as much as it is about protection from overburdening and pragmatism in delivering against customer expectations. We recognize there is risk in being too narrowly focused or overexposed to a single type of work or a single class of business risks. Balance recognizes that we must understand our capacity and our capabilities and allocate them across a range of customers, services, work types, and risk classes in order to have robustness and a survivable business. Balance respects the needs of a disparate set of stakeholders or of multiple customers who compete for scarce resources and available capacity.

Balance requires trust and respect amongst customers and other stakeholders. There needs to be support for fairness and consensus about what represents a fair share. To achieve this, we need greater levels of collaboration amongst all stakeholders.

Business Focus

Maturity Level 4 represents the point where think about long-term survival, robustness, and running a sustainable business. It isn't enough to satisfy customers. It isn't even enough to deliver on our vision, mission, or purpose as an organization. All of that would count for nothing if we entered bankruptcy and had to close. Business focus means that we must keep everything in balance—product and service design and quality, customer satisfaction, regulatory compliance, and meeting all other stakeholders' concerns. We must have the finances available to adequately capitalize our business. We must have trust with all of our stakeholders, including our investors and financiers.

A business-focused organization is one in which all employees understand the nature of the business and their contribution to it. Decisions are made and actions are taken based on their business impact, and facts and data are used to demonstrate that business impact.

The Kanban cadence of Operations Review can often be hard to adopt. This becomes much easier in a business-focused organization. An Operations Review begins with business reporting and data. Everyone in the organization becomes aware of the nature of the business and understands their contribution. The Operations Review is a strong mechanism for creating a business-focused organization. Valuing a focus on business, profits, and other socioeconomic objectives becomes an enabler for the Operations Review, which in turn delivers the business-focused organization necessary for achieving Maturity Level 4 and beyond.

Competition

At Maturity Level 4, we've already demonstrated that we can satisfy customers with fit-for-purpose products and services. Now we start to value competition because it is competition that drives us to even greater levels of achievement. At Maturity Level 4, competition becomes a stressor that motivates us to do better. If we aspire to Maturity Level 5, now is the time to start paying attention to our competition. Rivalry for supremacy can be a great thing—it can inspire us to levels of performance and achievement that we didn't believe were possible.

If we focus on competition too early, though, we'll never be fit-for-purpose. Early development requires a myopic focus on the customer. Once we've mastered basic customer satisfaction, outdoing competitors is how we ensure robustness and longevity.

Customer Intimacy

At Maturity Level 3, we valued customer service. We took an altruistic position of being in the service of the customer, and the fitness of our work was judged based on the customer's needs and expectations. At Maturity Level 4, we take that a step further. Now our task is to be intimate with the customer's context—to understand their purpose for selecting us and the risks that they manage. We need to know why the customer has asked us for something. Knowing why helps us to best tailor the product or service to the customer's needs. It tells us whether to focus on design, implementation, or service delivery, and to understand which level of service is required in each of these three categories. Customer intimacy is the means by which we acquire the customer's loyalty. When we supply a product or service uniquely fitting their needs, why would they ever look elsewhere? Customer intimacy enables us to keep customers for the long term. Our economic performance will improve dramatically as our cost of sale falls and the perceived value of a uniquely tailored product or service will enable us to charge higher prices and obtain improved margins. Valuing customer intimacy makes sound economic sense.

While researching the sequel to their book, *Fit for Purpose*,[2] David Anderson and Alexei Zheglov interviewed London taxi drivers about the new, all-electric TX taxi that replaced the diesel-powered TX4. The new model comes in part as a response to new regulation—the

---

2. David Anderson and Alexei Zheglov (Seattle: Blue Hole Press, 2nd edition, 2018).

Transport for London authority and the Greater London council want to clean up the air and reduce toxic emissions inside the city, so they've mandated a move to electric vehicles for public transport. The new taxis are more expensive, about $20,000 USD more expensive than the older diesel version. The drivers wonder who will pay this extra cost during the transition period. Fares cannot be any higher, as they are strictly regulated, and the fare is the same regardless of the engine or motor powering the vehicle. They also questioned the range. Today most London cabbies don't live in the freshly gentrified East End as they used to; instead, they live in the suburbs, perhaps sixty miles (100 km) from central London. They don't want to burn battery range commuting to work. Equally, they don't wish to be stranded, unable to return home at night or have to delay while they find a suitable charging point.

The new TX eCity electric model is larger than the older cabs. It has space for six paying passengers and more luggage space. It is also better equipped than older taxis, with modern features such as WiFi and touchless payment. Thus, the new design is fitter-for-purpose for the consumer taking a taxi ride, and it meets the regulatory authority's needs—offering an environmental improvement to everyone living in London. The new cabs are quieter and cleaner than ever before. However, the additional cost of the new design was not adequately thought through—the needs of the London Taxi Drivers Association (LTDA) as a stakeholder were not adequately taken into account. At the time of introduction in January 2018, no subsidy or tax incentives to switch were offered. Without this, drivers held off purchasing a replacement vehicle for as long as possible. In mid-2019, Nissan entered the market with a rival vehicle to the TX eCity. Recognizing its early mistake[3] the government introduced a £7,500 tax incentive, covering about 50 percent of the additional cost, in order to encourage faster adoption of the electric taxis. Greater London Council is behind schedule for the switch, and London major Sadiq Kahn is hoping that the new incentive will accelerate the obsolescence of the diesel-powered taxis.

To be fitter-for-purpose, a product or service must be fit-for-purpose for each and every stakeholder. Without that, there will be some failure in the market and expectations won't be met. A failure to fully recognize the needs of drivers, who are mostly owner-operators, means that against the goals of the whole program, the new TX electric taxi isn't entirely fit-for-purpose. A truly Maturity Level 4 organization would avoid this failure by taking all stakeholders' needs into account and delivering a product or service that is fit-for-purpose in every way.

Data-Driven Decision Making

Maturity Levels 0 through 2 can also best be characterized as "qualitative management"; less generous labels might be "superstitious" or even "emotional" decision making. Achieving Maturity Level 3 is when we begin to transition and the use of data and quantitative management emerge as an approach to decision making. To reach Maturity Level 4, we

---

3. https://www.theguardian.com/environment/2019/oct/23/first-100-electric-black-cab-for-120-years-launches-in-london

must openly value facts, data, process instrumentation, quantitative management, and scientific inquiry. At Maturity Level 4, we believe that we'll make consistently better decisions using facts, data, and models than we will with mere experience and emotional or pattern-driven decision making.

We recognize that emotional and experience-driven, pattern-based decision making is inherently fragile—it relies on the experiential learning of an individual. When personnel change, we lose the benefit of experience and we lose institutional memory. Outcomes regress while new staff gain experience to replace that which was lost. With a data-driven, quantitative, scientific culture, where we value facts and we keep logbooks and knowledge bases, we gain a robustness that makes us more resilient to changes in personnel.

Fairness

Every parent with more than one child understands the inherent human need for fairness. In a world of finite capital, finite resources, and limited personnel with a finite capacity for work, achieving balance means that we need to value and understand fairness. We need to value fairness if we are to answer questions such as, "What represents a fair share of capacity for this customer or risk category?" Valuing fairness is the antidote to greed and dysfunctional behavior. Fairness recognizes that you will treat others as you yourself expect to be treated.

Leadership Development

Leadership development is the next and final step in a maturing appreciation of leadership at Maturity Level 4. It started with taking initiative at Maturity Level 1 and progressed through acts of leadership at Maturity Level 2 and leadership at all levels at Maturity Level 3. Now, with Maturity Level 4, we must recognize that leadership isn't magic fairy dust, nor does it grow on trees, fall from Heaven, or happen by magic. While raw desire to be a leader may be genetically wired into some individuals and not others, we must recognize that leadership skill is not magically inherited, rather it is learned. People with natural leadership tendencies need to be trained and developed into better leaders. Leadership skill is gained through experience. Leaders need role models. They need mentors. And they need a model or codification of leadership behavior against which they can evaluate their own decision making.

Developing leaders takes time and costs money. If an organization doesn't value it, it won't happen. The alternative to not developing leaders is to assume that leaders can be acquired on the market. This means adopting an inherently heroic model of leadership. This is low-maturity behavior—Maturity Level 1 behavior. An organization that isn't prepared to develop its own talent and develop its own future leaders is condemned to low-maturity performance. It is not possible to achieve Maturity Level 4 in a sustainable manner without a commitment to leadership development.

Regulatory Compliance

For mature businesses, a healthy respect for regulatory compliance is merely table-stakes—the cost of doing business. In life- or safety-critical industries or in economically critical industries, regulation exists to protect the public, the economy, and civil society. Mature businesses recognize that regulations level the playing field: they create explicit fitness criteria for a product or service, and hence, define the cost floor and capital requirements to enter a market. Immature businesses might believe that flouting regulations gives them an advantage—lower costs, faster time-to-market—and it may open up market segments that were closed due to price and affordability. However, flagrant disregard of regulations is inherently fragile. A business can be closed down if the full power of the law is set against it. A recent example is Uber, the darling of the startup unicorns, which lost its license to operate in cities such as Austin, Texas, and London, England, as well as the entire country of Denmark. For businesses that aspire to be around a long time, learning to live with regulation and the costs and delays that it entails is all part and parcel of achieving a robust, fit-for-purpose, adequately risk-hedged enterprise.

7 Culture in High-Maturity Organizations

SCOPE	LEVEL	CULTURAL FOCUS
Task	0 Oblivious	Individualism
Deliverable	1 Team-Focused	Individual Heroics
Product/Service	2 Customer-Driven	Managerial Heroics
Product lines/Shared services	3 Fit-for-Purpose	(Customer) Purpose
Product lines/Services Portfolio	4 Risk-Hedged	Unity & Alignment
Business Lines Portfolio	5 Market Leader	Pursuit of Perfection
Business Lines Portfolio	6 Built for Survival	Reinvention

Figure 7.1 Attributes of the Culture pillar

For convenience, the seven levels of the Kanban Maturity Model are repeated in Figure 7.1. In this chapter we describe the values necessary to develop an organization that produces exceptional, market-leading results or manages to reinvent itself—what it does, how it does things, why it exists, and who it is. It is these qualities that define organizations at Maturity Levels 5 and 6. At Maturity Level 5, the organization produces market-leading products or offers market-leading services. It is capable of questioning how it does things and adopting new methods and techniques that provide an advantage. It is also capable of questioning what it does, the products and services it offers, and the market segments it serves. With a solid understanding of its identity and its purpose, a Maturity Level 5 organization can adapt to offer anything, delivered any way, as long as these things are congruent with its identity and purpose. Maturity Level 6 takes this adaptability and reinvention to a higher level. A Maturity Level 6 organization can question and reinvent why it exists and who it is. A Maturity Level 6 organization can happily take on a new identity, a new purpose, and completely replace old products, business units, and methods in a managed and controlled fashion that ensures that the enterprise survives disruption, political or social change, or discontinuous innovation.

Maturity Level 5 – Market Leader

At Maturity Level 5, customers, competitors, and others in an industry will refer to you as the benchmark, the best; they will emulate your techniques, your "how," and your products and services, your "what," will become a key objective for competitors. Your customers will be fiercely loyal and extremely proud. The market or product may even be named after you; for example, vacuum cleaners were for decades known as hoovers, because Hoover so dominated that market. To hoover became a verb in the English language. It is noteworthy that not only has Hoover disappeared as an independent company, sold to a Chinese firm in 2006, but use of the verb hoover has become arcane. A market-leading position isn't invincible. It is possible to be displaced as the market leader. For this reason, our model extends to Maturity Level 6, the ability to reinvent a business, to redefine its purpose and its identity. We discuss Level 6 later in this chapter.

Maturity Level 5 can be characterized by "the relentless pursuit of perfection." Maturity Level 5 is a world of marginal gains, of using data and science to extract every last ounce of efficiency from your product design, implementation, processes, and service delivery so as to optimize economic performance and achieve your business objectives. Maturity Level 5 affords you the ability to charge premium prices and earn greater margins than your competitors. This is possible not only because you are the best, but you are the best of a peer group that already delivers acceptable or superior customer experience and customer satisfaction.

It is also fair to state that many businesses do not aspire to, nor do they require to be, the market leader. For many people reading this book, Maturity Level 4 is where your organization needs to be. Maturity Level 4 should be your aspiration. There is no judgment in the maturity model—Maturity Level 4 is just fine if it fits with your business goals and objectives.

Equality of Opportunity

Equality of opportunity isn't simply fairness all grown up—equality of opportunity is necessary to provide resilience, robustness, and ultimately anti-fragility. Equality of opportunity isn't just about treating people fairly; it means that you proactively don't discriminate based on someone's educational background, ethnicity, race, religion, accent, dialect, appearance, socioeconomic background, parentage, relationships, or disability. Equality of opportunity recognizes that there is no monopoly on good ideas, innovations, or epiphanies. Rich people aren't better at innovation than poor people. Men aren't better at it than women. Someone with good grammar and pronunciation isn't better at innovation than a dyslexic with a regional dialect.

Equality of opportunity is best explained through an example, in this case from the relatively recent history of the nation of South Africa. The new republic of South Africa was formed between 1994 and 1997, between the first general election in which the majority black population was free to vote and the acceptance of the new constitution, which came into effect in 1997. Nelson Mandela was elected president and served a five-year term from 1994 to 1999. He was replaced by Thabo Mbeki. One of the greatest challenges facing the new state wasn't just the historical racism of the Apartheid era, but the deep social problems and poverty faced by millions of the majority black population. The first instinct of the government was to create policy favoring the appointment of blacks in government, civil service, education, and private businesses, known as Black Economic Empowerment (BEE).[1] Such policies are referred to as positive discrimination in the UK and affirmative action in America. Early into Thabo Mbeki's presidency, it was self-evident that the affirmative action to promote black people into high positions wasn't working. While corporations complained that the policy made them uncompetitive because they weren't able to hire the best person for the job, the deeper issue was that favoritism wasn't solving the wider economic issues. Giving a few black people top jobs wasn't helping millions of poor people living in shanty towns rise out of poverty. Positive discrimination had simply created a small, elite sector of rich black people driving Mercedeses and living in expensive, predominantly white neighborhoods.

In 2000, the government formed a commission, BEECom,[2] led by now-president Cyril Ramaphosa, that refined the policy to use a balanced scorecard of measures intended to make it more effective. This is known as Broad-based BBE (BBBEE),[3] enacted in 2003. Although Ramaphosa was a strong advocate of BBBEE, he also believed deeply in the ruling party's Freedom Charter,[4] and his interpretation of it known as nonracialism,[5] in which the best person for the job would be hired regardless of their skin color, an approach that encouraged people to be colorblind when selecting employees and civil servants. Some years later, Mbeki's government came to realize that equality of opportunity through the provision of higher education and economic opportunity were the keys to true broad-based black economic empowerment; specifically, this manifested through making tertiary education (college/university) free for everyone. The route out of poverty was education, coupled with the necessary balancing economic factor of job creation. For their newly well-educated young people there needed to be plentiful economic opportunity. The new policies took time to implement and

---

1. Anthony Butler, *Cyril Ramaphosa: the Road to Presidential Power* (Martlesham: James Currey, 2019).
2. ibid.
3. ibid.
4. https://en.wikipedia.org/wiki/Freedom_Charter
5. http://www.saha.org.za/nonracialism/about.htm

were brought into law by Jacob Zuma's government. Unfortunately, Zuma's leadership encouraged corruption and damaged the economy, limiting foreign investment. South Africa has struggled to provide quality opportunities for its energetic and well-educated young graduates. Nonracialism and equality of opportunity remain pivotal tenets of now-President Ramaphosa's government. The affirmative action of BBBEE continues[6] despite recognition of many flaws in its implementation. It would be politically difficult to remove; a very large, extremely poor portion of the electorate still expects some action in their favor. To his credit, Ramaphosa leads by example, promoting nonracialism by appointing nonblack people to prominent positions in his government and vociferously defending his choices as necessary for the future economic success of the nation. He believes that the route out of poverty for tens of millions of black people is to fight corruption and boost the economy by using the best available leadership regardless of their skin color or ethnicity.

If you aspire to be the best, or your organization must take on massively challenging tasks such as solving poverty in a nation with a checkered past and serious social problems, there can be no monopoly on good ideas, no bias toward where leadership, genius, innovation, and epiphany will emerge. Market-leading organizations nurture talent regardless of where it comes from.

Experimentation

Although experimentation may emerge in a business well before Maturity Level 5, it is impossible to achieve Maturity Level 5 without valuing it as core to your culture. As a cultural value, experimentation means that we are willing to take risks, that we are willing to try things out, but we do so in a measured fashion and with a scientific mindset. Experimentation means that we have a hypothesis and an expected outcome based on a model and that we develop a controlled way of testing our hypothesis, limiting our risk exposure. At Maturity Level 4, we valued data-driven decision making; now we take it further by valuing the scientific method.

Valuing experimentation teaches us that doing something—visible evidence of experiments happening, the presence of the practice of experimentation—is not the same as valuing something. We value experimentation and data-driven decision making over intuition and gut feeling. We value managing risk on investment rather than gambling. Valuing experimentation means that we have a hypothesis-driven culture, that commitments are made in multiple phases, and that our risk exposure is directly related to the quantity and quality of information we have available.

We observe the presence of valuing experimentation not just through evidence of experiments taking place, but by a refusal to make decisions without evidence derived through experimentation. Valuing experimentation is demonstrated by the evidence that we invest to purchase information, that we eliminate options through information acquisition, and that we generate options by having multiple hypotheses. We value experimentation

---

6. https://www.gov.za/sites/default/files/gcis_document/201409/37271act46of2013.pdf

through the active use of models to postulate outcomes and through the active use of feedback to refine and update the models we use. We invest in development and maintenance of models.

Perfectionism

Maturity Level 5 organizations are the fittest-for-purpose. Fittest-for-purpose simply means that we are the best. We achieve this through the relentless pursuit of perfection.

We meet or exceed all stakeholder needs and we do so in a manner that outperforms our competitors. We recognize that market-leading performance gives us the greatest resilience and robustness to changing customer needs. Fittest-for-purpose performance tends to move market expectations and serves to weaken competitors by redefining customer perception of acceptable quality.

To value being fittest-for-purpose means that we identify with being the best. We seek validation through recognition of exceptional performance. We invest to maintain a leadership position. We do this because we believe that the safest place to be, for the longest survival, is out in front. We might believe that if we aren't out in front, if we aren't leading, then we are going backward. This is particularly true in highly competitive industries, such as Formula 1 motor racing, or in the clandestine services and government digital agencies in a costly race with cybercriminals, terrorists, and nefarious and rogue nation states that might seek to damage our economies, societies, and public services. If you are reading this book and you hold a Top-Secret clearance or higher, your agency must aspire to Maturity Level 5.

Social Mobility

In general sociology, social mobility is a measure of the ability of someone to move up (or down) the socioeconomic ladder based on their ability. It is an indicator of equality of opportunity and the absence of bias in the culture. Because there is no monopoly on leadership or good ideas, social mobility is a necessary element of resilience and antifragility.

Highly visible examples of social mobility exist in recent American and British politics. Americans' sense of self, their identity as citizens of the United States, includes the belief that anyone born in the country can rise to become its leader. The recent evidence that this is still true is manifest through presidents like Bill Clinton, a poor kid from a single-parent family in Arkansas. Clinton's rise to the presidency is prima facie evidence that social mobility was alive and well in the United States in the 1990s. Less well known is the story of British premier John Major, again a poor kid who grew up in the circus.

In the corporate world, social mobility implies that someone can join the firm as a mailroom clerk and still rise to the position of chief executive, chairman of the board, or owner of the business. This concept was illustrated in a whimsical fashion in the movie *Grand Budapest Hotel*, where the bellboy rises through the ranks, though more by accident than design, to become the owner of the hotel.

Human beings are naturally wired to make sense of a complex world, and our brains are optimized to be efficient and avoid spending too much energy on any activity. Consequently, we tend to categorize the human beings we meet. This is often referred to as pigeonholing. While this is a natural human tendency, it introduces a major obstacle to social mobility within organizations. A competent middle manager gets labeled as an operations guy and therefore not a strategic thinker. Consequently, this very competent leader is passed over for promotion. Organizations must seek to avoid this natural human bias and tendency to pigeonhole people.

When David was a boy of eleven years old, he won a school prize. The prize was named for its benefactor, Lord Fleck,[7] the son of a coal miner in the small coastal town of Saltcoats in Ayrshire, Scotland. Fleck was educated as a chemist and rose to become the chairman of the board of ICI, at the time Britain's largest and richest company. ICI was an explosives, chemicals, and pharmaceuticals business and the great rival of America's DuPont. Alexander Fleck's career is evidence that, at the time, ICI was a high-maturity business capable of long-term survival. His rise through its ranks is evidence that ICI valued social mobility. The eventual demise of ICI has been well documented by the economist John Kay in his book *Obliquity*.[8] ICI lost its values and its identity and became a very fragile business. It took only fifteen years of poor leadership between 1991 and 2006 for it to disappear entirely. From market leader to gone in less than a generation. ICI serves as evidence that a market-leading position is hard to maintain. It requires the ability to find the right leaders, to promote the best people—wherever they may come from—and to hold those values to be inviolable.

Maturity Level 6 – Built for Survival

At Maturity Level 6, a company recognizes that although it has been good at what it does, its purpose for existing has been just and important, and it has a strong understanding of its identity, its role in the market, and its place in the world, it also recognizes that these things must change if it is to survive and continue. It must reinvent itself. It may require not just a change to how it works or what it does, but a deeper change to why it exists and fundamentally who it is and the role it plays in the world. Surviving through such deep changes is the ultimate challenge for any business, and great leadership is required to make it happen.

Maturity Level 6 can be characterized as "nothing is sacred." Maturity Level 6 is where it becomes acceptable to question everything about a business: its identity, its values, its purpose, its products and services, its business model and channels to market, and its processes and techniques; who, why, what, and how are all open targets for change. The goal is

---

7. https://en.wikipedia.org/wiki/Alexander_Fleck,_1st_Baron_Fleck
8. J. A. Kay, *Obliquity: Why Our Goals Are Best Achieved Indirectly* (New York: Penguin, 2012).

survival, continued relevance in a modern world, and a secure future for the workforce and in the wider society that depends on it for their livelihood, health, and wellbeing.

To succeed at Maturity Level 6, the organization must value long-term survival as well as tolerance and diversity.

Congruence and Integrity

A Maturity Level 6 organization values alignment of actions and decisions at all levels. At this maturity level, congruence means alignment and integrity of decision making in multiple dimensions:

- Tactical, operational, and strategic decisions are all aligned. From a ticket being pulled on a Kanban board to a board of directors' meeting on strategy and direction, we can trace the appropriateness of decisions made.
- From ideation to delivery, and from receipt of a customer request to receipt of that customer's cash, we have complete alignment.
- Our strategy is aligned with who we are and why we exist—our purpose.
- Our operational decisions are congruent with our goals and objectives. Our metrics are aligned with our objectives and drive the correct operational behavior and evolutionary change, enabling us to meet customers' and all other stakeholders' objectives.
- Our tactics are aligned with our values and, regardless of circumstances, we act with integrity and within the constraints of our own ethical and moral framework.
- We know who we are: we understand our identity, our history, our values. We know why we exist: we understand our purpose. We know what we do, and how we do it. All of our decisions and actions are aligned and congruent with our how, what, why, and who.
- We value congruence, because we understand that integrity is the ultimate consistent leadership attribute. Integrity is what gives us the energy and power to sustain market leadership and transcend market and economic disruption. We recognize that long-term survival is unlikely without integrity, and integrity is impossible without congruence.[9]

Long-Term Survival

Business survivability has become a key motivator for deeper Kanban adoption. We've seen this extensively in medium-size companies, often privately held, often family-owned, and in some cases, multi-generational family ownership. The owner-managers who value business survivability often represent patient capital. The current leader of the business, and (usually) patriarch of the family, is entrusted with its survival—the protection of the family wealth and the business that provides for the security and comfort of present and future generations.

---

9. Much of our thinking on congruence owes a debt to Gerald M. Weinberg's *Quality Software Management, Volume 3: Congruent Action* (New York: Dorset House, 1994).

What will ensure survivability in our fast-paced modern economy where disruptive new technologies seem to appear at an ever-faster pace? There is a need to move with agility; a need to sense and respond to changes in market sentiment, to changes in the political and economic environment; and a need to understand customers, why they selected you and your products and services, and how well you meet their needs and expectations. Business survivability comes from a focus on being continually fit-for-purpose and moving quickly, with agility, to provide new products and services as the market changes around you.

Owner-managers of medium-size companies from Canada to Belgium to Spain have been turning to Kanban as a means to improve their capability to manage in the complex modern economy. Some of the deepest Kanban implementations have been achieved in businesses that value their long-term survival. Kanban gives them the DNA to rapidly evolve their provision of services and their service delivery capability.

Tolerance and Diversity

Tolerance and diversity are two values but, like yin and yang, they must come together as a pair. You cannot encourage diversity without embracing tolerance. Tolerance without diversity is just a theory—it is without substance.

Diversity becomes essential at Maturity Level 6. It is impossible to imagine a business reinventing its identity without a diverse workforce to influence the new direction. Diversity refers to all manner of human differences, not merely gender, ethnicity, skin color, or sexual orientation. The wider the experience and cultural exposure of a workforce, the more likely it is to produce a broad pool of ideas—ideas that can be tested by the evolutionary forces in the marketplace. The primordial soup of ideas generated from a diverse workforce will survive and thrive, and the business will be reinvented with new purpose, new values, new identity, and a new role in the world.

To value tolerance, it is essential to be intolerant of intolerance. This means that actions and decisions must be congruent with the value of tolerance. Acts of intolerance, discrimination, bias, and injustice based on who is speaking, who is suggesting, who is attempting to lead, must be stamped out. The intolerant must be weeded out.

It takes great leadership energy to create a diverse and tolerant culture in the name of robustness and long-term survival. Diverse societies are loosely cohesive. They are harder to lead. They are harder to move with unity and alignment. They have greater inertia. They tend to cluster into factions, and politics and "own world" views will abound. It will always be easier to lead a homogenous, tight-knit group with similar values, views, shared and lived experience, goals, and aspirations. However, homogeneity is fragile. Homogenous groups are unlikely to sustain performance above Maturity Level 4, and their life expectancy is limited.

When IBM needed to reinvent itself in 1991 in order to survive, it didn't look inward; instead, it looked to hire an outsider, Lou Gerstner, as chairman and chief executive.

Gerstner was previously the CEO of Nabisco, the bakery company. In some ways he seemed an odd choice for chairman of IBM. He took over from John Akers, a career IBMer, whose tenure at the top resulted in many redundancies, and the loss of important staff and skills. From David's personal experience of knowing staff and managers at IBM's Greenock facility in the UK, Akers was not well liked by IBMers. The firm was in poor financial shape and bleeding cash, with less than six months' working capital remaining. Lou Gerstner was under extreme pressure to save the firm—personal pressure from the founding family, the Watsons, to hold it together and not break it up into bits, and conflicting pressure from activist shareholders. He famously said, "The last thing IBM needs now is a vision," while he set about improving how it executed its existing businesses. Gerstner was an evolutionary-change type of leader. Over a ten-year period he reinvented IBM as a professional services firm, relegating their mainframe computer business to merely a line of business and not the core identity of the firm. Gerstner's tenure at IBM is a classic, archetypal example, showing that survival often comes from introducing ideas from outside.

Many businesses will not aspire to Maturity Level 6. They lack the leadership. They lack the ability to truly embrace tolerance and diversity and all of the other values from the preceding levels. And in doing so, they will be admitting that they do not value long-term survival. W. Edwards Deming once said, "It is not necessary to change. Survival is not mandatory."[10] Pursuit of survival will always be a choice. For those who make that choice, we've laid out a map of the territory.

---

10. https://quotes.deming.org/authors/W._Edwards_Deming/quote/10081

8 | Culture Hacking

Writing in his memoir, *Who Says Elephants Can't Dance?*,[1] former IBM Chairman Lou Gerstner said the following:

> *Until I came to IBM, I probably would have told you that culture was just one among several important elements in any organization's makeup and success—along with vision, strategy, marketing, financials, and the like ... I came to see, in my time at IBM, that culture isn't just one aspect of the game, it is the game.*

Prior to joining IBM as chairman in 1991, Gerstner had been the CEO at Nabisco, famous in the United States for its cookies and crackers and more broadly around the world for breakfast cereals. Switching to a technology giant like IBM so late in his career was seen as risky, both for him and for the company. However, IBM needed a shake-up from the outside, and in hindsight, the board of directors did an outstanding job selecting Gerstner. In the quote above, Gerstner is reflecting on how his job at Nabisco as chief executive differed from his role at IBM. At IBM, he could delegate "vision, strategy, marketing, financials, and the like"; he had but one job, to change the culture.

> *Fixing culture is the most critical—and the most difficult—part of a corporate transformation. . . . In the end, management doesn't change culture. Management invites the workforce itself to change the culture.*

---

1. Louis V. Gerstner. *Who Says Elephants Can't Dance?: Leading a Great Enterprise through Dramatic Change.* New York: HarperBusiness, 2004.

Gerstner recognized that although it was his job to lead—to signal the appropriate culture, to set an example—culture is defined by the sum of decisions and actions taken and, one hopes, in congruence with espoused values. It is the workforce, from chief executive on down, that must change the culture by changing their behavior. They've got to want to do it. Gerstner saw his role as a culture hacker. David saw this firsthand while he worked at the IBM PC Company in the mid-1990s. In this chapter, we examine the codification and tools we have available to make culture hacking pragmatic and actionable.

Three Social Dimensions of Culture

The culture of a social group can be expressed in three dimensions: social innovation, social capital,[2] and social cohesion. Each of these dimensions represents a spectrum, a sliding scale. Any specific organization or social group's culture could be mapped to a specific location on each spectrum, providing a unique cultural or social profile. Figure 8.1 shows these three dimensions, oriented to illustrate the way that best encourages or enables change: a liberal, high-trust, tightly cohesive group is easier to lead and easier to catalyze change.

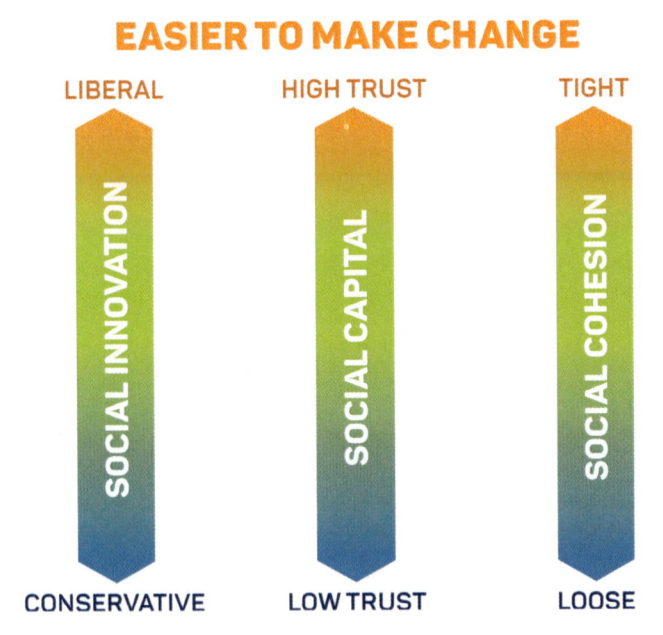

Figure 8.1 Three social dimensions of culture

We use this framework not only to make sense of existing culture but to recognize the cultural levers leaders have available at their disposal to make leading change easier. We look at each of the three in turn.

---

2. The term "social capital" was introduced into the lexicon of economics, political science, and sociology by Robert Putnam in his 1992 book *Making Democracy Work*. Putnam studied the cultures and economies of northern and southern Italy and concluded that the north was richer because people were more willing to trust and collaborate with people outside their immediate family groups, enabling them to raise capital, grow larger businesses, and achieve greater economies of scale.

Social Innovation

The spectrum of social innovation spans from ultra-conservative to extremely liberal. For some Americans reading this text, it may be necessary to remind you of the meanings of these words, as their usage in American politics can cloud the picture.

> **Conservative (adj.)** *averse to change or innovation and holding traditional values*
>
> **Liberal (adj.)** *willing to respect or accept behavior or opinions different from one's own; open to new ideas*

Liberal cultures tolerate diversity and readily accept change, while conservative ones do not. If you are lumbered with a conservative culture that is resistant to change, you can't simply change the culture by decree. Leadership by direction or command doesn't help: issuing an email memo to all staff declaring, "Henceforth, we shall be liberal" is unlikely to work. Nor can leaders magically inspire liberal culture and innovation. A speech telling people, "Go on, take a chance, think differently" is equally unlikely to work. Leaders can, however, signal liberal leanings through tolerance of diversity and by creating equality of opportunity. Leaders also can lead by example by behaving, dressing, and acting in unconventional ways, sending a signal that it is okay to be different.

Liberal culture naturally maps to the deeper levels of organizational maturity, specifically Maturity Levels 5 and 6 (ML5 and ML6). It would be really challenging to achieve the outcomes expected at ML5 and ML6 without a strongly liberal, innovative culture. In this respect, the KMM encapsulates the historical period of the Enlightenment[3] in its architecture. A built-for-survival, resilient, robust, antifragile organizational culture resembles a mature, liberal democracy as envisaged by 17th and 18th Century philosophers.

So, at lower maturity levels it is likely that the culture is more conservative, and that is an impediment to change, an impediment to improving outcomes and economics, and an impediment to deeper maturity.

It is important to note that our cultural assessment goes beyond simply making sense of the existing culture, although sense-making does enable appropriate practice adoption and provides guidance on selecting specific practices that are both suitable to an existing culture and likely to be adopted without a great deal of resistance. However, we would like to get beyond sense-making and ask what pragmatic, actionable guidance might be available to encourage a more liberal culture.

To consider this question, let us consider an example: Britain, and specifically London, post-World War II, was in an era of austerity and slow economic recovery. It was an era of stark contrasts: the coronation of Queen Elizabeth II, a young woman ascending the throne, signaling a bright new future, but as part of a centuries-old system and surrounded

---

3. https://en.wikipedia.org/wiki/Age_of_Enlightenment

by courtiers who were conservative and steeped in tradition. It was an era of stockbrokers in pinstripe suits, black shoes, and bowler hats. And yet it was also the era of the Mini (the car), the miniskirt, the Beatles, and the Rolling Stones, and later, Punk in the 1970s. If you were asked to recreate the culture equivalents that would provoke innovation like the Mini, the miniskirt, and both punk fashion and punk music, you might ask what cultural elements were necessary in the Britain of the 1950s through the 1970s that made this possible in what was otherwise often seen as a fairly conservative country steeped in tradition, pomp, and circumstance.

The Mini is considered the second most influential car of the 20th Century after the Model T Ford.[4] Minis are incredibly spacious on the inside given their small exterior size, just 10' x 4' x 4'. In fact, Minis are so spacious that they enabled a cultural meme: "How many [. . .] can you get in a Mini?" How many boy scouts? How many students? How many gymnasts? How many elephants? This was possible due to a number of innovations in the design: a wheel at every corner, providing incredible road holding and handling; a transverse mounted engine; front-wheel drive; and a gearbox engineered into the sump of the engine, using engine oil for lubrication. Only the last of these four hasn't become standard on small and medium-size cars of today. The Mini was perhaps the most unconventional car design of the century, and for its time, an incredible feat of engineering. It became an icon of 1960s London, popular with pop stars, actors, fashion models, and TV and radio personalities.

Mary Quant is the fashion designer credited with introducing the miniskirt (circa 1962). Quant apparently loved the Mini car and named her short skirts after the car.[5] Quant believed that short hem lengths signaled youthfulness, and that this was desirable in fashion. The miniskirt came to be associated with the general liberation of women during this time period. Freed from endless hours of household chores such as laundry by innovations such as the washing machine, and able to take control of their reproductive systems and plan their families with the advent of The Pill, women were freer than ever before to pursue careers. They could signal this new-found freedom by wearing miniskirts.

Malcolm McLaren[6] promoted and managed the punk rock band the Sex Pistols, who reached the height of their short but controversial reign over British popular culture with the anarchy-invoking song "God Save the Queen" in 1977, the year of Queen Elizabeth's Silver Jubilee (twenty-five-year anniversary as monarch). McLaren owned a boutique in London where Vivienne Westwood[7] first sold her now-iconic punk clothing of ripped t-shirts, Scottish plaid trousers, and black leather accessories. McLaren and Westwood, along with Sex Pistols frontman John Lydon (known at the time as Johnnie Rotten), eventually became part of the British Establishment. Westwood was knighted by the

---

4. https://en.wikipedia.org/wiki/Mini
5. https://en.wikipedia.org/wiki/Miniskirt
6. https://en.wikipedia.org/wiki/Malcolm_McLaren
7. https://en.wikipedia.org/wiki/Vivienne_Westwood

Queen, becoming a Dame of the British Empire, and not only did she design three outfits for Princess Eugenie, the Queen's granddaughter, to wear to the events surrounding Royal Wedding of Prince William and Catherine in 2011, she also designed the wedding dress for Carrie Bradshaw, the lead character in the TV series and film *Sex and the City*. Remarkable progress for young people who had been part of an anarchist/republican movement in the 1970s.

How do you create a culture that can produce such radical innovations as these? What had to be present? Tolerance. Freedom of speech. The rule of law. A high level of trust in the aforementioned tolerance, freedom of speech, and rule of law. Although McLaren was arrested once for an illegal publicity stunt on the River Thames outside the Houses of Parliament, his music and his band were not banned and none of them was thrown in jail. So, we must have explicit values. We must have congruent and aligned action. We must have explicit policies. We must have congruence and alignment of action with policy. We must mean what we say and say what we mean. We must tolerate diversity and create time, space, and attention for the weird. It must be a safe space for unconventional ideas. We must encourage a high-trust culture. We must have a fair and transparent justice system.

Social Capital

Social capital is the fancy academic term used by sociologists and political scientists for the level of trust in a society, culture, or social group. A high level of trust is associated with high-performing economies. Trust enables us to move quickly. Trust eliminates bureaucracy, avoiding the need for negotiation, contracts, audit, and arbitration. Trust reduces transaction costs of doing business and eliminates waste. Trust eliminates cost of delay by enabling things to happen faster. Trust enables greater resilience by removing constraints and smoothing a path to reinvention. "Trust is a means of dealing with complexity in an increasingly complex society."[8] In other words, trust is required if you want to scale. If you want to deliver large-scale business agility that enables Kanban adoption at large scale in your organization, you need to build trust.

Luckily, social capital is a well-understood and well-documented field. There are many well-defined, actionable means by which to build trust. We present here a comprehensive, though likely not exhaustive, list:

1. Transparency
2. Collaboration
3. Vulnerability
4. Keeping promises
5. Predictability
6. Consistency

---

8. Robert C. Solomon and Fernando Flores. *Building Trust in Business, Politics, Relationships, and Life*. New York: Oxford University Press, 2003.

7. Competence
8. Confidence
9. Simpler, flatter organizational structures with broadly defined roles and porous boundaries between responsibilities, allowing for job overlap and some role ambiguity
10. Event-driven; more frequent is more trustworthy
11. Build reputation
12. Explicit values
13. Explicitly defined boundaries of responsibility and empowerment
14. Explicit decision frameworks
15. Explicit policies
16. Tolerance of failure
17. Learning from failure
18. Transparent, equitable justice system
19. Acts of trust

We look at these briefly, one by one:

1. Transparency

When you hide nothing, you are trustworthy. Transparency also builds empathy. When something is visible, it engages the sensory perception, the limbic brain. Mirror neurons in the brain then enable the viewer to feel as others might feel. Seeing isn't just believing, seeing is feeling! Transparency (in the context of a kanban board) shows that you trust the viewer not to overreact, to use the information they gain wisely.

2. Collaboration

Working with others builds on transparency and creates empathy. It creates awareness of competence, but it also creates shared responsibility and accountability, social cohesion, and a sense of being all in it together—shared risk exposure, skin in the game.

3. Vulnerability

It is counterintuitive that in negotiations for peace, you must lower your shield rather than your spear. Showing vulnerability shows that you trust the other side not to attack you. Maintaining your spear communicates that you are strong, potent, and have bargaining power, but it is the vulnerability you exhibit by lowering your shield that kick-starts negotiating. Equally, raising your shield, or raising your defenses, communicates that you don't trust.

Defensiveness is an inherently untrustworthy human behavior, while an ability to show vulnerability is inherently human and signals trustworthiness.

4. Keeping Promises

When someone asks you to do something for them, and you not only do it, but do it well and meet their expectations, you gain a sense of achievement, pride in a job well done. Your brain rewards you with dopamine (see Chapter 18, Why Do People Resist Change?

for more on this). At the same time, the person who asked for the work receives an oxytocin hit, which trains their brain to trust you a little bit more.

5. Predictability

When others can anticipate your behavior, you are trustworthy. Meeting expectations is trustworthy.

6. Consistency

In the same way that predictability shows trustworthiness, consistency—behaving in the same consistent manner, given the same context—builds trust.

7. Competence

Exhibiting competence and doing so transparently allows others to trust you, to trust your abilities and to know that they can rely on you.

8. Confidence

Exhibiting well-founded confidence is trustworthy, but arrogance is not. There is a thin line between the two. To see you as confident, the viewer must have some understanding of your history, your narrative, your track record. People see confidence without competence or experience as arrogance.

There is a flip side to the trustworthiness of confidence—the confidence trickster—an individual so good at communicating confidence that they win trust undeservedly and exploit it for ill-gotten gain.

9. Simpler, Flatter Organizational Structures with Broadly Defined Roles and Porous Boundaries Between Responsibilities, Allowing for Job Overlap and Some Role Ambiguity

When people trust each other, they are more tolerant of role ambiguity, or more flexible and adaptable in both the role they are willing to play in a social group and the roles they are willing to let others play. Higher-trust cultures tend to have less need for the symbols of status such as job titles and adornments that indicate rank. Status is tacitly recognized.

10. Event-Driven; More Frequent Is More Trustworthy

Every trust event results in an oxytocin hit. Getting small doses more frequently is more powerful and builds a stronger trust relationship than seldom-occurring large doses.

11. Build Reputation

Having a history, a narrative of achievement, accomplishment, and success, or the opposite, such as failure, irrational behavior, or flakiness, builds reputation—positive or negative. A good reputation helps others see confidence for what it is rather than as arrogance.

12. Explicit Values

Making all policies explicit allows them to be held up to scrutiny. Explicit values enable consistency of behavior, allow people to anticipate behavior, and make a social group predictable—all aspects of trust.

13. Explicitly Defined Boundaries of Responsibility and Empowerment

Seek to remove ambiguity. Ambiguity causes delay because of uncertainty. When decision and action boundaries aren't clear, people delay due to uncertainty and fear.

14. Explicit Decision Frameworks

Trust in the framework. Trust in someone's ability to use the framework. Trust that when the framework is used, decisions are consistent and predictable. Know that if the framework is used appropriately and a resulting decision is sub-optimal or leads to undesirable outcomes, the framework needs to be updated. If the decision framework was not used, or was used inappropriately, then address the issue with the individual.

15. Explicit Policies

Writing in *The Why Axis*,[9] behavioral economists Uri Gneezy and John List report on twenty-plus years of research into the intractable problem of why women almost always get paid less than men for doing the same work. One of the well-documented reasons in the scientific literature is that women simply don't ask for as much money and don't negotiate as hard. Gneezy and List have shown that this is not the case in companies that have very explicitly listed policies on pay grades, pay ranges, and skills required to obtain that pay and grade. When the rules or policies are explicit, women are much better at speaking up and standing up for what is fair and just. Consequently, organizations with more explicit policies and less ambiguity are fairer, higher-trust organizations. The Kanban general practice of Make Policies Explicit is a direct way of improving the level of trust in your organization.

16. Tolerance of Failure

A high-trust culture is one that is free of fear. If failure is the consequence of following explicit values, explicitly defined boundaries of empowerment, and explicit decision frameworks, it is the framework, boundaries, or values that must be called into question, not the action of an individual. Individuals should feel safe to act within the rules without fear of punishment or consequences.

17. Learning from Failure

"Can we trust that it will never happen again?" High-trust cultures learn from failure and do their best to mitigate the impact or reduce the likelihood of a reoccurrence. We trust the commercial aviation industry because every time a jet aircraft falls out of the sky, they investigate, learn from failure, and take action to avoid reoccurrence and/or mitigate the impact should such an occurrence happen in the future.

18. Transparent, Equitable Justice System

Justice must be equitable in a high-trust system. If someone overstepped the boundaries of their empowerment, any punishment must be equivalent to their foolhardiness. The

---

9. Ûrî Genîzî and John A. List, *The Why Axis: Hidden Motives and the Undiscovered Economics of Everyday Life* (London: Random House Business Books, 2013).

justice system must be perceived as fair and it must be transparent and open to scrutiny. The justice system must be predictable, consistent, and competent.

19. Acts of Trust

Trust begets trust. Ultimately, unilateral disarmament is a viable strategy. To build trust, you must take a risk by trusting first. To be trusted, you reciprocate by trusting. Lower your shield and your enemy may lower their shield, too. Humans are wired to trust and to respond to trust by trusting. Competence in managing risk is inherently necessary in building a high-trust culture. To trust first, you expose yourself to risk. Competence in assessing that risk, of knowing the downside risk of trusting first, is vital to building a high trust culture.

Social Cohesion

Social cohesion describes the strength of the affinity in a social group—how tightly knit they are. Think of social cohesion as the gravity of an organization. If the cohesion is high, the gravitational force is strong and the group attracts new members.

The need to belong is inherent to the human condition. Maslow[10] ranked it third after physiological and safety concerns in his hierarchy of human needs (see Chapter 18, Why Do People Resist Change, for more about this). In fact, humans can be so determined to show conformity and maintain membership in a social group that it overrides their own values, beliefs, judgment, or moral compass. This can lead to significant undesirable outcomes: group-think errors, riots, ethnic cleansing, and war crimes. At a more immediate family level, it can manifest as delinquent teenagers who get into trouble with drugs, alcohol, abusing substances like glue, and committing petty crimes such as vandalism and shoplifting. The child's actions go against their family values, against their upbringing, but they are influenced by their peer group, the gang they hang out with. Tightly cohesive social groups can be problematic.

High social cohesion may be desirable for leading change and for coping in crises, but it comes with its own set of risks and side effects. The tightest groups are often referred to as cults. The high gravitational pull of cults makes them attractive homes for individuals in crisis, the "lost sheep." Leaders of highly cohesive social groups can be very charismatic and, ultimately, abusive. They take advantage of weakness in the "lost," who desperately need to belong and find a welcoming home in the cult.

How Can We Influence Social Cohesion?

Hacking social cohesion is actionable. There is a considerable body of knowledge of actions and decisions that strengthen or weaken social cohesion. Although presented in Table 8.1 as if they are binary choices, recognize that many of these policy choices are in fact a spectrum, shades of grey, rather than black and white.

---

10. https://en.wikipedia.org/wiki/Maslow%27s_hierarchy_of_needs

Table 8.1 Examples of actions that strengthen or weaken social cohesion

Strengthen	Weaken
Work in the office	Work remotely from home
Collaborate with colleagues	Work in isolation
Wear a uniform	No dress code
Charismatic leader	Introverted, distant leader
Strong rite of passage	No rite of passage
Clear definition of membership, or "in"	Fuzzy definition of membership, or "in"
Clearly defined social hierarchy	Loosely defined or implicit social hierarchy
Clearly defined roles and relationships	Loosely defined, implicit, or missing definitions of roles and relationships
Strong symbols, brands, and identity marks	No symbols, brands, or identity marks
Strong history and narrative	Weak history or narrative
Strong traditions	Weak or no traditions
Arcane tribal language	Plain language
Common enemy	No clear enemy
Strong sense of purpose	No sense of purpose
Clear external measures of success	No clear measures of success
Known source of power (e.g., intellectual property, patents, secret recipe)	No obvious source of power
Strong, equitable, trusted justice system	No justice system
Tribal homeland or place of refuge	Homeless
Loyalty	Lack of loyalty
Strong, selfless leader dedicated to the group's success	Weak or selfish leader

Actions taken that strengthen one or more attributes in the left-hand column enhance the social cohesion. Strongly cohesive social groups follow their leader. Hence, as long as the leader wants to make a change, everyone else quickly falls in line and follows the leader. To influence change in highly cohesive social groups, it is necessary to influence the alpha in the group, the leader.

Do Liberal, High-Trust, Tight-Knit Organizations Exist?

At the beginning of this chapter, we observed that we prefer to work with socially innovative, high-trust, highly cohesive organizations, as these give us the best and easiest conditions in which to lead change. As you've read through each of the three sections, you have perhaps recognized that these three dimensions of social-group culture are not entirely independent. Some actions in one dimension influence another. For example, a flatter structure with more ambiguous roles and responsibilities, and hence greater flexibility, is an attribute of a higher-trust group, but role ambiguity weakens social cohesion, and a flatter structure weakens loyalty, weakening social cohesion. So, is it impossible to excel in all three dimensions?

Our Kanban case study literature does, in fact, provide us with examples of organizations that excel at all three, namely, Tupalo[11], Visotech[12] and, to a lesser extent, mobile.de.[13] And the wider Kanban body of experience and community includes firms such as Jimdo. Based in Hamburg, Germany, Jimdo achieved a culture that excelled in all three dimensions at a scale of 250 people; author Stephen Bungay called them "The New Model Organisation."[14] The other examples are at a smaller scale of fewer than one hundred people. Is there an example of a liberal, high-trust, highly cohesive company at a much larger scale? We believe that Richard Branson's Virgin Group of companies does meet the criteria. At the time of writing, in the midst of the Coronavirus pandemic, the Virgin Group's resilience is being tested to its limit. With a portfolio of businesses in the travel and leisure sectors, which include airlines, a hotel chain, a cruise line, and a chain of fitness centers, Virgin has been hit hard. Without a doubt, changes will be necessary and Richard Branson's leadership and ability to steer them through the crisis and reinvent their business will be tested as never before.

Decision Filters

With the KMM, we recognize that desirable outcomes follow practice adoption, that practice adoption is impeded by cultural obstacles, and therefore, culture must lead; and to change culture, we must lead with values—as illustrated with the KMM cultural mantra in Figure 8.2. Values are made explicit in the KMM. So, it is necessary to provide pragmatic, actionable guidance on values adoption. We do this by introducing Decision Filters.

In 2008, shortly after starting his Kanban consulting business, David was working with BT (formerly British Telecom) in London. His sponsor, JP Rangaswami, was a senior executive, a direct report to the COO. At the time, BT was undergoing an Agile transformation, which involved training its UK technology staff in Extreme Programming (XP) and modifying their contracts with Indian services vendors such as WiPro, Infosys, and TCS to require them to use Agile methods. JP asked David, "What can we at the executive level do to help enable adoption of Agile across a business of this scale?" David replied with what he published in 2009 at the XP Conference, as the "Agile Decision Filter."

---

11. https://prod-kanbanuniversity-backend-store.s3-us-west-2.amazonaws.com/case-studies/Tupalo_EU.pdf
12. https://prod-kanbanuniversity-backend-store.s3-us-west-2.amazonaws.com/case-studies/Visotech-Final-Case-Study.pdf
13. https://prod-kanbanuniversity-backend-store.s3-us-west-2.amazonaws.com/case-studies/Mobile.de-Final-Case-Study.pdf
14. https://www.stephenbungay.com/news/97785/The-New-Model-Organisation/

Make progress with imperfect information rather than delay waiting for perfect information.

Act to encourage & maintain a high trust culture.

Treat WIP as a liability rather than an asset.

The Agile Decision Filter is designed to create a culture that encourages adoption of Agile software development methods and their specific practices. It is easy to remember—just three simple statements, three simple concepts. Yet it is powerful and captures the essence of the Agile movement. It works at the executive level and at all levels of management.

At that same time, for the XP Conference in 2009, David published the "Lean Decision Filter." This was an expansion of ideas from Merwan Mehta, David's co-author of a 2007 academic paper,[15] who shared that he often had to teach his students of Lean manufacturing to unlearn the concept that "Lean is waste elimination."[16] This stems from a shallow understanding, often derived from reading the 1995 book *Lean Thinking* by Jim Womack and Daniel Jones.[17] So, the first two statements of the Lean Decision Filter originated from a conversation between Merwan and David in 2007.

Value trumps Flow.

Flow trumps Waste Elimination.

Waste Elimination trumps Economy of Scale.

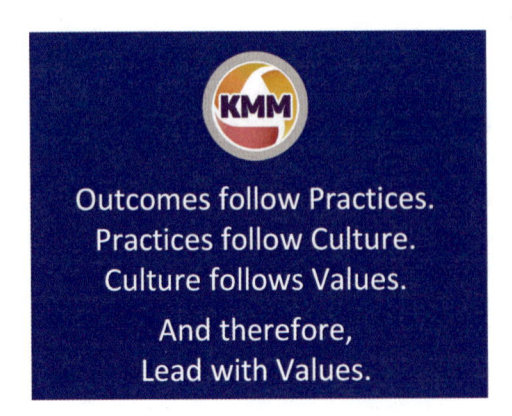

Outcomes follow Practices.
Practices follow Culture.
Culture follows Values.

And therefore,
Lead with Values.

Figure 8.2 The KMM cultural mantra

---

15. Merwan Mehta, David J Anderson, and David Raffo. "Providing Value to Customers in Software Development through Lean Principles." *Software Process: Improvement and Practice* 13, no. 1 (2008): 101–9. https://doi.org/10.1002/spip.367.

16. For further information about how Kanban compares with Lean, see Appendix B, Integration with Other Models and Methods.

17. James P. Womack and Daniel T. Jones, *Lean Thinking: Banish Waste and Create Wealth in Your Corporation* (New York: Free Press, 2003).

We expedite something valuable even though it impacts flow, delays other work, and makes our lead time distribution less predictable and fatter tailed. However, we prefer flow, smoothness, and predictability because it builds trust, shortens delivery times, increases optionality from deferred commitment, and eliminates opportunity cost of delay. Flow and its benefits in trust, risk management, and economic value creation outweigh the cost savings from waste elimination. Waste elimination means reducing overheads, transaction costs, and the coordination costs of doing business. We prefer to reduce these and make small batches or single-piece flow effective rather than pursue economy from large scale and large batches. Large scale and large batches are risky in an uncertain environment. Large scale drives us in the opposite direction, away from agility. Large scale causes us to commit early and move slowly. The consequence may be abandoned, aborted, or obsolete work, the waste from which far outweighs the benefits of lower unit costs from efficient large batches.

The Lean Decision Filter is more operational, while the Agile Decision Filter is a little more strategic in nature. Both provide simple, three-statement filters that are easy to remember, easy to implement, and if followed, will change the behavior in an organization and enable an Agile and Lean organization.

Our goal with the KMM is to publish a decision filter for every value. For now, we encourage you to create your own. Introduce the filters for just one, two, or three values at a time—values that you need to be in place to facilitate the next steps in your Kanban adoption. We give you one to get you started, the Flow Decision Filter:

Stop starting, start finishing!

Tribal Culture and Motivating Change

Ray Immelman's codification of tribal behavior in the workplace[18] gives us some unique insights into sociology and some pragmatic, actionable tools for culture hacking.

First, we look at the lower levels of Maslow's hierarchy of needs with regard to security.[19] We assess how secure individuals feel. Individual security includes job security, financial security, and the availability of health care, as well as having sufficient income to take care of food and shelter needs—to be living above the poverty line. Organizational security implies financial security, political security, and market security. If a business's products, markets, technologies, intellectual property, and sources of profits are under attack, the business isn't secure.

Next, we look at the higher levels of Maslow's hierarchy, the sense of belonging, of identity, of self-esteem, and of self-actualization, both as individuals and as social groups, tribes, and organizations.

---

18. Ray Immelman. *Great Boss, Dead Boss*. Gurnee, IL: Stewart Philip International, 2003.
19. https://en.wikipedia.org/wiki/Maslow%27s_hierarchy_of_needs

	Organization feels secure	**Organization feels threatened**
Individuals feel secure	• Process focus • Rules and regulations • Infighting and backstabbing • Lack of innovation • Risk averse • Conservative	• Cooperative effort to strengthen the tribe • Personal sacrifice • Symbols and symbolic actions become more important • Common enemy • Rituals practiced (to strengthen social cohesion)
Individuals feel insecure	• Resignation (leaves org) • Antagonism toward remaining staff or . . . • Organization ejects individual • Individual acts to harm the organization	• Everyone leaves the organization • Organization quickly dissolves • Individuals lay claim to tribal valuables • Look for a new organization to join

Figure 8.3 Organizational Security Matrix (adapted from Immelmann's Tribal Security Matrix)

In the first instance, like our three dimensions of social culture, these matrices, adapted from Immelman's originals to use plainer, more accessible language, help us make sense of the current situation (Figures 8.3 and 8.4). They are primarily sense-making tools that act to explain current behavior. However, they become culture hacking tools when we use them to guide leadership actions and behavior.

The desirable quadrant in these charts is always the upper-right quadrant. This represents the cultural sweet spot where the workforce is highly motivated and ready to embrace change. Leading change is easiest in the upper-right quadrant. However, disaster lies in the lower-right quadrant. Leaders who drive their cultures into the right columns of these Immelman matrices risk catastrophic failure of their business.

As David wrote, with Alexei Zheglov, in *Fit for Purpose*,[20] Bill Gates, at Microsoft, along with peers such as Lou Gerstner at IBM and Andy Grove at Intel, would encourage their workforces to "be paranoid." This is inherently tribal leadership from leaders who see themselves as culture hackers. By encouraging their workforces to "be paranoid," they (and specifically Gates) would say things like, "We could be innovated out of existence over a fifteen-year period." These leaders were moving their people into the right side of the Immelman matrices.

However, context is required. Microsoft employees are well paid—most definitely above the poverty line—and they enjoy great benefits, career opportunities, healthcare, and financial security. They have a mature employer, trained managers, and a human resources function capable of ensuring a safe, secure, respectful workplace. It would be reasonable to assume that the vast majority of the Microsoft workforce individually relate to the upper rows on these matrices—individually, they feel secure, dignified, recognized, respected, and

---

20. David J Anderson and Alexi Zheglov. *Fit for Purpose: How Modern Businesses Find, Satisfy, & Keep Customers*. Seattle: Blue Hole Press, 2018.

	Organization feels recognized and respected	**Organization feels ignored and disrespected**
Individuals feel they have dignity, recognition, respect, and status	• Clear outcome of organizational efforts • Highly motivated • Extreme loyalty • Strong encouragement and support • Individual heroics praised (at low maturity) or • Systemic improvements are recognized (at higher maturity)	• Urgency to change • Individuals hone skills • Tribal symbols are reaffirmed • Strategies are redefined • Relationships are refined and improved
Individuals feel they lack dignity, recognition, respect, and status	• Individual feels out of step with the culture, values, and group norms, tries to change their behavior and (re)integrate with the group or • Individual leaves to form a new organization	• Finger pointing and blame • Involve outsiders • Loss of focus • Promoting own world view • Infighting • Looking for new symbols of value

Figure 8.4 Organizational Self-image Matrix (adapted from Immelmann's Tribal Value Matrix)

their status reflects their experience and contribution. Although there may be a few employees who feel disgruntled, entitled, or otherwise fearful or insecure, the overwhelming majority relate to the upper rows of the matrices. David reflects back on his own career and time with Microsoft and remembers it as the most secure and respectful work environment he enjoyed in his career. For Bill Gates, it was safe to push the organization to "be paranoid."

So, to use the Immelman matrices as culture hacking tools and as means to guide leadership action—with the goal of moving the culture into the upper-right quadrants—it is necessary first to ensure that each individual feels secure and valued. Address issues of individual job security, financial security, and health first. Next, address issues of individual value, social belonging, feeling part of the tribe, having dignity, being welcomed as well as recognized and respected, and having both a clearly defined role and suitable status.

W. Edwards Deming told us to "first drive out fear"; Immelman paints nuance onto the face of fear and gives it deeper meaning. Drive out fear of losing a job, a home, and good health. Drive out fear of social isolation and lack of respect, dignity, status, or recognition. At the same time, don't pander to entitlement. Drive out entitlement by making explicit criteria for status, recognition, and respect. Make what you value explicit. Create transparency around the assessment criteria of your culture. Entitlement is a destructive behavior that damages your culture and hinders your organization's ability to mature and achieve the economic and business outcomes you desire. There is no room for entitlement in a high-trust culture.

Making the Culture Stick

In her fifteen years' experience with organizational change initiatives, Teodora has always been concerned with making changes stick, bringing continued benefits to the company. This concept of institutionalization, of the changes becoming "how we do things around here" such that they are passed from one generation of the workforce to another, eventually allowing the entire organization to churn and replace itself with new people, and yet the doctrines, processes, purpose and values remain, is vital to long-term survival, and core to achieving a return on investment in change.

The three pillars of the Kanban Maturity Model are designed to make cultural change stay. Organizational change is led by cultural values. People have to like and appreciate how they live in their organization. Practices strengthen these values and ensure that the culture does not revert to what it was before. To the best of our knowledge, the KMM is the first such organizational maturity architecture to encourage values-driven, culture-first change. The KMM's separation of transition practices, largely normative in nature and designed to encourage emergent structural social changes later, is also, to the best of our knowledge, unique. The KMM represents a new means to drive large-scale organizational change and make it stick.

Let us give a few examples:

- At Maturity Level 1, the practices of visualizing teamwork and policies sustain the value of Transparency. Establishing per-person, and later, team WIP limits and holding Kanban Meetings sustain the values of Collaboration and Taking Initiative.
- At Maturity Level 2, the practices of visualizing the defined workflow and defining the work types based on customer requests sustain the value of Customer Awareness. The practices of collecting flow-related data and managing blocking issues and WIP aging strengthen the value of Flow.
- Similarly, at Maturity Level 3, the practices of defining fit-for-purpose metrics, explicitly defining fitness-for-purpose, and managing it based on those metrics sustain the Fitness-for-Purpose value.

Together, cultural values and specific practices enable achieving a sustainable work pace and better business outcomes. These improvements motivate further evolution of culture, and the practices from the next maturity level make it stay.

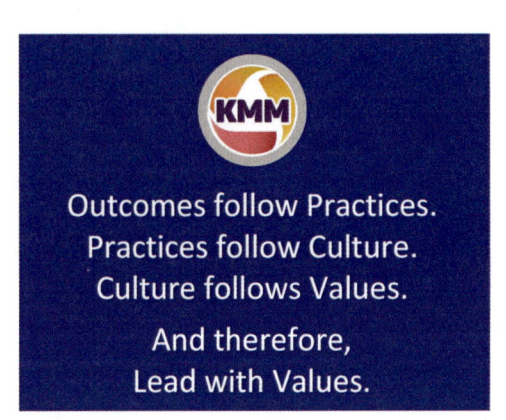

> Outcomes follow Practices.
> Practices follow Culture.
> Culture follows Values.
>
> And therefore,
> Lead with Values.

Part III | Practices

9 | KMM Architecture

The three pillars of the Kanban Maturity Model are Culture, Practices, and Outcomes; together, they describe how people live in an organization, how they do things there, and what the business of the organization looks like.

There are organizations in which managers make decisions, assign tasks to workers, and monitor their execution personally. People do their best individually or in teams to complete the requested work and cope with the frequently changing priorities. Visualizing and sharing what they are doing, as well as collaborating whenever necessary, is their way of managing work in order to meet deadlines and customer expectations. The business outcomes in organizations with this manner of thinking and working depend entirely on the knowledge, skills, and attitudes of the people who take part in it.

In other organizations, managers communicate the objectives for the business and involve the employees in defining the appropriate approaches for achieving them. People coordinate their activities—both within their own teams and with other teams—to deliver the best possible outcomes. To do this, they apply shared policies and use different means to provide visibility into the entire process of developing and delivering a product or service, including workflow-related data and on-time feedback to customers and other stakeholders. The business outcomes of organizations with these characteristics are consistent and predictable, and the entire organization is able to adapt quickly to changes in their business context—and might even be able to anticipate them.

Organizational Maturity Levels

The Kanban Maturity Model describes seven organizational maturity levels. Each maturity level is a collection of culture, practices, and business outcome characteristics.

Managed Evolution is woven into the KMM. It is about defining the approach that enables an organization to evolve toward their fitness-for-purpose while avoiding resistance and overreaching. The organizational maturity levels defined in the KMM can be seen as different stages in the evolution of the organizations that use the model's guidelines.

Kanban Maturity Model Architecture

The KMM architecture defines the foundational relationships among the three pillars of the model. Figure 9.1 provides an overview of the KMM architecture.

The three key components—Culture, Kanban Practices, and Outcomes—are shown in three adjacent areas. The vertical axis of the architecture plots the organizational maturity levels.

Specific Practices

Each of the general Kanban practices can be implemented with one or more specific practices. These practices may have varying levels of fidelity, which is generally related to the depth of organizational maturity. Therefore, the name and number of a specific practice reflects both its fidelity and the depth of maturity of the organization implementing the practice.

For example, Implement Feedback Loops has the following specific practices:

- FL 2.1 Conduct internal workflow replenishment meeting at ML2.
- FL 3.1 Conduct replenishment meeting at ML3.

These are effectively just two versions of the same practice with differing levels of fidelity.

The focus of FL 2.1 is internal, and the attendees tend to be the workers involved in the service delivery workflow or process. The selection of new work is determined by the workers, who pull from some predefined backlog.

With FL 3.1, the meeting now includes customers, and selection is generally made by the customers or by a consensus of all present stakeholders. The purpose of the meeting is the same regardless of implementation, but at the deeper maturity level there is a recognition that there are customers, there are risks that have to be managed, and that customers' expectations must be met. By including customers in the system replenishment and enabling them to affect the sequencing and scheduling of work through the system, risk is pushed upstream to people better informed to manage it appropriately. Hence, risk management is improved, and we recognize that the replenishment meeting (FL 3.1) is a deeper, more mature variation of an internal team replenishment meeting (FL 2.1).

The specific practices defined at each maturity level are derived from patterns observed in the field and are associated with organizations exhibiting the behaviors and outcomes associated with the corresponding maturity level.

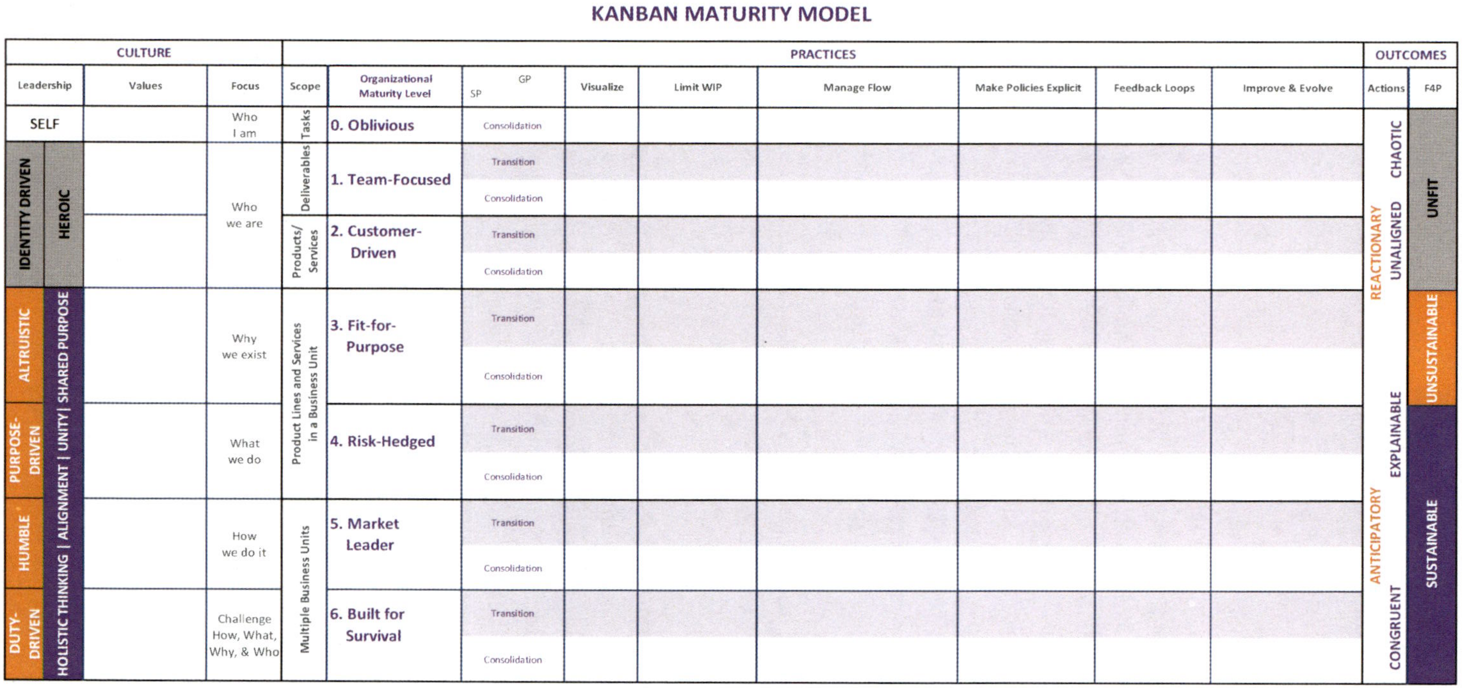

Kanban Maturity Model Architecture

KANBAN MATURITY MODEL

CULTURE					PRACTICES						OUTCOMES	
Leadership	Values	Focus	Scope	Organizational Maturity Level	SP / GP	Visualize	Limit WIP	Manage Flow	Make Policies Explicit	Feedback Loops	Improve & Evolve	Actions / F4P

Organizational Maturity Level	Focus	Scope
0. Oblivious	Who I am	Tasks
1. Team-Focused	Who we are	Deliverables
2. Customer-Driven		Products/Services
3. Fit-for-Purpose	Why we exist	Product Lines and Services in a Business Unit
4. Risk-Hedged	What we do	
5. Market Leader	How we do it	Multiple Business Units
6. Built for Survival	Challenge How, What, Why, & Who	

SP/GP stages: Consolidation / Transition (repeated per level)

Leadership (SELF):
- HEROIC
- HOLISTIC THINKING | ALIGNMENT | UNITY | SHARED PURPOSE

Values (IDENTITY DRIVEN / DUTY-DRIVEN):
- ALTRUISTIC
- PURPOSE-DRIVEN
- HUMBLE
- DUTY-DRIVEN

Outcomes / Actions:
- CHAOTIC — REACTIONARY — UNFIT
- UNALIGNED
- EXPLAINABLE — UNSUSTAINABLE
- ANTICIPATORY
- CONGRUENT — SUSTAINABLE

Figure 9.1 KMM Architecture

Transition and Consolidation Practices

To ensure a smooth evolution for an organization, the specific practices at Maturity Levels 1 through 6 are organized into two broad groupings:

- Transition practices
- Consolidation practices

The transition and consolidation practices together codify the mechanisms for successful evolution in alignment with the Evolutionary Change Model, which is described in more detail in Chapter 17 along with additional coaching guidance on how to apply it.

Transition practices serve to stress the organization just enough—avoiding resistance to change and overreaching—to lead to reflection and realization that the current state still can be improved. When an organization aspires to achieve the outcomes that characterize the next level of maturity, it can add transition practices to facilitate that. So long as the intent and the will to achieve the next level of depth in maturity are present, adopting and implementing these practices should meet with little or no resistance.

Consolidation practices are practices that are necessary to achieve the outcomes that define a maturity level. An organization at a lower maturity level tends to resist or repel them unless some preparatory work is done first. More precisely, introducing (or pushing) the transition practices causes the organization to evolve further and, therefore, pull and implement the consolidation practices.

Architectural Extensions

It is possible to extend the published KMM in two fashions: by mapping additional practices to the existing model and publishing them collectively as a Kanban Maturity Model eXtension (KMMX); and by extending the existing model with additional general practices and then mapping specific practices against these additional general practices and associated maturity levels. Several KMMXs are envisaged, based on the broader Kanban body of knowledge:

- KMMX for Project, Program, and Portfolio Management (PPPM)
- KMMX for Fit-for-Purpose (F4P)
- KMMX for Enterprise Services Planning (ESP)
- KMMX for Service-oriented Organizational Design (SOO)
- KMMX for Leadership

The KMMX for Project, Program, and Portfolio Management (PPPM) will map existing specific Kanban practices for personal, team, project, and portfolio-level kanban boards against the existing KMM and six general practices of the Kanban Method.

Although many practices from the Fit-for-Purpose Framework are included in the KMM published here, a specific extension will focus exclusively on the full set of practices from the framework and any that might emerge in subsequent sequels to the existing *Fit for Purpose* book. The second book in the series, titled *Built for Survival*, has clear, self-evident links to the higher maturity levels in the KMM.

The KMMX for Enterprise Services Planning will map approximately seventy specific ESP practices against the existing KMM—with each ESP-specific practice falling within the scope of an existing general practice of the Kanban Method.

An extension focused on service-oriented organizational design will focus on structural practices and organizational development necessary to enable a high-maturity service-oriented organization.

The KMMX for Leadership will map techniques for leadership development and culture hacking. It will extend the existing set of general practices.

We encourage you to publish your own mappings and extensions to favorite frameworks and methods, or internal corporate doctrine, creed, processes, or methodologies. For more information on developing your own extensions, visit kanbanmaturitymodel.com.

10 | Visualize

The Visualize practice applies to making all aspects of knowledge work visible—the system of managing work, the underlying policies, assumptions, guidelines, and constraints, as well as the work itself. Kanban boards visualize work items that are currently in progress, waiting to be processed, blocked, waiting on others, or behind schedule. This information about the status of work is important for making correct decisions about the work. Similarly, visualizing the policies for managing work, such as the ready-to-start and done criteria as well as the triage criteria, is crucial for understanding the process and developing the ability to improve and adapt to changes in the business environment.

In general, Kanban visualizes

- The work requests and their status
- The workflow
- The risks associated with the work
- The customer's and other stakeholders' expectations for the work
- The policies used for managing the work
- Who is doing the work, and with whom they are collaborating
- For intangible goods, or professional services domains, the goal is to use visualization to enable many of the management techniques that are normally afforded to physical environments and physical goods industries.

Goals of the General Practice

- To provide individuals, teams, and managers visibility on the work, the workflows, and the risks associated with it

- To facilitate the understanding of how the work really works in the process and the identification of problems in the workflow
- To engage sensory perception and move people emotionally
- To create greater transparency and encourage greater empathy
- To enable collaboration, better communication, and healthy debate; to challenge implicit understanding and to catalyze improvements
- To facilitate decision making and policy definition

Benefits from Applying the General Practice

- Makes visible that which is invisible
- Ensures clear and correct communication of information about work items
- Reduces overburdening by visualizing and limiting the work-in-progress to the capacity of the individuals that make up the kanban system
- Develops a shared understanding of objectives, work status, impediments, and risks
- Captures significant business risks associated with work items
- Facilitates timely and coherent decision making, collaboration, and knowledge sharing
- Develops trust
- Reduces disruptions
- Moves the focus from the worker to the work

Specific Practices Summary

Maturity Level		Visualize (VZ) Practices
ML0	Consolidation	**VZ 0.1** Visualize a person's work by means of a individual kanban board. **VZ 0.2** Visualize basic work item related information on a ticket.
ML1	Transition	**VZ 1.1** Visualize work for several people by means of an aggregated individual kanban board. **VZ 1.2** Visualize discovered initial policies. **VZ 1.3** Use avatars to visualize an individual's workload.
	Consolidation	**VZ 1.4** Visualize the work carried out by a team by means of a team kanban board. **VZ 1.5** Visualize basic policies.

Specific Practices Summary

Maturity Level		Visualize (VZ) Practices
ML2	Transition	**VZ 2.1** Visualize progress using a horizontal position on an emergent workflow kanban board. **VZ 2.2** Visualize work types by means of card colors or board rows. **VZ 2.3** Visualize blocked work items, defects, and rework. **VZ 2.4** Visualize work item aging. **VZ 2.5** Visualize dependencies on another service or system. **VZ 2.6** Visualize basic service policies. **VZ 2.6** Visualize dependencies on shared services using avatars. **VZ 2.7** Visualize basic service policies.
	Consolidation	**VZ 2.8** Visualize constant WIP (CONWIP) on an emergent workflow delivery kanban board. **VZ 2.9** Visualize concurrent or unordered activities with checkboxes on the ticket. **VZ 2.10** Visualize optional, unordered, potentially concurrent activities using two columns of checkboxes on the ticket. **VZ 2.11** Visualize optional multiple unordered, nonconcurrent activities performed by specialist teams using partial rows within a column on the board. **VZ 2.12** Visualize defined workflow using a kanban board. **VZ 2.13** Visualize multiple services by means of an aggregated service delivery overview board.
ML3	Transition	**VZ 3.1** Visualize Ready to Commit status, also known as Ready to Pull. **VZ 3.2** Visualize request acceptance criteria, also known as entry criteria. **VZ 3.3** Visualize workflow and team's work items by means of an aggregated teams kanban board. **VZ 3.4** Visualize Ideas development by means of an upstream (discovery) kanban board. **VZ 3.5** Visualize discarded options on an upstream (discovery) kanban board. **VZ 3.6** Visualize aborted work. **VZ 3.7** Visualize class of service using ticket colors, board rows, or ticket decorators. **VZ 3.8** Visualize parent-child and peer-to-peer dependencies. **VZ 3.9** Use a parking lot to visualize currently waiting or blocked work requests dependent on another service or system. **VZ 3.10** Visualize pull signals.
	Consolidation	**VZ 3.11** Visualize replenishment signals. **VZ 3.12** Visualize pull criteria (also known as pull policies, definition of done, or exit criteria). **VZ 3.13** Visualize what is pullable. **VZ 3.14** Visualize available capacity. **VZ 3.15** Visualize failure demand versus value demand. **VZ 3.16** Visualize target date or SLA. **VZ 3.17** Visualize dependencies on shared services using a column with a WIP limit

Maturity Level		Visualize (VZ) Practices
ML4	Transition	VZ 4.1 Visualize local cycle time. VZ 4.2 Use ticket decorators to indicate risk. VZ 4.3 Visualize risk classes with different swim lanes. VZ 4.4 Visualize split-and-merge workflows. VZ 4.5 Visualize waiting time in a dependencies parking lot. VZ 4.6 Visualize SLA exceeded in a dependencies parking lot.
	Consolidation	VZ 4.7 Visualize WIP limits in a dependencies parking lot. VZ 4.8 Visualize capacity allocation by work type. VZ 4.9 Visualize capacity allocation by class of service.
ML5	Transition	
	Consolidation	VZ 5.1 Visualize fixed teams and floating workers (shared resources) across aggregated services.

Specific Practice Descriptions

Maturity Level 0

The intent of Visualize at ML0 is to reduce individual overburdening and facilitate focusing on the right tasks, as well as defining appropriate work policies.

CONSOLIDATION PRACTICES

VZ 0.1 Visualize a person's work by means of a individual kanban board.

The individual kanban board visualizes an individual's work items and their state (see Figure 10.1).

TIP: Replenish the *Next* column by selecting work items from the *Backlog* column at a certain regular cadence, for example, weekly or daily. For a small number of *Backlog* tasks, the *Next* column can be replenished as soon as a work item is pulled into *In Progress* or on demand.

Figure 10.1   Individual kanban board

Implementation Guidelines

Visualize the tasks and their states on a individual kanban board.
A ticket represents a work item, typically a task.

- Each board column explicitly shows the task's states: Backlog (a list of all pending tasks), *Next*, *In Progress* (currently doing), and Done (completed tasks). The intent of the *Next* column is to relieve the person from overburdening or feeling crushed by the weight of the large number of tasks they have in the backlog, to let them focus on those tasks that are *In Progress*, and complete them without losing time due to multitasking. To use the language of Gestalt theory in psychology, items in the *Next* column, together with those in the *In Progress* column, are "open," while those in the *Backlog* and *Done* columns are "closed." The introduction of the *Next* column is required for this effect to be true; without it, the *Backlog* remains open, and consequently a psychological weight bears down on the individual.
- The numbers under the column names specify how many tickets can live in a column at any moment. Refer to LW 0.1 for how to establish personal WIP limits.

VZ 0.2 Visualize basic work item related information on a ticket.

The main benefits of having the tickets on a kanban board is that they visualize work and relevant information about it that is often invisible. The information visualized on a ticket has to facilitate quick understanding and decision making about the work that is represented on it.

Implementation Guidelines

- Use a kanban card (ticket) to represent a work item (Figure 10.2).
- Summarize key information about the task on the ticket: title, short summary, due date. Make sure that the title describes the outcome to be delivered. More detailed information about the tasks can be provided in other systems or in personal notes.
- Further, for better control of the work, note the date (and time, if necessary) when the work item was requested, when real work on it started, and when it was finished.
- Visualize whether the work item is waiting for external input, for example, from another worker, customer, or stakeholder.
- For better understanding and control of the work, annotate when and from whom it was requested and delivered.

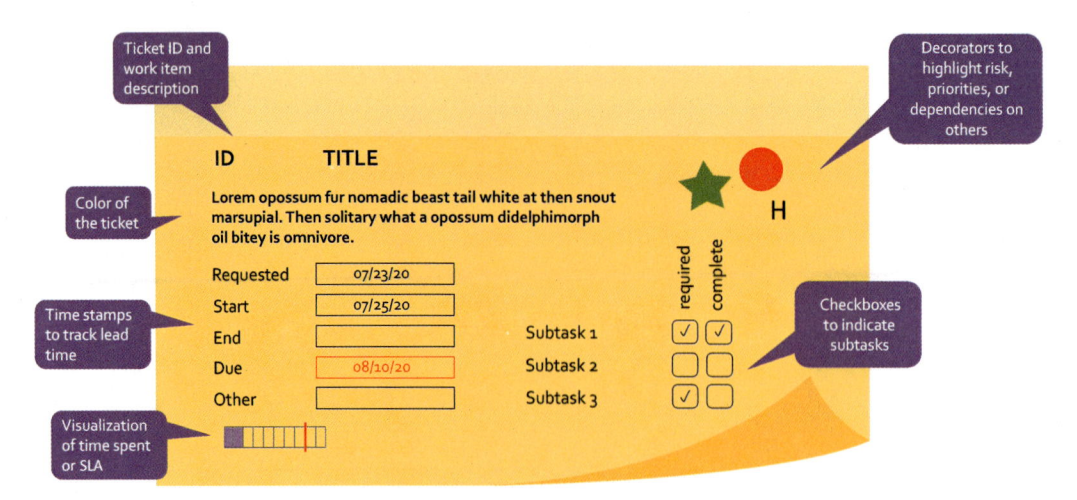

Figure 10.2 Example of a ticket design

Maturity Level 1

The intent of Visualize at ML1 is to develop the habits of collaborative work, improve the quality of work, and relieve overburdening at the team level by means of visualizing both the work conducted by all team members and the policies for managing it.

TRANSITION PRACTICES

VZ 1.1 Visualize work for several individuals by means of an aggregated individual kanban board.

Use the aggregated individual kanban board (Figure 10.3) to provide visibility to the work carried out by several people and to reduce multitasking and individuals' overburdening. Each person handles their own work items (tasks) visualized on the individual's swim lane.

This pattern is particularly useful for geographically distributed teams, as it clarifies what every team member is working on.

Implementation Guidelines

- Use *Backlog – Next – In Progress – Done* columns to indicate the stages of task development.
- Use separate swim lanes for each person's work items.

VZ 1.2 Visualize discovered initial policies.

The intent of visualizing initial policies is to make sure that all team members manage work the same way.

See XP 1.1 for how to discover and define initial policies.

Figure 10.3 Aggregated individual kanban board

Implementation Guidelines

There are different means to visualize policies, for instance:

- Put the policies in writing and post them next to the physical kanban board. Make sure that all who use the board see them easily and interpret them the same manner.
- The established per-person WIP limits (LW 1.1) are a group of policies. Visualize them as well, for example, under the column name, as shown in Figure 10.3. Feel free to use other forms of visualizing WIP limits as long as they are understood and agreed to by the individuals who use the kanban board.
- Define and visualize the policies in the digital kanban board if its functionality supports it.

VZ 1.3 Use avatars to visualize an individual's workload.

Figure 10.4 also shows a visualization of personal workload using avatars. This is another means of catalyzing the control of individuals' overburdening. Typically, one avatar is user per item of WIP. If the personal WIP limit, see LW 1.1, is three, then three avatars are used. In addition, the avatars indicate involvement in executing the work.

Implementation Guidelines

- For each team member, use an avatar to indicate which work items they are currently focused on.
- Different avatars can be used to indicate whether the person is accountable for the work item or is collaborating on it. In this case, each *In Progress* work item will have an avatar of the team member accountable for it and avatars for the collaborators.

- The accountable person may use a larger avatar, or some other agreed visualization for accountability.

CONSOLIDATION PRACTICES

VZ 1.4 Visualize the work carried out by a team by means of a team kanban board.

Using a team kanban board gradually shifts the focus from managing workers to managing work. Team kanban boards also help the team to concentrate on their work, start self-organizing, and reduce overburdening at a team level.

Implementation Guidelines

- Use a team kanban board (Figure 10.4) to visualize the team's work. Use the columns to represent the basic stages of the workflow: *Backlog – Next – In Progress – Done*.
- Visualize work items by means of cards.
- Position the cards in the column that represents the stage of development of the corresponding work item.
- Visualize WIP limits on active (*In Progress*) and committed (*Next*) work. Per-person WIP limits may also be in use; however, the column WIP limit shows the total number of cards that can reside in the column for all team members.
- Use avatars to visualize who is doing what—the current team focus. Each individual may have more than one avatar. The number of avatars per person usually corresponds to an agreed per-person WIP limit (see Figure 10.4).

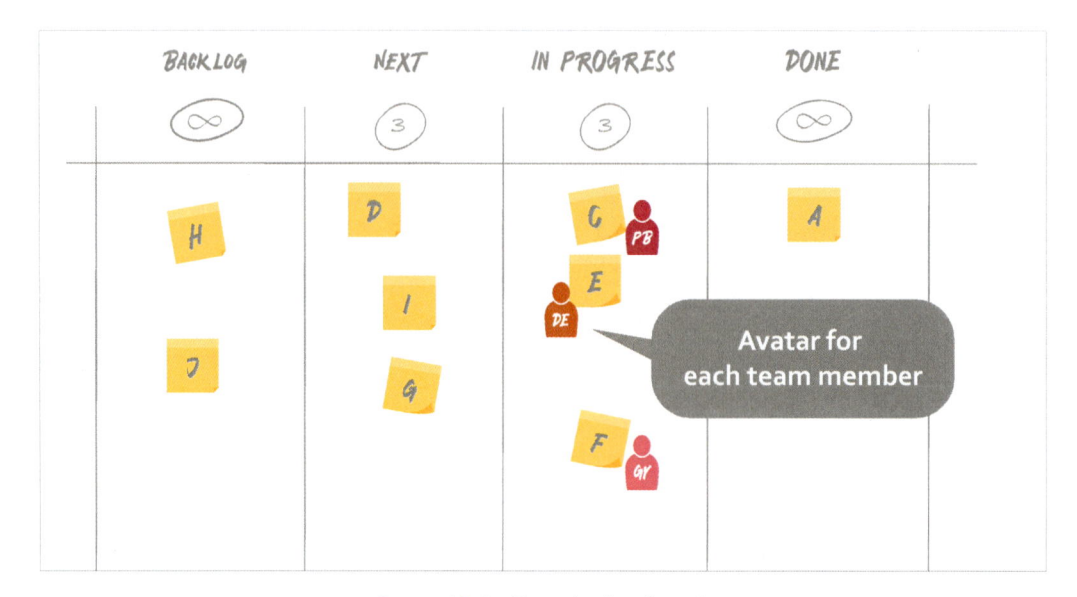

Figure 10.4 Team kanban board

VZ 1.5 Visualize basic policies.

The intent of visualizing basic policies is to ensure consistency in managing work. Team policies may also be known as working norms or team norms.

See XP 1.2 for how to define basic policies.

Implementation Guidelines

- Refer to XP 1.2 for revising and updating the policies that guide and coordinate the team's work.
- Make the policies immediately visible to people who use the kanban board.

Maturity Level 2

The intent of Visualize at ML2 is to facilitate introducing service orientation in the organization, allow the organization to start seeing work from a customer perspective, and enable the collaboration of different teams of specialists, sometimes coming from different business units, in the end-to-end delivery of a product or service to the customer. The specific practices at this maturity level also facilitate the understanding of the key factors that affect the flow of work and the fulfillment of the customer expectations, such as blockers, dependencies between teams, and rework. This information helps the involved teams take appropriate actions and improve both service delivery time and quality.

TRANSITION PRACTICES

VZ 2.1 Visualize progress using a horizontal position on an emergent workflow kanban board.

The intent of this practice is to help teams get a better understanding of the progress of their work. This practice is common when the workflow is poorly understood or emerging. Often the concept of "progress" is very qualitative in nature. However, thinking about "How done is it?" often helps the emergence of a defined workflow.

A simple way to implement a board with horizontal position for degree of progress is to make the *In Progress* column of the team kanban board wider and use the horizontal position of the ticket in the column to visualize two types of progress:

- Progress of a deliverable: the deliverable's percentage of completion
- Progress in the workflow: when the workflow is emergent (i.e., not yet formally defined) or there is no need to show it in detail (when the board is used mostly to report status and the consumers of the information are not those doing the work)

Implementation Guidelines

The emergent workflow kanban board is a rudimentary form of visualizing a workflow and the progress of work.

- Visualize the workflow by means of a wide *In Progress* column that shows the percentage of the work complete (Figure 10.5).

- Evaluate the completeness of the work items using whatever method works for your organization. It is common for this to be qualitative and opinion based. Position each ticket at the point in the *In Progress* column that represents the percentage of completion of the corresponding work item.
- As the team's understanding of the workflow gets deeper, the *In Progress* column can be split into columns that represent the main stages of the workflow.

The horizontal position of the ticket in the *In Progress* column shows the percentage of completion of the deliverable. Lines for 25, 50, and 75 percent of progress can be added as well, as a preliminary step before defining the workflow.

See VZ 2.8 as a possible next step in the board's evolution for the case of a downstream delivery workflow.

Figure 10.5   Emergent workflow kanban board

VZ 2.2 Visualize work types by means of card colors or board rows.

Using a signaling language shared and understood by all the people who use the kanban board is essential for having unambiguous, correct, and on-time communication.

Implementation Guidelines
- Establish a color scheme for visualizing work item types defined in MF 2.1.
- Alternatively, use separate rows on the kanban board to visualize different work types.

If work items are categorized by size, work items with different sizes can be represented on physical kanban boards by means of different-sized cards.

Figure 10.6 illustrates both alternatives.

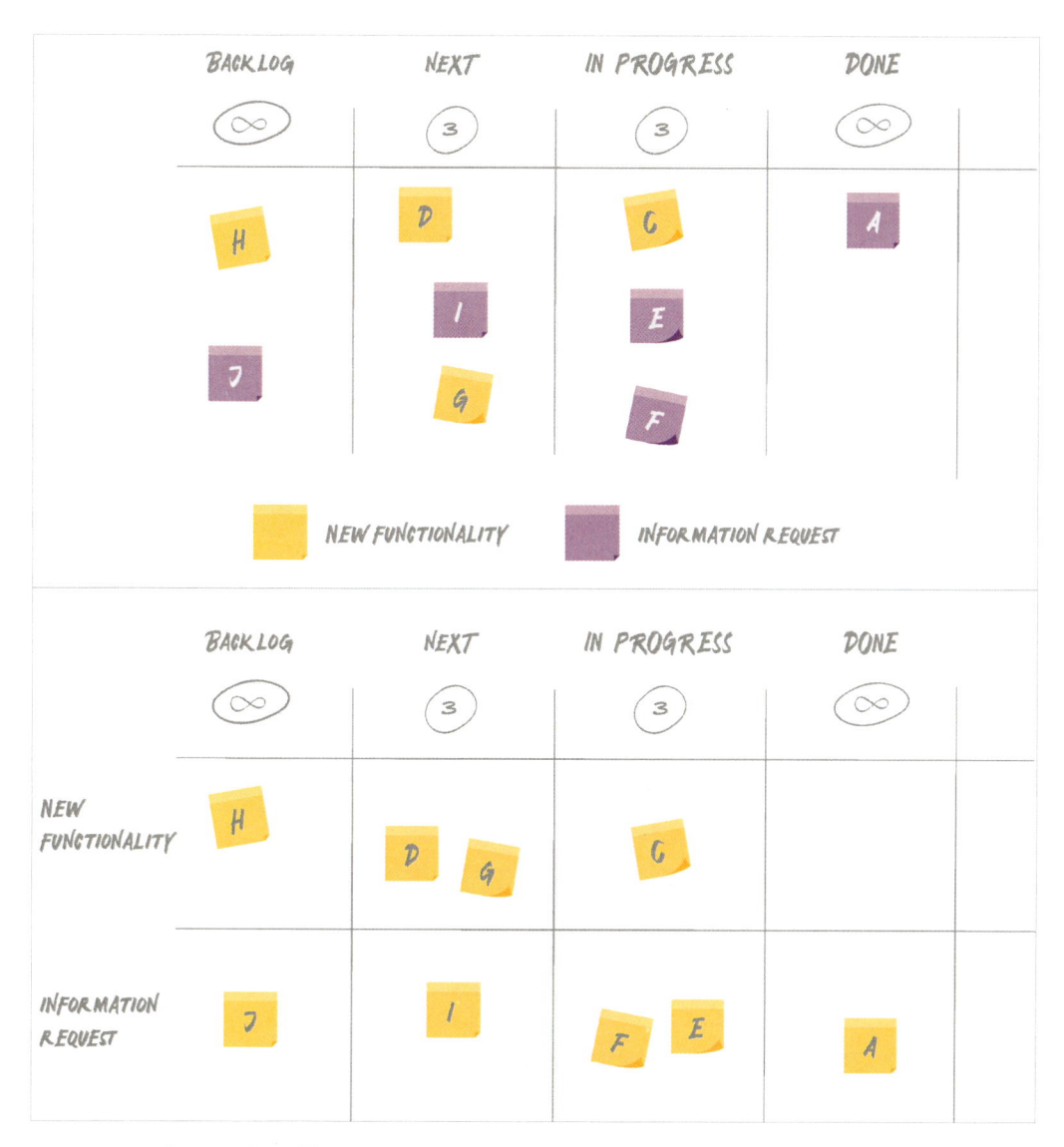

Figure 10.6 Visualizing work types by means of card colors or board rows.

VZ 2.3 Visualize blocked work items, defects, and rework.

Awareness is the first step toward improving the workflow and acting on the sources of delay.

A blocking issue is something that was not anticipated that prevents continuing work on a ticket, for example, waiting for information or permission; dependence on another team, customer, or provider; temporarily moving a team member with specific knowledge to another project or service; a need for additional information; and so on.

Blocking issues, as well as defects and other rework activities, reduce flow and cause delay of the product or service delivery. To lessen these effects, it is important to visualize them, understand what causes them, and resolve them quickly. In addition, collecting and analyzing information about the blockers is essential for identifying and adequately managing risks for future services and product development endeavors.

Implementation Guidelines

- Visualizing blockers:
  - Select a symbol or some manner to indicate that a work item is blocked.
  - There are different means to visualize blockers:
    - If you use a physical board, draw or stick the symbol manually on the blocked tickets.
    - With magnetic physical boards, the color of the magnet may be changed to indicate the blocked state.
    - Digital kanban tools provide visual means for showing that a work item is blocked.
    - Attach a ticket of a different color to the blocked one, as shown in Figure 10.7, explaining the reason for the blockage and additional data that would facilitate further analysis and learning—such as date of blockage, date of unblocking the ticket, main causes for the issue, who is assigned to resolve it, resolution effort, and so on.
  - Different symbols or colors of blocker tickets may be used to signal different reasons for the blockage or different sources of delay, for example, an issue internal to the system, one outside the system but inside the company, or one that is external to the company.
  - Different means can be used to visualize how much time has passed since a card was blocked. A simple way is to draw one dot per day on top of the blocker ticket. An alternative is to visualize the date when the card was blocked.

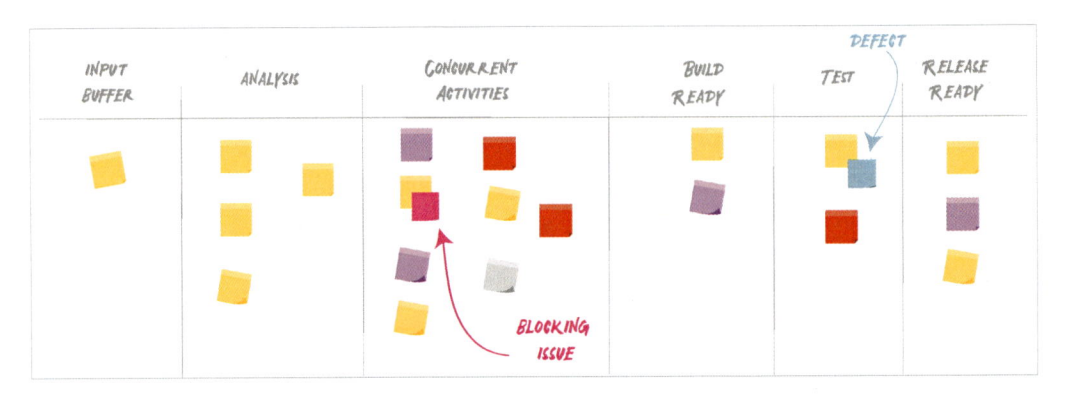

Figure 10.7   Kanban board showing blocked items using blocker tickets

- Visualizing defects and other rework types:
  - Design the rework ticket so as to visualize the following information:
    - ID of the work item with which the rework is associated
    - Title or brief description of the rework item
    - Date when the rework was generated
    - Due date
    - Severity
  - Use a separate color for rework tickets to make them easily visible.
  - Show on the ticket who carries out the rework, the same as for the other work items.

VZ 2.4 Visualize work item aging.

Work item age is the amount of time (e.g., days, hours) that has passed since the work item was committed. For an upstream part of the workflow, this is the amount of time since the idea was first introduced (see Figure 10.8).

Work item aging is an indicator of potential problems because the longer a work item is in progress, the higher the risk of not delivering on time, suffering change requests, or deciding to abort due to not meeting the customer's evolved expectations.

Implementation Guidelines

These are some alternatives for how to visualize aging:

- Use a time progress bar on the ticket, as shown in Figure 10.2. Visualize the time (e.g., in days or hours) since pulling the work item into the system. Mark one unit of the progress bar per unit of time.
- Annotate when the work item was committed as well as started (as in Figure 10.8).
- Ideally, track the age of the work item as well as the time it spends in each column of the workflow to understand which phase of the workflow contributes more to WIP aging.

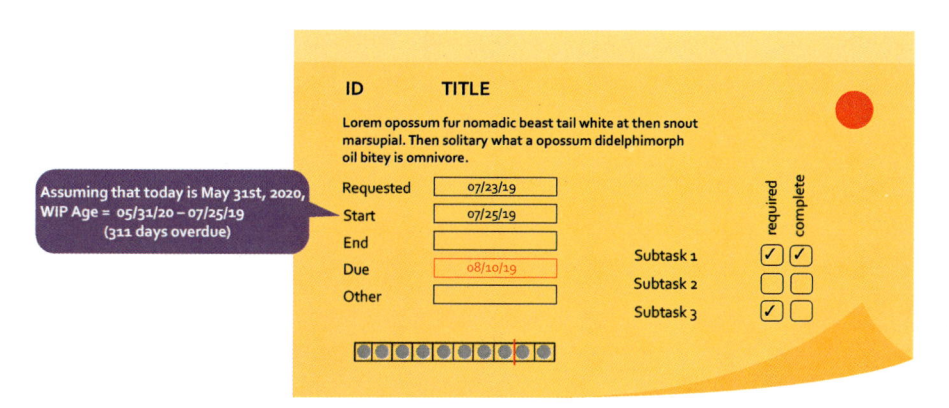

Figure 10.8 Visualizing age of WIP

- If there is an agreed SLA/SLE, one common approach is to decorate the ticket with, for example, a red triangle, once half of the SLA/SLE time has elapsed, and then enhance the decoration to, for example, a red star, to indicate that the whole SLA/SLE has passed and consequently the item is now late.
- Some kanban software solutions visualize aging by means of gradually dulling the color of the ticket to create a withering effect.

VZ 2.5 Visualize dependencies on another service or system.

Dependencies between work items typically occur when different individuals or teams are involved in doing the job. Not managing dependencies correctly increases risk for delays or quality issues. Therefore, it is important to visualize them consistently.

When there are dependencies on external groups (e.g., other teams, the customer, suppliers), it is appropriate to use a specified ticket color or a parking lot to visualize them.

Implementation Guidelines

- Use a tag with a predefined color and stick it on a work item to indicate that its further development depends on work that has been requested from an external group (Figure 10.9).
- Alternatively, designate a special area of the kanban board, a so-called parking lot, for putting the tickets that are waiting on other teams.

Figure 10.9 Visualizing dependencies on another service or system

VZ 2.6 Visualize dependencies on shared services using avatars.

It is common for specialist work to be supplied by people who are not assigned as permanent members of a workflow or a larger service delivery team. Rather, they represent shared services made available to multiple customer-facing services and workflow kanban boards.

You can represent the involvement of these specialists by using avatars on the board. There may be up to three types:

- Local to our project, service, or line of business but shared across multiple teams within that project, service, or line of business
- Internal to our organization but not assigned to our project, service, or line of business; often referred to as enterprise services (or resources)
- External to our organization, such as vendors who do specialist work that we don´t retain in-house, most likely because it is expensive, our demand is relatively low, and/or our need is infrequent

Implementation Guidelines

- As shown in Figure 10.10, use a small sticky note or magnetic card for each person from a shared service.
- Potentially, map the color of the card to the type of shared service as described above. Use consistent colors for:
  - Local shared resources (i.e., internal to your project or service)
  - Enterprise services
  - External vendors
- You may want to decorate the tickets with names and photographs or cartoon drawings depicting the specific individuals.

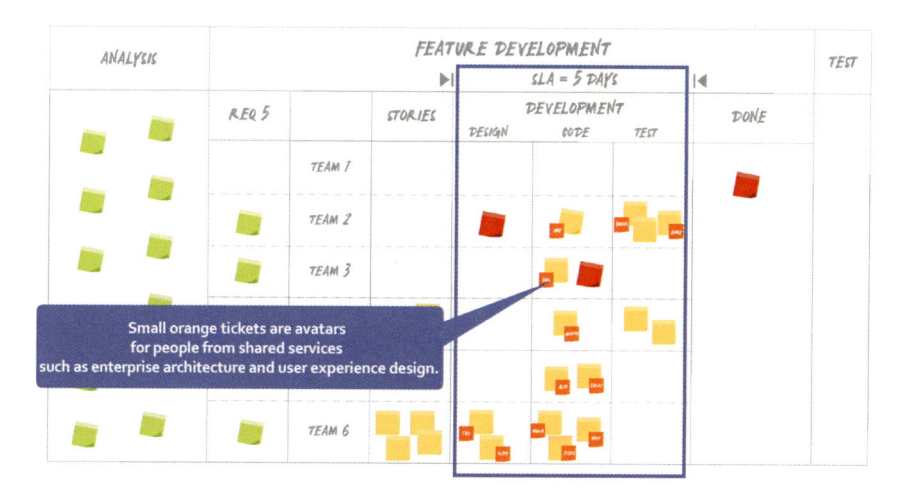

Figure 10.10 Using avatars to visualize dependency on a shared service

- An individual from a shared service may have multiple avatars on the board. As a Maturity Level 2 transition practice, we do not expect to limit the number of avatars, as there may not be any WIP limits at this stage. However, at deeper maturity levels, it is perfectly reasonable to set an individual WIP limit and limit the number of avatars for that individual to match the WIP limit.

VZ 2.7 Visualize basic service policies.

Visualizing policies helps to "Make Policies Explicit," one of the six general practices of the Kanban Method. Visualization helps to remind everyone of the agreed policy and encourages discussion of policies at feedback opportunities such as the Kanban Meeting (see FL 1.1). Visualizing policies also encourages a focus on quality and contributes to developing a shared understanding of the process and identifying improvement opportunities. See XP 2.2 for guidelines about how to define basic service policies.

Implementation Guidelines

Policies can be built into the design of a physical board, for example, by using physical space or tokens such a magnets or sticky clips to indicate kanbans. A capacity allocation for a work item type or a class of service can be displayed on a row of the board.

Policies or criteria that indicate that the work item can be pulled can be printed and displayed at the top or bottom of the column (as in Figure 10.11).

Expected delivery time or service level agreement may be visualized as progress bars on cards or on a legend printed and attached to the side of the board.

Digital kanban tools visualize policies in different manners, for example, by changing the color of a column if its WIP limit is exceeded, showing the criteria for "done" for a column at the bottom of that column, using a symbol for a blocked card and impeding its movement, stating the work item size on the card, and so on.

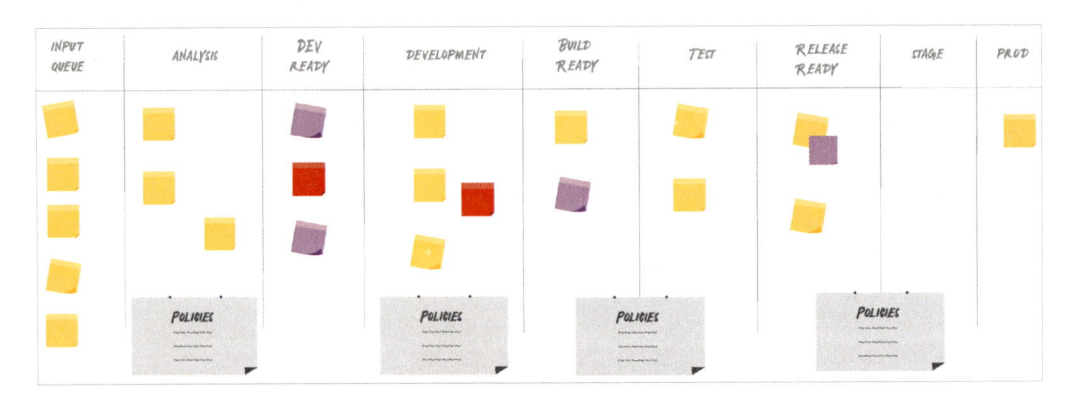

Figure 10.11   Visualization of basic service policies

Visualize – Maturity Level 2   133

CONSOLIDATION PRACTICES

VZ 2.8 Visualize constant WIP (CONWIP) on an emergent workflow delivery kanban board.

A delivery kanban board with a defined commitment point and constant WIP is a pull system with a basic definition of the workflow. Therefore, it allows the team to understand better how service delivery or product development really occurs.

Implementation Guidelines

- Refer to LW 2.1 for how to establish constant WIP limits. Visualize the established CONWIP for the system on a board such as the one shown in Figure 10.12.
- Establish the commitment point and visualize it on the kanban board. At this point, the customer is committed to receive the requested work, the team has a good understanding of the work to develop and also commits to deliver it. The lead time starts to count at this point.
- Using a CONWIP makes it possible to decouple the cadences of the Replenishment and Delivery Meetings as well as to get more precise lead times, as they are no longer tied to the replenishment cycle.
- This board design can be combined with the one in VZ 2.1 to offer a wide column for *In Progress* and visualization of progress using horizontal position.

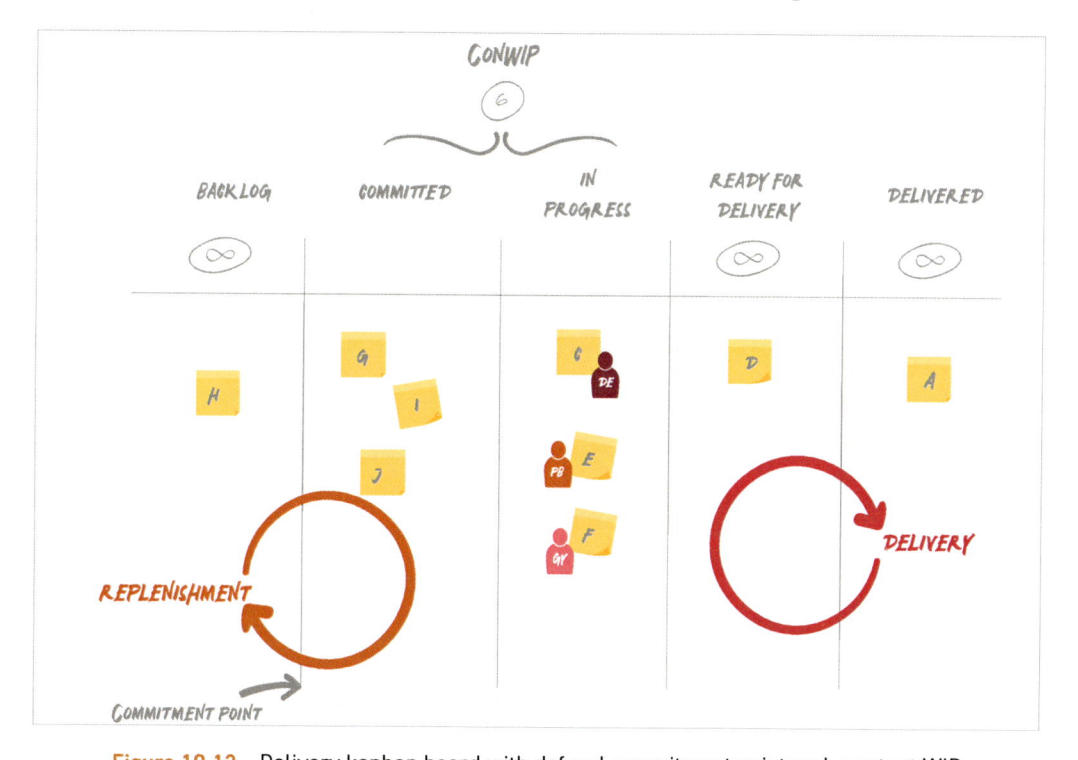

Figure 10.12 Delivery kanban board with defined commitment point and constant WIP

This practice is somewhat of an anomaly in the model, as it contains elements of ML1 (a team kanban board) and elements from Maturity Level 3 (a pull system, commitment point, and decoupled cadences). We've chosen to place it here in the model as a compromise. Its true placement would depend on scale; if the scale is a single team, then this ML2 placement is probably correct. However, if the scale were larger, and involved several teams with different specializations collaborating end-to-end, then we would consider this a ML3-Consolidation kanban system implementation.

VZ 2.9 Visualize unordered activities with checkboxes on the ticket.

The development of some work items might include a range of activities that can be performed by different people from the same team in any order, even concurrently. There is no particular sequence in which the activities have to be done. If these activities were represented by columns on a board, that would imply sequence or dependency that is unnecessarily constraining.

Implementation Guidelines

One way to represent and visualize the unordered activities is with checkboxes on the ticket, one checkbox for each activity. See the example in Figure 10.13. When all checkboxes are checked off, the work for this ticket in this column is considered completed and the ticket can pulled to the next column.

Figure 10.13 Visualize unordered activities with checkboxes.

VZ 2.10 Visualize optional, unordered, potentially concurrent activities using two columns of checkboxes on the ticket.

Compare Figure 10.14 to the pattern shown in VZ 2.9 (Figure 10.13), where all of the activities visualized on the ticket are required. In this example, the activities are optional.

Some analysis is required to determine whether each activity is required. This can be illustrated on the ticket. The analysis can be done up front or just in time either by the person who does the work or by another qualified person capable of assessing whether an activity is needed.

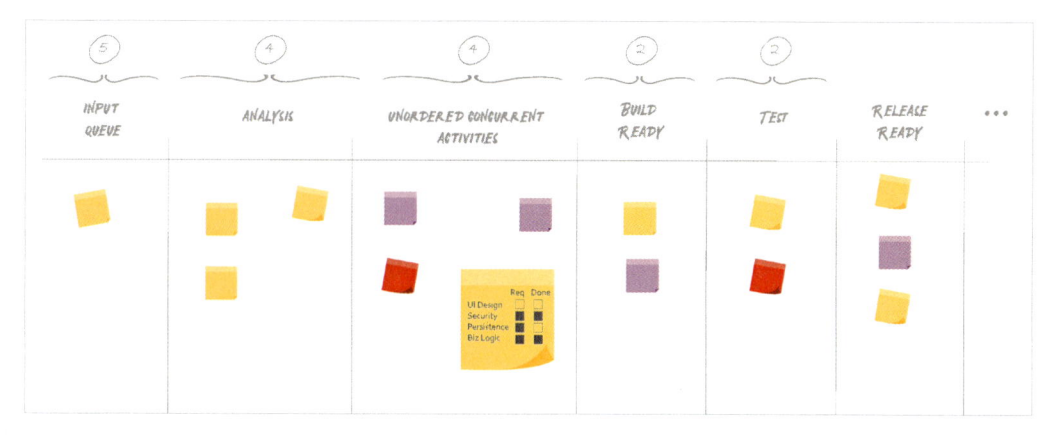

Figure 10.14 Visualize optional, unordered, potentially concurrent activities.

Implementation Guidelines
- List all the possible concurrent activities on the ticket with two columns of checkboxes labeled Required and Done.
- Indicate which activities are required using the checkboxes on the ticket. When all the Done boxes for required items are checked off, the card can be moved to the next column.

VZ 2.11 Visualize optional multiple unordered, nonconcurrent activities performed by specialist teams using partial rows within a column on the board.

The intent of this practice is to visualize a nonsequential series of activities performed by different specialists. The key is that the activities do not happen concurrently, unlike the patterns in VZ 2.9, and VZ 2.10. Either ticket design from VZ 2.9 or VZ 2.10 is possible with this board design. Use the ticket design from VZ 2.9 if all activities are required; use the alternate design from VZ 2.10 if some activities may be optional.

Implementation Guidelines
Because concurrent working is not possible, the ticket-based solution of VZ 2.9 and VZ 2.10 is not possible. Now the board design must resolve visualization of an unordered workflow:
- On the board, create partial rows spanning one or more activity columns where specialist services should be performed. Label each row to show which service it represents.

- If there is only one column of checkboxes, the ticket must move to each vertical area. Once the work in an area is completed, its box can be checked. This acts as a pull indicator—now the ticket can be pulled to one of the other areas. The ticket isn't moved to the *next* column until all checkboxes are completed.
- If there are two columns of checkboxes on the ticket, as in the example shown in Figure 10.15, during *Analysis* it is determined which activities are needed, shown with a column of Required checkboxes on the ticket. When an activity is complete, this is indicated by marking the corresponding *Done* checkbox. Once there is a full set of matching checkboxes, the item becomes pullable to the next column (*Build Ready* in Figure 10. 15).
- If appropriate, define different WIP limits for the specialist areas of the column and visualize them. This pattern is particularly popular if there is a belief that one specialist activity is a source of delay or is a capacity-constrained resource (or bottleneck).

Figure 10.15   Visualize multiple unordered, nonconcurrent activities performed by specialists.

VZ 2.12 Visualize defined workflow using a kanban board.

One of the main objectives of visualizing the end-to-end workflow is to provide information about the stage and status of work to facilitate decision making for all the people involved in the service delivery. In addition, visualizing the entire workflow establishes the background for a better understanding of how work works and defining appropriate improvement actions.

A defined workflow may be a superset of all states for the collection of work item types it visualizes. This takes into account that not all work items need to go through the same steps. At Maturity Level 2, there is a poor or non-existent concept of a commitment point, where optional ideas become committed requests. However, it may be implicitly understood that work items are discardable, or optional, in which case there is an "upstream" board. In other cases, it may be understood that the work items are irrefutable and committed, in which case there is a "downstream" board. In other cases, it might be a bit of both, but the concept of a firm and clear commitment point, where optional ideas cease to be optional and become committed for delivery, may be vague or nascent. There might be small differences in the design that indicate whether the board is upstream, downstream, or a bit of both.

Implementation Guidelines

- Model the end-to-end workflow to reflect all work item process stages as described in MF 2.3.
- Name the workflow stages for the dominant activity that is conducted in them to generate new information or move the work item toward completion.
- Visualize how multiple teams, functions, or specialists collaborate to deliver a customer-requested work order or idea.
- Visualize the workflow for each service delivered to customers as well as for each type of work item that the service works on.
- A service that includes the development of different types of work items with different workflows can be visualized on a single kanban board using columns for workflow states and rows for work types and indicating which columns are not relevant for a particular work type. For example, the Incident work items in Figure 10.16 start from the *Selected for Development* column and go directly into the *Testing* column, skipping the *Development* column.

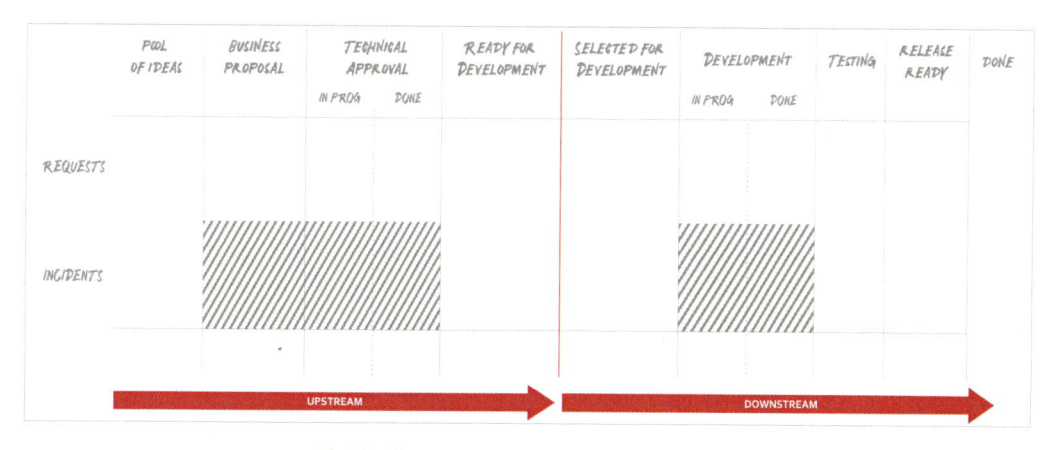

Figure 10.16   Example of upstream and downstream flow

10 | Visualize

VZ 2.13 Visualize multiple services by means of an aggregated service delivery overview board.

The intent of this practice is to visualize the progress of a collection of services. One or more service teams might be involved in the delivery of each one of these services. Like VZ 2.12, visualizing the state of different services on a common kanban board facilitates their joint management and coordination.

Implementation Guidelines

Figure 10.17 shows an example of an aggregated service delivery overview board.

- Each swim lane represents a service. Services have different demands, workflows, patterns of arrival, and governance policies, and they require different knowledge and skills. Some examples of services are Information Requests, Operations, and Application Change Requests.
- Each card represents a service request.
- The details about the development of each ticket could and should be on another board. This board visualizes only an overview of the overall state of the services.

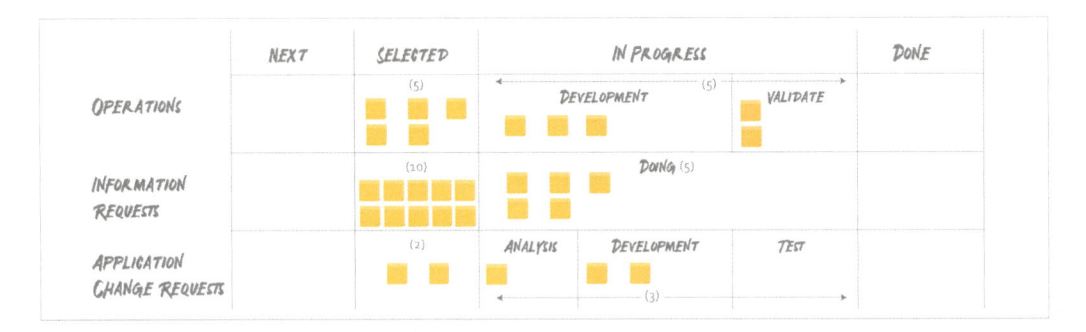

Figure 10.17   Aggregated service delivery overview kanban board

---

Maturity Level 3

The intent of Visualize at ML3 is to facilitate the development of deeper understanding of the end-to-end workflow in order to balance demand and capability, reduce the overall workload, and deliver fit-for-purpose services. The specific practices at this maturity level strengthen the culture of working that is aligned with and focused on meeting customer expectations in a sustainable manner.

TRANSITION PRACTICES

VZ 3.1 Visualize Ready to Commit status, also known as Ready to Pull.

The intent of this practice is to visualize the work items to be discussed and potentially committed to at the next Replenishment Meeting in order to facilitate and speed up the selection of work. Similarly, visualizing work items whose development in one state of the workflow is complete and that are ready to pull into the next state makes it easier to decide what to focus on next as soon as capacity is available.

Implementation Guidelines

Use a physical space or a column on the board to indicate which work requests are ready to be committed for future development and delivery. Alternatively, use a ticket decorator to communicate the ready-to-commit status.

For example, in Figure 10.18, the *Ready to Commit* column includes the requests that are ready to move on to be selected for further development and delivery. The *Next* column has a limit of five work items, and there is one left in it. Therefore, during the next Replenishment Meeting, four work items from the *Ready to Commit* column can be selected for work to begin on them in the next cycle.

Figure 10.18 Visualize *Ready to Commit* status

VZ 3.2 Visualize request acceptance criteria, also known as entry criteria.

Agreeing on and visualizing criteria for starting to work on an item aligns the customer's and the team's understanding of when the request is ready to be processed. Elaborating these criteria as a joint collaborative endeavor improves the comprehension of the entire process for both sides and speeds up decision making. Moreover, having these policies visualized leads to revising and adapting them appropriately so as to improve the entire process.

Implementation Guidelines

- Refer to XP 3.2 for defining request acceptance policies.
- Visualize the policies to be used to decide if a work item can be pulled into the input queue on the kanban board. Place them next to the board to make it easy to check them when needed.

For the case shown in Figure 10.18, these will be criteria for pulling work from *Ready to Commit* into the *Next* column, as well as criteria for pulling work from *Next* into *Development – Ongoing*, and from *Development – Done* into the *Testing – Ongoing* column. Logically, the available capacity (number of kanbans) is one of these criteria.

> **VZ 3.3** Visualize workflow and teams' work items by means of an aggregated teams kanban board.

A service-oriented organization that cares about meeting its customers' expectations manages end-to-end flow. It makes sure that handoffs between different teams do not affect the workflow negatively. In particular, work does not pile up excessively at the handoff point, and the team receiving work does not starve for work, either.

Figure 10.19 illustrates a kanban board that aggregates the boards of two teams, Development and Testing. A board in this style may also be known as an infinite *Done* queue board, because the *Done* sub-columns are unbounded.

In a design like this one, the *Development – Done* column is the handoff point. The *Done* sub-column doubles as the *Next* column for the following activity.

Transitioning to Maturity Level 3, the workers on this service delivery workflow start taking care that there are just enough work items in the *Development – Done* column to make sure that the testing team is neither starving for work nor getting overloaded. This is a step toward establishing and using a kanban system to ensure a smooth and balanced workflow.

Implementation Guidelines

Use an aggregated teams kanban board to visualize on a single board the work carried out by different teams on adjacent steps in a workflow, for example, *Development* and *Testing*, as shown in Figure 10.19.

- Visualize the WIP limits for the parts of the board that correspond to the team kanban systems.
- Sub-activities use the queue of delivered work from the first-step team as an input queue for the second-step team. Initially, this queue can remain unbounded.
- Refer to LW 3.1 for more details on establishing team- and activity-based WIP limits.

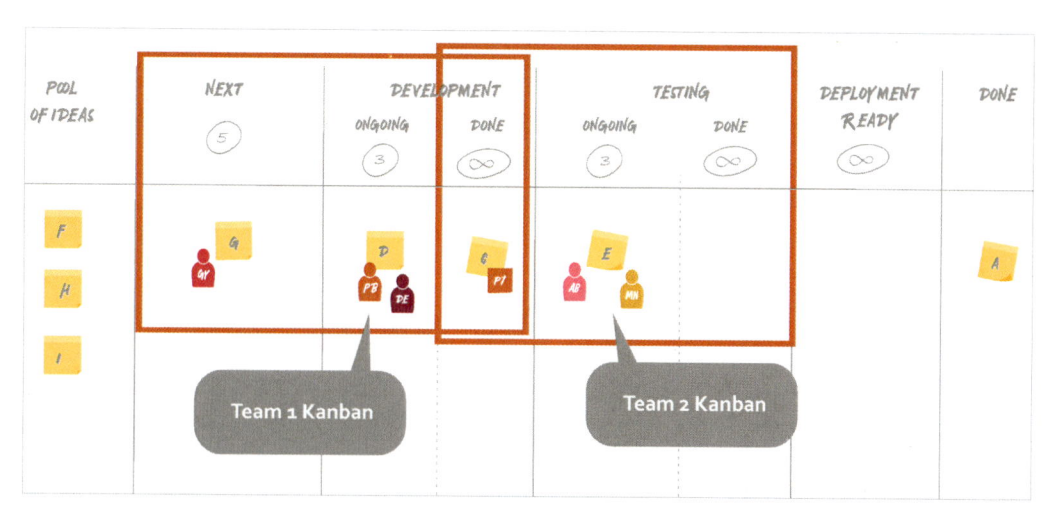

Figure 10.19 Aggregated teams kanban board

VZ 3.4 Visualize ideas development by means of an upstream (discovery) kanban board.

An option is an idea, request, or concept that is available for selection, development, and delivery. Options must be developed by learning about them, by gathering information from sources such as scientific research, market research, risk assessment, business analysis, and so on.

The process of elaborating ideas to be developed and delivered to customers and end users is in itself a triage process. Each idea goes through several steps of refinement before finally either being selected for development or discarded. Only viable options that are feasible to be developed with the available capacity downstream get committed to be delivered.

Refer to MF 2.3 for how to model the upstream workflow.

The intent of an upstream kanban board is to facilitate the development of a stream of ideas before they are converted into committed work. The upstream part of the workflow represents the steps through which an idea evolves and is converted into a committed request. Instead of handling a single unordered list of customer requests, the discovery kanban board allows the team to focus their efforts on elaborating options, concentrating first on those that can be replenished to the delivery team while elaborating further other alternatives.

Elaborating options often involves individuals who also work downstream, that is, those who also have assignments on the delivery kanban board. For instance, developers might work on a prototype or a proof of concept upstream and on implementing functionality downstream.

Creating a smooth flow of options without affecting the delivery workflow requires proper management of an individual's availability.

10 | Visualize

Implementation Guidelines

- Use an upstream kanban board to visualize the state of possible options (Figure 10.20). The commitment point separates the discovery kanban board from the delivery board. Only requests that the customer is sure they want delivered pass through the border between the two systems.
- Visualize the steps through which a request or idea evolves in its analysis and synthesis; for example, *Pool of Ideas – Risk Analysis – Requirements Analysis – Ready for Engineering*. In the *Pool of Ideas* stage, an idea is rather rough and unspecified. In the *Requirements Analysis* stage, the idea becomes coherent, clearer, and can be split into concrete smaller requests. In the *Ready for Engineering* stage, the requests defined from a business point of view are validated from technical perspective. Once this approval is obtained, a request is committed and is ready to be pulled into the downstream (delivery) kanban system.
- Use a ticket to visualize an idea (option).
- Use avatars to visualize the workload of individuals working upstream.
- If the individuals working upstream also work downstream, extend the per-person WIP limits to include the work items from the upstream kanban board as well as the downstream one.
- Often, discovery and delivery are performed by separate organizations, and in many larger enterprises these functions do not sit together. When physical boards are used, it is common for a discovery board to be separated from a delivery board. Hence, it is more natural to have two boards rather than just one.

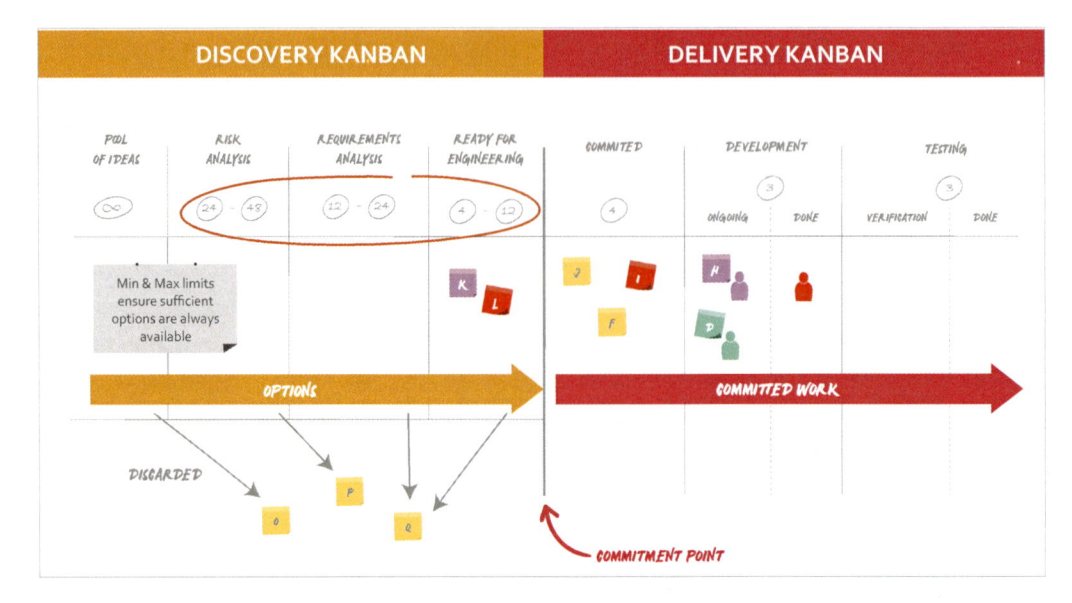

Figure 10.20 Upstream-downstream kanban board that includes discarded options

VZ 3.5 Visualize discarded options on an upstream (discovery) kanban board.

It is useful to visualize and then collect and study discarded options. This allows for reflection on whether alternatives might have been better choices and whether an option has been appropriately discarded.

Implementation Guidelines

- Create a space on an upstream/discovery kanban board or a bin to the left of the commitment point on a delivery kanban board and actively display recently discarded tickets. See Figures 10.20 and 10.21 for examples.
- Before removing the cards of the discarded options from the board, review and reflect on what you have learned from the experience.

VZ 3.6 Visualize aborted work.

Aborted work is work for which all of the following are true:

- It was committed, and a customer indicated they wished to take delivery.
- The delivery organization indicated that they were ready and committed to carrying out the work and delivering the finished work product.
- The work was started.
- For some reason, the work was aborted before completion.

Such work wastes capacity within the system and diminishes delivery capability. It is desirable to avoid starting work that does not make it to completion.

Implementation Guidelines

- Use a "waste bin" to collect all the tickets representing work items that are aborted (Figure 10.21).

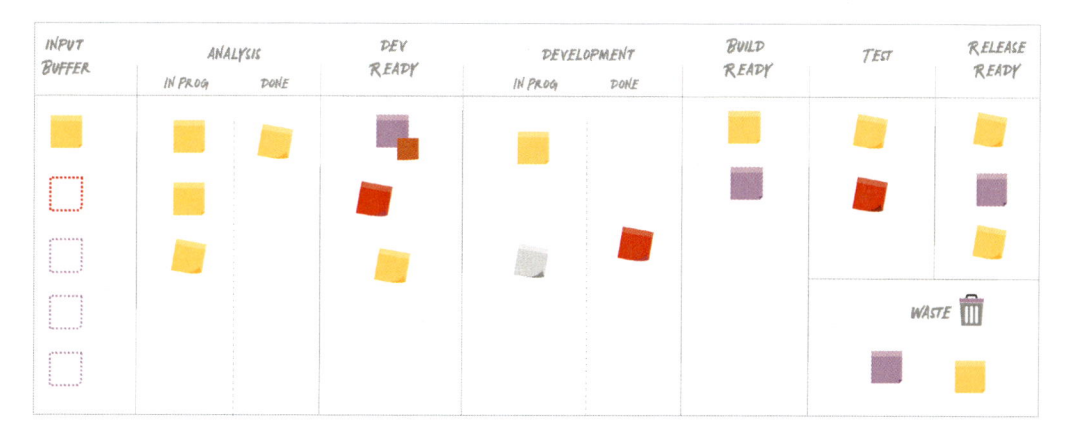

Figure 10.21 Waste bin for aborted work items

- Use graphs (e.g., pie charts, bar charts, Pareto diagrams) or spreadsheets to visualize the amount of aborted demand and the reasons the work was aborted.
- Analyze the causes of aborted demand.
- Plot on graphs the quantitative summary of the analysis.

Aborted demand has to be reported at the Replenishment Meeting and, optionally, at Service Delivery Review, Risk Review, and/or Operations Review.

VZ 3.7 Visualize class of service using ticket colors, board rows, or ticket decorators.

A class of service is a set of policies that describes how something should be treated. Policy is usually aligned to risks associated with an item, or perhaps the value or price paid to process the item. Multiple classes of service are commonly used to extract additional economic performance from a system or to align delivery with differing customer expectations. Assuming there is more than one way that work items are treated, it is useful to visualize the difference in anticipated treatment. Refer to XP 3.5 regarding defining classes of service.

Implementation Guidelines

Assign a color scheme for the defined classes of service. Typically, greater risks or higher levels of service are given warmer, or hot, colors such as red, orange, or white. Lower risks or less urgent items are given colder colors, such as pale blue or green. It is conventional to use pale yellow for the default, or Standard, class of service. This convention emerged due to the usual pale-yellow sticky notes so commonly used in physical kanban board implementations. See Figure 10.22 for an example.

If possible, create standard work policies for the use of colors in kanban boards across the entire business unit or organization. This enables managers and external stakeholders to correctly interpret the meaning of colors across all boards within the same product line or business unit.

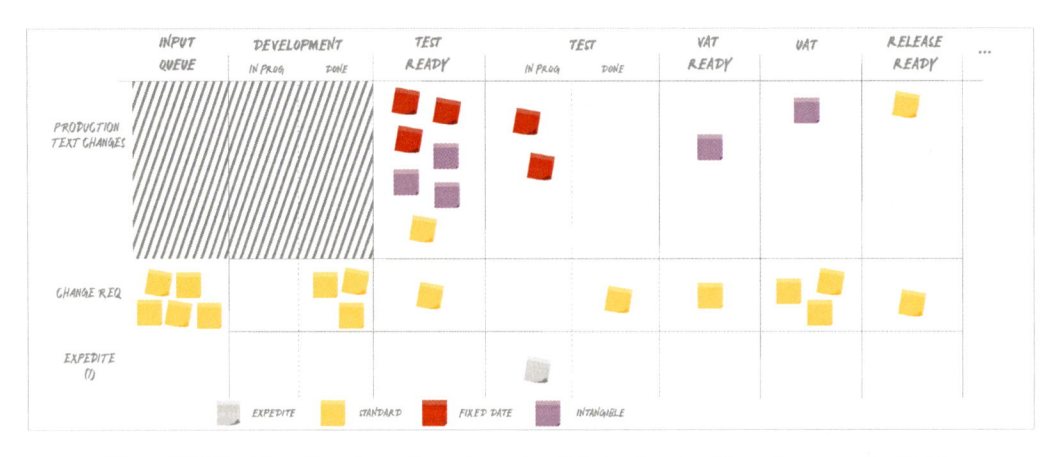

Figure 10.22 Visualize class of service using ticket colors and board rows; note that in this example, Expedite gets both a different color and its own row on the board.

Alternatively, use a horizontal lane on the board for each class of service, labeling the lane with each class's name. Often, this technique is used for Expedite requests, and such a lane is usually labeled with a nickname or common-language term such as *Express Lane* or *Express Service*. The choice to use a separate lane for Expedite offers two advantages:

1. It gives enhanced visual emphasis, which is especially useful if we assign a temporary (tiger) team to the expedite request.
2. It enables tickets in the Expedite lane to keep the color of its original class of service (e.g., if a Fixed Date item isn't selected early enough or serviced fast enough, it can be escalated to the Expedite lane, but maintaining its original class of service color provides evidence for a Service Delivery Review and an opportunity for learning (e.g., we had to expedite that item because [we didn't start it early enough]).

VZ 3.8 Visualize parent-child and peer-to-peer dependencies.

Parent-child dependencies emerge when a work item is broken down to the elements that comprise it. A parent work item is considered done only when all its child work items are successfully completed and integrated. Child work items can reside on different boards from their parent cards.

Peer-to-peer relationships define dependencies between work items at the same level. Typically, these are work items that have to be finished in a particular sequence or items that must be delivered together to enable something of customer value. Metaphorically, you cannot go skiing without both skis and boots—there is a mutual dependency between the boots and the skis in the context of a day of mountain skiing; however, the production and delivery of skis can happen entirely independently from the boots.

Implementation Guidelines

- Define a manner of visualizing each type of dependency: parent-child or peer-to-peer. It could be a symbol—for example, an up or down (or left or right) arrow whose direction indicates whether a work item is a child or a parent, or a predecessor or successor, respectively; the type of line (horizontal or vertical) can indicate the type of relationship (parent-child or peer-to-peer). Make sure that both cards show the symbol of the relationship and that they refer to each other; that is, the parent and child cards or the predecessor and successor cards. Figure 10.23 shows an example.
- Another way of visualizing parent-child dependencies is by means of a two-tiered board (Figure 10.24 on the next page).

Digital boards use different means or tags to visualize parent-child and peer-to-peer dependencies between work items.

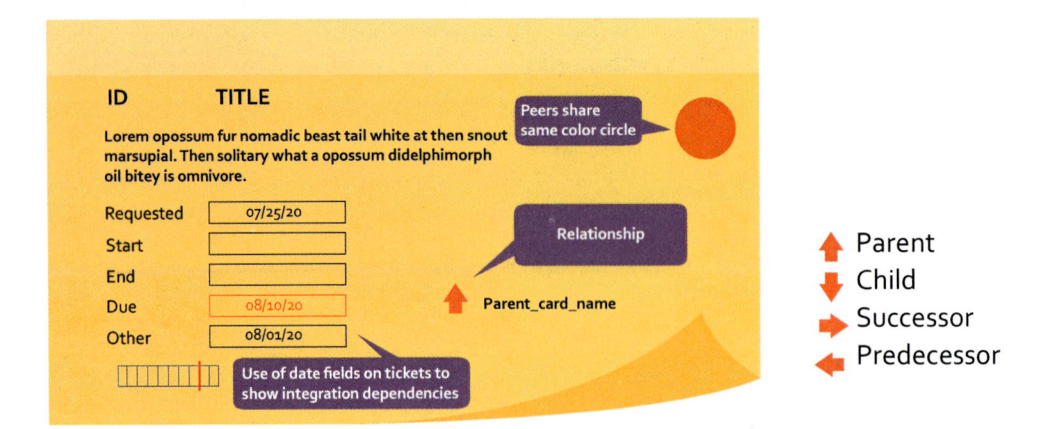

Figure 10.23 Visualize parent-child and peer-to-peer dependencies on a card

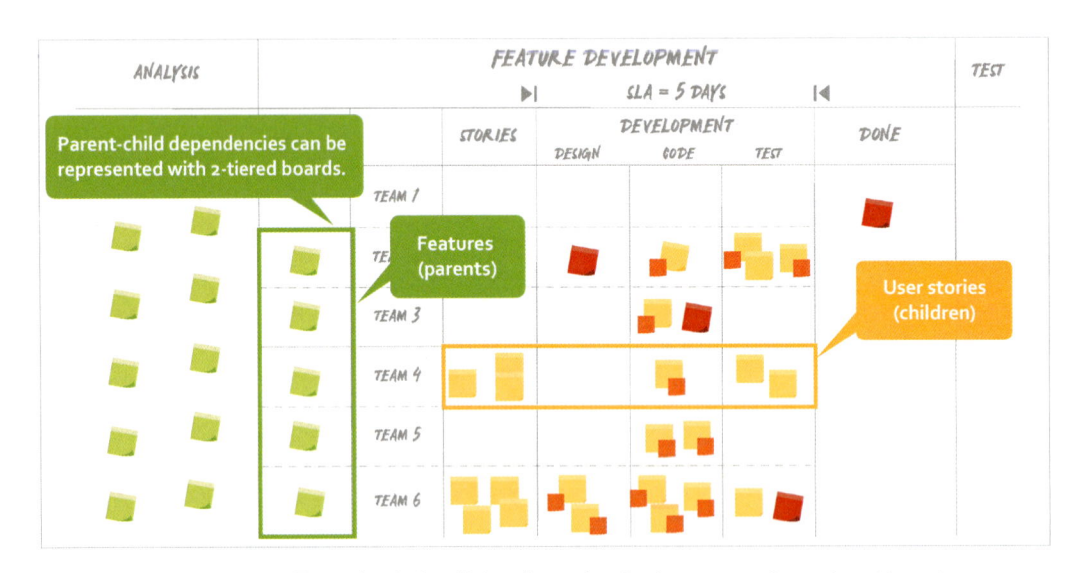

Figure 10.24 Example of visualizing dependencies by means of two-tiered board

VZ 3.9 Use a parking lot to visualize currently waiting or blocked work requests dependent on another service or system.

The intent of this practice is to manage situations when a work item is waiting on an external group (another service, customer, or supplier) and stays in this state for a certain amount of time (e.g., by a certain date). When little or nothing can be done to shorten the waiting, the ticket representing the work item can be moved to a "parking lot" until the end of the expected time.

Implementation Guidelines

- Designate a special area of the kanban board, a parking lot, for placing tickets that are currently waiting on an external group (see Figure 10.25).
- There are variants of this pattern that may involve spawning a new ticket with peer-to-peer dependency on the original. The new peer is placed in the parking lot, and a visual indicator, such as a smaller ticket of a similar color, is placed on the ticket that spawned the external request. See VZ 2.3 regarding visualizing blockers.
- Make sure to track the time the card spends in the parking lot.
- As soon as the agreed waiting time (service level expectation [SLE]) expires, mark and manage the work item as blocked.
- Consider creating explicit policy about managing dependencies, including WIP limits for the dependent items' parking lot and SLEs or service level agreements (SLAs) for the processing time of dependent items, as well as procedures for escalation when dependent items are taking too long and causing delay (see VZ 4.5 and VZ 4.7).

Figure 10.25 Visualize parking lot for dependencies on an external service

VZ 3.10 Visualize pull signals.

Kanban systems are pull systems with established commitment points for both replenishment and delivery. To ensure proper functioning of the kanban system, clear signals must be given for when a work item can be pulled.

Implementation Guidelines

There are different ways of visualizing pull signals, which are illustrated in Figure 10.26:

- By means of physical tokens or slots. Having a free magnet, or a slot, indicates that a work item can be pulled into the column.

- By virtual signals, created by the column WIP limits. Having fewer work item cards in a column than the visualized WIP limit for it creates the pull mechanism. A work item's card can be pulled into a column only when the number of work items currently in it is below the defined WIP limit for the column.

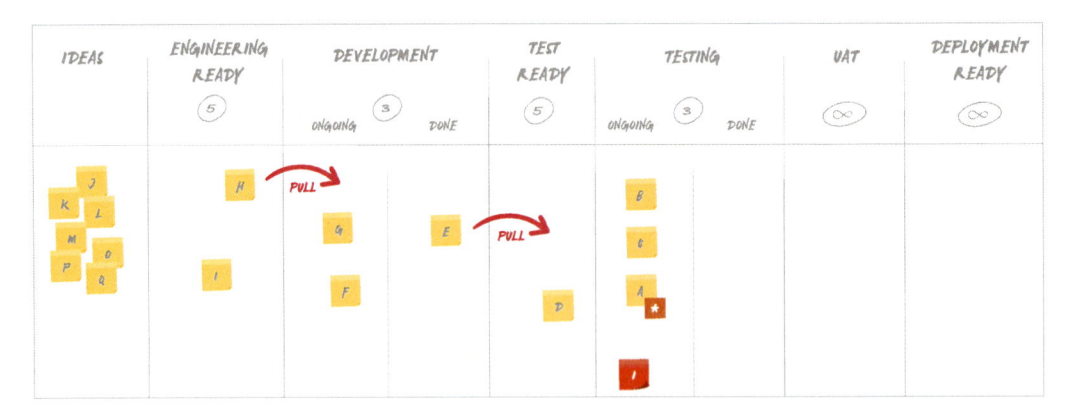

Figure 10.26 Tickets ready to pull to the next stage are shown in the *Done* sub-columns.

CONSOLIDATION PRACTICES

VZ 3.11 Visualize replenishment signals.

Replenishment is the action of reviewing the requested work items and selecting the ones to be pulled into the input buffer of the service system. Selection is made based on an understanding of available capacity, customer needs, defined classes of service, and established policies for capacity allocation.

Typically, Replenishment Meetings are conducted with a determined frequency. However, organizations that have easy access to customers and other stakeholders who need to be involved in the replenishment process can conduct it on an on-demand basis.

Implementation Guidelines

There are different ways to indicate the need for replenishment.

- Movable tokens, such as magnets on a magnetic whiteboard or physical slots, can represent replenishment signals (see Figure 10.27). Having a free magnet or physical slot indicates that there is available capacity and work can be pulled in from the *Ideas* column.
- A virtual kanban mechanism can be used to signal replenishment as well. Having fewer tickets in the *Engineering Ready* column than the established WIP limit for it (the bottom board in Figure 10.27) indicates the need for replenishment.

  A similar case is illustrated in Figure 10.25—the empty spaces in the *Input Buffer* indicate that it needs replenishment.

Figure 10.27 Different means for visualizing available capacity

VZ 3.12 Visualize pull criteria (also known as pull policies, definition of done, or exit criteria).

The intent of this practice is to create a shared understanding for all users of a kanban board of what constitutes a completed work item, when a kanban card can be pulled into the next column of a kanban system, or when a card can exit it. See XP 3.7 for more details about how to define pull criteria.

Implementation Guidelines

Exit criteria can be visualized in different ways:

- Post the list of exit criteria next to a physical kanban board or at the place where daily Kanban and Delivery Planning Meetings take place.
- Write the list of *Done* criteria above each column of the kanban board.
- Visualize the pull policies using relevant functionality of your digital kanban tool.

VZ 3.13 Visualize what is pullable.

The intent of this practice is to indicate visually when work on a work item is complete and it is ready to be pulled to the next stage (i.e., is pullable), as shown in different ways in Figure 10.27. This is a necessary step in instrumenting and measuring flow efficiency. Work that is waiting to be pulled is not flowing and could be delayed. This lack of flow needs to be visible in order to improve flow efficiency by reducing delay.

Implementation Guidelines

The approach to visualization may depend on the type of board:

- If a magnetic whiteboard is used, pullable can be signaled by switching to a green magnet.
- If columns with sub-states are used, it is common to use a *Done* sub-column (and sub-state) to signal that an item is pullable.
- It may also be possible to decorate the ticket with a tab or a bookmark sticky.
- If a set of checkboxes is used to track sub-activities, as seen in VZ 2.10, simply having a complete matching set of Required and Done checkboxes on the ticket may be sufficient to signal that it's pullable.
- Software tools have other ways of signaling that work is ready to pull, such as framing the ticket with a green border.
- It is important that the done, or pullable, condition is modeled as a separate state or sub-state. This enables both instrumentation for measuring working time versus waiting time and more accurate reporting of flow efficiency metrics.

VZ 3.14 Visualize available capacity.

Implementation Guidelines

There are different means to visualize the available capacity:

- Physical slots
- Movable tokens
- Virtual kanban

A free slot, magnet, or sticky clip in a column is a signal for pulling work from the column immediately before it. Having fewer cards in a column than the virtual kanban number also indicates that a work item can be pulled from the preceding column.

The physical slot kanban board is designed to serve teams that tend to deviate from established WIP limits. Therefore, it explicitly shows the places from where work items can be pulled.

On a movable tokens kanban board, the number of magnets represents the WIP limit. The color of the magnets shows the work item's status: in progress, done, or blocked. This board provides more flexibility to the team, as magnets can be moved, added, or removed dynamically. However, it also requires more discipline in handling the number of tokens to ensure the process delivers consistent outcomes.

The virtual kanban for a column is the difference between its WIP limit and the number of tickets in the column. For example, on the third board in Figure 10.27, the WIP limit for the *Test Ready* column is five, and there is one card in it, which means that there are four kanban (available capacity for four tickets).

VZ 3.15 Visualize failure demand versus value demand.

The intent of this practice is to facilitate properly managing failure demand and to develop insights on how it can be reduced or eliminated. Refer to MF 3.9 about how to measure and manage failure demand.

Implementation Guidelines
- Use ticket color or a ticket decorator to indicate which work items are failure demand. It may be appropriate to have an explicit work item type for failure demand and take actions to reduce this type of work.
- Analyze failure demand and graph the quantitative results summary.
- Discuss failure demand at Service Delivery Review, Risk Review, and/or Operations Review to drive corrective improvement actions intended to reduce it.

VZ 3.16 Visualize target date or SLA.

Establishing a target delivery time for a class of service eliminates the need to estimate, negotiate, and commit to each work item individually. Refer to XP 3.5 about defining classes of service.

Implementation Guidelines
Consider the following two alternatives for visualizing a target date (Figure 10.28):
- Indicate on the ticket the threshold date as per the SLA as well as the due date.
- Mark the threshold date on a progress bar (a row of cells, one for each day of the agreed time) such that elapsed time and remaining time until the threshold are clearly visible.

152 | **10** | Visualize

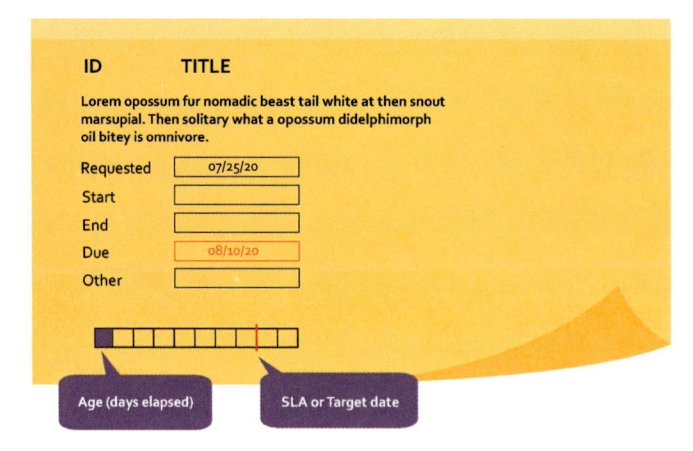

Figure 10.28 Ticket showing due date, progress bar, and SLA lead-time target

> **VZ 3.17** Visualize dependencies on shared services using a column with a WIP limit.

When using a two-tiered kanban board (VZ 3.8), it is common for some shared services to span the rows on the board, effectively offering the same shared service to each of the teams or service delivery workflows shown on the board.

We can tell that the activity is provided by a shared service because of the WIP limit at the top of the column, as shown in Figure 10.29. If the people with the skills were embedded in the teams for each row, then a WIP limit at top of the column would not make sense. The WIP limit represents the capacity allocated to the service (or kanban board) regardless of which team (or row) is requesting it.

There is an implication that the shared service is at least at Maturity Level 3, or perhaps even Maturity Level 4, as capacity is being allocated to this calling service as either a demand-shaping tactic (XP 4.1), or a risk-hedging tactic (MF 4.9).

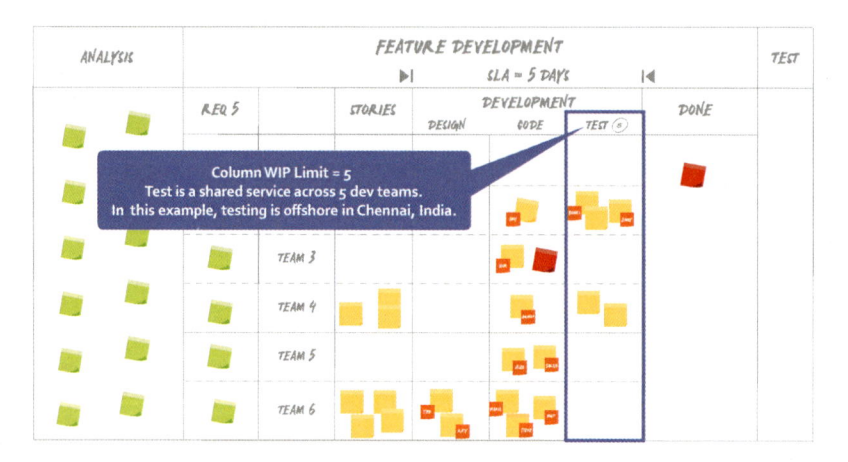

Figure 10.29 Visualizing dependencies on a shared service using a WIP-limited column

Implementation Guidelines
- On a multi-row, multiple-service, or two-tiered kanban board
  - From a design perspective, treat the shared service as if it were a team in the workflow. Give it a column on the board for its specific activity.
  - Set a WIP limit on the column according to the capacity the shared service has indicated is available to this workflow, kanban board, or customer-facing service.
  - The column and WIP limit the span rows on the board.
- It is likely that the shared service has its own kanban board and treats this calling service as a customer and its work requests as a work item type. The WIP limit on the column of this board should match to the WIP limit on the row of the shared service's board, as described in MF 4.9 and shown in Figure 12.13.

Maturity Level 4
TRANSITION PRACTICES

VZ 4.1 Visualize local cycle time.

Local cycle time is the amount of time a work item spends in a specific activity or a defined sequence of activities. For example, local cycle time for test is the time a work item spends in the *Testing* column. If *Development* comprises *Requirement Analysis*, *Design*, and *Implementation*, then the development cycle time is the time a work item spends in all these states before being pulled into *Testing*.

Knowing local cycle times is important for developing a deeper understanding of the entire workflow and for being able to identify the slowest parts of it (the bottlenecks) and the flow impediments.

It might also be interesting to study waiting time by measuring time in *Test* separately from time waiting in *Ready for Test*. These data contribute to calculating flow efficiency and also indicate which states impact flow efficiency the most, and hence, provide insight on where to focus improvement initiatives.

Implementation Guidelines
Alternative approaches can be used for visualizing local cycle time:
- Use dots next to the kanban cards to indicate the number of days they spend in a state (column), as shown in Figure 10.30. The total number of days spent in the column is then recorded in a cell on the ticket when the ticket is moved.
- Indicate on each card the date in and date out for the column in which local cycle time is being monitored.

The same ways for visualizing local cycle time can be used to visualize the time a work item is blocked, for example, waiting on an external group or a customer.

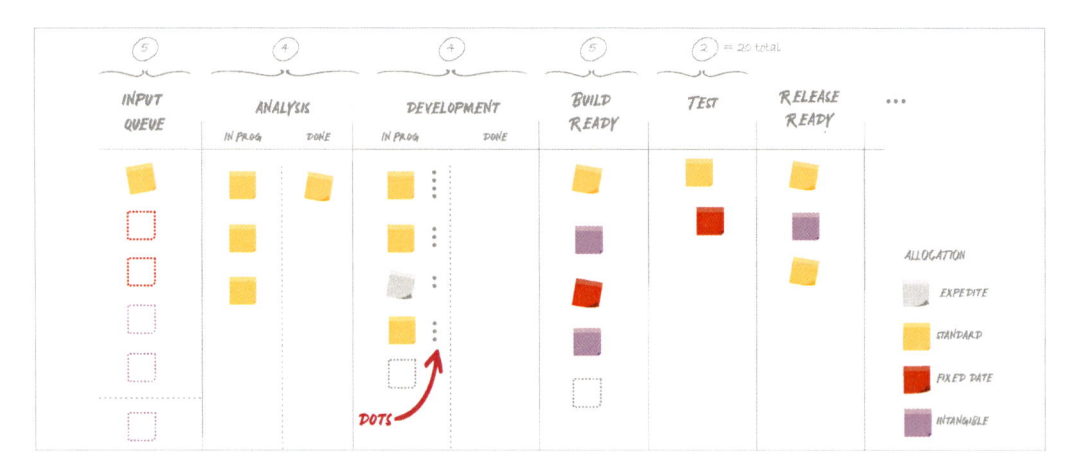

Figure 10.30 Visualizing local cycle time beside a ticket using dots or tallies

VZ 4.2 Use ticket decorators to indicate risk.

Risk is a multi-dimensional contextual problem. Proper risk visualization facilitates understanding the risk itself and how it could affect the outcome of the service, project, or business. Risk visualization facilitates democratization of risk management, enabling workers to make well-informed risk-reduction or mitigation decisions. Risk visualization is a means to greater empowerment and higher levels of trust.

Designated decorators on the kanban cards can indicate to team members which specific risks are present with an item, which will inform what actions are appropriate.

Some software kanban boards are capable of adding decorators to tickets and, in some cases, displaying entire risk profiles as Kiviat charts[1] on the ticket.

Implementation Guidelines

There are different ways to visualize risks associated with a work item (see Figure 10.31). Some possibilities follow:

- Use card colors to indicate risks associated with cost of delay (CoD), typically caused by schedule, budget, or scope change; for example, use white for Expedite, orange for Fixed-date, yellow for Standard, and purple for Intangible work items. Refer to XP 3.5 for defining classes of service.
- Visualize CoD-associated risks by designating a row on the kanban board for each class of service.
- Indicate the due date and actual end date for the work item to signal a delay risk.

---

1. Further explanation of risk profiling and the use of Kiviat charts for visualizing risk will be provided in the KMMX for Enterprise Services Planning (ESP).

- Use a row of cells, one for each day of the agreed time. Marking the age of the ticket on this row clearly shows the risk of not meeting the SLA.
- Use checkboxes to visualize technical or skill set risks related to the work item.

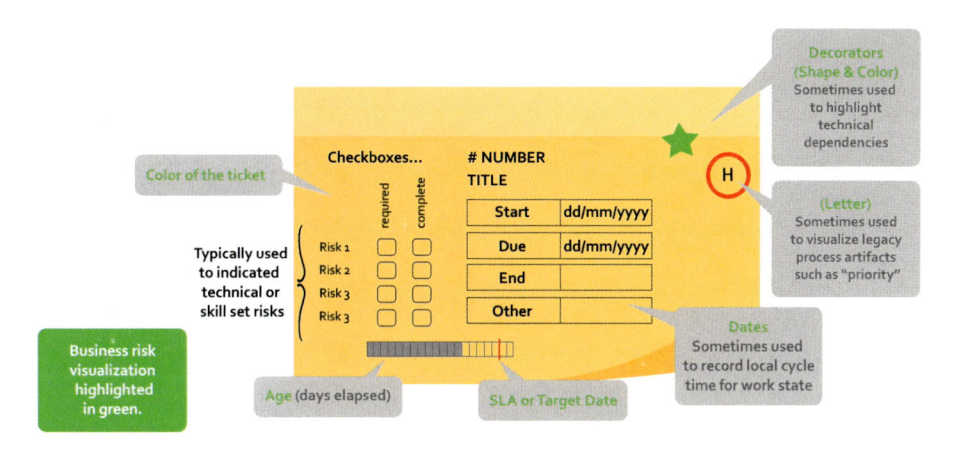

Figure 10.31 Using decorators to indicate risks

VZ 4.3 Visualize risk classes with different swim lanes.

Kanban boards have three very obvious dimensions available for communicating important information. The horizontal position tends to be used to communicate the sequence of workflow stages and an item's state of completion within the workflow. The vertical position and the ticket color are available to communicate the two risk dimensions that are considered most important, usually the source of or destination for the demand (generally indicated by a row on the board) and the class of service (usually visualized by ticket color). Less significant risks must be relegated to ticket decorators or left not visualized altogether.

Implementation Guidelines
- Decide the two most important risk dimensions to be managed. Typically, these are (1) source of demand (customer) or destination for the demand (deployment environment (e.g., iOS, Android, Web), and (2) urgency (class of service).
- Pick one of these two to be displayed using a vertical position on the board (e.g., source of demand).
- For each risk category in the taxonomy for the selected dimension, draw and label a swim lane on the board. All work items carrying that specific risk category are placed in the appropriate lane, as shown in Figure 10.32.
- Define what ticket colors to use to visualize each risk level for the second most important risk dimension.

Figure 10.32 Visualizing risk dimensions:
Horizontal axis: completion percentage **Vertical axis:** source of demand **Ticket color:** class of service

VZ 4.4 Visualize split-and-merge workflows.

Split-and-merge workflows occur when two or more activities or chains of activities need to happen in parallel. This pattern is most relevant when the parallel work is done by different sets of workers or is perceived as different or separate services. Sometimes, one or more of the parallel workflows are provided by external service providers. The parallel work is later merged into a single work product that continues to flow downstream for delivery. Conceptually, this is done on physical boards by splitting the ticket and then merging it back to a single ticket later. The arrival of the completed sub-elements must be coordinated so that the parallel work can be merged back into a single work item and work product. This is usually achieved with a holding buffer labeled *Done*, displayed as a single vertical column spanning the two or more rows for the parallel workflows.

Implementation Guidelines

Consider the following example, illustrated in Figure 10.33. Design and development happen in parallel with test plan design and automated test development. For those columns on the board, create two rows, one for deliverable design and development and the other for the test plan design and development. When a ticket is pulled into design and development, create a second ticket and place it in the other row, using the same index number, so that its peer or sibling can be identified and the pair merged into one after the activities are complete.

When sticky notes are used, the merge can be achieved by placing the second ticket at the bottom or behind the first ticket at the point of merging.

Software kanban boards do not support this split-and-merge concept. Instead, the implementation is done by creating two child tickets and using a two-tiered board solution.

The physical board for a split-and-merge workflow uses rows on the board to designate the split and the merge and the different workflows. The software solution delegates the split to the ticket types. There is no concept of merge—the child tickets simply complete and the parent ticket continues to flow across the board. With software, it may make sense to use different colors to show the different types of child tickets, for example, the mainline deliverable (design and development) as distinct from the second line deliverable (test plan design and automated test development). With the physical board, different workers move tickets in different lanes; with the software, different workers move different colors (types) of tickets within the same lane (Figure 10.33).

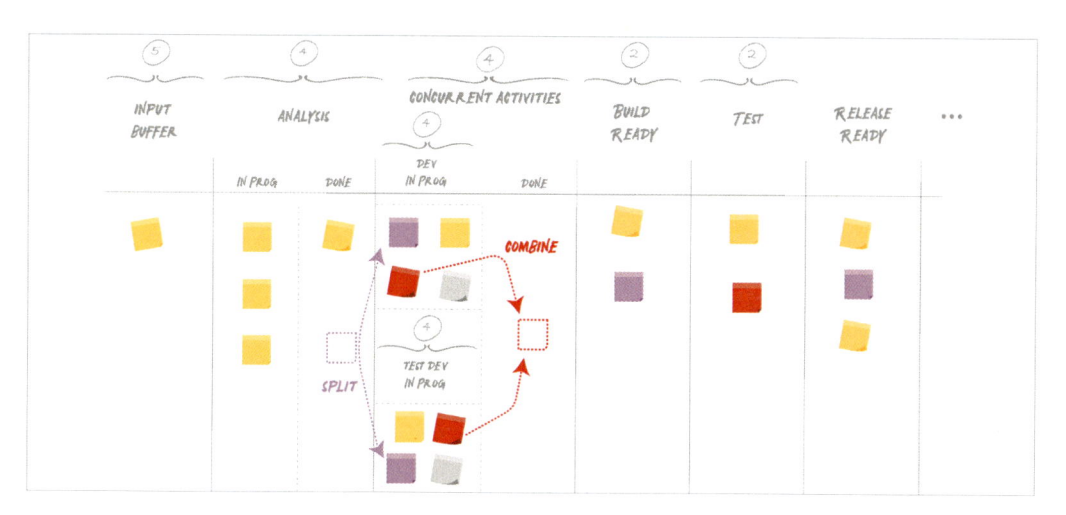

Figure 10.33 Visualizing a split-and-merge workflow

VZ 4.5 Visualize waiting time in a dependencies parking lot.

It is useful to record how long an item spends in a parking lot. Having this data can help to drive improvements at the Operations Review and at the network of interdependent kanban systems level of scale. Visualizing waiting might also motivate external groups to deliver in a more timely manner.

Implementation Guidelines

- Use dots or tally marks beside a waiting ticket to denote each day of waiting (Figure 10.34).
- When a dependent item returns, record the waiting time on the original ticket or the blocker ticket, as appropriate.

Figure 10.34 Recording waiting time for dependencies

VZ 4.6 Visualize SLA exceeded in a dependencies parking lot.

If an SLA or SLE exists with a dependent service, or kanban system, then it is useful to visualize when that SLA/SLE has been exceeded. This information can help to drive improvements at the Operations Review and for the global network of service systems. Visualizing late against an SLA might also prove a sufficient motivator for an external group to accelerate.

Implementation Guidelines

- Use a small blocker ticket in a bright color to indicate that a dependent request has taken longer than expected.
- When a dependent item returns, record the waiting time and the fact that the SLA/SLE was exceeded on the original ticket or the blocker ticket, as appropriate.

Figure 10.34 illustrates tracking time for blocked items using tally marks on the right-hand side of a ticket in the parking lot and then escalating with a pink blocker ticket if the dependent service fails to meet its SLA.

CONSOLIDATION PRACTICES

VZ 4.7 Visualize WIP limits in a dependencies parking lot.

A WIP limit on a dependency parking lot has the potential to stop flow altogether on a service delivery board. It is therefore a behavior of a deeper-maturity organization that is prepared to cope with the stress caused by unpredictable delivery from dependent services or has already resolved the predictability issue so that problems do not occur. However, establishing a limit on the number of work items waiting on others prevents the system from overflowing, which would affect delivery times as well as transaction and coordination costs.

Implementation Guidelines

- Build a place on the kanban board for a parking lot.
- Refer to LW 4.1 regarding establishing a WIP limit for the parking lot.
- Visualize the WIP limit on the parking lot as shown in Figure 10.35.

Figure 10.35 Visualizing WIP limit on a parking lot

VZ 4.8 Visualize capacity allocation by work type.

This practice is intended to facilitate demand shaping, reserving limited capacity of the pipeline for processing work of a certain type. This allocation is often tied to a strategy or a larger goal. For example, if an organization's marketing strategy is subscriber retention, it may wish to focus more on system maintenance and production defect fixes to discourage existing customers from leaving its SaaS platform. In that case, it would reduce capacity for change requests and increase it for maintenance and production defects.

Implementation Guidelines

- Identify the work types and decide how much capacity you want to allocate to each of them.
- Use different swim lanes on the kanban board to visualize the work types.
- Create a kanban WIP limit for each lane that corresponds to the allocated capacity per work type.

For example, Figure 10.36 illustrates the design of a kanban board on which three work types are visualized together and share a workflow: Change Requests, System Maintenance Work, and Production Defect Fixes.

Capacity is allocated to each service as follows: 60 percent (twelve cards) for Change Requests, 10 percent (two cards) for Maintenance and 30 percent (six cards) for Production Defects. Shared personnel can work on delivering any of these work types.

Figure 10.36 Capacity allocation by work types

VZ 4.9 Visualize capacity allocation by class of service.

This practice is intended to facilitate demand shaping, reserving limited capacity of the pipeline for processing work of a certain class of service. Typically, the objective of such capacity allocation is to ensure predictability and allow for optimal scheduling of delivered services. Usually, the capacity allocated to the lowest class of service is used as a risk hedge against arrival of planned or unplanned work with a higher class of service. The greater the variability in the arrival rate, or the more unpredictable the arrival of unplanned work, the greater the capacity allocation for the lowest level of service should be. See the example in Figure 10.36, the purple tickets.

Implementation Guidelines
- Visualize the classes of service using different ticket colors.
- Decide how to distribute the total WIP in the system across all the classes of service.

- Calculate the amount of WIP to use per color (class of service).
- An alternative approach is using a swim lane on the kanban board for each class of service.

Figure 10.37 illustrates an example of capacity allocation across four classes of service.

Figure 10.37 Capacity allocation by classes of service

Maturity Level 5
CORE PRACTICES

VZ 5.1 Visualize fixed teams and floating workers (shared resources) across aggregated services.

A flexible labor pool helps to smooth flow and provides agility in response to the ebb and flow of demand for work of given types or risks. A mixture of fixed teams and flexible floating workers who have generalist, or T-shaped, skill sets is a good solution for optimizing customer satisfaction and business agility.

Implementation Guidelines

- As shown in Figure 10.36, define a board with rows for specific work item types or specific categories of risk.
- Allocate specific teams to each work type and row on the board. Provide a column or space to write the names of each team member against the appropriate row. Indicate whether there is a team hierarchy or a member explicitly playing the Service Delivery Manager (SDM) role.

- For all other floating or flexible workers in the larger team or department, provide them with one or more avatars accordingly. Their avatars can be placed on any row on the board to indicate the tickets on which they are working or collaborating with fixed team members (see Figure 10.38).
- Assignments for floating workers can be discussed at the Kanban Meeting or specifically on an on-demand, or ad hoc, basis with team leads or SDMs.

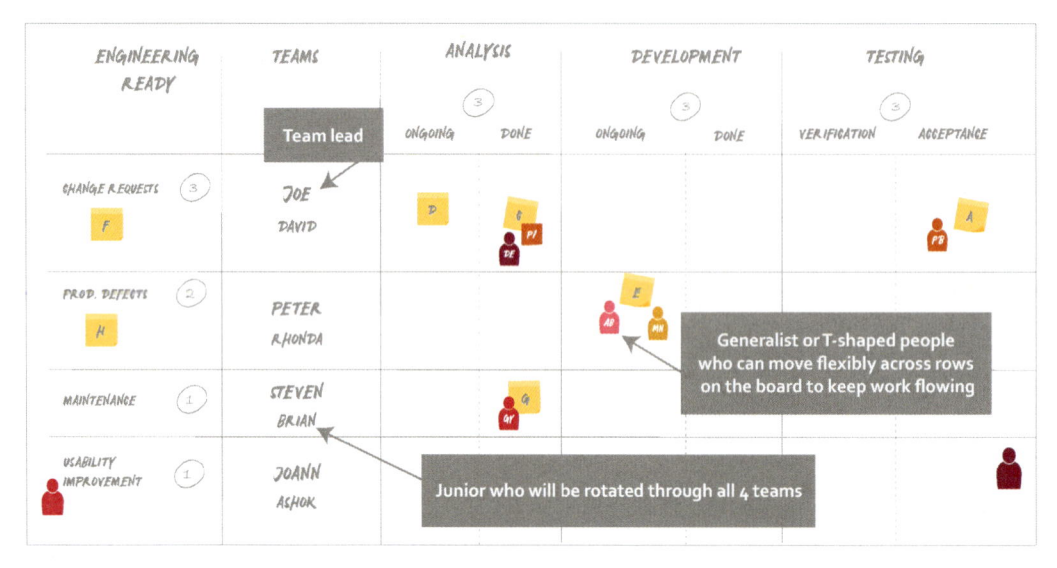

Figure 10.38 Example of a flexible labor pool pattern for improved system liquidity and smoother flow

11 | Limit Work-in-Progress

As customers, we all love receiving our requested products and services quickly and on time. Every business is interested in increasing their delivery rate, reducing their delivery time (time-to-market), rework time and cost, and improving their flow efficiency.

Traditional management methods are strongly focused on following a plan. This is the foundation for the belief that to ensure on-time delivery, work has to start on time, hence the need to push work. Little attention has been paid to the effects of having more work items than the available capacity can handle efficiently. Individuals tend to carry several work items to make sure that if one gets blocked, they stay busy working on another one. The adverse effects of multitasking on delivery time, on rework, and hence, on costs are either not known or not taken into consideration. In knowledge work, there is an additional difficulty, namely that it is hard to determine the available capacity unless it is visualized. Consequently, in organizations that carry out lots of work in parallel, people have the perception that workers are very busy, but their productivity is low.

Limiting work-in-progress (WIP) is about introducing signals (kanbans) that indicate whether capacity for starting work is available. This converts the push practice into a pull one, and it improves the flow of results as well as the delivery time.

Goals of the General Practice

- To relieve individuals, functions, and service delivery systems of overburdening
- To discourage excessive and damaging multitasking
- To accelerate flow, increase delivery rate, and reduce delivery time
- To encourage deferred commitment

- To establish a pull system on the workflow, either whole or in part
- To catalyze the development of triage capability

Benefits from Applying the General Practice

- Allows individuals and teams to focus on customer-valued work
- Helps the work flow smoothly through a kanban system, making delivery times more predictable
- Mitigates the effects of unevenness in arrival rate and flow of work
- Makes bottlenecks visible
- Makes visible delays due to non-instant availability of shared resources
- Amplifies the impact of blocking issues and encourage their early and swift resolution
- Improves value delivery rate, delivery times, and quality
- Stimulates conversations about problems in the process
- Fosters collaboration, causing people to work together on work items in order to finish them and free up capacity in the kanban system
- Facilitates achieving balance within and between kanban systems
- Facilitates understanding of the process
- Helps reduce or eliminate three core types of waste: *muri* (overburdening), resulting in poor quality and rework; *mura* (unevenness), resulting in long and unpredictable lead times, encouraging early starts and more WIP, or incurring unanticipated (opportunity) cost of delay; and *muda* (non-value-adding activities), resulting in additional costs and potential delays

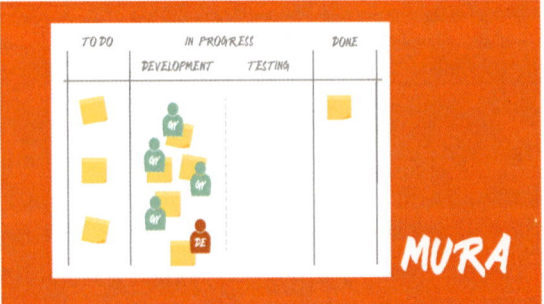

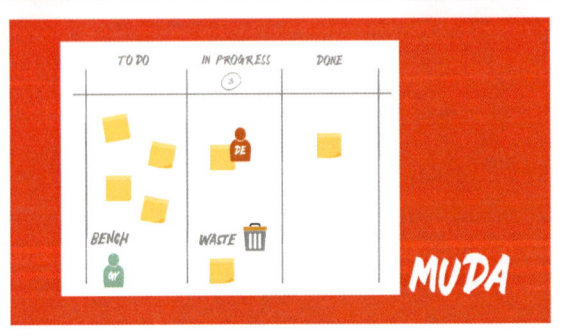

Specific Practices Summary

Maturity Level		Limit Work-in-Progress (LW) Practices
ML0	Consolidation	**LW 0.1** Establish personal WIP limits.
ML1	Transition	**LW 1.1** Establish per-person WIP limits.
	Consolidation	**LW 1.2** Establish team WIP limits.
ML2	Transition	
	Consolidation	**LW 2.1** Establish constant WIP (CONWIP) limits on an emergent workflow. **LW 2.2** Establish WIP limits on an aggregated service delivery overview board.
ML3	Transition	**LW 3.1** Establish activity-based WIP limits.
	Consolidation	**LW 3.2** Use an order point (minimum limit) for upstream replenishment. **LW 3.3** Use a maximum (max) limit to constrain upstream capacity. **LW 3.4** Bracket WIP limits across sub-states. **LW 3.5** Bracket WIP limits across activities. **LW 3.6** Create a full kanban system.
ML4	Transition	
	Consolidation	**LW 4.1** Limit WIP for a dependency parking lot. **LW 4.2** Limit WIP by type of work. **LW 4.3** Limit WIP by class of service.

Specific Practices Descriptions

Maturity Level 0

The intent of this practice at ML0 is to reduce an individual's overburdening, distractions, and multitasking, and to facilitate focusing on the right tasks. The immediately observed benefits are reduced delivery time and better quality of work.

CONSOLIDATION PRACTICES

LW 0.1 Establish personal WIP limits.

Limiting work-in-progress (WIP) restricts the number of started-but-not-finished work items. This reduces multitasking, and hence, the lead time for delivering work. The lower the WIP limit, the less multitasking, the shorter the time for delivering results, and the better the quality.

> Research in psychology suggests that two or three things in progress simultaneously is optimal, producing the best outcome for efficiency, quality, lead time, and completion rate. Regularly completing work provides a sense of achievement and motivation to continue.

Implementation Guidelines

- Establish the number of work items (tasks) that can reside in the *In Progress* and *Next* columns (Figure 10.1).
- Determine the WIP limit, empirically observing how many tickets are completed between two subsequent replenishments of the *Next* column.

Initially, the "personal tasks" list is unlimited—and usually long. A rule of thumb is to start limiting the WIP gradually until reaching the minimum optimal number of tasks in progress.

One approach could be to count the tasks you currently have in progress every day and average them over the last week or two; establish this number as an initial limit, and then gradually reduce the WIP limit while measuring your productivity. Continue reducing the limit as long as productivity increases.

Keep the size of the work items small enough to observe how they flow across the board. Small things achieved frequently have a greater positive impact than a large thing or batch of things completed infrequently.

Maturity Level 1

The intent of Limit WIP at ML1 is to have the team focus on the right work to do at a given moment in order to improve both work quality and delivery time as well as to reduce team overburdening and spread knowledge among team members.

TRANSITION PRACTICES

LW 1.1 Establish per-person WIP limits.

Implementation Guidelines

- Establish empirically the number of work items per person that can be in the *In Progress* column of a person's lane on the aggregated individual kanban board (VZ 1.1).
- Try to codify the size of an individual work item against a single unit of WIP; for example, no ticket should involve more than two days of work for an individual working without interruption.
- For teams that are used to managing work in terms of working hours or other units, an appropriate per-person WIP limit would be approximately the number of work items that can be delivered in a couple of days.

CONSOLIDATION PRACTICES

LW 1.2 Establish team WIP limits.

Unlike per-person WIP limits, establishing team WIP limits fosters collaboration, speeds up delivery, increases workflow efficiency, and facilitates knowledge sharing. In addition, team WIP limits build the culture of "delivering customer value together." Team members start collaborating on work items that require joint work, trying to understand and resolve them together. A team WIP limit is the first step toward viewing a group of individuals who collaborate together as a system. A team WIP limit aims to avoid overburdening the team as a system. Team WIP limits change the sociology from individualism to thinking as a small group—a team—"we are in this together."

Implementation Guidelines

- Empirically establish the WIP limit for the entire team. Pick a reasonable number, then adjust upward, if team members are idle because the WIP limit does not allow them to start work; adjust it downward if team members are multitasking.
- Observe what causes breaking the established team WIP limit. Make sure that team members do not start new work items or stay idle instead of swarming on larger tasks or tasks with associated issues.

Maturity Level 2

The intent of limiting WIP at ML2 is to reduce overburdening in the entire system that delivers a service. Several teams might be involved in the service delivery. Each delivers a service as part of the end-to-end service. If the entire workflow gets overloaded, the work starts piling up in the queues between the systems and the teams wait on one another longer. This increases delivery time and reduces delivery rate. Limiting WIP in the end-to-end service workflow creates a smoother flow and improves predictability, although unevenness in the teams' workload might occur.

CONSOLIDATION PRACTICES

LW 2.1 Establish constant WIP (CONWIP) limits on an emergent workflow.

The constant WIP (CONWIP) defines the number of work items that can be in the entire system, no matter what their type and size are. In the example in Figure 10.12 (on page 133), these are in the *Committed* and *In Progress* columns. This is a way to create a pull system in which a work item enters only when another one is complete and has exited the system. A CONWIP pull system keeps less tight control on the cards in each state (column) of the workflow; therefore we consider it a proto-kanban system. However, it provides the workflow relief from overburdening and allows the team to better understand how service delivery or product development really occurs. In addition, establishing a CONWIP makes it possible to cope with the concept of a timebox, which many teams struggle with. Ideally, the CONWIP is set large enough to keep the team busy until the next replenishment meeting, and the delivery meeting can have a different cadence. Lead times are no longer restricted to a single system cycle.

Implementation Guidelines

Determine the CONWIP by taking into account the team's ability to complete work during a replenishment cycle. The CONWIP is considered too high if some individuals multitask. The CONWIP is too restrictive if some remain idle after exploring the possibilities for collaboration.

LW 2.2 Establish WIP limits on an aggregated service delivery overview board.

The intent of this practice is to establish the foundation for achieving a smooth and balanced flow for the collection of services that involve one or more service teams. Refer to VZ 2.13 for an example of an aggregated service delivery overview board.

Implementation Guidelines

- Determine the WIP limit for the service with most restrictive customer expectations. In the example shown in Figure 10.17 (page 137), this could be the Operations service because it has to meet strict regulatory requirements and deadlines.
- Determine the WIP limits for the rest of the services, taking into account the remaining capacity and the delivery rate data for these services. Refer to MF 2.4 regarding defining and collecting flow-related metrics.
- Discuss adjusting the WIP limits at the Flow Review (FL 2.4).
- Visualize the established WIP limits on an aggregated service delivery overview board (Figure 10.17).

Maturity Level 3
TRANSITION PRACTICES

LW 3.1 Establish activity-based WIP limits.

Establishing WIP limits for each column of a kanban system that represents a different activity (i.e., work performed by a different group of specialists) helps to achieve balance across the entire workflow, avoiding overloading some parts of it while others are idle. The less the flow fluctuates, the higher the predictability of the delivered products and services is, which leads to higher customer satisfaction.

Implementation Guidelines

- Use Little's Law (MF 3.5) to establish the number of work items that can reside in a column that represents a particular activity. All work items in the column, blocked or not, count as WIP.
- As a rule of thumb, a group of people working in a workflow state (column) should produce approximately as many work items as the next state (next column) can

process in the same time period. This enables a smooth and predictable flow with less fluctuation of workload and performance.
- If the column for an activity is split into *In Progress* and *Done* sub-columns, the WIP limit includes the number of complete work items in this state that have not yet been pulled into the next state, that is, the *Done* sub-column for the activity.
- When a WIP limit for a column is established and there are several lanes within it (e.g., one per work type), the WIP limit is the total number of work items in all lanes unless specific WIP limits for each lane are established.
- The established WIP limit might need to be exceeded occasionally to handle an expedite/urgent item. Use such events to reflect on the benefits of limiting WIP.
- A commonly asked question is "how do I calculate the WIP limit?" The answer is often unsatisfactory to many people: at Toyota, the process is empirical—someone makes their best guess and then they adjust from there. David has gone as far as to suggest that in sixteen years of practice and touring the world observing implementations, it is unusual to see a WIP of more than ten, while a WIP of one is rare. So, given this evidence, start with five and adjust from there.
- Other methods exist based on policy, such as "one per person plus three blockers"; it may even be possible to use a local implementation of Little's Law, looking at the local cycle time (which should be Gaussian distributed) and the arrival rate to calculate a WIP limit. However, this assumes that you have some flexibility of staffing levels. Another approach is to start with what you have now and slowly reduce until you start to inflict idle time and other delays on the system's flow. The best advice is not to get too hung up on WIP limits and recognize that the system can adjust based on feedback.

CONSOLIDATION PRACTICES

LW 3.2 Use an order point (minimum limit) for upstream replenishment.

The minimum (min) limit for an upstream kanban board ensures a steady flow of ideas and options. Downstream functions should never starve for lack of input; the min limit upstream serves to prevent this. Hitting the min limit point is a signal for replenishment—it demands the upstream system to produce more.

Consider the following example: Your family consumes between three and five boxes of cereal per week and you can buy cereal on demand providing you have one day of notice (i.e., if we hit the limit this morning, the cereal will be replenished by tomorrow night). So we need two days of buffer stock. What is the minimum number of boxes you need in your cupboard to ensure that you will not run out of cereal? The answer is two boxes. When the third from last is opened, it should send the signal to replenish.

Description

In general, order points are about ensuring enough choice. For example, if an input buffer (a *Ready* buffer) is properly sized, then it is possible that it will be empty at the Replenishment Meeting. Therefore, the upstream column must have at least this many items ready to pull. So, if the input buffer for the kanban system has a WIP of five, then the upstream system must have at least five. But is this enough? Don't we want some choice at our Replenishment Meeting? Don't we want to be able to pick from a slightly bigger set? If yes, then five is insufficient; we need to send the signal to replenish earlier, so maybe a WIP of ten, ensuring that we always have at least two choices for every slot in the *Ready* buffer.

LW 3.3 Use a maximum (max) limit to constrain upstream capacity.

Each ticket on an upstream kanban board represents an option, a potential request for the downstream team. The max limit serves to protect the upstream people from overburdening. Workers developing options—performing experiments, designing, discovering and studying new information—might suffer from overburdening and multitasking if too many options are In Progress together. A max limit prevents such overburdening from becoming troublesome. In addition, establishing a max WIP limit prevents the entire system from overproduction, that is, excessive production of options that get discarded later.

Implementation Guidelines

Determine how many options above the min order point are needed to ensure both of the following are true:

- The discard rate is directly affected by the amount of uncertainty. In a high-uncertainty environment, the discard rate might be 90 percent. In a low-uncertainty environment, it might be less than 5 percent. The upstream WIP needs to reflect this. If the *Ready* buffer is five in a high-uncertainty environment, then you might expect an upstream WIP of at least fifty, with forty-five of them being discarded.
- It is necessary to ensure that the upstream activity is adequately staffed to accommodate the expected discard rate. The more innovative the business, the more focus and resources are needed upstream.

LW 3.4 Bracket WIP limits across sub-states.

Often, teams use a *Done* (or *Ready for . . .*) sub-column to visualize that a completed work item is ready to be pulled to the next column. For example, as shown on Figure 11.1, when testing a work item is finished, the kanban card that represents it is moved to the *Done* sub-column of the *Test* column, which is a queue.

It is a common mistake to view as separate the *In Progress* and *Done* states of a column and use individual WIP limits for them when, in fact, the *Done* state merely signals that an item is "pullable." The correct solution is to visualize the WIP limit across both states, explicitly showing that the two sub-columns comprise a single activity.

It is desirable to avoid unbounded queues or buffers, as this breaks the integrity of the pull system and has consequences of long and less predictable lead times.

Implementation Guidelines

- Use the guidelines in LW 3.1 to set the WIP limit for an activity.
- Do not treat sub-states and sub-columns as different activities.
- Bracket a WIP limit across the sub-columns and sub-states for a given activity.

Note With some alternative methods to visually signal that an item is pullable when an activity is completed, this technique of bracketing WIP limits can be obviated. For example, some software tools signal pullable by bordering the ticket with bright green. In such designs there are no *In Progress* and *Done* sub-columns.

Figure 11.1 Bracket WIP limits for different sub-states

LW 3.5 Bracket WIP limits across activities.

The technique from LW 3.4 can be extended across multiple activity columns, as shown in Figure 11.2. This is routinely done when work is "flowed" through several activities by generalist workers who do not concede ownership of a ticket when a single activity is completed. As there is no pull between activities when work is flowed by a generalist or craft worker, there is no need for separate WIP limits—the same people are doing the work in the bracketed columns. Within the bracket, handoffs do not happen, and pull is not necessary.

11 | Limit Work-in-Progress

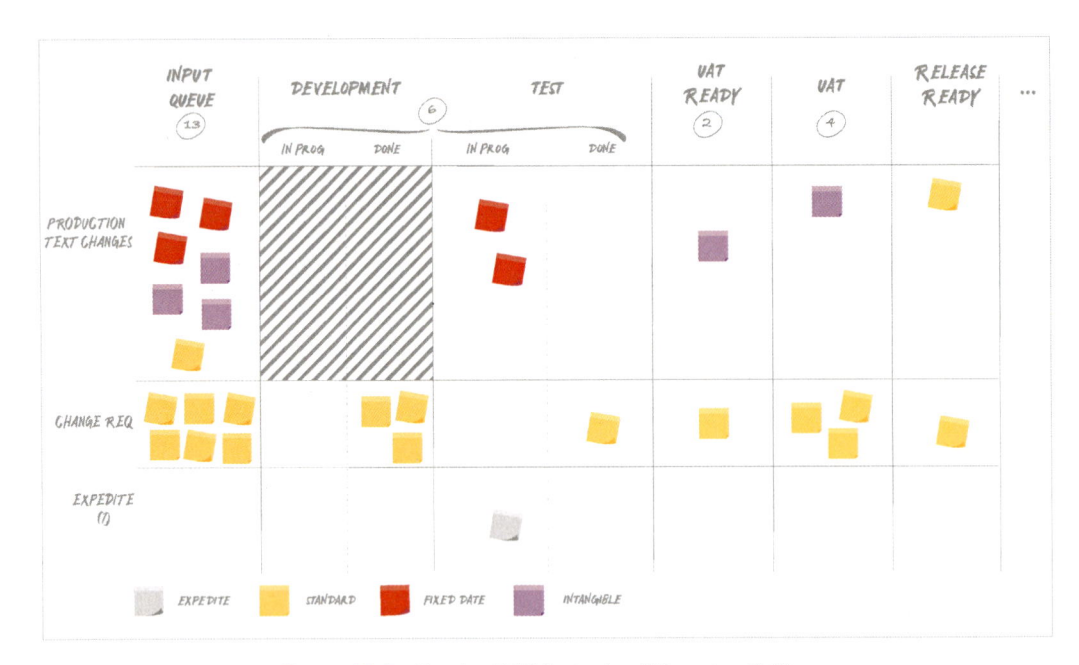

Figure 11.2 Bracket WIP limits for different activities

Tickets will flow between development and test because the same worker performs both activities. There is no queuing or handoff. Once a ticket is tested, it moves into the *UAT Ready* buffer, a hand off, to queue and wait to be pulled into user acceptance testing.

Implementation Guidelines
- Determine the WIP limit, typically with a policy such as "three per person and three in addition."
- It may be useful to have a per-person WIP limit–type policy, possibly with avatars for visualization (LW 1.1, VZ 1.3).
- Bracket a WIP limit across a set of activity columns typically performed by a single worker.

LW 3.6 Create a full kanban system.

The intent of this practice is to establish a full kanban system; using such a system allows organizations to control their flow of work, defer commitment, establish triage policies, and pull work into the system only when there is available capacity to handle it.

Description
A kanban system for managing work has the following characteristics:
- It is a pull system, that is, a work item is started only when it is requested and there is capacity for delivering it. The WIP limits (kanbans) are used to represent available

capacity. Having fewer work items in a column (stage) than the established WIP limit is a signal for pulling work from the previous column in the workflow.
- A kanban board is used to model the workflow (MF 2.3) for each work type and to visualize the work in progress, the ready-to-start work, and the delivered work.
- Tickets are used to represent work items and visualize information necessary for decision making, such as class of service, due date, risk, blockage, which specialist is working on it, and so on. See Chapter 10, Visualize, for specific practices and more details about designing tickets.
- The work in the kanban system is managed based on established explicit policies and using flow-related metrics. Policies include WIP limits, classes of service, triage policies, and so on. See the Chapter 13, Make Policies Explicit, for more details.
- It uses two-phase commitment, separating the commitment to start the work from the commitment to deliver it (MF3.14).

Maturity Level 4

CONSOLIDATION PRACTICES

LW 4.1 Limit WIP for a dependency parking lot.

A dependency parking lot, as shown in Figure 10.35 (page 159), buffers work between one kanban system and another. If the dependent system exhibits stability and predictable lead times, then it is possible to limit WIP in a dependency buffer without causing too much stress. Even if the dependent system doesn't exhibit stability and predictability, a WIP limit can still be set for the buffer to avoid losing sight of the stopped work. The WIP limit acts as a stressor, potentially causing upstream stalling within the kanban system. This stress can be discussed at a Service Delivery Review (FL 3.4) and escalated at an Operations Review (FL 4.2).

Implementation Guidelines
- Estimate buffer sizing, or the value for the parking lot's WIP limit, using Little's Law. If we know the average arrival rate in the calling kanban system and the average lead time from the called (dependent) system, we can calculate the average WIP. The WIP limit should be set slightly higher than the average WIP.
- WIP tends to vary over time and exhibit a Gaussian distribution. Assuming the dependency parking lot buffer was previously unbounded, a study of historical data will suggest an upper limit, and the new WIP limit should be set somewhere between the upper limit and the mean calculated using Little's Law.
- Adjust the WIP limit empirically; it should be a topic of discussion at Service Delivery Reviews until a stable value has been realized.

LW 4.2 Limit WIP by type of work.

Use a WIP limit for each type of work. This is typically coupled with a capacity allocation risk-hedging strategy. The WIP limit implements the risk-hedging policies.

Implementation Guidelines

- For example, if for risk-management reasons we wish to allocate 25 percent of capacity to a certain type of WIP, say, product defect fixes, and our WIP limit for our kanban system is twenty, then we set the WIP limit for production defect fixes at five.
- While it is typical to visualize this using a row on a kanban board, note that this is not required. A WIP limit by type of work can be enforced without needing to visualize the work type with a specific row on the board. Alternatives include using the color of the tickets to connote the type of work.

LW 4.3 Limit WIP by class of service.

Use a WIP limit for each class of service. This is typically coupled with a capacity allocation risk-hedging strategy. The WIP limit implements the risk-hedging policies.

Implementation Guidelines

- For example, if for risk management reasons we wish to allocate 25 percent of capacity to a certain class of service, say, Intangible, and our WIP limit for our kanban system is twenty, then the WIP limit for Intangible class items should be five.
- Although it is typical to visualize this using a row on a kanban board, note that this is not required. A WIP limit by class of service can be enforced without needing to visualize the class of service with a specific row on the board. Alternatives include using ticket color to connote class of service. This was already a common practice with early implementations in 2007.

12 | Manage Flow

Effectively managing a business, an organization, work, or people suggests two things: that your goal is to achieve success, overcoming unexpected and challenging circumstances without overburdening people; and that you take care of the available resources (time, money, staff, and other resources), deal carefully with them, and do not waste them.

Successful management requires analysis of the current situation, fast decision making, and taking relevant actions to adapt quickly to changes in the business context.

The Kanban Method applies the systems thinking approach to managing work and organizations. Understanding and managing the flow of work is an essential element of this approach.

Goal of the General Practice

The goal of Manage Flow is to achieve fast, smooth, sustainable, and predictable creation and delivery of customer value, minimizing risk and cost of delay.

Benefits from Applying the General Practice

- Develops a deep understanding of the types of demand and how they are processed to deliver customer value
- Identifies impediments in the workflow and determine how to eliminate them.
- Improves delivery predictability
- Improves workflow efficiency
- Establishes classes of service

- Develops a quantitative understanding of the entire process and how to use it to manage better the capacity of the kanban systems, the workflow, and customer satisfaction
- Improves forecasting
- Improves risk management
- Improves optionality by enabling ever-later deferral of commitment

Specific Practices Summary

Maturity Level		Manage Flow (MF) Practice
ML0	Consolidation	**MF 0.1** Categorize tasks based on the nature of the work and its urgency, importance, and impact.
ML1	Transition	No specific practices at ML1; same as ML0, but at a team level.
	Consolidation	
ML2	Transition	**MF 2.1** Define work types based on customer requests. **MF 2.2** Define basic services. **MF 2.3** Map upstream and downstream flow. **MF 2.4** Collect flow-related data (e.g., lead time). **MF 2.5** Capture the desired delivery date.
	Consolidation	**MF 2.6** Manage blocking issues. **MF 2.7** Manage defects and other rework types. **MF 2.8** Manage aging WIP. **MF 2.9** Implement Flow Manager role.
ML3	Transition	**MF 3.1** Organize around the knowledge discovery process. **MF 3.2** Defer commitment (decide before the last responsible moment). **MF 3.3** Measure and analyze the service's fitness-for-purpose. **MF 3.4** Use cumulative flow diagrams to monitor queues. **MF 3.5** Use Little's Law. **MF 3.6** Report rudimentary flow efficiency. **MF 3.7** Gradually eliminate infinite buffers. **MF 3.8** Actively close upstream requests that meet the discard criteria. **MF 3.9** Analyze and report on aborted work. **MF 3.10** Use classes of service to affect selection. **MF 3.11** Analyze and report on failure demand.
	Consolidation	**MF 3.12** Develop triage discipline. **MF 3.13** Manage peer-to-peer and parent-child dependencies. **MF 3.14** Use two-phase commit. **MF 3.15** Establish a service level agreement (SLA). **MF 3.16** Determine the due date. **MF 3.17** Forecast delivery. **MF 3.18** Apply qualitative Real Options Thinking. **MF 3.19** Implement Service Delivery Manager role. **MF 3.20** Implement Service Request Manager role.

Maturity Level		Manage Flow (MF) Practice
ML4	Transition	MF 4.1 Collect and report detailed flow efficiency analysis. MF 4.2 Use explicit buffers to smooth flow. MF 4.3 Analyze to anticipate dependencies. MF 4.4 Establish refutable versus irrefutable demand. MF 4.5 Use classes of dependency management according to cost of delay. MF 4.6 Use classes of booking in a dynamic reservation system.
	Consolidation	MF 4.7 Determine a reference class data set. MF 4.8 Forecast using reference classes, Monte Carlo simulations, and other models. MF 4.9 Allocate capacity by work type. MF 4.10 Allocate capacity by class of service. MF 4.11 Assess forecasting models for robustness. MF 4.12 Make appropriate use of forecasting. MF 4.13 Use statistical methods for decision making.
ML5	Transition	
	Consolidation	MF 5.1 Use hybrid fixed service teams together with a flexible labor pool.

Specific Practices Descriptions

Maturity Level 0

The intent of Manage Flow at ML0 is to understand what work a person is doing and to facilitate defining the rules for managing an individual's tasks.

CONSOLIDATION PRACTICES

MF 0.1 Categorize tasks based on the nature of the work and its urgency, importance, and impact.

Implementation Guidelines

Categorize tasks, taking into consideration the following aspects:
- The nature of the work that must be done—think about the essence of the task, the qualifications or skills needed, and the scale and complexity of the task. Following are examples of task categories based on the nature of the job:
  - For software development: specify requirements, implement features, fix bugs.
  - For administrative work: issue invoices, write reports.
  - For marketing: write copy, create marketing campaigns, prepare publications for social media.
    - Urgency: how soon a task must be delivered to avoid negative consequences
    - Importance: the significance or value of the outcome; for example, core business development, internal improvement, billable work, other

Maturity Level 2

The intent of Manage Flow at Maturity Level 2 is to develop the basic skills to manage work and flow, taking into account customers' expectations.

TRANSITION PRACTICES

MF 2.1 Define work types based on customer requests.

Defining work item types based on customer requests helps to understand the demand from a customer perspective and to focus management activities on developing and delivering outcomes expected by the customer or end user.

Implementation Guidelines

Identify work types, taking into consideration the following aspects of the work:
- Source of demand: the types of customers who may request work, for example, internal or external; the types of end users
- Customer requests (even if unreasonable): for example, receive information, resolve an incident, obtain a particular report, get a new feature for a software application, and so on
- Expected outcome of the work: for example, the type of product or service
- Specialist skills required: for example, development, marketing, or commercial

MF 2.2 Define basic services.

A service fulfills a customer request. Through a series of activities, it delivers a tangible or intangible (or both) outcome to the customer. At the lowest level of granularity, a type of work can be considered a service; for example, resolving an incident and providing information can be seen as services. A service might include several activities (mini-services or work types) that an organization performs but that are invisible to the customer. For example, renewing a passport is a service that responds to the customer's need to have a valid personal identification document. Delivering this customer request, however, involves updating the customer's personal data, taking an actual photo, paying a fee, printing the new passport, rendering the old one unusable, and delivering the valid passport to the person. All these are types of work or internal services that must be conducted in a well synchronized manner to respond to the customer request.

Implementation Guidelines
- Analyze the customer requests you receive. Take into account what customers ask for, their market segment, characteristics of the customer's business, service trends and patterns, and so on.

- Analyze your organization's strategy; that is, what kind of service your business is interested in providing and to what types of market segments or customers.
- Analyze the skills and capabilities you need for delivering the services that meet customer expectations.
- Define a catalog of basic services, that is, a list of agreed service definitions. Consider the range of customer needs and requests in light of your organization's objectives and capabilities.

Defining the services aligns the business goals of the organization and the provided services. At Maturity Level 3, the service catalog is extended with additional information about the services, such as service levels, degrees of detail or quality, prices, negotiable terms and conditions, and so on.

MF 2.3 Map upstream and downstream flow.

The workflow defines the sequencing of activities and/or the work item states that result in delivered products or services. The workflow definition encompasses all stages of developing and delivering work from an original idea to the final value realization. The upstream, or discovery, part of the workflow includes the phases through which an idea passes on its way to elaboration, analysis, and definition until the point of committing to its development or discarding it. The downstream, or delivery, part of the workflow includes the stages of developing and delivering committed work.

Mapping the workflow is essential for understanding what it takes to get a work item from its inception to delivery and for identifying appropriate adjustments to improve it.

Implementation Guidelines

- Sketch the sequence of stages though which a type of work evolves from idea (usually named *Pool of Ideas* or *Backlog*) to complete (usually called *Done*). Any method is acceptable, for example, flowchart, stick-figure drawing, state chart, or simply listing the states horizontally.
- List the activities that are performed to advance a work item from one state to the next. Use the corresponding verbs that describe the essence of the activities. Avoid the temptation to state which role (who) is responsible for doing a job; instead, focus on what must be done in a particular state.
- Designate a column on a kanban board for each phase of the workflow.
- The upstream part of the workflow represents the steps through which an idea evolves and converts into a committed request, for example, *Business Proposal – Technical Approval – Ready for Development*.

- The delivery part of the workflow visualizes the steps through which a committed work element develops into a value-adding deliverable, such as *Development – Testing – Release*.
- Refer to VZ 2.12 regarding visualizing the delivery and discovery workflows.

MF 2.4 Collect flow-related data (e.g., lead time).

Refer to XP 2.1 about how to define flow-related metrics. Correctly collecting the right data is essential for analyzing the flow-related metrics and making informed decisions. Refer to Appendix C for a detailed explanation of lead time.

Implementation Guidelines

- Instrument your system to collect data. You can do this using physical tickets, snapshots of boards, or a software tracking tool.
- See XP 2.1 for a full list of metrics to record and report. At ML2, it generally isn't possible to get a clean measure of lead time as defined in Kanban, that is, from the commitment point to the point of being ready for delivery. This is because there is rarely a cleanly defined commitment point at ML2 (refer to XP 3.6 for details about establishing a commitment point). We simply accept that lead time measures in Maturity Level 2 organizations are unreliable and as a consequence, they shouldn't be compared with other services/kanban boards. Low-maturity, unreliable metrics should never be used for benchmarking or comparison across services, teams, or organizations.
- As much as possible, facilitate integrating data collection with normal work. Provide appropriate guidance about what types of data are needed and how to register them, with what frequency, and with what tools to store the information.
- Check data correctness as close to the point of collection as possible.
- As much as possible, facilitate automatic data collection.

MF 2.5 Capture the desired delivery date.

The desired delivery date is the ideal date on which service delivery happens. It is typically defined by the customer, the market, or the business environment. Knowing it is important for making decisions about the sequencing of work items. However, it is important that the correct information about the due date is used and not one that has been intentionally modified for whatever reason (e.g., to make sure that the work item is delivered on time or not forgotten).

Implementation Guidelines

- Review regulatory requirements for indication of desired delivery date.
- Desired delivery date may be a window of time—such as a month of the year or a quarter of the calendar year—not necessarily a single specific date.

- Review customer requirements for specification of due date or expected delivery time (e.g., five days after receiving a request).
- Refer to VZ 0.2 about visualizing desired delivery date.

CONSOLIDATION PRACTICES

MF 2.6 Manage blocking issues.

Blockers contain information that is valuable for improving the flow and reducing delivery time. Therefore, they must be analyzed, and relevant improvement actions must be taken.

Implementation Guidelines

- Use different colors to mark blocked tickets to indicate the type of dependency (e.g., waiting on us, waiting on an external group, or another type of dependency relevant for you).
- Review the status of all blockers at the daily Kanban Meeting. If the team is unable to resolve an issue, escalate it to the appropriate management level. See XP 2.4 regarding how to define policies for escalating blocking issues.
- Periodically analyze the blocking issues. In particular, identify the categories of blockage causes, the frequency of occurrence, and the range of blocked time per cause to understand the impact of the blockage on delivery time. Use appropriate graphic reports, such as bar charts of open and closed issues per time period, histogram of blocked time, histogram of blockage causes, cumulative flow diagram of blockers, root-cause analysis diagrams, and so on, to analyze the blockers.
- Define actions to eliminate the blockage causes and reduce the blocked time.
- Update the policies for resolving or escalating blocking issues (XP 2.4).

MF 2.7 Manage defects and other rework types.

Defects and rework are well-known types of waste. Fixing defects, which are usually unforeseen or underestimated, requires additional resources and time and therefore causes many adverse effects, such as:
- Delays for the developed product or service they belong to and those who depend on it
- Longer tail in the distribution of lead times, and hence, poorer predictability of delivery
- Increased costs
- Assuming some defects leak to customers, reduced value, and hence, reduced customer satisfaction
- Reduced value due to opportunity cost of delay while defects are fixed or other rework is performed
- Additional maintenance or support demand
- Missed business opportunities

Defects are mainly associated with errors in the final product or service. However, there are other types of rework that produce similar effects on product or service delivery. These are, for example, rework of request specifications or product design due to insufficient communication with the customer or other team members or rework of project plans and reports due to using incomplete or inexact data.

Organizations new to managing defects and rework usually do not have explicit policies about managing rework. See XP 2.5 for guidelines about establishing policies for managing defects and other rework types.

Deeper-maturity organizations treat rework as first-class work items and count them against the WIP limit. Excessive rework, then, has the impact of halting the pull of new work until quality issues in current work are resolved.

Implementation Guidelines

- Track defects and other rework items.
- Record the reason for the defect or type of rework.
- Track the rework item's state for reporting and further analysis.
- Analyze defect and rework data. In particular, categorize the defects and rework types and analyze their frequency and pattern of occurrence as well as their impact in terms of time and cost on the product or service delivery. Use graphics such as bar charts, histograms, run charts, or control charts to do the analysis.
- Report defects and rework analysis results at the Flow Review.
- Define actions to reduce defects and rework and then execute them.
- Update the policies for managing defects and other rework types accordingly.

MF 2.8 Manage aging WIP.

Knowledge work is perishable. Started work that is not delivered to the customer within a reasonable amount of time is waste.

Implementation Guidelines

- Take note of the time when a work item is requested as well as when real work on it starts.
- Monitor the elapsed time since the work item was requested. Make sure that it fits with the customer's expectations and respects the established policies for managing WIP aging as defined in XP 2.3.
- Take actions to reduce WIP aging (e.g., setting alarms for items that pass a certain threshold of time or creating filters that allow quick identification of high-age WIP).

MF 2.9 Implement Flow Manager role.

An ML2 organization develops customer awareness and an initial understanding of the importance of flow and introduces the Kanban service delivery principles. This creates the need for introducing the role of a Flow Manager to oversee these aspects of work. Note that Flow Manager is a role to be played and not necessarily a job title or a new position in the organization. The means for implementing a role should be adjusted according to organizational culture. This is discussed in Chapter 19, Barriers to Adoption.

Implementation Guidelines

- The Flow Manager (FM) is responsible for the following:
  - Create the consciousness that the service team is delivering a service to identified customers.
  - Ensure that flow metrics are collected (MF 2.4).
  - Facilitate the workflow Kanban Meeting.
  - Facilitate the understanding of customer requests.
  - Facilitate the resolution of blockers, rework, and aging WIP–related issues that are escalated from the service team.
- A typical approach to implementing this role is to assign it to a team member who has volunteered for it and has appropriate knowledge and skills to do the job.

At ML3, this role evolves into the Service Delivery Manager role (MF 3.19).

Maturity Level 3

The focus of Manage Flow at Maturity Level 3 is on achieving both smooth flow at large scale and services that are fit-for-purpose from a customer perspective. Therefore, the specific practices are directed at shaping demand, balancing demand and capability based on data, and managing options.

TRANSITION PRACTICES

MF 3.1 Organize around the knowledge discovery process.

Kanban requires that you start with what you do now rather than first reorganizing into some new organizational structure. Ultimately, one goal of the Kanban Method is to engineer organizational resilience and agility by adopting a service orientation—to be an organization designed and built of services that are readily orchestrated and assembled into novel, customer-facing services with little impact or delay. A first step on this journey is to start thinking in terms of services and to encourage collaboration across organizational units to provide a customer-facing service.

A kanban board should always visualize the customer-facing service. It should visualize the series or sequence of knowledge or information-discovery activities that take an idea or a request to a finished and deliverable work product. The kanban board serves to facilitate cooperation amongst different organizational units that may need to collaborate to produce the desired product for the customer. The Kanban Meeting and other cadences provide a means for such cooperation and collaboration. Figure 12.1 illustrates a generic organizational hierarchy and shows how a customer request must flow across the nodes of the organizational network. The kanban board illustrates how to visualize this flow on a single board. The board is at the service level, and people from different organizational units and different teams must come together to facilitate the flow of work in the service delivery workflow.

This is the first step toward a truly service-oriented organization, desired at Maturity Levels 5 and 6.

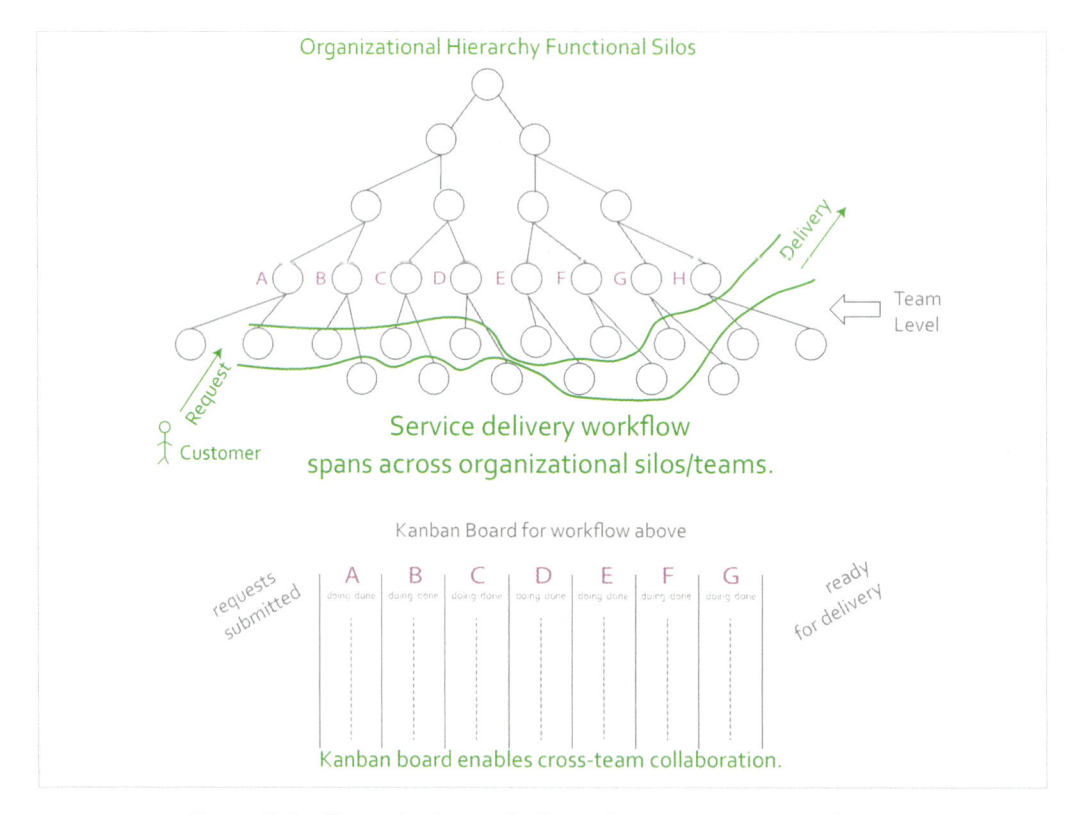

Figure 12.1   Illustrating how a single service spans organizational units

Implementation Guidelines
- See your organization as an ecosystem of interdependent services.
- Map the workflow for each individual service, focusing on the dominant activities at each knowledge discovery phase as described in MF 2.3.
- Organize workers around this knowledge discovery process.
- Map the overall, end-to-end workflow across the interdependent services, taking into account the dominant activities at each phase, and manage the flow of work items through it.

- Define a commitment point in the workflow (i.e., the point in the workflow at which the customer commits to accept the requested work item and the delivery team agrees to pull the ticket, start working on it, and deliver it).
- Appoint Service Request and Service Delivery Managers (SRM and SDM) to manage the flow upstream and downstream of the commitment point.
- The SRM and SDM roles may be played by someone within the existing hierarchy or may come from a new organizational unit formed to provide the required customer-facing service.
- When a service is identified, ask, "Who is responsible and accountable for receiving the customer's order and ensuring delivery?" This is the role of the SDM. If there isn't someone, this role needs to be created.
- If the process involves some discovery and interaction with customers in order to decide what to do, as is common with advertising, architecture, or other creative services, there may need to be a service request manager, often an account manager or a producer who acts as the liaison with the customer during the upstream stages while the work is still optional. This may be true whether the work is billable or not.

MF 3.2 Defer commitment (decide before the last responsible moment).

Deferring commitment means not committing early. Instead, waiting to decide on an item until more information is available. Deferring commitment should reduce the amounts of both aborted work and rework. It should also increase the discard rate, as more information may mean that an idea is rejected rather than aborted later. The more frequent the cadence of the Replenishment Meeting, the more it enables deferred commitment. For example, if we have weekly replenishment and we know that a go/no-go decision is not required for another ten days, we can safely defer a decision until the next meeting. Deferring commitment implies that we should not decide until (1) we are sure we want to do something and (2) we have as much information as possible that may affect the decision to do it or not.

However, every option has an expiry date, the point at which it is no longer viable to make a positive choice. The point just prior to that is referred to as the last responsible moment. However, as discussed in Appendices D and E, while an option has an expiry date—a point at which it no longer makes sense to do it—we generally don't control the delivery date; instead, we control the decision to start an item. For the purposes of triage, selection, and kanban system replenishment, we have chosen to define the Last Responsible Moment (LRM) as the 50th percentile of the lead time prior to the desired delivery date (DDD). Beyond that point, we call it "irresponsibly late."

Deferring commitment until the LRM comes with a tradeoff: we probably have to treat that item with a higher class of service, probably Fixed Date class of service, whereas if we start it earlier we can trade some certainty and quality of information, and possibly rework or risk of aborting, for a lower class of service, such as Standard or Intangible.

In general, we want to avoid committing early and to encourage acquiring more knowledge to ensure that we commit to items that will not be aborted later. However, we do not want every item deferred until the LRM. Doing so would load too much risk onto our delivery capability.

Deferring commitment brings several benefits:

- Buys more time to refine understanding and improve certainty on requirements, design, and implementation
- Reduces the chances for changes to the requested work or the promised deadline
- Reduces the probability of aborting requested work items
- Reduces the overhead for managing modifications, reprioritization, and replanning
- Reduces the coordination cost for holding meetings

Implementation Guidelines

- Establish criteria for committing work items, that is, for letting them pass through the commitment point of the kanban system between the pending and in-progress work. Refer to VZ 3.1 and VZ 3.2 for visualizing the *Ready to Commit* status and entry criteria, respectively.
- Use a WIP limit on the *Selected* state (column). This limits the amount of committed work and forces everything else to remain uncommitted or be actively discarded.
- Develop the notion that deferred does not imply "never." This is often facilitated by developing an explicit policy around the requirements for commitment, also known as the definition of ready.
- Apply a triage mechanism at a regular cadence—usually during the Replenishment Meeting. Divide new work requests into three categories: now, later, and never (i.e., discarded). For the "later" category, state approximately when the work item can be started.
- Agree on a definition for the Last Responsible Moment.

We have provided a definition for LRM; however, you are welcome to create your own. The concept of LRM is quite tricky. For example, even if an item is delivered late, how much of its value can still be realized for it to be considered worthwhile? This is extremely contextual. Hence, although there may be a desired delivery date (DDD), there is probably also a point at which there is no longer any point (PNP). In that case, we then need to adjust this for the lead time and accept that lead time is a probability distribution. Hence, we can never be deterministic about LRM. The solution provided in Appendices D and E is a conservative compromise designed for adoption by Maturity Level 2 organizations as a relatively safe but useful definition of LRM. More mature organizations may get more sophisticated about LRM, and at Maturity Level 4 or deeper, it may be possible to define a specific LRM for each work item based on its risks, cost of delay profile, value lifecycle, and the lead time distribution for delivery.

MF 3.3 Measure and analyze the service's fitness-for-purpose.

Periodic analysis of a service's fitness-for-purpose provides the feedback organizations need to enable making good decisions for improving their customers' level of satisfaction, as well as to identify and adapt to changes in customers' expectations. Refer to XP 3.1 for defining Fit-for-Purpose–related metrics for a service.

Implementation Guidelines
- Analyze a service's fitness-for-purpose.
  - For each KPI, identify the causes' data points that do not reach or exceed the established thresholds. Analyze the causes and the impacts for those cases.
  - Analyze the qualitative, or narrative, information about the service.
- Analyze the balance between demand and capability for a particular service.
  - Analyze the number of service requests received for a given time period (e.g., day/week/month). Different time periods will reveal different amounts of demand. Identify whether there are patterns of demand, seasonality, or particular causes that led to an increase or decrease in demand.
  - Analyze the number of delivered service requests for a time period (throughput). Compare the amount of received versus delivered demand per time period and annotate any findings that need to be discussed at Flow Review.
- Categorize key causes that affect the service's fitness-for-purpose and identify improvement actions.
- Define actions to address the identified causes.
  Overall, there are two types of approaches for addressing imbalance between demand and capability (see Figure 12.2):
  - Shape demand: Visualize explicit work types; add policies for capacity allocation across provided services; eliminate causes of failure demand and disruptive or speculative demand; use risk profiling and policies to bifurcate demand (e.g., if the user interface design service is overburdened, use risk assessment to allow business analysts or programmers to design low-risk areas of an application).
  - Optimize flow: Limit WIP; focus on disruptions and sources of delay (blockers, rework, high WIP, waiting in queues); improve flow efficiency.
- Bring the analysis results and suggested improvements to the Flow Review and the Improvement Suggestions Review.

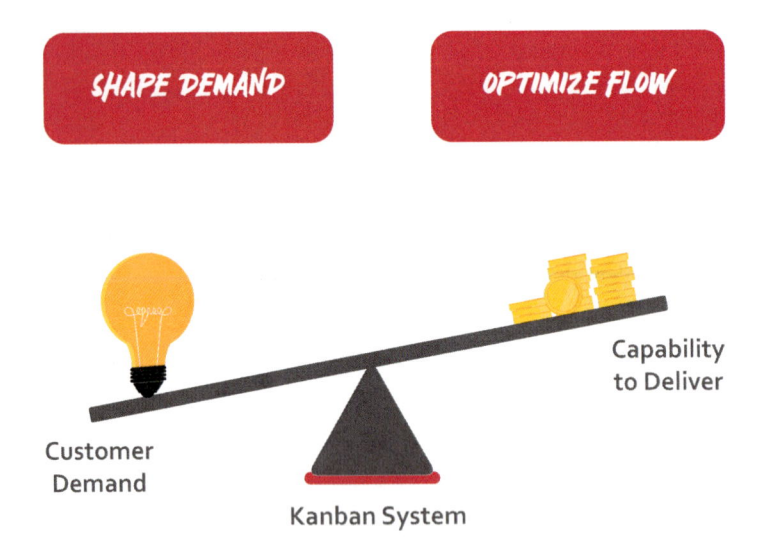

Figure 12.2 General approaches for addressing imbalance between demand and capability

MF 3.4 Use cumulative flow diagrams to monitor queues.

The cumulative flow diagram (CFD) is one of the most useful tools for managing queues. The diagram uses calendar time as its horizontal axis and cumulative quantity as its vertical axis.

The vertical distance between two subsequent lines on the CFD represents the amount of work in the corresponding state of the workflow on that date. In Figure 12.3, the vertical distance between the *Committed* state of the kanban system and the *Delivered* one on a particular date is the work that has been started but not completed yet; that is, the work-in-progress, or the queue size in the entire kanban system on that date.

The horizontal distance between the arrival and delivery (or departure) lines shows the average time that it took for a work item to get processed through the system, or the average delivery time (lead time).

The slope of the departure line indicates the average capacity of the process to empty the queue, or the average delivery rate.

The benefit of using a CFD is that it can be constructed continuously, not only when a work item is finished. The CFD is the only graphic that alerts to potential delivery delays; therefore, it is a valuable tool for service delivery managers.

Implementation Guidelines

- Plot the cumulative arrivals for a state of the workflow on a date on the horizontal axis.
- Color the bands to distinguish the amount of work-in-progress in each state (optional).
- Observe the distance between the lines on the CFD:

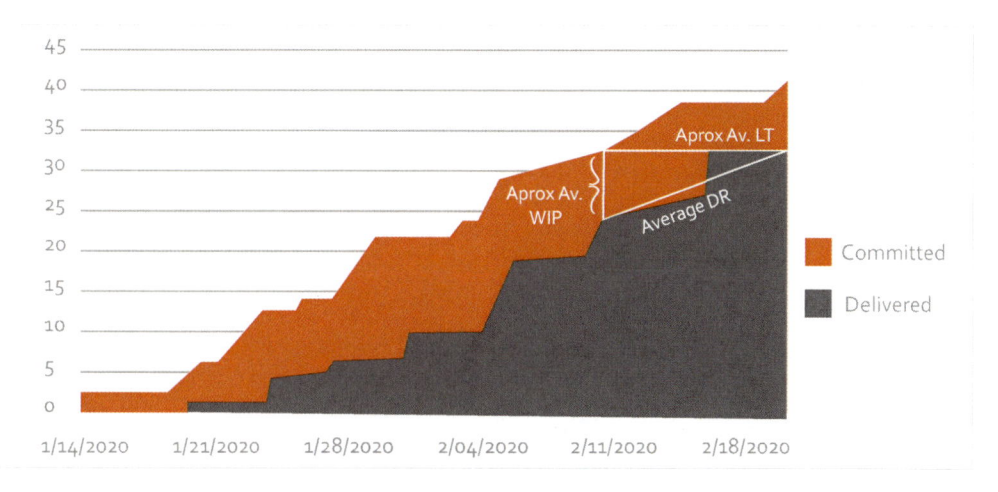

Figure 12.3 Cumulative flow diagram

- If they stay parallel overall (in knowledge work they never stay absolutely parallel), there is equilibrium between the demand and capability; that is, the system is stable and work delivery is predictable.
- If the work's arrival increases faster than its departure (the slope of the arrival line is higher than that of the delivery line), this means that more work-in-progress has accumulated, and the balance between demand and capability is broken due to excess demand. There is a risk of delay of work delivery.
- If the work's arrival rate stays stable but the slope of the delivery line decreases, this means that work is getting stuck in the process due to reduced or insufficient capability. Again, there is a risk of delay of work delivery.
* Identify changes in the patterns of demand and capability.
* Recognize emerging bottlenecks (they appear as bulges in the diagram) and their growth rate.
* Take corresponding actions quickly.

MF 3.5 Use Little's Law.

Little's Law, as used in the Kanban Method, defines the relationship that exists in a stable flow system in which all work items that are selected are delivered. More precisely,

$$\overline{Delivery\ Rate} = \frac{\overline{WIP}}{\overline{Lead\ Time}}$$

The overline denotes arithmetic mean. Figure 12.3 illustrates the parameters on a cumulative flow diagram.

In managing knowledge work, the intent of using Little's Law is as follows:

- Make a quick and inexpensive forecast of one of the parameters when the other two are available.

    For instance, calculate the required average WIP based on the average delivery rate (or throughput) and average lead time over a long period of time. Use the resulting WIP value for planning necessary resource levels.
- Understand the impact of changing one of the parameters.
- Uncover and define the right policies for managing the work that ensure a stable and predictable flow. Subsequently, observe improvements in the team's behaviors, such as consistent prioritization, collaboration, and focus on improving system design and performance so as to better satisfy customer expectations.

What is important to understand, however, is that for Little's Law to be useful, the kanban system must be stable; more precisely, the following assumptions must be fulfilled:

- All measurement units must be consistent. If lead time is measured in weeks, throughput must be measured in work items per week, and WIP must be measured in the same work items. For example, throughput is measured in requests per week and WIP is measured in requests, not in tasks that must be done to complete the requests.
- The average arrival rate is equal to the average delivery rate (i.e., the amount of work entering the system should be equal to the amount of work exiting the system over a long period of time). This is achieved by means of the WIP limit policy (i.e., a work item can be pulled into the system only after another work item has exited the system).
- All work that enters the system leaves the system. Work that enters the system and exits it abnormally affects the arrival- and delivery-rate metrics and hence, the quality of the prediction.
- The average age of WIP is constant over the observed period of time. This addresses the risk of suffering the consequences of restarting the work on a work item that had been forgotten in the system for a long time.
- The system is not converging (i.e., the amount of WIP is the same at the beginning and the end of the time period). If the WIP is trending up or down, the system is not stable.

All of these assumptions must be met to have confidence in the calculations made using Little's Law.

The larger the divergence from the stated assumptions, the less reliable the forecast and conclusions are. Instability of a kanban system would manifest as turbulence in the flow. It is typically caused by unpredictable arrival patterns; large batches of work; unavailability of shared resources; delays due to external dependencies; unforeseen circumstances; or an unusual mix of work items, either by their size or class of service. Turbulent systems are unpredictable, and Little's Law is inappropriate under those conditions.

Manage Flow – Maturity Level 3

Implementation Guidelines

Use Little's Law for the following purposes:

- Establish WIP limits and resource levels to enable meeting expected delivery time (lead time).
- Define appropriate policies for managing the workflow.
- Establish a stable kanban system and ensure predictable flow.
- Improve team behaviors.
- Forecast lead time and delivery rate.

MF 3.6 Report rudimentary flow efficiency.

The flow efficiency indicates how good a process's performance is. It shows the percentage of time a work item "flows" (i.e., is actively processed, not waiting in queues or blocked).

$$\overline{Flow\ efficiency} = \frac{\overline{Work\ time}}{\overline{Lead\ time}} \cdot 100\%$$

The work time is the amount of time a work item spends in active processing, independent of how many people work on it. For example, the work time for a particular surgery is two hours, no matter how many doctors are performing it.

> Delivering services that meet and exceed customer expectations is the key purpose of a business. Therefore, the improvement actions must be driven by the Fit-for-Purpose indicators, not only by the flow efficiency indicator.

The difference between the work time and the lead time is the time that a work item spends in queues (waiting to be pulled into the next active state and processed) or is blocked. For example, the lead time, or total elapsed time, for a surgery that effectively takes two hours could be four hours.

Internal queues between states in a kanban system act as buffers. They smooth flow and improve delivery predictability. However, they also increase lead time and thus reduce flow efficiency.

Flow efficiency should not be confused with resource efficiency. Resource efficiency is the percentage of time a resource (person or machine) spends working actively, not staying idle. Exclusive focus on resource efficiency leads to keeping people busy regardless of whether there is a smooth flow of results.

Organizations interested in increasing the efficiency of their processes wisely use this indicator.

Implementation Guidelines

- Collect the work time data per work type and calculate the average.
    - Use the collected lead time data to calculate the average lead time per work type.
- Calculate the flow efficiency using the above formula.

- Analyze which buffers can be reduced and which other sources of delay can be eliminated to decrease the lead time and improve flow efficiency. Refer to MF 3.7 for guidelines about how to gradually eliminate infinite buffers.
- Take actions to improve the current kanban system design and policies to deliver services in a more efficient way.

MF 3.7 Gradually eliminate infinite buffers.

Buffers are used for many purposes in kanban systems:
- Storing work so that it is instantly available to pull in between replenishment intervals, for example, an input queue
- Storing work for shared resources, normally not instantly available but not capacity constrained, for example, approvals
- Storing work between activities in a workflow so that the activities before and after the buffer can operate at their own speed and with their own variability in local cycle times, for example, "ready for the next stage"
- Storing work in front of a bottleneck such that the bottleneck will never be idle despite variability in work arrival
- As a proxy for, or ghost of, work sent to another system or service, either inside the business or external to it, while the work waits to be completed
- Storing work in front of a batch transfer within the system; transfer triggered by quantity in the buffer or a cadence of time

> Eliminating infinite buffers between dependent systems evolves the organization from a network of independently operating, locally optimizing services to an interdependent network of services. Such a network is constrained by the slowest moving activity within the slowest service in the network. However, proper management of the entire network of services as a true end-to-end pull system—from customer commitment to delivery—enables predictable service delivery at large scale.

In summary, buffers are used to store inputs to the system, outputs from the system, and work between activities within the workflow of the system to make sure that they do not remain idle. They are also used to manage dependencies on external services and bottlenecks.

However, infinite buffers (also known as unbounded queues) between the functions break kanban systems and have an adverse effect on flow. Therefore, full-service delivery workflow kanban systems do not contain infinite buffers.

Eliminating infinite buffers (unbounded queues) is a core discipline for achieving smooth flow at large scale.

Implementation Guidelines

These are several approaches for eliminating infinite buffers:
- Bracket an activity and its *Done* queue with a single WIP limit to create a pull system, as explained in LW 3.4.

- Couple dependent services with dependent kanban systems, thus eliminating the infinite buffers between them (VZ 3.3), the unbounded queues in parking lots, as well as those in areas of work sent out to another system.
- Ideally, buffers should be sized to cope with the upper limit of the natural variation in the arrival rate of work from upstream. This requires a quantitative understanding of the variability of the demand, which is fully obtained at Maturity Level 4. Until it is available, use an empirical approach to size the buffer and set WIP limits for an activity. Pick a reasonable number and adjust it upward if the downstream system starves frequently due to a lack of pullable work; adjust it downward if the buffer is never completely exhausted, even for the briefest amount of time.

The benefits of properly sized buffers are a smooth, predictable flow and shorter lead times. Accurate WIP limits and buffer sizing depend on the stability of the overall system. If local cycle times fail to exhibit stability, it will be impossible to establish consistent WIP limits. Stable system capability (MF 3.4) is a necessary condition for improved efficiency.[1]

MF 3.8 Actively close upstream requests that meet the discard criteria.

The intent of this practice is to focus the upstream work on viable requests. See XP 3.3 regarding defining work request discarding policies.

Implementation Guidelines

- Review the upstream requests and close all that meet the established discard criteria.
- Periodically analyze the causes for discarding options and take appropriate actions as necessary.

MF 3.9 Analyze and report on aborted work.

Aborted work is committed work that has consumed team effort and has not been delivered to the customer. Aborted work usually occurs because commitment was made too early, with insufficient information. Working on a committed item until it is aborted impedes developing and delivering other valuable requests to the customer. Therefore, such work is waste, failure demand.

The intent of this practice is to understand the causes for aborting committed work so that they can be appropriately addressed.

Implementation Guidelines

- Explicitly identify aborted work items. Collect the tickets that represent them and annotate the reasons for aborting for subsequent analysis.

---

1. A fuller explanation of system stability and its impact is provided in Enterprise Services Planning.

- Move the aborted work items to the Done state of the kanban system. Do not remove or delete the tickets from the board, as this will affect the metrics necessary for applying Little's Law.
- Periodically analyze the causes for aborting work items after the replenishment commitment point.
- Develop an aborted work report.
- Explicitly quantify the impact of the aborted work.
- Report the aborted work items' analysis results at the Flow Review.
- Through an Improvement Suggestions Review, consider revising entry and triage criteria to reduce the future possibility of aborted work.

MF 3.10 Use classes of service to affect selection.

Generically, a class of service is defined by a set of policies that determine how something should be treated. With kanban systems and workflows, one key aspect of a class of service indicates how the item should flow, or the priority that it should be given as it is pulled across the kanban board.

Lower-maturity organizations are advised to stick with the canonical set of four classes of service that originally evolved during an early Kanban implementation in 2007. These four classes are focused on urgency and priority of pull through the system: Expedite, Fixed Date, Standard, and Intangible. These are described in detail in Appendices D and E. Typically, the policies for the Standard class of service involve first-in-first-out (FIFO) queuing of Standard class tickets, or a policy to always pull the oldest available Standard class ticket.

As a general rule, any class of service with policies other than FIFO queuing negatively affects flow and adds delivery risk to a kanban system. When multiple classes of service are present, the tail of the lead time distribution is longer and fatter. Classes of service are used as a tradeoff: we trade predictability for a focus on value or risk. Classes of service are used to mitigate or react to the business or to other external risks associated with a work item. The more urgent, critical, or valuable an item, the higher its class of service is likely to be.

More mature organizations may find it necessary to define their own custom classes of service based on a detailed understanding of risks and tradeoffs.

Implementation Guidelines
- Visualize the classes of service as described in VZ 3.7.
- Use the class of service information to decide which work item to start next as well as which work items to select for the input queue at the Replenishment Meeting.
- Establish limits on the number of work items per class of service to ensure a balanced system, avoiding trends to processing mainly urgent work items.

- Use the lower class of service to compensate for variability in the number of work items in the higher classes of service.

MF 3.11 Analyze and report on failure demand.

Failure demand represents demand generated as a consequence of previous poor-quality deliverables or demand that never should have been received. Failure demand is avoidable if initial quality is better matched to customer expectations. Some examples of failure demand include the following:

- Defect-fixing requests
- Rework due to usability problems
- Rework due to poor design or not understanding customer needs
- Features requested by users because other functionality did not work (workarounds)
- Demand that never should have been accepted

Implementation Guidelines

- Explicitly visualize work items that represent failure demand. Refer to VZ 3.15 for how to do that.
- Collect the tickets that represent failure demand (or register them in whatever tool you use) for deep analysis of the root causes and the parts of the processes that produce it.
- Periodically analyze and quantify the amount of failure demand and its impact.
- Report the analysis results at the Service Delivery Review.
- Through a review at an appropriate level, such as Service Delivery, Risk, or Operations Review, consider revising policies in order to reduce the failure demand.

CONSOLIDATION PRACTICES

MF 3.12 Develop triage discipline.

The intent of triage is to avoid overburdening a system as well as to provide some rudimentary prioritization, or selection and sequencing criteria. Work should be separated into three basic categories: now, later, and never. Items for later may receive some further categorization. In those cases, it is important to establish what and approximately when. Setting expectations for approximately when has the psychological benefit of alleviating anxiety over the belief that "if not now, then never."

With Kanban, triage is mainly applied to the pool of options prior to the commitment point, and specifically to items that are ready to commit. Appendix D provides a deep introduction to triage and using Triage Tables.

Implementation Guidelines

- Go through newly arrived items and decide if each should be committed, deferred, or discarded.
- Apply triage periodically to any newly arrived items, typically during a Replenishment Meeting.
- Triage can be simplified, or its impact lessened, by introducing policies such as a guillotine for older items; that is, items older than a specific amount of time, for example, six months, are automatically discarded.
- Triage is most commonly associated with prioritizing defects for fixing. It can be equally applied to new work requests and managing blocking issues.

MF 3.13 Manage peer-to-peer and parent-child dependencies.

Dependencies increase risk of delay. Therefore, properly visualizing and managing them is important for meeting customer expectations.

Implementation Guidelines

The following approaches can be used for managing dependencies:

- Visualize them. See VZ 3.8 regarding visualizing peer-to-peer and parent-child dependencies.
- Use a separate kanban board for managing dependencies on third parties, such as suppliers, other teams, specialists, or external organizations.
- Periodically monitor the status of the child or related work item to make sure that delivering it does not put at risk delivering the dependent work item.
- Regularly analyze dependence-related blockers. Identify the causes and take actions to prevent them from occurring in the future.
- Schedule periodic meetings with representatives of each kanban system to facilitate communication and to resolve issues relating to dependencies.
- Escalate dependencies that cannot be managed within the service delivery workflow team to the Service Delivery Manager.

MF 3.14 Use two-phase commit.

The kanban system should use a two-phase commitment approach to improve customer satisfaction and better manage customer expectations:

1. The first commit phase happens when an item is selected and pulled into the kanban system at the Replenishment Meeting—the commitment to do the work.
2. The second commit phase happens later, once the ticket is sufficiently far along in the workflow that its arrival in the ready-for-delivery buffer can be predicted with a high confidence level. This enables a commitment to a specific delivery date.

Mature kanban implementations should separate the commitment to do the work from the commitment to deliver on a specific day. This better manages the psychology of the customer: they get a high level of confidence that the work is started and that it will be delivered—a promise you can keep—at the first phase of commitment; later, they get a precise, specific delivery date, one for which you have high confidence that you can hit and hence, keep the promise you are making. Using a two-phase commit—separating your promise to deliver from your promise to deliver on a specific day—makes two promises you can keep rather than a single, tightly coupled promise for a piece of work and a delivery date—a promise that you would likely break, ruining your trust relationship with the customer.

Think of two-phase commit like an engagement and a wedding. The first phase of the commitment is a promise to get married, an engagement to marry. Later, the wedding is planned, and a specific wedding date is set. This is the second phase of the commitment: booking the wedding ceremony. Now, planning the wedding ceremony and inviting guests can occur. It is unusual for an engagement to happen simultaneously with setting a date for the wedding and booking the venue, catering, and so forth. Two-phase commitment is a natural approach that we use in everyday life to manage uncertainty and set expectations.

Using two- or multi-phase commitments is a means to manage customer expectations. It is popular with, for example, furniture retailers, which rarely keep much stock on hand and need to order items from a warehouse or manufacturer. They often promise only approximate delivery dates, such as ten to thirteen weeks, and then, as the delivery date gets closer and more certain, they add precision to their forecast and their promise—your dining table will be delivered in week thirty-one. Then, later, they'll say that your dining table is scheduled for delivery on Tuesday of week thirty-one and, finally, perhaps a day or two prior to that, the delivery truck will arrive with your dining table between eleven a.m. and one p.m. on Tuesday.

Implementation Guidelines
- The first phase of commitment happens at the Replenishment Meeting (FL 3.2).
- Clearly communicate that replenishment commitment is a commitment to get started and to deliver at some point in the future—a commitment to do the work.
- The second commitment phase happens during the Delivery Planning Meeting (FL 3.3).
- The second commitment phase commits to a specific delivery date, so now a specific piece of work is scheduled as part of a specific delivery.
- After the second phase of commitment, items should be tagged with the target delivery date and have their class of service bumped up to Fixed Date to ensure that everyone involved understands that a specific date commitment has been made.

MF 3.15 Establish a service level agreement (SLA).

Being unable to meet delivery expectations due to poor estimation is one of the most frequently communicated sources of internal dissatisfaction. Estimating the delivery time of a work item in an environment that changes frequently due to different factors consumes considerable capacity of the people involved in the work processes, reducing their ability to do value-adding work, while the outcome of the effort to estimate is often highly inaccurate. Re-estimating usually disrupts the foreseen sequence of the tasks, delays other work items, and affects the budget of the service. In addition, failure to deliver on time causes customer dissatisfaction. Therefore, delivering within the given estimate is one of the most common pain points for organizations.

A pragmatic approach to eliminate this problem is to stop estimating and instead use historical data and a probability density function for historical lead times to establish a service level agreement (SLA) based on a probability of delivering within a given time period. This use of data and statistics frees up capacity, increases delivery rate (throughput), and improves predictability. Furthermore, the customer sees the service provider as trustworthy and reliable.

Implementation Guidelines
- Define an SLA per service (as an SLA per work item type).
- If appropriate, define SLAs per customer (particularly if a specific customer is given a customized class of service tuned to specific business risks affecting their delivery expectations).
- Use the histogram of lead time for the service (MF 2.4) to determine the service level target. For example, using the 85th percentile of the histogram gives a forecast of the delivery time that, based on historical data, would be unmet in only 15 percent of the cases. This means on-time delivery should be possible for six out of every seven work items. For professional services, intangible goods work, this six out of seven success rate has proved to be within the psychological tolerance of most customers.
- Compare this service level with the customer's expectations (XP 3.1). If they are misaligned, this indicates that current capabilities are unfit-for-purpose. Consequently, define appropriate actions to reconcile them. This can be achieved by lowering the customer's expectations through adjustment of the SLA (e.g., rather than an 85 percent on-time promise, perhaps a 70 percent on-time promise is viable) or through the harder challenge of process improvements and service delivery changes to left-shift the probability density of the distribution of lead times.
- Add the established service level agreement to the policies for the process.
- Refer to VZ 3.16 regarding how to visualize the target date or SLA.

MF 3.16 Determine the due date.

The concept of a due date reflects a customer expectation—a promise that has been made. A due date and a desired delivery date (see MF 2.5) may be the same thing, in which case it is called a deadline or a fixed date. Generally, we use the term "deadline" to imply an artificially imposed date, by a customer, as a control mechanism—the customer doesn't trust the service delivery and is using the deadline as a forcing function. This is common at Maturity Level 2. A fixed date is used to reflect an externality such as a public holiday, a regulatory date, or some other event that is normally beyond the control of either the service delivery organization or the customer. A fixed date is a risk that the customer is managing, whereas a deadline represents the customer shifting the risk to the delivery organization.

As trust improves, it should be possible to replace deadlines with service level expectations or, in a more formal, bureaucratic, and conservative culture, a service level agreement (SLA, a contract). In which case, the "due date" is defined by the replenishment commitment point plus the expectation of the service level. Due dates are now about ensuring trustworthy, predictable service delivery. They represent a benchmark, or target, for healthy operation of the service.

Implementation Guidelines

If a service level expectation (SLE) or a service level agreement (SLA) exists, determine the due date by taking into account the following information:

- The date on which you commit to deliver the work item
- An understanding of the lead time for the type of work (See XP3.6 for more details about defining lead time.)
- The terms of the SLE or SLA
- Due date = commit date + SLA

If there is no service level expectation or agreement, then it is likely that there is a deadline:

- Record the due date as equivalent to the desired delivery date.
- Identify whether the due date is an artificially imposed customer deadline or an externally driven date—and therefore a risk that the customer is managing.
- Deadlines represent risk transference, while external fixed dates represent risk sharing. Risk sharing is required to reach Maturity Level 3 and beyond. Raising awareness of low-trust behavior via a Service Delivery Review with the customer present may be one way to encourage gradual improvement in the relationship and develop the trust needed to consolidate Maturity Level 3.

MF 3.17 Forecast delivery.

A forecast is a prediction of what will happen in the future. There are two basic types of delivery forecasts:

- *When will it be done?* Forecast when delivery of a fixed scope of work will be made.
- *How much can I expect?* Forecast how much work will be delivered on a fixed and known delivery date.

Unlike estimating, which tends to use a reductionist and deterministic approach, forecasting uses a probabilistic, non-deterministic approach. Consequently, forecasting is cheaper, faster, and often more accurate than estimating. We might think of estimating as a white-box approach that requires a lot of analysis and guesswork, while forecasting takes a black-box approach that relies on factual historical data to model a probability distribution.

Forecasts are based on an understanding of historical patterns, collection of historical data, use of models, and an assumption that system capability and process performance in the near future will continue to reflect the recent past. This is known as the equilibrium assumption, specifically referring to the concept of a period of equilibrium in the observed capability, usually as a consequence of stability in the kanban system.

Forecasts should provide a range of probable outcomes. For a fixed scope, a forecast should provide the earliest anticipated date and the latest anticipated date. Ideally, a probability distribution function showing the probability of any specific date within the range should be provided. For a fixed delivery date, a forecast should provide the smallest anticipated scope complete and the largest anticipated scope complete, again, ideally, with a probability distribution function showing the probability of any one outcome within the range.

Maturity Level 3 organizations have delivery rate (or throughput) data, work item lead time data, and local cycle time data for each individual state in a workflow.

Implementation Guidelines

- Check the stability of the system as described in MF 3.5.
- To forecast the delivery of a single work item, use a histogram of the lead time data for its type and class of service; then report a percentile that you feel comfortable with, for example, the 85th percentile. The lead time indicated at the 85th percentile suggests a six out of seven chance of delivering on or before that date.
- Make a scatterplot diagram of the lead time for a type of work and take, for example, the 85th percentile. Subtract the obtained delivery time estimate from the expected delivery time. If a work item is started before this point in time, there is an 85 percent or better chance of it being delivered on time. Otherwise, the chance of delivering on time is lower.

- If the kanban system is stable, use Little's Law for forecasting. Little's Law is a function of averages, and therefore it can forecast only average (mean) outcomes, not a range. It requires that its input data exhibit a Gaussian distribution.
- If the input data is Pareto distributed (that is, sub-exponential with a long, fat tail), as is typical at lower maturity levels, then simple forecasts using functions of averages, such as Little's Law, are not possible. With fat-tailed data sets, what is required is an algorithmic simulation approach such as a Monte Carlo simulation (see MF 4.8).
- However, there is a dilemma. To use a Monte Carlo simulation, the input data set—the reference class data—must exhibit stability; it must come from a period of stable volatility—an equilibrium. Monte Carlo simulation is described at Maturity Level 4 because it typically requires a Level 4 organization to provide the stability in the kanban systems, together with the mathematical capabilities, to be able to analyze and ensure suitable input data. Therefore, the dilemma: low-maturity organizations with fat-tailed lead time distributions need Monte Carlo simulation in order to forecast, but they cannot use Monte Carlo reliably because they cannot ensure either stability in the reference class data set or the likelihood that the equilibrium assumption remains true during the forecast period. The solution to this dilemma is to find an alternative means to build trust rather than trying to make promises based on elaborate and exotic techniques, which are ultimately unreliable and will not result in improved trust. Instead, focus on simplifying the promises being made to build trust—the two-phase commit approach in the Kanban Method, deferring delivery commitments until later, is a better, more reliable means for lower-maturity organizations to build trust.

MF 3.18 Apply qualitative Real Options Thinking.

General literature on Real Options Theory describes it as the application of financial option theory to real-world problems. It often goes further and describes it as the application of the option pricing algorithm.[2]

However, there is a much simpler notion of real options, or just options, thinking. To have options is to have choices. So, a qualitative understanding of real options means that there is explicit recognition of choices and a decision either to discard a choice or to pursue it by investing further. Simple analogies can be drawn to examples such as picking a spouse. There is a progression from mixing socially with several prospects to dating exclusively, resulting in a discard or escalate decision. Escalation may involve engagement or moving in together. Further time may go by and again a discard or escalate decision occurs involving marriage. Later there may be a decision about whether to start a family. And so on.

---

2. Robert C. Merton, Myron S. Scholes, and Fischer Black developed a pioneering formula for the valuation of stock options and received the Nobel Prize in Economics for it in 1997.

Each of these decision points, when there is either a discard or an increased investment to develop the option further, represents an embedded option.

Chris Matts and Olav Maassen, in their wider work on risk management, and specifically in their book *Commitment*,[3] have provided a lot of valuable guidance on qualitative assessment and the use of the Real Options Theory. Their aphorism

"Options have value. Options Expire. Never decide early unless you know why."

is just one example of how skills in options theory can be developed without a need for a quantitative mathematical understanding.

Real Options Theory relates directly to deferred commitment—never decide early unless you know why—and the general concepts of commitment, choice, and triage. For organizations adopting Kanban where there is some basic capability in triage, deferred commitment, and an understanding of the meaning of commitment and its implications, developing knowledge, experience, and capability with Real Options Theory is the next step toward deeper and more powerful risk management.

Implementation Guidelines

- Develop a qualitative understanding of Real Options Theory.
    Ask questions such as:
    - When should we decide?
        This question suggests defining the last responsible moment or understanding the expiry date of an option (or choice).
    - How much should we invest before we reach a decision point?
        This question suggests emergence of a skill in options pricing.
- Recognize that you would need to invest more (time, money, or resources) when the uncertainty is high, and much less when the uncertainty is low.
    - Ask yourself, "How much would I pay to know [this piece of information] or [the answer to this question]?" This helps you gauge the price you are willing to pay for an option.
- Recognize also that cost of rework can be traded for option pricing. Ask yourself whether an option is reversible and what the consequences are of reversing it. For example, a marriage can be reversed with a divorce, but this comes with a cost. Releasing a product to market that has to be recalled or reworked and replaced may have unacceptable consequences, in which case, it is worth paying more for the option up front. On the other hand, if the consequences of problems in the market are perceived as minor, then the option price would be lower; it would be better to proceed, and course correct later. In general, the Agile software development movement has made the assumption that consequences of problems

---

3. Olav Maassen, Chris Matts, and Chris Geary, *Commitment: Novel about Managing Project Risk* (Amsterdam: Hathaway te Brake Publications, 2016).

or failure after launch are minor, and that options should be cheap or free (see the Agile Decision Filter in Chapter 8, Culture Hacking).
- Prepare for developing a quantitative understanding of the Real Options Theory. Although a qualitative understanding may be a skill that can become pervasive and democratized across the wider workforce, a more advanced quantitative understanding may be a niche for specialist risk analysts. A broad understanding of options theory across a workforce enables much more advanced risk-management decisions at deeper maturity levels. The workforce will understand why a decision was made even if they don't understand the precise details. Developing a broad understanding of options theory is an enabler of deeper-maturity, optimizing behavior. It enables unity and alignment behind decisions, and it provides language to frame decisions and thus achieve consensus and agreement. Triage becomes more effective with a workforce skilled in qualitative real options assessment.

MF 3.19 Implement Service Delivery Manager role.

A fit-for-purpose organization manages work effectively through the entire value stream, both upstream and downstream. This naturally leads to the emergence of two roles, Service Delivery Manager (SDM) and Service Request Manager (SRM) (see Figure 12.5).

The intent of this practice is to describe the functions of the Service Delivery Manager. The title of the role can vary in each organization, and the functions need to be adjusted to the nature of the services that are managed. For instance, the title of the person responsible for managing the service of incident resolution could be Support Manager; the title of the role responsible for developing a specific product and delivering it to the customer within certain time and budget constraints might be Project Manager.

Implementation Guidelines

The SDM oversees the delivery of a fit-for-purpose service, ensuring a smooth flow through the kanban system and conducting appropriate actions to improve the service.

The SDM is a higher-maturity version of the Flow Manager (MF 2.9).

- Typical functions of the SDM include the following:
  - Manage the downstream flow of work, that is, the delivery of selected items to customers.
  - Facilitate the Delivery Planning Meeting (FL 3.3).
  - Run the Service Delivery Review (FL 3.4).
  - Guide the identification, analysis, and resolution of impediments in the workflow such as blockers, rework, and aging work items.
  - Oversee dependency management and assignable causes for delay in service deliveries that failed to meet customer expectations or SLAs.

12 | Manage Flow

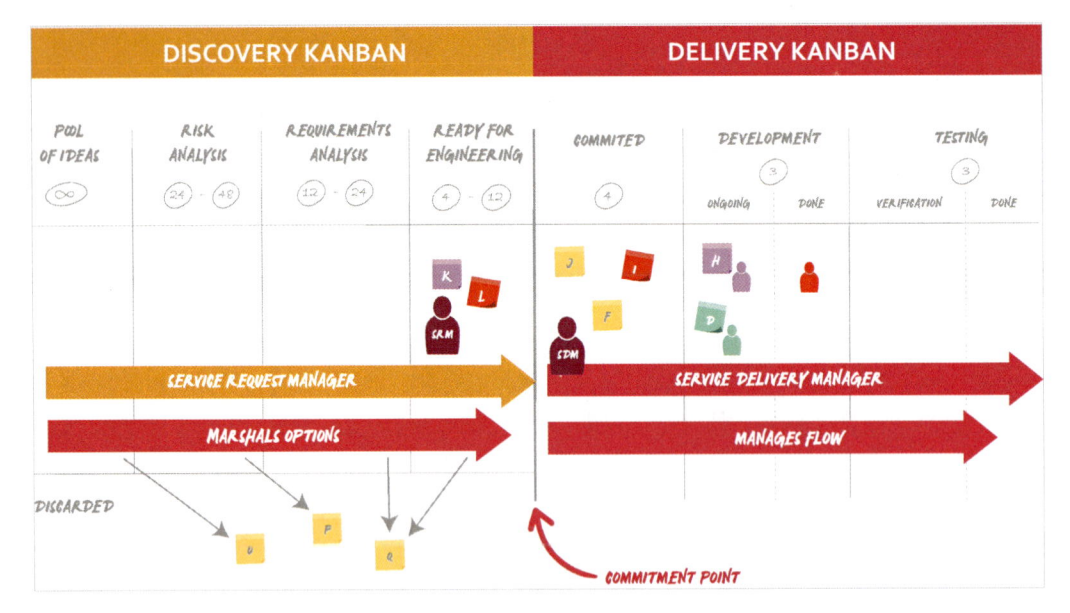

Figure 12.4 Service Request Manager and Service Delivery Manager roles

- There are different alternatives for introducing the Service Delivery Manager role in an organization. Depending on the organization's culture, the role of the SDM can be introduced as an individual or a group responsibility, a job title, or a position in the organizational structure. For advice and guidance on implementing roles in your organization, see Chapter 19, Barriers to Adoption.

MF 3.20 Implement Service Request Manager role.

The intent of this practice is to describe the functions of the Service Request Manager (SRM). In general, the SRM acts as both the service delivery manager and risk manager for upstream activities.

Implementation Guidelines
- Typical functions of the SRM include the following:
  - Develop an understanding of customers' needs and expectations.
  - Oversee the development of a consistent request elaboration process, agreed by all stakeholders. This includes defining explicit policies for triage, managing options upstream, qualitatively evaluating options, and discarding upstream requests.
  - Facilitate the Service Request Review (FL 3.5).
  - Facilitate, select, and order work items at the Replenishment Meeting.
- At higher maturity levels, the SRM facilitates the upstream Risk Review and participates in the Operations Review.

- The SRM ensures that the decisions made align with the organization's strategic objectives. Therefore, a solid understanding of the business, as well as well-developed communication and negotiation skills, are essential.
- Similar to the SDM role, the SRM role could be implemented as an individual or group responsibility, job title, or a position in the organizational structure.

Refer to Chapter 19 for coaching guidance on how to implement roles.

Maturity Level 4

The focus of Managing Flow at Maturity Level 4 is on optimizing the flow of work for higher efficiency and better economic outcomes. The specific practices at this level further develop the capabilities of an organization to smooth flow, manage optionality and capacity, anticipate dependencies, and forecast by means of predictive models.

TRANSITION PRACTICES

MF 4.1 Collect and report detailed flow efficiency analysis.

Flow efficiency is the metric that measures the percentage of time a work item spends in valuable, value-adding activities versus its total lead time.

$$\overline{Flow\ efficiency} = \frac{\overline{Work\ time}}{\overline{Lead\ time}} \cdot 100\%$$

Maturity Level 4 organizations look for higher fidelity and greater accuracy of collected data. They analyze the data to improve economic results, mainly considering two parameters:

- Earlier delivery avoids cost of delay.
- Shorter lead time improves optionality; hence, better flow efficiency improves optionality upstream and enables greater deferred commitment and, potentially, lower WIP in the system.

Implementation Guidelines

- Identify and label each state in the workflow as a work state or a wait state.
    Ideally, if it is a work state, identify the quantity of multitasking or time-slicing happening to work in that state. For example, a ticket may spend three days in a work state, but if a worker was multitasking across three items, the ticket probably received only around one day of work rather than three days. Because of this anomaly, most software solutions tend to overstate flow efficiency. They tend to report the full amount of time spent in activity states and credit it all as value-adding work. This is almost never true, and hence, the current state of the art in reporting flow efficiency is generous in nature.

Additionally, flow efficiency tends to be overstated in low-maturity implementations in which there is no signal that an item is pullable and no concept of "ready for the next stage" as a separate state. As a general rule, if your kanban board doesn't support *Done* sub-columns to signal "ready to pull," a Maturity Level 3 transition practice, it is unlikely that you can reliably report flow efficiency.

  - There is a simple but very useful hack for flow efficiency: ask how long Expedite class of service tickets take and how long regular, Standard class of service tickets take on average. Divide the Expedite class's lead time by the Standard class's lead time. This gives you a pretty good sense of the flow efficiency, as Expedites generally spend very little time waiting and have very high flow efficiency—their lead time consists almost entirely of working time.

- Record the time spent in each state.

  This can be done manually. For example, place dots or pins next to a ticket for each day it remains in a column on a kanban board (its state in the workflow) and, when it moves, count the dots or pins and record the number. Repeat this procedure for each column on the board and for every ticket on the board. Software systems simply timestamp when a ticket enters and leaves a given state, and the time spent in that state can be calculated by subtracting one from the other. Some adjustment for the percentage of the twenty-four-hour calendar day spent working may be desirable. For example, there may be a default that no day is longer than eight hours. At the time of writing, it is not known how effective commercial software packages are at calculating and reporting flow efficiency. However, regardless of accuracy, they are at least consistent from one ticket to the next and therefore useful for relative comparison within the same workflow, service, or kanban board. It is, however, dangerous to compare flow efficiency metrics across organizations or to try and use them for benchmarking or comparative assessment.

- Calculate flow efficiency.

  The primary use of flow efficiency is to help understand where improvements can be made. With low flow efficiency, values of less than 15 percent, the most improvement comes from eliminating delay. Do this by reducing the WIP in the system, by reducing queues and buffers, and by focusing on trimming the tail of the lead time distribution by improving capability at blocker management, issue management and resolution, and dependency management. If flow efficiency is quite high, say, greater than 30 percent, you may need a stronger focus on new working practices. Working practices are always domain specific, and hence, it isn't possible in a Kanban Method or a KMM text to give specific advice and guidance on that. In general, look for practices that can lower cycle times without affecting quality, or that improve quality and are "first time right." Such improvements always have a positive effect on the lead time and the tail of the distribution.

- Report flow efficiency analysis results at Service Delivery Review. Flow efficiency has historically proven to be a very poor improvement-driver metric. Treat it more as a health indicator.

MF 4.2 Use explicit buffers to smooth flow.

Bottlenecks and shared resources (or non-instant availability resources or services) impact and impede flow. Flow can be smoothed by placing an explicit buffer in front of a bottleneck or non-instant availability shared resource or service. Sizing the buffer must be treated differently for each case.

Implementation Guidelines

- Smooth the flow in a bottleneck.
    - Place the buffer in front of it to prevent the bottleneck from starving.

      The buffer just upstream of the bottleneck is intended to hold work so that there is always something available to the bottleneck. The purpose is to make sure that the bottleneck is fully exploited, operating at maximum utilization. This maximizes the throughput, or delivery rate, of work through the overall system. It also prevents upstream activities from stalling because of a lack of downstream kanban at or just before the bottleneck. The buffer both smooths flow upstream and absorbs uneven upstream flow, ensuring instant availability of work at the bottleneck, smoothing flow downstream.
    - Size the buffer such that potential variability in cycle times upstream, or variability of cycle time in the bottleneck, never creates a situation in which the bottleneck is without work.

      For example, imagine a bottleneck with a local cycle time of 0.25 days to 1.0 days, with an average of 0.5 days, or a throughput of 2.0 work items per day. The upstream function has a cycle time of 0.2 days to 0.8 days, with an average of 0.4 days, or a throughput potential of 2.5 per day. However, the upstream function has a series of quite long or large items and in the past two days has produced only one item, with another half-finished and due to be pullable by the bottleneck midday tomorrow. Meanwhile, the bottleneck has been running quickly and has produced six items in the past two days. This was possible because the buffer in front of the bottleneck contained at least five items that were pullable and had already completed the previous upstream step.

      Although it is technically possible to calculate buffer sizes mathematically, the more pragmatic approach is empirical adjustment. Create the buffer as part of the workflow design and select a starting kanban limit, say three. If the bottleneck suffers idleness, adjust it upward. If the buffer never runs dry, or empties for just a short time, then it is probably too large, so adjust it downward.

Such adjustments may be necessary for several weeks until a stable operating value is reached.
- Smooth the flow through a non-instant availability resource or shared service.
  - Ask how often the resource is available. For example, daily. And for how long is the availability? For example, one hour per day.
  - Ask, what is the maximum reasonable throughput in one hour?
  - Choose a buffer size that prevents the resource from starving but that does not turn it into a bottleneck.

    Throughput, or delivery rate data, tend to be Gaussian distributed. For example, two to eight items, with a mean of four. The distribution has a skewed bell curve. If we were to choose a buffer size of eight, we should be completely safe. However, this might result in turning the non-instant availability, shared resource into a bottleneck. Perhaps a size of six or seven is better.
  - Once again, empirical adjustment is the most pragmatic approach. Start with a reasonable number and adjust. If your shared resource is underutilized, then increase the buffer size. If your shared resource is unable to empty the buffer during a period of availability, then reduce the buffer size.

MF 4.3 Analyze to anticipate dependencies.

Will a work request produce additional knock-on requests of other services? Being able to anticipate dependent demand and schedule it in advance may improve predictability and inform commitment. Without analysis to inform whether a dependency is likely, the network of services—our system of systems—is operating in a purely reactionary fashion.

Unplanned, unscheduled, or unanticipated dependent demand is likely to lead to longer lead times, less predictability, poorer timeliness, and less fit-for-purpose service delivery. It is hard to maintain deeper maturity behavior in a purely reactionary mode of operation.

Description

There are two forms of analysis to establish whether a dependent request is likely or necessary—the probabilistic approach and the deterministic approach.

The probabilistic approach is fast and cheap and therefore preferred. However, it gives us a mere probability of whether a dependency exists and may result in some sub-optimal behavior when we guess one way and the result goes the other way. For example, if we believe there is a low probability of a dependency and so ignore that chance and then the dependent request emerges later, our system or network of services must react to late-breaking information.

With the probabilistic approach, historical data for this type of work is analyzed for whether it spawned dependent requests in the past. Historical data is used to predict the future. If, for example, every second ticket has historically needed a dependency, then there is a 50 percent chance that this ticket will generate one.

For example, we run an advertising agency, and one of our services is to design ad campaigns. When a customer requests a campaign, what is the probability that the campaign will generate a need for custom photography rather than use stock images?

The deterministic approach involves business analysis, systems analysis, and decomposition of the request into a likely design in order to assess what additional services may be needed. For another example, will the new features in our investment banking application require API changes to our trading platform? We can "determine" this through analysis and design work. This deterministic approach isn't foolproof. Business and systems analysis is never perfect, and designs tend to change during implementation. So, there is still a probabilistic element to our determinism. We may believe that our analysis and design say there is a dependency, but historically, this analysis has been only 85 percent accurate. So, even the expensive and time-consuming deterministic approach merely gives us a confidence level and does not eliminate changes and operating in reactionary mode altogether.

As a general rule, we want to use the probabilistic approach where it is most effective and accurate and the deterministic approach only when the impact and costs of a mistake are severe. With our banking example, if failing to detect the need for an API change in our trading platform caused a delay in deploying our new investment banking application, and that caused us to miss a deadline for new legal requirements, and then, due to the regulatory nature of that industry, we suffered a denial of trade, then the consequences of failing to detect the dependency were severe. As a result, we might prefer to start earlier, invest time and money in deterministically analyzing whether a dependency exists, and have far greater confidence in our planning.

MF 4.4 Establish refutable versus irrefutable demand.

Refutable, or discretionary, demand means that requests for work can be refuted, denied, or declined. When work is refutable, all three triage options—now, later, and not at all—are available. "Not at all" implies that the request can be denied. Discretionary work need not be accepted by the service provider. Discretionary work is optional work. It represents a real option in an upstream, or Discovery Kanban, workflow. It occurs prior to the commitment point.

Irrefutable work is not discretionary. There is no option to decline it. A full triage decision is not possible. Only the now and later options exist with irrefutable work.

Work is irrefutable because it is already committed, and the decision to commit to it was made somewhere else, by someone else, often at a much higher pay grade.

Irrefutable demand represents a problem, because it is often a source of overburdening, and hence, a root cause of disappointment and service delivery that isn't fit-for-purpose.

Irrefutable demand can also be of a legal or regulatory nature and hence, if we committed to being in that line of business, then we must abide by the laws and regulations in the territories in which we operate. Meeting such demand is table stakes for entering the market. At the point of service delivery, the work is irrefutable.

Other irrefutable demand can happen because a feature, function, component, sub-system, or system is table stakes and is required for a fit-for-purpose design. For example, a car must have wheels and tires. If we are in the business of designing and manufacturing cars, then we must include wheels and tires, and the request for them isn't refutable.

The final category of irrefutable demand is that it is mission critical. For example, if we are an ecommerce trading house and our website crashes, then the request to repair it and bring it back to full operation is irrefutable—such a request is related to our mission. We cannot trade on the World Wide Web without a website.

In general, demand directly related to the identity of our business—our why, our vision, mission, and purpose for existence—is irrefutable.

However, there is often a perception of irrefutability when, in fact, the work is refutable. Or the irrefutable work still has some elasticity or fungibility to its definition. Perceived irrefutable demand is often something that can be challenged. The first step in challenging it is to identify it. List it. Measure it. Assess its impact.

If previously perceived irrefutable demand can be challenged and its irrefutability changed or modified in terms of fidelity or timeliness, then we have an opportunity to better manage flow.

Implementation Guidelines

Create explicit policy for whether demand is refutable or not, and identify services that work only on irrefutable demand and hence, cannot be fully triaged. Use the descriptions above to help craft policy around irrefutability and whether a full triage of now, later, or not at all is available for a given service. For a service with no option to refute requests, a focus on scheduling and smoothing demand by pushing requests until later based on their costs of delay is necessary. A careful demand analysis with anticipation of spikes in demand is advisable.

Services that cannot refute demand may need capacity augmentation through the provision of the staff liquidity pattern (see VZ 5.1). Alternatively, spikes in demand may need to be rerouted based on a risk assessment using a demand shaping threshold (XP 4.1), allowing a tradeoff in fidelity or quality to avoid overburdening a service. Bifurcation of demand, for example, allowing programmers to design the UI for a screen rather than using a professional UX designer, is a good way to manage irrefutable demand spikes on internal shared services.

MF 4.5 Use classes of dependency management according to cost of delay.

Dependency discovery and management can be expensive. It is possible to minimize the economic and productivity impact of managing for dependencies by utilizing classes of service based on cost of delay. When a request isn't urgent, it makes sense to let dependency discovery happen dynamically and manage the dependency using established Kanban visualization and flow management techniques. When cost of delay is low, there is no need to invest time and energy up front to detect, plan for, schedule, and manage dependencies. It is important to understand that all requests should not be treated homogeneously from a dependency management perspective. Classes of dependency management are possible based on the cost of delay and class of service of the original request.

Description

We have identified six classes of dependencies management based on cost of delay and the four classes of service of the originating request. They are: Don't Care, Trusted Availability, Tail-Risk Mitigation, Fixed Date, Guaranteed On-Time, and Expedite. It is necessary to make upfront dependency discovery—planning for dependencies and advanced management—only when the originating request has a Fixed Date class of service. Recognizing and understanding this creates significant economic and productivity improvements.

Table 12.1 shows the class of service for the originating customer request on the calling service, the necessary class of service for the dependency work item on the called service, the class of dependency management, and the class of reservation needed on both the calling and called services. What follows is a detailed explanation of each of the six classes of dependency management.

Table 12.1 Six Classes of Dependency Management

Class of Dependency Management	Calling Service Ticket	Called Service Ticket	Calling Service Reservation	Called Service Reservation	Nature of Dependency Management
1. Don't Care	Intangible	Intangible	Optional Standby	None	No dependency management; dynamic, just-in-time dependency discovery
2. Trusted Availability	Standard w/ SLE	Standard	Optional Standby	None	Dynamic, just-in-time dependency discovery; capacity allocation on called service to guarantee service when needed
3. Tail-Risk Mitigation	Standard w/ Deadline	Fixed Date	Optional Reserved	Standby	Standby class of reservation (just in case); dynamic, just-in-time dependency discovery; use filtered lead time distribution—assume dependency exists to determine start time and calling service ticket's class of service.
4. Fixed Date	Fixed Date	Fixed Date with high-priority start	Reserved	Reserved	Up-front dependency detection, with reserved class booking on called service; definition of ready requires up-front analysis and a reserved class booking.
5. Guaranteed On-Time	Fixed Date w/ zero tolerance for delay	Fixed Date w/ guaranteed start	Guaranteed	Guaranteed	Up-front dependency detection, with guaranteed class of booking on called service; definition of ready requires up-front analysis and a guaranteed called service reservation.
6. Expedite	Expedite	Expedite	None	None	No dependency management; dynamic dependency discovery; expedite dependencies when discovered.

Class 1 Dependency Management: Don't Care

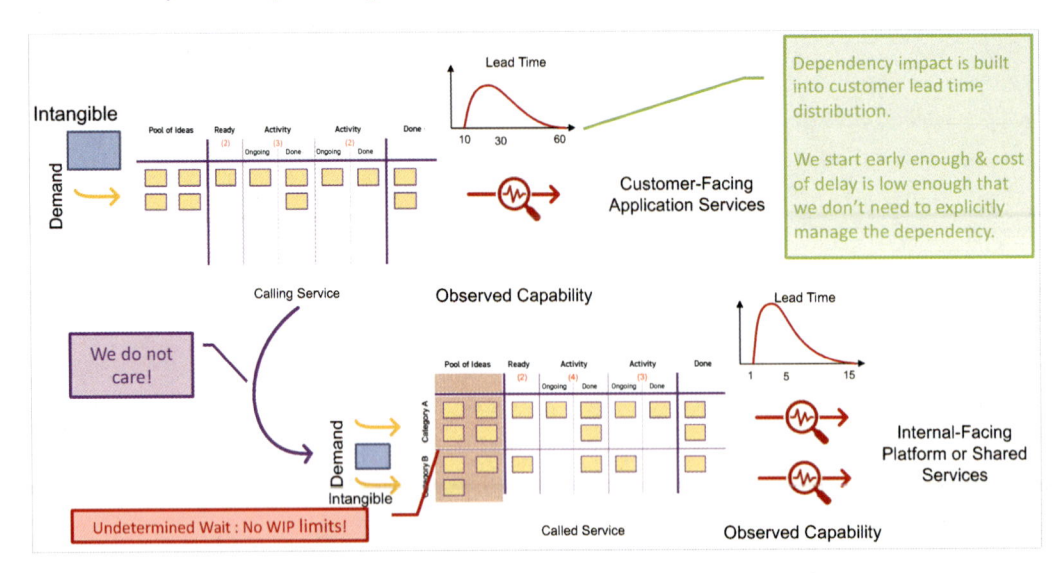

Figure 12.5 Don't Care dependency management

Since the cost of delay is very low, there is no need to actively manage dependencies; simply let them happen if they do. Class 1 dependency management, as modeled in Figure 12.5, is characterized as follows:

- Chance of dependency occurrence is probabilistic.
- Use probabilistic scheduling—if it happens, it happens!
- Lead time distributions already account for dependency delays.
  - No attempt to discover dependencies
- There is low risk of incurring any significant cost of delay, or:
- We can start early enough that we don't care about lead time tail risk.
- So, just do it, don't worry about dependencies. Let them happen if they do!
- No reservation is needed for the calling service or the called service.

Class 2 Dependency Management: Trusted Availability

The cost of delay is low, but trusted delivery implies it is within an SLA/SLE. Class 2 dependency management, modeled in Figure 12.6, works as follows:

- There is a probabilistic chance of a dependency occurrence.
- Use probabilistic scheduling.
- We care about tail risk due to cost of delay in the calling service (e.g., a change request for IT system maintenance). Tail risk is increased when a dependency exists, for example, on database administrators (the called service).
- There is no attempt to determine whether a specific dependency occurs or when specific capacity will be required on the called service.

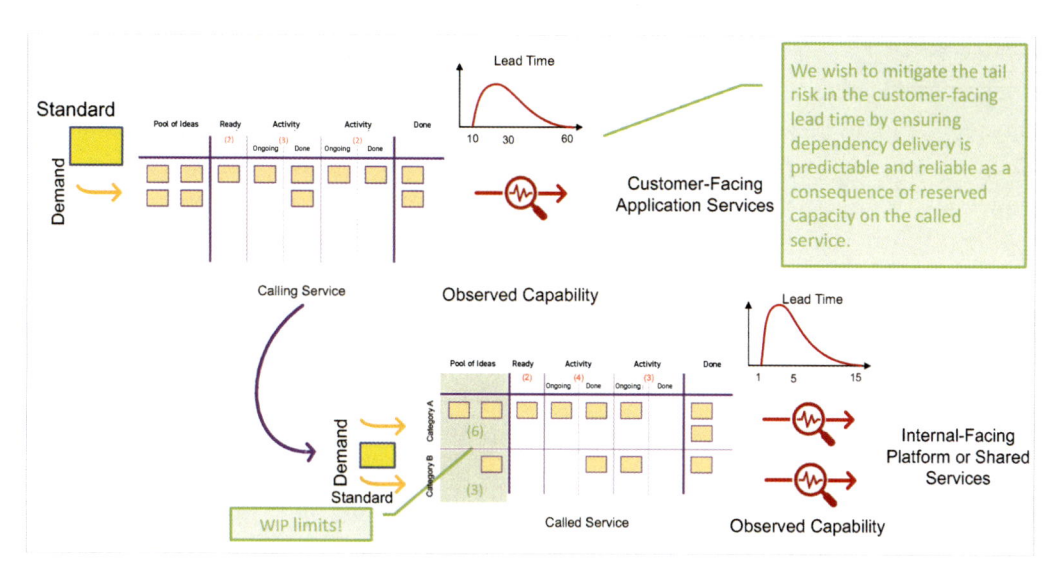

Figure 12.6 Trusted Availability dependency management

- It needs reliable service and predictable queuing on the called service (e.g., the called service has an SLE).
- Allocate capacity on the called service for probabilistically anticipated demand. Use outcome-driven design to design for anticipated demand with STATIK.[4] Little's Law (MF 3.5) provides average delivery capability, defining a WIP limit for capacity.
- Demand shaping. Shape demand from the calling service against average delivery capability. Avoid overburdening the called service.
- Track lead time on the called service from request submission, as the request is already committed. By definition, demand on the called service is irrefutable. It is push demand. Lead time distribution and SLA take into account queuing time delay at the front end of the called service.
- If a dynamic booking system is implemented on the calling (customer-facing) service, then schedule a slot on the calling service sufficiently far ahead of the desired delivery date to account for the tail of its lead time distribution.
- Use Standby class of service for the reservation (i.e., we'd like to start this early if possible and capacity is available).

---

4. STATIK, meaning Systems Thinking Approach to Introducing Kanban, is a process for designing a kanban system for managing service delivery and the work to be performed as part of it, and improving it continuously. It defines eight steps for each identified service: (1) Understand what makes the service fit-for-purpose for the customer. (2) Understand sources of dissatisfaction with the current system. (3) Analyze demand. (4) Analyze capability. (5) Model workflow. (6) Discover classes of services. (7) Design the kanban system. (8) Socialize the system and board design and negotiate implementation.

Class 3 Dependency Management: Tail-Risk Mitigation

In Class 3 dependency management, modeled in Figure 12.7, the cost of delay is worth managing, and there is a desire to avoid excessive cost of delay in the 85th through the 100th percentiles of the lead time. Therefore, we hedge the risk and assume a dependency exists. This has the effect of encouraging us to start the item earlier. We are trading off early start (earlier commitment) for the economic benefit of not having to detect and actively manage a dependency up front. Class 3 dependency management works as follows:

- Use probabilistic scheduling for any dependency, but assume one exists.
- Use filtered lead time to facilitate scheduling and selection (encourages earlier start).
- Trade off an earlier start against the economic cost of detecting and actively managing the dependency. If dependency detection is cheap and easy, why not do it, and defer commitment until later? Notice the relationship to option pricing and Real Options thinking.
- Capacity must be available on the called system when it is needed to provide prompt, trustworthy, predictable, reliable service delivery for the dependency.
- Use capacity allocation and demand shaping on the called service.
- Introduce a reservation system for the called system.
- Book a *Standby* slot on the called system. No reservation on the calling system is needed because the filtered calling system lead time distribution accounts for the effect of the dependency.

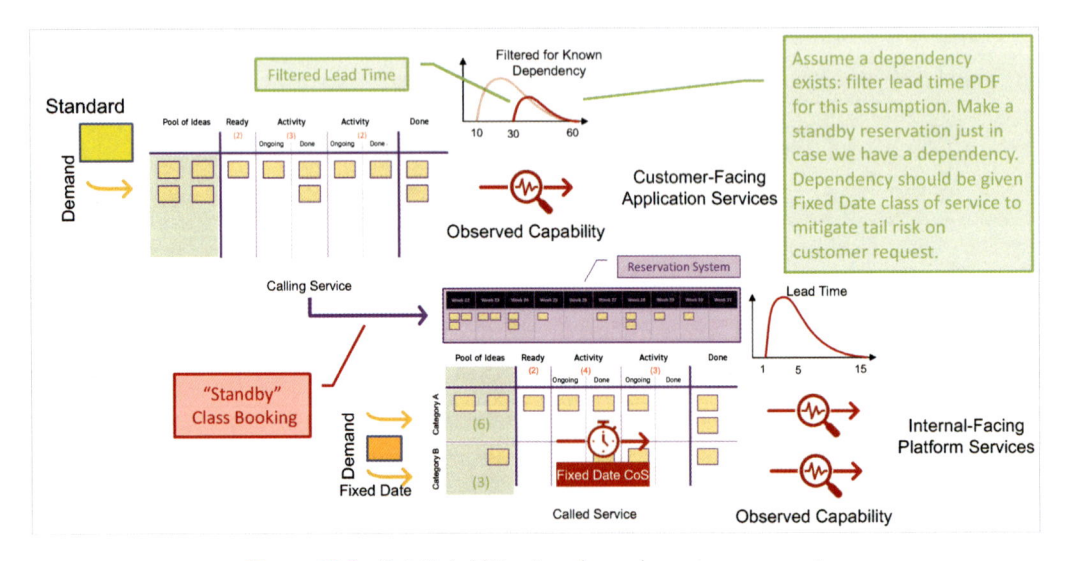

Figure 12.7 Tail Risk-Mitigation dependency management

Class 4 Dependency Management: Fixed Date

For Class 4, Fixed Date dependency management (see Figure 12.8), there is a significant cost of delay. There is a need to deliver on or before a deadline associated with an external event. It is now necessary to determine in advance whether or not a dependency exists. Any dependency is actively managed using a filtered lead time distribution and a reservation on the called system. Class 4 Dependency Management works as follows:

- Implement a reservation system on the calling (customer-facing) service.
- Make a Reserved class booking for the customer's work item.
- Cost of delay is significant or critical, or deferred commitment is valuable (as arrival of additional information to mitigate other risks is required to facilitate [in/out] selection decisions), or it was simply not possible to start early enough to mitigate tail risk.
- Treat as Class 3 and, in addition:
  - Anticipate approximately when the dependency will occur.
  - Forecast time from commitment to when the dependency will occur.
  - Book a Reserved class kanban in the dynamic reservation system for the calling service.
  - Book a Reserved class kanban in the dynamic reservation system for the called service.
- The calling service's definition of ready requires a booking on the called service. A confirmed booking for the dependency is necessary as the initial pull criterion at replenishment.

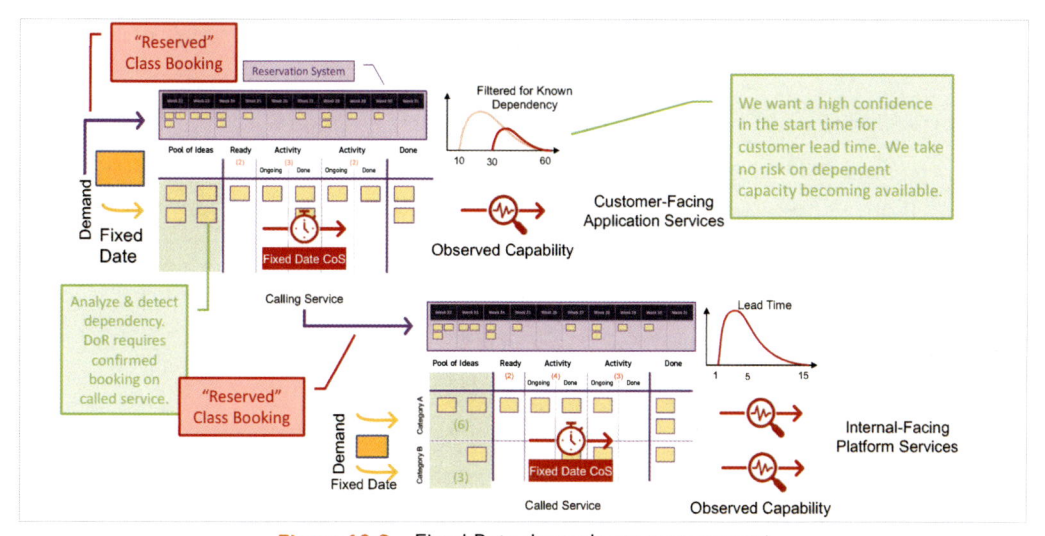

Figure 12.8 Fixed Date dependency management

Class 5 Dependency Management: Guaranteed On-Time

Class 5 dependency management, depicted in Figure 12.9, is the most expensive and should be used when there is zero tolerance for late delivery: the cost of delay is significant and occurs dramatically on a known date in the future. Use Class 5 dependency management when there is no margin for error with the delivery schedule. Class 5 dependency management works as Class 4 does, but with the following addition:

- Definition of ready is tightened to Guaranteed class booking in the reservation system for the work items on both the calling and the called services.

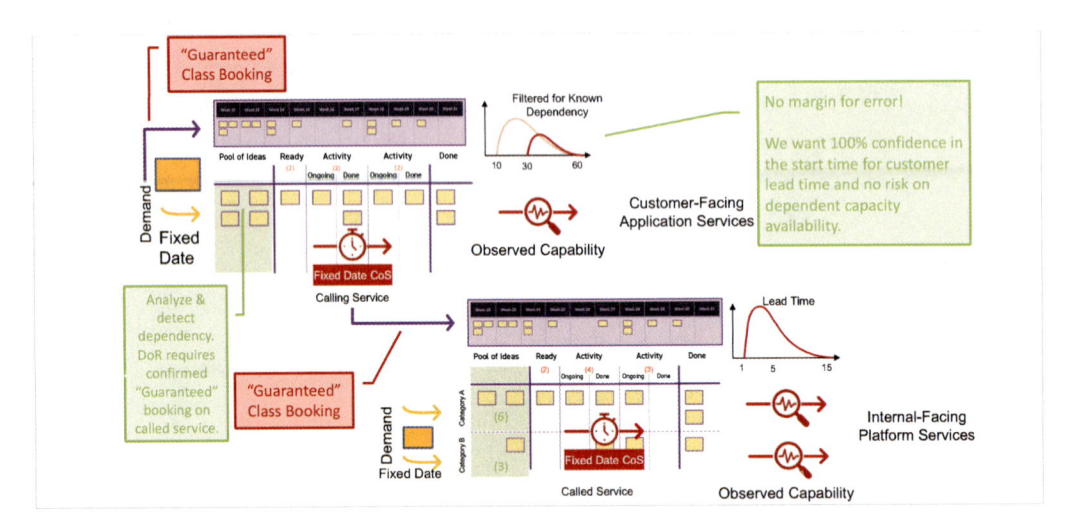

Figure 12.9 Guaranteed On-Time dependency management

Class 6 Dependency Management: Expedite

For Class 6 (modeled in Figure 12.10), the work is urgent and critical and must be delivered as soon as possible. We need to expedite the customer-requested tickets and all the dependent tickets that it spawns. Class 6 dependency management works as follows:

- We do not care about dependency management: Just do it!
- Just-in-time dynamic dependency discovery is done.
- All dependent requests receive Expedite class of service.
- Reservation systems are not used.
- No upfront dependency detection is done.

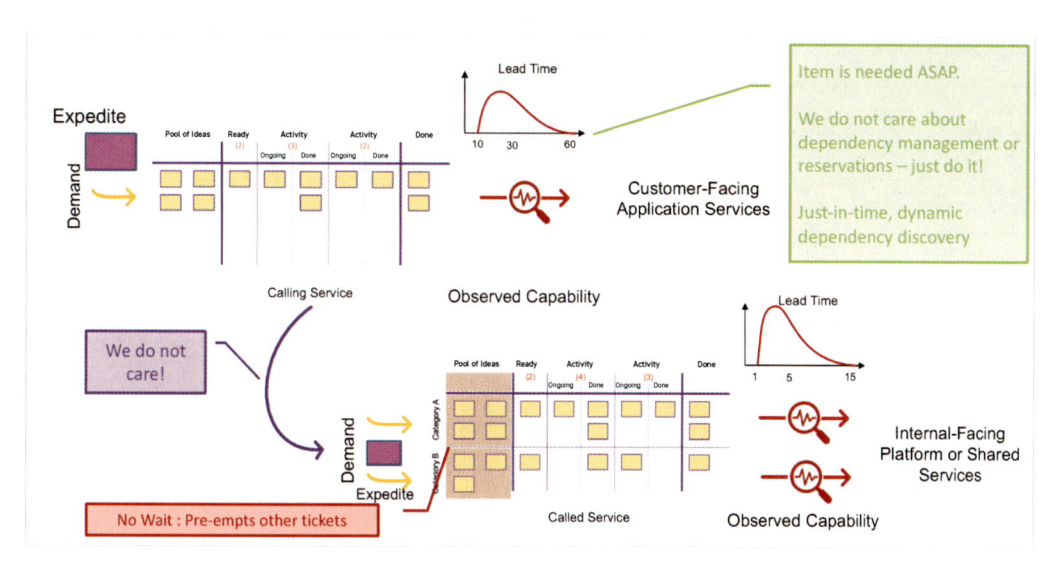

Figure 12.10 Expedite dependency management

MF 4.6 Use classes of booking in a dynamic reservation system.

A reservation system permits making bookings for the kanban system based on a calendar. Reservation systems provide a means to schedule the start of work. Adding classes of reservation (or booking classes) to the reservation system provides an improved means for managing uncertainty. The concept is not new. Airlines have used classes of reservation to manage risk for years.

For example, three basic classes of reservation exist when flying on full-service airlines: guaranteed seat, standby, and shuttle service. A guaranteed seat on a scheduled flight is just like it sounds—you are guaranteed to get on and have a seat and you probably know the specific seat number. Standby implies that you don't have a guaranteed seat but instead you will stand by at the boarding gate and wait for availability, taking the best remaining seat available before departure. A shuttle service ticket is less common, but it occurs on London-to-New York and Madrid-to-Barcelona routes. A shuttle ticket is more expensive than business class. It guarantees you'll be on the next available flight after check-in without a reservation. You just show up and hop on the next flight—like a bus, but with a guaranteed seat. Cost of delay, or uncertainty of schedule risk, can be managed through classes of booking.

Description

A booking or reservation system is usually a visual board adjacent to a kanban board with a space for each time period between Replenishment Meetings. Tickets are placed into the slots to make a reservation, essentially guaranteeing that a work item will be started at that time, or at least be given the opportunity to start based on its booking class.

Figure 12.11 shows a basic reservation system board adjacent to a kanban board. The slots in each time period on the calendar should be equivalent to the average (mean) delivery rate from the kanban system.

If we introduce classes of reservation, we can allocate capacity for different classes as a means of hedging risk. This is shown in Figure 12.12.

The total number of reservable kanban must not exceed the average delivery rate of the kanban system. The figure shows real data from a firm in northern Germany, courtesy of flow.hamburg. The average delivery rate is twenty work items per week. These twenty are allocated into three tranches for three classes of booking: Guaranteed, meaning that this item will definitely start on this week; Reserved, meaning that it will start that week if there is available capacity; and Standby, meaning that it will be considered with other items from the backlog if there is available capacity, but there is a strong preference for starting it due to its recognized cost of delay. In this example, the minimum delivery rate is eight items per week, hence the Guaranteed class of booking has an allocation of eight. The difference between the mean of twenty and the minimum of eight is twelve, and those twelve are split evenly to give six for Reserved and six for Standby classes of booking. This is just an example, but it communicates the concept and might be typical of a risk-hedging strategy for schedule and dependency uncertainty using a dynamic reservation system.

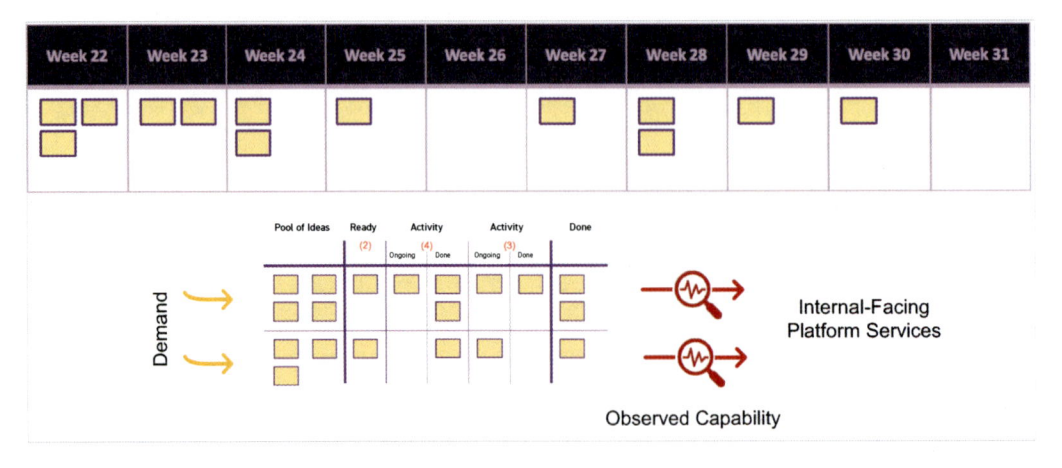

Figure 12.11 Reservation system board[5]

---

5. First reported by Sami Honkonen in 2011; https://www.slideshare.net/AGILEMinds/sami-honkonen-scheduling-work-in-kanban

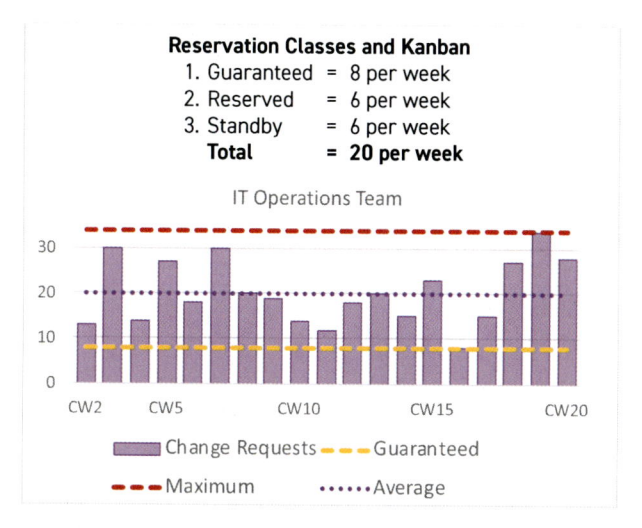

Figure 12.12 Three classes of booking with capacity allocation
Real data from an IT operations team in Hamburg, Germany
(courtesy of Susanne & Andreas Bartel, flow.hamburg Gbr)

CONSOLIDATION PRACTICES

MF 4.7 Determine a reference class data set.

Where simulation algorithms are used to forecast future outcomes and the algorithm relies on a bootstrap data set selected from historical observations, it is important that the policies for selecting the reference class data set are made explicit.

Implementation Guidelines

- Extract a reference class data set from a period of equilibrium, a period without turbulence. Where the historical data set—the run series or the time series—does not exhibit stability (has no period without turbulence), then using reference class forecasting and bootstrap data for simulation algorithms is not mathematically valid.
- Make explicit the policies for selecting the reference data set for the bootstrap of the simulation algorithm. These policies can be assessed to demonstrate the robustness of the forecasting model (MF 4.11).

MF 4.8 Forecast using reference classes, Monte Carlo simulations, and other models.

- At deeper maturity levels, forecasts should be delivered with an explanation of the method used and an assessment of its robustness. The robustness of the forecasting method is an indicator of the trustworthiness, or confidence, that can be given to the prediction.

Description

Simulations, such as Monte Carlo, require parametric probability distribution functions derived from a "best fit" to historical data patterns, or a simple bootstrap reference data set sampled from a stable period of equilibrium. Simplistically, a reference data set could be "the last thirty data points."

It should be declared whether the simulation uses a parametric function or a bootstrap data set. The model error and simulation error can then be assessed. Model error refers to how well the parametric function fits, or resembles, the actual historically observed data. Simulation error refers to gaps in the bootstrap data set in comparison to a close fit, continuous, parametric function. Such gaps represent values that will never occur in the simulation, while they almost certainly will occur in real life, and hence, their absence produces simulation errors.

In the Kanban community it is widely held that bootstrap algorithms are more pragmatic—it is easy to acquire historical data to bootstrap a simulation—and that the simulation error is generally not greater than any model error would be if a best-fit parametric probability distribution function were selected instead.

Simulations can be run using throughput data for an entire system, with a granularity of each day or week of system operation. This is a rather coarse, or crude, simulation with low fidelity, and we don't recommend it. Throughput or delivery rate data is Gaussian distributed, and the bootstrap data set should have at least 1,000 data points to have high confidence in the model.

A better approach is to randomly simulate lead time—from start to completion of every ticket. Lead time data is either sub-exponential (fat-tailed) or super-exponential (thin-tailed), but not Gaussian. The mathematical properties change dramatically. It might be acceptable to have only thirty historical data points for a sufficiently robust bootstrap data set.

A yet higher-fidelity simulation might simulate the movement of every ticket on a kanban board by randomly estimating the local cycle time that each ticket spends in each state in the workflow.

MF 4.9 Allocate capacity by work type.

The intent of this practice is to ensure that capacity is properly allocated to the work types or services offered by the organization (Figure 12.13).

Which work to continue or start depends on a business decision about what services to offer and the available capacity.

Implementation Guidelines

- Decide how to distribute the capacity among the work types or services.
- Use rows of the kanban board to visualize work types or services.

- Indicate the WIP limit on each row of a kanban board.
- Active work-in-progress in any row of the board should not exceed the limit indicated.

This approach creates a pull system for each row on the board.

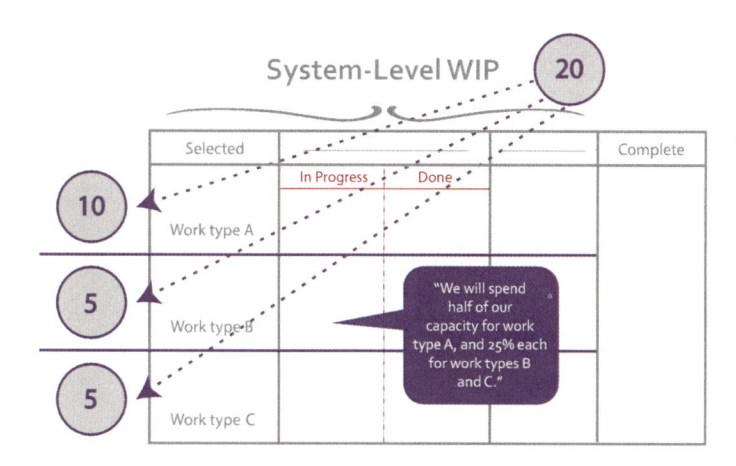

Figure 12.13 Capacity allocation by work type

MF 4.10 Allocate capacity by class of service.

The intent of this practice is to ensure that enough capacity is available for providing the established classes of service.

Implementation Guidelines

- Allocate capacity to classes of service, which prevents too many items that are urgent or critical (or both) from entering the system; otherwise, the system's routine ability to deliver will be severely affected. For example, allocate 20 percent of the available capacity for Fixed Date, 50 percent for Standard work, 30 percent for Intangible items, and 5 percent for processing Expedite work items when necessary. That 5 percent is an overallocation, exceeding the WIP limit; allocating 30 percent for Intangible items is a risk hedge against Expedite demand. Any additional unforseen, unplanned demand would require decreasing the number of Intangibles to make room for those items.
- Indicate the WIP limit per class of service in a legend and make it visible (e.g., on the board or next to it), as shown in Figure 12.14.
- Active work-in-progress for each class of service should not exceed the limit indicated.
- Replenish the input queue with work items of classes of service that fit the agreed distribution.

Figure 12.14   Capacity allocation by class of service

This approach creates a pull system per class of service. It can be used to allocate capacity by other risks as well.

MF 4.11 Assess forecasting models for robustness.

Models and simulation algorithms for forecasting should be subjected to sensitivity analysis, and the limits of usefulness of the model or simulation should be understood and defined.

Implementation Guidelines

There are some anomalies or dichotomies inherent in mathematics. When quantitative mathematical models are used, it is important to know their limits or their sensitivity to unexpected input data. For example:

- Models that assume Gaussian-distributed data sets are highly sensitive to the assumption of the alpha (or spread in the bell curve) within the data. To have a high level of confidence in the alpha, it is necessary to have a large data set—perhaps 1,000 to 2,000 data points. When a small number of data points is available, say thirty, and the data is known to be from a domain that is typically Gaussian distributed, it is dangerous to make assumptions about the precise nature of the distribution—its mean, median, and mode values—and its spread (or alpha). Derivative conclusions, such as a reasonable number of data points required to create convergence to a mean, that is, how many data points are required to provide a meaningful result for the Central Limit Theorem, may be even more misleading.

- Models that assume Pareto-distributed data sets are actually quite robust—just a few random data points, five to ten, may be all that are required to define a good enough model. However, with Pareto distributions, the concept of a mean is meaningless—a useless notion.
- Monte Carlo simulations that rely on Gaussian-distributed data sets actually require large numbers of data points to provide forecasts with a high confidence level, while the same simulation algorithm used in a different domain exhibiting a Pareto-distributed data set would provide a high-confidence forecast with very few data points.

Mathematical sensitivity analysis for forecasting equations and simulations should be performed and reported on against the expected nature of data in the domain. As new data arrives, it should be continually analyzed to see whether it falls within expected ranges and whether the emerging data set falls within a reasonable variance of the distribution function used in the forecast equation or simulation.

One emerging technique is continual reforecasting, using all new data as it arrives, to build up a set of real data used in bootstrapping a discrete (rather than parametric) simulation. This provides useful insights for robustness and sensitivity analysis. For example, what did our forecast tell us about a possible range of delivery dates for our project before we started it versus what our forecast is telling us now that we have completed half of the project work? By analyzing how the forecasted range of completion dates has changed, the robustness of the original forecast can be assessed.

However, there is a need to understand the stability of the system, and therefore, the validity of the simulation from the actual received data. If the data set exhibits turbulence, also known as volatility of volatility, then the actual data cannot be considered a stable reference class data set from which to forecast future outcomes. More mature models will take this into account.

Statistical models can also be assessed for other behavioral attributes. For example, a model that assumes its input data represents a small random sample from a bigger data population, for example, seven random data points from a set of 2,000, is sensitive to the randomness of the sample as well as to the number of random samples. If the real-world situation is that we don't have a random sample from a larger data population—in fact, all we have are the first seven data points—any model we use is exposed to the risk that the first seven data points are not representative of the entire data population.

Use of statistical quantitative models without thorough sensitivity and robustness analysis is likely to result in shallow maturity results—low predictability—and actual outcomes at unreasonable or unfit levels of variance from the original predictions. Use of statistical methods can provide a veneer of deeper maturity when, in fact, it is merely misdirection. Using statistical models and quantitative analysis is in itself not an indicator of a deep-maturity organization. Deep-maturity organizations are typically capable of delivering against both customer and economic expectations. This practice of assessing models in use for robustness and sensitivity is an important component of competent quantitative management.

> **MF 4.12** Make appropriate use of forecasting.

Description

The appropriateness and applicability of models, mathematical equations, and statistical techniques should be known and understood, and using such models should be appropriate in context.

For example, the popular Little's Law equation from queuing theory, which states that the average delivery rate is equal to the average work-in-progress divided by the average lead time, is a function of averages—each of the three algebraic components is an average. Little's Law was conceived in a domain where distribution of data points was assumed to be Gaussian in nature. This underlying assumption makes using the arithmetic mean an appropriate choice, and in domains where the spread of the bell curve, the alpha, is relatively low, very few data points are required to use Little's Law to forecast an outcome in the near future with acceptable accuracy.

As soon as the data set available, such as that for the lead time, is not Gaussian in nature, but rather super-exponential—it resembles a Weibull function with a shape parameter $1.0 < \kappa < 2.0$—more data points are required for the arithmetic mean to be meaningful and a reasonable assumption. Hence, Little's Law is less effective over short time horizons. It is still useful when projecting seventy to one hundred data points into the future, though.

If the data set for lead time falls below exponential, exhibiting a Weibull function with shape parameter $\kappa < 1.0$, then convergence to the arithmetic mean within a reasonable error margin is unlikely for at least 2,000 to 10,000 data points. For all practical purposes, Little's Law is not appropriate or useful as a forecasting tool under these circumstances.

Lead time distributions with long fat tails, where the data set resembles a Weibull function with shape kappa, $\kappa < 1.0$, are common in IT operations and other IT services and in any domain with excessive numbers of dependencies on other services, especially if these are external to the organization.

Shallow-maturity organizations tend to use mathematical models such as Little's Law blindly and fail to understand when those models let them down. This type of usage is superstitious and tends to lead to a belief that the equation is magical. When it works, all is well; and when it doesn't, there may be an emotional reaction that results in discarding the practice. Deeper maturity organizations understand when it is appropriate to use a model such as Little's Law and apply it correctly in relevant situations while deploying alternative techniques in others.

Develop a basic capability to analyze and understand data sets and probability distribution functions (PDFs) that are in one of five data distribution domains:
- Gaussian (Weibull, 2.0 <= κ <= 4.0)
- Super-Exponential (Weibull, 1.0 < κ < 2.0)
- Exponential (Weibull, κ = 1.0)
- Sub-Exponential (Weibull 0.7 < κ < 1.0)
- Pareto (fat-tailed power laws)

Nassim Nicholas Taleb refers to the range of κ > 1.0 as Mediocristan[6] because averages are useful and practical, and generally risk management is quite easy, whereas he calls the range of κ < 1.0 Extremistan because averages are not useful or practical, and risk management is far more challenging.

Select forecasting tools, statistical models, simulation algorithms, and quantitative analysis methods that are appropriate for each of these data-distribution domains. For example, the concept known as the Lindy Effect[7] for predicting the life expectancy of a current product based on its previous period of survival—an ability that relies on a decreasing hazard/mortality rate and an assessment of its health (e.g., its fitness-for-purpose)—is appropriate in a Pareto-distributed domain for nonperishable tangible or nontangible goods, such as the life expectancy of a Broadway musical or the career of a pop star.[8] Making a Lindy Effect assumption or forecast in a domain with a Gaussian-distributed life expectancy would be inappropriate due to the perishable nature of the entity.

Deep-maturity organizations should be able to provide a defensible mathematical analysis for their choices of forecasting models.

Forecasting requires a feedback loop to monitor its effectiveness and the robustness of the mathematical models in use. We recommend that this is done with the Risk Review.

MF 4.13 Use statistical methods for decision making.

Making an informed decision based on objective statistical analysis of probability and impact is key behavior expected at Maturity Level 4. Adopt the use of statistical mathematic models and analysis in order to make decisions.

Description

For example, a customer desires delivery within sixty days. What is the probability that we can meet the customer's expectation and deliver on or before their expected due date?

---

6. Nassim Nicholas Taleb, *The Black Swan: The Impact of the Highly Improbable* (New York: Random House, 2012).
7. https://en.wikipedia.org/wiki/Lindy_effect
8. Note: The career of a pop star, or group, can exceed the actual lifetime of the individual(s) (e.g., Elvis Presley, John Lennon, Michael Jackson).

If this question is answered through statistical analysis of historical data used to create a lead time histogram or an approximate, "best fit" parametric probability distribution function (PDF), then quantitative decision making is present.

For example, if recent historical data suggests an 80 percent probability that we can meet the sixty-day delivery expectation, we have a four in five chance of meeting expectations and being seen as fit-for-purpose. A risk-management decision can now be made regarding whether the 20 percent chance of failing to meet this customer's expectation is a risk worth taking. A decision one way or another is likely to be highly influenced by the consequences of late delivery. If the consequences are severe, such as a denial-of-trade restriction from a regulatory authority, we may choose to refuse the request and exit that business, or we may choose to provide a higher class of service to accelerate the development and reduce the lead time. If the consequences are minor, such as an uncomfortable meeting with senior leaders from the customer's organization, we may choose to carry the risk and suffer the consequences.

Maturity Level 5

CONSOLIDATION PRACTICES

MF 5.1 Use hybrid fixed service teams together with a flexible labor pool.

Description

Labor pool (or staffing) liquidity is an important attribute for minimizing delay and maintaining smooth flow. The kanban board design pattern illustrated in Figure 10.38 on page 162 visualizes this concept. Small teams that provide a single or limited range of services are organizationally merged into a larger group that offers a much wider range of services (servicing a greater number of work item types).

Each service offered occupies a lane on the board. Approximately half of the workforce from this merged larger group is allocated as a fixed-service team to undertake work of the types intended for that row on the board. One member of the team is designated as the Service Delivery Manager and carries the accountability and responsibility for taking the customer's order, accepting the work, making a commitment to deliver, managing the flow, and ensuring delivery occurs.

The remaining half of the larger group workforce are not allocated to specific services. They represent a floating pool of labor available to do any work for which they have the skills. This floating labor pool can be used to augment any one of the fixed-service teams. These workers have avatars for the board; an avatar is placed to show where they are currently working, which service they are assisting.

The labor pool liquidity pattern provides an advantage when there is ebb and flow in demand for any specific work item type or service offered, and where there may be limited resources and availability for specialist skills and a specialist can't be embedded in each individual service team. The labor pool liquidity pattern helps improve staff utilization at times when they might otherwise be underutilized due to an ebb in demand for the type of work their team services.

Aggregating teams into larger, multi-service groups with a floating labor pool is a means to improve both effectiveness and efficiency and to optimize the organization's performance. This pattern enables both resource efficiency and flow efficiency. Empirical observations suggest that this pattern works at the following scale: four to six small teams merged into one multi-service group offering six to eight services, with a total of twenty to forty staff members split into one floating labor pool that represents 40 to 60 percent of the total staff; each dedicated service team consists of a minimum of two staff members, often three or four.

An advanced version of this practice can also incorporate an explicit career-development path. New hires, essentially apprentices, enter as team members on one fixed-service team. After an agreed period, these junior members rotate to another fixed-service team. This pattern repeats until they've worked in all the different services. At this point, these apprentices have acquired all the skills and experience necessary to work as part of the floating labor pool. They are now eligible for a switch to the floating pool, with a promotion and pay grade increase. The floating labor pool consists of journeymen workers who have all the skills and experience required to be effective when assisting on any of the services.

From time to time, new Service Delivery Managers will be required to lead fixed-service teams. A floating labor pool worker asked to take on a Service Delivery Manager role should be given a promotion and a pay raise. Service Delivery Managers carry accountability and responsibility for the service delivery capability of their team. They are also responsible and accountable for the development of new junior personnel obtaining experience working on the team as part of their rotation and journey toward promotion to the floating labor pool. For these additional responsibilities, the Service Delivery Manager position should carry additional status and remuneration acknowledging the additional responsibilities.

13 | Make Policies Explicit

Kanban is a method for managing and continuously improving services. A fundamental element of the method is using kanban systems for managing knowledge work. A kanban system models how work is developed and delivered. Policies are part of the kanban system. They define how work is done at each step of the process, how it is visualized, how decisions are made, and what the appropriate relationships are, both within the service organization and with its customers. Making policies explicit is essential for growing a fit-for-purpose organization.

Goal of the General Practice

Establish clear rules for managing work that allow for developing a better understanding of the entire process and improving it further with consensus.

Benefits from Applying the General Practice

- Establishes explicit rules and criteria for making decisions related to work items, process, and customer service
- Manages dependencies between an organization's business units and with other groups
- Establishes criteria and guidelines for managing risks
- Aligns strategy and capability

Specific Practices Summary

Maturity Level		Make Policies Explicit (XP) Practice
ML0	Consolidation	**XP 0.1** Make the rules for the individual kanban explicit.
ML1	Transition	**XP 1.1** Discover initial policies.
	Consolidation	**XP 1.2** Define basic policies.
ML2	Transition	**XP 2.1** Define flow-related metrics (e.g., lead time). **XP 2.2** Define basic service policies.
	Consolidation	**XP 2.3** Define policies for managing aging WIP. **XP 2.4** Define policies for managing blocking issues. **XP 2.5** Define policies for managing defects and other rework types. **XP 2.6** Define basic policies for dependency management.
ML3	Transition	**XP 3.1** Define Fit-for-Purpose–related metrics. **XP 3.2** Explicitly define request acceptance criteria. **XP 3.3** Define policies for discarding requests upstream. **XP 3.4** Define criteria for aborted work. **XP 3.5** Define basic classes of service based on qualitative cost of delay.
	Consolidation	**XP 3.6** Establish a commitment point. **XP 3.7** Explicitly define pull criteria. **XP 3.8** Establish a delivery point and a delivery buffer. **XP 3.9** Establish customer expectations for each work item or class of work items. **XP 3.10** Explicitly define fitness-for-purpose and manage it based on metrics.
ML4	Transition	
	Consolidation	**XP 4.1** Establish demand-shaping policies. **XP 4.2** Establish SLA on dependent services.

Specific Practices Descriptions

Maturity Level 0

The intent of this practice at Maturity Level 0 is to discover and define the policies for an individual to use to better manage their work and deliver good results.

CONSOLIDATION PRACTICES

XP 0.1 Make the rules for the individual kanban explicit.

The intent of the rules (policies) is to make it easier for an individual to organize their work and carry it out with less stress.

Implementation Guidelines

Define individual kanban policies, which typically include the following:

- Initial guiding rules for deciding what to focus on based on the task categories defined in MF 0.1
- A limit on the number of tasks that the individual can have in progress
- A cadence for making a personal reflection

Making these rules explicit helps an individual apply them consistently and learn how to make them more coherent, meaningful, and useful for managing their work.

Maturity Level 1

The intent of Make Policies Explicit at Maturity Level 1 is to initiate defining and unifying the rules a team uses to guide them in making decisions about the work they do.

TRANSITION PRACTICES

XP 1.1 Discover initial policies.

People working together often assume that they do the same job the same way, and then they are surprised to find that this is not always true. Policies define the rules to apply during process execution. They govern the behavior of individuals and teams. Therefore, it is important to set them up with consensus and to respect them.

The intent of this specific practice is to uncover implicit policies and make them explicit.

Implementation Guidelines

- List the rules for managing work that are currently used.
- List the practices that the team decides to apply in their daily routine, for example, have a daily Kanban meeting.
- Revise the lists of practices and rules and discover gaps among the policies.
- Fill in the gaps as necessary to align the policies.
- Make sure that the policies are clear so that all team members interpret and understand them the same way.

CONSOLIDATION PRACTICES

XP 1.2 Define basic policies.

The basic policies are a consolidated, refined version of the initial policies. They include the fundamental elements necessary for the team to make decisions in the concrete work context, and they serve as a baseline for further improvement.

Implementation Guidelines

- Involve all team members in defining basic policies to guide their work process. The policies typically address the following aspects, among other relevant ones:
    - Per-person WIP limits
    - Team WIP limits
    - Conditions under which WIP limits may be exceeded
    - Frequency and criteria for replenishing the *Next* column of the team kanban board (Figure 10.4 on page 124)
    - Other rules to guide decision making related to the type of work as well as interactions within the team

Maturity Level 2

The focus of this general practice at Maturity Level 2 is on introducing the service delivery principles of the Kanban Method, strengthening the inter-team coordination in an end-to-end service workflow, and developing a shared consciousness about the need to manage the flow of work and address issues related to blockers, defects, and rework.

TRANSITION PRACTICES

XP 2.1 Define flow-related metrics (e.g., lead time).

Managing flow requires metrics that facilitate understanding how value flows through the system and what impedes flow, and discovering how flow can be improved to meet the desired business outcomes. This understanding establishes the foundation for introducing the practice of continuous improvement in the pursuit of delivering services that fit customer expectations.

The intent of this practice is to define which metrics are needed for managing and improving flow. See MF 2.4 for guidelines on instrumenting, collecting, and reporting these metrics. Refer to Appendix C for a detailed explanation of lead time.

Implementation Guidelines

Blockers, WIP aging, rework, and long delivery times in any state of the workflow directly affect flow and overall service delivery time. Therefore, studying them is important for improving flow, meeting customer expectations, and acquiring knowledge about risks related to the managed services.

The following metrics are typically used to understand and manage flow:

- Demand- and capability-related metrics
    - Number of work items received during a time period per work type and customer
    - Patterns of demand arrival from the identified sources; for example, continuous, random, seasonal (e.g., the first week of each month, in May and June every year)

- Delivery rate, or the number of work items delivered during a period of time
- Customer or system lead time, as defined in XP 3.6, "Establish a commitment point," and explained in detail in Appendix C, Understanding Lead Time.
- Amount of WIP in the system (ideally visualized with a cumulative flow diagram, MF 3.4)
- Additional information that would help analyze demand and capability, such as work type, customer type, work size or complexity, and so on
- Blocker-related metrics:
  - Date and time of blocking and unblocking the work item
  - Type of blocker (e.g., internal to our system, external to our system but internal to the organization, or external to the organization)
  - Blockage cause, or the reason a work item is blocked
  - Any additional information that would help you analyze blockers' impact on the service, such as the affected customer, the qualifications and skills of whoever should be involved in resolving the issue, or other context-related information
- Due-date performance
  - Delivered within due-date expectations or not
- WIP aging–related metrics
  - Time since requested
  - Time in progress
  - Reason item does not progress further
- Defects and other rework type–related metrics
  - Date and time of creating, starting, and finishing the rework or defect fixing
  - Type of defect or rework
  - Cause of the defect or rework
  - Any additional information that would help you analyze the rework or defect's impact on the service, such as the affected customer, the qualifications and skills of whoever must be involved in resolving the issue, or other context-related information
- Time stamps for receiving request from the customer, starting to work on it actively, and delivering it

Refer to VZ 2.3 for details about how to visualize blocked work items, rework, and defects.

XP 2.2 Define basic service policies.

The basic service policies define the essential requirements associated with a service delivery. These must be defined for each individual service based on its characteristics and the current understanding of who the customer is and what they expect. Defining clear service policies adds clarity to the decision-making process and facilitates the delivery of more valuable outcomes.

Implementation Guidelines

For each service identified in MF 2.2, define the following aspects:
- Service description, that is, characteristics that distinguish this service from other services
- Initial criteria for determining the urgency of a work item
- Requirements related to the service delivery, for example, meeting certain deadlines
- Cadence of the internal team Replenishment Meeting for this service

CONSOLIDATION PRACTICES

XP 2.3 Define policies for managing aging WIP.

Not controlling the amount of time an item spends in WIP affects the work item's delivery time and the predictability of that type of work, and it creates risks for rework due to changes in customer requirements and expectations. Policies for managing aging WIP ensure that all work is delivered within a reasonable time and that no work item stays in progress for an excessively long time, causing additional management and rework effort.

Implementation Guidelines

- Define an acceptable amount of time for processing a work item based on customer's or service-level expectations.
- Define how and to whom to escalate work items that exceed this time limit.
- Periodically analyze the causes of WIP aging and revise policies as needed to prevent those causes from reoccurring.

XP 2.4 Define policies for managing blocking issues.

Blockers generate waiting, which is a type of waste in a process, and they contribute to increased inventory. Fast resolution of blocking issues is essential for improving flow, delivery time, and predictability of work, as well as for reducing delays and rework.

Implementation Guidelines

Define the policies for managing blocking issues based on an understanding of what causes them and their impact.
- Define how blockages are visualized and what information is recorded about the blocking issues for appropriate management and further analysis.
    Because of their negative effects on service delivery, blocked work items usually are marked by means of a symbol or a sticky note of a preselected color. They stay in the swim lane and column in which they are blocked, and they add to the WIP for that column. This might create tension because it impedes pulling work into the column, but it also encourages fast resolution of blockages.

Blockages that need to wait until a certain future date before being resolved (e.g., a deadline established by the customer or a regulation) can be moved to a parking lot until that date.
- Define what kind of blockage data is collected. Typically, this is the date and time of blocking the work item, the date and time of unblocking, and the cause.
- Define what kind of blocking issues can be resolved autonomously by the teams.
- Define what kind of blocking issues have to be escalated to what organizational role and by what means.
- The policy for escalating blocking issues has to be agreed on collaboratively by those involved and the affected stakeholders, and it must be documented and made explicit to the workers who use that policy.
- Periodically revise the established policies to reflect the outcomes and the knowledge gained from analyzing the blockers.

XP 2.5 Define policies for managing defects and other rework types.

Defects and rework are other types of waste in the process that strongly affect delivery time, predictability, budget, and customer satisfaction. Therefore, policies for managing defects and rework need to be established and periodically revised to ensure learning from experience and improving performance.

Implementation Guidelines
- Define how rework is visualized and handled:
  - Decide whether a rework ticket should be attached to the work item that spawned it, and hence, remain in the same work state (e.g., *Test*) where the problem was discovered, or whether it should be sent backward to the column of the activity that needs to be reworked (e.g., *Design*). At Maturity Level 2, it is typical that the rework ticket is sent backward, and often it doesn't count against the WIP limit. Higher-maturity organizations keep the rework ticket attached to its parent. This has the effect of "stopping the line" and ensures a timely and effective defect fix.
  - Define what data about the defect or rework is collected for appropriate management and further analysis; typically, this is the defect's cause and the amount of time for the rework. Higher-maturity organizations collect information about the effort dedicated to the rework so they can analyze the economic impact of the rework on the project or service budget.
- Define what analysis of the defects and rework must be done, who does it, and with what frequency.
- Periodically revise the established policies to reflect the outcomes and knowledge gained from the performed analysis.

> **XP 2.6** Define basic policies for dependency management.

One type of dependency that needs to be managed in Maturity Level 2 organizations is dependency between and among teams that together are part of a larger service team that delivers a service to a customer.

The intent of this practice is to ensure a coordinated, end-to-end flow of a service involving multiple service teams.

Implementation Guidelines

- Identify the points of handoffs between service teams. Handoffs might generate different types of waste (rework, waiting, duplication of effort) due to transmitting incomplete or partially correct information.
- Define and agree on basic policies that ensure that handoffs between service teams are done effectively and on time. These include policies about the following:
  - Using and understanding a service delivery kanban board or an aggregated service delivery overview board that allows different teams to see a summary of the work they are carrying out together
  - How to visualize which work item is ready to be pulled by another service team
  - What information needs to be passed to the team conducting the next step in the workflow
  - Expected delivery time
  - Information that helps in selecting work items in the appropriate order
- Use the policies during the Workflow Kanban Meeting (FL 2.2) to make correct decisions about what to do first and then what next.
- Use the policies at the Workflow Replenishment Meeting (FL 2.1) to determine when to start something and how to handle any possible dependencies.
- Periodically revise the policies to reduce delays caused by handoffs, the number of handoffs, and the length of delivery time.

See Appendix F, Dependencies Management, for additional guidelines on managing dependencies. More mature organizations might define and use classes of dependency management and classes of reservation (or classes of booking, if you prefer this alternative language) as well as dynamic reservation systems as part of an overall dependency management strategy.

Maturity Level 3

The intent of Make Policies Explicit at Maturity Level 3 is to elaborate and establish policies that enable effective delivery of products and services that meet customer expectations, balance demand and capability, and foster a culture of continuous improvement.

TRANSITION PRACTICES

XP 3.1 Define Fit-for-Purpose-related metrics.

A fit-for-purpose organization continually satisfies its customers by means of services designed, implemented, and delivered in a sustainable manner.

The fitness-for-purpose must be managed overall and per service, based on both quantitative and qualitative (narrative) information.

Implementation Guidelines

- For each service, define fit-for-purpose metrics and indicators. These are key performance indicators (KPIs), derived from the criteria that customers use to decide whether they request the service or not, or from sources of customer dissatisfaction; for example:
  - Customer lead time per class of service: the time between receiving the customer's request and delivering on it[1]
  - Quality of the service: the rate of requests delivered without needing rework
  - Service cost
  - Additional customer expectations
- For each fitness criterion, define lower and upper limits within which the service is considered fit-for-purpose. Obtaining values above or below these thresholds means either exceeding customer expectations or underserving the customer.
- Monitor general health indicators that show the sustainability of the service level from the internal organization's point of view, or sources of internal dissatisfaction, such as the following:
  - Throughput, or the number of work items delivered for a defined period of time
  - System lead time, or the amount of time between committing and delivering a work item
  - Blockage time per cause
  - Rework time per cause
  - Degree of priority changes or interruptions, or other causes of work stoppage
  - Additional metrics that help you understand the sustainability of a particular service

    For each general health indicator, define a trading range within which the system or organization would be considered healthy—effectively upper and lower limits that, if exceeded, would signal that improvement intervention and actions are needed.

    Overall, getting values beyond the acceptable limits of the general health indicators is a red flag for a risk of deteriorating the service's fitness-for-purpose.
- Implement improvement drivers when necessary. These are indicators aligned with the fitness criteria or general health indicators to drive improvements. For each

---

1. Refer to Appendix C for a deep exploration of lead time.

improvement driver, there should be a target that, when achieved, should trigger switching off the improvement driver and ending the improvement initiative.
- Be careful of vanity metrics—those that make people feel good and for which more is always better, such as happiness. Vanity metrics can be formally documented, perhaps with some indication of the social, or emotional, need for the metric. In general, there should be no targets, no ideal trading range, no thresholds, and no goals associated with any vanity metric.
- For each of the established metrics, define what data must be collected, how to collect it (by means of what tools), who will collect the data, and with what frequency. Clarifying all aspects of data collection is key to ensuring that all data collectors have the same understanding, which reduces the chances of disparate results among collectors.
- Define what kind of qualitative analysis to make and what decisions will be made based on the derived observations and conclusions.
- Clearly communicate the purpose of the metrics and how the data will be analyzed and used. Clear communication is fundamental to eliminating wrong interpretations by the workers, collecting the correct data, and thus deriving an accurate understanding about the service and what actions are necessary.

XP 3.2 Explicitly define request acceptance criteria.

Establishing explicit policies for accepting upstream requests facilitates the process of deciding which options to pull into the ready-to-start stage of the delivery kanban system.

Implementation Guidelines

- Decide what information the customer request must include to initiate the delivery process. The following criteria are typically used:
    - It is complete.
    - It is clear.
    - It is coherent with other requests.
    - It is testable.
    - It has defined user acceptance criteria.
- Make sure that enough capacity is available to commit to delivering the work item within the expected time.
- Refer to VZ 3.2 regarding visualizing the request acceptance criteria.

XP 3.3 Define policies for discarding requests upstream.

Frequently, organizations have a large number of submitted ideas that linger without attention for months, or even years. There is never enough capacity to start working on all of the ideas and get them done. Plenty get discarded some time later because they no longer interest the customers or fit the organization's business. However, the elaboration, development, and management of some of these ideas have already consumed significant time and effort (Figure 13.1).

Acknowledging this fact shows significant progress. It is useful to define explicit policies for actively closing aged options before the kanban system's commitment point (i.e., upstream). This allows the organization to focus on ideas that are expected to bring more value to customers and to avoid discarding work items in later stages of their development, which wastes time and resources.

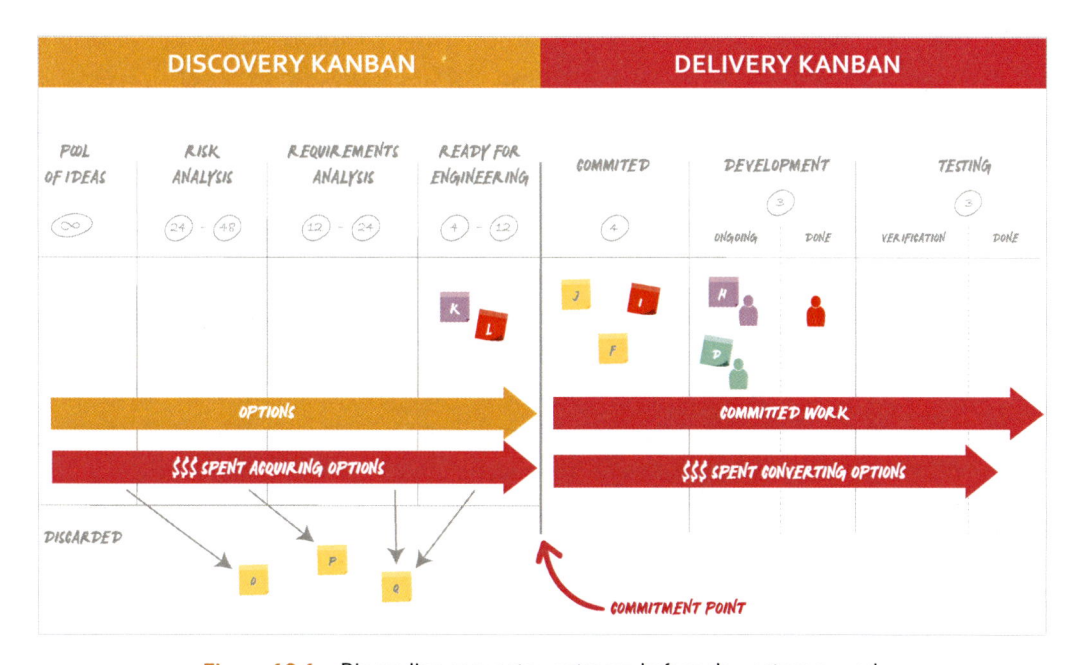

Figure 13.1 Discarding requests upstream before downstream work

Implementation Guidelines
- Agree with customers and other stakeholders what age or other conditions qualify an option to be discarded. For example, an idea submitted more than a year ago that has not been started yet is discarded; an option that requires high development effort and is expected to bring little customer or business value is discarded.
- Define these policies explicitly.
- Use these policies for proper management of upstream work.

XP 3.4 Define criteria for aborted work.

Work items can be aborted after the commitment point. This is undesirable behavior, as we shouldn't have committed if the item wasn't going to be completed. Explicit policy is needed to label an item "aborted" and move it to the waste bin. For example:

- The customer has changed their mind.
- New information has emerged and the business case is no longer viable—the item will cost too much to complete, take too long to complete, or the anticipated value was overestimated and is no longer realistic.
- The item is technically infeasible.

In such cases, the entire effort of elaborating the idea, developing it, and managing the job is wasted. Additionally, the team lost opportunities to deliver other customer requests earlier. Aborted work is wasteful. Therefore, organizations should study the causes of aborted work in order to learn how these errors might be better avoided in future. Avoiding selecting work that will be aborted later increases capacity, improves predictability, left shifts and trims the tail of the lead time probability distribution, and improves the flow of value. These are all important contributions to realizing Maturity Level 3. Reducing and eliminating aborted work is a key means of eliminating waste and improving efficiency at Maturity Levels 4 and 5.

Implementation Guidelines

- Collect the tickets of aborted work items.
- Analyze the causes and/or considerations for abandoning these work items.
- Infer criteria or symptoms of work items that can help to identify a risk of aborting them at the commitment point or as early as possible in the workflow.
- Agree with the customer on how to manage the act of aborting a committed work item.

XP 3.5 Define basic classes of service based on qualitative cost of delay.

A class of service is defined by a set of policies that describe how a piece of work should be treated. The intent of defining classes of service is to better manage customer satisfaction by tuning the service level to both the customer's expectations and the business's priorities. Offering a variety of classes of service improves risk management and economic outcomes.

Organizations at Maturity Level 2 and below typically treat all work homogeneously, or have no explicit policies on classes of service; hence, they visualize them all the same way, with the possible exception of an Expedite class of service. Organizations that rely on individual or managerial heroics often need a process to facilitate the heroic effort—an explicit definition of an expedite class of service facilitates this.

A more sophisticated understanding of risk, customer expectations, and the possibilities enabled through multiple classes of service emerges in the transition to Maturity Level 3. Organizations transitioning to Maturity Level 3 typically focus classes of service on policy providing guidance on priority of pull. This aligns directly to the urgency of an item. Urgency may be understood only in a qualitative manner.

Make Policies Explicit – Maturity Level 3

At Maturity Level 3, it is typical to have an explicit understanding of customer expectations (or fitness criteria for service delivery) and align the classes of service to these expectations.

In deeper-maturity organizations, Maturity Level 4 and beyond, classes of service are aligned to sets of business risks and are used to optimize economic performance as well as to ensure customer satisfaction.

Implementation Guidelines

- For each class of service, define the policies to be used for selecting and processing work items while they are in the kanban system. These can be related to risks of delay or cost of delay, the organization's image, or other business-related criteria. Four archetypes of class of service based on cost of delay are widely used (see Figure 13.2):
  - **Standard** The largest portion of the work should be in this class. The selection criterion is typically first-in, first-out (FIFO) queuing, or earliest start date first.
  - **Fixed Date** There is a hard date beyond which there is a severe cost of delay, such as a fine, a concrete expense, a lost business opportunity, or another reason for which the cost of delay increases drastically, and therefore missing the date is unacceptable.
    - Queuing discipline, selection, and pull are judged (usually qualitatively) against the delivery date. Items are effectively given a higher priority if there is a strong chance of missing the required delivery date. There is a tendency to delay starting fixed date items until "just in time," deferring commitment until they must be given priority in order to be completed on time.
    - Deeper-maturity organizations may develop quantitative means to determine start dates for such work items and choose to start some of them earlier than necessary to avoid needing to give them priority over other items.

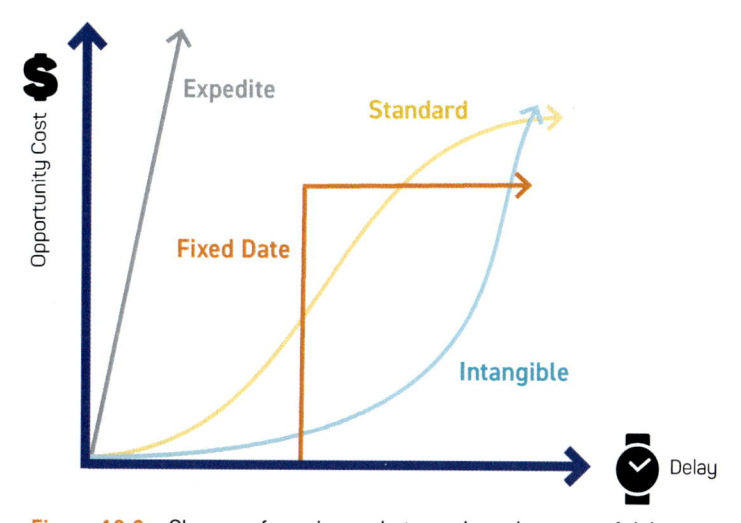

Figure 13.2 Classes of service archetypes based on cost of delay

- **Expedite** These work items are urgent, associated with a high cost of delay. Usually, they are given override priority and as many staff and other resources as may be necessary, jumping to the head of every queue, preempting existing work-in-progress.
- **Intangible** These work items are currently of low urgency, but important. Often, they involve a severe cost of delay in the distant future. This is work that must be done and is important for long-term survival and consistent economic outcomes. Urgency will change in the future if the work is not addressed early.
• For each class of service, establish a threshold expectation for lead time. These must be based on historical data and customer expectations and must be properly aligned with the business risks they are managing.
  - A threshold expectation should have two parts: a number of days (or hours) within which the work items should be delivered and a probability, or percentage of work items that should hit the expectations, for example, 85 percent within thirty days.
  - It is important that the threshold can be achieved under normal circumstances and missed only due to a specific cause.
• Require that all team members and external stakeholders know and understand the classes of service, their threshold lead times and probabilities, as well as the rest of the associated policies.
• Define how classes of service are visualized (see VZ 3.7 for more details).
• A class of service for an item is selected along with the item when it is pulled into the kanban system.

CONSOLIDATION PRACTICES

XP 3.6 Establish a commitment point.

To say that a work item is committed, it must meet two conditions: (1) the customer has a strong expectation that the work on their request should now proceed to delivery and is committed to receive (and pay for) the output; (2) the service team has available capacity to carry out the job and commits to pull the ticket, start working on it, and deliver the work.

The point in the process at which the transition between the stages of uncommitted and committed work occurs, typically as a result of a Replenishment Meeting (FL 3.2), is referred to as the commitment point (Figure 13.3).

At Maturity Level 3, we expect the commitment to be synchronous (i.e., the customer and the delivery organization agree and commit together at the same time—effectively, a handshake). Asynchronous commitment at Maturity Level 3 or higher would be an exception, and there would need to be an explicit reason for it, such as time-zone inconvenience (e.g., an upstream team on the West Coast of the US separated from a downstream delivery team in India with a twelve and a half-hour time difference).

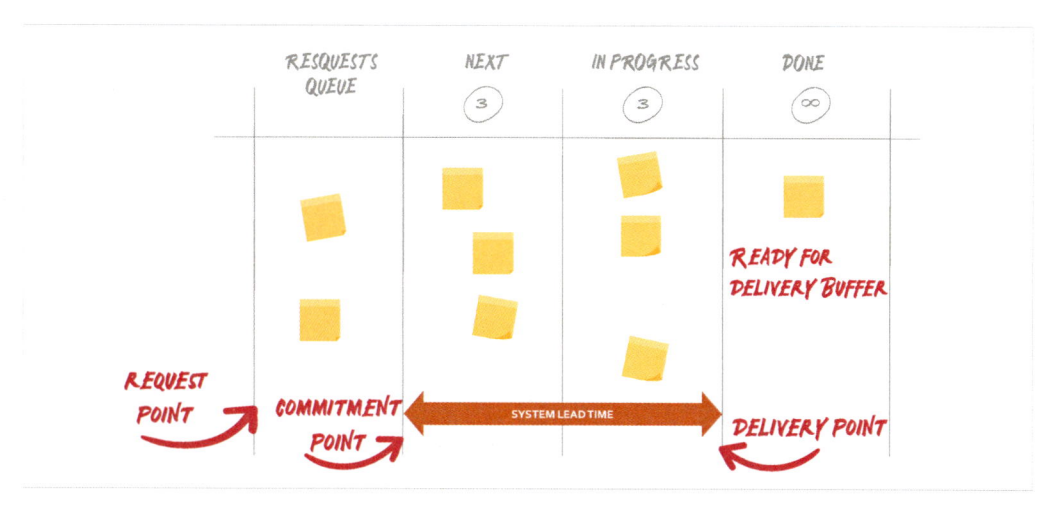

Figure 13.3 Commitment and delivery points

At Maturity Level 2 and below, asynchronous commitment is common. Consequently, the customer might believe that an item is committed when the delivery team does not feel the same way about it.

System lead time is the time that passes from the point when the delivery team agrees to pull the ticket and start working on it until the ticket is ready for delivery (i.e., has reached the delivery point). The delivery team is not responsible for any delays incurred by the customer when an item is ready for delivery.

Customer lead time is the time that passes from the point when the customer believes their order has been accepted (i.e., it has reached the request point) until the item is ready for delivery.

The delivery point is described in XP 3.8. Refer to Appendix C, Understanding Lead Time, for a detailed explanation.

Implementation Guidelines

- Indicate the commitment point on a kanban board, for example, by means of a vertical line before the first column of the delivery part of the workflow.
- Agree with the customer that this is the commitment point and that the system lead time starts running here.
- Define criteria for committing work, which must be met for a request to pass through the commitment point. Refer to XP 3.2 for more details on establishing acceptance criteria.

Making the commitment point explicit brings clarity and transparency to the decision-making process. Removing ambiguity about the request point and the commitment point and clarifying the meaning of "to be committed" makes the customer lead time and system lead time the same. Hence, the term "lead time" becomes sufficient to refer to either of them, as it has the same meaning for both the customer (upstream) and the service delivery organization (downstream).

Refer to FL 3.2 for more details about conducting Replenishment Meetings.

XP 3.7 Explicitly define pull criteria.

The pull criteria are essential for using the kanban system properly. They define conditions that must be fulfilled for a work item to be pulled into the next stage of the workflow. Having these criteria explicitly defined allows the people who use the kanban system to make coherent decisions autonomously. As a whole, this contributes to establishing a more consistent, more effective, and less costly management process.

Implementation Guidelines

- Identify what conditions need to be true for a work item to pull it into the next column of the kanban system. These criteria are also known as definition of done or exit criteria. Some examples of pull criteria are the following:
    - WIP limit for the next column
    - WIP limit for the lane
    - Criteria for completing the work item in its current state (criteria for done)
    - Class of service of the work item
    - Age of the work item
    - Expected due date for the work item
    - Additional considerations related to the work item type
- Achieve consensus on the pull criteria.
- Revise the established pull criteria periodically or as needed to improve the flow of work.

XP 3.8 Establish a delivery point and a delivery buffer.

Establish the point in the workflow where work items would be considered complete and ready for a customer to take delivery. Create explicit policy to define where the responsibility lies for switching the work item from the delivery organization to the customer. This may entail some sort of acceptance testing criteria, a sign-off, or related testable criteria that determine that the delivery organization has nothing more to contribute other than facilitating a handoff, delivery, installation, commissioning, and so forth, enabling the customer to take delivery and make use of the item.

While on-demand delivery of single items is possible, it is unusual except in higher-maturity organizations or in technology and IT services in which automated configuration management and deployment technology facilitates what is known as continuous integration. Typically, deliveries are batched and made either on a scheduled, periodic cadence or triggered by the batch size. Either way, it is necessary to buffer delivery. Usually, this is done by providing a *Ready for Delivery* state in the workflow and a matching column on the kanban board. Sometimes this state is simply called *Done*.

Implementation Guidelines

- Determine the point in the workflow at which the delivery organization's contribution is complete.
- Determine the criteria for a "definition of done," also known as the definition of "ready for delivery": these are the gating criteria that limit work items from exiting the kanban system and entering the *Ready for Delivery* buffer.
- Size the delivery buffer.
    - If you have on-demand, automated delivery, the delivery buffer may be unnecessary or have a WIP limit of one.
    - If you have a buffer size–triggered delivery, determine the batch size that makes economic sense for delivery and set the WIP limit accordingly. When the buffer fills up, it triggers a delivery.
    - If you have a periodic delivery cadence, model the average delivery rate and a higher percentile, such as the 85th percentile, of the delivery rate, and calculate how many items are likely to arrive for delivery in up to six out of seven delivery cycles. Using Little's Law, determine the buffer size. It is not usual for the delivery buffer to be unbounded.
- Visualize the delivery point and the delivery buffer with its WIP limit on a kanban board, as shown previously in Figure 13.3. Note that if the delivery buffer is unbounded, it is conventional to illustrate this with a infinity symbol for the WIP limit. Refer to MF 3.14 about using two-phase commit for delivery commitment.

XP 3.9 Establish customer expectations for each work item or class of work items.

To ensure that customer expectations are properly understood for a given product or service, relevant customer acceptance criteria must be defined. They remove ambiguity and prevent misunderstandings with respect to customer satisfaction.

Implementation Guidelines

- Define customer acceptance criteria for each work item type. Customer acceptance criteria include the following characteristics:
    - A set of conditions to be fulfilled by the product or service in specified scenarios
    - A definition of the scope of the work item to be delivered
    - Other relevant characteristics related to delivery time and quality as well as non-functional and safety requirements
- Determine what kinds of tests must be performed on the work item to ensure it meets customer expectations.

- Make sure that the customer acceptance criteria are defined, agreed, and understood equally by the team and the customer.
- Align the metrics defined in XP 3.1 with the customer's expectations.

XP 3.10 Explicitly define fitness-for-purpose and manage it based on metrics.

Fit-for-purpose means that a customer's expectations are met by a product or service with respect to a specific purpose they held when placing the order for a piece of work. The Fit-for-Purpose Framework[2] defines three dimensions for fitness-for-purpose, namely, Design, Implementation, and Service Delivery.

Implementation Guidelines

- Define fitness criteria for each of these three dimensions. The fitness criteria are selection criteria that the customer uses to choose one product or service over another.
- For each fitness criterion, define a threshold level that represents "fit," and therefore selection of the product or service, or satisfaction with the product or service delivered.
- For Design, define a level of nonfunctional quality with a threshold that represents "good enough" for each feature, component, sub-system, assembly, or whole. Optionally, define an additional threshold that represents "beyond expectations." Each feature needed for a given purpose defines a function requirement and, in turn, each feature should have a quality or fidelity threshold representing an acceptable level of performance.

    The nonfunctional, cross-functional, or fidelity definitions represent the required implementation level. Service delivery has criteria such as lead time, predictability, and timeliness with their own thresholds.
- For each market segment, where segments are defined based on a customer's purpose, define a set of fitness criteria that establishes the threshold of fit-for-purpose.

    In Kanban, each work item type defines or represents an offered service. Hence, each work item type needs explicit fitness criteria. Each class of service represents the service level required to mitigate the risks associated with a particular customer's purpose, so each class of service needs a set of fitness criteria as well.
- Once the fitness criteria are established, create a two-dimensional matrix with work types in each row, classes of service in each column, and a set of fitness criteria in each relevant cell in the table, as in the example in Table 13.1.

---

2. David J Anderson and Alexei Zheglov. *Fit for Purpose: How Modern Businesses Find, Satisfy, & Keep Customers*, 2e. Seattle: Blue Hole Press, 2018.

Table 13.1 Example of Fit-for-Purpose Criteria Matrix

| | Class of Service ||
	Standard	Expedite
Work Item Type A	[Fitness criteria for work items of type A, delivered with Standard class of service]	[Fitness criteria for work items of type A, delivered with Expedite class of service]
Work Item Type B	[Fitness criteria for work items of type B, delivered with Standard class of service]	[Fitness criteria for work items of type B, delivered with Expedite class of service]
Work Item Type C	[Fitness criteria for work items of type C, delivered with Standard class of service]	[Fitness criteria for work items of type C, delivered with Expedite class of service]

Maturity Level 4

At this maturity level, an organization is fit-for-purpose, both inwardly and outwardly. It designs, develops, and delivers products and services that consistently satisfy customers' expectations. In addition, it meets stakeholders' and regulatory authorities' requirements in a sustainable manner. The explicit policies of a Maturity Level 4 organization are focused on managing all aspects of a fit-for-purpose organization.

CONSOLIDATION PRACTICES

XP 4.1 Establish demand-shaping policies.

Description

A demand-shaping policy is a statement restricting the quantity and arrival rate of a given type of work or class of service. It is generally done to facilitate capacity allocation for work of different types or different classes of service where there is contention—or a deliberate design choice—to create a shared resource or labor pool servicing multiple customers with a variety of demand types and classes.

Examples

- Any given customer is limited to three expedite class of service requests per calendar quarter.
- Bug fixes are limited to thirty per month.

Demand shaping policies help create balance. They provide risk management by balancing a portfolio of risk classes in the work-in-progress pool. They focus triage discipline down to a level of individual types of work or specific classes of service. As a consequence, they create stress that drives behavioral change.

For example, a restriction of three expedite requests per quarter may cause an organization to be more proactive and place orders or make requests earlier such that work that historically might have been expedited at the last moment is actually started early and is completed using standard service levels. Such restrictions often result in not just limiting expedite requests to three per quarter; rather, they reduce them to less than three on average. This is explained through deferred commitment. Customers, product managers, service request managers, and product owners, knowing that their allocation of expedite requests is limited, hold on to them until as late as possible. They then try hard to start other work early, knowing that they hold an expedite request up their sleeve for some late-breaking, important, and urgent opportunity that arises toward the end of the quarter. If such opportunities never materialize, the available expedite request goes unused.

XP 4.2 Establish SLA on dependent services.

To maintain stability of flow in a kanban system that creates dependent work to other services, it is necessary to limit the WIP waiting for any given dependent service. As illustrated by Little's Law, in order to set a WIP limit, we need some consistent expectation of lead time from the dependent service.

Implementation Guidelines

- Gather historical data from requests sent to the dependent service.
- Plot a histogram or probability distribution function (PDF) of the lead time data. Lead time should be measured from commitment—usually submission by mutual agreement—until the finished work is delivered back for integration.
- From this data, establish a service level expectation or make a service level agreement by mutual agreement.

14 | Implement Feedback Loops

Kanban adopts a holistic, complexity-science approach to managing processes and evolving organizations. Fundamentally, this means that we can think of an organization as a service-oriented network of interconnected services. The nodes in the network interrelate in different ways to deliver as a whole on a specific common purpose. What is essential is that achieving that purpose depends on multiple successful interactions among the individual services that comprise the network. In other words, the behaviors and outcomes of the organization depend on timely reception of meaningful feedback that ensures that the dependencies among services and the work within each service are managed appropriately.

Goal of the General Practice

The goal of the Implement Feedback Loops general practice is to enable reflection against desired outcomes and enable the opportunity for adjustments, changes, and mutations to policies, processes, workflows, and working practices. Implementing Feedback Loops is a key element enabling evolutionary change (see Chapter 17, Evolutionary Change Model).

Benefits from Applying the General Practice

- Provides empirical observation and adjustment
- Drives evolutionary change
- Enables the achievement of fitness-for-purpose
- Establishes coherent end-to-end process management
- Encourages the use of metrics
- Makes objectives and goals explicit
- Develops unity and alignment

Overview

Kanban defines two sets of feedback loops (illustrated in Figure 14.1) that include the following:

- Feedback loops focused on managing and improving the work process of a single service:
  - Kanban Meeting
  - Replenishment Meeting
  - Delivery Planning Meeting
  - Service Delivery Review
  - Service Request Review
- Feedback loops focused on improving the performance of a network of services through refining the policies for managing the interdependencies among the individual services:
  - Operations Review
  - Risk Review
  - Strategy Review

The feedback loops also strengthen stakeholders' learning capabilities and enable the organization's evolution by means of managed experiments (see Chapter 15, Improve and Evolve).

The periodic meetings and reviews conducted to receive feedback and decide how to act on it are known as Kanban Cadences. The right cadence, or frequency, of each meeting is context dependent and is essential for the organization to function properly and deliver good outcomes. Establishing a fixed cadence for the meetings also reduces the coordination costs for holding them.

Note that three of the cadences are meetings and the other five are reviews. The meetings are focused on managing the work that is conducted—resolving impediments in the process and ensuring that the outcomes meet customer expectations. The reviews are assessments of the performance of the system, or the system of systems, whose objective is to identify opportunities for improvement.

It is important to understand that although Kanban defines eight cadences, this does not mean that eight new meetings have to be added to the already existing ones in an organization. The correct approach is to find out how the topics addressed in the Kanban cadences fit best into an organization's current management meetings.

Figure 14.1 illustrates the principal meetings and reviews. However, as organizational maturity evolves, preliminary forms of these cadences emerge and various meetings are held. The specific practices in this chapter describe all the forms of the Kanban cadences corresponding to their organizational maturity levels.

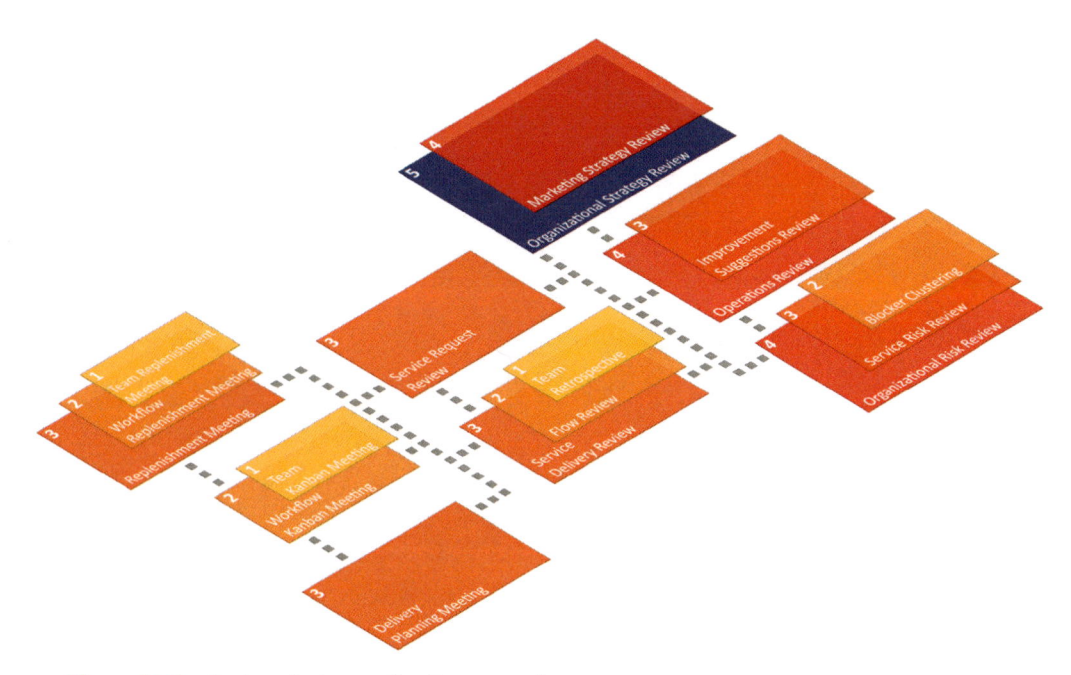

Figure 14.1 Kanban Cadences (feedback loops) showing communication channels among them

Specific Practices Summary

Maturity Level		Implement Feedback Loops (FL) Practice
ML0	Consolidation	**FL 0.1** Engage in personal reflection.
ML1	Transition	**FL 1.1** Conduct Team Kanban Meeting.
	Consolidation	**FL 1.2** Conduct Team Retrospective. **FL 1.3** Conduct Team Replenishment Meeting.
ML2	Transition	**FL 2.1** Conduct Workflow Replenishment Meeting.
	Consolidation	**FL 2.2** Conduct Workflow Kanban Meeting. **FL 2.3** Conduct Blocker Clustering. **FL 2.4** Conduct Flow Review.
ML3	Transition	**FL 3.1** Conduct Improvement Suggestions Review.
	Consolidation	**FL 3.2** Conduct Replenishment Meeting. **FL 3.3** Conduct Delivery Planning Meeting. **FL 3.4** Conduct Service Delivery Review (downstream). **FL 3.5** Conduct Service Request Review (upstream). **FL 3.6** Conduct Service Risk Review.
ML4	Transition	**FL 4.1** Conduct Organizational Risk Review. **FL 4.2** Conduct Operations Review. **FL 4.3** Conduct Marketing Strategy Review.
ML5	Consolidation	**FL 5.1** Conduct Organizational Strategy Review.

Specific Practice Descriptions

Maturity Level 0

The aim of Implement Feedback Loops at Maturity Level 0 is to create the habit of developing an understanding of the actual situation of work before taking actions.

CONSOLIDATION PRACTICES

FL 0.1 Engage in personal reflection.

The intent of personal reflection is to help an individual to learn from their own experience and discover ways to improve.

Implementation Guidelines

- Review the tickets of the finished work items and reflect on what factors influenced completing them.
- Reflect on whether the priorities allow for balance between work needs and emotional well-being.
- If established WIP limits were exceeded, reflect on what caused that and whether it was justified.
- Think about whether the size of the tickets is small enough to allow both seeing progress with the work and identifying potential problems soon enough.
- Check if all work is visualized on the board.
- Reflect on other aspects that influence your work.
- Identify improvements and take appropriate actions. If suitable, update the defined policies.

Maturity Level 1

The aim of Implement Feedback Loops at Maturity Level 1 is twofold: to ensure that all team members have the same understanding of the status of the work and so can make the right decisions about what to do; and to develop a shared understanding of the emergent process and facilitate defining and refining the work practices. The cadences for Maturity Level 1 are shown in Figure 14.2.

TRANSITION PRACTICES

FL 1.1 Conduct Team Kanban Meeting.

The intent of the Kanban Meeting is to create a collaborative conversation about the status of the work, the impediments in the workflow, and problems in the emergent process—such as overloading some individuals—as well as to define appropriate actions for resolving the identified issues.

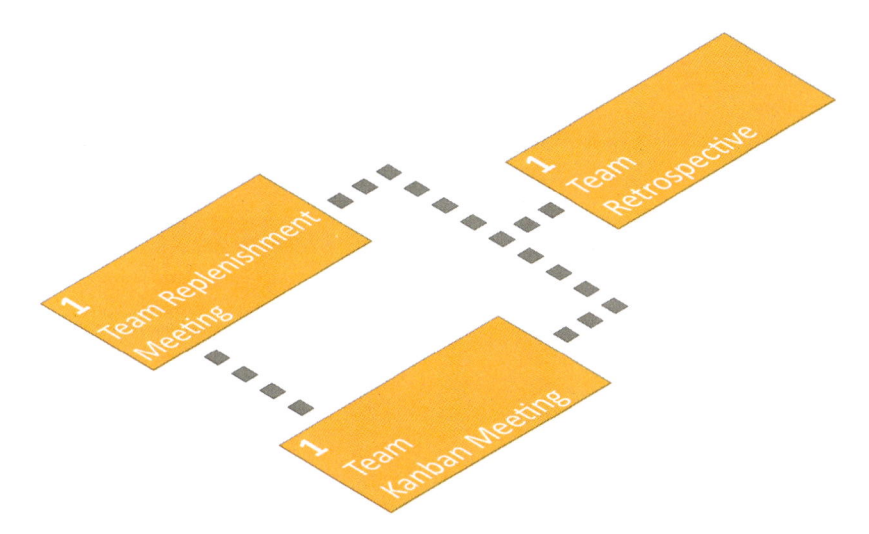

Figure 14.2 Maturity Level 1 cadences

- The Team Lead, Process Owner, or a person with a responsibility and accountability for the delivered work usually facilitates the meeting. However, it is a good practice to rotate the facilitator so that every team member knows how to run a Kanban Meeting.

Implementation Guidelines
- Hold the Kanban Meeting daily, always at the same time, to coordinate the work within the team and to facilitate self-organization.
    - Conduct the meeting in front of the kanban board. Make sure that all team members update the status of their work items and show them on the board before the meeting.
    - Walk the board from right (the part that is closest to completed work) to left (the part with not started work).
    - Report the status of each ticket, each work item on the board. Kanban Meetings always focus on the work, rather than the workload of individual people. Iterate across the tickets on the board, not around the group of people attending the meeting.
    - Keep the Kanban Meeting short by focusing the conversation on completing work items and resolving issues such as possible delays, blockages, technical problems, lack of information, and so on.
- Treat issues that require more time after the meeting, involving only the team members who can contribute to resolving them.

CONSOLIDATION PRACTICES

FL 1.2 Conduct Team Retrospective.

The intent of this specific practice is to have the team reflect on how they work and which aspects of the process could be improved to get better outcomes. To foster learning, it is useful to do the retrospectives with a reasonable frequency (e.g., biweekly or monthly).

Implementation Guidelines

Different forms of a Team Retrospective can be used. However, the key aspects are as follows:

- Identify up to three aspects of the current work practices that need to be improved (e.g., too much time spent on Kanban Meetings, additional work that is not visualized on the kanban board but consumes team's capacity, and so on).
  As an alternative, list the current work management practices and occurrences or facts that fall into some of the following categories:
    - Enjoyable/useful/worth repeating
    - Annoying/not useful/avoid, if possible
    - Missing/consider doing
    - Ideas/worth exploring further
    - Related to current policies
    - Related to sources of dissatisfaction
- Conduct the meeting in front of the kanban board; focusing on the completed work items helps recall what has happened since the last retrospective.
- Categorize the collected feedback and analyze the most important issues.
- Assign actions, defining deadlines and expected outcomes.
- Revise the actual versus expected outcomes once the actions are completed.
- Limit the time for the meeting; one hour might be appropriate.

FL 1.3 Conduct Team Replenishment Meeting.

The intent of the internal Team Replenishment Meeting is to select work items from the backlog to commit next, and to replenish the queue for delivery until the next Replenishment Meeting.

The typical cadence of this meeting is weekly, or as needed, based on the arrival rate of new information. At an internal team level, the meeting is usually facilitated by the team lead or the person who is in contact with the customer.

Implementation Guidelines

- Discuss topics related to the requested work:
    - Information about work items ready to be pulled into the system
    - Dependencies on other work items and technical risks associated with implementing the potentially selected work items

- Information needed to facilitate implementing the potentially selected work items
 - Decisions about the order in which to pull the selected requests
- Select requests and then pull them into the *Next to Start* column of the kanban board (Figure 10.4 on page 124).

Maturity Level 2

The aim of Implement Feedback Loops at Maturity Level 2 is to develop the skills to manage basic feedback information about the delivered services and the workflow—in particular, information visualized on the kanban boards and basic metrics related to fulfilling customer requests. The cadences for Maturity Level 2 are shown in Figure 14.3.

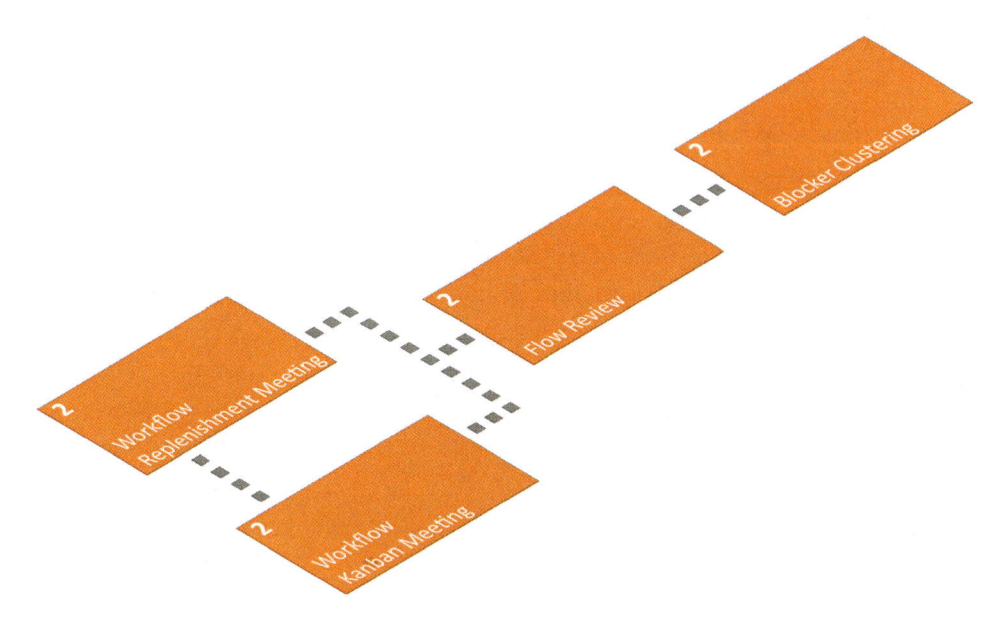

Figure 14.3 Maturity Level 2 cadences

TRANSITION PRACTICES

FL 2.1 Conduct Workflow Replenishment Meeting.

The intent of the internal Workflow Replenishment Meeting is to allow the service team (or the team of teams involved in the end-to-end service workflow) to select work requests and refill the *Next-to-Start* column of their kanban board so that they do not run out of work before the next Replenishment Meeting.

Implementation Guidelines
- Involve leads or representatives of the service teams who take part in the entire workflow. If possible, involve the customer in the Workflow Replenishment Meeting.
- Select requests solicited by the customer and placed in the *Requested Work* column.

- Make sure that the service team understands the requested work.
- Take into account technical aspects and dependencies among service teams when selecting a request to be pulled into the *Next-to-Start* column.

CONSOLIDATION PRACTICES

FL 2.2 Conduct Workflow Kanban Meeting.

The Workflow Kanban Meeting is a higher-maturity version of the Team Kanban Meeting (FL 1.1). Its scope includes the end-to-end workflow of a service or project. The intent of the practice is to involve the respective service teams in a collaborative conversation about the status of the work, queues between stages of the workflow, and problems that affect the flow of work. The identified issues are resolved after the meeting by team members with relevant knowledge and skills.

Implementation Guidelines

- Hold the Workflow Kanban Meeting with regular frequency (e.g., weekly) to reduce coordination effort.
- Conduct the meeting in front of the kanban board that visualizes the complete workflow (VZ 2.12). Make sure that the board is updated and shows the real status of the work.
- Report the status of each ticket, each work item on the board. Kanban Meetings always focus on the work, rather than the workload of individual people. Iterate across the tickets on the board, not around the group of people attending the meeting.
- Walk the board from right (the part that is closest to completed work) to left (the part with not started work).
- Keep the meeting short by focusing the conversation on completing work items and resolving issues such as possible delays, technical problems, lack of information, and so on.
- In some cases, it might be appropriate to combine the internal Workflow Replenishment Meeting and the Kanban Meeting.
- Service team members have access to the end-to-end workflow kanban board at any time. If they find issues in the workflow for which discussion cannot wait until the next Workflow Kanban Meeting, they take initiative to signal and resolve them at once.

FL 2.3 Conduct Blocker Clustering.

Blockages affect flow, delivery time, and predictability. Therefore, the intent of this practice is to study the main reasons for the blockers and their impact in terms of lead time. This practice is the basis for understanding and mitigating risks.

Implementation Guidelines

- Collect and categorize the blocker tickets by blockage reason (e.g., missing information from the customer, waiting on another team, lack of access to a system, etc.). See Figure 14.4 for an example.
- For each category of blockers, analyze the range of time it takes to resolve the issues.
- Reflect on the outcome of this analysis. Refer to IE 2.4 for how to define actions to improve flow.

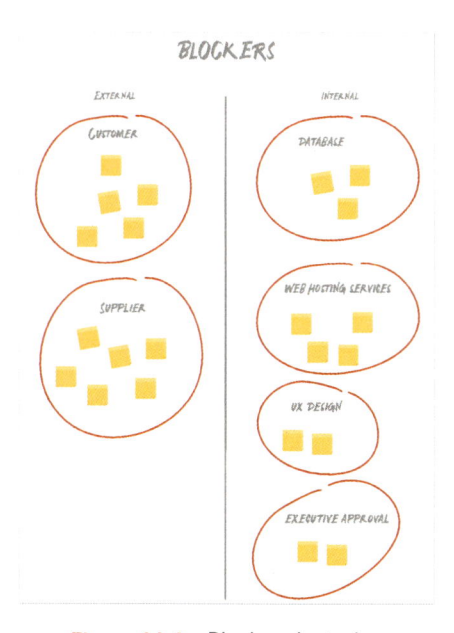

Figure 14.4 Blocker clustering

FL 2.4 Conduct Flow Review.

The intent of the Flow Review (FR) is to develop an initial understanding of the delivered service and use it to facilitate work planning and thereby improve predictability.

Flow Review is a degenerate form of Service Delivery Review (FL 3.4). The difference is that an FR is inward facing; it looks at capability without considering customer needs or expectations. With an FR, more is usually better, and the intent is to become as effective as possible.

Flow Reviews develop the quantitative understanding of the current capability of the service team. If a target is defined and known, it might be compared to the system capability to trigger improvement actions. At this level of organizational maturity, the service team is not so concerned with where the target came from—it may simply be a goal set by a manager to encourage improvement. Tying objectives to real customer expectations and business risks emerges at Maturity Level 3 and is reviewed in the Service Delivery Review, described in FL 3.4.

A Flow Review is typically held twice a month, facilitated by the Flow Manager or their immediate superior. Other participants are typically the workers from the service delivery workflow who can contribute to analyzing and understanding certain events in the workflow, such as long-time blockages or work items spending a long time in progress. There is little or no external representation at this meeting.

Implementation Guidelines

- Prior to the meeting, review progress and system capability data derived from the kanban board or tracking system, such as the following:
  - Distribution of demand per work type
  - Average arrival rate of the demand: the average number of requests for a period of time per work type
  - Average delivery rate (throughput): the average number of completed work items for a period of time per type of work, using the same unit of time for both the arrival and delivery rates
  - Average lead time per type of work: the amount of time between selecting an item to work on and delivering it to the customer
  - Average customer lead time per type of work: the time measured from the moment the customer placed the request to the moment it was delivered
  - Range of blocker time per blocker cause (see MF 2.4 for more details)
  - Range of defect and rework time per cause
  - Highly aged work items
- During the meeting, reflect on the collected data and analyze the cases for which there was a perception of poor service, or a failure to meet customer expectations, if known.
- Define actions to improve the flow. Start with defining actions for reducing blocker time, rework, or WIP aging, as described in MF 2.4.
- Provide feedback and communicate decisions to the service team and their immediate manager.

Maturity Level 3

The focus of Implement Feedback Loops at Maturity Level 3 is on how to facilitate a flow of information that ensures fitness-for-purpose from a customer perspective, that is, continual delivery on customer expectations in a sustainable manner. Maturity Level 3 cadences are shown in Figure 14.5.

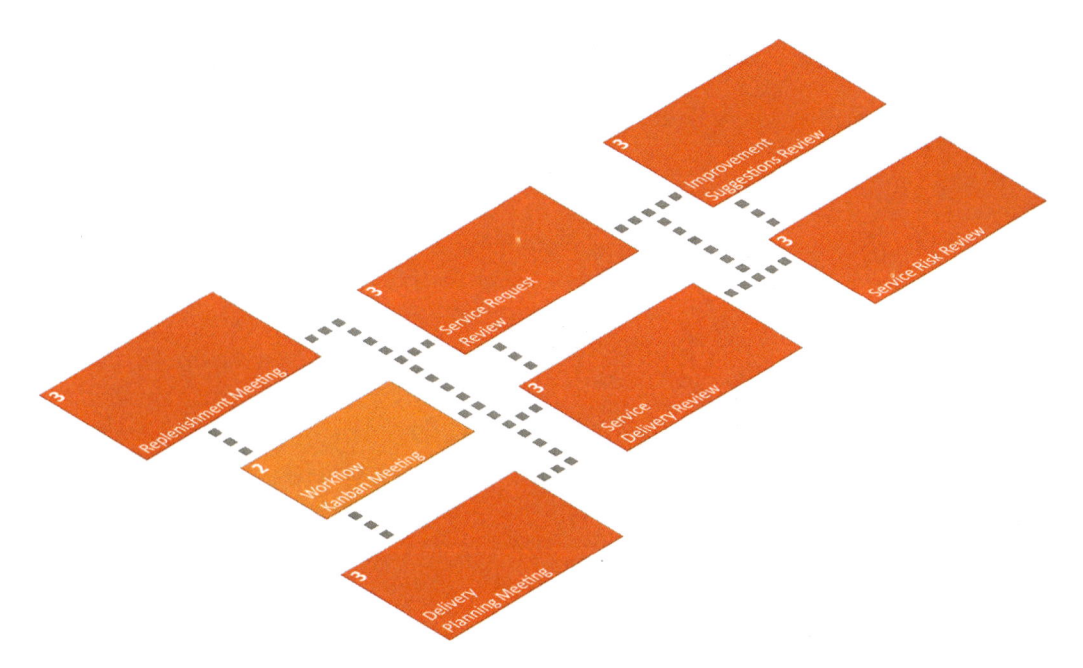

Figure 14.5 Maturity Level 3 cadences

TRANSITION PRACTICES

FL 3.1 Conduct Improvement Suggestions Review.

The concept of an employee suggestion box is an old idea. In a Kanban implementation, it tends to take a more visual form. There might be a lane on a kanban board for process improvement–related work, or perhaps just as a visual bin for collecting the suggestions. There might be a WIP limit or capacity allocation for process improvements in progress.

An Improvement Suggestion Review is effectively a triage meeting for selecting which improvements should be implemented now versus later or not at all. Hence, it is a special version of a Replenishment Meeting. Attendees tend to be internal to the workflow or service delivery, although some organizations involve the entire service team.

Implementation Guidelines

- Examine new suggestion tickets one by one.
- If there is available capacity (free kanban), some of the suggestions can be selected to be implemented now, while others are triaged for later or discarded.
- Evaluate each suggestion for its impact on the overall performance of the system and the nature of the cost of delay.

CONSOLIDATION PRACTICES

> **FL 3.2** Conduct Replenishment Meeting.

The purpose of the Replenishment Meeting is to decide, together with the customer and business stakeholders, which work requests to select for the next period, until the next Replenishment Meeting. The selection of work items takes into account the information about the service capability and the available capacity; this is brought to the meeting by representatives of the service team.

The typical participants in a Replenishment Meeting are the customer, decision makers, and other relevant stakeholders.

The Replenishment Meeting should have an established cadence. Two factors must be taken into account when determining the frequency of the meeting: the arrival rate of new requests and the cost of holding the meeting. More frequent meetings with customers and business stakeholders enable making appropriate decisions based on the current business situation. Therefore, more frequent replenishment is more Agile. On-demand replenishment is most Agile.

Implementation Guidelines

- Prepare the Replenishment Meeting:
    - Identify what requests are available and need to be discussed at the meeting. Collect and visualize these requests in a queue to be reviewed during the meeting.
    - Prepare data and information needed for the meeting, such as service-related data.
- Conduct the Replenishment Meeting:
    - Discuss what requests and combination of requests can be selected for delivery before the next Replenishment Meeting.
    - Select requests and pull them into the *Selected for Delivery* column of the kanban system. Make sure that the selected items meet the acceptance criteria. Document what criteria or additional considerations for selecting requests are being used if these differ from the established policies.
- Bring Replenishment Meeting–related observations to the Service Delivery Review for further analysis of the system.
- The essential aspect of the Replenishment Meeting is that this is the point at which the customer commits that they want the outcome of the requested work, and the service team commits to deliver it within the customer's expectations. Before this point, the customer's requests are considered options that can still be discarded. Refer to XP 3.5 for more details about establishing the commitment point.

FL 3.3 Conduct Delivery Planning Meeting.

The intent of the Delivery Planning Meeting is to plan and commit both outcomes and delivery date to the customer. Typically, Delivery Planning Meetings have a cadence and are held at regular intervals, for example, every two weeks. In more mature implementations, or cases with either sporadic deliveries or very high transaction costs of delivery, the meeting may be triggered by a kanban (i.e., a ready-for-delivery buffer that fills up and, once full, it triggers the meeting.

At a Delivery Planning Meeting, the delivery organization commits to releasing finished work for acceptance and delivery on a specific delivery date. Typically, a Service Delivery Manager (SDM) facilitates the meeting. Any other interested parties should be invited, including those who receive and accept the delivery, and anyone involved in the logistics of making the delivery. Specialists are present for their technical knowledge and risk-assessment capabilities. Managers are present so that decisions can be made as soon as possible.

The participants in the Replenishment and Delivery Planning Meetings, as well as the transaction and coordination costs for them, are likely to be different. Therefore, decoupling Replenishment from Delivery Planning makes sense and improves agility.

Implementation Guidelines

- Prepare the meeting:
  - Determine the invitee list—people who can provide information, make decisions, or take actions related to delivery.
  - Review the state of the work items that are potentially available to deliver. Information about this comes from the daily Kanban Meeting.
  - Review feedback from Service Risk Reviews to assess how it might affect delivery.
- Define the frequency of the meeting. The transaction and coordination costs of delivery constrain and define the delivery planning cadence.
- Conduct the meeting:
  - For the current state of the work items on the board, forecast which of them will be ready for delivery before the release date. Do the forecast based on the established forecasting method, such as trends or moving averages of collected service-related data. More mature organizations can use a simulation to project the probability that a ticket will arrive in the ready-for-delivery buffer on or before the scheduled delivery date.
  - For tickets near the margin of confident delivery, re-evaluate the probability of finishing them by the release date and consider changing their class of service to Fixed Date, with the scheduled delivery date as the fixed date for the ticket.

- Taking into account the above-mentioned considerations, make the final decision about which work items to commit for delivery. Prepare the feedback for the next Service Risk Management Meeting.
- Bring Delivery Planning Meeting–related issues to the Service Delivery Review and Risk Review.

FL 3.4 Conduct Service Delivery Review (downstream).

The intent of the Service Delivery Review (SDR) is to examine and improve the effectiveness of a selected service. It is typically held twice a month, facilitated by the Service Delivery Manager. Other participants include the corresponding Service Request Manager, representatives of delivery teams, customers, and other external stakeholders, if necessary.

Implementation Guidelines

- Prepare the review:
    - Review progress and service performance data.
    - Review feedback from daily Kanban Meetings that might need to be discussed at the SDR.
    - Review decisions made at Operations and Risk Reviews (or similar meetings).
- Conduct the review:
    - Compare current service delivery capability to customer expectations and other fitness criteria metrics.
    - Analyze shortfalls and causes for not meeting service level expectations.
    - Discuss possible actions that enable balancing demand and capability, as well as hedging risks appropriately.
    - Identify opportunities to improve the delivered service.
    - Define actions.
    - Prepare feedback for the Operations Review.
- After the review:
    - Communicate decisions.
    - Schedule and execute defined actions.

FL 3.5 Conduct Service Request Review (upstream).

The intent of the Service Request Review is to understand the status of the requests on the upstream kanban board and select those that need to be moved across the commitment point and those to be elaborated (analyzed or synthesized) further.

Typically, participants in the Service Request Review are the customers or their representatives. The frequency of the review can be biweekly or monthly and must be established based on the transaction and coordination costs associated with conducting the review (IE 3.2).

Implementation Guidelines
- Prepare the review:
  - Review the status of the work requests that have been elaborated.
- Conduct the meeting:
  - Walk the discovery board from right to left.
  - Items to the right may be ready to commit. Items further to the left may be ready to promote to the next level.
  - Identify the requests that are ready to commit. Take into account the following aspects when making the selections:
    - Request acceptance criteria (XP 3.2)
    - Proper diversity of options for each work type or customer
    - Dependencies among the requests
    - Important dates and delivery times
    - Available capacity of the delivery kanban system as reported by the Service Delivery Manager
    - Cost of delay and required class of service of the item, and how this affects dependencies
  - Identify items that may be ready to promote to the next stage, should be shelved until circumstances change or new information arrives, or should be discarded.
  - Make sure that enough work requests are selected to guarantee that the delivery kanban system does not starve. Likewise, each upstream stage needs enough options to ensure choice downstream. There should always be a certain discard rate.
  - Review the discard rate. Is it in line with expectations? High uncertainty should mean a higher discard rate, perhaps as high as 90 percent, while low uncertainty should mean a low discard rate, perhaps as low as 1 percent. If the discard rate is out of line with expectations, there are two possible problems: insufficiently good ideas or ineffective means to evaluate good versus bad options to be promoted to the next stage. Refer the results to a Risk Review.

FL 3.6 Conduct Service Risk Review.

The intent of the Service Risk Review is to understand and respond to risks to effective delivery of products and services.

This review is typically held monthly and is facilitated by a Service Delivery Manager, Service Request Manager, director, or alternatively, by a Kanban coach. Other participants include anyone with information or experience of recent blockers, project and program managers, customer-facing managers, and managers from dependent services.

The scope of the review is one or more kanban systems being used for the service delivery.

Implementation Guidelines
- Prepare the review:
    - Review the status of the issues and risks from previous Service Delivery Review, Service Request Review, and Delivery Planning Meetings.
    - Prepare the list of potential problems to be discussed at the review.
    - Risk review can consider both downstream delivery and upstream discovery workflows.
- Conduct the review:
    - Categorize the identified risks.
    - Analyze the likelihood and impact of the risks for meeting customer expectations identified in the Delivery Planning Meetings, Service Delivery Review, and Service Request Review.
    - Analyze other relevant aspects of the identified risks, for example, those that address non-functional or safety expectations of the customers.
    - Define appropriate actions to mitigate the identified risks based on the outcome of analyzing them.
- After the review, communicate decisions as appropriate and make sure that affected artifacts (kanban system designs, policies, etc.) are properly updated.

Maturity Level 4

Maturity Level 4 organizations focus their attention on managing effectively the dependencies among the services, as well as the anticipated risks, to achieve robustness at the enterprise level. Maturity Level 4 cadences are shown in Figure 14.6.

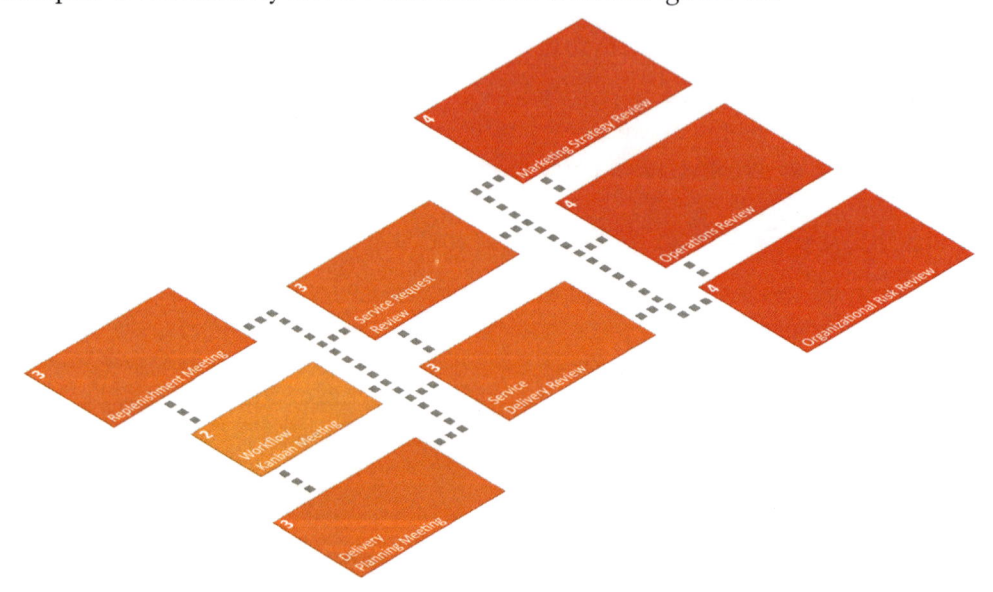

Figure 14.6 Maturity Level 4 cadences

TRANSITION PRACTICES

FL 4.1 Conduct Organizational Risk Review.

The intent of the Organizational Risk Review is to understand and hedge risks related to product lines and service portfolios, meeting stakeholders' expectations as well as those of the entire business.

This review is typically held monthly and is facilitated by a Service Delivery Manager, Service Request Manager, or director. Other participants include anyone with information or experience of recent blockers, business unit managers, customer-facing managers, and product and service line managers.

The scope of the review is one or more product or service lines, similar to the Operations Review.

Implementation Guidelines

- Prepare the review:
  - Review the status of the issues and risks from previous Operations Review, Service Delivery Review, Service Request Review, and Delivery Planning Meetings.
  - Prepare the list of potential problems to be discussed at the review.
- Conduct the review:
  - Define the parameters and the corresponding scales for analyzing the risks; for example, technical, market, delay impact, urgency, and so on. Figure 14.7 illustrates a sample risk framework with five dimensions: market role, lifecycle, urgency, delay impact, and technical risk.

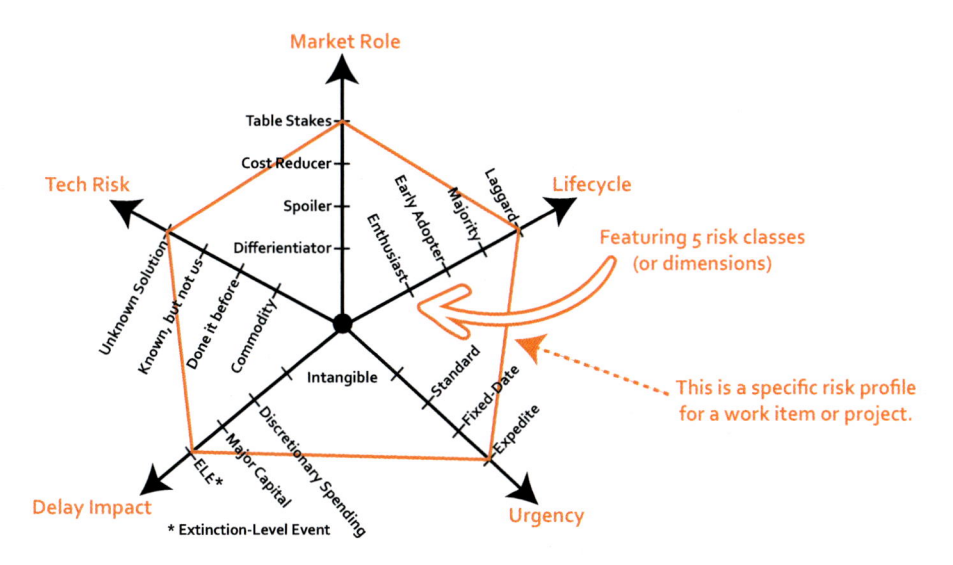

Figure 14.7 Example of a Risk Assessment Framework and a risk profile for a work item

- Analyze each risk using the dimensions of your organization's risk framework.
- Visualize the risk profiles (e.g., as shown in Figure 14.7).
- Cluster the risks according to the required mitigation actions.
- Define relevant risk-hedging or risk-reduction actions, or contingency plans. These might affect the established policies and classes of service.
- For upstream workflows, consider the options' pricing strategies: high uncertainty, pay more for options—more time, more staff, more resources; low uncertainty, pay less for options—less time, less staff, less resources. Typically, cycle time in an upstream state (or column of a board) should be time-bound by risk-management option pricing strategy.
- For upstream, consider the option triage policies and thresholds to: invest—promote the option to the next stage; shelve—leave an option pending more time, changes in circumstances, or new information arriving; or discard—the option is poor and not worthy of further investment.
- After the Review, communicate decisions as appropriate and make sure that affected artifacts (kanban system designs, policies, etc.) are properly updated.

FL 4.2 Conduct Operations Review.

The intent of an Operations Review is to do the following:
- Look at performance, capability, and dependencies among multiple kanban systems.
- Understand dependencies; expose interdependent effects.
- Hold *kaizen* (continuous improvement) events suggested by attendees.
- Assign improvement opportunities.

Typically, the scope of an Operations Review covers the work of a product unit, a business unit, or a large department or function within an enterprise.

Operations Reviews are a level up from Service Delivery Reviews. The primary focus should be on the interactions between services rather than the independent service nodes within the network. Operations Reviews should be outward looking and business focused. The intent is to ask, Who are our customers? What do they ask of us? What are their expectations and why? as well as, How well do we serve them? Do we meet their expectations?

Operations Review is, like Service Delivery Review, a disciplined review of demand and capability. At this level, demand and capability are examined for each kanban system within a dependent network of services. Particular focus should be on dependencies and dependent effects. Operations Review is relevant only when the scope is large enough and at least more than one kanban system exists.

We recommend that Operations Reviews happen monthly. A balance must be struck to establish the right cadence. Too often carries too much overhead, and there is little learning from one meeting to the next, while insufficiently often is also problematic. When meetings aren't held often enough, there is too much to discuss and the meeting goes on too long, while attendees struggle to have strong memories of events several months earlier. The frequency also affects the effectiveness of the feedback loop. Waiting too long between Operations Reviews means it is longer before action can be taken to correct an undesirable effect. Empirically, one month has emerged as the best default cadence.

Operations Review should be hosted and facilitated by a Service Delivery Director or a vice president responsible for the product or business unit being reviewed. Participants should include Service Delivery Managers and Service Request Managers for each kanban system; senior management with responsibilities beyond the product or business unit being reviewed; head of PMO; senior business owners or customer representatives; downstream mid-level managers—those accountable for receiving completed work; functional managers responsible for activities within the network of services; senior individual contributors representing each kanban system; and product, portfolio, and project managers.

Establishing policy around who should be invited and attend an Operations Review is an important step in producing an effective review.

Implementation Guidelines

- Prepare the following inputs for the review:
    - Summary findings from Service Delivery Reviews and Service Request Reviews for all kanban systems in the network
    - Business performance information from Strategy Review, such as financial reports and customer satisfaction surveys
    - Status of ongoing improvement initiatives from Risk Review about system-wide changes
- Develop the following outputs during the review:
    - A list of improvement suggestions, actions, decisions, or required changes to strategy, with designated owners sent to Service Delivery Review, Service Request Review, and Strategy Review
    - Dependent impact on tail risk for a lead time distribution, sent to Risk Review to inform prioritizing risks for reduction, mitigation, or contingency planning
- Record the meeting by a scribe. It is common for the scribe to be a process coach, but any specifically designated person who is not the facilitator and host is acceptable.

An Operations Review is expensive, and it is important that the best use is made of the time and that the meeting runs on schedule. It should be an orchestrated production with a strictly scheduled and timed agenda.

FL 4.3 Conduct Marketing Strategy Review.

A Marketing Strategy Review is a regular meeting of leaders in the marketing function of the business to review and assess the following:
- Current markets
- Go-to-market strategies
- KPIs

It should be driven by product management or service design executives and attended by senior marketing executives plus representatives from strategic planning, sales, marketing, portfolio management, risk management, service delivery, and customer care.

We recommend that Marketing Strategy Reviews happen quarterly, as many business, political, and economic environments change quickly. The cadence of the meeting should be a matter for its attendees to decide and should be tuned to specific circumstances. If quarterly isn't the right cadence, the organization must pick a frequency that is appropriate.

The Marketing Strategy Review aligns closely with the use of the Fit-for-Purpose Framework. The purpose is to review market segmentation and go-to-market strategy while ensuring that the right metrics are being used to focus the organization and drive improvements in design, implementation, and service delivery.

How does an organization choose an appropriate frequency for a Marketing Strategy Review? New information should have arrived since the last meeting. No new information implies there is nothing new to discuss. So how fast is new information relating to strategy, markets, marketing, and capabilities available to the people who attend the review? How often do you receive feedback from Fit-for-Purpose surveys, or from narrative clustering exercises from frontline staff? Equally, the period between meetings shouldn't be so long that the quantity of material to discuss, review, analyze, and act upon is so great that the meeting takes too long—days rather than hours. So, a balance must be struck—often enough that the meeting doesn't carry too much overhead and place a burden on the attendees, but sufficiently spaced such that new and valuable information is available to discuss. Quarterly is a good default frequency in the absence of analysis of information arrival rate or experiencing the meeting as burdensome. The cadence of a Marketing Strategy Review can be adjusted dynamically based on experience and tuned to the business, market, political, and economic conditions within which an organization is operating.

A Marketing Strategy Review agenda should include the following:
- Market segmentation analysis:
  - Which markets are we in?
  - Which segments do we serve, and with which products or services?
  - In each segment, are we a leader/innovator or a follower?
  - What is our strategic position in each segment? Are we differentiated? A cost leader? A niche player protected by a high barrier to entry? Or are we "stuck in the middle" with a clear position?

- Fit-for-Purpose assessment (see below)

A Marketing Strategy Review may include a Fit-for-Purpose review. If the Fit-for-Purpose Framework is in use within the organization, it provides information regarding customer purpose, market segmentation, fitness criteria for customer selection, and thresholds for customer satisfaction. Based on customer surveys or frontline reporting via customer narrative clustering, each market segment can be analyzed to see which are well-served, over-served, or under-served. Equally, determine whether target segments are well-, over-, or under-served, and whether non-targets—customers that we were not expecting—are well-, over-, or under-served.

The Fit-for-Purpose Review enables strategic decisions about market segmentation, targeting, and market actions to encourage or discourage specific segments, such as adjusting pricing or where to target advertising spending.

FL 5.1 Conduct Organizational Strategy Review.

A Organizational Strategy Review contains all the elements of a Marketing Strategy Review (see FL 4.3) and extends its scope to review and assess the following:
- Current markets
- Strategic position
- Go-to-market strategies
- KPIs
- Capabilities
- Alignment of strategy and capability

It should be attended by senior executives and representatives from strategic planning, sales, marketing, portfolio management, risk management, service delivery, and customer care.

We recommend that Organizational Strategy Reviews happen quarterly, as many business, political, and economic environments change quickly. The cadence of the meeting should be a matter for its attendees to decide and should be tuned to specific circumstances. If quarterly isn't the right cadence, the organization must pick a frequency that is appropriate.

How does an organization choose an appropriate frequency for an Organizational Strategy Review? New information should have arrived since the last meeting. No new information implies there is nothing new to discuss. So how fast is new information relating to strategy, markets, marketing, and capabilities available to the people who attend the review? Equally, the period between meetings shouldn't be so long that the quantity of material to discuss, review, analyze, and act upon is so great that the meeting takes too long—days rather than hours. So, a balance must be struck—often enough that the meeting doesn't carry too much overhead and place a burden on the attendees, but sufficiently spaced such that new and valuable information is available to discuss. Quarterly is a good default frequency in the absence of analysis of information arrival rate or experiencing the meeting as burdensome. The cadence of an Organizational Strategy Review can be adjusted dynamically based on experience and tuned to the business, market, political, and economic conditions within which an organization is operating.

An Organizational Strategy Review agenda should include all the elements of a Marketing Strategy Review plus the following:

- Analysis of corporate identity (Who are we?)
- Analysis of risk exposure by service, product, or business unit (How resilient is each part of our business?):
  - Fragile
  - Resilient
  - Robust
  - Antifragile
- Survivability assessment:
  - Is our identity still relevant and will it continue to be so?
  - If our identity needs to change, what is the time frame, and how might we go about it?
  - If we are in the midst of a strategic shift in corporate identity, how is it progressing, and is the intended result still relevant?
- Capability assessment (from the Operations Review):
  - Current markets
  - Strategic position
  - Go-to-market strategies
  - KPIs
  - Capabilities
  - Alignment of strategy and capability
- Strategy versus capability review:
  - How well aligned is our strategy to our capability?
  - Are our people set up for success?
  - Is our strategy within our capability, or are we overreaching?

At Maturity Levels 5 and 6, the fidelity of the Strategy Review and the quality of the leadership are higher. At Maturity Level 5, the organization focuses on how business is done, seeking congruence, equality of opportunities, perfectionism, and market leadership. Therefore, developing the market-segmentation and go-to-market strategies becomes central for the Strategy Review. Maturity Level 6 is about long-term survival—questioning the how, what, why, and who—and reinvention. At this level, we expect to see profound survivability assessment and consistent alignment around the strategic decisions.

15 | Improve Collaboratively, Evolve Experimentally

Kanban is a method that continually improves both the process and the organization that uses it. In contrast with other methods, it starts from the process and organizational situation as it is now and pursues continual and incremental improvement using an evolutionary approach. The evolutionary approach means taking advantage of the organization's current strengths, avoiding resistance, and making decisions and actions that increase fitness-for-purpose while dampening ineffective activities and waste.

Improve collaboratively stands on the premise that developing a complete and correct understanding of the actual situation requires a collaborative collection of observations and insights from people at different positions in the process and the organization. This profound comprehension is fundamental for defining the right steps for improvement.

Evolve experimentally conveys the idea that chosen changes are guided by models and have a hypothesis, even if purely qualitative in nature, about the anticipated outcome. The scientific method is used to identify ideas, validate them in a controlled manner, and draw conclusions based on data and solid arguments.

Goal of the General Practice

The goal of Improve Collaboratively, Evolve Experimentally is to build a shared comprehension of the purpose, process, and associated problems; suggest improvement actions based on scientific models and methods; and reach agreement by consensus in order to evolve continually.

Benefits from Applying the General Practice

- Promotes learning via the process of defining an improvement experiment—foreseeing the outcome—and comparing actual and expected results
- Helps people understand the impact of decisions made
- Improves risk management at all organizational levels
- Continually develops fit-for-purpose capabilities

Specific Practices Summary

Maturity Level		Improve Collaboratively, Evolve Experimentally (IE) Practice	
ML2	Transition	IE 2.1	Identify sources of dissatisfaction.
	Consolidation	IE 2.2	Identify sources of delay.
		IE 2.3	Revise problematic policies.
		IE 2.4	Define actions to develop basic understanding of the process and improve flow.
ML3	Transition	IE 3.1	Solicit change and improvement suggestions.
		IE 3.2	Identify transaction and coordination costs.
	Consolidation	IE 3.3	Analyze blocker likelihood and impact.
		IE 3.4	Analyze lead time tail risk.
		IE 3.5	After meetings: Discuss a problem spontaneously; then bring it to the Service Delivery Review.
ML4	Transition	IE 4.1	Develop qualitative understanding of chance versus assignable cause for process performance variation.
	Consolidation		
ML5	Transition	IE 5.1	Identify bottlenecks.
		IE 5.2	Identify impact of shared resources.
		IE 5.3	Develop quantitative understanding of chance versus assignable cause for process performance variation.
	Consolidation	IE 5.4	Exploit, subordinate to, and elevate bottlenecks.
		IE 5.5	Exploit, subordinate to, and elevate shared resources.
		IE 5.6	After meetings: Discuss – Suggest – Take actions – Seek forgiveness.
ML6	Transition		
	Consolidation	IE 6.1	After meetings: Take congruent actions with confidence.

Specific Practice Descriptions

Maturity Level 2

The intent of the practices at ML2 is to establish the foundation for continual improvement, namely, developing an understanding of the sources of internal and external dissatisfaction and defining initial actions to address them.

TRANSITION PRACTICES

IE 2.1 Identify sources of dissatisfaction.

Understanding sources of dissatisfaction is fundamental for service design, kanban system design, policy definition, and offered classes of service. If the identified sources of dissatisfaction are addressed properly, the outcome should be services that are fit-for-purpose.

Implementation Guidelines

Identifying sources of dissatisfaction is done in two steps:

1. Identify reasons for customer dissatisfaction: Why customers are unhappy? What do they complain about? Consider as a customer the recipient of the outcome of the service, independent of whether they are internal or external to the organization.
2. Identify internal sources of dissatisfaction: What prevents teams and individuals from delivering professional results and meeting customer expectations? What affects their personal job satisfaction?

Once the sources of dissatisfaction have been identified, define appropriate actions for addressing them. These actions might include changes to service interfaces such as the Replenishment Meeting, or changes to the kanban system design or its corresponding policies (e.g., information necessary for initiating a service, the definitions of "done," etc.). On occasion, dissatisfaction may come from poor quality workmanship, which may indicate a need for training, learning new skills, or a change in personnel.

CONSOLIDATION PRACTICES

IE 2.2 Identify sources of delay.

There might be a variety of causes for delays of work items, services, or projects, such as dependency on another service or external vendor, unexpected rework, lengthy approval of a deliverable, and so on. Organizations that develop service orientation and customer focus pay special attention to their response or delivery time to customer requests. Therefore, identifying the sources of delay becomes fundamental for understanding delays, learning, and defining appropriate actions.

Implementation Guidelines

- List all work items, services, or projects that were delayed for a meaningful period of time.
- List the causes for blockages, rework, waiting in queues at handoffs (dependencies on other teams or individuals), and waiting on clients or vendors.
- Cluster the identified causes.
- Identify the range of impacts of the identified sources on the service or project's delivery time.
- Decide which causes to address first and how.

    You might decide to address first the causes with high impact on delivery time, even though they might not occur very often. Alternatively, you could decide to resolve first the causes that happen more frequently, and therefore, their total impact is high even though their individual contribution to the delay is not that large. A third approach could be addressing the causes by type, for example, defining actions to reduce waiting time on another service team.

Visualizing causes such as blockages, waiting on another service or team, work item age, defects, and rework are all means for fast identification and resolution of the causes for delay, thereby reducing delivery time.

IE 2.3 Revise problematic policies.

It is common for a service to be governed by a set of policies that evolve over time. As circumstances change, the appropriateness of some of these policies might have to be revised. The intent of this practice is to facilitate the definition of policies that lead to improving the performance of the entire system rather than addressing only a local part of it without observing overall effect.

Implementation Guidelines

- Collect observations of how an outcome is produced and how policies affect decision making and the delivery process. For this, pay attention to what your board reveals (visualizes) and what outcomes result from your current ways of managing work.
- Study the outcomes of Team Retrospectives (FL 1.2), the identified sources of dissatisfaction (IE 2.1), as well as the analysis of the causes for delay (IE 2.2). From those, identify policies that need to be modified or added.
- Seek both internal and external improvements:
  - Internal: Reduce individual and team's overloading as well as imbalances among other teams' workloads.
  - External: Reduce rework, resolve blocking issues faster, and speed up delivery.
- Draw conclusions about how to update the selected problematic policies.

IE 2.4 Define actions to develop basic understanding of the process and improve flow.

An essential component of the Kanban Method and KMM is understanding the system and the environment in which it works. Adopting the collaborative and experimental approach to understanding and improving the process and the flow speeds up learning and enables teams to develop adaptability to changes in their context.

The intent of this practice is to develop a basic comprehension of the what, why, who, and how of the process so that everyone involved in it understands the reasons for the defined improvement actions.

Implementation Guidelines

- Based on the results of the Flow Review (FL 2.3), the understanding of the sources of delay (IE 2.2), and the problematic policies (IE 2.3), decide what changes to policies to introduce and what results you expect to observe as effects of introducing the modifications.
- Listen to people's narrations that complement the collected data and observations to develop a better understanding of the context and the individuals who take part in the process. Use this understanding to fine-tune your approach for suggesting and implementing improvements.
- Make only a few changes at a time to facilitate studying their effects.
- Allow a reasonable time, not too long, for the actions to produce results that can be analyzed.
- Provide the necessary support for the adoption of the modified policies.
- Compare expected and obtained results and reflect on what hindered or enabled achieving the desired outcome—improving the flow and the capability of the kanban system.
- Decide which policies to keep and which you still need to adjust to reach deeper understanding and improvement of process and flow.

Maturity Level 3

At Maturity Level 3, the Improve and Evolve activities are focused on involving anyone who works in a service delivery workflow in submitting improvement ideas. Improvement actions are defined based on a deep understanding of the process as well as the transaction and coordination costs associated with it.

TRANSITION PRACTICES

IE 3.1 Solicit change and improvement suggestions.

The intent of this practice is to collect insights and feedback about the process and service delivery from different perspectives in order to focus the improvement actions on the right issues. This action democratizes the overall evolution of the organization, as anyone working in a service delivery workflow or a kanban system is invited to submit improvement ideas and proposals.

Implementation Guidelines

There are different forms of soliciting and collecting change and improvement suggestions:

- Individuals involved in service delivery have a good understanding of the process and can identify what slows down or hinders its execution and what affects the fulfillment of a customer's expectations. Ask them to reflect on this, for example, in their Team Retrospective, and provide feedback.
- Collect improvement ideas from external sources, such as a coach's advice, trusted literature references, and working groups or communities of the practice.
- Designate an *Improvements* lane on the kanban board or add a *Suggestion Box* area or bin. Invite everyone to post suggestions on it.
- Bring the collected ideas to the Improvement Suggestions Review (FL 3.1).

> **IE 3.2** Identify transaction and coordination costs.

Managing knowledge work involves coordination tasks in addition to purely executing management activities. Coordination costs are costs associated with facilitating a decision already made. For example, once a work item is selected and committed to the kanban system, any actions taken to coordinate workers, required resources and equipment, and external dependencies such as vendors are all coordination costs. The cost should be measured as the time spent, and any out-of-pocket discretionary spending, on facilitation: include the time of the person who organizes a meeting, which includes finding a time slot that fits the schedules of all participants, arranging a room, catering, if necessary, coordinating the agenda, making the corresponding travel arrangements, and so on.

Transaction costs are costs associated with making a decision or taking an action. Replenishment is a transaction cost for a kanban system. Making or taking delivery of finished work is a transaction cost of committing to undertake and complete the work. The transaction cost of replenishment, for example, can be measured as the total cost of holding a meeting, incurred by all participants. This includes the time that each participant dedicates to preparing their part of the meeting (reports, data, presentations, and so on) as well as concluding it (saving the information obtained in the meeting in the right place and defining, communicating, and launching relevant actions). The costs of making a batch transfer of work, or of a handoff down the workflow from commitment to final delivery, are also transaction costs.

High coordination and transaction costs raise the unit cost of completing a work item. They are overheads. The higher the coordination and transaction costs, the lower the economic efficiency of the service. Therefore, organizations are interested in minimizing these costs. Defining a fixed cadence for the meetings is a straightforward approach to reducing coordination costs. If effectiveness of a meeting can be maintained but its length can be shorter, this reduces transaction costs. Using visual and collaborative workspaces enables having the right conversation with the right data at the right moment (i.e., it also reduces transaction costs).

The intent of this practice is to instill the understanding of transaction and coordination costs as a first step to reducing them.

Implementation Guidelines
- Some organizations have detailed time records of how employees spend their working hours. Use this information to obtain an idea of the volume of transaction and coordination costs.
- Alternatively, register the data during some short period of time (e.g., two weeks), and extrapolate an estimate for a longer period (e.g., a month or a year) per project or service.
- Identify and make an explicit list of coordination costs associated with meetings, feedback mechanisms, batch transfers, deliveries, and handoffs.
- Identify and make an explicit list of transaction costs associated with meetings, feedback mechanisms, batch transfers, deliveries, and handoffs.
- An effective way to identify how to reduce transaction and coordination costs is to ask, if an activity is truly value-adding, would they do more of it? If the answer is no, then consider what actions would contribute to reducing setup, cleanup, facilitation effort, and meeting time.
- Consider elements that contribute to costs such as scheduling or setting an agenda (coordination costs). Can these be reduced or eliminated by having a regularly scheduled meeting with a set cadence and a fixed agenda?

To develop a sense of the amount of transaction and coordination costs, images like those in Figure 15.1 can be elaborated in collaboration with the people who need to be involved in optimizing them.
- Monitor the actual incurred costs and actively seek to reduce costs through suitable policy changes, system design changes, and risk management decisions.
- These costs should be monitored as a health indicator metric, and action should be taken if they exceed a defined limit.

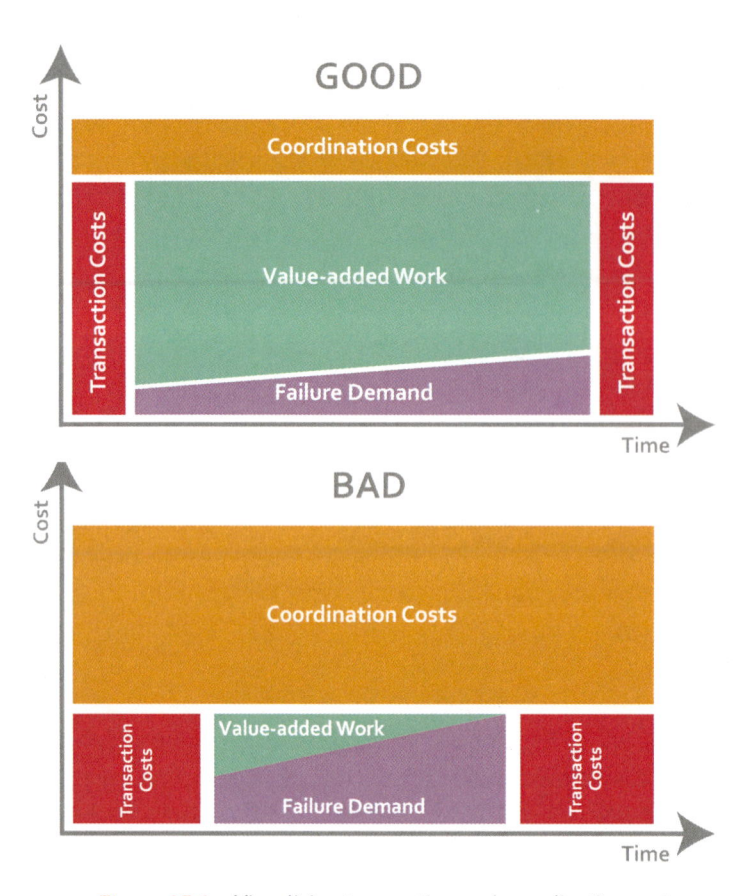

Figure 15.1 Visualizing transaction and coordination costs

CONSOLIDATION PRACTICES

IE 3.3 Analyze blocker likelihood and impact.

The blocker tickets possess valuable information for reducing delays and improving dependencies management. They can be harvested from a kanban board once per month and analyzed. The process of analyzing them is called blocker clustering.

The intent of this practice is to get a deeper understanding of the causes of blockages in the workflow, their likelihood, and their impact, and to define appropriate improvement actions.

Implementation Guidelines
- Collect blocker tickets during a specified period (e.g., a month). Make sure that each ticket records the reason for the blockage and the number of days blocked.
- Cluster the tickets by causes, as described in IE 2.2. Add complementary information such as class of service of the work items.

- Calculate the average impact of a blocker by cause.

$$\overline{Impact} = \frac{\sum_{\kappa=1}^{n\,(cause)} days\ blocked(\kappa)}{Total\ number\ of\ tickets\ per\ cause\ for\ the\ period}$$

- Calculate the average likelihood.

$$\overline{Likelihood} = \frac{Number\ of\ blocker\ tickets\ per\ cause}{Total\ number\ of\ tickets\ processed\ for\ the\ period}$$

- Use the insights from blocker analysis and the values for $\overline{Impact}$ and $\overline{Likelihood}$ to calculate the magnitude of the risk for a certain event to occur.

$$Risk = \overline{Likelihood} \cdot \overline{Impact}$$

IE 3.4 Analyze lead time tail risk.

The lead time metric indicates how predictably an organization delivers against expectations. Understanding the distribution of the lead time for class of service enables evaluating the risk of late delivery.

Implementation Guidelines

- Plot the lead time for a work item type or a class of service on a histogram (Figure 15.2).
- Using a histogram for analyzing lead time is more useful than using its mean because it provides more complete information about the time it took to deliver work items, including outliers.

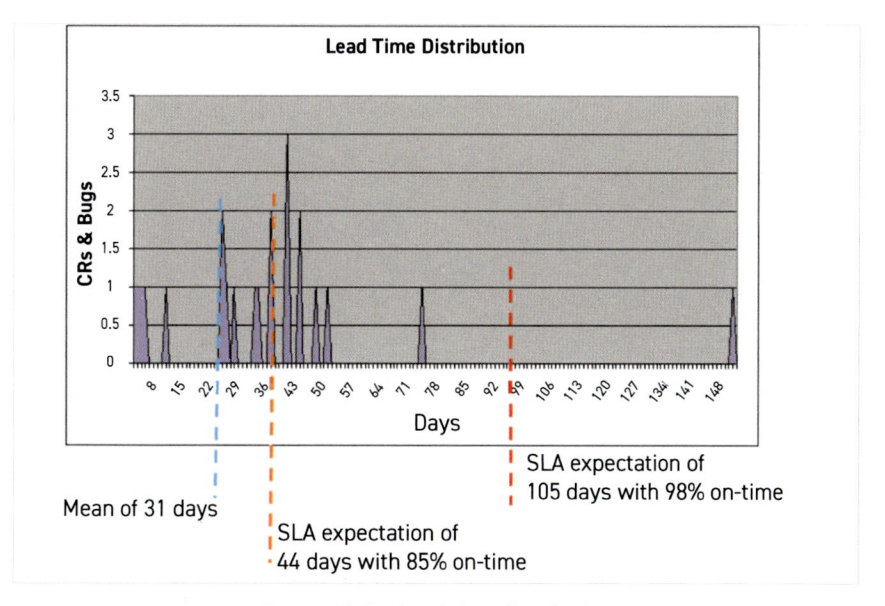

Figure 15.2 Lead time distribution

- To evaluate the risk of delay, identify what percentage of work items can be delivered within customer expectations. For example, based on the data in Figure 15.2, 85 percent of the work items could be delivered in forty-four days. If this were the customer expectation, evaluate what the risk of delivering 15 percent of the work behind deadline means to the organization.

> **IE 3.5** After-meetings: Discuss a problem spontaneously; then bring it to the Service Delivery Review.

After meetings refer to the spontaneous assembly of a small group of individuals involved in the resolution of an issue or an identified weakness in the process or in the kanban system design. Specifically, the spontaneous assembly is after the Kanban Meeting. In industrial engineering literature, after meetings are often referred to as spontaneous quality circles and are seen as self-organizing and self-initiating—there is no specific managerial or leadership role in convening an after meeting. After meetings are not scheduled, nor is there an agenda or invitee list. After meetings could occur periodically until a solution or an improvement idea is developed. However, they are not to be confused with formal approaches to collaborative improvement, such as A3 Thinking.

Implementation Guidelines

- Identify the issue to resolve.
- Discuss possible solutions.
- Decide which solution to implement.
- If the solution affects the design of the kanban system or changes to the policies, present the idea at the Service Delivery Review for further approval and implementation.

Maturity Level 4

The intent of Improve Collaboratively, Evolve Experimentally at Maturity Level 4 is to start developing profound knowledge of the causes of process variation so as to achieve balanced economic outcomes and be able to perform appropriate risk hedging.

TRANSITION PRACTICES

> **IE 4.1** Develop qualitative understanding of chance versus assignable cause for process performance variation.

Understanding workflow variation and the causes of it is central to improving the performance of the process and the system.

This is best illustrated by an example . . .

A golf tournament takes place on a course by the ocean on the west coast of Ireland. The course has a par of 72 strokes. This means that on a typical day, a good golfer should complete the eighteen holes using only 72 strokes—72 swings of a club, regardless of the club's design—wood, iron, putter, and so forth. The course designer was most likely a fairly good golfer and familiar with the weather conditions on the west coast of Ireland. The course design is such that, on average, a good golfer should score 72, perhaps over ten to twenty iterations of playing the course.

If we hold a tournament with, say, a hundred competitors, and some, but not all of them, are good golfers, we might expect a range of scores—perhaps from a low of 67 (5 under the par of 72) to a high of 85 (13 over par). The average is probably a couple of shots over par, around 74. This indicates that the course is well designed to offer a suitable challenge to a range of experienced golfers. This spread from 67 to 85 with an average of 74 is said to be the common cause variation of the course, played by golfers of sufficient standard to hold a handicap ranking and qualify to enter the tournament.

Now, imagine that the tournament is held on a glorious summer day, with hardly a breath of wind, and that this weather was unexpected, following some days of wind and rain. The underfoot conditions are dry, but soft, so the golf balls do not run far after impact. In glorious weather, with no wind, and ground conditions that hold the ball reliably, the players can attack the course. Consequently, the best score is a 61 (11 under par, and a new course record), while the average score is 70 (2 under par), and the worst score of the day is 80 (just 8 over par). The skewed results are quite obviously a consequence of the beautiful weather conditions, and these conditions can be characterized as special, or assignable, in terms of how they influenced the results.

Equally, on a bad weather day, with howling wind and heavy rain, the scores might be affected in the opposite direction. The best score of the day is 74, the average is 77, and the highest recorded scorecard shows a 95, while some competitors simply failed to return a scorecard at all. Once again, the weather has affected the scores—the range of scores and the average—and once again the weather can be characterized as the special, or assignable, cause or reason for the change in observed behavior.

Developing a skill at qualitative assessment of common versus special cause variation is important. In the example of the golf tournament on the west coast of Ireland, after the new course record is set on a glorious summer day, should the club pay to have the course redesigned to increase its level of difficultly (usually achieved by making the holes longer and increasing the overall distance for the full course)? The answer, of course, is no. This is intuitive. We understand that the course played easy on an unusually fine day in summer, and it was merely coincidence that the tournament was played on the same day.

We intuitively take the correct action. We do not redesign the system in response to special cause variation.

The causes for process variation that are produced by natural interactions among the components of the process or the system are called common, or chance, cause for process variation. Examples of such causes are policies, individuals, skills, tools, management decisions, and so on. Common cause sources of process performance variation can be identified by analyzing the design or implementation of a workflow. For instance, the delay or wait states (e.g., *Ready for Design*) in the workflow can be identified and potentially flagged or visualized as such. This is a core enabler for gathering flow efficiency data and using them to improve the flow and the system.

A cause of process variation that is associated with some transient circumstances, usually external ones, and is not an inherent part of a process is known as special, or assignable, cause of process variation. Examples of such causes are events that are beyond the control of the system, like having the operations system down due to exceptionally bad weather conditions, delay of delivery due to a general strike, and so on.

Implementation Guidelines

- Identify whether a source of variation is special/assignable (e.g., weather, power outage, general strike, vendor outage, transportation-related, and so forth) or whether it is common/chance cause variation as a result of the "rules of the game"—the design and policies of the system (e.g., careful placement of the holes on the greens of a golf course can make the course easier or harder, or narrowing the fairways by not cutting the grass also makes the course harder by requiring much more accurate tee shots).
- Special/assignable cause variation can be controlled by means of risk-management and issue-management strategy and policies. For each special/assignable-cause issue, it should be possible to make a probability and impact assessment and devise risk reduction or risk mitigation to reduce the likelihood, or the impact, or to make contingency plans to undertake in the event of an occurrence. Contingency plans can include temporary fixes, workarounds, or recovery actions.
- When the common cause variation is beyond acceptable bounds, then we should redesign the system that produced the observed data. In Kanban, this means redesigning the kanban system, changing explicit policies, or changing classes of service, WIP limits, work item type definitions, capacity allocations, and so forth. This should happen only in response to obviously common/chance cause variation. When there is a special, or assignable, cause variation, we need to take alternative action. We need to use risk assessment and management techniques to determine the likelihood and the impact of an occurrence and then assess whether we wish to reduce the likelihood, mitigate the impact, or make contingency plans in the event of such an occurrence.
- All improvement actions, policy changes, and modifications to the design of a kanban system, or a network of kanban systems, including such things as the cadence of a feedback mechanism such as Operations Review, should be cataloged, and the motivation behind the change documented.

- Risk management actions such as risk reduction, mitigation, or contingency should be recorded against the anticipated event, its likelihood, and its impact.

There should be clear alignment between risk management interventions to address special cause variation and system design changes (policy changes) made to address common cause variation.

Where there has been inappropriate action taken, that is, a system redesign resulted from a special cause variation (W. Edwards Deming classified this as management mistake number two), then a learning opportunity has occurred. Operations Review is a good forum to discuss inappropriate action due to wrongly identifying common versus special cause variation.

When the opposite is true, that there were no changes in the system design and its explicit policies when undesirable behavior was clearly a common failing rather than a specific, special, external event out of the control of management (W. Edwards Deming classified this as management mistake number one), then another learning opportunity has occurred.

An organization should strive to eliminate instances of Deming's mistake numbers one and two and show that action and intervention are congruent with the nature of the problem, even when that nature was qualitatively assessed, such as the weather in the anecdotal golf example.

Maturity Level 5

TRANSITION PRACTICES

IE 5.1 Identify bottlenecks.

Bottlenecks constrain and limit the flow of value. In general, a bottleneck is a point in a process flow where work items accumulate while waiting to be processed. Identifying the bottleneck and its type is essential for improving the flow and efficiently delivering more value to the customer. In order to properly identify bottlenecks, we need stability in the system; we need to see stable volatility in the internal function of the system, such as local cycle times, system throughput, and the volume of pull transactions in the system (see Implementation Guidelines in IE 5.3).

Implementation Guidelines

- Identify the bottleneck in the process. There are two ways to identify a bottleneck:
    - In an unconstrained system with no WIP limits, a pile of work should accumulate in front on the bottleneck. Meanwhile, process steps downstream of the bottleneck should regularly be idle, or starved of work. This is readily observed in a cumulative flow diagram by a divergent, expanding band of color—a growing queue of work (see Figure 15.3).

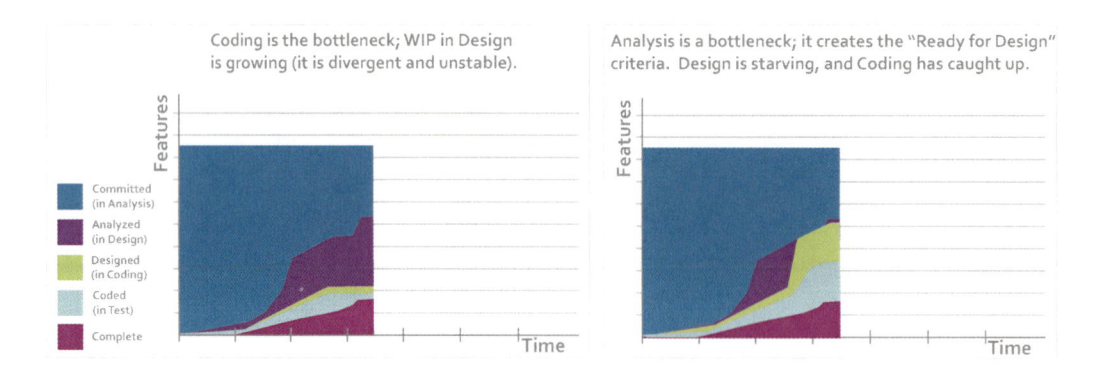

Figure 15.3 Cumulative flow diagrams showing bottlenecks

- In a constrained system with WIP limits (a Kanban system), bottlenecks are harder to spot. The bottleneck will typically be the process step immediately upstream of the first observed starvation point in the workflow. This is more easily observed in a cumulative flow diagram where as band of color disappears due to zero work in that stage of the workflow.
- A bottleneck can also be defined as the step in the workflow that has the longest average local cycle time.

- Validate that the bottleneck is correctly diagnosed and isn't in fact a non-instantly available shared resource (see IE 5.2):
  - Bottlenecks are always capacity constrained. For example, in a twenty-four-hour period, a function has capacity to process twenty items. If thirty items are arriving in the same period, then demand exceeds capability to supply, and the function is definitively a bottleneck.
  - It is possible for a non-instant availability shared resource to also be a bottleneck and vice versa; they are not mutually exclusive.
- Bottlenecks should always be downstream from the commitment point. The reason for this is that we never want to waste precious bottleneck resources on work that will be discarded or aborted later. This concept is known as exploiting the bottleneck. If your bottleneck is upstream of your commitment point, then, by definition, your downstream delivery organization has slack capacity. This is costly and wasteful. However, often this slack capacity is invisible because the downstream workers are asked to assist the upstream workers with analysis, estimation, planning, prototyping, and so forth. This tends to make the downstream service delivery unpredictable and unfit-for-purpose because the downstream workers are being pre-empted to do upstream work. As a general rule, if it is possible, or even desirable, to discard or abort work in your bottleneck, then your commitment point is in the wrong place.
- Bottlenecks should always be buffered to ensure exploitation. The buffer should be immediately upstream of the bottleneck and should be sized to adequately

buffer variation in arrival rate. The goal of a bottleneck buffer is to ensure that the bottleneck is fully exploited and never suffers idle time.

See IE 5.5 for information about resolving bottlenecks.

IE 5.2 Identify the impact of shared resources.

Shared resources (and shared services) are also known as non-instant availability resources. They might not be instantly available because they are also utilized by another service.

Shared resources are often available on a regular cadence. In this case, their availability is subject to time-slicing, with each "owner" receiving a slice of time in a given period, for example, one day per week or two hours per day.

The impact of shared resources, or shared services, is primarily delay. The impact can be measured as the period of availability and the frequency of availability versus no availability. So, for example, availability of two hours per day in an eight-hour workday is 25 percent availability.

Implementation Guidelines

Calculate the arrival rate of work and determine its nature.

For example, if the arrival rate is two items per hour and its nature is both Gaussian and stochastic, we can infer that, on average, sixteen items arrive during an eight-hour workday. If the shared resource is available only two hours per day, then, on average, that resource must be capable of processing all sixteen within a two-hour period, or the function is a bottleneck. Items arriving while the shared resource is available are processed within two hours, and those arriving at another time wait, on average, three hours (half of six hours) until the resource is available again.

Shared resources cause some delay, introducing variability into lead time distributions, and their delays must be buffered immediately upstream. This buffer looks similar to a buffer for a bottleneck, but it serves a different purpose: a bottleneck buffer buffers variability in arrival rate with the goal of maximizing the exploitation of the bottleneck by always keeping it busy; while a buffer for a non-instant availability resource buffers the variation introduced by the non-instant availability.

See IE 5.5 regarding resolving shared resources–related problems.

IE 5.3 Develop quantitative understanding of chance versus assignable cause for process performance variation.

The intent of this practice is to establish the quantitative understanding of process performance in support of achieving the expectations of customers and stakeholders as well as the strategic business objectives. In order to properly identify special/assignable cause variation in a statistical manner, we need stability in the system. We need to see stable volatility in the internal function of the system, such as local cycle times, system throughput, and the volume of pull transactions in the system (see Implementation Guidelines).

Implementation Guidelines

- Use time or run series data showing a rate (or first derivative of an absolute count) for general health indicators (e.g., heart rate or pulse), improvement drivers, and fitness criteria metrics.
- Identify common and special causes for process variation.
- Examine the data for stability using its volatility (the second derivative of the time or run series) and its turbulence (the volatility of the volatility, or the fourth derivative of the time or run series). See Figure 15.4 for an example.

    Stable systems should be devoid of turbulence. Periods of time between spikes of turbulence are known as volatility regimes. It may be possible to determine the bounds of variation within a given volatility regime where all the data points are generated by common or chance cause variation in the system performing under normal circumstances. Data points outlying these bounds should be characterized by annotations indicating special or assignable cause events.

    Pay attention to the nature of the recorded data set. There should be a clear understanding of leading versus lagging indicators (e.g., WIP is a leading indicator, while lead time is a lagging indicator). With lagging indicators, attention must be paid to the period of the lag and whether an assignable, special cause event happened within that period and had an impact on the value of one or more data points.

- Seek to define bounds of variation that indicate normal (chance, or common cause) variation for the current volatility regime. The result should provide automatic mathematical triggers to indicate out-of-bounds behavior, special cause problems, and/or changes in the volatility regime pre-empted by turbulent data.[1]

    Typically, special cause events outside of the system's design or control, or changes to system design, result in turbulence followed by resumption of a new volatility regime. Once changes settle in, the system performs within new limits.

---

1. At the time of writing (2020), David has been examining the applicability of statistical process control (SPC), taken from manufacturing industry, since the publication of his first book in 2003. After seventeen years, it is still unclear how applicable SPC methods are to intangible goods, knowledge-worker industries. The essence of the problem is whether the method produces too many false positives and false negatives. Given that there are very few Maturity Level 4 or 5 organizations, and very little reliable data has been reported, it is still impossible at this time to make a definitive statement on whether the technique is valid or not. For the method to work properly, the implication is that any outage—any special/assignable cause variation—will push the result into the statistical margins. With manufacturing, where a simple process might take thirty seconds and is Gaussian distributed with a narrow alpha, an outage might easily be two minutes. In that scenario, it is easy to see that a special cause variation pushes the cycle time well into the tail of the Gaussian distribution. With knowledge work, we don't yet have this confidence of understanding. If you reach Maturity Level 5 with your organization, we invite you to help us pioneer the thorough understanding of the methods of Shewhart, Deming, Chambers, and Wheeler for the field of intangible goods, professional services, and knowledge-worker industries.

A quantitative analysis may reveal the impact of changes that were not recognized or understood. For example, a change of a department manager, without any explicit changes to strategy, values, or policies, may result in turbulence and changes in system performance. When this happens, it is an indication that intangibles are present. For example, the new manager may be seen as soft on discipline, and consequently some workers cease to follow policy and operating parameters. Without a quantitative analysis, the very subtle impacts of this loss of discipline may be undetectable.

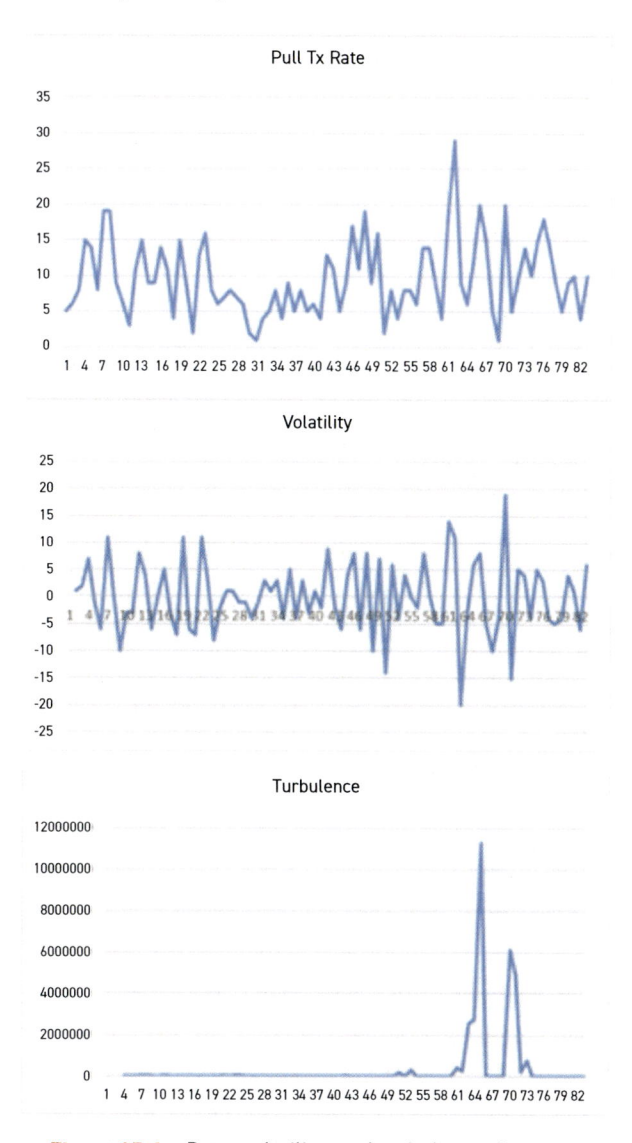

Figure 15.4   Rate, volatility, and turbulence diagrams

CONSOLIDATION PRACTICES

IE 5.4 Exploit, subordinate to, and elevate bottlenecks.

The intent of this practice is to correctly manage capacity-constrained resources, often referred to in plain language as bottlenecks.

See IE 5.1 regarding identifying bottlenecks and non-instant availability shared resources.

Implementation Guidelines

The following steps help in resolving the identified bottlenecks:

1. Decide how to exploit the bottleneck:
   - Exploit capacity-constrained resources by means of actions such as these:
     - Buffer work so that the bottleneck is never starved of work to do.
     - Ensure that a bottleneck never works on something twice. There is no slack for rework.
     - Ensure high quality in the bottleneck, such that the same work will never be reworked by the bottleneck.
     - Ensure that a bottleneck never works on something that will be discarded or aborted later. Ensure the bottleneck is downstream from the commitment point.
     - Change the policies to control better the work performed by the bottleneck resource. Classes of service can be used for this purpose.
     - Use bifurcation: this is a special case of class of service in which the lower-risk work is routed around the bottleneck. The idea is that other workers with slack capacity perform the work, perhaps at a lower fidelity or level of quality. Make sure, however, that the risks are adequately managed.
     - Limit the interruptions on the bottleneck. Ideally, a bottleneck should never be interrupted, pre-empted, or delayed. This may require providing redundancy to insure 100 percent availability.
     - Swarm on resolving problems in the bottleneck. If there is an outage in the bottleneck, then it is all-hands-on-deck to resolve it.
2. Subordinate any other actions in the value stream to enable exploiting and protecting the bottleneck or the non-instant availability resource.
   - Ensure high quality upstream of the bottleneck, such that the same work will never be reworked by the bottleneck.
   - Accept slack capacity downstream of the bottleneck.
   - Do not optimize for resource efficiency; optimize for flow efficiency.
   - Use slack capacity to perform low-risk work that has been rerouted to avoid the bottleneck.

- Allow new work to enter the system only at the rate the bottleneck completes new work. Implement a pull system known as Drum-Buffer-Rope.
3. Elevate the bottleneck—this should always be the last option because it requires investment and time to implement:
    - Adding more people and tools/machines to increase capacity
    - Partial or total automation of the bottleneck activity to increase its capacity and/or eliminate non-instant availability
    - Training (especially on new methods, techniques, tools, or machinery) to improve quality, reduce cycle times, and increase throughput

IE 5.5 Exploit, subordinate to, and elevate shared resources.

The correct management of shared resources makes flow smoother and increases throughput. Shared resources are generally not instantly available, and the effect of waiting for availability makes them resemble bottlenecks. How they are managed is similar though subtly different, as they are not, at least initially, capacity constrained.

See IE 5.1 regarding identifying bottlenecks and non-instant availability shared resources.

Implementation Guidelines

1. Exploit the shared resource:
    - Make sure that the resource does only the designated work.
    - Buffer work so that work queues for the availability and the upstream function aren't stalled because of non-instant availability.
    - Change the policies to control better the work performed by the shared resource. Classes of service can be used for this purpose.
    - Use bifurcation: this is a special case of class of service in which lower-risk work is routed around the bottleneck. The idea is that non-specialist workers with slack capacity perform the work, perhaps at a lower fidelity or level of quality. Make sure, however, that the risks are adequately managed.
    - Limit the interruptions of the resource. Do not allow multitasking or pre-emption while the resource is available.
2. Elevate the shared resource:
    Buffering non-instant availability of shared resources can be viewed as a symptomatic fix—addressing the observed symptoms without attempting to address the root cause. The root cause of non-instant availability is lack of instant availability. Its fix is instant availability, and it can be achieved by different means:
    - Replace the shared resource with (instantly available) automation.
    - Provide contingent, slack resources that are instantly available on demand.
    - Seek greater or more frequent availability. For example, one hour per day could be changed to two half-hours per day. This halves the delay impact and

halves the buffer sizing requirements. Three periods of twenty minutes per day is even better. Often, the frequency is determined by the transaction costs of switching, and this ultimately limits the possible frequency. By separately addressing the transaction costs of switching (see IE 3.2), greater frequency may be enabled without providing automation or contingent staffing or additional resources.
- Add more people and/or tools or machines, and assign them to the workflow as non-shared, dedicated resources. This trades delay for cost.

IE 5.6 After-meetings: Discuss – Suggest – Take actions – Seek forgiveness.

At ML5, after meetings are focused on improving the performance of the organization. Spontaneous action is taken and later reported to more senior managers. Those taking action seek validation that their action was acceptable, while also reporting that the action has taken place, so that more senior leaders know about it and avoid wasting further time, energy, or resources on the topic.

Implementation Guidelines

- Typically, following a Kanban Meeting, form a group with a shared affinity for a recognized problem or process performance issue.
- Discuss the matter based on collected evidence, both qualitative and anecdotal as well as quantitative.
- Evaluate possible options.
- Make a decision.
- Take action and experiment with whatever change was made, taking responsibility for it.
- Once the action is completed, report to more senior managers the fact that it has happened, why, and its likely impact.
- Seek forgiveness if the expected improvement does not occur.

Maturity Level 6

CONSOLIDATION PRACTICES

IE 6.1 After meetings: Take congruent actions with confidence.

Spontaneous action can be taken with confidence when strategy, values, and objectives are explicit, institutionalized, and universally understood and supported.

Implementation Guidelines

Confident, congruent action can occur when a spontaneously formed group pursues an improvement action in full knowledge that it aligns with strategy, organizational values, and current operating parameters expressed as a set of metrics defining fitness criteria, improvement targets, and health indicators with bounded ranges.

There is no need to seek forgiveness, as it is self-evident that actions are bounded by strategy, values, and current operating parameters. There is overt trust that those empowered to take action do so within understood constraints, while those taking the action understand that they are empowered to do so within known and understood constraints.

Individual actions or decisions are never questioned in isolation. When, retrospectively, a failure or poor decision appears to have occurred, the focus is always on redefining strategy, values, or operating parameters, or in better communicating existing strategy, values, and operating parameters.

At Maturity Level 6, spontaneous congruent action is not validated post hoc by seeking forgiveness, nor is it delayed and validated prior to action by seeking permission. At Maturity Level 6, action simply happens. If the action taken produces an unsatisfactory outcome, it is succeeded by further action and double-loop learning to examine whether strategy, values, or operating parameters need to change.

In some ways, deep maturity behavior, on the surface, resembles low, shallow maturity behavior—it appears unconstrained. The difference lies in the ability to reflect on effectiveness of action, compare it to expectations, and modify the models, frameworks, rules, policies, and parameters being used. A Level 6 organization has the ability to redefine its understanding of the world and modify its behavior accordingly. Deep Maturity Level 6 behavior is characterized by double-loop learning and is always reflecting on outcomes against the framework of strategy, values, and operating procedures and parameters, explicitly defined and broadly communicated.

Part IV: Managed Evolution & the Pursuit of Organizational Agility

16 | Why Pursue Evolutionary Change?

Social psychologists divide the types of changes we experience as individuals into two categories—normative and structural.

A normative change is a change to the way we do something, or to a tool we use, or perhaps to a scaling challenge. If we like running, and we often run five kilometers, then choosing to run a marathon represents a normative change—it is still running, but just farther. While attributes of pace, strength, endurance, and fitness may need to be different for five kilometers versus a marathon, we're still runners, and most likely how others relate to us will be unchanged.

A structural change is one in which our relationships to others are altered: we get a promotion at work or a reward that changes our status, level of respect, or recognition. When you change jobs, move to a new neighborhood, get married, when you experience the birth of your first child, get divorced, experience the death of a family member or beloved pet, all of these things represent structural changes. To a greater or lesser extent, humans experience structural change as a form of crisis. Psychologists use the word "crisis" in a very specific manner. It means that as a consequence of structural changes, we suffer role anxiety or financial uncertainty, which causes status-, respect-, recognition-, or dignity-related anxiety, and so forth.

Whenever we experience uncertainty in relation to other people, we suffer stress and anxiety—a psychological crisis. In times of crisis, people often turn to others for support. Sometimes these people are family members, or friends, or trusted colleagues; at other times they may be trained professionals, such as members of the clergy, life coaches, therapists, or clinical psychologists. In neuropsychological terms, when we are in crisis, our brains are being rewired: synapses are being weakened or strengthened; neural pathways are being modified. We experience this as pain. There are common language terms for this pain we experience when we encounter common forms of structural change: grief, for example, is the pain we feel due to the loss of a family member, friend, or colleague; denial, the pain we feel when we realize that what we believe to be true is being challenged by experience, data, science, or other evidence.

Structural	Normative
• Changes to the social structure • Changes in relationships • Changes in status • Changes in identity • Changes in group structures • Changes in organizations • Traumatic and painful • Always causes some level of psychological crisis	• Changes in methods, tools, and practices that do not affect social relationships, status, identity, respect, or dignity • Might lead to emergent structural change (small changes)

Social psychologists divide forms of social change into four basic categories: stability, inertia, incremental, and dramatic. Structural change is always dramatic; the only question is the degree of the drama (see Table 16.1). For example, the birth of a first child is a structural change for a couple, and possibly also for their parents, who just became grandparents for the first time, and so forth. However, that isn't of the same order of magnitude as the structural changes that come from war, ethnic cleansing, mass migration of refugees, or from the homelessness and perhaps unemployment that follow from natural disasters such as earthquakes, floods, volcanic explosions, and storms such as hurricanes or tornados, and, of course, as we've been writing this manuscript, from a pandemic. Structural change is always dramatic, but the degree of drama varies.

"Stability," as the name implies, suggests that people are happy and that there is no pressure for any changes. It tends to coincide with what is known in evolutionary biology as a period of equilibrium. While (environmental) conditions may exhibit some volatility, some variation, the swings are within known and understood upper and lower bounds—there is a concept of average, and with that average the range of variability above and below it is stable. People, their social groups, such as in business and their families, and the activities performed in day-to-day life are adapted to these stable conditions, and the volatility is anticipated and understood. People living in places such as Kansas City, Missouri; Winnipeg, in the Canadian province of Manitoba; or Novosibirsk, in the Russian province of Siberia, are adapted to temperature swings that vary from approximately −36°C to 36°C (−32.8°F to 96.8°F) during the course of a year. Despite these huge temperature swings, this extreme volatility to environmental conditions, life goes on—the people and their lifestyles have evolved and adapted to it.

Table 16.1 Effects of Structural Change[1]

Stability	Inertia	Incremental	Dramatic
Happy people	Frustrated people	Dissatisfied people	Disrupted people
No Pressure	Distraction, sympathy, (group) therapy; limit impact to prevent dissatisfaction.	Seeking slow incremental change; consequently little resistance and little anxiety	Anxiety, fear, stress, crisis
No Change	No Change	Change	Change
		Initially, normative, and not threatening to status, respect, recognition, or dignity; structural changes may emerge.	Normative change with implications for social status, respect, recognition, or dignity; or structural change to the social order or hierarchy
		Kanban	Agile
		Changes to "how" and "what"; emergent structural change is voluntary and is "pulled."	Changes to "who" and "why"

Periods of equilibrium can apply to environments and ecosystems, to economies, to governments and systems of governance, to social structures, to cultures, and to ways of life. When there is a schism in the equilibrium, known as a punctuation point, which may be preceded by a period of turbulence—volatile volatility—it is usually followed by a short period of chaos and a continued period of turbulence until a new normal—a new equilibrium, a new period of stable volatility—is achieved.

Periods of equilibrium, or stability, may not rule out the metaphorical equivalent of a global warming problem. That is when, although there appears to be stability, there are underlying problems which, if left unchecked, will eventually lead to turbulence and a dramatic event—a punctuation point—and the emergence of a new regime following a stabilizing period of chaos and further turbulence. In social terms, these periods of global warming with the current equilibrium, are known as inertia. Socially, it represents frustration, leading to dissatisfaction, often driven out of a lack of respect, status, or recognition, resulting in undignified living. In a larger, political sense, such inertia eventually leads to revolutions, military coups, civil wars, or, in a more democratic world, referenda for independence or secession. In a commercial, corporate world, inertia tends to lead to dramatic changes, such as changes in leadership, reorganization, divestiture, splits, mergers, or economic crises resulting in bankruptcy protection filings, refinancing, or changes in ownership or, in worst cases, bankruptcy,

---

1. This material was adapted and simplified from Roxane de la Sablonnière, "Toward a Psychology of Social Change: A Typology of Social Change," *Frontiers in Social Psychology* (March 2, 2017), https://doi.org/10.3389/fpsyg.2017.00397.

closure, or a switch to public ownership. The 2008 financial crisis, brought on by years of fiscal imprudence and the financial bubble fueled by a mortgage-backed securities derivatives market based on fixed-income products such as home loans, is an archetypal example of a global warming problem during a long period of financial and economic equilibrium, which eventually popped, causing a significant crisis.

"Incremental" change is the term social psychologists use for small changes that are normative in nature. The change is motivated out of dissatisfaction and is either growth or improvement related, or recessive in nature. Positive, growth and improvement related changes could be societal in nature, such as pursuit of a fairer and more just society, or economic, such as seeking a better quality of life, better healthcare, child care, school system, or pensions and provisions for the elderly, or it might be personal or related to a social group such as family, church, professional society, or employer. Recessive motivations seek to reduce an undesirable effect in society, such as racial or gender discrimination.

Changes that are initially normative do not meet with resistance. They do not cause structural changes. They do not affect the status, recognition, respect, or dignity of the person adopting them. They do not threaten identity. Incremental social change is the world of evolutionary change. When David first introduced the Kanban Method, between 2004 and 2007, he referred to it as "incremental change." His entire motivation had been to find an incremental method to improve organizational agility rather than the forced, dramatic, structural social change he observed with all the Agile methods he had seen. With Agile methods, everyone got a new role, a new job title; the organization was reorganized into new social structures such as cross-functional teams, and the means for assessing and attributing status, recognition, respect, and dignity were all dramatically changed.

> *"People do not resist change, they resist being changed."*
> —Peter Senge, *The Fifth Discipline*

Peter Senge explained why workers resist workplace changes in his seminal text on Systems Thinking, *The Fifth Discipline*. Humans resist dramatic, structural social change.[2] The anxiety, stress, and fear that they suffer due to changes in role, relationships with others, status, respect, recognition, and, ultimately, their dignity, as a consequence of workplace change means that the vast majority of workers are inherently resistant to it and oppose new ways of working. David realized that if you were to be truly Agile in your approach to organizational agility, you needed an incremental method—a way of introducing change

---

2. An academic understanding of this concept emerged contemporaneously in 2002 and is known in social psychology literature as Identity Threat Theory. The paper, "Contending with Group Image: The psychology of stereotype and social identity threat," by Claude M. Steele, Steven J. Spencer, and Joshua Aaronson (https://www.sciencedirect.com/science/article/pii/S0065260102800090), is widely cited as the origin, although the authors acknowledge earlier work by others dating from 1995. It would be reasonable to suggest that the Kanban Method's approach to change and the curriculum for Kanban Coaching Professionals are rooted in Identity Threat Theory.

that was non-threatening, a way to change that allowed you to start with what you do now and evolve from there. Identify your number one problem—your top source of dissatisfaction, your prime impediment to achieving your goals—and fix it. Once the first problem is fixed, then number two gets promoted; iterate and repeat.

By 2008, David realized that many people were misinterpreting the term "incremental." They assumed that incremental change implied step-by-step adoption of a known, defined, prescribed solution, such as "the twelve steps to Extreme Programming." The assumption was that if you adopted one practice out of twelve, and then the next, and the next, you were incrementally approaching adoption of the entire method. This was never what David intended with Kanban. He came to realize that his intent was evolutionary in nature: define an outcome that is desired or acceptable, and then make changes to delivery processes until the outcome is achieved, until the process is fit-for-purpose. Kanban is an evolutionary change method, and indeed, what social psychologists mean by the term "incremental" is that it is evolutionary in nature.

Evolutionary, incremental, normative changes do not rule out emergent structural changes. For example, in 2007, if someone suggested that you replace your feature phone (a flip-phone or candy-bar design) with a smartphone, you might have asked, does it do voice calls and text messaging? Yes. So, it is still a phone! The adoption of smartphones was a normative change. However, smartphones, and the 3G networks they ran on, allowed us to download applications. Our smartphones had cameras and GPS location-positioning devices. Suddenly the combination enabled an explosion of new social media and social interaction behaviors that were undreamt of previously. Dramatic, structural social change happened as an emergent consequence of what were initially normative changes.

We have observed this kind of emergent social behavior with Kanban implementations since 2007. For example, in the implementation that David led at Corbis, in Seattle, the one that provided the archetypal definition of the Kanban Method described in the book *Kanban: Successful Evolutionary Change for Your Technology Business*, we saw emergent social change as job titles were eliminated and functions were merged. Corbis had a business analysis function and a separate systems analysis function. On their Kanban boards, these two functions were represented by separate, adjacent columns on the boards. It was suggested that flow would improve if systems analysts helped the business analysts define requirements, thus enabling better, cleaner requirements that would flow more smoothly downstream. And in turn, it was suggested that business analysts pair with systems analysts to provide instantly available responses to disambiguate requirements, thus ensuring proper design. Collaboration across the functions and the columns on the board smoothed flow and improved the system, moving it toward the shared goal of more work finished faster, to the greater satisfaction of customers.

Over time, it became clear that the pairing was enabling cross-skilling, and the team members themselves then suggested that there was no longer a need for two job titles, that just a single title, analyst, was sufficient. This was the first emergent structural change that resulted from what was initially only a normative, incremental change without social consequences. What followed was a simplification of the kanban board design, with one column removed, and a simple *Analysis* column, now with two subtasks of business analysis and systems analysis required on each ticket. This eliminated WIP and queuing from the system and reduced the average lead time of forty-four days to approximately thirty days—a huge win in achieving a shared goal. It then became easy to reorganize and merge the two departments—a much more dramatic social change in the organization—as the groundwork had already been laid. The reality was that already there was no social separation between business and systems analysts, so there was no need for an organizational separation. The functions of business analysis (describing business requirements) and systems analysis (describing impact on systems design, architecture, and infrastructure) were still being performed.

The whole process took five months. Five months for an evolutionary change to happen naturally, without resistance. Five months for a change that sticks, that is institutionalized, and that is widely accepted. The alternative—forcing a reorganization, forcing a change in job titles, and a directed command to cross-train and cross-skill—would have met with resistance, resentment, and dysfunctional, passive-aggressive behavior. It is likely that it would have failed to institutionalize while imposing anxiety, stress, and fear—imposing psychological crisis upon the workers.

In 2019, several teams in the Finance area of the global bank BBVA were using Kanban for managing their teamwork. The teams were providing services to larger processes (services). However, they each belonged to separate specialized business units and therefore, nobody was in charge of managing the end-to-end processes. When Teodora suggested that they start managing the flow in the end-to-end processes, the answer from the head of business execution (BEx) was "This would take us five years. It is not appropriate to introduce a new management position now."[3]

Instead of introducing a new role, they started visualizing the end-to-end process and defining policies for effectively resolving blockers and dependencies between teams. This is an example of normative change. The head of BEx took the initiative and facilitated defining policies. Poor management of dependencies among teams from different business units was one of the strongest sources of dissatisfaction, so nobody objected to the definition of these policies. Eight months later, three teams from three business units were cooperating in managing the first end-to-end process focused on delivering value to customers as quickly as possible. The head of BEx gradually ceded his role of Flow Manager to one of the team process owners. Three months after that, the same pattern was applied

---

3. Teodora Bozheva and Juan José Gil Bilbao, "BBVA: Developing agility with KMM," Enterprise Agility Everywhere 2020.

to a second end-to-end service, and at the time of finishing this book, the next process to take on has already been identified.

Structural change was achieved by means of a few normative changes.

The reason to pursue evolutionary change is that it avoids the psychological crisis that ensues from dramatic social change. Consequently, changes are more likely to institutionalize. Evolutionary change is the humane approach to change. Agile methods have always pursued aggressive, dramatic social change. They are designed to throw the workforce into psychological crisis. The self-prescribed antidote to this is to fill the workplace with Agile coaches cast in the self-image of life coaches and dilettante therapists—they are needed as a direct consequence of the choice to invoke crisis in the workforce.

Kanban avoids invoking crisis in workers. It avoids the need for coaches as therapists. It creates the natural internal pull for change that sticks. Consequently, Kanban is far cheaper to implement and institutionalize than any Agile method. China Merchants Bank (CMB) ran a comparative study of adopting Kanban alongside Scrum. They showed that Kanban produced better, faster results, at a mere one-150th of the cost per employee.[4] Scrum continually failed to institutionalize and continued to need constant coaching at a ratio of one coach for every fourteen employees, or 7 percent of fixed costs. Consequently, CMB rolled out Kanban across five locations in China and a total of 3,500 staff while maintaining their CMMI Maturity Level 4 appraisal.

Evolutionary Relics

An evolutionary relic is an attribute left behind by evolution that no longer serves any purpose but for which there isn't a mechanism to remove it. Such relics appear in our own bodies and are known collectively as vestigial organs.[5] Our coccyx bone on the end of our spine is the obviated connector for a tail, and our appendix is left over from a herbivore species from which we evolved into modern humans. There is some argument that our gallbladder may be a similar relic. It seems we aren't quite sure what it is for, but just like our appendix, if it goes wrong it can be rather serious and life-threatening. Evolutionary processes leave behind artifacts and behaviors that are hard to explain and serve no purpose.

Paul Klipp, an American from Chicago living in Krakow, Poland, and founder of Kanbanery, a kanban software tool, explained the concept in his blog[6] on March 6, 2013, after attending the Kanban Coaching Professional (KCP) Masterclass. That blog post is reprinted on the next page.

---

4. https://djaa.com/is-agile-costing-you-too-much/
5. https://scienceoxford.com/vestigial-organs/
6. http://paulklipp.com/blog/evolutionary-change-better-than-a-kick-in-the-nuts/ Used with kind permission.

I'll enlist the help of a giraffe. His name's Fred.

Like all mammals, Fred has a larynx controlled by his brain, and Fred is the product of evolutionary change. Fred's larynx is just inches from his brain, because it's at the top of his neck and so is his head, as you might expect. Fred's getting impatient, so he bellows for me to get to the damn point. His brain got impatient first and sent the impulse to bellow right down that nerve to his larynx. A short trip? Not really. Silly evolution decided that the best way to route a nerve between one thing on the top of his neck and another thing on the top of his neck was to wrap it around his aorta first.

Here's Fred's laryngeal nerve; it's about 15 feet long.

Now, who decided THAT was a good idea?

That's where evolution gets you. It's a hell of a lot better than being a fish, at least from the giraffe's point of view, but the evolutionary path from fish to giraffe has some constraints. The corresponding nerve in a fish makes sense. A straight line between a fish's brain and its gills passes the heart, so the nerve crossing behind the heart is pretty sensible. Here's the thing, though. Evolution starts with the existing processes and systems and changes them incrementally. Re-routing a nerve is not an incremental change; it's a revolutionary change.

If true evolutionary processes are at work, awkward solutions evolve over time. You wouldn't intentionally design a nerve to run down a giraffe's neck and back up again. It isn't logical or efficient, but it is robust. The concept of survival of the fittest in evolutionary biology indicates that a solution was fit for its environment. For us, we seek to evolve fit-for-purpose business services. Being fit-for-purpose likely indicates an ability to survive and continue. The ability to respond to stress in the environment and continuously evolve to remain fit for that ever-changing environment is what Nassim Nicholas Taleb labeled anti-fragility. Kanban, as a method to wire a business with evolutionary DNA, provides a means to anti-fragility.

Meanwhile, if you walk into a company and everything seems too neat and tidy, all of the processes are efficient, lean, and devoid of artifacts or activities that seem to serve little purpose, have little or no value, and may have been obviated by circumstances or new techniques, you are likely looking a designed environment—the process consultants have been in, designed a new process, installed it (perhaps through the use of position power), and then left. These designed solutions are fragile, and the businesses using them are fragile. Why?

When resistance is overcome by using positional power, it is highly likely that employees are acquiescing, while their behavior is actually passive-aggressive. When management's attention turns to something else, the employees quietly revert to the old ways. They had no ownership in the changes, and they haven't internalized them. It hasn't become "how we do things around here." It isn't part of their identity individually or as a group. Evolutionary change is robust, while designed-and-managed change is fragile.

The J-Curve Effect

Traditional change management and process improvement follows a model developed by James McKinsey, of McKinsey & Company, during the 1920s. This established one of the definitive consulting engagement models, and it has proven robust and resilient for around one hundred years. We, however, feel this model is outmoded and incompatible with the modern 21st Century workplace and with modern professional services and knowledge-worker industries. The McKinsey model starts by mapping the existing process as currently performed. The consultants then choose a defined process or design a new, preferred process. A plan is then made to "transition" the organization from the current mode of working to the new, desired process design or definition. This model works nicely for both the sponsor and the consultants because it is entirely deterministic. There is a clearly defined outcome—a new process design to adopt—and a clearly defined plan can be made to map the journey from the current process to the future process. There is a clear definition of done—the future process has been adopted, and this can be validated by observing the practice's adoption. The sponsor can see that the work is complete, and the consultant knows when to send their invoice. The problem is that in the 21st Century, this approach rarely produces the desired outcomes—the defined or designed process rarely delivers the intended outcomes. It may be that in as many as 85 percent of cases, the desired, anticipated results are not realized. To understand the reasons for this, we must first understand the approach a little more deeply.

In the first model, shown in Figure 16.1, they select a defined and prescribed process from an existing catalog. The consultant's role is foremost to understand context and appropriateness and, acting ethically, to make an appropriate recommendation. All too often, however, this approach is implemented more like a Procrustean bed, where the organization's context is changed to fit the prescribed process rather than the process tailored to fit the client's situation.

Figure 16.1 The McKinsey model for change

It is rare that the defined, prescribed process is a perfect match for the organizational context to which it is being applied. Effectively, the Procrustean bed problem is always present to some extent. The founder of the Agile method Scrum, Ken Schwaber, wrote the following:

> *"An enterprise can use Scrum as a tool to become the best product development and management organization in its market. Scrum will highlight every deficiency and impediment that the enterprise has so the enterprise can fix them and change into such an organization.*
>
> *Whenever an enterprise modifies or only partially implements Scrum, it is hiding or obscuring one or more dysfunctionalities that restrict its competence in product development and management."*[7]

It is clear from this quote and the rest of the paper it is taken from that Schwaber intends Scrum to be used to invoke dramatic social change.

More recently, consulting firms have become enamored of the Spotify model, which described some organizational design pattern present at the internet music streaming service Spotify during the early 2010s. Large consulting businesses have been encouraging their clients the world over to switch to the Spotify model. On hearing this, David asks them, Are you an internet radio business? Do you operate an online music streaming service? Do you lose more than a billion dollars per year? In which ways do you feel that the Spotify model is an appropriate choice for your business? Do you wish to follow them and copy their billion-dollar losses each year?

Changing context is hard! People don't like it. Context change means dramatic social change. Inherently, humans in the workforce resist context change in their workplace. Additionally, the nature of the business may not easily lend itself to such context change. The media industry had widespread early adoption of Kanban—from TV news, newspapers, and movie studios to online media and content businesses such as Yahoo! People in the media business quickly realized that Scrum, with its required context that everything happens in synchronized two-week increments, called Sprints, was not appropriate—breaking news announcements cannot wait for the next sprint. Almost all industries have constraining

---

7. http://static1.1.sqspcdn.com/static/f/447037/6486484/1270930467650/Scrum+Is+Hard+and+Disruptive.pdf

elements in the nature of their business. The natural philosophy of their environment determines what is appropriate or not.

There is a variant of this first McKinsey model that involves tailoring a specific process design chosen from a large catalog of definitions. This effectively creates a hybrid of both defined and designed approaches. This process-tailoring approach became popular in the 1990s, and the Agile movement was in part a rebellion against its more outrageous excesses. The concept is simple: there is a large reference catalog of process elements and the consultants select the elements needed to right-size a solution to their client's context. Alistair Cockburn referred to this as the "shrink to fit" approach. This approach appeals to the consultant, who gets to play the role of "smartest guy in the room," and to the process wizard, who knows the contents of the reference tome intimately. The failings of the approach were widely recognized in the late 1990s: too slow, too fragile (it depends on the skills of the consultant and process designer), and it tended to deliver something too heavy, with designs that were too difficult to adopt. You might actually recognize this as the overreaching problem which, in part, the KMM is designed to avoid. Someone who is paid to be the smartest guy in the room tends to want to show off and demonstrate "value for money" to justify their large fees. Consequently, overreaching tends to result in transition failures.

In contrast, Cockburn characterized Agile methods as "stretch to fit." In his view, Agile methods were frameworks, incomplete structures, the skeleton of a process to which more had to be added to fit a given context. The problem was that what was missing, the "more" to be added, was left as an exercise for the reader, and the typical Agile practitioner had no skill or expertise or models with which to envisage what was missing and needed to be added. Twenty-plus years of Agile methods have demonstrated that "stretch to fit" isn't a viable option. David describes the Kanban Method as a mechanism with which your existing processes can evolve to fit your needs. Kanban works at the meta level—it isn't a process definition, a methodology, or a framework; instead, it contains a mechanism with which to wire your organization to evolve its own unique process solutions tailored to your specific context. With evolutionary change, there is no intelligent designer, no smartest guy in the room. And hence, Kanban didn't fit the existing consulting engagement model, the model that had persisted successfully since James McKinsey introduced it in the 1920s.

In the second model, the consultants get to show off how smart they are by designing a solution tailored to solve the problems and produce the desired outcome the client seeks. There are often frameworks for performing such designs—Lean value stream mapping is a good example. A value stream is drawn from analysis of the current organization, and activities are labeled value adding or non–value adding (waste). The waste is then designed out, and the process shortened. The goal is to deliver shorter lead times at lower cost. This model has proven effective in well-defined, deterministic production, manufacturing, and distribution situations. We, however, believe that it is inappropriate for professional services and knowledge-worker processes.

If your job title is project manager or risk manager, everything you do would be classified as waste by the Lean consultants mapping the value stream. But don't worry, as the waste will then be subcategorized as necessary and unnecessary, and only the unnecessary waste will be designed out. Put yourself in the shoes of such a project or risk manager: how do they feel? Try to empathize with their feelings. Value stream mapping meets with resistance from the workforce, who feel that they are being attacked and disrespected, that they stand to lose social status, respect, and even dignity as a consequence of being labeled waste.

However, the bigger issue with the McKinsey transition model is the transition itself, and the so-called J-curve effect.

How we wish change worked?

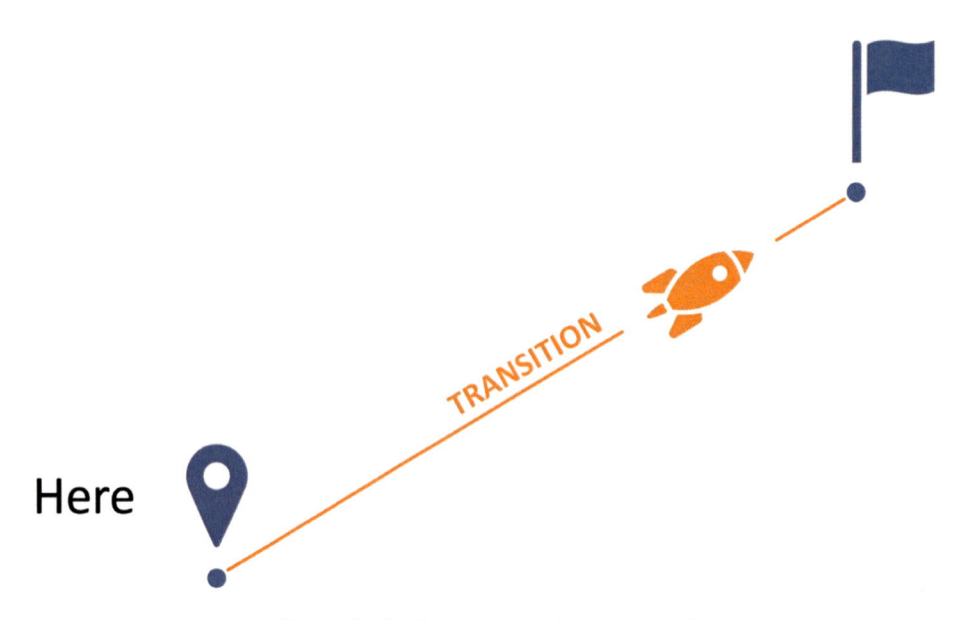

Figure 16.2   How we wish change worked

Wishful thinking (modeled in Figure 16.2) wants to assume that transitioning from where we are now to some newly designed, tailored, or selected process definition would run smoothly and directly, and that there would be no downside risk or impact. David worked for a company vice president in 2003, during his time with Motorola, who asked him, with an entirely straight face, to double the productivity of the product development team, but that there must be no downside, no slowing down at all, as it would be unacceptable to report any slowdown to the wider organization. This is not how change actually works. While we're hoping to make things better, things always get worse for a while.

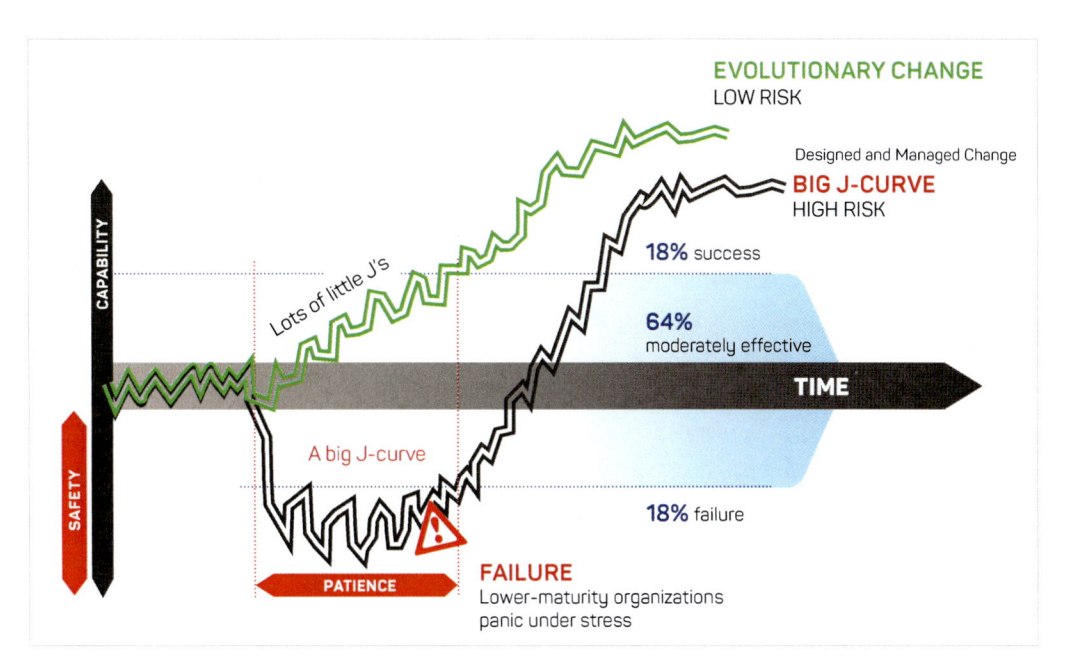

Figure 16.3 How capability is affected by change initiatives over time

The graph in Figure 16.3 shows a current level of capability; this could be some specific metric, such as the delivery rate of software features, expressed as features per week. For whatever reason, this rate isn't good enough, and consultants have been called in to lead an initiative to transition to a new way of working. The goal is to achieve the level of capability shown in the upper-right section of the graph.

To illustrate the basic truth in this picture, David often asks software developers, "Imagine for a moment that your big boss complains that development isn't happening quickly enough and gives your manager permission to hire two more developers so that you will speed up. What happens next?" And the answer is always that they go slower. Why? Who writes the job description? Who reads the CVs? Who interviews the candidates? Once a successful candidate is chosen, who onboards them and how does onboarding work? How does a new person become a productive member of the team? The answers to all of these questions illustrate that the team is distracted during the transition period, and consequently, their productivity is affected negatively. Things get worse before they get better.

How bad can they get? How much of a drop in capability is acceptable? This is represented on the portion of the graph marked Safety. How far can things drop before someone is punished?

How long does it take to recover from the initial impact? How resilient are we? How quickly do we bounce back? This is shown on the graph in the area marked Patience, the bottom of the J-curve.

Now ask yourself, how patient and tolerant are the leadership team in our organization? Together, safety and patience combine into the concept of executive tolerance. How bad can it get before they intervene? How long do we have to show that the changes are working before they shut it down? If things get too bad, or take too long, or some combination thereof, the change agent gets fired. The consultants are gone—made scapegoats, who take the blame for the failure. Things reset, and then, at some point, another transition is started.

In 2018, Teodora met with a European insurance company operating in Spain. They were conducting an Agile transformation, applying their headquarters' blueprint. However, they found it an inappropriate tool for managing their services, the core of their business, and therefore they wanted to start learning to use Kanban. Managers from both the Spanish branch and headquarters took the first trainings with Teodora. Three people from another country's human resources department were also invited to one of the first trainings so they could understand the method and the changes to the job descriptions and responsibilities that would be introduced as a consequence. When they realized that Kanban applied the evolutionary approach to change, the CIO said, "Knowing this would have saved us two years of fighting with resistance." The point is that their blueprint was based on the assumption that building an Agile organization starts with introducing the corresponding organizational structure. Precisely this first step happened to be the key obstacle to making progress.[8]

The truth is that low-maturity organizations tend to have very low-maturity leaders with low tolerance thresholds. Low-maturity organizations are not capable of managing big transition initiatives with deep J-curves. For low-maturity organizations, an evolutionary, incremental approach involving lots of little J-curves is much more likely to succeed.

The Project Management Institute (PMI) reported in 2014[9] that only 18 percent of large change initiatives succeed and deliver on their expectations (i.e., only 18 percent make it to the top of the J-curve). The same report states that 18 percent fail, as illustrated with our J-curve graph, leaving the remaining 64 percent described as moderately effective; that is, they failed to deliver on expectations and failed to reach the desired goal and, most likely, failed to justify the time, expense, and disruption they inflicted.

The PMI cites the following main success indicators for change management initiatives:
- Having well-defined milestones and metrics
- Having senior management committed to change
- Establishing and communicating concrete ownership and accountability
- Using standardized project management practices
- Having engaged executive sponsors

---

8. At the time of writing this book, the Spanish branch of the company uses the KMM to develop the agility of their service business units, and we expect them to present their experience in the coming months.
9. https://www.pmi.org/-/media/pmi/documents/public/pdf/learning/thought-leadership/pulse/organizational-change-management.pdf?sc_lang_temp=en

A simple shorthand summation is that high-maturity organizations manage change initiatives more successfully than low-maturity organizations. Low-maturity organizations aren't good at managing change, and to mature into a high-maturity organization, they must change. We can conclude from this that low-maturity organizations must choose small changes and implement them incrementally. The Kanban Maturity Model provides a roadmap and guidance that make this possible.

The challenge has been the engagement model. How do you know when you are done? Evolutionary change has no end point, no practice definitions with which to validate that the transition is complete. You can't use the McKinsey engagement model with Kanban. So, what do you do? How do you bound a Kanban initiative? How do you measure progress and success? You use the Kanban Maturity Model.

The KMM is organized into seven maturity levels, which are defined by observable outcomes. At Maturity Level 3, the observable outcome is fitness-for-purpose—customer expectations are met. Therefore, you are done when your processes have evolved sufficiently that you deliver on this goal. When your Service Delivery Review shows that you have consistently met customer expectations, it means that this service is now at Maturity Level 3. You can report that progress. Report the achievement of ML3 as a completed goal. You can celebrate this achievement and your celebrations are rightfully deserved. You drive an organizational transition initiative using the Kanban Maturity Model, and you celebrate success as your organization matures and exhibits the desirable outcomes that map against each of the organizational maturity levels.

17 | Evolutionary Change Model

Evolutionary change doesn't happen in nice, clean, periodic increments. Instead, it happens in what is known as punctuated equilibrium. The world can be trundling along with an environment and weather patterns much as they were last year, a decade ago, a century ago, a millennium ago and so on, and then—Bam!—an asteroid hits the planet and everything changes suddenly. The asteroid impact is the punctuation point; what follows it is an immediate, though short, period of chaos followed by a period of stabilization while a new normal emerges, and then things settle down again into a new, different period of equilibrium.

In human history, punctuation points are events such as military coups, for example, the attempted coup in Turkey in 2016. During the coup itself, chaos reigns. No one knows who is in charge or which side is winning. Either the coup is successful, and by morning a new government is emerging or, as in this example, the coup fails, and the incumbent regime reasserts its power and leadership and uses the event as justification to make sweeping changes.

Periods of equilibrium are said to be stable, but this does not mean that they are without variation. Stable means that there is stable volatility, that things vary within known and understood upper and lower bounds—that the environmental conditions are predictable, with a known range of uncertainty, and consequently the system, environment, or context is trustworthy. When there is unstable volatility—volatility of the volatility, also known as turbulence—then the system, environment, or context is described as unstable, or without stability. Such an environment is untrustworthy.

Often, if a disruptive event, or a punctuation point, can be anticipated or foreseen, or at least speculation can exist about it—metaphorically, some astronomers have telescopes and can see the asteroid coming, and some of them are convinced that an impact is inevitable, while others speculate that it may be a near miss—then a period of turbulence might emerge prior to the punctuation point. Financial regulatory authorities use a means of mathematical interpretation of turbulence to detect insider trading in stocks and shares prior to punctuation points. If no one can see the asteroid coming, trading patterns prior to impact should be normal, or stable, within the bounds of known volatility.

In evolutionary biology, punctuated equilibrium drives evolutionary change through selection of mutations, or versions of species. As a broad general rule, the species fittest for the environment and best adapted to current conditions is the one that thrives during a period of equilibrium. However, on the other side of a punctuation point, with a new environment, new weather patterns, and a new period of stability with a new regime of volatility, different attributes may be desirable. These attributes get selected, and it is a new species or variant of an existing one that now thrives in the new equilibrium. The punctuation point itself need not cause the mutations. It is much more likely that the mutation was latent in the gene pool, and the changes emerging after the disruption enable those formerly latent attributes to shine, and succeed.

We can understand this concept through the parable of *Rudolph the Red-Nosed Reindeer*. Rudolph is a mutant—he has a very shiny red nose. The reindeer are a conservative, tight-knit, intolerant culture, and Rudolph is different. His differentness causes Rudolph to be ostracized from the herd, and he wanders off hoping to find a new life, a new purpose, and a new place to belong. As would be true in nature, a lone individual, separated from the herd, is at risk from predators. Rudolph, luckily, survives his encounter with the Abominable Snowman, and eventually he finds sanctuary on the Island of Misfit Toys.

Then there is a disruptive change in the environment—the weather on Christmas Eve is foggy. Santa cannot see to navigate his sleigh and deliver the presents to all the girls and boys around the world. Consequently, Santa now values Rudolph's red nose. He invites Rudolph to join the team as the lead reindeer, lighting the way to navigate the sleigh through the foggy night. Rudolph saves Christmas for all the girls and boys.

All of a sudden, on the other side of the punctuation point, red noses are now a valuable attribute. To have a red nose is to be Santa's favorite. There is social status associated with it. Consequently, red noses get selected, and gradually the number of red-nosed reindeer grows until the entire team working for Santa all have red noses.

The lesson here is that the mutation, the capability, already existed, but it wasn't considered useful and wasn't being selected. Red noses weren't part of the fitness criteria for Santa's reindeer. After a disruptive punctuation point, the fitness criteria change. What was best before is unlikely to be best afterward. The period of emergence after a punctuation point gives mutations—changes—a chance to show their fitness and get selected.

Periods of equilibrium, periods of stable volatility, do not rule out, metaphorically speaking, a global warming problem. An inherent system failure may be growing, slowly, slowly, for a long time, not making any noticeable difference until eventually it causes a schism—and a catastrophic failure. For example, a product development team doesn't pay careful attention to the internal quality of their program code and system architecture such that their code base becomes more and more unmanageable; as each new version of the product is released, the code becomes harder and harder to work with, and the cycle times between releases get longer and longer. We see examples of this in our case study literature, such as Nemetschek Scia.[1] Eventually, the code base is in such poor condition that the product needs to be abandoned and the business needs to start from scratch with a new version. David experienced this early in his career, at Motorola's mobile phone division; they were forced to abandon the code base for their mobile phone operating system several times over the course of approximately a decade, each time starting again with a new technology platform and/or a new programming language. The schism caused by an unaddressed global warming problem is a self-inflicted, unintentional, undesirable punctuation point.

Referring back to our social psychology classification of changes from Chapter 16, we can equate the following:

- Stable equilibrium = Stability
- Equilibrium with an underlying global warming problem = Inertia
- Punctuation point = Dramatic social change
- Equilibrium with an underlying problem and action taken to rectify it = Incremental change

Insert a Punctuation Point as a Last Resort, Not as a Starting Point

As we explained in the previous chapter, the Kanban Method's approach to social change is always incremental (evolutionary). With the Kanban Method, we believe in making changes incrementally, with the current equilibrium. Most other change management approaches recommend introducing punctuation points and then inserting the desired changes during the emergent periods immediately following them. That is, most change management and organizational transition initiatives take a dramatic social change approach using artificial punctuation points. This makes it easier to insert desired changes at the expense of social psychological well-being and with the risk of possible collateral damage, not to mention the possible unknown side effects that emerge after the punctuation point.

---

1. https://prod-kanbanuniversity-backend-store.s3-us-west-2.amazonaws.com/case-studies/SCIA-dist.pdf

Punctuation Points

Punctuation points in the history of an organization are always good opportunities to introduce change. If you are lucky enough to have a convenient punctuation point, it is a gift. Use it! Take full advantage! Punctuation points can take many forms:

- Launch of a first product
- Taking an investment round
- Arrival of a new CEO or leader
- Key employee exit (typically, a founder or a creator of intellectual property, such as a chief scientist or a lead designer)
- Merger, acquisition, divestiture, or takeover
- IPO (initial public offering of company stock—taking a company public from previous private ownership)
- Regulatory, legal, political, or major economic changes (such as a financial crisis)
- Outsourcing and/or offshoring work
- Company reorganization
- Retrenchment
- Arrival of a new disruptive competitor or business model (such as budget airlines)
- Arrival of a disruptive innovation into a market (such as commercial jet aircraft into the flying boat and ocean liner transportation business during the 1950s)

Famously, there is the concept of the first one hundred days, sometimes called the honeymoon period. It is used, for example, to refer to the tenure of a new president or head of state or a new leader in an organization. The one hundred days starts with the punctuation point and runs for approximately three months. During this period, everyone is adjusting to the turmoil, and the new leader gets to blame their predecessor or the conditions that existed before they took control. As a consequence of the punctuation point—or the conditions that existed prior to it (metaphorically, a global warming condition), a period of inertia that provokes some engineered punctuation point such as a reorganization of a business—the new leader has an opportunity make changes without much resistance. Punctuation point changes almost always represent dramatic social change and invoke some form of psychological crisis amongst the workforce. The resilience of the people and the resilience of the organization (the social group) determine whether they stick together and see the crisis through to a new period of equilibrium, or disintegrate and disperse. The number of employees that departs as a consequence of a punctuated change is essentially the collateral damage of the change—the cost of making the change. It is always up to the leaders and decision makers to determine whether the benefits justify that cost.

Leading Change in Periods of Equilibrium

With Kanban, we believe in creating punctuation points as a last resort. We resort to dramatic social change only when all else fails. Making changes during a period of equilibrium is harder. To motivate people to change, they must recognize that there are problems, and they must have an emotional motivation to change. Many business leaders and change management consultants consider this too challenging—they don't have the patience for it. Ironically, and in comparison, political leaders almost always have to pursue incremental social change to evolve their nations economically and socially: they need to find ways to motivate their population to get onboard with necessary changes. Usually, politicians cannot act without the political will of the electorate and their support for their actions.

In the Kanban Method, we have codified a holistic approach to leading change in periods of equilibrium, and the Kanban Maturity Model and its architecture play a significant role in confidently delivering incremental social change.

Stressors, Reflection Mechanisms, and Acts of Leadership

The cartoon from the cover of *Kanban: Successful Evolutionary Change for your Technology Business* (Figure 17.1), illustrates the three main elements needed to drive evolutionary change—incremental social change in times of equilibrium—namely:

- A stressor
- A reflection mechanism
- An act of leadership

Figure 17.1   Cartoon from the cover of *Kanban* (the blue book; 2010)

The conversation shows that there is stress in the environment; things are not flowing smoothly: "I'm stuck," "I'm too busy," and "I'm idle." The visualization of the kanban board and the social forum of their daily Kanban Meeting provide the reflection mechanism—a way to articulate and reflect upon their stress. However, it takes the third element, and the fourth character in the cartoon, who says, "Let's do something about it!" to provide the stimulus—the act of leadership to catalyze the conversation and action that follow. Without the act of leadership as the third element, there is social inertia—frustration with the status quo without a catalyst for change. Without the third element, without leadership, the Kanban Meeting serves only as a therapy session, and the individuals are victims, trapped in their circumstances, unable to take responsibility or ownership or to cope with their situation.

Stressors, Reflection Mechanisms, Normative Changes, and Transition

In the KMM architecture, the transition sub-levels prepare the ground for consolidation to the next level of maturity. By their nature, specific practices in a transition sub-level should be normative and easy to adopt without much resistance; they generally can be pushed into the environment without significant disruption and play a role as stressors, with the goal of engaging people emotionally and motivating support for further changes.

The Kanban Method has codified a set of reflection mechanisms, known as the Kanban Cadences, namely:

- Kanban Meeting
- Replenishment Meeting
- Delivery Planning Meeting
- Service Delivery Review
- Risk Review
- Operations Review
- Strategy Review

For the most part, these are introduced at the relevant transition sub-level to act as the reflection mechanism needed to catalyze the demand for further change. Where one of the cadences appears in a consolidation sub-level, it is because we've recognized that introducing it meets with considerable resistance. The most notable and challenging of these is the Operations Review. Operations Review challenges an organization to have transparency across organizational units, to build trust across a wider network, and to cooperate and collaborate across that network for a shared goal and the greater good. This creates social stress and anxiety, and it requires leadership at higher levels to provide support, to signal that it is valued, and to encourage participation. The truth is that it isn't always pleasant to hold a mirror up to reality. And hence, reflection mechanisms can and do meet with adoption resistance.

The third element, leadership, is the magic fairy dust that makes it all work. We have been working on codifying a blueprint for leadership, and a leadership development extension for the KMM is in the works. It is the one critical element that remains missing from this otherwise comprehensive text on organizational change.

The KMM Uses a Sports Coaching Model

The KMM uses a sports coaching model, and its specific practices map is the playbook. Sports coaches are charged with improving their players' capability, developing their skills. The coach must inflict just enough stress and discomfort to make their players unhappy with the status quo and motivated to overcome their fears and anxieties so they can take their athletic prowess to the next level. Too much stress might break a player, causing them to regress—or abandon the sport altogether. The challenge for the sports coach is to use judgment to apply just enough stress to catalyze improvement. The KMM is designed to provide this with transition sub-level practices tuned to be just stressful enough to engage people emotionally and motivate change, instilling ambition to reach the next level.

The Evolutionary Change Model

Figure 17.1 shows the KMM Evolutionary Change Model. The model is intended to map to any level of the KMM from ML1 to ML5 and illustrates how to use the specific practices in the KMM to manage evolutionary, incremental change. The model assumes that maturity levels represent sustainable equilibria. Hence, the model is designed to disrupt existing equilibrium at a current maturity level and bring the organization to a new, stable equilibrium at the next level of maturity. It assumes a happy, stable equilibrium, a comfort zone at the current level of maturity. Unless the organization is already at Maturity Level 4, we contend that any stable, happy state is due to hubris, arrogance, lack of ambition, or lack of self-belief. Lower maturity levels should not represent comfort zones.

Fostering Willingness to Improve

The upper half of the KMM Evolutionary Change Model illustrates how to use the transition sub-level practices to foster willingness to improve. Transition sub-level practices are intended to be "pushed" into the organization. There is some risk of collateral damage: a risk of losing people and a risk of undesirable, destructive, and socially cancerous behaviors. These are illustrated in Tables 17.1 and 17.2.

17 | Evolutionary Change Model

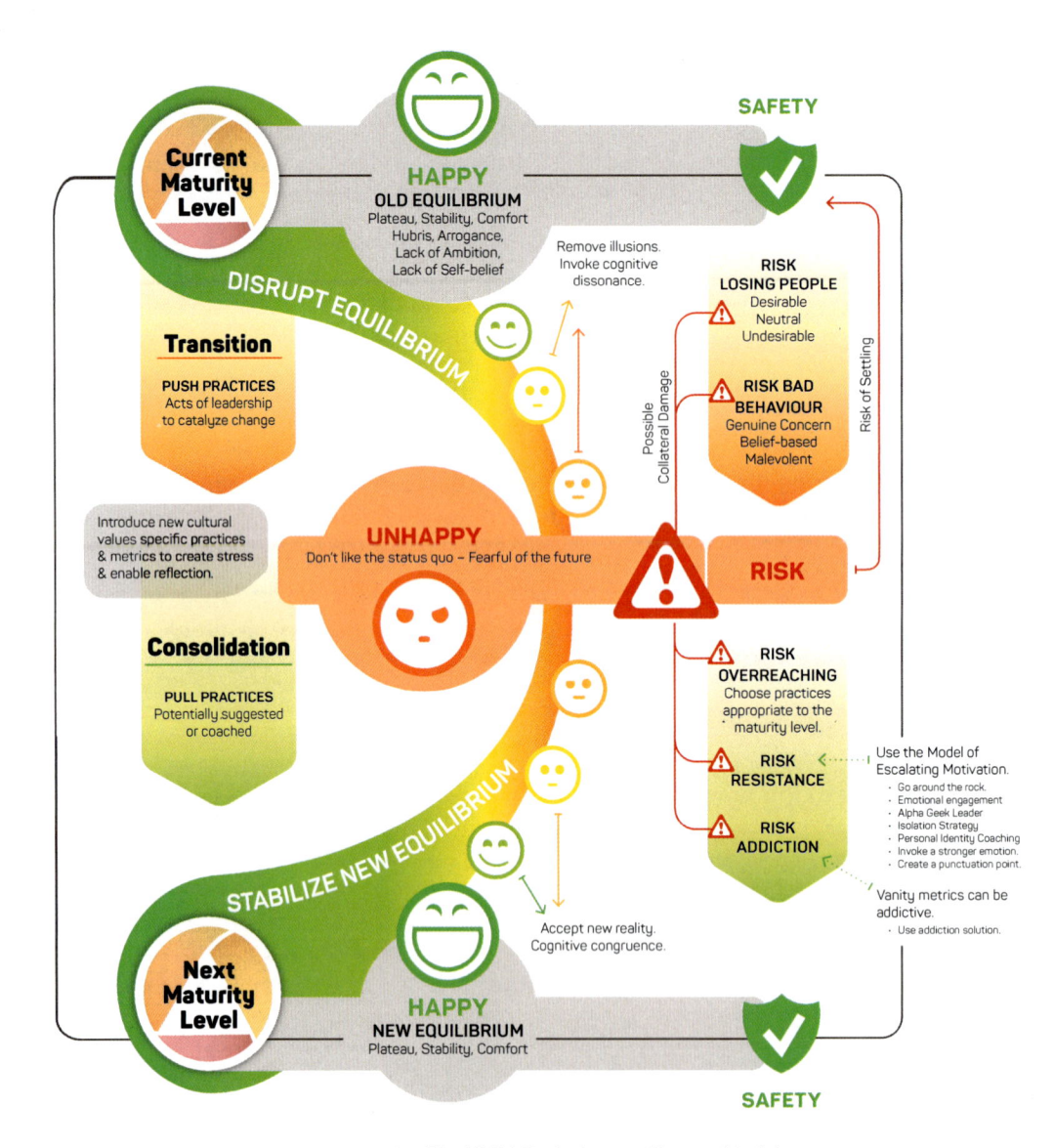

Figure 17.2 The KMM Evolutionary Change Model

Sometimes it is desirable for ineffective or problematic people to leave. However, it is important to be sure that their leaving doesn't create a hardship. It's also wise to ensure that their exit is amicable, and that they leave with dignity, respect, and recognition for their contribution, however small.

Table 17.1 Transition Sub-Level Practices: Risk of Losing People

Risk of Losing People		
Desirable	**Neutral**	**Undesirable**
No problem—there's no loss if the person leaves. Another could take on the work.	There is cost to rehiring, but no significant loss of ability.	Their tacit knowledge or ability can't be replaced.
Mitigations		
Make sure that's true! Help create an amicable exit.	Stand by the values and let it all unfold.	Address their complaints directly and negotiate.

Sometimes people may be considered easily replaceable, their skills a fungible commodity; for example, the Java programming game developers in the Posit Science case study[2]—hiring more Java programmers in San Francisco should be easy enough. But make sure that is the case before showing someone the door.

Other times it would be undesirable to lose people because they are vital to the business—the Ph.D. neuroscientists who did the research work at Posit Science are a good example. Consequently, as happened in the case study, their objections and complaints had to be addressed directly and a solution negotiated.

Table 17.2 Transition Sub-Level Practices: Poor Behavior

Outbursts, Disruption, Sabotage, and Conflict		
Genuine Concern	**Belief**	**Malevolence**
Their objections are valid, and resistance is to mistakes or loss.	Deeply anchored beliefs in dogma, best practices, etc., trigger responses.	Behavior is personal, vindictive, ad hominem, tribal, destructive, etc.
Mitigations		
Listen to and address their concerns. (Satisfied detractors become advocates.)	Appeal to higher authority. Frame changes in terms of common values.	Engage in conflict resolution, build trust. Escalate to management.

Resistance may come from genuine concern and love for the organization and its mission. Listen to, recognize, and address these concerns. A satisfied detractor may become an advocate. They weren't necessarily against what you proposed, but equally, they couldn't support it. Sometimes they simply need to understand it.

Some objections and bad behavior may be belief-based, rooted in superstition: "We've always done it this way; why change now?" What people may see as an attack on deeply anchored beliefs, dogma, and practices that have become core to the identity of individuals and entire social groups can trigger highly emotional responses.

---

2. https://prod-kanbanuniversity-backend-store.s3-us-west-2.amazonaws.com/case-studies/Posit_US.pdf

The response here should be to appeal to a higher authority, a higher calling, more strategic goals and objectives. Seek to frame the changes in terms of common values, shared purpose, and collective goals. An individual detractor opposing proposed changes may become a neutral, passive conformist. Although they remain skeptical of the proposals, they do not stand in the way.

People whose malevolent behavior actively seeks to undermine changes, sometimes resulting in personal attacks—though not necessarily physical—often question the motives, character, and qualifications of the change agent as a way to undermine their proposals. Such an individual may act to harm the organization, or those who are a part of it. This behavior must not be tolerated. It must always be escalated to senior management and brought to the attention of professional human resources staff, if available. If the individual is sufficiently valuable, introduce professional conflict resolution to rebuild a broken trust relationship. Others who are less crucial to the organization may need to be removed before their bad example spreads.

Risk of Settling

There is the possibility that the anxiety, stress, and fear of change are too great, that there is a "risk of settling," of regressing to the comfort zone of the established status quo. While the KMM is designed to alleviate psychological effects such as structural tension, for some people, even small changes may seem overwhelming. Counter these with leadership and by offering emotional and material help to the individual(s) struggling with anxiety and structural tension over the changes. At this stage, look for a neutral, if skeptical, position from those who are not actively advocates. It's important to avoid having the detractors form a social group around the affinity of shared anxiety. Leadership must communicate that the outcomes achieved with the status quo are unacceptable and that there is no going back. We are not suggesting that, like Roman generals, you burn the bridges to prevent retreat, but you must send signals that neither the current performance nor regression is acceptable. Individuals may need coaching to free them from psychological concerns about their identity, their capabilities, or the practices they perform as part of their role. Ideally, these concerns don't emerge until the consolidation stage of the maturity level transformation, by which time it should be a given that turning back is not a viable option.

Pulling Further Changes

Assuming the upper half of the Evolutionary Change Model has done its job, and you have used the transition sub-level practices to disrupt the status quo and shake people out of their comfort zone, it is up to you, as change agent, advisor, and coach, to help take things further, once invited to do so. Now is the time to suggest further improvements. Coach the adoption of practices that are likely to evoke resistance.

We see in the Posit Science case study that Janice Linden-Reed initially had to back off from implementing a Maturity Level 3 kanban system. Exhibiting patience, she gains agreement on a Maturity Level 2 implementation with some Maturity Level 3 transition practices in place. Six to eight months later she is invited to take things further with the request, "Is there more we can do?"

Consolidation sub-level practices should be pulled. There should be an invitation both to suggest them and to coach their adoption.

Risks and Challenges to Consolidating Changes

Risk of Overreaching

As identified in the Preface, one of the key motivations for the Kanban Maturity Model was its use as a tool to avoid the overreaching problem. Overreaching happens when practices being introduced are so stressful to the organization that they break the elastic of resilience and cause a regression. Often, this involves a lot of emotion and discomfort as, technically speaking, the fight-or-flight response (explained in the next chapter) is invoked in some or many of the people affected by the change. Assuming that the KMM is being used as designed, we believe the risks of overreaching are adequately mitigated.

Risk of Inertia due to Addiction

Sometimes our organization needs to lose some bad behaviors, and this is a challenge because people have become socially addicted to them. Addiction to some existing, undesirable behaviors and practices causes inertia and increases resistance to change. A common example is reporting "velocity" in so-called story points by adopters of Agile methods such as Scrum. When a metric can't be directly related to a customer's selection criteria or an evolutionary change fitness criterion, or can't be identified as driving a specific improvement initiative or as a general health indicator, it is almost certainly a vanity metric. Vanity metrics can be related to emotional deficiencies and a strong desire for self-assurance. They are, in and of themselves, a strong indicator of a low-maturity culture, with low resilience and low self-esteem.

Leadership is needed to overcome unsatisfactory addictive behaviors. Addicts are addicts. One approach to overcoming addiction is to substitute a healthier addiction for the harmful one. For example, can you switch a drug addict or alcoholic to a healthier addiction such as fitness? In the books *Trainspotting* and *Porno*, (transformed as the movies *Trainspotting* and *T2*), author Irvine Welsh provides a thinly disguised self-portrait of his own addictions and how he overcame them by becoming addicted to writing. Hence, leaders can encourage replacing the addictive behaviors with more wholesome practices.

Addiction to a habit that produces a reward, "I feel good because our velocity went up," can be replaced with addiction to some alternative practice that produces a greater reward. Rewards can be social and emotional in nature. Rewards can appeal to Thymos or Eros.

Rewards can produce dopamine, oxytocin, or serotonin hits. These concepts are more fully elaborated in the following chapter as part of the Human Condition.

Addictive bad behaviors can also be hacked by leaders who signal that they no longer value them, that there will be no social status (reward) from continuing them. Alleviating addiction to undesirable behaviors requires leadership.

Risk of Emotional Resistance (from the Humans Involved in the Changes)

Motivating change in periods of equilibrium is challenging. People resist change for emotional reasons, which is explained more fully in the following chapter. We have a codified playbook of approaches for motivating change during periods of equilibrium. We explain these escalating strategies in full at the end of the next chapter, after a thorough investigation into why resistance to change is always emotional and why such resistance is core to the human condition.

18 | Why Do People Resist Change?

The Human Condition

To understand how people react to change, we need to understand more about the human condition and how the human brain works. Philosophers have been studying the human condition since ancient times. We'll start with Plato and his ideas on the human psyche and the human soul from the *Republic*, books I and IV, although Plato was influenced by Homer before him. See Table 18.1 for a simplified map of the human condition.

Daniel Kahneman, writing more recently in his seminal text on neuroscience and behavioral economics, *Thinking Fast and Slow*, divided our brain into two basic systems he calls System 1 and System 2, the emotional and the logical. In our view, System 1, the emotional part of the brain, should be subdivided into two or even three parts.

The word "emotion" entered the lexicon of the English language in 1579[1] during the Scientific Revolution,[2] which preceded The Enlightenment, or Age of Reason,[3] in the 17th and 18th Centuries. The term "emotion" was adapted from the French *émouvoir* (translated as "to move") as a convenient shorthand and catchall term for all passions, sentiments, and affections. Plato described the human psyche, and later the human soul, as having three parts: he called these logos (reason), eros (desire), and thymos (passion, or spirit). Scientists in the 16th Century came to subdivide eros into two subcategories, sentiments and affections. Only in the recent past has the new field of neuroscience shown how prescient this insight was: the neurotransmitter for sentiments is dopamine, while affection is controlled by oxytocin. Meanwhile, the spirit, thymos, is controlled by serotonin levels in the brain.

1. https://en.wikipedia.org/wiki/Emotion
2. https://en.wikipedia.org/wiki/Scientific_Revolution
3. https://en.wikipedia.org/wiki/Age_of_Enlightenment

Table 18.1 Mapping the human condition (a simplified though useful model)

Brain	Limbic			Neocortex
	Hypothalamus	Amygdala Hippocampus		Prefrontal Cortex
Plato	Desire/Appetite	Spirit		Reason
Psyche (*Republic* I)	Eros	Thymos		Logos
Soul (*Republic* IV)	Epithymos	Thymos		Nous
Enlightenment	Emotion			Logic
Kahneman	System 1			System 2
Scientific Revolution/ Age of Reason	Sentiment	Affection	Passion	
Examples of Emotions	Like Achievement Pride	Desire Lust Trust	Dignity Respect Recognition Status Identity Entitlement	
		Love		
Neurotransmitter	Dopamine	Oxytocin	Serotonin	

Plato was remarkably accurate in his observations, given the era in which he lived (428–348 BCE), in that we now know that desires, eros, are controlled by the hypothalamus in the brain, while the spirit, thymos, is controlled by the broader limbic system. To complete the picture, desire is also referred to as appetite, and indeed, the hypothalamus does provide the control mechanism for appetite.

If we compare these insights to Maslow's Hierarchy of Needs[4] we see that eros, the desires or appetites, map to the lower three levels—physiological, safety, and love and belonging—while thymos, the spirit, maps to Maslow's higher levels, namely esteem and self-actualization, with belonging representing the bridge between them. A sense of belonging helps form a sense of self, enhancing our sense of identity. Hence, belonging plays a role in thymos as well as eros. In the fourth book of *The Republic*, Plato renamed eros as epithymos, meaning "over the thymos," or perhaps "controlling the thymos." Maslow perceived that needs lower in the hierarchy take precedence over those at higher levels (i.e., if you are malnourished and don't have a safe place to be, it's difficult to work toward anything other than getting those basic needs met), and hence, Plato's observations concur with Maslow's. The hypothalamus performs a function similar to a servo-controller, regulating desires such as appetite, so interpreting epi to mean "control over" has some foundation in neurology. A simpler and more structural interpretation comes from the translation of *epi* as "before," so "before the thymos." In the architecture of the brain, the

---

4. https://en.wikipedia.org/wiki/Maslow%27s_hierarchy_of_needs

hypothalamus comes before the hippocampus and amygdala in the limbic system, and again, Plato's nearly 2,500-year old observations seem astoundingly accurate.

Plato used the metaphor that the human psyche was a two-horse chariot, with Logos as the driver, and Eros and Thymos as the horses, being driven. Eros was the stronger, more volatile, less predictable horse, while perhaps Thymos was the more determined and stubborn. The hypothalamus is the controller for many bodily functions, and Plato's sense of this power was correct. However, it seems that it is the stubbornness of Thymos that makes leading and driving change in organizations so challenging. This stubbornness is in the nature of the amygdala in the limbic system, essentially a network of wiring. Daniel Kahneman described the limbic brain, System 1, as fast to judgment yet slow to learn. It is slow to learn because to learn it must be rewired. Writing in *Blink!* Malcolm Gladwell uses the metaphor that System 1 (eros and thymos) is the circuit board, while System 2 (logos) is the central processing unit (CPU). For System 2 to change, you simply load a new program into the memory. For System 1 to change, you must rewire the circuit board, a more difficult and longer-lasting task. For the amygdala, thymos, to adapt and change, it must be rewired. This rewiring happens as a chemical process in the brain, and it can take hours, days, weeks, months, or in extreme cases, years. While cognitive agility, our ability to rewire our amygdala, almost certainly exhibits as a spectrum across humans, some of us are more readily capable of adapting our sense of self, our sense of identity, and our social affiliations—are more readily able to rewire our limbic systems—than others. The reality is that the nature of the human condition means that changing who we are and how we relate to others is a painful, slow, chemical process. The nature of the human condition is that thymos is stubborn, and resistance to change is, therefore, always identity related.

> *"People do not resist change, they resist being changed."*
> —Peter Senge, The Fifth Discipline

Peter Senge directs us to thymos. We resist our identity being changed. We resist changes that may affect our status, recognition, respect, or dignity. Daniel Kahneman's work teaches us that it is System 1—the limbic brain, the emotions—we must affect if we are to move people to change. The words "move" and "emotion" have similar etymology. The word "emotion" is from the Latin root *emovere*, meaning "to move out." We must move people emotionally to overcome their resistance to change because that resistance is rooted in emotions, specifically their spirit and their desires. Kahneman points out that you do not appeal to System 2—the logical inference engine, the prefrontal cortex, logos—to overcome emotional objections. System 2 is like an advisor; while it can signal the control it would like, the emotional brain does as it pleases.

So, people resist change because it affects them emotionally—their spirit, their sense of identity, and their sense of belonging, as well as their affections, their love and sentiments, and their pride. If we are to lead change, we must seek to avoid invoking these emotions, or we must use emotional engagement as a means to overcome the objections. The primary approach in the Kanban Method is to avoid invoking such emotions and instead pick normative changes that do not attack thymos. Secondly, we invoke some stress, just enough stress to motivate change, but not so much as to throw the people affected into crisis. The hypothalamus regulates stress reactions in the body. Hence, stress motivates eros, providing we do not flood the system with too much stress. In neuropsychology, the concept of flooding is known to cause the "fight-or-flight response,"[5] also known as the acute stress response, or hyperarousal. This starts in the amygdala, part of the limbic system (thymos), and it triggers a response in the hypothalamus, eros, causing it to emit the hormone and neurotransmitter ACTH. None of this is desirable in the workplace. Tension and conflict (fight) is bad enough, but the collateral damage of people becoming withdrawn, disengaged, remote, self-isolated, and ultimately departing (flight) may be worse.

As we detail in the previous chapter, the Evolutionary Change Model (EVM) within the Kanban Maturity Model codifies how to use the recommended approach to change in the Kanban Method—first, to avoid invoking emotional resistance with normative changes, and second, to engage people emotionally by invoking just enough stress to motivate change and improvement without causing an acute stress response and the subsequent disruption and damage that can inflict on the workplace culture and sociology.

Resistance to Practice Adoption

We have observed common patterns of resistance, and innately human reactions, to practice adoption. Let's examine them:

- **Individual or organizational identity being changed or attacked** The adoption of a new practice significantly changes the roles and/or responsibilities of one or more people working within a workflow, system, or process; or people perceive the introduction of the practice as attacking an existing role and diminishing that role or obviating a skill from which individuals may derive self-esteem, professional pride, status, or their self-image. For example, if simulation and probabilistic forecasting are introduced, replacing a former planning and estimation practice, the person responsible for leading planning or estimation may feel attacked or diminished by the switch. Alternatively, if such a practice is a tribal ritual associated with the identity of a social group, such as Planning Poker in Scrum, an entire team may feel attacked by the suggestion that this ritual is no longer needed. This problem is rooted in affiliation with Scrum as a social group rather than Scrum as an organizational tool. Hence, attitudes affect whether a change in practices is viewed as an attack and meets with resistance. It is important to assess whether a practice is related to a sense of identity—that using the practice demonstrates

---

5. https://en.wikipedia.org/wiki/Fight-or-flight_response

membership in a social group. A narrow sense of identity is constraining. For example, a certain violin player doesn't want to play the viola because that would be a drop in status. However, a musician might be happy to play a violin or a viola. The musician sees both as instruments—as tools to use—while the violinist sees her instrument as an extension of herself.

- **Fear of incompetence** An individual may be competent in performing a practice at the current level, but a higher-fidelity version of the practice at the next maturity level requires them to learn new skills or gain new knowledge and understanding. The person fears being seen as incompetent, even temporarily, at this new level and resists adoption. For example, forecasting using linear regression of a mean, assuming Gaussian distribution of data in a sample set, and the applicability of the Central Limit Theorem may be easy to learn and use, and an individual may be competent in applying it, even if some of that application is inappropriate. Switching to a more robust method of forecasting, such as Monte Carlo simulation, and using properly sampled reference class data requires the individual to acquire both new knowledge and new skills, and a deeper understanding of mathematics. They may resist this for fear of appearing incompetent or of being unable to master the new skill. Loss of mastery affects self-esteem and self-image and can result in emotional resistance to adoption.

   A variant of this fear is the **fear of losing control** over a situation when the person carries high responsibility for the business outcomes. For example, the IT area of a large insurance company is developing and maintaining the software applications for the other eleven business areas. The head of IT is aware that the traditional management practices are not effective. However, due to her high responsibility for the operation of the entire business, she is concerned that introducing Kanban might cause her to lose control over the development process and projects and fail to deliver on business expectations.

- **Failure to understand the causation between a practice and an outcome** For example, limiting WIP is a typical challenge for individuals and organizations just starting with Kanban. Limiting WIP is intuitively associated with underutilizing the resources or saying no to the customer. Neither of these alternatives is emotionally acceptable until people have had some practice and have evidence that limiting WIP to the available capacity is beneficial.

   Similarly, achieving Maturity Level 3 requires that organizations deliver within expectations, which also requires that they set expectations appropriately. This necessitates abandoning existing deterministic, reductionist planning methods that use speculative estimation techniques and replacing them with analysis and probabilistic forecasting methods. Failing to recognize that expectations were not met because the input to the planning process was speculative and without basis in fact reflects core individual immaturity, which results in resistance to adoption.

- **Failure to appreciate scale** Practices that work well with teams of three or four people may hinder larger teams, creating too many lines of communication and too much overhead. Practices that work for a department of thirty may not work for a product unit of 150 or a business unit of four product units numbering 600 individuals. Failing to recognize that the scale has changed or that practices loved at small scale are not effective at large scale is, again, a failure of individual maturity that results in resistance to adoption.
- **Failure to recognize a maturing market and match organizational maturity to the market appropriately** In an immature, early lifecycle market, technology is emerging, designs are emerging, implementations are emerging, and delivery channels and service levels are both emerging. As a consequence, processes are evolving and managing them needs to be loosely constrained. In an early market, it is acceptable for product designs to lack the right features, for quality to be poor, and for service delivery to be inconsistent or delivery channels unreliable. Early markets may require and reward heroic effort as part of being reactionary to the evolving and emerging nature of the ecosystem in the market. If the organization is staffed with individuals who act heroically and are rewarded for it, heroism becomes core to their identity, their self-image, their self-esteem, and the culture of the organization—they are Maturity Level 1 people in a Maturity Level 1 organization delivering to an immature market. When the market matures, the organization needs to mature with it. Mainstream buyers expect reliability and predictability. They want to work with trustworthy suppliers. If individuals fail to mature and modify their behavior to be congruent with market conditions, they will continue to behave as Maturity Level 1 individuals in an organization that now needs to be at Maturity Level 3 or 4. If leaders fail to signal a change in organizational culture and a move away from valuing individual heroics to a more holistic, systems-thinking, collaborative, aligned organization, maturity will not improve, and new mainstream customers will be dissatisfied. Adoption of higher-maturity practices obviates the need for heroes, and hence, the heroes often resist adoption, feeling it as an attack on their identity.

Escalating Motivation for Change

Although motivating change in periods of equilibrium is challenging, we have a codified playbook of approaches to help you do just that. These are sequenced in order of difficulty and risk—personal risk to the change agent and risk to the organization from collateral damage and side effects.

1. Go Around the Rock

Borrowing from Taoism and the philosophy of the martial artist Bruce Lee, "Kanban should be like water." Writing in his book published posthumously by his wife, Linda, *Striking Thoughts*, Bruce Lee tells us that water flows around the rock. The rock is a metaphor for resistance. In his case, the resistance comes from the opponent in hand-to-hand combat. In our case, the resistance to change is always emotional. The reasons for this are rooted deep in the human condition, as explained at the beginning of this chapter.

We have several strategies for going around the rock. The first is to choose normative changes that do not affect the social order and hierarchy nor challenge people's self-image, self-esteem, or identity, nor threaten the respect, recognition, status, or dignity of those involved. Choosing the Kanban Method—and choosing to pursue incremental social change and evolutionary organizational change—is the first strategic choice to go around the rock. Transition practices in the KMM are intended to be normative. Transition sublevel practices are the second way to go around the rock.

We also have means of mitigating what some might see as identity-challenging changes that invoke emotional resistance.

1a. Better Version of Yourself, Not a New Identity

When asked to adopt new ways of working that at first glance appear to affect the self-image, self-esteem, or social status of an individual, changes can be introduced with language that conveys "doing this will make you better at being who you are"—a better version of yourself, not a new identity. For example, a project manager who spends her time fighting fires, running down issues, and holding meetings to react to unfolding events, and who prides herself as "the queen of firefighting," can be encouraged to change behavior by using values. If a senior figure, a leader, communicates that we no longer value this reactionary, firefighting behavior, and that instead we value more mature, anticipatory behavior such as risk management, it becomes clear that social status, respect, recognition, and reward are attached to these new behaviors. What is important is that the changes are couched in the language of "this is what mature, experienced project managers do." Challenge an individual's self-concept and then challenge them to live up to it. There may, however, be structural tension, or anxiety, about making the switch. Emotional and material help such as training, coaching, mentoring, and reassurances of preservation of status may be needed.

A product owner with a self-view as "the uber prioritizer" who plays a heroic role, perhaps cast as it is in the definition of the Scrum framework as "the single wringable neck" or "the single throat to choke"—the hero who is responsible for making all of the value-oriented decision making—must be encouraged out of this low-maturity self-image and inherently fragile organizational role. We do this by communicating that we don't value this fragile, "bus factor = 1" heroic behavior. Instead, we value facilitating the Replenishment Meeting and collaborative decision making as well as taking ownership of replenishment policies, capacity allocation policies, risk assessment frameworks, and triage thresholds. While these practice behaviors are all theoretically normative in nature, there is a key difference—the product owner is no longer the sole decision maker for prioritization. Instead, they own the decisions that enable good prioritization, such as the replenishment cadence, Replenishment Meeting participation, risk assessment and triage, and risk hedging, as well as balance and fairness–enabling practices such as capacity allocation and demand shaping. The product owner doesn't get a new job title; rather, what we expect of a good and effective product owner changes.

What happens next depends a lot on whether the individual values their social status in your organization more than they value their identity as a member of the Scrum community and their social status within that community. If they value their position in the wider professional community of Scrum practitioners, it's likely they will resist your requests to change their behavior out of fear of losing status in the Scrum world through nonconformance with what they perceive as good product owner behavior based on their training and the established tribal norms of Scrum. Consequently, and referring to the Immelman matrices from Chapter 8, they will feel not only out of step with your expectations and the organization's needs but also undervalued and possibly disrespected. They will face the difficult choice of either changing their behavior to integrate with your needs or resigning their position. Those who value their broader professional identity and status within the Scrum community will leave, and you should choose to let them go. Accept that they weren't willing to fulfill your needs and expectations and that keeping them will only hinder your organization's development and achieving its goals. If they do leave, this is a minor punctuation point, and it gives you an opportunity to make a change. You should not replace the product owner with another; instead, hire specifically for a (service) request manager. When you are offered a punctuation point, accept it as a gift and exploit it.

1b. Red Squirrel, Grey Squirrel

Survival of the fittest! Evolutionary theory in action—let two species compete against each other.

Rather than ask someone to stop an existing practice to which they have an emotional attachment, simply ask them to augment their existing practice with an additional one. The additional practice needs to be seen as adding value. If it truly is adding value—helping someone do their job, perform their role, be their best self—it is unlikely to meet with resistance. We call this the "red squirrel, grey squirrel" strategy , and it helps us to go around the rock.

In the XIT case study[6] outlined in *Kanban: Successful Evolutionary Change for Your Technology Business* (the blue book), project manager and change agent Dragos Dumitriu didn't ask the product managers to change the way they worked. Their practice of

---

6. This case study will be published on the Kanban University website in the fall of 2020 (https://resources.kanban.university/case-studies/).

calculating return on investment (ROI) using business value and cost would stay. This is the red squirrel—the incumbent way of doing things. The product managers were encouraged to continue to make business cases and calculate ROI using their own estimates of business value, while the IT engineers estimated costs. They continued to column-sort their spreadsheets to provide a stack ranking of change requests from highest to lowest ROI, creating a prioritized list.

Meanwhile, they'd bought into deferred commitment—they had no objection to switching to weekly Replenishment Meetings and dropping the time-consuming monthly planning meeting.

However, as soon as they'd start with Kanban, their prioritization work would instantly become an evolutionary relic. Why? At a replenishment conference call, they might be asked to pick the one item they'd most like for delivery within the next twenty-five days. This isn't a request for the item with the highest return on investment; rather, it is a request based on urgency, or timeliness. It is a request based on cost of delay. An item deemed important, but perhaps not with the highest ROI, likely gets selected; for example, "Support Puerto Rican address format on the employee information form within the employee records application." This isn't a request with a particularly high ROI. How do we even calculate the business value of such a request or put a dollar value on it? Even if we do cook up some method to devise a number, it's unlikely to produce the highest ROI. And yet, it gets picked! Why? Because the Puerto Rico office is scheduled to open at the end of next month and we need to be able to record details about the new employees hired for that office.

Kanban replenishment questions are about urgency and timeless, not return on investment. Product managers may have a spreadsheet filled with data stack ranked and column-sorted by the ROI calculation, but when it comes to the crunch, and making a decision during the replenishment conference call, the item they most want for delivery in twenty-five days or less is not the item in row two of the spreadsheet. Consistently, their top picks are coming from farther down their list.

Their efforts to prioritize have been obviated. They are now selecting items from their pool of available options based on the cost of delay of those items. What is the cost of delaying opening the new Puerto Rico office because we can't onboard the employees? Cost of delay isn't the same as return on investment. Effectively, both methods are now in use—cost of delay and return on investment. One has obviated the other. The practice of calculating return on investment has become an evolutionary relic.

This approach of leaving (some) existing practices in place while introducing new practices to replace them is a standard technique in applying evolutionary change. Effectively, ROI and cost of delay are two species for the purpose of prioritization or, to use less ambiguous, more precise language, the scheduling and sequencing of work. These two methods—the incumbent and the insurgent—will compete in the same way that two biological species compete to be fittest for their environment.

ROI is the red squirrel, while cost of delay plays the role of the grey squirrel. This metaphor is based on the introduction of grey squirrels from North America to the British Isles in the late 19th Century. Red squirrels are native to most of Eurasia, with a range from Portugal to Mongolia, including the British Isles. They have been in decline in Europe for centuries, initially through hunting and a shrinking habitat. Their decline, especially in the British Isles, has been rapid since the latter half of the 20th Century. This accelerated decline is widely due to the arrival of grey squirrels. The confusingly named Eastern Gray (note the spelling with an *a*) is actually an invader from North America, where it takes its name from its territory and the extent of its range along the Eastern Seaboard of the continent and inland to the Midwest. Herbrand Russell, the eleventh Duke of Bedford,[7] takes the blame for the introduction of greys to the British Isles. He introduced them from New Jersey to his Bedfordshire home, Woburn Abbey, in 1890.[8] However, it is believed that greys didn't start to spread widely in the British Isles until 1911, when the Duke of Birmingham is said to have gifted a pair as a wedding present. Starting from the south of England, greys spread throughout the British Isles, including to Ireland, where they appear to have been introduced by another aristocratic family to their stately home relatively soon after Russell introduced them in England.

Grey squirrels are significantly larger and more aggressive than the red ones, particularly during springtime, and they compete for nuts and other food. However, for decades it was believed that the bigger issue was that greys carried the squirrel pox virus. This disease is deadly to red squirrels, whose population has been in severe decline. In the UK, most of the red squirrel population is now isolated in Scotland, Cornwall, and on the islands of Anglesey in Wales and Wight in the South of England. What happened with the squirrels is known in biology as a disease-mediated invasion (DMI).

However, recent studies[9,10] suggest a different explanation. Where reds and greys cohabitate, the reds suffer anxiety and stress competing for nuts with the larger, more aggressive greys. This stress has been shown to lower the immune system of reds and, with lower immunity, they fall prey to the virus.

---

7. http://www.telegraph.co.uk/news/earth/wildlife/12122377/11th-Duke-of-Bedford-blamed-for-unstoppable-grey-squirrel-invasion.html; http://www.bbc.com/news/uk-england-beds-bucks-herts-35417747; http://www3.imperial.ac.uk/newsandeventspggrp/imperialcollege/newssummary/news_25-1-2016-15-38-49; https://www.ft.com/content/6d9fd8f0-c9ff-11e5-be0b-b7ece4e953a0
8. Note: Some sources quote 1870 as the original date, and we've been unable to reconcile conflicting, authoritative sources. It is safe to say "late 19th Century" but being more specific is challenging.
9. https://www.animalaid.org.uk/wp-content/uploads/2017/02/historygreysquirrels.pdf
10. http://www.italian-journal-of-mammalogy.it/A-review-of-the-competitive-effects-of-alien-grey-squirrels-on-behaviour-activity,77444,0,2.html

Red squirrels continue to thrive in mountainous areas, the reason for which wasn't understood until recently. It was assumed that greys were somehow unfit for the mountains. However, in the mountains, squirrels face a predator known as the pine marten. Red squirrels, native to the territory, can smell pine martens coming, and hence, avoid them.[11] Grey squirrels, not adapted to detect the presence of the pine marten, are picked off as prey. It seems that red squirrels are (relatively) safe in the mountains, so it's likely that their population will not be totally annihilated.

We use the red squirrel, grey squirrel metaphor to describe the concept of introducing an alternative and letting it compete side by side with the incumbent.

We go around the rock by not asking people to give up their current practices. Instead, we ask that they augment them with an additional practice that adds value for them. If the new practice, such as selecting and sequencing work based on urgency or timeliness (through an understanding of cost of delay), is successful, then we expect the older practice of sequencing based on ROI to die out. However, in stubborn environments, often where there is a tightly knit, highly cohesive social group with a conservative, risk-averse culture, or where a practice is particularly strongly associated with the identity, self-esteem, ego, or social group status of individuals, the old practice tends to stick around. Even though the old practice has been obviated and no longer plays a role in successful outcomes, it survives. Time spent on it is wasteful overhead, and yet it remains. It's an evolutionary relic—something hard to explain that has been left behind by evolutionary changes in action.

2. Engage People Emotionally

To influence the limbic brain, which includes the amygdala, the hippocampus, and the hypothalamus, we must engage people emotionally. And we must give this emotional engagement time to work. The amygdala must be rewired, so we must exhibit patience. Kanban has many types of tools to engage people emotionally:

Visual

Kanban boards visualize work, workflow, and, potentially, so much more: blockers, customers, urgency (class of service), and risk. Visualization helps us see the flow.

Social/Collaboration

The Kanban Meeting and the other cadences are social in nature and encourage cooperation and collaboration. Kanban is inherently designed to build trust. Social collaboration helps us to encourage flow.

Tactile

Physical boards engage people emotionally because they involve physical movement—walking to the board, physically moving tickets. The act of grabbing, feeling, and moving

---

11. https://www.bbc.com/news/science-environment-5163709

a ticket engages the human with the work—even when the ticket is an abstract metaphor for that work. Tactile engagement helps us feel the flow.

Narrative

At each Kanban Meeting, we engage with the unfolding story of the board, the flow of tickets. The growing narrative helps us know the flow.

Experiential Immersion

Pilots are trained in flight simulators. They learn how to cope with crises in a safe-to-fail environment. Flight attendants are trained in mock-ups of aircraft cabins "set ablaze" and filled with smoke. They learn how to evacuate a burning aircraft through doing it in a safe-to-fail environment. North Sea oil workers are trained to evacuate downed helicopters in the safe-to-fail environment of a swimming pool in Aberdeen, Scotland, where they live through the simulated ditching and capsizing of their aircraft in the dark. We learn how to cope with a crisis through simulation and practice—experiential immersion.

The use of simulation games in Kanban training helps people "feel" Kanban. We don't persuade them to adopt it using logic. We move them emotionally. Simulations engage eros and thymos. Only logos is persuaded by logic.

Form Empathy

Throughout history, all great politicians the world over have been good at forming empathy. To understand how to do it, read great political speeches, study great politicians. David has tested this across the world in Brazil, Russia, India, China, and South Africa (the BRICS), as well as in Australia, New Zealand, and throughout Europe and North America. Regardless of location, everyone agrees that great politicians are good at empathy.

Every story ever written, every joke ever told, every speech, every presentation, every movie, and every TV drama all follow the same core format: they have a beginning, a middle, and an end. The purpose of the beginning is always to form empathy with the audience and engage them emotionally for the meat of the story to come. The successful ones do this well; the others often fall flat.

If you want to motivate and inspire people to change, you have to form empathy.

One dictionary we consulted broadly defines empathy as the ability to understand and share the feelings of others. We find this definition inadequate. True empathy is the ability to walk in the shoes of others: to feel as they feel, to think as they think, to understand your sense of self as they do. If you can feel empathy in this deeper fashion, you can learn to anticipate the "rocks," know where the objections will arise, and understand why they do. To go around the rock, you must have empathy. To move people emotionally, you must instill true empathy in them.

The transparency of Kanban helps form empathy. The narratives of Service Delivery Reviews and Operations Reviews help to form empathy. The tension of scarcity at

Replenishment Meetings, the pushing back of a WIP limit, and the concept of a capacity all help form empathy. The exposure to business risks and the urgency information of cost of delay and classes of service help to form empathy. Kanban is designed to engender empathy.

3. Flip the Alpha

A highly cohesive social group follows the leader. Use the culture-hacking tools from Chapter 8 to tighten the social cohesion. Identify the leader of the pack, and use the tactics from strategy #2 (Engage People Emotionally) to engage and move that person emotionally. Everything else will follow.

4. Coached Identity Change

When the self-image of your head of project management is "queen of firefighting" and you need her to reinvent herself as "queen of risk management," you may need to engage the services of an occupational therapist—a trained, certified psychologist—if you are ever going to get beyond Maturity Level 2.

When you need to implement the service delivery manager role or the service request manager role, and the individual who seems like the best fit is resisting, you need to engage with a professional occupational psychologist. If coaching the "better version of you" from strategy #1 (Go Around the Rock), has failed, you need to engage professional help.

Why do you need a professional psychologist? Because you are messing around with the wiring of someone's brain. This isn't for amateurs or dilettantes. This is properly the work of a trained professional who understands the possible negative impacts of the approach they pursue.

Coached identity change is time consuming, painful, and expensive, so use it sparingly and on people whom you've determined you really need to retain. Humans feel the chemical process of rewiring the amygdala as pain. Let the infliction of that pain come from an outsider—a professional psychologist.

People who have gone through coached identity change—people who've successfully graduated from personal therapy—often love the new version of themselves. However, they never forget the pain they went through to get there. They often resent the person who inflicted that pain upon them. It is better for that person to be an outsider who leaves once the job is done.

5. Counter Emotional Resistance with Stronger Emotions

In his only textbook, *What Is This Thing Called Theory of Constraints and How Should It Be Implemented?*[12] published in 1990, Dr. Eli Goldratt devotes the second half of the book to

---

12. Eliyahu M. Goldratt, *What Is This Thing Called Theory of Constraints and How Should It Be Implemented?* (Croton-on-Hudson, NY, NY: North River Press, 1990). All of Goldratt's other books were allegories.

the topic, "What if the constraint on improving your organization is emotional resistance from the people in the organization?" Goldratt poses this as a question, as if it has only a slim probability of being true, when the reality of the human condition means that, to some extent, it is always true.

To summarize half a book in a single sentence, Goldratt suggests that the antidote to emotional resistance is to motivate change by invoking a stronger emotion. David used to run classroom workshops on this topic, asking groups of participants to list strong emotions and then categorize them as either positive or negative.

Figure 18.1 shows the result of one such group exercise.

Positive	Negative
Passion	Anxiety
Excitement	Fear
Happiness	Hate
Love	Anger
Loss/grief	Shame
Achievement	Humiliation
Pride	Embarrassment

Figure 18.1 Examples of positive and negative emotions

Notice that the list of strong positive emotions covers all three categories of sentiments, affections, and passions. Both eros and thymos are represented. Interestingly, loss/grief is listed as positive even though any of us would also associate it with pain. When asked, the group explained that to feel loss, you must have loved someone. "Grief is the price we pay for love" is a quotation attributed to Queen Elizabeth II[13] following the tragedy of September 11, 2001, in New York City.

Invoking passion, excitement, achievement, or pride seems like a viable strategy in the workplace. Love and happiness are more nuanced and complex in nature. An inspirational speech by a strong and charismatic leader may invoke passion, pride, excitement, hope, or a sense of achievement, but you cannot incite someone to love or to feel happy.

The list of negative emotions is grim reading. All too often we've seen weak leaders use fear as a motivator. Although people will act upon fear, we've seen from the Immelman matrices that fear-based motivation in the workplace may not have the desired consequences—the collateral damage could be huge. Meanwhile, hate must be avoided at all times. It is simply never appropriate. When it is alleged that a leader such as Steve

---

13. https://www.telegraph.co.uk/news/worldnews/northamerica/usa/1341155/Grief-is-price-of-love-says-the-Queen.html

Ballmer, of Microsoft, said "I f***ing hate that Eric Schmidt," referring to his peer at Google/Alphabet, he is obviously speaking out of frustration, and the words aren't motivational, only demanding of sympathy. As for anger, shame, humiliation, and embarrassment, these may have their place in some contexts, but they are extremely dangerous to use in the workplace. If your name is Sir Alex Ferguson, former manager of Manchester United, and you are in the locker room at halftime, and your job is to motivate a lackluster David Beckham, who was out on the town the night before and hasn't played well in the first half, then perhaps some anger, shame, humiliation, and embarrassment are called for. In fact, Ferguson was famous for this, and the players even had a nickname for it, calling it "the hairdryer treatment" due to the proximity with which the anger, shame, humiliation, and embarrassment were delivered. If you aren't a drill sergeant or a world-famous sports team coach, it is probably best to avoid using negative emotion to counteract emotional reactions to change in the workplace.

6. Create a Punctuation Point

If you've reached this far and you've tried all the other plays in our playbook—you've tried culture hacking and you've tried all five means listed above—and still you aren't making progress, it may be time to take the "nuclear option" and blow things up by introducing your own punctuation point. When all else has failed, it is time to reorganize, fire someone, outsource work, restructure, or introduce any other form of dramatic social change, such as giving people new job titles, changing the means by which people are recognized and rewarded, reshuffling the social order, or promoting some people or demoting others. When everything else has failed, it is time for your "Moneyball Moment."[14]

---

14. Moneyball Moment has become an expression implying a disruptive punctuation point and shakeup. It references the actions of Billy Beane, General Manager of the Oakland Athletics baseball team, mid-season 2002, the first year in which he was using a data-driven, statistical approach to selecting players for the roster. This approach is known as "Moneyball," after the book and film of the same name. The "Moneyball Moment" refers to a point in the summer when the new strategy didn't appear to be working and Beane decided to shake things up, trading three of his best players and sending five others down to the minor leagues. While many commentators thought Beane had given up, the punctuation point had a dramatic effect. The Athletics followed that with, at the time, the longest winning streak in Major League Baseball history and qualified for the end-of-season playoffs.

19 | Barriers to Adoption

While we have been able to codify the organizational maturity model and correlate patterns of Kanban implementation to maturity levels, we have also seen patterns of resistance and inertia that hinder deeper adoption of Kanban and achieving higher levels of maturity. We are sharing these commonly occurring barriers to adoption so that you might anticipate them and have some means to mitigate their effects.

Generally Observed Barriers to Adoption

Impediments to achieving a next level of organizational maturity are often due to an insufficiency or lack of a sociological or psychological element, or the absence of an important value, in the culture of the organization, such as the following.

- Lack of leadership
- Lack of understanding
- Lack of holistic thinking
- Lack of agreement
- Lack of trust or insufficient empathy
- Lack of respect
- Lack of customer focus or a service-orientation
- Failure to value flow

Transition practices and the Kanban values are there to mitigate these sociological, psychological, and cultural challenges that impede achieving a subsequent level of organizational maturity. The Kanban values are mapped against the maturity levels on the model, and leaders must be prepared to introduce these values to the culture of the organization to enable the next level of depth in maturity.

As a general rule, transition practices do not affect identity or the emotional state of individuals and are safe and easy to adopt. Transition practices for Maturity Level 3 can be introduced at Maturity Level 2 in an organization that aspires to Maturity Level 3. However, the main practices of Maturity Level 3, at the consolidation sub-level, are likely to meet with resistance in a Maturity Level 2 organization.

Transition practices are often designed to lay the groundwork and modify the social conditions to enable adoption of the main practices of a given maturity level. The main practices are required to deliver the outcome that defines the level, such as "consistency of outcome"—reliable, repeatable, service delivery within customer expectations—that characterizes Maturity Level 3.

Breadth of Adoption as a Mitigation of Inertia

Breadth of Kanban adoption also helps remove impediments to greater depth of organizational maturity. For example, making policies explicit raises the level of social capital by defining the boundaries and constraints on action. Empowerment is enabled by explicit policies and hence, trust is increased. Thus, as we expand the breadth of Kanban general practice adoption, we anticipate that the depth of organizational maturity will deepen.

Visualization and metrics help with understanding. If the impediment to adoption of main practices at the next level is due to a lack of understanding, then implementing additional visualization or reporting additional metrics that "shine a light" on the problem will help with understanding and create demand for the main practice otherwise resisted. So, additional visualization or reporting practices act as transition practices to implement the main practice.

Visualization and transparency also create empathy and trust. Both empathy and trust are core enablers of everything else.

There may be a need to justify why a group of individuals needs to act as a team. A team may simply be a social group with some affinity around shared identity and some need for accountability or supervision. In this case, we see the aggregated individual kanban pattern.

In other cases, the need for collaborative teamwork comes from a task being too big or too intimidating for an individual to undertake it alone. As soon as we have a need for collaboration, we see the team kanban pattern emerge.

When there is a lack of social capital or social cohesion, transition practices are required to engineer more social capital and the social structure as well as a mechanism to encourage collaboration. We see this with the transition pattern from an aggregated individual kanban to a service-oriented, collaborative team kanban. At this point, the lanes are renamed; instead of individuals, the lanes now represent the services provided and the work item types processed, and they use avatars to distinguish flexible, multi-skilled workers from those who are more narrowly skilled and dedicated to a single service (see Figure 19.1). By implication, a worker with an avatar is seen as socially superior to those who merely have their name on a single row of the board. By creating social pressure for individuals to improve and broaden their skills, this change results in a broader, more skilled, more liquid labor pool. The benefit is faster, smoother flow. What enables this pattern is service-oriented thinking, coupled with the oblique approach of introducing a practice known to socially engineer demand for a desirable outcome—a more broadly skilled workforce, encouraged by attributing status to flexibility and cross-skilling, a managerial focus on work to be done and customer satisfaction, and a move away from managing individuals.

Making policies explicit and defining boundaries and constraints also helps with understanding. A clearer definition of the rules may enable main practices at the next level.

Figure 19.1   Example of a flexible labor pool pattern

The Need for Individual Maturity

Between maturity Levels 3 and 4, there is a distinct shift from qualitative measures and decision frameworks to quantitative measures and analysis. In neuropsychological terms, there is a shift to System 2 (logical inference thinking in the pre-frontal cortex) from System 1 (emotional pattern matching in the limbic brain or amygdala). A level of individual maturity is required to enable this transition. In some cases, it will be individuals who impede achieving a deeper level of maturity. From time to time it may be necessary to move or remove individuals who lack the emotional agility to operate comfortably at deeper maturity levels.

Deeper maturity demands individuals with altruistic, service-driven motivation. It requires individuals who don't just take responsibility for action, but accept accountability for outcomes.

Accountability doesn't happen by magic—it requires feedback mechanisms to reflect on outcomes and individual actions. Mature individuals accept that their behavior has an impact on outcomes for the collective social group and organization. A lot is written about the need for leadership. The inherent desire to be a leader isn't wired into every individual, and leadership development is a large topic—one that we have deferred on with this edition of the KMM. However, do not underestimate what can be achieved by wiring an organization for accountability. Proper feedback loops designed to reflect on outcomes, and how those outcomes were affected by action, will take you a long way. Breadth of Kanban practice adoption, with a focus on using feedback loops to drive accountability, is an oblique means to encourage more leadership.

Values as a Mitigation of Inertia

A lack of leadership and a failure to create *Einheit*—unity and alignment behind a sense of purpose—is an impediment to achieving Maturity Level 3 or deeper.

A lack of holistic thinking is an impediment to achieving Maturity Level 2, and this becomes more and more acute the deeper the attempted implementation is. To achieve Maturity Levels 3 and deeper, the organization needs to think in terms of services as systems and the organization as an organic, living organism, a network of interdependent services. Understanding that local actions, or inactions, may have a ripple effect across the network is critical to improving outcomes. A move away from local selfishness—thinking about oneself or one's immediate team or organizational unit—does not by itself contribute to the collective effort in the service of customers and other stakeholders. An inherent move toward selfless action is needed to improve the performance of the organization as a whole. It is necessary to think in terms of systems and to use metrics that drive holistic improvement rather than local optima.

A lack of customer focus is an impediment to achieving Maturity Level 3. Again, this becomes more and more acute the deeper the attempted implementation or the greater the scale of the implementation. To achieve Levels 3 and deeper, an organization needs to think in terms of services and see the organization as a network of interdependent services, while always keeping the end customer, their needs, expectations, purpose, and risks they may be managing, in mind.

A failure to value flow impedes achievement of Maturity Level 3. Unevenness of flow results in a lack of predictability and an inability to deliver on expectations and promises. This impacts trust, and a lack of trust retards some other practices, such as pull and deferred commitment, which are needed to respect WIP limits and maintain a system without overburdening it. A failure to value flow can result in a vicious cycle that causes maturity to regress.

Agreement requires trust, respect, and explicit policies. Without agreement, there cannot be disciplined implementation of WIP limits, which affects flow, resulting in unevenness and overburdening.

Without respect, the operation of the systems and processes is dysfunctional and unreliable. Maturity Level 3 cannot be achieved without a cultural value of respect. Some specific practices are engineered to mitigate a lack of respect, or to increase the level of respect, enabling an organization to get to the next level.

In low-maturity environments, a lack of respect can be mitigated or countermanded with legislation—explicit policies, strictly enforced. While such countermeasures may be effective in some situations, they don't reflect the core Kanban values.

To achieve Maturity Level 4, there needs to be respect for the shareholders and the concept that there is a business, an economic entity, that requires making profits in order to exist. Without respect for the owners who have placed capital at risk, there will be scant regard for margins, profitability, cost controls, and so forth. There will be no drive to achieve deep maturity at Levels 5 and 6 if the long-term survival of the business isn't explicitly valued.

Skin in the Game

It is common for founders or founding families to value long-term survival. Their interests are aligned with the lowest paid and least mobile of the workforce. It is often the middle managers who are least vested in long-term survival—there is nothing in it for them, no shared interests, and their skill set and relative wealth make them highly mobile and resilient to partial or total business failure. To enable Levels 5 and 6, it is necessary that senior leaders align the interests of middle management and give them "skin in the game" of long-term survival. Traditionally, this was done using corporate pension plans rather than the more common employer-subsidized individual contributor systems preferred in modern businesses. Other approaches usually involve employee ownership, including stock grants or stock options with vesting periods typically exceeding five years. Such systems have had limited success in creating a middle-ranking workforce truly vested in long-term corporate survival. Leaders need to think deeply about how to align the interests of highly mobile, economically secure middle managers if deep maturity is to be achieved and sustained. Loyalty needs to go both ways in an organization.

The Organizational Dilemma of Social Status, Trust, and Loyalty

Typically, high-trust organizations have a flat structure with fewer job titles and pay grades than is usual, and a simpler social structure. Deeper hierarchies are associated with lower-trust organizations with greater bureaucracy—slow-moving, seek-permission cultures. However, deep hierarchies encourage loyalty, while shallow ones discourage it, as individuals quit to find accelerated social status elsewhere. This is a core organizational maturity dilemma: to have high maturity, you need high trust and high loyalty, and yet they seem mutually exclusive.

What might be the resolution to this dilemma? Clearly, Level 5 and 6 organizations do exist.

There must be more than just pay grades or job titles that enable accumulation of social status. The social engineering in the organizational design requires a multi-faceted and highly nuanced approach to conferring recognition.

While a simple, flat structure with few pay grades and job titles might be attractive, it may also be somewhat naïve. Is it possible to have a deeper hierarchy without a loss of trust and a move to a conservative, seek-permission, highly bureaucratic culture? We believe so! Use transparency, explicit policies, and a fair and equitable justice system; create empowerment; create the means for reputation to flourish. Leaders can use every means at their disposal to encourage loyalty—shared purpose and a strong sense of identity, history, and narrative—a hero's journey of struggle against adversity, exhibiting resilience until a robust, admired brand emerges—all of these things encourage loyalty. Consider rewarding loyalty and attributing social status to it. Value loyalty to the organization, to the mission, and to the organization's values: attribute virtue, integrity, and dignity to it.

Barriers to Maturity Level 2

> *"Every team reports that they deliver on their commitments, but I know that customers are waiting longer than six months for delivery."*
> —Agile coach, Internet Equipment Manufacturer,
> Boston, United States

This statement was whispered to David in a corridor outside a large meeting because the individual involved didn't feel safe bringing it up in a public forum. David's host was a 600-person business unit that made two products. They had strongly adopted Scrum and had been using it for six years. By their vice president's own admission, the unit's performance had plateaued for at least the previous two years, and further improvements weren't emerging.

We can diagnose this situation as follows:

- Lack of service orientation
- Localized metrics and objectives, not instrumented for or reporting lead time
- No customer-recognizable work items
- Lack of collaboration across service delivery workflow
- Clearly, Maturity Level 1; and what we might advise is:

- Participate in a STATIK workshop for the end-to-end workflow, as well as for the teams involved in it.
- Define customer-recognizable work item types.
- Implement a service-oriented workflow board.
- Institute Flow Review.
- Use flow-related metrics to revise the imposed SLAs (in the second case) and the existing policies.

Common Barriers to Maturity Level 2

We recognize the following commonly recurring obstacles to achieving Maturity Level 2:

1. Not starting with a customer-facing service
2. Lack of service orientation or customer focus
3. Copying an organizational blueprint
4. Forced to use an organization's standard process
5. Managers not trained in Kanban
6. Lack of a Flow Manager
7. Legacy tooling

We look at these in turn.

1. Not Starting with a Customer-Facing Service

When there isn't an end customer, people often struggle to define meaningful work item types. When a customer is present, it is easier to identify a customer request as a work item type.

A customer-facing service also means that we have refutable demand—we can say no to a request. Consequently, a full triage of now, later, or not at all is available. The need to start with a customer-facing service was standard guidance for Kanban coaches until a recent empirical example from Best Day, a travel company based in Mexico. Best Day focused initially on a shared service, exclusively with irrefutable demand, and yet improved the customer-facing service to a fit-for-purpose level of performance without directly addressing the customer-facing service.

Regardless of the outstanding achievements of the coaches at Best Day, starting with a customer-facing service provides greater options, more flexibility, and fewer constraints, and it is more likely to lead to success.

2. Lack of Service Orientation or Customer Focus

As an extension of the first issue, no one is asking, whom do we serve? Nor do they have a purpose with an external, altruistic focus. There is no customer. They are not in service to anyone. If there is a purpose, its benefits are internal and probably self-serving.

Twelve experienced Kanban coaches who participated in the KMM Beta Program in 2018 and 2019 shared the observation that the majority of organizations conducting Agile transformations are stuck at Maturity Level 1. They have largely introduced Agile practices at the team level but struggle with scaling beyond it.

Introducing the principles of Service Delivery and Service Oriented Organization is key for connecting the motivation for the organizational initiative (the why) and the introduced practices (the what).

3. Copying an Organizational Blueprint

In recent years, the most common example is the Spotify Model. The attractiveness of a prescribed organizational design and dramatic social change—with a big J-curve—persists. However, these blueprints often come with organizational charts but miss the dynamics of how those organizational units must interact, cooperate, and collaborate. There is no cultural dimension to an organizational blueprint.

An organization that copies a blueprint does not recognize themselves (who we are). There is no business-related purpose in the copied blueprint that is meaningful to the organization (why we exist). Therefore, copying such a blueprint essentially imposes both an organizational structure and practices that do not fit the organization's identity, culture, or management style and thus hurts more than it helps.

4. Forced to Use an Organization's Standard Process

We see this mostly in Industrial-era companies using management techniques developed between the 18th and 20th Centuries. They have a mindset that they can pilot a new process in one location, on one line, and then replicate it all over the world across many lines of business. They do not comprehend that knowledge work does not benefit from this kind of economy of scale. In knowledge work, the workflows have inherently different risks and unique dynamics. Each professional service workflow must evolve its own unique solution.

5. Managers Not Trained in Kanban

Despite a decade of selling Kanban as a management method and operating a management-training business, labeling what we do as management guidance and education, Kanban continues to be seen as an Agile method, an element within the Agile movement. Agile is something managers impose on their workers using consultants and Agile coaches. Viewing Kanban as "just another Agile method to be imposed on our workforce" has blinded many managers to the true power of Kanban, denying their organizations the extensive economic benefits it can produce.

In three independent conversations with senior managers of three companies (two insurance companies and a hospital) who were already running their Agile transformations, Teodora observed the same pattern: the managers were associating Kanban with a visual board only. What struck them most was to learn that (1) Kanban uses an evolutionary, not a drastic, approach to change; (2) Kanban practices enable effective management of the workflow all the way from a customer request to delivery; and (3) the Kanban feedback loops link strategic, operations, and line management in a simple and straightforward manner. This broadened their understanding of Agile at the enterprise level and led to revising and integrating their current approaches by using the KMM.

6. Lack of a Flow Manager

When no one is responsible and accountable for keeping the work moving, it tends to fester in the buffers between siloed teams. While a Scrum Sprint may take only two weeks, the customer may wait more than six months to take delivery. A flow manager would ensure that this doesn't happen.

7. Legacy Tooling

Many companies that do have instrumentation to track knowledge work are using tools that were not designed for flow, or for evolutionary change, or for a service-oriented mindset. Many of the most popular tools, such as Jira from Atlassian, do not track and report metrics such as lead time; nor are they architected to support evolutionary change. Insistence on continued use of legacy management tools has a severe economic impact.

The most commonly quoted reason for sticking with a legacy tool such as Jira is, "It was so incredibly painful to adopt this tool that we don't ever want to go through that pain again." There is a natural cognitive bias to project the pain inflicted by the current tool onto other tools. This projection is entirely irrational, and yet entirely human. There are, however, approaches that "go around the rock"; these include, but aren't limited to adding Kanban-friendly reporting tools, like Nave, as a plug-in to Jira. Ramsey Solutions adopted Nave at the beginning of 2020. They are regularly seeing flow efficiencies greater than 60 percent throughout their entire value stream.[1] Nave supports most of the Kanban Cadences and can greatly improve Jira as a tool suitable for instrumenting a Kanban implementation.

Barriers to Maturity Level 3

> *"I haven't looked at the lead time chart in months."*
> —Software Development Manager, Telecom Equipment Manufacturer, Beijing, China

This quotation comes from a teleconference David was holding with managers involved in a large-scale Kanban adoption. The organization was stalled at Maturity Level 2. Still, at their scale, this business had gained significantly from adopting Kanban and advancing to Maturity Level 2.

A student in one of Teodora's classes shared the following:

---

1. https://getnave.com/customer-success-stories/ramsey-solutions.php

> *"Our customers are happy overall. We usually meet our SLAs. However, it is typically at the cost of lots of individuals' effort or a manager's ability to quickly resolve issues that arise between our departments. Nobody is in charge of customer requests end-to-end."*

Again, this is an organization stalled at Maturity Level 2, relying on heroic management effort, often invoking heroic individual efforts at the local team level. There is no systemic approach to accountability; instead, individual managers take it upon themselves to ensure good service to customers with whom they have some special relationship.

We can diagnose these situations with the following questions:

- Is there a Service Delivery Manager?
- Are customer expectations understood and communicated?
- Does Service Delivery Review happen?
- Is there any blocker management?
- Is blocker likelihood and impact being reported?
- Is there a Service Risk Review?
- Is the lead time distribution thin- or fat-tailed?

It is impossible to achieve Maturity Level 3 without paying attention to lead time. What we might advise here is:

- Instrument and report lead time.
- Implement Service Delivery Manager role.
- Conduct Service Delivery Review.
- Collect and analyze blocker metrics.
- Conduct Service Risk Reviews.
- Articulate customer expectations better and get a deeper understanding of them based on fitness criteria.

Common Barriers to Maturity Level 3

We recognize the following commonly recurring obstacles to achieving Maturity Level 3:

1. Lack of purpose
2. "We are just order takers."
3. Silos, local metrics and reporting, lack of customer-oriented KPIs
4. Lack of role responsible and accountable for ensuring that customer orders meet expectations—the Service Delivery Manager
5. Regime change: evolving "informal" collaboration across silos eradicated after reorganization
6. "All our demand is fixed date."
7. "All our demand is irrefutable."

8. Lack of qualitative understanding of business risks
9. Lack of mathematical literacy
10. Lack of skills in negotiation or forming business agreements
11. Legacy tooling
12. "We need a tool before we can get started."

We look at these in turn.

1. Lack of Purpose

If we don't know why, it is hard to align disparate groups and get them to cooperate, collaborate, and move in the same direction. It is purpose that enables us to drive effective delivery and bring together workers from different organizational units to cooperate on a workflow kanban system. It is purpose that enables service-orientation without reorganization.

It is also purpose that enables resilience. If we've taken a blow, it is a sense of purpose that gives us the energy and drive to pick ourselves up and try again.

It is purpose that provides the guiding objectives for feedback and adjustment. Feedback mechanisms cannot drive worthwhile evolutionary change without a purpose to guide them.

One of the insights from the participants in the KMM Beta Program was that the lack of a clearly stated purpose, meaningful for the enterprise and the business, is one reason that organizations do not progress further than Maturity Level 2. This observation also explains the finding in the "13th Annual State of Agile Report"[2] that 97 percent of the respondent organizations practice Agile development methods, but only 6 percent of them report that Agile practices are enabling greater adaptability to market conditions.

We use the Fit-for-Purpose Framework to understand both a customer's purpose and the value of customer service to focus our organization on the purpose of fulfilling customer needs and expectations. Understanding how we help our customers gives us a sense of contribution; it brings meaning to our lives.

2. "We Are Just Order Takers."

David has seen this problem at a global bank and at a global telecom equipment and mobile phone manufacturer: the idea that the IT services organization, or the product development organization, is simply a collection of engineers who know nothing of the business and should be told what to do. With no stewardship, the engineering delivery organization is disenfranchised. They are not partners in delivering the best outcome. Rather, they are treated like vendors, in a low-trust, low-maturity fashion, with the implication that their services are fungible and that they can be easily replaced with an external vendor.

---

2. https://stateofagile.com/#ufh-i-613553418-13th-annual-state-of-agile-report/7027494

This is wrong on so many levels: low trust, poor asymmetrical risk management, vulnerability to abusive and bullying behavior—these lead to very poor decision making and a delivery organization that is set up to fail and to take the blame for failing. The overall outcome is poor performance, disappointed customers, and a spiral of blame and low-trust responses, which leads to ever more bureaucracy and oversight, with poorer and poorer service and longer and longer delivery times.

3. Silos

In some hierarchical organizations, the only collaboration and cooperation is at the executive committee or board of directors' level. To get anything done, requests and memos need to be copied up several layers of management, with direct requests of these senior people to intervene. Often, senior people are reluctant to intervene across organizational boundaries (outside of their own silo). Little progress is made and only ever so slowly.

Silos tend to feature metrics and reporting that focus on localized activities—things that are easily observed, instrumented, and reported. They tend to be activity related and report whether people in the business are fully utilized. It is likely that efficiency is measured as a percentage of worker utilization.

In general, a siloed organization is not using customer-oriented KPIs. Accountability for customer experience, customer satisfaction, and customer service is lacking. The organization is successful in the market more as a coincidence, or despite itself, or because of a strong brand, strong or near-monopoly position in the market, customer loyalty, or some other structural reason such as barrier to entry for competitors. These things have led to complacency. Siloed organizations often have complacent cultures.

4. Lack of Service Delivery Manager

No one is responsible and accountable for taking a customer's order and ensuring its delivery. Consequently, it doesn't happen within expectations—typically, no one knows the expectations, or if they do, there is an assumption that it is someone else's job to ensure that expectations are met.

5. Regime Change

A successful informal system had developed despite the usual organizational challenges. New senior leadership arrives and, having no visibility on to the informal but functional system for meeting customer expectations, they "go nuclear" with a reorganization—designed, managed, dramatic social change—and they blow up a functional system that was meeting customer expectations. Not knowing what they had, they are mystified about how they might have broken it.

6. "All Our Demand Is Fixed Date."

Most businesses we have encountered over ten to fifteen years do have some genuine fixed-date demand: their business is seasonal in nature and events such as holidays drive their calendar; or they work in a regulated industry, and regulations change, with deadlines to enforce compliance; or there are major contractual obligations with milestones and payments attached. But typically, businesses we meet seldom have more than 15 percent genuine fixed-date demand.

If everything you are requested to do has a fixed date attached to it, it is because the requestor doesn't trust you. They are using a deadline as a means to drive and control your behavior. Deadlines are inherently low-maturity behavior.

So, when you have dysfunctional behavior due to a lack of trust, look to build trust.

Educate your customers about cost of delay and help them understand scheduling and early or late start and how those relate to classes of service. See Appendixes D and E at the end of this book for guidance.

7. "All Our Demand Is Irrefutable."

Again, there are circumstances in which all the demand for an internal shared service is likely to be irrefutable. These requests happen because someone two or three degrees of separation removed in the network of interdependent services accepted a customer request. However, although a request may be irrefutable, can it be scheduled? Do we know the cost of delay of the original customer request, and therefore, can we determine the urgency and cost of delay of this request, at least in a qualitative, class-of-service fashion?

Regulatory requirements are mandatory and irrefutable. We are either in a business or we aren't. If we are, we must deliver the mandatory functionality. However, if we know we need it, can we commit early and use the Intangible cost of delay class of service?

We service urgent and critical tasks such as recovering outages in production systems. Our demand is irrefutable and urgent and must be expedited. If this is the case, the volume and nature of this demand must be risk hedged with a capacity allocation of intangible cost of delay items. If we have regulatory demand that we can start early, we can use those intangible class of service items as our risk hedge against expedite requests.

Irrefutable demand means that the triage options of now, later, and not at all are reduced to a bifurcation of now or later. This ability to schedule irrefutable demand later based on understanding cost of delay means that we can smooth flow, improve predictability, and build trust.

8. Lack of Qualitative Risk Management

The ability to analyze risks using fact-based taxonomies and to establish Kiviat charts, mapping a risk profile for an item based on facts, enables effective triage decisions.

Qualitative risk management is a core skill that instills confidence and trust, and it removes the anxiety and fear that drive a "push" mentality that demands early commitment.

Quantitative understanding of cost of delay, using triage tables and classes of service, can feed into a more complete risk assessment framework (Kiviat chart) and a triage bar or demand-shaping threshold to filter demand into the three categories of now, later, and not at all.

9. Lack of Mathematical Literacy

At Maturity Level 3, we need a broad base of workers and managers who understand some fundamental mathematics. We need them to understand that "average" is an ambiguous term, and that mode, median, and mean are the same only in a perfect bell-curve distribution. They need also to understand distribution curves and histograms and that "the risk is always in the tail."

Understanding both lead time distributions and what causes a fat tail is essential for defining correct actions to improve delivery time and customer satisfaction and to adjust policies so as to increase an organization's agility.

10. Lack of Negotiation Skills

Writing in *Leading Geeks*,[3] Paul Glen, an occupational psychologist who studied the workforces of Microsoft, Oracle, and Sun Microsystems in the 1990s, wrote, "Geeks don't negotiate, they solve puzzles." Your delivery organization probably isn't good at negotiating; your businesspeople, however, went to business school and took a two-credit class in negotiation. Geeks likely want to design the perfect Kanban system to solve all of the problems, while the customers, unless they were involved in the STATIK workshop that facilitated the design, are not vested in the solution—they don't understand it and they don't trust it.

When seeking buy-in to Kanban implementations, it is important to engage the customer side, and this can be done through negotiation.

We recommend that you start from a position of humility and a desire to repair a broken trust relationship. Apologize for past failings. State that you wish to provide better service and that to do so, you are making some changes. As a consequence, how you interface with other parts of your business will change. Now, open your negotiations by revealing your design with only the standard class of service.

The purpose of this is to show that you are open to improving and that you take responsibility for past failings. However, the standard class of service is unlikely to meet all your customer's needs all the time. They also likely have business risks and the kinds of demand that require fixed date and expedite classes of service.

---

3. Paul Glen, David H. Maister, and Warren G. Bennis. *Leading Geeks: How to Manage and Lead the People Who Deliver Technology*. San Francisco: Jossey Bass, 2002.

Let your customer object. Ask them to explain. Respond by offering a higher class of service, and possibly a guaranteed capacity allocation. This technique brings your customers into the design process. They are now vested in the solution and feel that they had a direct influence on the outcome. Now they have skin in the game.

11. Legacy Tooling

This hasn't gone away. It was a problem at Maturity Level 2 and it becomes a greater problem at Maturity Level 3. There simply aren't enough good tools that have the correct metrics to facilitate the Kanban Method and all the Kanban Cadences.

The same guidance given for Maturity Level 2 holds true; it is simply more important than ever.

Organizations that are serious about their evolution through KMM should include in their tool selection process the criterion of facilitating the Kanban practices at least up to Maturity Level 4.

12. "We Need a Tool Before We Can Get Started."

David first heard this objection while talking to a very experienced senior executive at a Swedish bank. Actually, the half-day discussion was about creating a service-oriented organization and managing it with Enterprise Services Planning. What was on the table was a high-maturity implementation. The executive involved was very excited and not only seemed to understand the applicability and efficacy of such a solution, he quickly moved into the mode of thinking how to operationalize it. Suddenly he paused and said, "Of course, we are going to need a tool to aggregate all the data into a single system before we can get started." He then began making plans to propose a project to the annual planning meeting to create a new IT system to aggregate work item tracking data from disparate sources across the bank. Once this was in place, they'd be able to consider getting started during the following annual planning cycle. In other words, it would be eighteen months and two sets of portfolio planning and governance meetings before we could start offering Kanban services to the IT department. The result: the idea disappeared into a black hole.

The reality is that you don't need fancy tools to get started. You can manually collect start and end dates and aggregate data in spreadsheets to calculate cumulative flow diagrams and lead time histograms. As this work is distributed, though it does involve some time commitment from both workers and line managers, collecting basic Kanban metrics at enterprise scale is something you could start doing next Monday. Don't let the geek tendency to seek a technology solution to every problem generate inertia that prevents you from getting started.

Barriers to Maturity Level 4

> *"We just put out a release on time, met our commitments, but our product management team reacted with WTF is this?"*
> —Software Development Manager, Mobile Application, Berlin, Germany

This comes from our mobile.de case study.[4] The team already had a successful iOS application for iPhone, and they had expanded so they could produce an Android version. The first release of the Android app surprised and disappointed the marketing sponsors. When the team responded defensively, "But everything we did was transparently available on our Kanban board. Why didn't you say something earlier?" the humbling response was, "We have no idea what the tickets on that board mean." The problem lay in the nature of the "user story" work items being tracked. They were too fine-grained and not meaningful to customers.

We can diagnose this situation as follows:

- Work items not meaningful nor understood by customers
- Asynchronous commitment
- Pull from partially committed "buffer," no Replenishment Meeting

Although they had achieved Maturity Level 3 for their iOS app, some practices we would expect to see, such as synchronous commitment at a Replenishment Meeting that involved customers, were not present. They regressed to Maturity Level 2 when stressed with the additional scale of the Android application. They will never be able to achieve a sustainable level of customer satisfaction unless they progress to Maturity Level 4. What we might advise is:

- Set up a two-tiered Kanban board.
- Introduce a new, coarse-grained work item type.
- Use synchronous commitment.
- Institute full Replenishment Meetings with customers present and synchronous commitment.
- Require that customers commit to coarse-grained work items.

Common Barriers to Maturity Level 4

We recognize the following commonly recurring obstacles to achieving Maturity Level 4:

1. Lack of customer intimacy
2. Lack of strategic direction or risk-hedged allocation of investment

---

4. https://prod-kanbanuniversity-backend-store.s3-us-west-2.amazonaws.com/case-studies/Mobile.de-Final-Case-Study.pdf

3. Lack of alignment and congruence with strategy and values
4. Lack of quantitative understanding of business risks
5. Lack of mathematical literacy
6. Lack of risk-management literacy
7. Lack of confidence, planning, and scheduling at scale

We look at these in turn.

1. Lack of Customer Intimacy

With the Fit-for-Purpose Framework, we define customer intimacy as knowing why a customer chooses to do business with you and understanding their context, or the risks they are managing. Customer intimacy goes beyond taking orders and fulfilling expectations on a transactional basis. There is an assumption of a long-term relationship and hence, a need for trust. Understanding why enables a more symmetrical commitment, a share in risks, and the ability to design a product or service that meets and anticipates their needs.

2. Lack of Strategic Direction

Sometimes a firm has strategic objectives and a direction, but they are very poor at communicating it. Other times, it is simply lacking: there is an understanding of "who we are" and "what we do," but there is a lack of purpose, a lack of "why are we here."

3. Lack of Alignment and Congruence with Strategy and Values

Strategy and values exist, are explicitly defined and communicated, but there is no feedback mechanism to hold people accountable and to train the organization to make good decisions that are aligned and congruent. Congruence is a skill; it must be learned and practiced. Feedback mechanisms, such as Operations Review and Strategy Review, are needed to reflect on the congruence of decisions and actions.

4. Lack of Quantitative Understanding of Business Risks

At Maturity Level 4, we expect some degree of quantitative risk management, particularly with external business risk, not just internal delivery or technical risks. Is this an Extremistan or Mediocristan business? What is the nature and pattern of demand and how is it distributed? Can we use averages and functions of averages for planning, forecasting, reporting, and decision making? And if so, how many data points represent a good average, regressed close enough to the true mean value? Are we using the correct approaches to managing risks given the nature of our business? Are we partitioning business risks according to their nature? Are we using Real Option Theory to price risk and investment in our upstream Discovery Kanban? And so forth.

5. Lack of Mathematical Literacy

Lack of mathematical literacy came up at Maturity Level 3. At Level 4, we need a deeper understanding of mathematics. We need an understanding of the probability distribution functions, the exponential function, Pareto functions, and both Gaussian and Weibull functions. We need an understanding of stable volatility and periods of equilibrium, and knowledge of how to sample reference class data for iterative simulation algorithms such as Monte Carlo.

6. Lack of Risk-Management Literacy

We expect an understanding of mathematical functions (curves) related to risk management and knowledge of concavity, linearity, and convexity in payoff functions. We expect some ability to use calculus and understand derivatives, integrals, and convolutions. Although we don't need this level of quantitative analysis capability in all employees, there needs to be someone in an Enterprise Risk Management (ERM) role capable of offering mathematical and risk assessment assistance within the organization.

7. Lack of Confidence, Planning, and Scheduling at Scale

There is an inherent fear and lack of trust at scale that leads to anxiety and demand for items to be committed early. This can lead to too much work-in-progress and consequent waste from abandonment and/or aborted work that should have been deferred until later. Using cost of delay, classes of service, classes of dependency management, dynamic reservation systems, and classes of booking contributes to creating a trustworthy system that meets expectations, at scale, across entire networks of interdependent services.

Implementing Roles

We've seen that the Flow Manager role, and its more mature implementations, the Service Request Manager and Service Delivery Manager, are required to achieve Maturity Level 2, then 3, and beyond.

However, the means of implementation has varied across different organizations over the last fifteen years. David first documented the notion that there are no roles in Kanban, and his definitive work on the topic, *Kanban: Successful Evolutionary Change for Your Technology Business*, made no mention of roles. The assumption was that with Kanban implementations, people keep the roles they already have and that responsibilities are only slightly modified as a consequence of specific practices.

However, what we now call low-maturity implementations persisted, and it became evident that the pattern of low-maturity implementations involved a failure to take responsibility—responsibility for flow and for delivering on customer expectations. This led to a change of guidance: if no one was responsible for these two crucial roles—Flow Manager and Service Delivery Manager—it was necessary to assign them. This led to another change in the guidance: we added all three roles—Flow Manager, Service Request Manager, and Service Delivery Manager—to the KMM in October 2019, prompting the 1.1 release of the model. However, it was clear from the history of Kanban and the case study literature that individuals often played these roles without a job title change; rather, they took on some additional responsibilities. This was true in early case studies such as Microsoft XIT, Corbis, and Posit Science. However, in others, it was necessary to give people the job titles and, in some extreme cases, to change the organizational structure and formally add the role and responsibilities as part of the business's reporting structure.

We decided to examine these examples through the lens of the cultural dimensions of the KMM. This enabled us to make sense of the variety of ways the roles had been implemented.

1. The group shares responsibility.
2. An individual takes on additional responsibilities within the scope of their current job.
3. An individual is formally given the Flow Manager or Service Delivery Manager job title.
4. A new organizational structure is introduced, formally creating a new position and reporting structure.

These four ways of implementing the roles and responsibilities for flow and meeting customer expectations are shown in Figure 19.2, mapped against the three social dimensions of the KMM culture pillar.

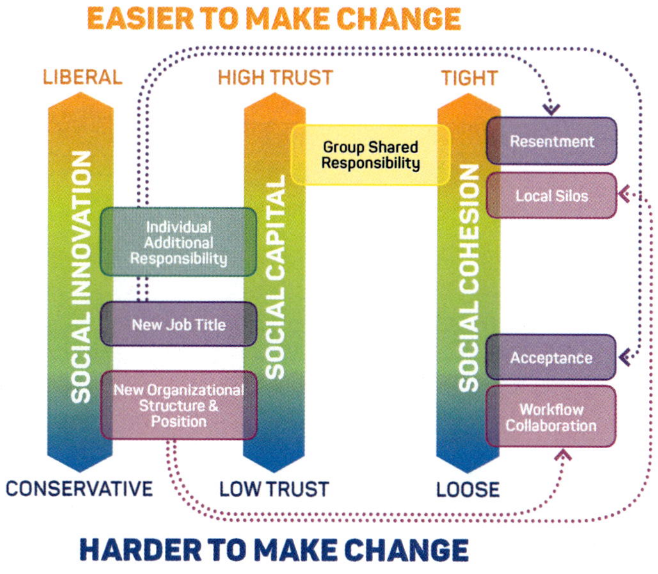

Figure 19.2 Implementation of roles based on culture

1. Group Shared Responsibility

We see group shared responsibility in case studies such as Tupalo.[5] It correlates with very tightly cohesive, high-trust organizations, and we have seen it only at small scale.

We believe that social cohesion is incredibly important for making this work. There must be a feeling of "We're all in this together." We do not believe that social innovation is important, because a high-trust, tight-knit, conservative group that knows they need to take responsibility is as likely to do so as a liberal group with the same realization. The conservative group needs only that the leader is on board with the plan to signal permission that it is okay to play along. A more liberal group probably doesn't require a signal from a central authority figure.

2. Individual Additional Responsibility

This was the norm in the early case studies, such as at Microsoft XIT with Dragos Dumitriu, the project manager at Corbis, where David assigned the responsibility to team leads and function managers reporting to him. Because individuals took on additional responsibility in all of the early case studies, the need for the specific roles remained largely invisible for many years.

The cultural attributes that correlate with this style of implementation are found in a pocket of higher trust within the business unit or department, and a reasonably liberal, tolerant, and experimental culture. All the early case studies were in California or Washington State on the West Coast (or left coast, as it is often nicknamed) of the United States.

We believe that social cohesion isn't an important parameter, because the additional responsibilities are given to an individual.

3. New Job Title

Someone must be given a job title when formal recognition of their responsibilities is required for others to give them due respect, and hence cooperate with them. This is necessary in more conservative, less-trusting cultures. The job title removes ambiguity in a conservative culture that doesn't cope well with such role ambiguity, while it signals authority in a less-trusting culture.

However, the social cohesiveness of the group may create side effects. In a loosely cohesive culture, acceptance is likely. If the social structure isn't too strong and too formal, then no one else feels threatened as a consequence of the new role. One person's change of title doesn't threaten the status, recognition, or respect paid to the others. Thymos is not threatened when one person takes on a new title in a loosely cohesive group.

In a more tightly knit group, there may be social consequences—others may resent the change. For example, in 2007 David assigned new responsibilities to one of a tight-knit group of three database analysts. He made one of them solely responsible for internal

---

5. https://prod-kanbanuniversity-backend-store.s3-us-west-2.amazonaws.com/case-studies/Tupalo_EU.pdf

reporting and preparing data extractions and reports for Operations Review. This seemed like a fairly simple matter of assigning work and responsibilities to a worker within his department. However, some days later one of the other database analysts was in David's office complaining about the change. "This wasn't done properly. This is a new job that should have been listed on the company's intranet job site. The position should have been open for anyone to apply and each candidate should have been interviewed and the best person selected." This was the right and proper process—the fair process. It was also the bureaucratic and slow-moving process.

While on the face of it this behavior was conservative in nature, what actually happened is that there was a perception within the group that changing one person's responsibilities shook up the social order, that status and recognition were given to one and not to the others. The fact that the director of the business unit made this change bestowed status and recognition upon the chosen one, and this was perceived as unfair.

Thymos is offended!

4. New Position and Organizational Structure

The reference case study for this fourth choice is the work Christophe Achouiantz did with Sandvik in Sweden. Christophe is best known for his book, *The Kanban Kick-start Field Guide*,[6] and a series of articles describing his use of Kanban in the approximately 150-year-old mining industry equipment company. Christophe presented at the 2016 Kanban Conference in San Diego,[7] where he discussed his two-year battle to achieve cross-workflow cooperation amongst teams in a highly siloed, conservative, old industrial company.

This fourth option actually reflects the guidance David published in his first book, *Agile Management for Software Engineering*,[8] in 2003. To gain cooperation across a workflow, the function managers, or team leads, should report to a second-line manager, who has responsibility for flow through that series of functions and has responsibility for ensuring delivery within customer expectations. *Agile Management for Software Engineering* predated David's pursuit of an evolutionary approach to change. In fact, it was while he was writing the book that he had the epiphany that he was writing the wrong book, solving the wrong problem—that prescriptive, defined Agile methodologies were always going to meet with human resistance, and that what was really needed was an incremental approach, an evolutionary approach.

Ironically, that book contained prescriptive advice on reorganization. Our guidance now is that you reorganize as a last—rather than a first—resort and that you can use the cultural pillar of the model to make sense of the situation and predict the scope of reorganization that may or may not be necessary. A new position and a reorganization

---

6. http://bit.ly/KanbanFieldGuide
7. https://resources.kanban.university/project/the-sandvik-it-story/
8. David J Anderson, *Agile Management for Software Engineering: Applying the Theory of Constraints for Business Results* (Upper Saddle River: Prentice Hall, 2003).

of reporting structures represent dramatic social change. There will be a J-curve effect. Christophe pursued this approach at Sandvik as a last resort when all else had failed. Don't allow a superficial cultural assessment give you permission to rush into abandoning incremental social change and pursuing emergent structural change. Making dramatic social changes stick is challenging. Does your organization have the resilience and patience to see the changes through?

A more recent example comes from the BBVA case study, detailed in Chapter 4, Case Study: BBVA Finance Division (Spain). Initially, when they started managing end-to-end (E2E) processes, the head of Business Execution (BEx) took the role of Flow Manager. They did not introduce a new organizational position, nor a new job title. The head of BEx executed this role until the policies for managing work among the teams that belonged to different administrative departments (disciplines) were established and the teams successfully adopted feedback loops and the use of flow-related metrics. This noticeably increased the level of trust among the teams and tightened their cohesion. Gradually, the head of BEx was able to let go of some of the management of the E2E process, and eventually a Process Owner of one of the teams took on the additional responsibility of Flow Manager.

20 | Building Resilience

Writing in *Forbes*[1] shortly after the global lockdown in response to the novel coronavirus and Covid-19, Julian Birkinshaw[2] of London Business School suggests that the new imperative for senior leaders isn't enterprise agility; rather, it is now enterprise resilience.

How can you build resilience and how does the KMM help?

Four Principles of Resilience

Julian Birkinshaw offers us four principles of resilience:

1. From Bureaucracy to Emergence
2. From Formalization to Personalization
3. From Efficiency to Reliability
4. From Profit to Meaning

We look at how the KMM helps with each of these in turn.

1. From Bureaucracy to Emergence

The transition from Maturity Level 0 to 1 often is where highly bureaucratic organizations allow looser affiliation and collaborative teamwork to emerge. Maturity level 1 Kanban patterns reflect these emergent, ill-defined workflows, policies, goals, and objectives.

From Maturity Level 2 onward, the concept is that a services-oriented organization, implemented as cooperative workflows across organizational boundaries, can quickly orchestrate and compose new services and new service delivery workflows, which allows for

---

1. https://www.forbes.com/sites/lbsbusinessstrategyreview/2020/03/28/the-new-boardroom-imperative-from-agility-to-resilience/#2164fe386711
2. https://www.london.edu/faculty-and-research/faculty-profiles/b/birkinshaw-j

a grander form of emergence. Solve a problem quickly, using the organization you have now, and let the bureaucracy and the organizational design catch up later. The core idea with Kanban implemented at scale, as a Service-Oriented Organization (SOO), is core to resilience, adaptability, and responsiveness.

A study by Arie de Geus showed that "two hallmarks of resilient companies are their sensitivity to the world around them, and a tolerance of new ideas."[3] In Kanban, we use the Fit-for-Purpose Framework to give us sensitivity to the world around us; and we use the cultural values and culture hacking ideas built into the KMM at higher maturity levels to move the culture toward being more liberal and tolerant.

"Resilient organizations build leadership at all levels, with those on the front line having the competence and authority to act."[4] Leadership at all levels is a core value in the KMM, and the culture elements and practices to empower competent people to act, in a trusted manner, are built into the KMM and the specific practices of Kanban and Enterprise Services Planning.

2. From Formalization to Personalization

Birkinshaw makes a strong argument that individuals must take more responsibility for their roles—and their actions. Rather than formal regulation and a need to constrain people who are assumed to be untrustworthy, we need people whom we trust to act in a trustworthy manner because they have personal skin in the game. Birkinshaw's argument is strongly aligned with that of Nicholas Nassim Taleb in his book *Skin in the Game*, the sequel to his earlier work, *Antifragile*, which directly addresses resilience, robustness, and reinvention.

Taking responsibility is a core concept in the KMM from Maturity Level 3 on. Having ownership while acting within formal boundaries and known practices for optimal risk management, Birkinshaw suggests that "humble checklists" used by pilots and surgeons are core to resilience. We could extend that further to include decision frameworks, decision filters, and any and all explicit policies. It is vital to have feedback mechanisms, such as Risk Review, Operations Review, and Strategy Review, to reflect upon such guidelines, frameworks, policies, and checklists to ensure that they are effective. Again, the Kanban Method has these mechanisms built in. Kanban empowers people to act, to take ownership and responsibility, and to enjoy the reward brought about by their actions, and it delivers empowerment and self-actualization without loss of control.

3. From Efficiency to Reliability

Efficiency has been subjugated within the KMM since its inception. Efficiency and economic improvements appear in the model at Maturity Level 4 and become a focus at

---

3. Arie de Geus, *The Living Company*: Boston, MA: Harvard Business School Press, 2002.
4. https://www.forbes.com/sites/lbsbusinessstrategyreview/2020/03/28/the-new-boardroom-imperative-from-agility-to-resilience/#2164fe386711

Maturity Level 5. Efficiencies can be achieved only after fitness-for-purpose, when proper balance and risk hedging are in place. Efficiency introduced too early is inherently fragile and leaves the organization open to ruin in conditions of extreme stress. The KMM is designed for resilience from the ground up—reliable, trustworthy, fit-for-purpose service delivery and a robust, balanced approach to risk hedging and meeting the needs of all stakeholders.

4. From Profit to Meaning

This has been a general trend in business writing and leadership guidance in the 21st Century. As Richard Branson has said, "Some people believe firms exist to make profits. They have that backwards, firms make profits in order to exist."[5] In other words, there must always be a calling, a higher purpose. The KMM uses purpose as a leadership tool to drive unity, alignment, and congruence, but most importantly, cooperation across organizational boundaries. Purpose enables us to move quickly. A strong sense of purpose is needed for resilience. Purpose is what drives us to get back up off the floor and fight on.

Anticipatory Rather than Merely Reactionary

Lastly, Birkinshaw observes that "resilient organisations are far *less* tolerant of things like test-and-learn, pivoting, iterative development and failure of any sort. Many of the 'Lean start-up' principles, for example, would be anathema to an organisation that puts true resilience at its heart."[6] In other words, anticipatory behavior is resilient! The KMM models the growing switch from reactionary to anticipatory behavior as organizational maturity deepens. Anticipatory risk-management practices are built into the model. Although probing for information is necessary in an emergent condition—such as emerging from crisis—experimental probing takes time and costs money. This can exhaust the resilience of an organization. David has a friend in London whose firm was fired by a client after wasting £2 million on Lean UX experiments, rather than delivering a website design. Resilient firms use modelling techniques such as the Fit-for-Purpose Framework to anticipate customer needs. The answer to a question such as, "Will the new feature be viewed as an improvement by our customers?" shouldn't be something that is left to experimental probing of the market. Models can be used to provide high probabilities of such choices proving correct. There is greater resilience from not spending time and money with experiments when trustworthy information is available from a model. High-maturity organizations use models to improve their resilience.

---

5. Richard Branson, *Screw Business as Usual* (New York: Portfolio/Penguin, 2017), quoting Ray Anderson of Interface Inc. (https://www.goodreads.com/quotes/6997142-for-those-who-think-business-exists-to-make-a-profit)

6. https://www.forbes.com/sites/lbsbusinessstrategyreview/2020/03/28/the-new-boardroom-imperative-from-agility-to-resilience/#2164fe386711

Coping with Crisis

In his recent book, *Upheaval*,[7] Jared Diamond examines resilience at the nation-state level. In this work, he uses a twelve-point list of attributes borrowed from the field of clinical psychology. These attributes are used by psychologists to predict how well an individual will cope with a psychological crisis. Diamond is cautious to suggest that the case studies in his book, all from countries with which he is very familiar—he has lived and worked there, speaks the language, and has many friends there—are just a small sample. He does not make any scientifically robust claims about his analysis. Nevertheless, we are fans of Diamond's earlier works, such as *Collapse*, and he has inspired elements of the KMM's cultural model as well as our approach to Kanban coaching. It was Diamond's work that made it clear that a more liberal culture is required for resilience and reinvention. Hence, despite Diamond's own caution about applying his crisis theory to nation-states, we believe that the same thinking can be applied to organizations.

Here are the twelve criteria used to evaluate how well an individual or an organization can cope with crisis:

1. Acknowledge that there is a crisis.
2. Accept responsibility.
   - Take ownership.
   - Don't play the victim.
3. Build a fence.
   - Ring-fence the good.
   - Focus on the problems.
4. Get emotional and material help:
   - Both normative and structural
5. Use models or archetypes:
   - Case studies
   - Experience reports
6. Develop ego strength (resilience).
7. Do an honest self-appraisal.
8. Learn from a previous experience of crisis:
   - Institutional memory
9. Exhibit patience.
10. Maintain flexibility:
    - Who, Why, What, and How
11. Explicit values are communicated.
12. There is freedom from constraints.

---

7. Jared M. Diamond, *Upheaval: Turning Points for Nations in Crisis* (New York, NY: Back Bay Books, Little Brown and Company, 2020).

For those who have read this volume from the front cover, you should instantly realize that the KMM helps with numbers 2 through 11, fully ten of the twelve points. Let's look at the exceptions first. Can Kanban also help with those?

1. Acknowledge that there is a crisis.

This depends on the leaders in the organization. No framework can take them out of denial or make them accept a situation. However, the KMM is still likely to help. "There is no wishful thinking in Kanban" is core value, and the Kanban Method, along with the KMM's specific practices, provides lots of data to reflect back reality. The feedback mechanisms of the Kanban Cadences provide reflection opportunities. It is hard to stay in denial when you are surrounded by elements of Kanban in action.

12. Freedom from Constraints

Organizational constraints can include regulatory constraints, geographic and political constraints, financial constraints, linguistic constraints, and constraints of skills and capabilities.

For example, when the de Havilland Comet 4 was finally capable of flying across the Atlantic Ocean without falling out of the sky, in 1958,[8] it spelled the end of the transatlantic ocean liner business. Larger businesses, such as P & O, with a portfolio of other shipping interests, could continue, but for smaller, pure-play ocean liner firms operating just one or two ships out of ports like Liverpool or Belfast, the arrival of commercial, transatlantic air travel spelled the end. They were constrained. They could not reinvent themselves as an airline. Equally, the leisure cruising market was yet to emerge. In 1958, the world was still recovering from the austerity of World War II and its aftermath.

There are some constraints with which Kanban simply can't help.

The Enterprise Services Planning body of knowledge does, however, include guidance on corporate strategy and identity. Developing a broad sense of identity is a means to create freedom from constraints and to increase resilience. This is best illustrated by the example of David's own business, the best-known part of which is Kanban University, which licenses Kanban training globally through a network of training and consulting partner companies. The name, identity, and nature of this business is quite constrained. However, the novel coronavirus crisis caused the business to move to an online delivery model and to issue revised training materials designed for online delivery, so Kanban University has shown some resilience despite the constrained nature of its identity.

David's group of businesses comprises a number of other brands and trading entities, including the David J Anderson School of Management and the physical training centers in Seattle and Bilbao, which are free to offer any form of management training and leadership development, not just Kanban. The holding company is known as Mauvius Group. "Mauvius" is a made-up word, formed by conflating the color mauve and the geometric

---

8. https://en.wikipedia.org/wiki/De_Havilland_Comet#Variants

shape Möbius Band: mauve + Möbius = Mauvius. The name is unconstrained. It can mean whatever David wants it to mean. Mauvius Group can be anything it wants to be. Other brands in the group include Blue Hole Press and Kanban University Press, both publishing imprints, which are constrained as publishing businesses, while Mauvisoft is the new mobile application software business. By its nature, it is constrained to be a software company, and as part of the Mauvius Group, it rightly provides software tools that amplify the effectiveness of training and guidance issued by the other businesses in the group. David created resilience across the group of businesses and his portfolio of business interests, although some of the specific business units are more constrained than others.

How Kanban and the KMM Help You Cope with Crisis

Let's look at the other ten attributes to understand fully how Kanban and the KMM help build resilience and enable organizations to better cope with crisis.

2. Accept Responsibility.

Maturity Levels 0 through 2 represent abdication of responsibility or a lack of ownership, or some sense of being victims of circumstance. "Oblivious" implies abdication, or denial. Internally focused behavior at Maturity Levels 1 and 2 implies that the outside is imposing its will upon the organization—pushing work onto it, overburdening it. Accepting responsibility would immediately start to drive adoption of behavior and practices that lead to Maturity Level 3 and beyond.

An organization already at Maturity Level 3 would accept responsibility for its own survival in a crisis and would act to do something about it.

3. Build a Fence.

The very nature of the Kanban Method, and its core principle of "start with what you do now," helps to build a fence. Managed evolution is an approach that seeks only to mutate that which isn't working well, while preserving that which is.

4. Get Emotional and Material Help.

The Kanban University partner network—including the network of Accredited Kanban Consultants, the Kanban Leadership Retreats, and the global Kanban community consisting of 300-plus local and regional meet-up groups—are all places to go looking for help. Books like this one and others can provide inspiration and pragmatic, actionable advice. Kanban tool vendors such as Kanbanize, Swift Kanban, and Nave have all published extensive literature, most of it freely available online.

5. Use Models or Archetypes.

The Kanban Method is a model-driven approach. The KMM is a model. The Fit-for-Purpose Framework is a model. The collection of Kanban and KMM case studies provides archetypes for inspiration. The extensive body of experience reports presented at ten or more years of Kanban conferences around the world provides yet more experience as well as a vast network of people to turn to for advice and support.

6. Ego Strength (Resilience)

We have known for some years that organizational maturity maps directly to an ability to cope with stress, anxiety, and crisis. Under stress, low-maturity organizations tend to lose their discipline, panic, and regress, while high-maturity organizations maintain their discipline and unity—and emerge stronger.

Organizational maturity is a direct analogy to organizational resilience, or social ego strength. High-maturity organizations cope better with crisis.

7. Honest Self-Appraisal

Kanban requires honest self-appraisal from the first encounter with STATIK (systems thinking approach to implementing Kanban) when introducing a workflow kanban system at Maturity Level 2 or 3. Kanban encourages continuous, honest self-appraisal through a focus on externally facing metrics and customer satisfaction, using the Kanban Cadences as feedback mechanisms. Levels in the KMM are defined by observable outcomes. There is no hiding behind practice adoption or affiliation with a belief system.

8. Previous Experience of Crisis

The KMM explicitly encourages institutional memory through the explicit value of narrative. By making time and space to collect, share, and tell the organization's story, previous experience of crises can be preserved in the folklore and legend of the firm.

Kanban and the KMM also encourage loyalty and long-tenured staff by creating a great place to work, providing work that has meaning and purpose, and fostering an environment in which everyone can continue to develop and learn.

9. Patience

Kanban coaching is all about patience. Managed evolutionary change—using the Evolutionary Change Model and the transition sub-level practices—is all about practicing patience so that changes for the better institutionalize. An organization that believes in evolutionary change is a patient organization.

10. Flexibility

The Kanban Maturity Model encourages organizations to show flexibility, to challenge how they do things, what they do, why they do it, and who they are. The KMM actively encourages reinvention and provides the wiring for the organization to enable reinvention. The cultural dimensions and culture-hacking tools provide the means to create a social culture that is flexible, open to change, and prepared to reinvent itself.

11. Explicit Values

The Kanban Method is a values-based approach to improved service delivery and organizational improvement. The KMM explicitly maps values to maturity levels and operationalizes them with decision filters.

The House of Resilience

We believe that resilience is the imperative for organizations in this third decade of the 21st Century. We agree with authors like Julian Birkinshaw, Nassim Taleb, and Jared Diamond. We also believe that resilient, modern, intangible goods; professional services; and knowledge worker organizations can be built on adopting the Kanban Method as a fundamental foundation of that resilience. The pillars of the modern resilient business are a Service-Oriented Organization (SOO), Fitness-for-Purpose (F4P), Enterprise Services Planning (ESP), and Organizational Maturity delivered using the KMM, depicted in Figure 20.1.

Organizational maturity is directly related to social ego strength and organizational resilience. Use the Kanban Maturity Model as your roadmap to build a resilient modern business.

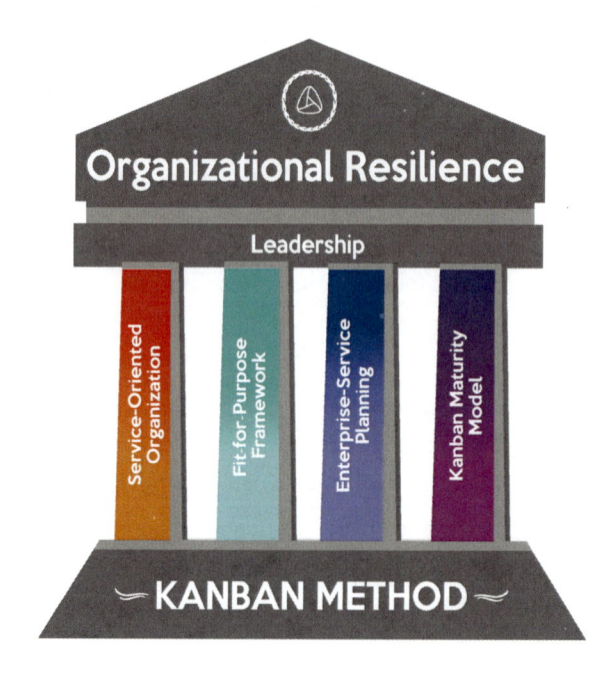

Figure 20.1 The House of Organizational Resilience

Appendices

A | The Kanban Method

Kanban's Three Agendas

Kanban recognizes three types of motivation for getting started with the method, known as the three agendas.
- The **Sustainability** agenda looks inward at the organization and is concerned with the following:
  - Achieving relief from overburdening
  - Producing better quality
  - Taking professional pride in individuals' work and in customer satisfaction
- The **Service Orientation** agenda looks outward from the organization and focuses on performance and customer satisfaction. It addresses management concerns about the following:
  - Committing to delivery and meeting deadlines with confidence
  - Making management decisions with confidence
  - Ensuring a reliable, predictable, and faster service delivery
- The **Survivability** agenda looks to the future and at developing resilience and competitiveness:
  - Making promises that the business can keep
  - Leading the business's strategy and positioning

Service Delivery Principles

Your organization is a network of interdependent services with policies that determine its behavior (see Figure A.1).

Therefore:

1. Understand and focus on the customer's needs and expectations.
2. Manage the work; let workers self-organize around it.
3. Regularly review the network and its policies to improve outcomes.

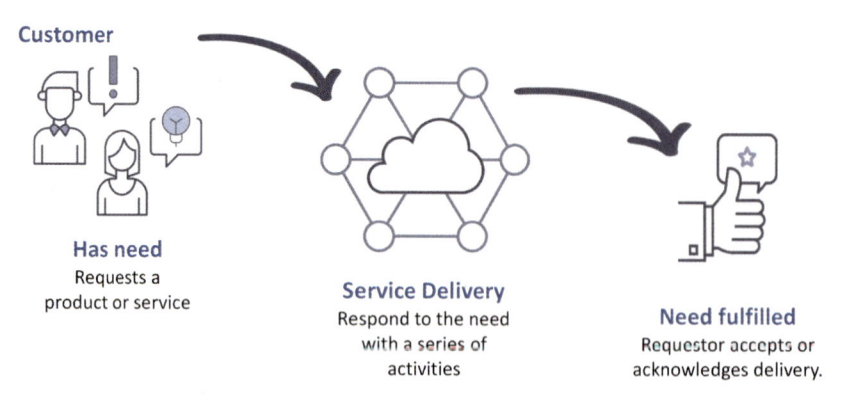

Figure A.1 Conceptually, a modern intangible-goods, services-sector business viewed as a network of services

Kanban Scaling Principles

1. Scale up in a service-oriented fashion one service at a time (Figure A.2 models a network of services).
2. Design each kanban system from the first principles using the systems thinking approach to introducing Kanban (STATIK). Do not attempt to design a grand solution at enterprise scale.
3. Use the Kanban Cadences as the management system that enables balance, which leads to better enterprise services delivery.

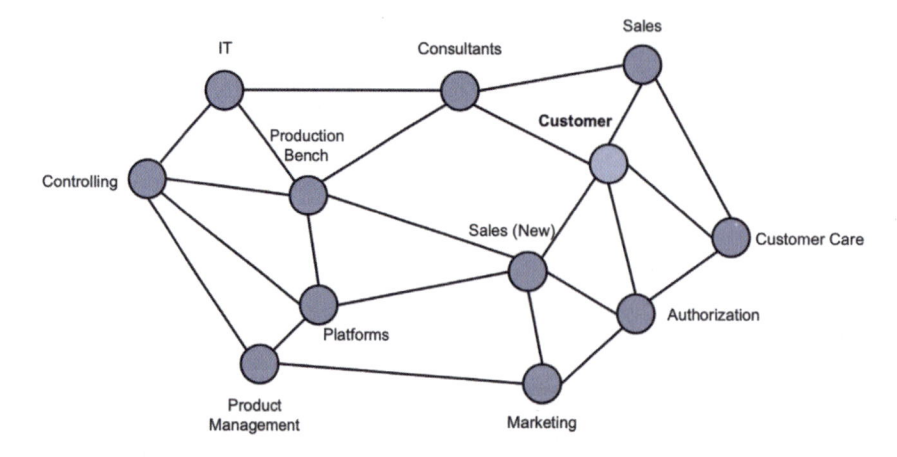

Figure A.2 A network of services modeled at a German bank

Change Management Principles

1. Start with what you do now:
   - Understanding current processes, as actually practiced
   - Respecting existing roles, responsibilities, and job titles
2. Gain agreement to pursue improvement through evolutionary change.
3. Encourage acts of leadership at all levels.

Kanban General Practices

1. Visualize.
2. Limit work-in-progress (with kanban).
3. Manage flow.
4. Make policies explicit.
5. Implement feedback loops.
6. Improve collaboratively, evolve experimentally using models and scientific methods.

STATIK

0. Identify Services.

For each service:

1. Understand what makes the service fit-for-purpose.
2. Understand sources of dissatisfaction regarding current delivery system.
3. Analyze sources of and nature of demand.
4. Analyze current delivery capability.
5. Model the service delivery workflow.
6. Identify and define classes of service.
7. Design the kanban system.
8. Socialize design and negotiate implementation.

B | Integration with Other Models and Methods

The KMM is a model for evolving an organization's culture and management practices to improve customer satisfaction and enable greater business outcomes, resilience, and reinvention. Cultural values and Kanban practices are blended in such a way as to create fast, smooth, and efficient flow of value; improve transparency and collaboration; reduce overburdening of individuals; and achieve predictable delivery on customer expectations. As such, it certainly stands on its own, but it also integrates well with other models that an organization may already be using.

Integration with Lean/TPS

The Kanban Method is arguably much closer to the Toyota Way management system and its Toyota Production System than to Western-authored literature on Lean. Arguably, the Kanban Method is a means to implement the management system and culture of Toyota into professional services, knowledge-worker businesses. Lean literature tends to focus on eliminating waste; value-stream mapping; and industrial engineers designing out wasteful, non-value-adding steps and then deploying new processes into organizations using a managed approach to change. Lean as practiced by American and other Western consulting firms generally does not replicate the employee-empowered "*kaizen* culture" of continuous improvement and fails to take an evolutionary and incremental approach to change driven by shop-floor workers and line managers. The Kanban Method, by comparison, does achieve this *kaizen* culture and replicates the empowered employee–driven approach to change, producing incremental and evolutionary improvement.

Toyota uses three words, which are all translated as "waste" in Western Lean literature: *muda*, meaning non–value adding, *mura*, meaning unevenness, and *muri*, meaning overburdening. Lean has tended to focus on *muda* removal, or reduction of non-value-adding activities. This was relatively effective in industrial, tangible-goods businesses. However, with intangible goods, professional services businesses, many roles are not considered value adding. For example, everything a project manager does would be labeled as non–value adding. If it is known and understood that Lean consultants have arrived to "eliminate waste," people in non-value-adding roles become fearful and resistant.

The Kanban Method differentiates itself from Lean by pursuing *muri*, then *mura*, first relieving individuals, teams, and workflows of overburdening, then focusing on a faster, smoother, even flow. This approach works better with human psychology. First, workers are able to take greater pride in their work and, psychologically, they are relieved of the existential overhead of thinking about too many pieces of work that have been started but remain open and incomplete. Second, by improving predictability, customer satisfaction improves, and workers gain a greater sense of purpose and mastery of their work. Workers like to be relieved of overburdening and they like their workload to flow evenly. Workers do not like to be labeled as "waste."

The Kanban Maturity Model provides a clear and clean integration with Toyota's system. Maturity Levels 0 through 2 are primarily focused on *muri*—relief from overburdening at the individual, team, and workflow levels. Maturity Level 3 is focused on *mura*—achieving evenness of flow. Maturity Level 4 introduces a focus on *muda*, as non-value-adding activities and transaction and coordination costs are reduced to improve economic performance. Maturity Level 5 produces a full implementation of *kaizen* culture with enterprise scale, evolutionary improvements being driven from the ground up, in pursuit of ever more fit-for-purpose products and services. Maturity Level 6 delivers on effective strategy deployment, or *hoshin kanri*, by providing the means to question the how, what, why, and who of the enterprise and, through leadership, strategic planning, and communication of intent, redefine any or all of these.

Integration with the Real World Risk Model

Nassim Nicholas Taleb introduced a taxonomy for assessing the risk exposure of individuals and corporations with his series of books known collectively as The Incerto: *Fooled by Randomness*, *The Black Swan*, *Antifragile*, and *Skin In The Game*. In 2015, he formed the Real World Risk Institute with a goal of democratizing risk management. For this reason, we've chosen to name Taleb's model the Real World Risk Model as a means to refer to its elements collectively.

Taleb uses four adjectives to define the risk exposure of four types of entities: fragile, resilient, robust, and antifragile.

A fragile entity is so exposed to the occurrence of a relatively probable event that, if the event occurs, the entity will cease to exist or suffer a financial bankruptcy.

A resilient entity lives in an environment with a high probability of an undesirable event that, were it to occur, would inflict a severe blow to the entity. However, it doesn't die from the severe blow and is capable of picking itself up, brushing itself off, healing its wounds, and recovering.

A robust entity has prepared itself such that it expects bad things to happen and, when they do, it is sufficiently well prepared that it rebuffs or deflects any damage and carries on relatively unharmed from the impact of the event.

An antifragile entity is one that responds to the stress of undesirable events by changing, adapting, and improving. An antifragile organization strives to be continually fit-for-purpose and has the ability to mutate in response to changing externalities that threaten its existence.

These ideas map to the Kanban Maturity Model as follows:

- Organizations at Maturity Levels 0 through 2 are fragile. They are extremely exposed to risks and have little to no concept of risk nor capability at risk management. They are exposed to single points of failure such that a single leader, manager, or individual contributor must play the role of hero during periods of stress.
- Maturity Level 3 organizations have an emerging capability at risk management, primarily focused on trimming the tail of lead time distributions to improve predictability. Level 3 organizations also have a strong sense of purpose. They have unity and alignment behind that sense of purpose. Level 3 organizations have a reason to pick themselves up, shake themselves down, and carry on after the impact of an undesirable event. Level 3 organizations are not exposed to single points of failure nor reliant on single individuals for their survival. Level 3 organizations have resilience.
- At Maturity Level 4, the superior proficiency in quantitative analysis of processes and capabilities, coupled with qualitative analysis techniques in managing business risks and other externalities, enables risk hedging through capacity allocation, demand shaping, class of service provisions, real option pricing, advanced scheduling with dynamic reservation systems, and other capabilities within the Enterprise Services Planning (ESP) body of knowledge. Because Level 4 organizations are adequately risk hedged, they are robust. At Maturity Level 5, the robustness is improved. Level 5 organizations can rebuff bigger impacts through their superior economic performance.
- Antifragility, the ability to mutate as a response to stress from the environment, starts to emerge as early as Maturity Level 3 or 4. However, the full capability isn't realized until Maturity Level 6. It comes from the feedback loops of Strategy

Review and Operations Review and the cultural ability to question how, what, why, and who. Level 6 organizations can reinvent themselves, reinventing their purpose and identity, if necessary, in response to stresses from the market. As such, they have long-term survivability. They are antifragile. Maturity Levels 3 and 4 organizations exhibit lesser forms of antifragility, capable of reinventing their processes and their product or service offerings while sticking rigidly to their original purpose and identity.

Integration with Agendashift

Agendashift is a change-management approach developed by Mike Burrows. It is outcome oriented, values based, and framework agnostic. Its non-prescriptive form inspires collaborative generation of alternatives for improving a particular organizational situation and then collaborating on the agreed actions.

The three main components of Agendashift are the following:

1. The *True North* statement:
   Everyone is able to work consistently at their best:
   - Individuals, teams, between teams, across the organization
   - Right conversations, right people, best possible moment
   - Needs anticipated, met at just the right time
2. The Agendashift delivery assessment, which is an organizational values-assessment tool
3. The set of the following principles:
   1. Start with needs.
   2. Agree on outcomes.
   3. Keep the agenda for change visible.
   4. Manage options, testing assumptions.
   5. Organize for clarity, speed, and mutual accountability.

Both the KMM and Agendashift are *outcome oriented* and *values based*.

Consultants familiar with Agendashift can use the Delivery Assessment Survey to complement their KMM-based understanding of the organizations they work with. More precisely, they can use it to comprehend better the strengths of the following values in the organization: Transparency, Balance, Collaboration, Customer Focus, Flow, Leadership, Understanding, Agreement, and Respect.

In addition, the following Agendashift workshops can be used with the KMM to define the roadmap for organizational change:

- **Discovery** Understanding where we are, current and future needs, and where we'd like to be
- **Exploration** Identifying change opportunities
- **Mapping** Visualizing our plans

- **Elaboration** Generating and framing actions
- **Operation** Making sure that progress is made

Integration with Mission Command

The Mission Command/Maneuver Warfare/*Auftragstaktik* is a doctrine or system of command (system of giving orders) taught to military officers throughout the NATO forces. It is most strongly associated with the US Marine Corps. Mission Command originated in the Prussian armies of the 19th Century; it was developed to enable armies to move quickly, and in a coordinated fashion, as both the scale increased and the effectiveness of weaponry improved dramatically. Mission Command creates empowerment without loss of control. It enables trust at large scale and coordination of action from organizational units acting with autonomy.

A key concept in Mission Command is that of *Einheit*, meaning unity and alignment. The German-language term is rooted in the origins of the method with Helmut von Moltke, a key figure in the Prussian military throughout most of the 19th Century. With Kanban, *Einheit* is required to achieve Maturity Level 3 at any scale larger than a small team. It should be introduced by leaders in Maturity Level 2 organizations. The *Einheit*, or unity of purpose, should be focused on the customer—their work orders, their demands, and their expectations. The Kanban value of Customer Service is required to provide the unity and alignment. Leaders must learn to communicate the goal clearly—to serve the customer better, with a better product, designed better, implemented better, and with better service delivery.

Integration with Capability Maturity Model Integration® (CMMI) v2.0

CMMI® v2.0 is a collection of best practices, organized in Practice Areas that are focused on improving process consistency to achieve business objectives related to performance, quality, cost, schedule, and functionality. The Practice Areas integrate content from the former CMMI for Development, for Services, and for Acquisition models in addition to the People–CMM model. In this way, CMMI 2.0 aims to provide a holistic view, allowing organizations to select the areas of improvement that are most relevant for them. The primary focus of the model as a whole is on improving an organization's business benefits, performance, and ultimately, the customers' needs.

The practices define what to do to improve performance, leaving the organizations to discover and decide how they will implement them.

Practice areas that deal with improving performance and activities in a specific domain are organized into capability areas. Similarly, four categories of capability areas are defined that address common challenges businesses face when developing a product or delivering a service.

The categories and the capability areas grouped under them are as follows:
1. Doing
    - Ensuring quality
    - Engineering and developing products
    - Delivering and managing services
    - Selecting and managing suppliers
2. Managing
    - Planning and managing work
    - Managing business resilience
    - Managing the workforce
3. Improving
    - Improving performance
    - Building and sustaining capability
4. Enabling
    - Supporting implementation
    - Managing safety
    - Managing security

A total of forty-two practice areas make up the CMMI 2.0 model.

The organizations select the practice areas that are important for them. They can achieve a different capability level for each of the selected practice areas. The capability level is determined by the performance and the amount of improvement gained in an individual practice area.

Maturity Levels are determined by the capability improvements in a predefined set of practice areas. CMMI 2.0 defines six maturity levels:

0. Incomplete
   Incomplete approach to meeting the intent of the Practice Area (PA)
1. Initial
   Initial approach to meeting the intent of the PA
2. Managed
   Simple but complete set of practices that address the full intent of the PA
3. Defined
   Uses organizational standards and tailoring to address project and work characteristics
4. Quantitatively Managed
   Uses statistical and other quantitative techniques to achieve quality and process performance objectives for the PA of focus
5. Optimizing
   Optimizes achievement of quality and process performance objectives

As with the KMM, each maturity level builds on the previous one.

The KMM practices develop teams' sense of unity and purpose across the workflow. The practices are focused on balancing demand and capability of the system and optimizing the value stream and economic outcomes by means of a strong prioritization and triage discipline.

The KMM defines seven maturity levels. It extends the CMMI levels with ML6, which is about developing a congruent business capable of reinventing itself in adverse circumstances. The names of the maturity levels characterize the entire organization, not only their process perspective. Specifically, the maturity levels are:

- ML0 Oblivious
- ML1 Team-Focused
- ML2 Customer-Driven
- ML3 Fit-for-Purpose
- ML4 Risk-Hedged
- ML5 Market Leader
- ML6 Built for Survival

KMM complements the CMMI Capability Areas in the following ways:

- Doing
  - Kanban introduces the service-oriented approach to managing work. This implies that service delivery and project development are seen through a collection of interdependent services; for example: design a feature, develop functionality, test functionality, and so on. Each service must be appropriately staffed and managed in order to deliver, on time, the expected outcome to the next service in the value chain.
  - The essence of Kanban, and hence, the KMM, is delivering services that meet customer expectations in a sustainable manner and further developing business capabilities to hedge risks, build market leadership, and achieve long-term survival.
  - Communication at a team level becomes fluent once the habit of conducting the Kanban Meetings is established. The visual aspects of the kanban systems and the Kanban Cadences facilitate communication and alignment not only between different teams but also with stakeholders, as well as with people at different hierarchy levels within the organization.
  - Establishing team norms and shared processes, and coordination within and among integrated teams, are an organic result of using integrated kanban boards.
- Managing and Enabling
  - Visual kanban boards facilitate real-time understanding of the current state of projects and services, issues that impede their development and delivery, dependencies on other stakeholders, and risks of delay. The time needed for obtaining status reports and coordinating meetings shrinks significantly.

- Having a real-time, visual, and shared understanding of the status of the individual projects and services focuses monitoring and control activities on what affects the value delivery flow and how to resolve the impediments.
- Kanban establishes explicit policies for prioritizing and managing work. Therefore, team members have autonomy to decide what work to do next, so the project manager's job becomes more about resolving blocking issues, ensuring smooth flow between stages, scheduling, and coordinating with stakeholders and other teams. The Service Manager's job includes proper capacity allocation to ensure that demand is processed in a timely manner.
- Instead of using discrete task estimation, in Kanban the delivery date of a work item is forecast based on historical data of lead time for the corresponding work type as well as by using Little's Law.
- Kanban uses classes of service that are defined based on understanding the business risks associated with the work items, particularly their cost of delay.
- Risk evaluation is based on previous blocker clustering and analysis, which brings a thorough understanding of the impediments for the workflow and eliminates the ambiguity of the probability and impact parameters.

- Improving
  - The purpose of improving the flow of valuable work and delivering on customer expectations is to focus the process-improvement effort on the aspects that are important to the business. This involves eliminating unnecessary over-processing and reducing transaction and coordination costs. In addition, it implies appropriately integrating individual processes or sub-processes to streamline accomplishing the expected outcome.
  - A positive consequence of this value-driven process improvement is that people understand the need for establishing defined processes and see the value of continuously improving them. This facilitates process adoption and reduces the effort of managing change.
  - Project- and service-level processes are defined directly on kanban boards. Service-specific performance metrics are supported directly from kanban board data.
  - Process performance objectives at the project, service, and organizational levels are supported directly from kanban data.

Using CMMI and KMM practices together helps product-development and service-delivery organizations increase process agility and better align business and process objectives.

In addition, the Kanban principle "Start with what you do now, respecting current roles and responsibilities" facilitates its adoption and is, in fact, a critical enabling factor for organizations with well-defined hierarchical structures that pursue agility but are not keen on making a radical change and restructuring.

C | Understanding Lead Time

Understanding lead time is necessary as a means to break out from Maturity Level 1, Team-Focused, and move to Maturity Level 2, Customer-Driven, and then beyond to Maturity Level 3, Fit-for-Purpose. Lead time isn't a single number; rather, it is a probability distribution because the time something takes from commitment to delivery is always non-deterministic. Effectively managing a professional-services business requires a basic understanding of mathematics not typically included in the curriculum for secondary education. The nature of the observed probability density functions (PDFs) associated with lead time is also not commonly taught in undergraduate-level one- or two-credit classes in statistics. Hence, it is necessary to provide some mathematical background to underpin the application of lead time distribution functions to real-world problems such as forecasting and managing cost of delay risk.

Definition

We define lead time as starting at the mutually agreed commitment point and continuing until an item is ready for delivery. In other words, we start counting lead time from the point when a customer can legitimately expect us to work on an item until we can legitimately expect the customer to take delivery. Any additional waiting time on the delivery end is not counted. This definition is unambiguous and works consistently for any workflow or service.

You should, however, recognize that this definition works reliably at Maturity Level 3 and deeper, while at lower maturity levels it is problematic. At lower maturity levels, the commitment point is often ambiguous and at best asynchronous; that is, the customer or the upstream part of the workflow commits a request before the delivery or downstream service workflow is ready to commit. In this type of asynchronous commitment, we measure lead time from the second half of the commitment, the point when the delivery workflow pulls the item into WIP. In Maturity Level 2 workflows, often there isn't a strong concept of commitment, and hence, there is a tendency to measure lead time from the point a work item is submitted. This is legitimate for internal shared services and other similar systems where the work is irrefutable.

For clarity, and most relevant in a lower-maturity world or a maturing and slowly scaling-out Kanban implementation, we use the terms "customer lead time," as defined above, and "system lead time," as a degenerate form, describing the time from when an item is pulled until it is ready for delivery. Customer lead time (or just plain lead time in a higher-maturity implementation) is a fitness criterion, while system lead time can only ever be a health indicator or an improvement driver. The difference between customer lead time and system lead time is always a non-deterministic period of waiting on the front end, the time between when the customer submits a request—or believes it was committed—to when it is actually pulled into the kanban system and actually is committed. In a Maturity Level 3 or deeper kanban implementation with synchronous commitment, customer lead time equals system lead time: they are equivalent. The effect of a difference in customer versus system lead time is that the customer lead time suffers from a longer, fatter tail, and possibly also has a higher value for location, all of which is explained in the next section.

The term "lead time," therefore, can be explained this way: "If you know when you need to take delivery, the lead time is the amount of time in advance you need to place an order to expect delivery on or before when you need the item" or, simply, the period of time that commitment must precede delivery.

Nature of Lead Time

The inconvenient truth is that lead time is not a single number; rather, it is a random number defined by a probability distribution function.[1] The good news is that by recognizing the shape of the lead time distribution, we can learn a lot about the nature of the work and the delivery risks associated with it. This enables us to make effective risk-management and planning decisions that provide for a reasonably optimal economic outcome given the uncertainty involved.

Figure C.1 shows two histograms of lead time data from real kanban system implementations. The x axis shows the number of days of lead time, and the y axis shows the number of occurrences of that time within the sample data set (the number of items pulled through the kanban system). The one on the left is from an IT operations group and the one on the right is from a software product development team. The one on the left is said to be

---

1. Technically, it's a probability density function.

fat tailed: there is a long, visible tail stretching out to the right along the *x* axis. Generally speaking, fat tailed is undesirable, risky, and makes planning difficult. The one on the right is said to be thin tailed: there isn't a long, visible tail running off to the right along the *x* axis. This naming convention can seem counterintuitive to non-mathematicians. The truth is that mathematically, these tails run to infinity. Hence, if you can see the tail, it must be fat—a thin tail is effectively invisible along the *x* axis. These concepts of fat-tailed and thin-tailed lead time distributions are very important. Knowing which one you have in your kanban system makes a vital difference in planning, risk management, and the likelihood of achieving customer satisfaction and being viewed as a trustworthy service provider.

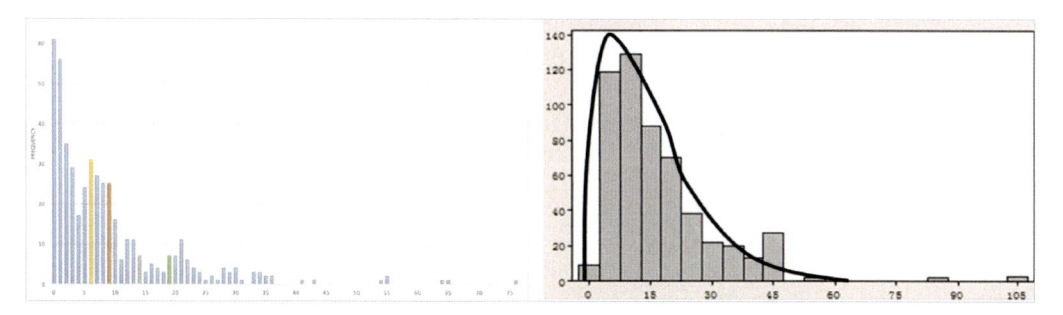

Figure C.1 Two examples of lead time distributions

Assuming you have single-modal data (see below), there are some simple ratios that indicate the likelihood that you have a thin-tailed or fat-tailed distribution:

$$\frac{(98\%ile - location)}{(50\%ile - location)} >= 5.6 => \textit{fat tailed}$$

$$\frac{(98\%ile - location)}{(50\%ile - location)} < 5.6 => \textit{thin tailed}$$

For convenience, you will sometimes see these written in a simplified form, assuming location = 0 and that the 98 percent is effectively the end of the tail you can see. Hence,

$$\frac{tail}{median} >= 5.6 => \textit{fat tailed}$$

$$\frac{tail}{median} < 5.6 => \textit{thin tailed}$$

These appear in the poster for Triage Tables available from Kanban University.
A further sanity check is available for thin-tailed distributions,

$$\frac{(98\%ile - location)}{mode - location} < 16 => \textit{thin tailed}$$

or simplified as

$$\frac{tail}{mode} < 16 => \textit{thin tailed}$$

This formula is not valid for fat-tailed distributions.

These results are produced through a thorough analysis of the behavior and attributes of the Weibull function, which is not included here.

Interpreting a Curve

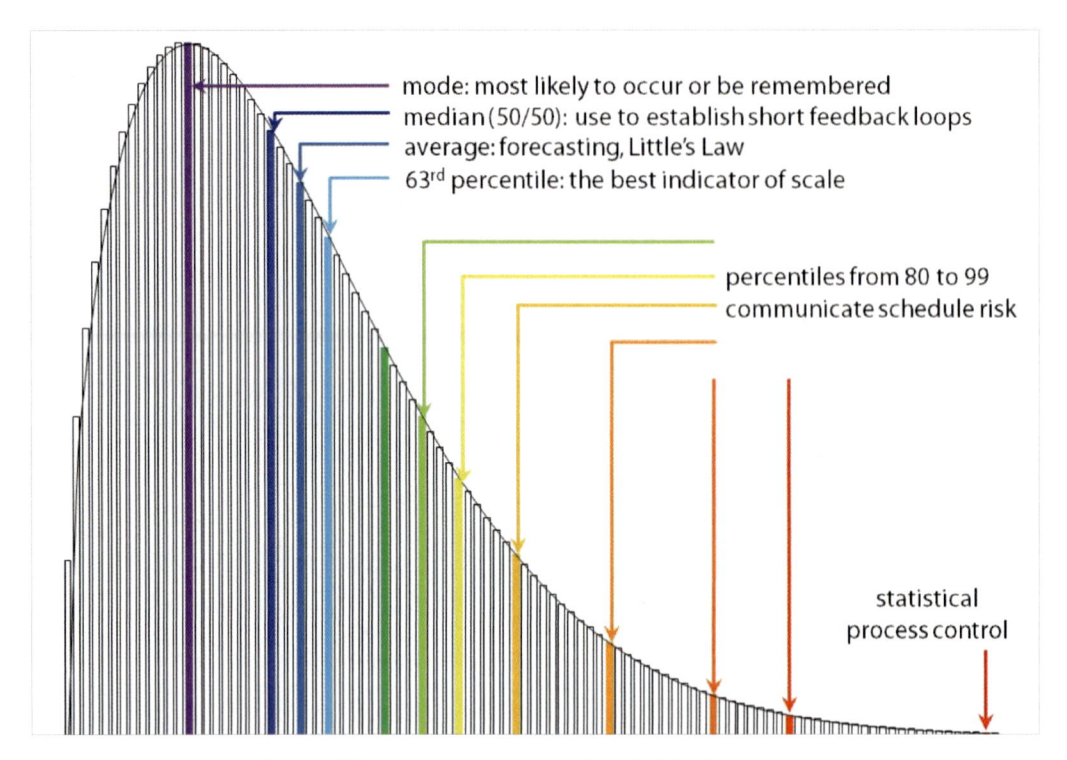

Figure C.2 Interpreting a lead time distribution curve

The mode is the top of the hill (purple in Figure C.2), the most commonly occurring lead time in the data set. The psychological impact is that it is the most memorable. If the mode is fifteen days, and you ask someone how long things typically take, they are likely to answer that it's usually around fifteen days because this is the most memorable, dominant result.

The median is the 50th percentile. If the median is twenty days, it means that half of the items processed took less than twenty days, while the other half took twenty or more days. This leads to the psychological result of "on average, things take twenty days" because half take less than twenty, the other half more. When humans use the term "average" to report a phenomenon they experience physically, emotionally, and with their sensory perception and limbic brain, they are almost certainly reporting their experience of the median.

The mean is the arithmetic average: sum up the value of all the data points and divide by the number of points. In plain language, the word "average" is usually used to refer to this arithmetic mean. Humans use this term correctly when they are referring to something they experience as mathematics and are processing with the logical brain, their prefrontal cortex. The mean tends to accelerate away from the mode and the median as the tail extends farther to the right with higher data points (work items with longer lead times). A fat tail affects the mean much more than it affects the median and is unlikely to impact the mode at all. Understanding this is important for planning, risk management, and customer satisfaction.

Planning is affected because simple forecasting equations, such as Little's Law and the use of regression to the mean, require using the mean. Just a few high-value data points skew the mean upward and may dramatically affect the accuracy of a forecast.

It is important to remember this simple mantra, "The risk is always in the tail." Fat-tailed distributions require a different approach to managing risk. The next section explains this in greater depth.

Fat tails affect customer satisfaction. The impact of a single long lead time, a single high-value data point, can destroy customer trust. For example, one item has a mode of ten, a median of twenty, and a mean of thirty; as a customer, I ask, "When will my request be ready?" and I am told, "We usually process items in fifteen to twenty days." I then wait 155 days—or ten times longer than I'd been told to expect. Burned by this one bad experience, I no longer trust the service delivery. Consequently, every future request I make will have a deadline attached to it and penalties for failure to deliver.

Figure C.2 also illustrates a set of percentile points as the tail stretches to the right; for example, the 85th percentile, or the value where 85 percent of the data points are to the left (and lower), while 15 percent are to the right and of higher value. This is illustrated again in Figure C.3. The curve in Figure C.2 is said to be right skewed. Again, this may seem counterintuitive, as the bulk of the distribution appears to be on the left.

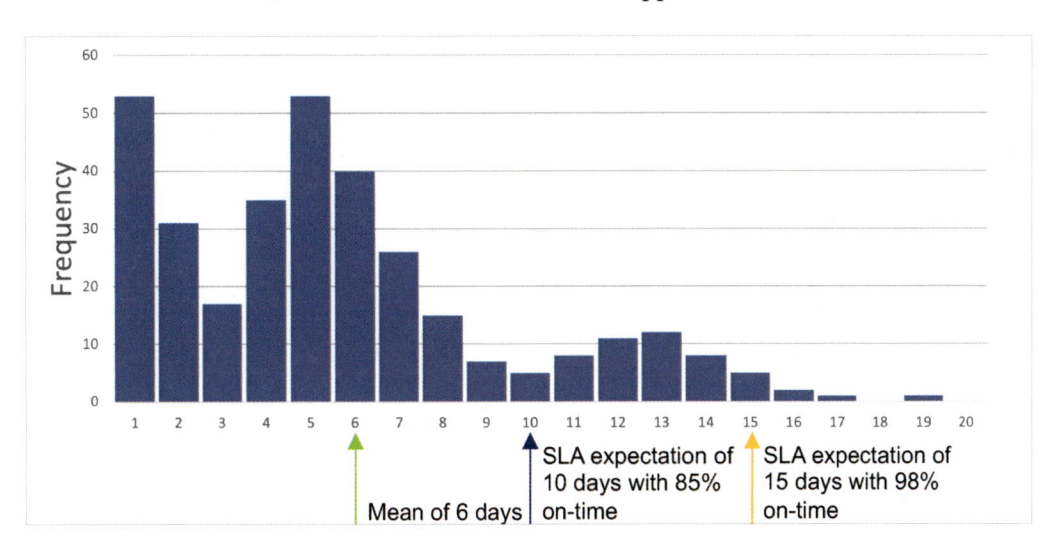

Figure C.3 Lead time distribution showing service level agreements

Figure C.3 shows a mean of six days, and the 85th percentile is ten days, indicating that six out of seven items are completed in ten days or less, while one in seven takes longer. The 98th percentile of fifteen days indicates that only one item in fifty takes longer than this. We find that for most knowledge work—intangible goods industries—there is a psychological acceptance level of six out of seven. Therefore, the 85th percentile is a very powerful tool. Trust can be established by delivering six out of seven items within a promised period (e.g., ten days), providing the impact of missing the promised date is not severe. So, psychologically, I can trust a service with six out of seven on-time deliveries within a service level expectation (SLE), providing the tail is thin and the penalty for exceeding ten days is only a few days more. Thin-tailed lead time distributions are trustworthy; fat-tailed distributions are not.

Multi-Modal Data

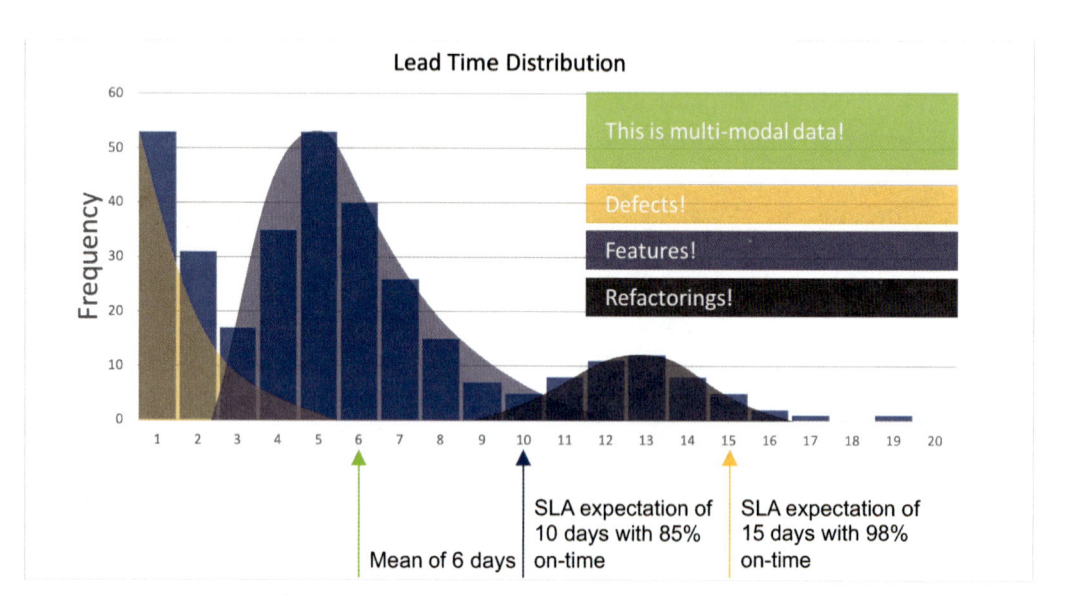

Figure C.4 Multi-modal data

If a curve has several peaks, it is said to be multi-modal. When this occurs in a kanban system's lead time distribution, it is usually an indication of multiple work item types. In the example in Figure C.4, there are three types: defect fixes, new features, and code and systems architecture refactoring. When this occurs, it is much better to filter the data set for only one work item type and obtain multiple lead time curves, each of which has only one peak and is therefore single modal.

Figure C.5 shows how the data in Figure C.4 look once filtered for each type of work.

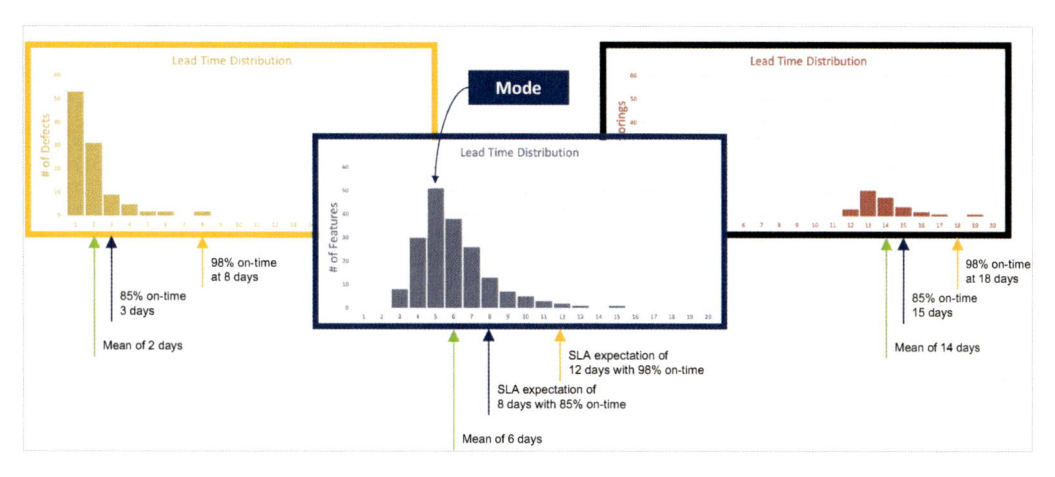

Figure C.5 Filtering the data by work item type

It is important to be able to report the current capability for a kanban system. A single number isn't an acceptable answer. Three pieces of data are required:

1. The mode to median: Most items are completed in approximately fifteen (mode) to twenty (median) days.
2. A high percentile, such as the 85th: Six out of seven items are completed within thirty (85th percentile) days.
3. Is it a thin- or fat-tailed distribution?

In order to use functions of averages such as Little's Law for forecasting or capacity allocation, it is necessary that the concept of an average is a meaningful number within a pragmatic quantity of data points. This is not the case for a fat-tailed distribution. Fat tails exclude us from using techniques such as capacity allocation and linear regression of delivery rate for forecasting. The mathematical explanation behind these observations follows.

Mathematical Properties of Lead Time Curves

As hinted at above in the advice for recognizing thin-tailed versus fat-tailed lead time distributions, lead time curves have been observed to have a set of mathematical properties that map from the rather Gaussian range of bell curve–like functions through to the Pareto range of power-law functions. The work of Troy Magennis revealed that the Weibull function provided a very useful means to map this range of curves using a single parameterized equation. This groundbreaking discovery proved immensely useful in helping us understand the mathematical properties of lead time and as a means to classify and categorize risk. It gave us a way to understand when equations of averages are appropriate, both in planning and forecasting and in product and risk management. This section explains the mathematical properties of Gaussian and Pareto curves, as well as the Weibull function, which integrates both into a single spectrum.

The Weibull Function

The Weibull distribution function, shown in Figure C.6, is named after Swedish mathematician Waloddi Weibull.[2] It turns out to be exceptionally useful, allowing us to map an entire universe of risk and probability distributions. The Weibull function enables us to model the entire set of domains that we see in project, program, portfolio, service delivery, and product management, namely, Gaussian, Super-exponential, and Pareto, by varying the shape parameter kappa (κ):

$$2.0 < \kappa <= 4.0 \quad \text{Gaussian range}$$
$$1.0 < \kappa <= 2.0 \quad \text{Super-exponential range}$$
$$\kappa = 1.0 \quad \text{Exponential function}$$
$$\kappa < 1.0 \quad \text{Pareto range}$$

$$f(x; \lambda, \kappa) = \begin{cases} \frac{\kappa}{\lambda} \left(\frac{x}{\lambda}\right)^{\kappa-1} e^{(x/\lambda)^{\kappa}} & x \geq 0, \\ 0 & x < 0, \end{cases}$$

Figure C.6 Weibull distribution function

Further, we like to divide the Pareto range into near-exponential, or sub-exponential, and the more extreme power laws of the full Pareto range. For example, a sub-exponential distribution may have a mode of 1 and a tail stretching to 100 (or 1×10^2). In this range, using established project management and process improvement techniques, it's possible to affect the distribution, modifying it to become super-exponential. More extreme Pareto distributions may have tails with values such as 1×10^{13}. In such an extreme domain, it is not possible to hack the distribution function into the super-exponential range, and an entirely different set of risk-management approaches must be deployed. Figure C.7 shows four domains, breaking the Pareto range into the sub-exponential (hackable) range and the extreme power law range.

In an ideal world, where a worker is never pre-empted, never interrupted, never multitasks, and is never blocked, the length of time to complete pieces of work of a similar type is Gaussian distributed. However, the real world isn't like that. Workers are interrupted and work does get blocked and delayed. As there is no such thing as negative delay, all delays add to the time needed to complete work, and the consequence is that all lead time distributions are right skewed. In a mature, well-managed kanban system with smooth flow, the lead time distribution tends to be in the super-exponential range, with a kappa (κ) in the range 1.4 to 1.6. We often use κ = 1.5 as a good approximation or guess for the shape of a Maturity Level 3 or 4 kanban system. In the right-hand chart of Figure C.1, κ = 1.4.

---

2. https://en.wikipedia.org/wiki/Weibull_distribution

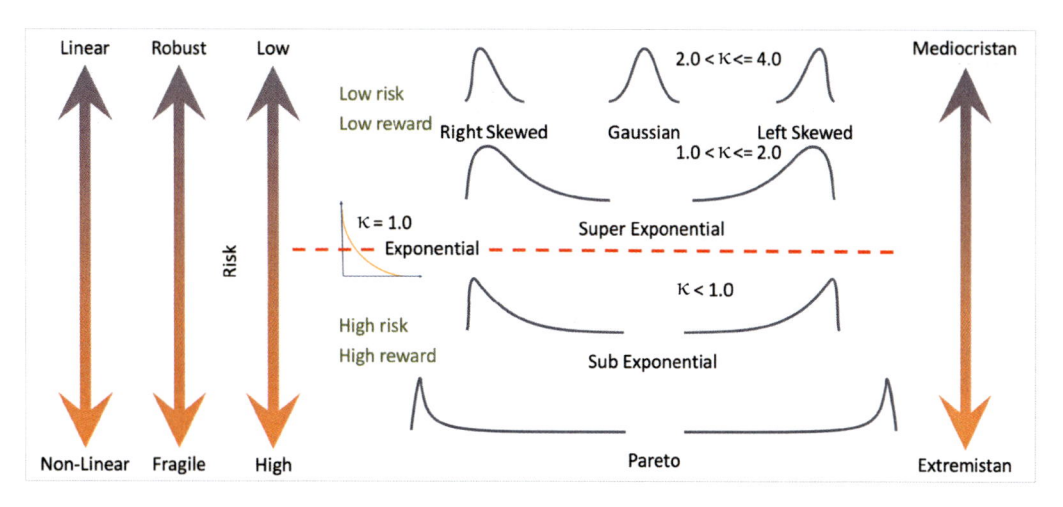

Figure C.7 Four domains of Pareto distributions

In less mature workflows, Maturity Level 2, the lead time tends to be sub-exponential, as flow is not well managed. In complex networks of interdependent services with lots of dependencies, work tends to get delayed often and the lead time tends to be sub-exponential. In the left-hand chart of Figure C.1, κ = 0.8.

To better understand the risks and what management practices are needed to mitigate them, we need to understand a little more about the mathematical properties of these ranges of probability distributions.

Gaussian Range

The key property of the Gaussian range is that both the head and tail of the function are asymptotic to the *x* axis (Figure C.8). Gaussian functions depart from the *x* axis and arrive back to the *x* axis. In a perfect bell curve, κ = 4.0. In skewed curves, kappa is in the range 2.0 < κ < 4.0; closer to 2.0 creates a greater skew.

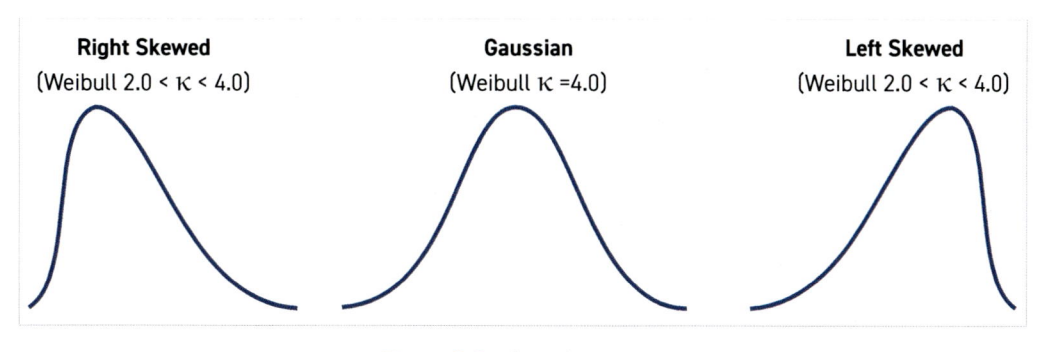

Figure C.8 Gaussian curves

The central limit theorem (also known as the law of large numbers) applies and is useful in this range. Regression to the mean within a 5 to 10 percent error is typically possible with fifteen to thirty data points, depending on the amount of skew. Gaussian-distributed data, on average, produces a linear line. Hence, linear regression is a reasonable technique. In risk management, Gaussian-distributed data sets and linear payoff functions, or risk functions, are synonymous. This is why Gaussian distributions are considered boring—Mediocristan.

The pro of Gaussian data is that it is easy to work with, easy to model, and simple to forecast with linear regression. The con, however, is counterintuitive. We need a large number of data points to have confidence in the range, or spread, of the function—its alpha—and to have confidence in the value of the mean.

Figure C.9 shows the spread of the Gaussian curve and its attribute alpha, α, describing its spread or range. The greater the alpha, the more data points are needed to regress within a reasonable variance of the mean. Models of real-world phenomena that exhibit Gaussian properties are sensitive to the value of alpha. Forecasts can be damagingly inaccurate if the wrong assumptions for mean and alpha are made. It can be necessary to have 1,000 to 2,000 data points in order to have strong confidence in the value of alpha.

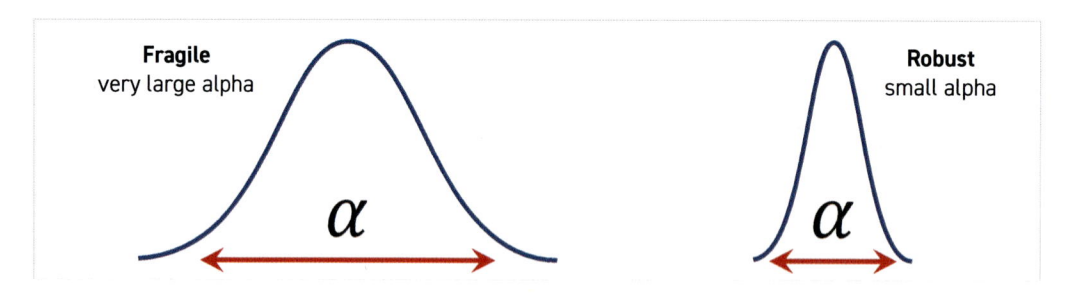

Figure C.9 Alphas of Gaussian curves

This creates an interesting dichotomy for Gaussian data; we need very few current data points to model and forecast, and the forecasting can be done with simple algebra. However, we need a much larger set of data points to have confidence in our model—our estimate of the shape of the curve. This makes working with Gaussian data problematic in real life. There is risk of model error—risk that we assume a narrow alpha when, in fact, we have a much broader one. When that happens, project plans are wildly inaccurate.

In real life, we know that kanban system delivery rates (also known as productivity rate, velocity, or throughput rate) are Gaussian distributed. We also know that the liquidity of a kanban system, the volatility in the rate of pull within the system, is Gaussian distributed. So, the rate of movement of work items is Gaussian at both a fine-grained level within the system and at the whole system level. This is a useful property when it comes to sizing input buffers, or reservation systems, or dependency buffers (parking lots).

Typical Gaussian functions observed in service delivery and project management look like the one in Figure C.10, right skewed and exhibiting a spread of two times above and below the mean.

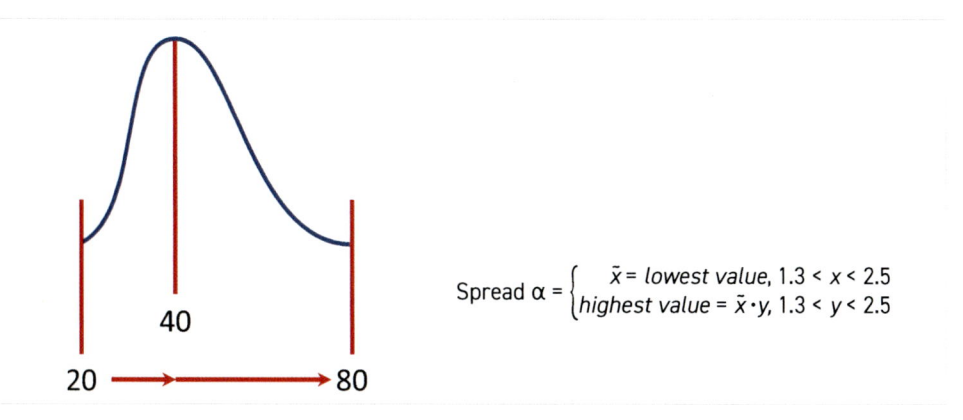

Spread $\alpha = \begin{cases} \tilde{x} = \text{lowest value}, 1.3 < x < 2.5 \\ \text{highest value} = \tilde{x} \cdot y, 1.3 < y < 2.5 \end{cases}$

Figure C.10 Right-skewed Gaussian curve

(Service) Delivery Rates typically exhibit an alpha in a range where the median = $x \times$ lowest value, $1.3 < x < 2.5$, and the highest value = median × y, $1.3 < y < 2.5$. For alphas in this range, sixteen to thirty data points are sufficient for the central limit theorem to produce a relative error in regression to the mean of less than 10 percent. Or, linear regression of the mean value, twenty to twenty-five data points into the future are sufficient to produce a plan that is "fit-for-purpose." #noEstimates works when you project approximately twenty-five data points into the future. If you have weekly velocity data, then a forecast over six months (twenty-six data points) will be accurate using linear regression; there is no added benefit from a Monte Carlo simulation.

Super-Exponential Range

The key property of the super-exponential range is that both the head and tail of the function are asymptotic to different axes, the head to the y axis, the tail to the x axis. Super-exponential functions depart from the axis and arrive back to the x axis. They have kappa in the range $1.0 < \kappa \leq 2.0$, as shown in Figure C.11. A kappa closer to 1.0 has a longer, fatter tail. Super-exponential functions aggregate to Gaussian with enough data points, and the concept of an average, or mean, is still meaningful.

Super Exponential
Weibull ($1.0 < \kappa < 2.0$)

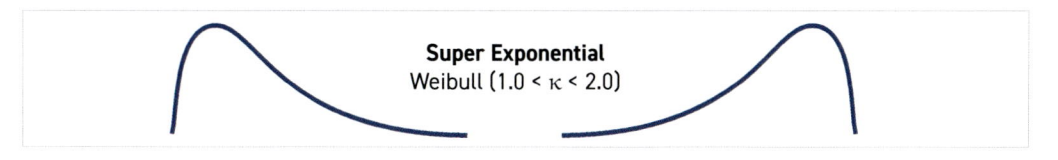

Figure C.11 Super-exponential range of Gaussian function

As shown in Figure C.11, the mode to tail ratio should be less than 16 and the median to tail ratio should be less than 6, assuming a location of 0. On the pro side, it is less sensitive to errors in alpha and hence, useful for modeling from relatively small data sets—eleven historical data points are often good enough, approximately thirty data points produce robust results with little model error (i.e., we have high confidence in the shape of the curve). The con is that linear regression of mean isn't useful until you have around eighty or more data points. Hence, it is riskier to use it with Little's Law—an equation of averages. For example, if we plan to use Little's Law to establish a capacity allocation, and on a monthly basis we need to meet our customer expectations about six months out of every seven, then we would want to know that the average throughput through that lane of the kanban board is at least eighty items per month. This would give us robust, predictable, trustworthy results. If we have lower throughput, we expose ourselves to some fragility—some risk that we will let customers down more often than is desirable.

Lead time distributions from well-managed kanban systems are usually super-exponential. Kanban system lead times tend to have κ ~= 1.5. Troy Magennis has reported that Scrum lead times measured only within a sprint tend to have κ ~= 1.2 (longer tailed, riskier than kanban). It is unclear what might cause this phenomenon at what is essentially a Maturity Level 1, team level, workflow. The most reasonable explanation is a lack of "focus." In Scrum, "focus" is a proxy for controlling WIP. Guidance is that a team shouldn't start too much all at the same time. A lack of focus increases multitasking and hence, fattens the tail of the lead time distribution. Note: this data reported by Troy Magennis did not reflect customer lead time, only local system lead time within a Scrum sprint tracking system.

In general, this super-exponential curve shape is associated with lead times for work with few external dependencies.

Figure C.12 shows the results of a simulation performed by Alexei Zheglov, mapping the median sample error for regression to the mean of a super-exponential distribution with κ = 1.5, using the popular and well-established central limit theorem and a new formula from Nicholas Nassim Taleb, known as the pre-asymptotic formula. The pre-asymptotic formula assumes that you have data points—at either end of the function—in the asymptotic range, close to the axes. In other words, it is a more conservative function, assuming that the set of data points you have so far is from the more extreme part of the range you might expect. The y axis shows the median error, and it is desirable to get this below 10 percent for psychological reasons, for example:

> "How long will my project take to complete?"
> "50 days."

Our experience of executive tolerance for error in such promises is 5 to 15 percent and hence, 10 percent is the midpoint, or median executive tolerance threshold. So, we want to know how many items need to be in the project in order for our forecast to lie in the forty-five to fifty-five days range, or within a 10 percent error of our estimate of fifty days.

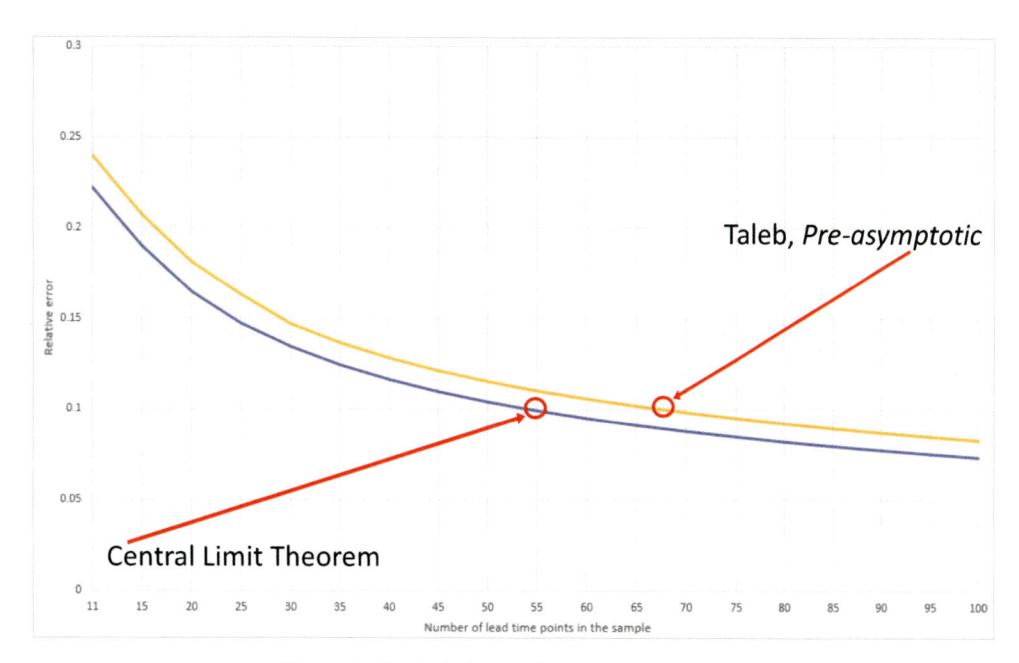

Figure C.12 Relative lead time averaging error

The result of the simulation in Figure C.12 suggests that fifty-five data points are needed with the central limit theorem. The more conservative pre-asymptotic formula produces a result of sixty-eight. Given that the kappa of the super-exponential function may be lower than $\kappa = 1.5$, our general guidance is that eighty to one hundred data points are needed for regression to the mean to be a useful technique when lead times are distributed in the super-exponential range. It is possible to trade down to twenty-nine data points for just a 5 percent relative error (i.e., +/−15 percent of the mean with half the data points).

Recommendation In the super-exponential range, you need seventy to one hundred data points for the concept of an average to be a meaningful value with an acceptable psychological tolerance for error.

Recommendation Little's Law is valid as a forecasting tool for kanban systems exhibiting a super-exponential lead time probability distribution, providing you expect at least 70 tickets to flow through your kanban board within the period of time that you are forecasting.

This is a highly important result! It means that Maturity Level 3 or deeper kanban systems exhibiting thin-tailed lead time distributions in the super-exponential range can be used to facilitate:

- Batch processing forecasts (e.g., project schedules) using linear regression of the delivery rate
- Buffer sizing, including input buffers and parking lots for dependencies

- Capacity allocation for demand shaping or risk hedging
- Sizing of booking/reservation systems
- Capacity allocation for classes of booking/reservation in a dynamic reservation system

Alexei Zheglov has described the super-exponential range as the sweet spot of project management forecasting, because only eleven to thirty data points are needed for extremely high model confidence, while fewer than one hundred data points are needed for high confidence in simple arithmetic forecasting techniques such as linear regression. He has also gone on to say that by far the most important thing any organization can do to improve its resilience—its customer satisfaction, its fitness-for-purpose, its robustness—and manage risk is first to instrument for lead time and then to focus on trimming the tail of the lead time distribution. This is the job of the Flow Manager role at Maturity Level 2, and it is vital to achieving Maturity Level 3 and deeper.

Approximately Exponential

The exponential function can be modeled with the Weibull equation using kappa, κ = 1.0. It represents the inflection point between the world of Mediocristan—the super-exponential and Gaussian probability distribution range—and the world of Extremistan, the world of Pareto distribution and power laws. Even close to the exponential function, simple forecasting is possible if we are willing to trade a little relative forecasting error . . .

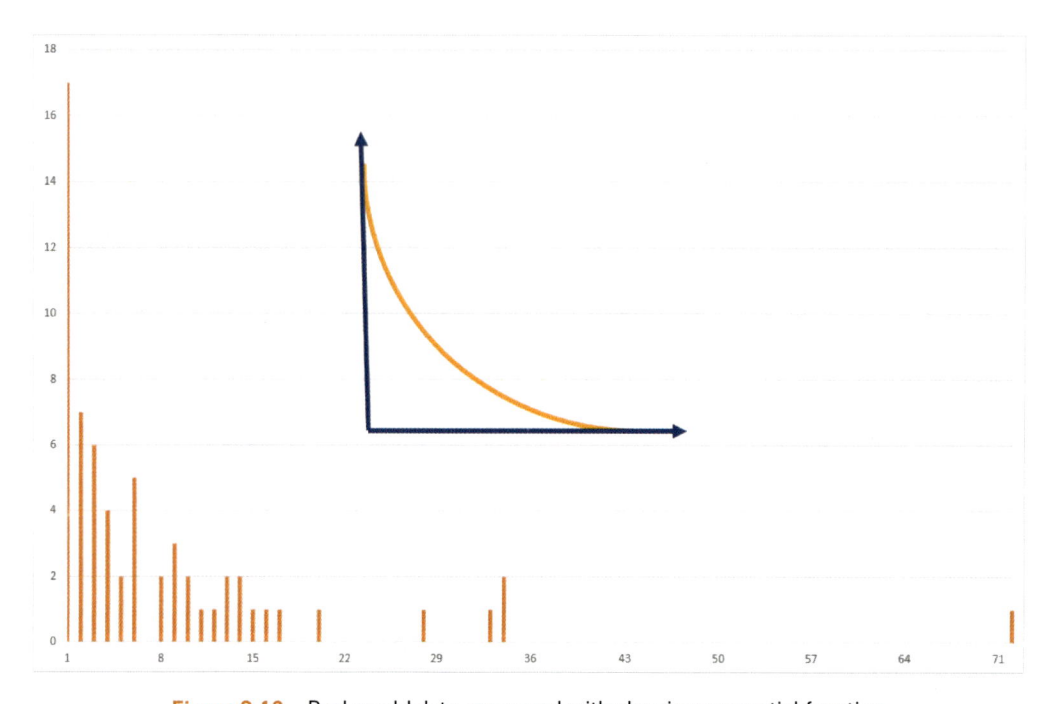

Figure C.13   Real-world data compared with classic exponential function

Figure C.13 shows a real-world data set, with the canonical exponential function inlaid in the picture. Excluding the outlier data point of seventy-two days, which originated from the bootstrap of the project and therefore does not come from a period of equilibrium and stable volatility, the remaining data points exhibit a distribution very close to, or an approximation of, the exponential function.

Figure C.14 shows the cumulative flow diagram for the same project.[3] For 150 data points, observation gives us 150 items in 154 days, or .97 per day, and Little's Law gives us 0.83 per day for an average WIP of 5.2 and observed lead time mean of 6.3, or a 15 percent relative forecasting error.

Recommendation Simple arithmetic forecasting remains possible at or close to the exponential distribution for lead time when the number of data points—the number of work items flowing through the kanban system—exceeds 150 in the relevant time period. The corollary of which is to say that for exponential-, super-exponential-, and Gaussian-distributed data sets, algorithmic, iterative techniques such as Monte Carlo are not required.

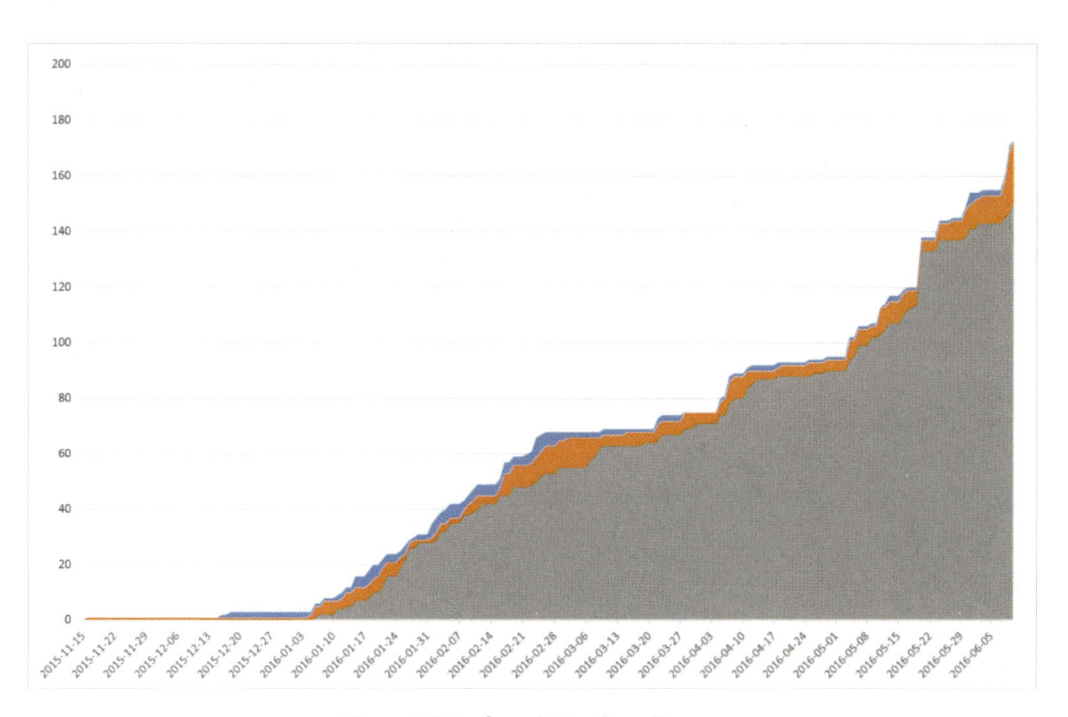

Figure C.14 Cumulative flow diagram

---

3. Both C.13 and C.14 courtesy of Andreas Bartel, flow.hamburg

Sub-Exponential Range

The sub-exponential range, shown in Figure C.15, is part of the Pareto range of power laws. We are choosing to break it out separately as we believe that the range of power laws, relatively close to the exponential function, are "hackable." In other words, there are pragmatic actions we can take to trim the tail and hack the distribution into the desirable super-exponential range.

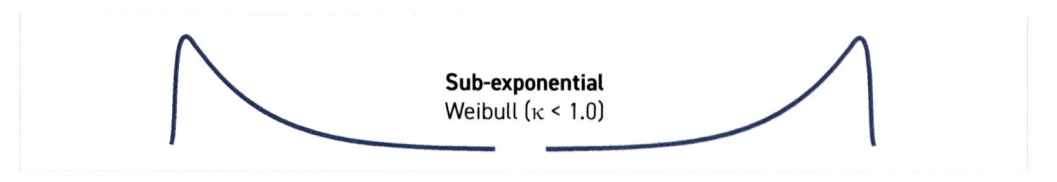

Figure C.15   Sub-exponential range

Sub-exponential functions are modeled as Weibull, with kappa in the range of $0.7 < \kappa < 1.0$. We consider these semi-fat tailed because the tail can be hacked through our actions. The median to tail ratio is typically in the range of six to one hundred times. If the median is five, we expect a tail in the range of thirty to five hundred, and not measured in thousands or tens of thousands or even higher. Lead time distributions for IT operations work are often sub-exponential. In general, this shape is associated with lead times for work with many external dependencies.

The pro for this function is that it is even less sensitive to errors in alpha and hence, is useful for modeling from relatively small data sets—eleven historical data points should produce robust results for estimating the shape of the curve. However, the con is that linear regression of the mean isn't useful at all. At around eighty data points it fails to get within 20 percent of the mean. Alexei Zheglov's simulation, plotted in Figure C.16, demonstrates that at least 2,000 data points are required to reduce the error to within psychological tolerances. Because of this, fat-tailed data sets should not be used with Little's Law—an equation of averages.

Recommendation In the sub-exponential range, arithmetic forecasting techniques, such as linear regression and the use of Little's Law, are not valid for buffer sizing, capacity allocation, reservation system sizing, and dependency parking lots. Although sub-exponential range data sets are suitable for iterative simulation techniques such as Monte Carlo, we do not believe that the range of outcomes from the simulations represent useful, pragmatic, actionable guidance. For example, simulating a range of WIP limits to use for a capacity allocation on a kanban board is not useful. In a context where a single number is needed, we need to be able to depend on the arithmetic mean. Therefore, the guidance is simple: Focus on trimming the tail of the lead time distribution using techniques such as blocker clustering, root cause analysis, risk mitigation and reduction, and reducing multitasking and pre-empting of work that causes delay. Reduce and limit WIP to discourage multitasking and pre-empting, and focus on quality and first-time right with the intent of avoiding rework and kanban tickets that cycle backward on the board, which result in longer lead times. In other words, use specific practices from Maturity Level 2 and Maturity Level 3 to control and eliminate the tail and hack the distribution into the super-exponential range.

Figure C.16 shows a chart, similar to the one in Figure C.12, displaying the mean relative error for regression to the mean, this time for a sub-exponential Weibull distribution with kappa, $\kappa = 0.8$. At one hundred data points, the median error is only just under 20 percent. In other words, if you forecast that a project with one hundred items to deliver takes fifty days, you have only a one in two chance that it will take between forty and sixty days, and you have a one in four chance that it will take more than sixty days. These are not good odds, psychologically speaking. It is unlikely that you can operate a trustworthy service delivery with such a forecast. This simulation showed extreme asymptotic behavior to the x axis and failed to fall below a 10 percent median error until it had 2,000 data points. Raphael Douady[4] advised Alexei Zheglov that 10,000 data points may be needed to make safe estimates and for the concept of a mean to be a meaningful idea.

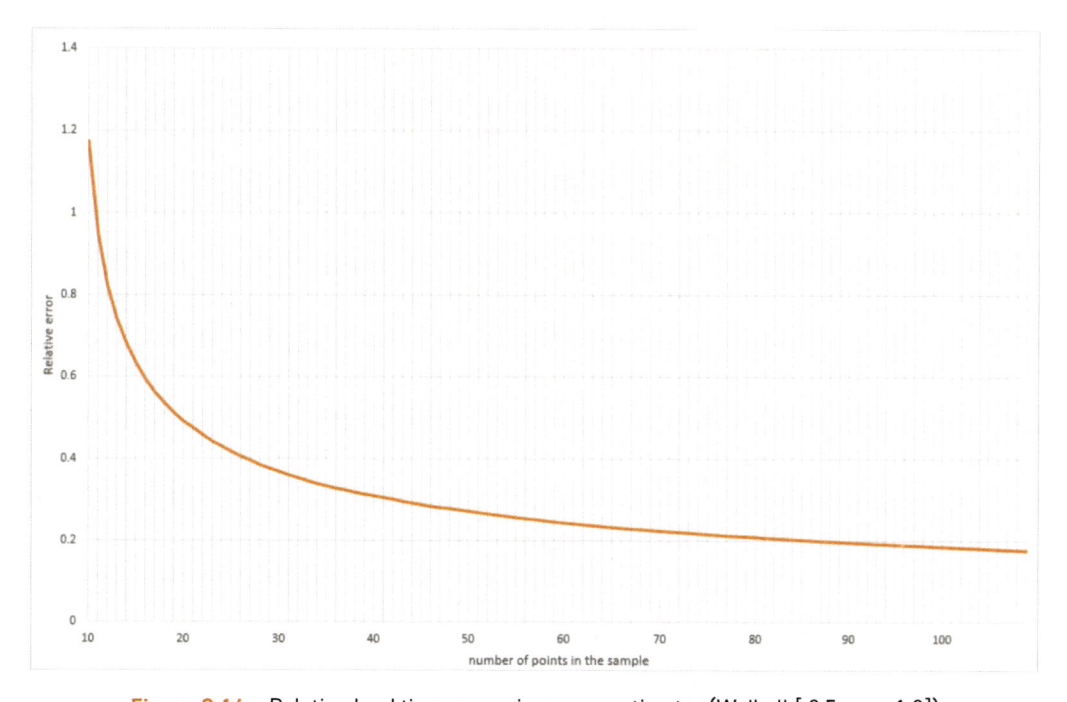

Figure C.16 Relative lead time averaging error estimator (Weibull [$0.5 < \kappa < 1.0$])

---

4. https://en.wikipedia.org/wiki/Raphael_Douady

The simple advice is that if you find yourself in the sub-exponential domain, averages are meaningless. Any technique or equation that requires an average is invalid. The implications of this are quite profound, as it implies that pretty much all published and well-established guidance on project management, portfolio management, and product management does not work in Extremistan (the sub-exponential domain). For example, the standard project management and product management guidance on prioritization by return on investment using the equation

$$ROI = \frac{Value}{Cost}$$

simply cannot be used if there is any possibility that either the value or the cost is sub-exponentially (Pareto) distributed. In domains such as publishing, music publishing, computer games, and almost any market with a network effect, such as social media platforms, operating systems, and business productivity tools, such approaches to prioritization are invalid. An equation such as ROI implicitly assumes average value and average cost. There is an implicit assumption of Gaussian distribution for a range of value, and a range of cost, and that these ranges regress to the mean within a reasonable number of data points for the given market or business domain.

This text is not the forum to explore the answers to this problem. If this interests you, we encourage you to follow new and future publications in the fields of Fit-for-Purpose and Enterprise Services Planning.

Pareto Range

Pareto class distributions are often referred to as power laws. These are very fat tailed and represent high risk. Hence the nickname Extremistan. In this range, tails exceed one hundred times the mode, ranging out to values such as 10^{13}. Although these distributions can be hacked through action, it is almost impossible to hack them into the super-exponential range. For example, the Pareto-distributed movie industry uses hacks such as the star system, franchises, sequels, and cross-licensing from books, comics, and other entertainment media such as games, theater, opera, and music to improve the chances of success. However, of all the movie franchises, only James Bond has successfully crossed into Mediocristan and achieved a sustainable concept of an "average" James Bond movie in terms of box office receipts, one that spans punctuation points, with changes of actor and script writers. For those who have counter-argued that *Star Wars* is a similar franchise that has crossed into Mediocristan, we counter with *Solo*, officially the first movie in the *Star Wars* franchise to flop.[5] As general advice, you can't hack the Pareto range into the Gaussian range, and hence, an entirely different approach to risk management is needed. Fortunately, Pareto distributions rarely, if ever, appear in project management or service

---

5. https://www.vanityfair.com/hollywood/2018/06/solo-star-wars-box-office-flop

delivery problems. Pareto distributions do exist in product management problems such as payoff uncertainty; for example, how much will our next book make? Is it the next *Harry Potter*? Or will it sell fewer than 300[6] copies? Pareto distribution problems are also known as black swan[7] problems. Project management and service delivery domains don't involve black swans, but product and portfolio management can.

---

6. Approximately 300 copies is the mean total sales of any specific book title on Amazon.com.
7. According to Taleb, a black swan event is an event that almost never happens, but when it does, it has major consequences. https://en.wikipedia.org/wiki/Black_swan_theory

D | Triage

Triage is a well-established technique used in emergency rooms in hospitals around the world. When a new patient arrives in an ambulance, a duty nurse immediately assesses whether the patient needs to be seen now or can wait until later, and if later, roughly when, and what preparation may be needed.

Deciding on Now, Later—and If So, When—or Not at All

The technique originates from the Crimean War fought in the 1850s and 1860s, contemporaneous with the American Civil War. At the time, the new battlefield technology was the rifled barrel. Rifles, though in short supply and expensive, were a devastating weapon compared to the single-shot musket that preceded them. Consequently, the death and injury rate in these wars was far greater than in any past war. As a further consequence, the field hospitals in Crimea were overwhelmed with injured soldiers dying from their battle wounds. There were not enough doctors, operating tables, beds, medicines, or nurses to care for the wounded, so some form of prioritizing had to be developed. They used triage to separate the wounded into three categories: now—if we treat this wounded soldier immediately, we can save his life; later—this soldier needs attention here in the field hospital but will not die within the next few minutes; and not at all—either this soldier will die regardless of what we do or he is only mildly wounded and can be transported behind the lines to a hospital farther away from the battle front.

    The art and science of triage is therefore based on a metaphorical, or analogous, understanding of "the rate the patient is bleeding to death." The rate of blood loss leading to a fatality is quite literally the "cost of delay." If we delay for minutes or hours, how much blood does the patient lose? How much closer are they to death? Effective triage requires us to understand the cost of delay, which is covered in depth in Appendix E, Cost of Delay.

Triage is a technique that works for managing the queuing of work for any scarce resource or service with limited capacity. As soon as we have a WIP-limited pull system, a kanban system, we need to triage. The work in the system is the work we are doing now, while work queuing upstream is work for later; and if we discard an option, that is work that we decided not to do at all. Upstream Kanban, or analysis required for a definition of ready, or the discussions at a Replenishment Meeting can all be used to implement an effective triage discipline.

Because most businesses do not understand the cost of delay with regard to their work, and because they do not yet have an analogous mapping to the rate at which the patient is bleeding to death, they struggle to adopt a WIP-limited pull system. They struggle to adopt triage and be comfortable with the concept that commitment can be deferred, that some work can—and should—wait until later.

To help with triage, we have developed a set of Triage Tables to enable the user to effectively prioritize work without needing to understand cost of delay in any depth. Only a few basic pieces of factual data are required to use the tables effectively and look up the required class of service to determine the appropriate time to start an item. The prerequisites for using Triage Tables are an understanding of lead time (by way of a lead time histogram) and knowing both the range for the lead time and the nature of its probability distribution: whether it is thin tailed (super-exponential) or fat tailed (sub-exponential/Pareto). These are explained fully in Appendix C, Understanding Lead Time.

Using Triage Tables, Step 1: What is the nature of the value acquisition lifecycle (VAL)?

Table D.1 shows eleven different patterns of value acquisition over time.

The impulse function (1) implies that there is a one-off opportunity to reap a benefit (make money), and after that the chance is gone.

The bell curve function models the well-established technology adoption lifecycle pattern attributed to the work of Everett Rodgers in the 1970s. Two versions of this curve are shown: the first version (4) has no catch up, implying that there is a network effect in the marketplace that gives the first mover an advantage that cannot be taken away later. This network-effect, first-mover advantage is often associated with technology platforms such as operating systems, productivity suites, mobile telephony standards, messaging and communications tools, and social media networking. The second version (5) has no such first-mover advantage, and second and subsequent movers can catch up to and even overtake an early market mover.

Table D.1 Patterns of Value Acquisition Lifecycles

#	Pattern	
1.	**One-off opportunity with an expiry date** The impulse function implies that there is a one-off opportunity to gain a benefit (make money) and after that opportunity, the chance is gone. *A customer with a remaining annual budget approaches you to spend the money before the new fiscal year. You either take the opportunity before the expiry date or lose the sale.*	
2.	**Very front loaded** 80 percent of the benefit is realized in the first 20 percent of the lifecycle. *A ski manufacturer issues new models every year in November, and most of the skis are sold in the first three months of what is a one-year lifecycle.*	
3.	**Front loaded** 80 percent of the benefit is realized in the first 50 percent of the lifecycle. *A bicycle manufacturer, as in the previous example, issues new bicycles every year in November–December (and insists retailers take half of the year's inventory then, making for very cramped bike shops in December), and the majority of sales happen in the beginning of the season—for holiday buying and on into spring—and drop off toward the end of the summer.*	
4.	**Bell curve, no catch up** A bell curve with "no catch up" implies that there is a network effect in the marketplace that gives the first mover an advantage that cannot be taken away later. *This network-effect, first-mover advantage is often associated with technology platforms such as operating systems, productivity suites, mobile telephony standards, messaging and communications tools, and social media networking.*	
5.	**Bell curve with catch up** A bell curve with catch up has no first-mover advantage, and second and subsequent movers can catch up and even overtake an early market mover. *The first car manufacturer that introduced LED lights in the market had an advantage, and it took one year for a second manufacturer to offer the same technology. Then it took several years for other market players to catch up. Nevertheless, the first player didn't have a lock-in market effect, and it didn't affect competitors' sales.*	

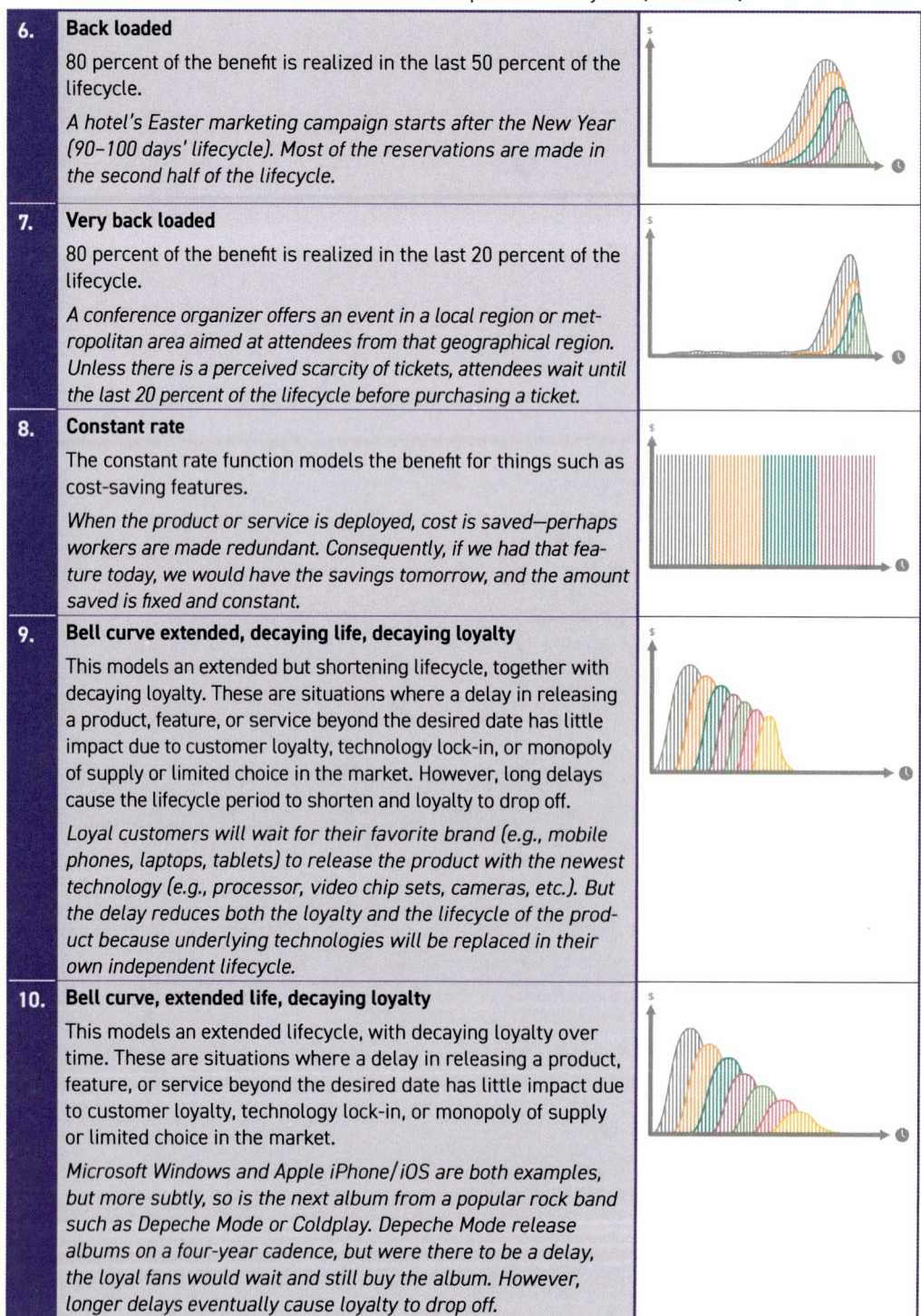

Table D.1 Patterns of Value Acquisition Lifecycles (continued)

6.	**Back loaded** 80 percent of the benefit is realized in the last 50 percent of the lifecycle. *A hotel's Easter marketing campaign starts after the New Year (90–100 days' lifecycle). Most of the reservations are made in the second half of the lifecycle.*	
7.	**Very back loaded** 80 percent of the benefit is realized in the last 20 percent of the lifecycle. *A conference organizer offers an event in a local region or metropolitan area aimed at attendees from that geographical region. Unless there is a perceived scarcity of tickets, attendees wait until the last 20 percent of the lifecycle before purchasing a ticket.*	
8.	**Constant rate** The constant rate function models the benefit for things such as cost-saving features. *When the product or service is deployed, cost is saved—perhaps workers are made redundant. Consequently, if we had that feature today, we would have the savings tomorrow, and the amount saved is fixed and constant.*	
9.	**Bell curve extended, decaying life, decaying loyalty** This models an extended but shortening lifecycle, together with decaying loyalty. These are situations where a delay in releasing a product, feature, or service beyond the desired date has little impact due to customer loyalty, technology lock-in, or monopoly of supply or limited choice in the market. However, long delays cause the lifecycle period to shorten and loyalty to drop off. *Loyal customers will wait for their favorite brand (e.g., mobile phones, laptops, tablets) to release the product with the newest technology (e.g., processor, video chip sets, cameras, etc.). But the delay reduces both the loyalty and the lifecycle of the product because underlying technologies will be replaced in their own independent lifecycle.*	
10.	**Bell curve, extended life, decaying loyalty** This models an extended lifecycle, with decaying loyalty over time. These are situations where a delay in releasing a product, feature, or service beyond the desired date has little impact due to customer loyalty, technology lock-in, or monopoly of supply or limited choice in the market. *Microsoft Windows and Apple iPhone/iOS are both examples, but more subtly, so is the next album from a popular rock band such as Depeche Mode or Coldplay. Depeche Mode release albums on a four-year cadence, but were there to be a delay, the loyal fans would wait and still buy the album. However, longer delays eventually cause loyalty to drop off.*	

Table D.1 Patterns of Value Acquisition Lifecycles (continued)

11.	**Last-minute decay**
	Immediate benefits regardless of the delay; however, last-minute results in a rapid drop-off in realized benefits.
	This models a business such as promoting a pop concert for a popular artist, such as Taylor Swift. If the tickets go on sale today, the whole stadium is sold out within hours. If we delay a week or a month, we still sell out. The perception of scarcity means that the sales are immediate regardless of the delay, unless we wait until the last minute without announcing the event.

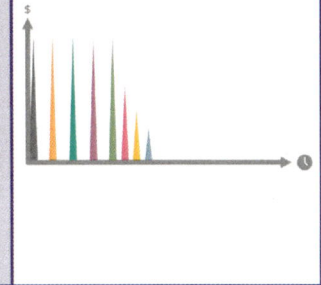

Several skewed versions of a bell curve are also shown, ranging from very front loaded (products for which 80 percent of the benefit is realized in the first 20 percent of the lifecycle) to very back loaded (products for which 80 percent of the benefit doesn't occur until the last 20 percent of the lifecycle), with varying amounts in between. Different products and businesses have different adoption lifecycles, which are often affected by seasonality, perception of scarcity, or a need to plan in advance.

For example, a ski manufacturer issues new models every year in November, and most of the skis are sold in the first three months of what is a one-year lifecycle. This is an example of a very front-loaded value acquisition function (2). Conversely, a conference organizer offers an event in a local region or metropolitan area aimed at attendees from that geographical region and, unless there is a perceived scarcity of tickets, attendees will wait until the last 20 percent of the lifecycle before purchasing their tickets. This is an example of a very back-loaded value acquisition function (7).

The constant-rate function (8) models the benefit for things such as cost-saving features. When the product or service is deployed, cost is saved, perhaps because workers are made redundant. Consequently, if we had that feature today we would have the savings tomorrow, and the amount saved is fixed and constant.

There are two functions that model extended lifecycles. These model situations in which a delay in releasing a product, feature, or service beyond the desired date has little impact due to customer loyalty, technology lock-in, or a monopoly of supply/limited choice in the market. Microsoft Windows and Apple iPhone/iOS are both examples, but more subtly, so is the next album from a popular rock band, such as Depeche Mode or Coldplay. Depeche Mode release albums on a four-year cadence, but were there to be a delay, their loyal fans would wait and still buy the album. However, as time goes by, loyalty drops off. The two curves model extended life with decaying loyalty over time (10) and extended but shortening life, also with decaying loyalty (9).

Finally, there is a last-minute decay function (11). This models a business such as promoting a concert for a popular artist, such as Taylor Swift. If the tickets go on sale today, the whole stadium sells out within hours.[1] If we delay a week or a month, we still sell out. The perception of scarcity means that the sales are immediate, regardless of the delay, unless we wait until the last minute to announce the event. This business model was originally inspired by Wine on the Waterfront, in Port Angeles, Washington, USA, the location where significant parts of the manuscript for *Fit for Purpose* were written. If the owner, Chef Stephen McNabb, announced in advance that he was cooking a special meal, tickets for the night in question would sell out within hours. The restaurant had limited capacity, and only twenty-two seats[2] could be reserved. However, on evenings when Steve waited until five o'clock to announce via Facebook that he'd be cooking that night, then only a few diehard, regular customers would attend. Potential customers for a gourmet dinner simply couldn't react in time.

So, Step 1 is to pick the value adoption function that applies to a work item waiting for the Kanban system.

Step 2: Select the Shelf-Life Ratio

Figure D.1 shows five ratios of lead time range to length of the lifecycle. If you have a fat-tailed lead time with a long tail, there are other aspects of the Triage Tables method to adjust for the risk that the visible tail, and hence the known range of lead time, could be exceeded.

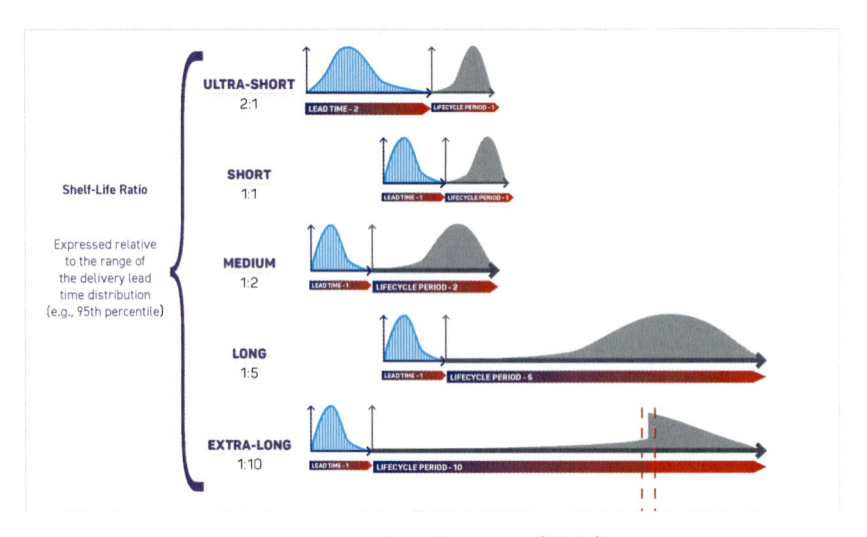

Figure D.1 Shelf-life ratios (SLRs)

An example of an ultra-short shelf-life ratio (SLR) comes from David's early career, working at IBM writing BIOS code for PC servers. IBM's personal computer (PC) company designed and manufactured PCs for the corporate market and ThinkPad-branded

---

1. As we go to press, the world is still in the grip of the coronavirus crisis and stadium shows are unlikely in 2020 or for some extended period beyond that.
2. The correct industry term for this is "covers."

laptops from their two PC division facilities in Raleigh, NC, and Greenock, in Scotland. It took a whole year to design a new model, incorporating chipsets and other physical innovations and design elements as they became available from suppliers. However, each model of PC or ThinkPad was designed to have a shelf life of only three months and be replaced with the next one. Consequently, IBM had four design teams working in parallel and staggered to complete a design every three months.

An example of a short SLR comes from our Kanban case study with Blizzard Sport, the ski manufacturer in Austria. New models of skis are released each year, and a whole year is used to design and manufacture each new model. It was a Blizzard executive who gave us the ratios of short equals one product cycle, medium is two to four cycles, and long is five or more cycles. To this set we added ultra-short and extra-long to complete the mathematical logarithm, giving us 0.5, 1, 2, 5, and 10 as a set of five.

If you know the lead time range, and you know the lifecycle period—and you should—then you can quickly select the SLR. This completes Step 2.

Step 3: Default Class of Service

Table D.2 on the next page is the first Triage Table. Use the results from steps 1 and 2 to index rows and columns on the table and select the default class of service for the work item from the cell cross-referenced in the table. For example, if you have an evenly loaded (bell curve) adoption lifecycle for your product, no first-mover advantage, and a medium SLR, select the Standard class of service for the ticket.

Step 4: How Classes of Service Relate to Cost of Delay

Table D.3 (also on the next page) shows the four canonical classes of service that first emerged in the Corbis implementation of the Kanban Method in 2007. These were documented in *Kanban* (the blue book, published in 2010) and have been taught in Kanban University training ever since. The cost of delay function shapes were not included in the 2010 book, as there was some doubt over their mathematical validity. More recently, we now have rigorous mathematical proof of the validity of these function shapes, explained in Appendix E, Cost of Delay. Not shown in these sketches are the ranges of the x and y axes. The origin point is intended to communicate "now" or "today."

The four classes of service are named by default as follows:

- **Expedite** There is an immediate, steeply rising (opportunity) cost of any delay.
- **Fixed Date** At a date in the relatively near future, within twice the range of the lead time distribution, we expect a step function impact (or a sloping S-curve function very close to a step function) on a known and very specific day. This is typical of seasonal demand or specific named events, such as sports tournaments or public holidays.

Table D.2 Triage Table for Selecting Class of Service

VALUE ACQUISITION LIFECYCLE (VAL)	SHELF-LIFE RATIO					
	Instant	Ultra-Short	Short	Medium	Long	Extra-Long
One-Off Opportunity	FIXED DATE					
Very Front-Loaded		FIXED DATE	FIXED DATE	FIXED DATE	FIXED DATE	STANDARD
Front-Loaded		FIXED DATE	FIXED DATE	FIXED DATE	STANDARD	STANDARD
Bell Curve #1 (1st-mover advantage)		FIXED DATE	FIXED DATE	STANDARD	STANDARD	STANDARD
Bell Curve #2 (with catch-up)		FIXED DATE	STANDARD	STANDARD	STANDARD	INTANGIBLE
Back-Loaded		STANDARD	STANDARD	STANDARD	INTANGIBLE	INTANGIBLE
Very Back-Loaded		STANDARD	STANDARD	INTANGIBLE	INTANGIBLE	INTANGIBLE
Constant Rate		STANDARD	INTANGIBLE	INTANGIBLE	INTANGIBLE	INTANGIBLE
Extended Life #1		STANDARD	INTANGIBLE	INTANGIBLE	INTANGIBLE	INTANGIBLE
Extended Life #2		INTANGIBLE	INTANGIBLE	INTANGIBLE	INTANGIBLE	INTANGIBLE
Last-Minute Decay		INTANGIBLE	INTANGIBLE	INTANGIBLE	INTANGIBLE	INTANGIBLE

Table D.3 Canonical Set of Classes of Service and Their Relationship to Cost of Delay

Color	Cost of Delay	Class of Service and Its Policies
(white)		**Expedite** Critical and immediate cost of delay; it can exceed other kanban limit (bumps other work).
(orange)		**Fixed Date** Cost of delay goes up significantly after deadline.
(yellow)		**Standard** Increasing urgency, cost of delay is shallow but accelerates before levelling out
(blue)		**Intangible** Cost of delay may be significant but is not incurred until significantly later (if at all).

- **Standard** The cost of delay rises over a period defined by the range of the lead time and the range of the lifecycle, initially in a convex pattern that eventually becomes concave. The shape is an S-curve over a medium to long period of time.
- **Intangible** As the name suggests, the cost of delay is intangible or insignificant for a period longer than one to two cycles of the lead time range. While we model the Intangible class of service as having a convex function shape, we learned that these are, in fact, also S-curve functions. Intangible class of service work is commonly observed as platform upgrades, incorporating new components or technologies into an existing design, or redesigning, reworking, or generally maintaining the system for a product or service or its design or source code.

With respect purely to cost of delay risk, we now know that this set of four classes of service provides sufficient coverage to adequately manage the temporal risks related to delay and its impact over time. It is no surprise, then, that this set of four classes of service has proven robust for thirteen years and is in broad usage in Kanban implementations globally.

Step 4 is merely a validation step. Given the indicated class of service from Step 3, does the meaning and explanation of the class of service match your understanding of the real business risks associated with the work item in question?

Step 5: Start Date Range

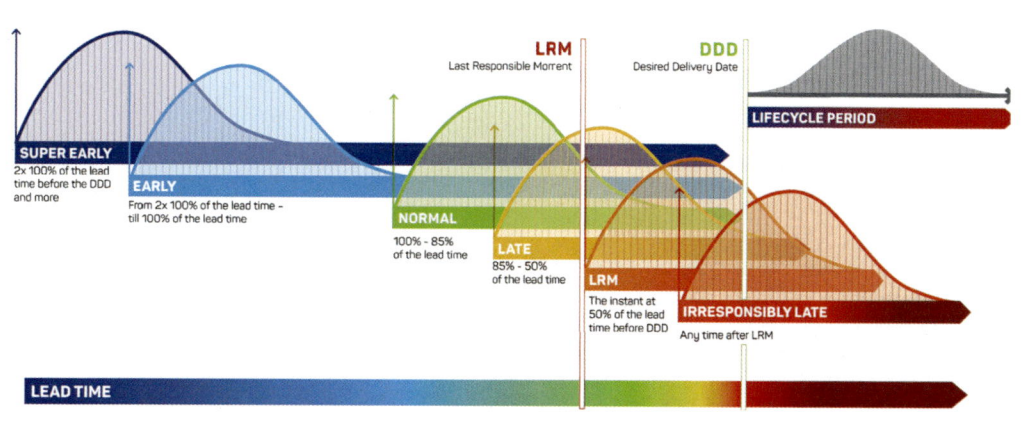

Figure D.2 Visualization of start date relative to desired delivery date and value acquisition lifecycle

Figure D.2 shows a visualization for the start date ranges relative to the desired delivery date and lifecycle of the opportunity for a medium SLR work item. The actual ranges are explained in Table D.4 on the next page. To use this table, you must first know the desired delivery date (DDD) of the work item. This is the ideal date to take delivery. For example, a cost-saving feature can have impact tomorrow if we receive it today, and hence, the DDD is today. However, for many items that are seasonal in nature or tied to specific windows of opportunity for a product or service, the DDD is in the future. A marketing campaign for Easter-themed items would not be launched during the year-end holiday season. The DDD is likely to be sometime in January, for example, the third Tuesday in January, because we always launch campaigns on Tuesday, and we want about ninety days of life from our Easter campaign.

Super Early is more than two times the 98th percentile of the lead time distribution range before the DDD, or before the item is needed. Early is more than one full lead time range before the DDD, while the Normal range lies in the tail—the 100th percentile down to the 85th percentile of the lead time distribution range prior to the DDD.

Beyond this, we consider that we are starting later than would be ideal. The Late range is from the 85th percentile of the lead time distribution to the 50th percentile (or median). We consider the median, where there is only a one in two chance of on-time delivery, to be the last responsible moment (LRM). This gives mathematical meaning to a term that has been in common usage, without any rigorous definition, in the Lean literature for twenty to thirty years. Beyond the LRM, we consider that an item is being started Irresponsibly Late.[3]

Using today's date and the desired delivery date, together with the known lead time range, use the start date range table (Table D.4) to determine the start date range. This completes Step 5.

If your lead time distribution is thin tailed (super-exponential), go to Step 6. If your lead time distribution is fat-tailed (sub-exponential/Pareto), go to Step 7.

Table D.4 Start Date Ranges

Super Early	Start < (DDD − 2 × lead time range)
Early	(DDD − 2 × lead time range) < start < (DDD − lead time range)
Normal	(DDD − lead time range) < start < (DDD − 0.85 × lead time range)
Late	(DDD − 0.85 × lead time range) < start < (DDD − 0.50 × lead time range)
Last Responsible Moment	DDD − 0.50 × lead time range
Irresponsibly Late	Start > LRM

---

3. Defining LRM as the 50th percentile before the DDD is quite a coarse approach. It is, however, pragmatic, and easy to implement, while providing a reasonably conservative risk-management approach. A more nuanced concept of LRM might be to provide a 50 percent chance of at least 80 percent of the value being realized. This requires a more sophisticated set of Triage Tables based on an as yet incomplete mathematical model. However, expect our guidance on LRM to change in 2021. Changes will be incorporated into the Mauvisoft Menta Triage DS mobile application and to the Triage Tables poster available from Kanban University, and to the KMM Plus online platform. Please check these sources for our latest guidance.

Step 6: Determining the Triage Table Modifier for a Predictable (Thin-Tailed) Lead Time Distribution

Figure D.3 shows examples of thin-tailed and fat-tailed lead time distributions. A deeper explanation of thin-tailed and fat-tailed lead time distributions is provided in Appendix C, Understanding Lead Time. Use these sketches to determine which type your actual data most resembles. If you have a thin-tailed distribution, use Table D.5 in Step 7; otherwise, for your fat-tailed distribution, use Table D.6 in Step 7.

Assuming you have single-modal data (see below), there are some simple ratios that indicate the likelihood that you have a thin-tailed or fat-tailed distribution:

$$\frac{(98\%ile - location)}{(50\%ile - location)} >= 5.6 \Rightarrow \textit{fat tailed}$$

$$\frac{(98\%ile - location)}{(50\%ile - location)} < 5.6 \Rightarrow \textit{thin tailed}$$

For convenience, you will sometimes see these written in a simplified form, assuming location = 0 and that the 98 percent is effectively the end of the tail you can see. Hence,

$$\frac{tail}{median} >= 5.6 \Rightarrow \textit{fat tailed}$$

$$\frac{tail}{median} < 5.6 \Rightarrow \textit{thin tailed}$$

These appear in the poster for Triage Tables available from Kanban University. A further sanity check is available for thin-tailed distributions,

$$\frac{(98\%ile - location)}{mode - location} < 16 \Rightarrow \textit{thin tailed}$$

or simplified as

$$\frac{tail}{mode} < 16 \Rightarrow \textit{thin tailed}$$

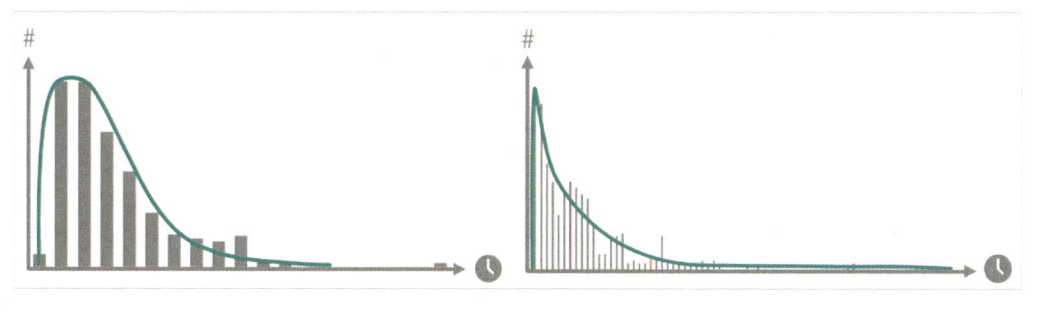

Figure D.3 Examples of thin-tailed (left) and fat-tailed (right) lead time distributions

Step 7: Determining the Triage Table Modifier

To use Table D.5 or Table D.6, you must first know your customer's expectations with respect to the desired delivery date. Are they laissez-faire and unconcerned? Is the date merely advisory, or there isn't really a specific date, and one was simply invented for the purpose of this exercise? Could we say they don't mind when it is delivered, so long as it eventually happens? If so, then our customer expectation is Don't Care. Or is there an SLA/SLE in place with the customer, and hence, if we start an item, there is an expectation that we deliver it within that time? If so, then our customer expectation is Within SLA/SLE. Or does the desired delivery date come with a demand of a deadline? The deadline may be real, as in a fixed date for an external event or something seasonal in nature, or it may simply be an instrument of a low-trust environment—the deadline is being used to squeeze us, as a stressor to drive action, or somehow to hold us accountable in an otherwise low-trust culture. Regardless of the reason, if the customer demands a deadline, we should account for it. When there is a genuinely high cost of delay beyond the desired delivery date, the customer may have Zero Tolerance. This is a more extreme form of deadline—when there is zero tolerance for delay, everyone understands the consequences and the impact on our business if we fail to meet the deadline. We are likely to sacrifice many other work items in order to achieve the date.

Note The use of deadlines with a predictable, thin-tailed lead time service delivery should be relatively rare. Predictable, thin-tailed delivery suggests that there should be a high level of trust. Deadlines are likely to be used only for genuine, high cost of delay reasons and not for dysfunctional, internal political, or lack of trust reasons.

Finally, the customer expectation may be as soon as possible (ASAP), in which case, if we choose to do the work, we need to expedite the request.

Use the start date range from Step 5 and the customer expectation to look up the class of service modifier on table D.5 or D.6. This will change the result from step 3. If the modifier names a class of service such as Intangible or Expedite, you should switch the item to the class of service indicated in Table D.5 or Table D.6, and proceed to Step 8. If the relevant cell in Table D.5 or Table D.6 directs you to move Up, Down, or Don't Change, use these instructions to modify your result from Step 3 and Triage Table D.2 for selecting class of service.

Step 8: Look up the Modified Class of Service on the Triage Table

Revisit the Triage Table D.2 from Step 3 and modify the cross-referenced cell, moving up, down, or left according to the advice from Step 6 or 7, as shown in Table D.7. Use the same cross-referenced cell from Step 3, and now modify it according to the advice from the table in Step 6 or 7. Move up or down one, two, or three cells as advised, and left one cell if so advised. If you move off the top or the left of the table, use Fixed Date; if you move off the bottom of the table, use Intangible. If you are still on the table, read the class of service from the new, modified position on the table. This is the start date–adjusted class of service to use for the work item if you decide to start it today.

Step 7.A Triage Table Modifiers for a Thin-Tailed Lead Time

Table D.5 Mediocristan (thin-tailed) Triage Table Modifier

START DATE	CUSTOMER EXPECTATIONS	CLASS OF SERVICE
NOW	ASAP	EXPEDITE
IRRESPONSIBLY LATE	WITHIN SLA/SLE	UP 3
LAST RESPONSIBLE MOMENT	WITHIN SLA/SLE	UP 2
LATE	WITHIN SLA/SLE	UP 1
NORMAL	WITHIN SLA/SLE	DON'T CHANGE
EARLY	WITHIN SLA/SLE	DOWN 1
SUPER-EARLY	WITHIN SLA/SLE	DOWN 2
IRRESPONSIBLY LATE	ZERO TOLERANCE	EXPEDITE
LAST RESPONSIBLE MOMENT	DEADLINE	UP 2
LATE	DEADLINE	UP 1
NORMAL	DEADLINE	DON'T CHANGE
EARLY	DEADLINE	DOWN 1
SUPER-EARLY	DEADLINE	DOWN 2
DON'T CARE	DON'T CARE	INTANGIBLE

Appendix D | Triage

Step 7.B Triage Table Modifiers for a Fat-Tailed Lead Time

Table D.6 Extremistan (fat-tailed) Triage Table Modifier

START DATE	CUSTOMER EXPECTATIONS	CLASS OF SERVICE
NOW	ASAP	EXPEDITE
IRRESPONSIBLY LATE	WITHIN SLA/SLE	LEFT 1 & UP 3
LAST RESPONSIBLE MOMENT	WITHIN SLA/SLE	LEFT 1 & UP 2
LATE	WITHIN SLA/SLE	LEFT 1 & UP 1
NORMAL	WITHIN SLA/SLE	LEFT 1
EARLY	WITHIN SLA/SLE	DON'T CHANGE
SUPER-EARLY	WITHIN SLA/SLE	DOWN 1
IRRESPONSIBLY LATE	ZERO TOLERANCE	EXPEDITE
LAST RESPONSIBLE MOMENT	DEADLINE	EXPEDITE
LATE	DEADLINE	EXPEDITE
NORMAL	DEADLINE	FIXED DATE
EARLY	DEADLINE	FIXED DATE
SUPER-EARLY	DEADLINE	STANDARD
DON'T CARE	DON'T CARE	INTANGIBLE

Table D.7 Modifying the Triage Table cell

VALUE ACQUISITION LIFECYCLE (VAL)	SHELF-LIFE RATIO					
	Instant	Ultra-Short	Short	Medium	Long	Extra-Long
One-Off Opportunity	FIXED DATE					
Very Front-Loaded		FIXED DATE	FIXED DATE	FIXED DATE	FIXED DATE	STANDARD
Front-Loaded		FIXED DATE	FIXED DATE	FIXED DATE	STANDARD	STANDARD
Bell Curve #1 (1st-mover advantage)		FIXED DATE	FIXED DATE	STANDARD	STANDARD	STANDARD
Bell Curve #2 (with catch-up)		FIXED DATE	STANDARD	STANDARD	STANDARD	INTANGIBLE
Back-Loaded		STANDARD	STANDARD	STANDARD	INTANGIBLE	INTANGIBLE
Very Back-Loaded		STANDARD	STANDARD	INTANGIBLE	INTANGIBLE	INTANGIBLE
Constant Rate		STANDARD	INTANGIBLE	INTANGIBLE	INTANGIBLE	INTANGIBLE
Extended Life #1		STANDARD	INTANGIBLE	INTANGIBLE	INTANGIBLE	INTANGIBLE
Extended Life #2		INTANGIBLE	INTANGIBLE	INTANGIBLE	INTANGIBLE	INTANGIBLE
Last-Minute Decay		INTANGIBLE	INTANGIBLE	INTANGIBLE	INTANGIBLE	INTANGIBLE

The Four Dimensions of Priority

"Priority" can mean whether something is selected (or chosen) and hence, "given priority." It can also suggest the sequencing, order, or queuing discipline in which a set of items are to be worked on. Priority can also indicate when something should be scheduled: now; later, and if so, when; or not at all. Additionally, priority can define how something is treated once it is in the system: its class of service.

Triage tables are designed to help with the latter two aspects of priority. They are designed to help you schedule work and determine the class of service to be applied to a piece of work given its scheduled start date.

The Kanban and Enterprise Services Planning bodies of knowledge suggest that sequencing work is not desirable except when related to dependencies.[4] Selecting an item of work, assigning it to a specific kanban, and pulling it into the system as work-in-progress (WIP) requires additional knowledge of the item and its risks, not merely its urgency and cost of delay. The risk-assessment framework recommended for solving tricky selection decisions is taught in the Kanban Coaching Practices and the Enterprise Services Planning training classes from Kanban University and will be described in a future book for the relevant KMM extensions.

However, using the Triage Tables to provide solid guidance for scheduling and determining class of service should go a long way toward resolving customer anxiety when introducing an end-to-end pull system at Maturity Level 3.

---

4. See Appendix F, Dependency Management.

E | Cost of Delay

The Triage Tables approach to deciding when and with which class of service to treat a work item has a solid mathematical foundation. This chapter explains the mathematics behind cost of delay.

Prerequisite

The prerequisite for any of these calculations is the knowledge that the payoff from the work item, project, product, feature, or service has a Gaussian or super-exponential payoff probability distribution function. To use Nassim Nicholas Taleb's vernacular, the payoff lies in Mediocristan. If the payoff has a Pareto (sub-exponential, power-law) probability distribution, as is typical in publishing and media such as music, movies, and computer games, this approach and the entire triage approach may be invalid. Markets, products, and services with power-law distributed payoffs can be described, using Taleb's vernacular, as being in Extremistan. All Extremistan work items should be treated as Intangible class of service and capacity should be allocated for them. When they are started becomes irrelevant, as the actual payoff is unknown and unknowable. The manuscript a publisher is holding might be the next *Harry Potter*, or it may be a flop that sells 300 copies in total over a ten-year lifespan. In Extremistan, there is no concept of "value." All general advice on product and portfolio management, all advice on calculating return on investment (ROI), requires us to have a concept of an "average payoff." The concept of value for the purposes of mathematical calculations requires us to understand that the variable in the equation, for example, ROI = value/cost is, in fact, an average. It should correctly read: average ROI = average value/average cost, where the numerator and denominator represent the mean values from two distinct probability distribution functions, one for value and the other for cost. In Extremistan, the concept of an average is meaningless, and hence, traditional prioritization methods, such as stack ranking by ROI, are inappropriate. This is also true for cost of delay. Cost of delay and triage to determine now versus later or not at all are appropriate only with a Mediocristan probability distribution for our payoff function. In the example shown in Figure E.1, we believe that our marketing promotion will realize, on average, 1,000 nights booked. Such an estimate should be based on historical data for similar promotions and an observation that the probability distribution from past promotions exhibited a super-exponential distribution function, ideally mapping to the Gaussian range of functions.

Put simply, cost of delay is for Mediocristan payoff opportunities; for Extremistan payoff opportunities, we should treat them as Intangible class of service items and allocate capacity for them. We should treat Extremistan payoff opportunities as a beauty contest or a lottery. Whether or not they have significant value is entirely random. Completely different product management guidance and techniques are required in Extremistan. However, a more rational approach to selection, scheduling, and determining class of service is possible for work items in Mediocristan.

It is, therefore, a core skill for any product manager, product owner, service request manager, or marketing person to know whether they are dealing with an opportunity that has a super-exponential/Gaussian payoff probability or a sub-exponential, power-law distributed, Pareto payoff opportunity. It is important to be able to separate out the items that can be managed using a triage function from those that can't. It is highly likely that most work items waiting for delivery do lie in Mediocristan. A full analysis of the product management challenge in Extremistan is left for a future text.

The remainder of this chapter provides the mathematical definition of cost of delay and explains why four classes of service provide entirely adequate coverage of temporal risk.

Calculating Delivery Delay Cost

Figure E.1 shows how value accumulates over time for a business feature, product, or service. In this case, the example models a hotel chain's marketing campaign to sell rooms over the Easter holiday weekend. There is a specific, ideal, desired delivery date, perhaps the second Tuesday in January. This happens because no one promotes Easter until after the New Year, and our business always launches promotions on Tuesdays. Consequently, we wish to launch on January 10. If we achieve this, we have approximately ninety-five days to run this promotion before Easter arrives. An adequately experienced marketing manager should be able to sketch the Value Acquistion Lifecycle function and put together some rough numbers, either the average total sales or the peak sales and, with a little mathematical comprehension of the shape of the function, one number—total sales—can be deduced from the other—peak sales—or vice-versa. Consequently, from a sketch like this we learn the length of the opportunity's lifecycle, how the rate of value acquisition changes over time, and an approximate number for the average value anticipated if the work item is delivered on or before the desired delivery date, that is, delivered without incurring a delay.

Next, we must consider what happens if the desired delivery date is missed. Figure E.2 introduces a delay and shows the consequential actual sales of hotel rooms. The remaining red area on the chart illustrates the difference between the anticipated results and the actual results. This red area in the aggregate is known as the "delay cost."

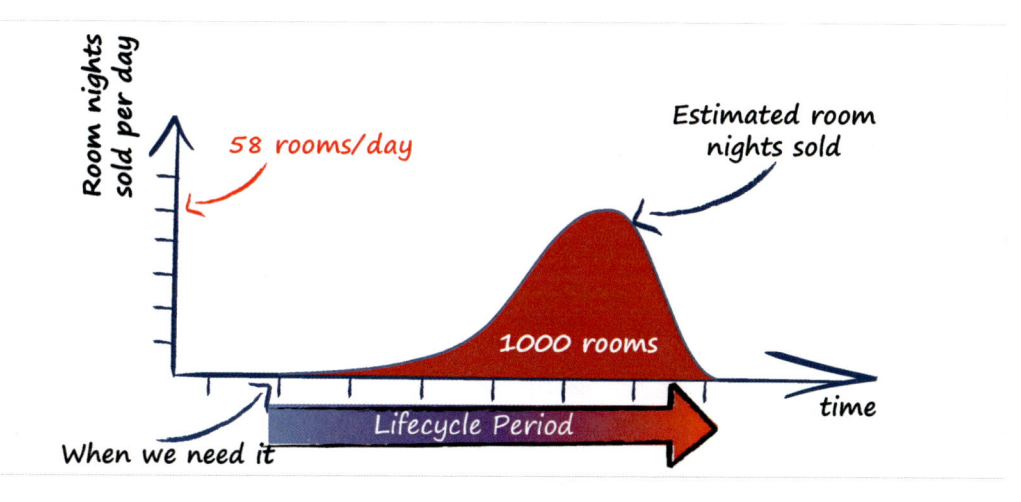

Figure E.1 The Value Acquisition Lifecycle for a hotel chain's Easter marketing campaign

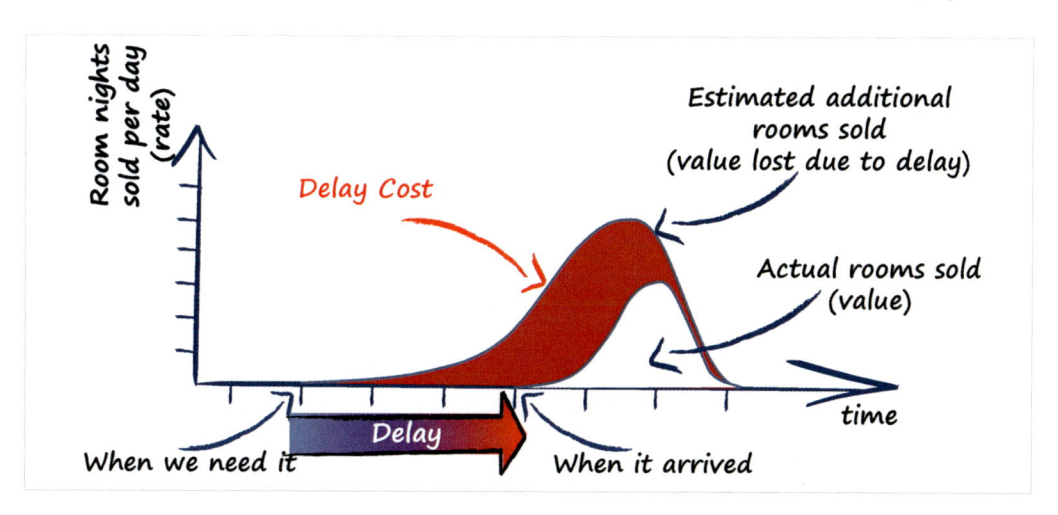

Figure E.2 Value Acquisition Lifecycle function showing a delay in delivery

Figure E.3 illustrates how delay cost increases as the length of the delay increases. In this case, we are using five discrete intervals of twenty days against a total lifecycle period of one hundred days. Very specifically, we are modeling delay in delivery, and hence, very specifically, we are illustrating the growing Delivery Delay Cost.

Appendix E | Cost of Delay

Figure E.4 plots the Delivery Delay Cost function, which shows how the delivery delay cost changes as the delay increases. The shape of this function is said to be concave to the *y* axis and asymptotic to the value of 1,000. People experienced in risk management will recognize that concave payoff functions represent high risk.

Now that we understand the mechanism for devising the Delivery Delay Cost function, we can plot it for a whole range of possible Value Acquisition Lifecycle (VAL) functions.

Figure E.5 shows the Delivery Delay Cost functions for each of the VAL functions shown in Figure E.6.[1] Figure E.7 shows all of these modeled on the same graph.

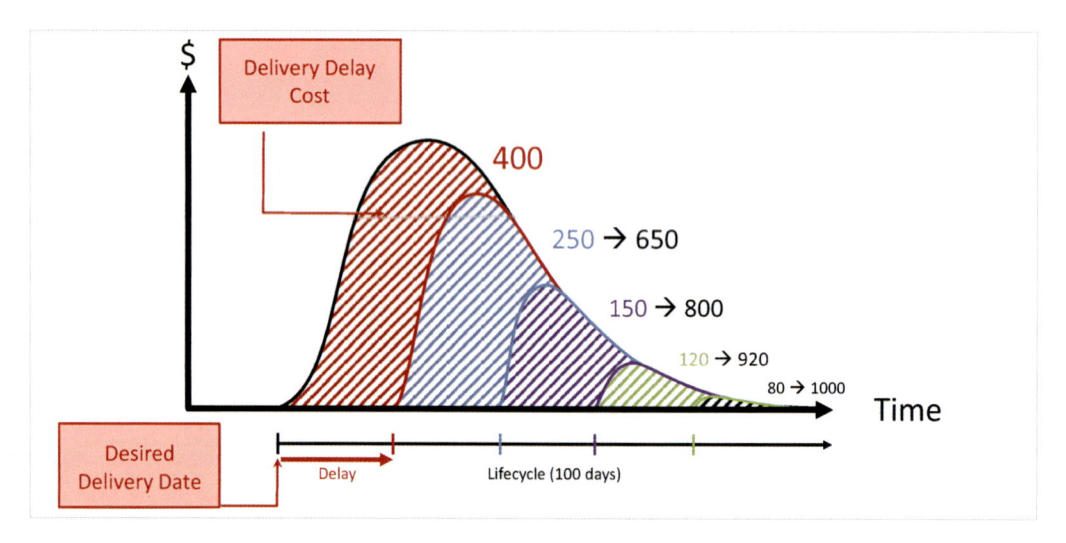

Figure E.3 Increasing delay, increasing aggregate delay cost

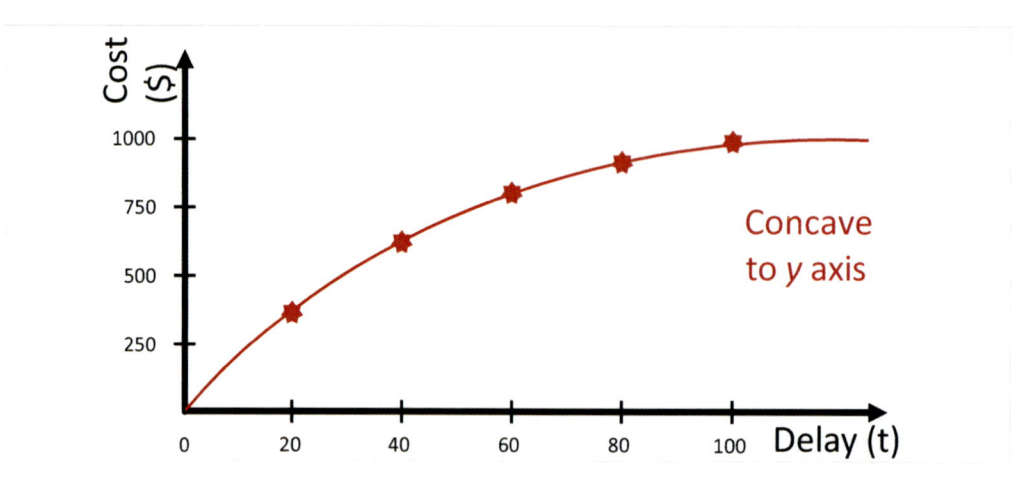

Figure E.4 Delivery Delay Cost function showing delivery delay cost against increasing delay

---

1. See Appendix D, Triage, for a full explanation of the typical business models represented by each pattern.

Calculating Delivery Delay Cost 423

Figure E.5 Patterns of Value Acquisition Lifecycle functions and their delay cost patterns

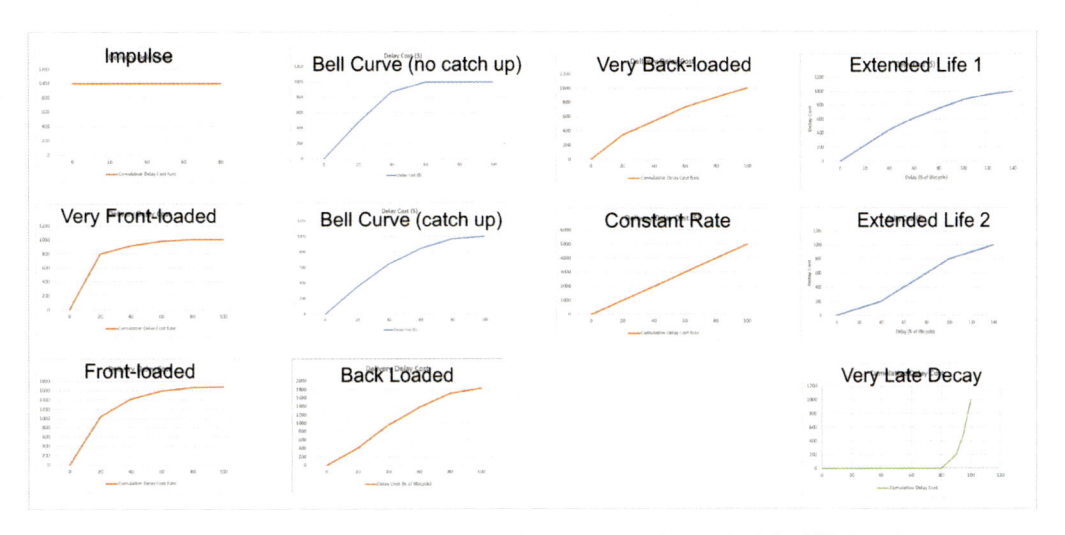

Figure E.6 Patterns of Delivery Delay Cost functions for each of the VAL functions

What we see is that from the Impulse function—a single one-off opportunity with a fixed delivery date—to the Very Late Decay function, we have a broad spectrum of risk from extremely concave through convex. The Linear function represents the case in which the cost of delivery delay increases at a constant rate.

We can make several statements given this evidence:

1. Given a fixed lifecycle period, any VAL function other than a Fixed Rate produces a concave delivery delay cost and is therefore riskier than the Constant Rate Value function. We can refer to this entire set as being in the super-linear risk range.

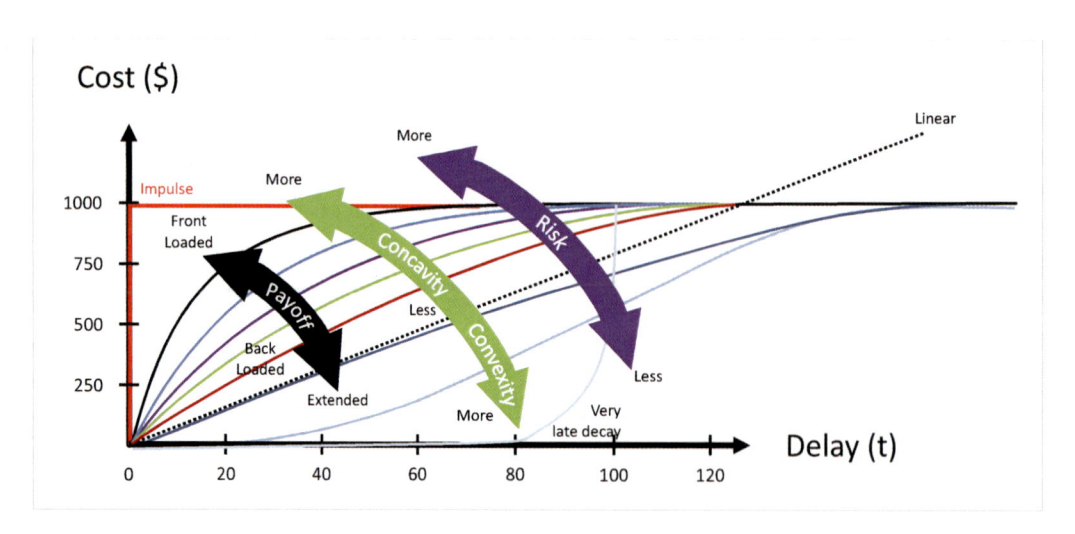

Figure E.7 Patterns of Delivery Delay Cost functions

2. Whenever there is the possibility of extended life due to loyalty, lock-in, monopoly of supply, or regulatory barriers, the Delivery Delay Cost function falls below the Linear function. We can refer to this set of Extended Life functions as being in the sub-linear risk range. We can further summarize by saying that loyalty and lock-in greatly reduce cost of delay risk.
3. Whenever there is a late decay in the value being delivered, the Delivery Delay Cost function exhibits partial or complete convexity. To summarize, very late decaying value greatly reduces cost of delay risk and has an even greater impact on risk reduction than loyalty or lock-in.

So, how does all of this mathematical explanation relate to triage, scheduling, and selection? Although Value Acquisition Lifecycle functions are relatively easy to understand and are often intuitive for someone experienced in a business domain, Delivery Delay Cost functions are not intuitive. A businessperson might be able to sketch a Value Acquisition Lifecycle function and a pattern of decay in adoption due to delay, or to pick one from a pattern catalog, but it isn't realistic to expect businesspeople to intuitively know Delay Cost functions. Hence, for a triage method to be effective, it must be based on the value acquisition lifecycle and a business domain understanding of how delay affects value realization or product adoption. It is not reasonable to ask businesspeople, product managers, service delivery managers, and marketing professionals to know and understand Delivery Delay Cost functions, which are effectively just an intermediate step in calculating cost of delay risk and divining advice on scheduling and class of service. The remainder of this chapter explains how we get from a Delivery Delay Cost function to solid, mathematically sound guidance on scheduling and class of service.

Calculating the Probable Cost of Delay in Starting (PCoDS)

Although understanding delivery delay cost is useful, it isn't particularly actionable. We do not control when an item is finished; rather, our decision making revolves around whether and when to start an item. The actionable decision guidance, therefore, has to revolve around when to start. And if we choose not to start an item, what is its probable cost of delay until the next opportunity to make a decision to start? In a typical Kanban system with a replenishment cadence, the delay is therefore equivalent to the time between replenishment meetings. If on-demand replenishment is implemented, the average time between pull signals and selection of new work is the reciprocal of the delivery rate. So, in a typical system with weekly replenishment, if we don't choose an item at today's meeting, our next chance to choose is one week from today. Hence, we are interested in the probable cost of delay over the next week. We can't put an absolute value on the cost of delay, because the period of delay in delivery, if any at all, is undetermined. This happens because lead time is a probability distribution, not a deterministic number. Hence, actual cost of delay is always uncertain because the amount of delay in any delivery is always uncertain.

To understand the probable cost of delay in starting, we must convolve the Lead Time Distribution function with the Delivery Delay Cost function, as shown in Figure E.8. Convolution is a mathematical operation or algorithm that involves passing one function over another and multiplying them together.

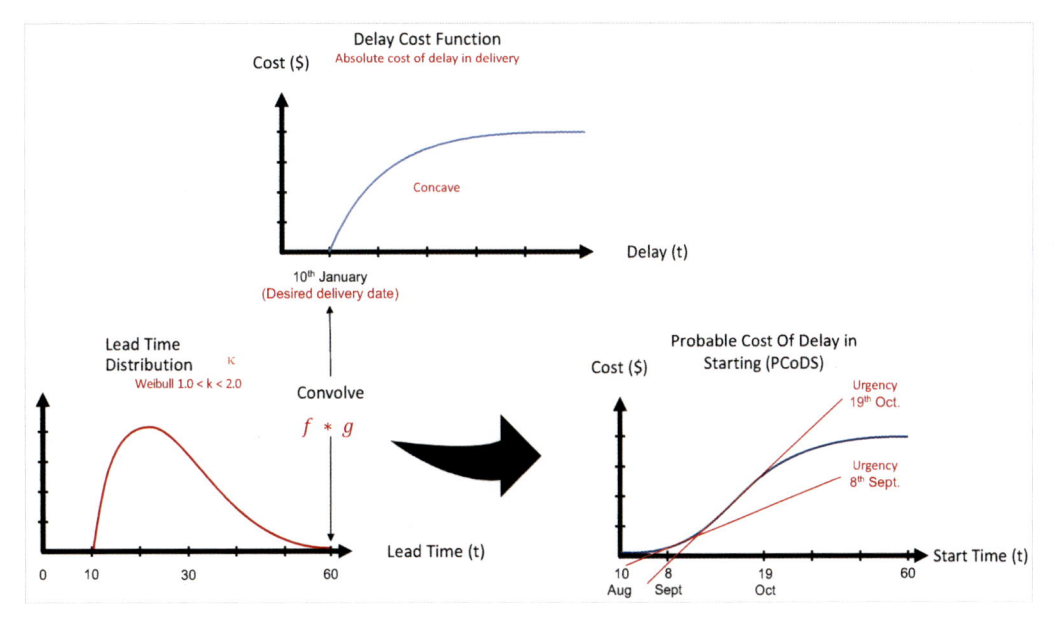

Figure E.8 Convolving Delivery Delay Cost with Lead Time Distribution to produce a Probable Cost of Delay in Starting (PCoDS)

The resulting function from the convolution is an S-curve. The Probable Cost of Delay in Starting (PCoDS) function illustrates the probable worst-case cost of delay for any given start date. Illustrated in Figure E.8 is a desired delivery date of September 23; the convolved function (bottom right) shows us that there is little cost of delay in August, but the cost of delay starts to rise steeply in early to mid-September. This graph also illustrates the concept of urgency. Urgency is defined as how much cost will be incurred in the immediate future if we don't start something on a specific date. Urgency is mathematically defined as the slope of the function on any given day, technically known as the derivative. This is written mathematically as $\frac{d}{dt}(PCoDS)$.

The graph shows that the urgency on September 8 is noticeable but not severe, whereas by October 19 the urgency has risen dramatically. The rate of loss of opportunity is much greater on October 19 than on September 8.

Figure E.9 shows the PCoDS functions for the patterns of Delivery Delay Cost functions shown in Figure E.6 for each of the Value Acquisition Lifecycle functions. The one-off business opportunity produces a J-curve, whereas all of the other functions result in S-curves; the green line shows the S-curve produced by the constant rate cost of delay, the Linear function in Figure E.7.

Figure E.10 illustrates the super-linear riskier cost of delay originating from the concave Delivery Delay Cost functions with a fixed lifecycle. Figure E.11 illustrates the sub-linear low cost of delay risk originating from extended life due to loyalty or lock-in or from convex Delivery Delay Cost functions.

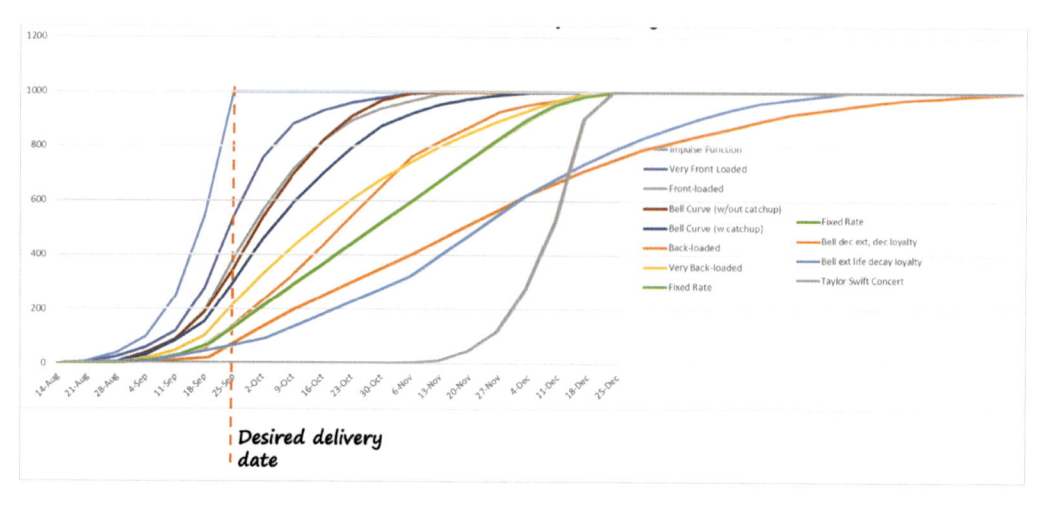

Figure E.9 Patterns of Probable Cost of Delay in Starting

Calculating the Probable Cost of Delay in Starting (PCoDS) 427

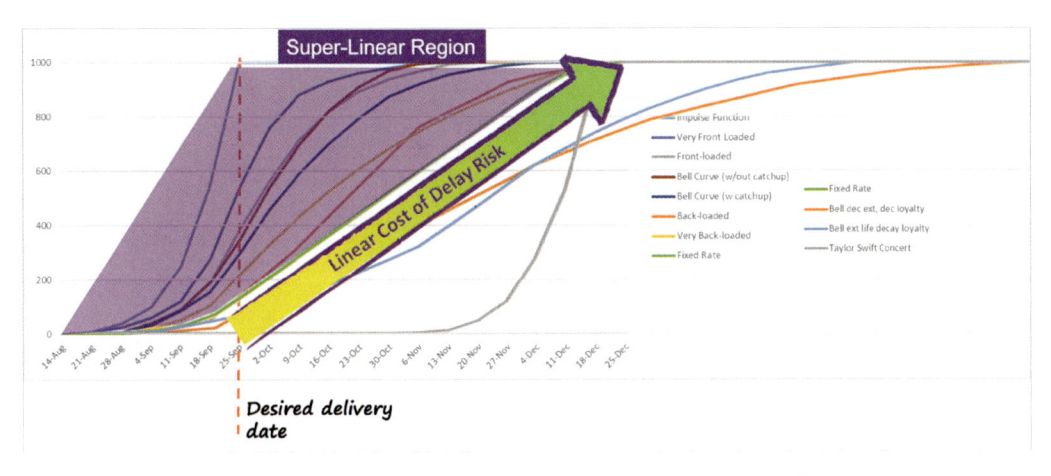

Figure E.10 Super-Linear region of Probable Cost of Delay in Starting

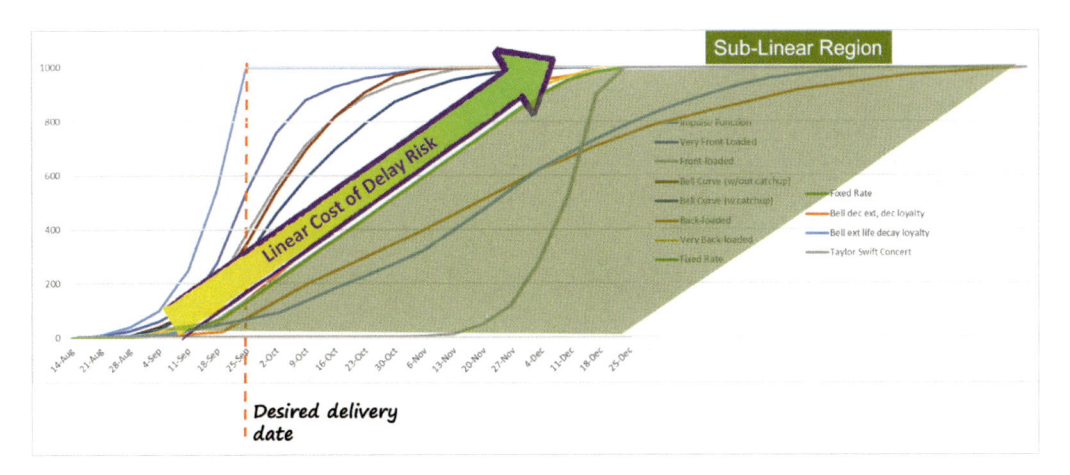

Figure E.11 Sub-Linear region of Probable Cost of Delay in Starting

Table E.1 repeats the classes of service from Appendix D. These classes of service emerged empirically during 2007 at Corbis, a Seattle-based company owned by Bill Gates of Microsoft.

Table E.1 Canonical Set of Classes of Service and Their Relationship to Cost of Delay

Color	Cost of Delay	Class of Service and Its Policies
	↗	**Expedite** Critical and immediate cost of delay; it can exceed other kanban limit (bumps other work).
	↗	**Fixed Date** Cost of delay goes up significantly after deadline.
	↗	**Standard** Increasing urgency, cost of delay is shallow but accelerates before levelling out
	↗	**Intangible** Cost of delay may be significant but is not incurred until significantly later (if at all).

In 2009, David analyzed the usage of these field-proven classes of service and created the four Cost of Delay function sketches shown in Table E.1. At the time, these were essentially based only on intuition, and there was no solid mathematical proof. However, we now have the mathematical proof that these sketches are correct, and our understanding of the domain gives us confidence that these four classes of service are sufficient to differentiate the cost of delay and urgency risk dimensions for adequately managing and hedging risk.

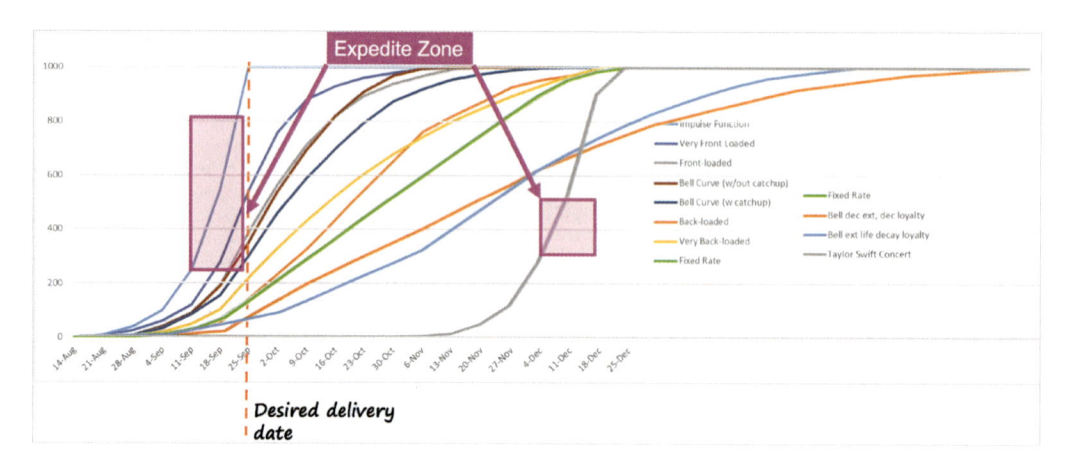

Figure E.12 The Expedite zones on the Probable Cost of Delay in Starting functions

Figure E.12 illustrates the regions on the PCoDS functions where there is a steep slope, that is, a significant value for the derivative. Expedite is a different animal from the other classes of service because the need for it is based on the derivative of the PCoDS function, not on the overall shape of the PCoDS function. It is therefore much more challenging to know when to expedite, and it is considerably trickier to provide generic guidance on it versus the other classes of service. The best advice is that you will know it when you see it. If you understand that a significant amount of the value of an opportunity will be lost in the next few days or weeks, then expediting is required. If there is no other means to hit a deadline against which there is a significant penalty, an item must be expedited. Expediting is necessary because the timing for the start of the work coincides with a steep slope in the PCoDS function.

Figure E.13 shows the square wave function shape associated with a one-off business opportunity with a deadline, the Impulse Value Acquisition Lifecycle function, as well as other VAL functions with significant concavity, such as the Very Front-loaded function. Work items from these categories of Value Acquistion Lifecycle functions produce PCoDS functions that lie in the Fixed Date class of service zone.

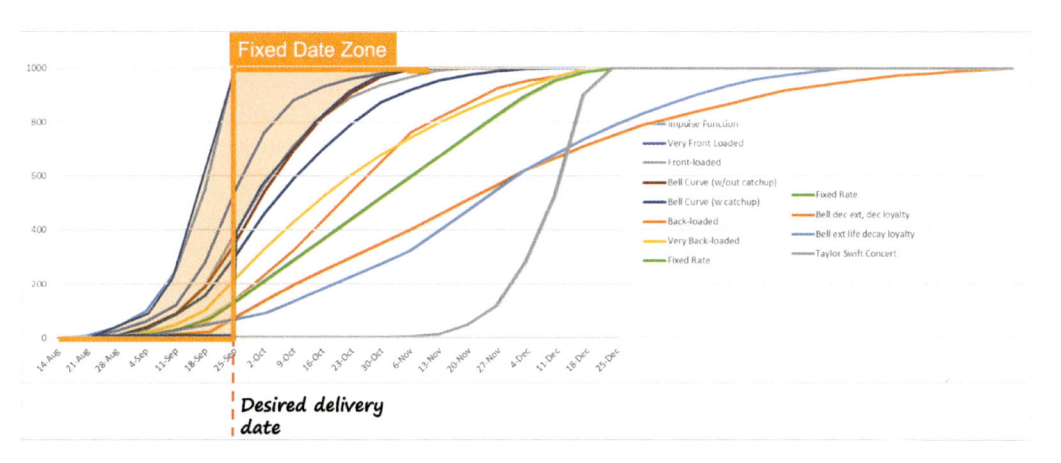

Figure E.13 Fixed Date function shape and Probable Cost of Delay in Starting risk zone

Figure E.14 shows the S-curve function shapes associated with many of the fixed lifecycle business models. Notice that anything to the left of the Linear function is in this zone.

Figure E.14 Standard class of service Probable Cost of Delay in Starting risk zone

Figure E.15 shows that the convex J-curve originally envisioned for the Intangible class of service is in fact an S-curve unwinding over a long time period. This zone also includes all extended-life business models with inherently lower cost of delay even though they are S-curves similar to the Standard class of service PCoDS functions.

Figure E.16 illustrates all four classes of service mapped against the patterns of PCoDS functions. This image shows in a single frame that the original intuition from 2009 regarding classes of service and their Cost of Delay function shapes was correct. The result of this generates some regret, as David chose not to include these functions in the first edition of *Kanban: Successful Evolutionary Change for Your Technology Business*, published in May 2010. At the time, David didn't have a solid mathematical explanation to defend the shapes and therefore hesitated to include them in the manuscript. However, the concept was being test-run simultaneously with clients such as Posit Science in San Francisco. Later in 2010, David became convinced that the technique was useful, and it was adopted into Kanban University training classes. However, this is the first time this material is being published with a full explanation. In the eleven years since 2009, it has become clear that the concept of classes of service, represented by the four types that first emerged at Corbis in 2007, is incredibly robust. It is therefore no surprise that a defensible mathematical proof emerged that provided a scientific basis for their value and utility.

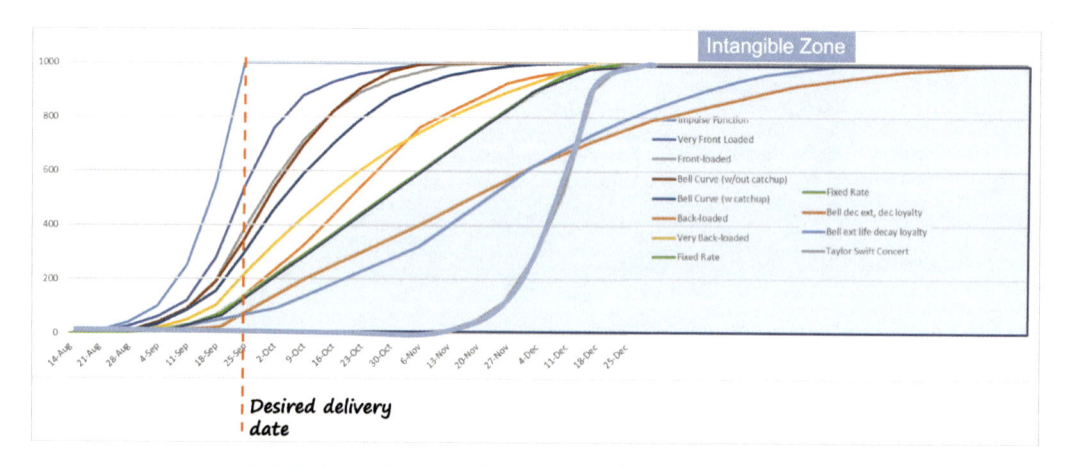

Figure E.15 Intangible cost of delay class of service PCoDS risk zones

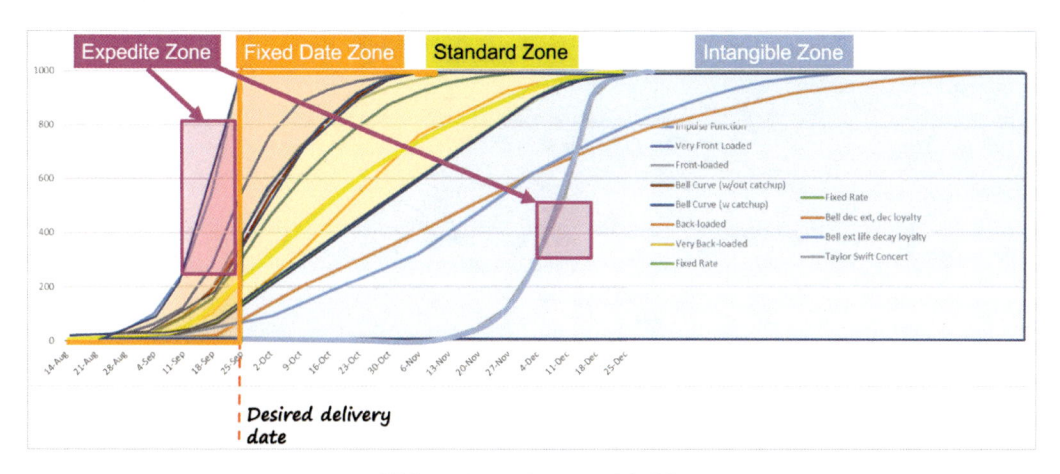

Figure E.16 All four class of service PCoDS function zones

Shelf-Life Ratio

Figure E.17 on the next page repeats Figure D.1 from Appendix D, Triage. It shows five ratios of lead time range compared to the lifecycle length. We suggest using the 98th percentile of the lead time range. The point is to avoid unrealistic values for the range for fat-tailed sub-exponential distributions. If you have a fat-tailed lead time with a long tail, use the separate modifier table, Table D6 in Appendix D, which is designed to account for this additional risk.

The five ratios use the approximate mathematical logarithm used for money/currency in most countries other than the United States and Canada. Money is logarithmic in nature in most nations because issuing coins and notes in these denominations is very efficient: 0.5, 1, 2, 5, 10, 20, and 50 (coins) and 1, 2, 5, 10, 20, 50, and 100 (notes). Logarithmic money reduces the need for a large amount of currency in circulation and makes giving change from cash registers easier. Logarithms occur regularly in nature, and this logarithmic distribution of shelf-life ratios is designed to provide suitable separation of risk and a set of five values in the taxonomy that make it easy to pick the right one and have confidence in the selection.

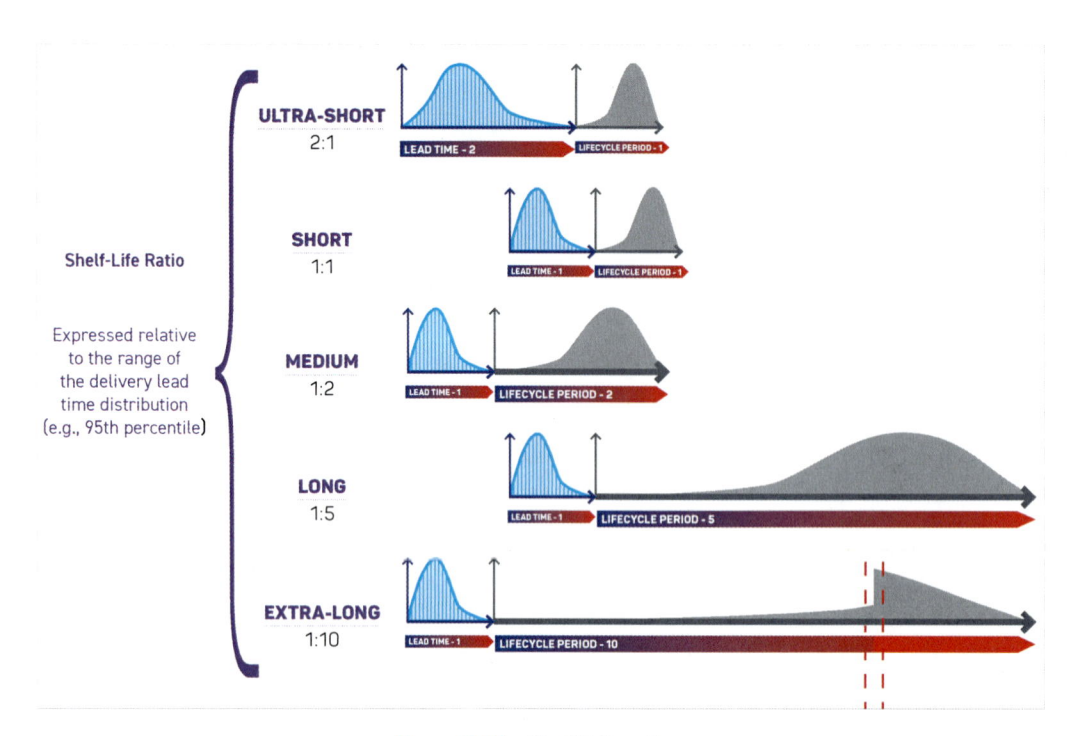

Figure E.17 Shelf-Life ratios

Triage Table Configuration

Table E.2 shows the Triage Table, Table D.2 from Appendix D, with the addition of markers indicating the cost of delay risk. The shelf-life ratios from Figure E.17 range from extremely concave for the ultra-short ratio to very shallow concavity over a long period of time; hence, left to right, the table's columns show high risk through low risk. The rows list the Value Acquisition Lifecycle functions ranked by the concavity of their Delivery Delay Cost functions, with highest risk at the top and lowest at the bottom. Hence, the upper-left portion of the table indicates the highest cost of delay risk, bottom right the lowest. The table's cells show the relevant class of service (taken from an appropriate mapping of PCoDS functions similar to those in Figure E.9 and Figure E.16). This provides three clear zones sloping diagonally upward left to right: a Fixed Date zone; a Standard class of service zone; and an Intangible cost of delay zone. Expedite does not appear on the table because the need to expedite is derived from the derivative of the PCoDS function and requires knowing the precise start date versus the desired delivery date as well as on-the-spot knowledge or understanding of "How much of this opportunity will we lose over the next few days or weeks?" As stated before, providing table-driven guidance on expediting is extremely challenging.

Table E.2 Class of Service Triage Table Illustrating Concavity/Convexity (riskiness)

VALUE ACQUISITION LIFECYCLE (VAL)	Instant	Ultra-Short	Short	Medium	Long	Extra-Long
One-Off Opportunity	FIXED DATE					
Very Front-Loaded		FIXED DATE	FIXED DATE	FIXED DATE	FIXED DATE	STANDARD
Front-Loaded		FIXED DATE	FIXED DATE	FIXED DATE	STANDARD	STANDARD
Bell Curve #1 (1st-mover advantage)		FIXED DATE	FIXED DATE	STANDARD	STANDARD	STANDARD
Bell Curve #2 (with catch-up)		FIXED DATE	STANDARD	STANDARD	STANDARD	INTANGIBLE
Back-Loaded		STANDARD	STANDARD	STANDARD	INTANGIBLE	INTANGIBLE
Very Back-Loaded		STANDARD	STANDARD	INTANGIBLE	INTANGIBLE	INTANGIBLE
Constant Rate		STANDARD	INTANGIBLE	INTANGIBLE	INTANGIBLE	INTANGIBLE
Extended Life #1		STANDARD	INTANGIBLE	INTANGIBLE	INTANGIBLE	INTANGIBLE
Extended Life #2		INTANGIBLE	INTANGIBLE	INTANGIBLE	INTANGIBLE	INTANGIBLE
Last-Minute Decay		INTANGIBLE	INTANGIBLE	INTANGIBLE	INTANGIBLE	INTANGIBLE

SHELF-LIFE RATIO

CONCAVITY / CONVEXITY

Adjusting the Class of Service Based on Start Date

Tables D.5 and D.6 in Appendix D provide guidance on modifying the position in the Triage Table based upon the start date range shown in Figure D.2 in Appendix D. The concept is actually a simple one: if you start early, the cost of delay risk is greatly reduced; if you start late, the cost of delay risk is increased. Increased risk means increased concavity, whereas decreased risk means reduced concavity. Hence, the modified risk of an early start can be modeled by shifting the position on the Triage Table down or to the right; likewise, the modified risk of a late start can be modeled by shifting the position on the Triage Table up or to the left, as shown in Figure E.18.[2]

---

2. At the time of writing, some research continues to optimize this guidance, so modified guidance may be issued in the fourth quarter of 2020 if the research illuminates any anomalies.

Appendix E | Cost of Delay

VALUE ACQUISITION LIFECYCLE (VAL)	SHELF-LIFE RATIO					
	Instant	Ultra-Short	Short	Medium	Long	Extra-Long
One-Off Opportunity	FIXED DATE					
Very Front-Loaded		FIXED DATE	FIXED DATE	FIXED DATE	FIXED DATE	STANDARD
Front-Loaded		FIXED DATE	FIXED DATE	FIXED DATE	STANDARD	STANDARD
Bell Curve #1 (1st-mover advantage)		FIXED DATE	FIXED DATE	STANDARD	STANDARD	STANDARD
Bell Curve #2 (with catch-up)		FIXED DATE	STANDARD	STANDARD	STANDARD	INTANGIBLE
Back-Loaded		STANDARD	STANDARD	STANDARD	INTANGIBLE	INTANGIBLE
Very Back-Loaded		STANDARD	STANDARD	INTANGIBLE	INTANGIBLE	INTANGIBLE
Constant Rate		STANDARD	INTANGIBLE	INTANGIBLE	INTANGIBLE	INTANGIBLE
Extended Life #1		STANDARD	INTANGIBLE	INTANGIBLE	INTANGIBLE	INTANGIBLE
Extended Life #2		INTANGIBLE	INTANGIBLE	INTANGIBLE	INTANGIBLE	INTANGIBLE
Last-Minute Decay		INTANGIBLE	INTANGIBLE	INTANGIBLE	INTANGIBLE	INTANGIBLE

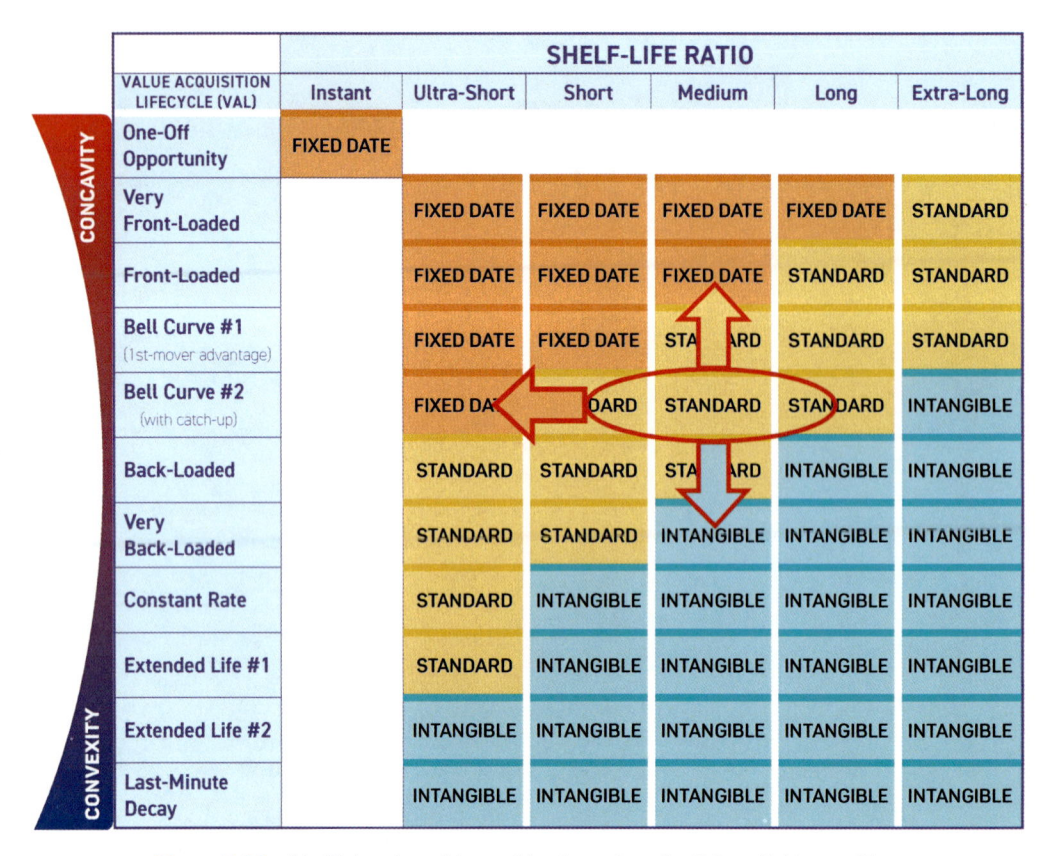

Figure E.18 Modifying the table position based on the Triage Table modifier

F | Dependency Management

The chance that a work request involves additional dependent work—that it invokes other services, whether internal or external to the organization, and that it can be delayed due to these dependencies—causes considerable anxiety. If dependencies exist, there is greater delivery risk, and work should be started earlier to ensure delivery on or before its desired delivery date, thus avoiding any cost of delay.

Often, customers are anxious about dependencies, and they push for early commitment, early start, and certainty regarding delivery. A common approach to handling dependencies involves a lot of upfront analysis and planning to detect and manage them. There is a tendency to treat all dependencies homogeneously in a fashion that is expensive and often creates a brittle dependency graph of fixed start and finish dates in the style of a Gantt or PERT chart, even when these tools are not explicitly used. Cost of delay and classes of service, as described in Appendixes D and E, give us insights into cheaper, faster, more economical, dynamic methods to manage dependencies without all of the expensive upfront analysis and planning. Dependencies should not be managed homogeneously; they should be managed according to the cost of delay and the required class of service for a work item.

To manage dependencies in an efficient and cost-effective manner with Kanban, we utilize a dynamic scheduling or reservation system—a technique we are borrowing from complex scheduling problems with lots of dependencies and timing uncertainty, such as the commercial airline industry. We also utilize "class of dependency" management—the concept of classes of service applied to the domain of managing dependencies. Together, these two new techniques, combined with our existing methods of Triage Tables and classes of service for kanban work items, give us a very powerful, properly risk-adjusted approach to dependency management. The dramatic benefit of this is that it is necessary to proactively manage dependencies only for Fixed Date class of service items. Typically, true Fixed Date items account for 10 to 20 percent of demand in a kanban system. Hence, we learn that we can avoid expensive, upfront dependency analysis and planning for 80 percent of our demand. This realization delivers a significant economic boost.

Reservation Systems

A reservation system permits making bookings for the kanban system based on a calendar. Reservation systems provide a means to schedule the start of work. Adding classes of reservation (or booking classes) to the reservation system provides an improved means for managing uncertainty. The concept is not new. Airlines have used classes of reservation to manage risk for years.

For example, three basic classes of reservation exist when flying on full-service airlines: guaranteed seat, standby, and shuttle service. A guaranteed seat on a scheduled flight is just like it sounds—you are guaranteed to get on and have a seat and you probably know the specific seat number. Standby implies that you don't have a guaranteed seat but instead you will "stand by" at the boarding gate and wait for availability, taking the best remaining seat available before departure. A shuttle service ticket is less common, but it occurs on London-to-New York and Madrid-to-Barcelona routes. A shuttle ticket is more expensive than business class. It guarantees you'll be on the next available flight after check-in, without a reservation. You just show up and hop on the next flight—like a bus but with a guaranteed seat. Cost of delay, or uncertainty of schedule risk, can be managed through classes of booking.

A booking or reservation system is usually a visual board adjacent to a kanban board with a space for each time period between Replenishment Meetings. Tickets are placed into the slots to make a reservation, essentially guaranteeing that a work item will be started at that time, or at least be given the opportunity to start based on its booking class.

Figure F.1 shows a basic reservation system board adjacent to a kanban board. The slots in each time period on the calendar should be equivalent to the average (mean) delivery rate from the kanban system.

If we introduce classes of reservation, we can allocate capacity for different classes as a means of hedging risk. This is shown in Figure F.2.

The total number of reservable kanban must not exceed the average delivery rate of the kanban system. Figure F.2 shows real data from a firm in northern Germany, courtesy of flow.hamburg. The average delivery rate is twenty work items per week. The twenty are allocated into three tranches for three classes of booking: Guaranteed, Reserved, and Standby. These are described in Table F.1.

Reservation Systems

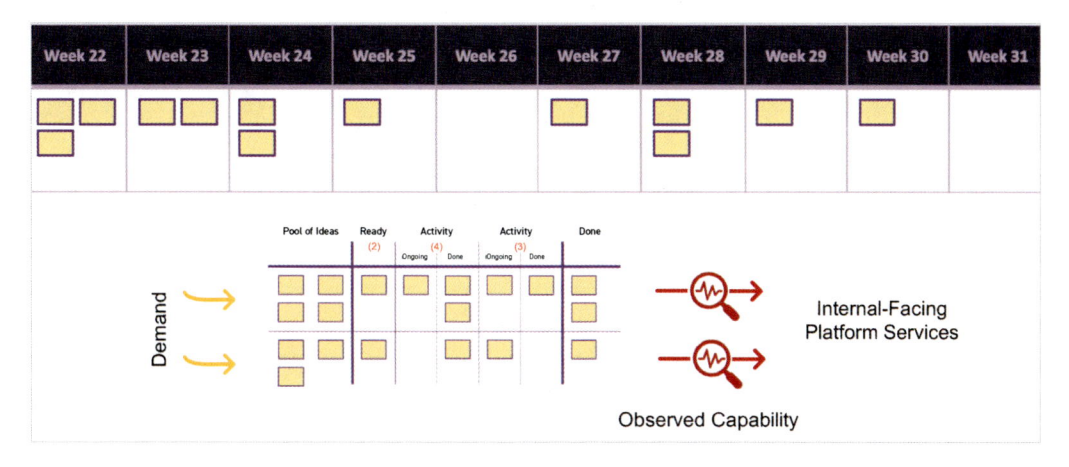

Figure F.1 Basic reservation system board[1]

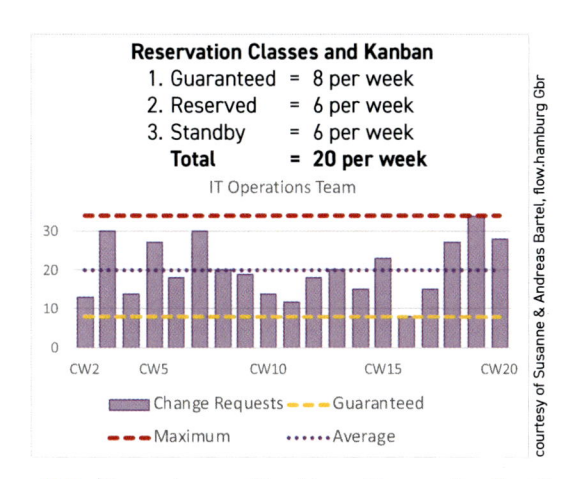

Figure F.2 Three classes of booking with capacity allocation[2]

Table F.1 Classes of Booking

Class of Booking	Description
Guaranteed	An item is guaranteed to start on this date.
Reserved	If capacity is available, this item will be started on this date.
Standby	If additional capacity is available, this item will be considered for selection against other items in the Ready buffer upstream of commitment. It will be given strong preference. If it isn't successful, its class of booking may be elevated to Reserved at the next or a subsequent opportunity.

---

1. First reported by Sami Honkonen in 2011; https://www.slideshare.net/AGILEMinds/sami-honkonen-scheduling-work-in-kanban
2. Real data from an IT operations team in Hamburg, Germany

In this example, the minimum delivery rate is eight items per week, hence the Guaranteed class of booking has an allocation of eight. The difference between the mean of twenty and the minimum of eight is twelve, and those twelve are split evenly to give six for Reserved and six for Standby classes of booking. This is just an example, but it communicates the concept and might be typical of a risk-hedging strategy for schedule and dependency uncertainty using a dynamic reservation system. You are free to adapt your own classes of reservation and/or capacity allocation strategy to suit your own unique circumstances.

Classes of Dependency Management

It is possible to minimize the economic and productivity impacts of managing for dependencies by utilizing classes of service based on cost of delay. When a request isn't urgent, it makes sense to let dependency discovery happen dynamically and manage the dependency using established Kanban visualization and flow management techniques. When cost of delay is low, there is no need to invest time and energy up front to detect, plan for, schedule, and manage dependencies. It is important to understand that not all requests should be treated homogeneously from a dependency management perspective.

We have identified six classes of dependency management based on cost of delay and the four classes of service of the originating request. They are: Don't Care, Trusted Availability, Tail-Risk Mitigation, Fixed Date, Guaranteed On-Time, and Expedite. It is necessary to make upfront dependency discovery—planning for dependencies and advanced management—only when the originating request has a Fixed Date class of service. Recognizing and understanding this creates significant economic and productivity improvement.

Table F.2 shows the class of service for the originating customer request on the calling service, the necessary class of service for the dependency work item on the called service, the class of dependency management, and the class of reservation needed on both the calling and called services.

The six classes of dependency management are described below. It is worth taking a moment to consider why we have six classes of dependency management though only four classes of service for kanban work items.

Classes 2 and 3 model items that have a probable cost of delay starting in the standard zone, as shown in Figure E.14 in Appendix E. However, the customer has different expectations for delivery. For Class 2, the expectation is within a service level agreement (SLA) or a softer service level expectation (SLE) that would typically describe a lead time expectation in days with some due-date performance expectation such as 85 percent on-time delivery. For Class 3, the expectations are tighter—there is a deadline or specific date for delivery. There are two typical reasons for this: this is a low-trust relationship and the customer is unwilling to agree to an SLA/SLE-type of contract with the delivery service;

or this item is part of a bigger, dependent network of items—perhaps sub-systems in a systems engineering project—and integration testing dates have been agreed. Hence, complex dependencies in big projects involving hardware, software, physical resources, and perhaps specific geographic locations may need to use date-driven planning. Although the work is being started early enough that it can be processed as Standard class, there is a need to deliver within a reasonable expectation. If there is an SLA, we must hit it. We must mitigate any risk of being in the tail of the lead time distribution. Hence, any dependencies must be managed such that they do not push our item into the tail of the lead time distribution. There must be no unexpected delays from a dependency.

Classes 4 and 5 are separated by the concept that Class 4 is merely a work item in the Fixed Date Zone, Figure E.13 in Appendix E, while Class 5 Dependency Management has a unit step impact function on a specific date, as illustrated by the heavy orange function line in the same figure. So, Class 5 should be used for items with a known and specific impact on a given day, such as a fine for failure to meet new regulations in a regulated industry such as banking, civil aviation, immigration, oil and gas, and so on.

Table F.2 Six Classes of Dependency Management

Class of Dependency Management	Calling Service Ticket	Called Service Ticket	Calling Service Reservation	Called Service Reservation	Nature of Dependency Management
1. Don't Care	Intangible	Intangible	Optional Standby	None	No dependency management; dynamic, just-in-time dependency discovery
2. Trusted Availability	Standard w/ SLE	Standard	Optional Standby	None	Dynamic, just-in-time dependency discovery; capacity allocation on called service to guarantee service when needed
3. Tail-Risk Mitigation	Standard w/ Deadline	Fixed Date	Optional Reserved	Standby	Standby class of reservation (just in case); dynamic, just-in-time dependency discovery; use filtered lead time distribution—assume dependency exists to determine start time and calling service ticket's class of service.
4. Fixed Date	Fixed Date	Fixed Date with high-priority start	Reserved	Reserved	Up-front dependency detection, with reserved class booking on called service; definition of ready requires up-front analysis and a reserved class booking.
5. Guaranteed On-Time	Fixed Date w/ zero tolerance for delay	Fixed Date w/ guaranteed start	Guaranteed	Guaranteed	Up-front dependency detection, with guaranteed class of booking on called service; definition of ready requires up-front analysis and a guaranteed called service reservation.
6. Expedite	Expedite	Expedite	None	None	No dependency management; dynamic dependency discovery; expedite dependencies when discovered.

Class 1 Dependency Management: Don't Care

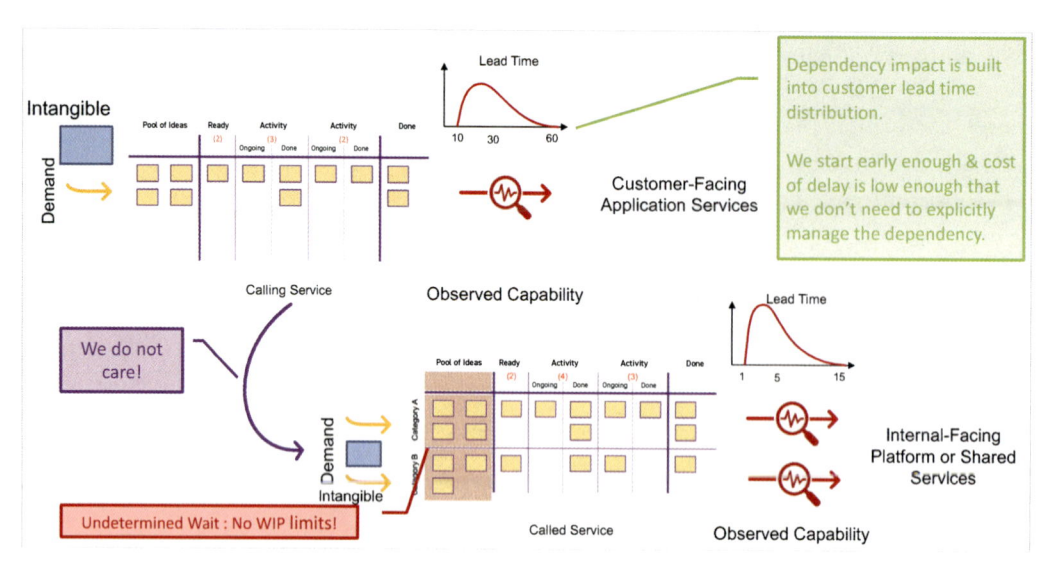

Figure F.3 Don't Care dependency management

The cost of delay is very low; hence, there is no need to actively manage dependencies; simply let them happen if they do. Class 1 Dependency Management, as modeled in Figure F.3, works as follows:

- Chance of dependency occurrence is probabilistic.
- Use probabilistic scheduling—if it happens, it happens!
- Lead time distributions already account for dependency delays.
  - No attempt to discover dependencies
- There is low risk of incurring any significant cost of delay, or
- We can start early enough that we don't care about lead time tail risk.
- So, just do it, don't worry about dependencies. Let them happen if they do!
- No reservation is needed for the calling service or the called service.

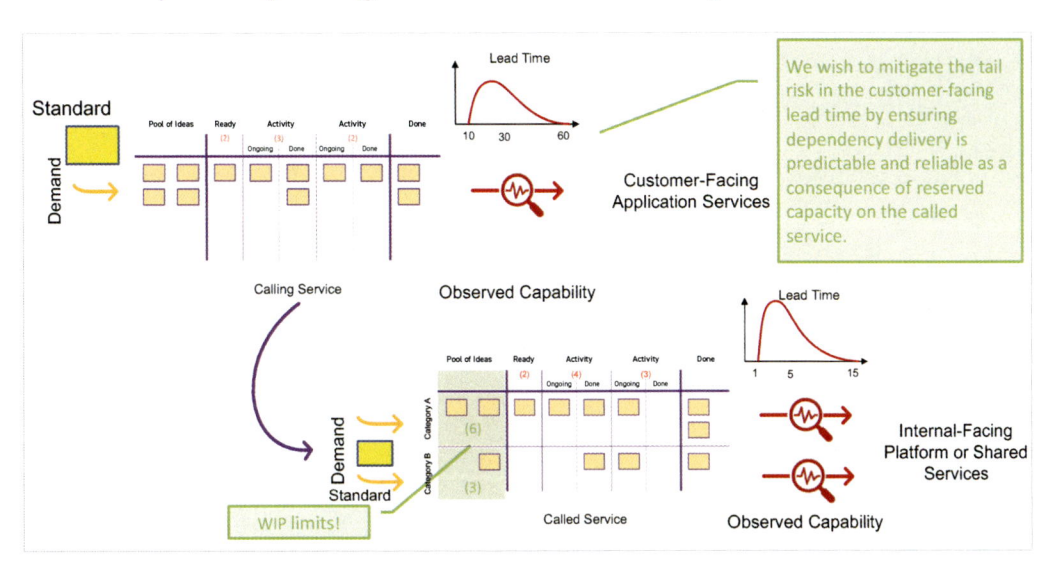

Class 2 Dependency Management: Trusted Availability

Figure F.4 Trusted Availability dependency management

The cost of delay is low, but trusted delivery implies it is within an SLA/SLE. Class 2 dependency management, modeled in Figure F.4, works as follows:

- There is a probabilistic chance of a dependency occurrence.
- Use probabilistic scheduling.
- We care about tail risk due to cost of delay in the calling service (e.g., a change request for IT system maintenance). Tail risk is increased when a dependency exists, for example, on database administrators (the called service).
- There is no attempt to determine whether a specific dependency occurs or when specific capacity will be required on the called service.
- It needs reliable service and predictable queuing on the called service (e.g., the called service has an SLE).
- Allocate capacity on the called service for probabilistically anticipated demand. Use outcome-driven design to design for anticipated demand with STATIK.[3] Little's Law (MF 3.6) provides average delivery capability, defining a WIP limit for capacity.

---

3. STATIK, meaning Systems Thinking Approach to Introducing Kanban, is a process for designing a kanban system for managing service delivery and the work that is to be performed as part of it, and improving it continuously. It defines eight steps, conducted for each identified service: (1) Understand what makes the service fit-for-purpose for the customer. (2) Understand sources of dissatisfaction with the current system. (3) Analyze demand. (4) Analyze capability. (5) Model workflow. (6) Discover classes of services. (7) Design the kanban system. (8) Socialize the system and board design and negotiate implementation.

- Demand shaping. Shape demand from the calling service against average delivery capability. Avoid overburdening the called service.
- Track lead time on the called service from request submission, as the request is already committed. By definition, demand on the called service is irrefutable. It is push demand. Lead time distribution and SLA take into account queuing time delay at the front end of the called service.
- If a dynamic booking system is implemented on the calling (customer-facing) service, then schedule a slot on the calling service sufficiently far ahead of the desired delivery date to account for the tail of its lead time distribution.
- Use Standby class of service for the reservation (i.e., we'd like to start this early if possible and if capacity is available).

Class 3 Dependency Management: Tail-Risk Mitigation

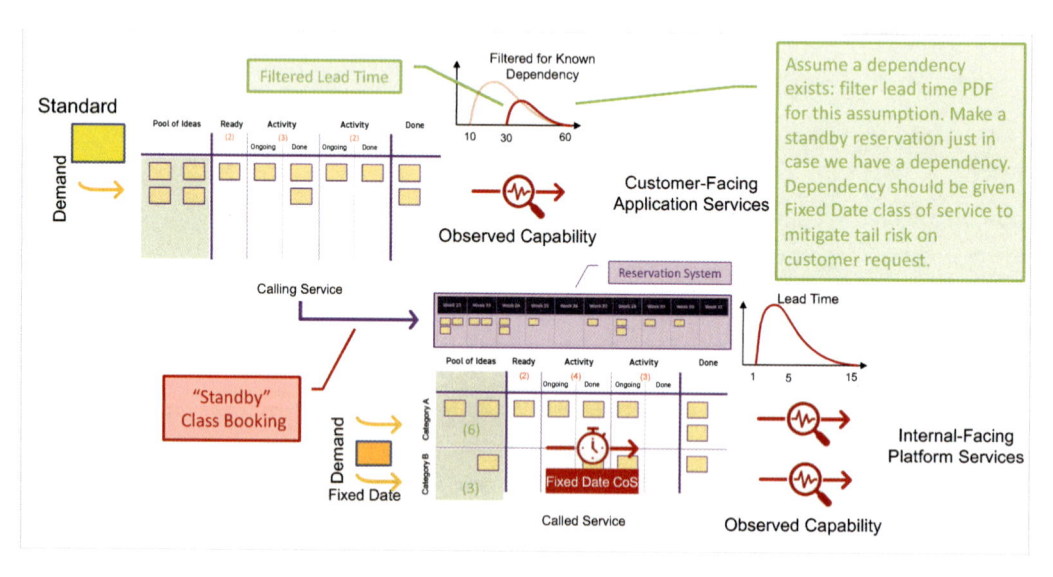

Figure F.5 Tail Risk-Mitigation dependency management

In Class 3 dependency management, modeled in Figure F.5, the cost of delay is worth managing, and there is a desire to avoid excessive cost of delay in the 85th through the 100th percentiles of the lead time. Therefore, we hedge the risk and assume a dependency exists. This has the effect of encouraging us to start the item earlier. We are trading off early start (earlier commitment) for the economic benefit of not having to detect and actively manage a dependency up front. Class 3 dependency management works as follows:

- Use probabilistic scheduling for any dependency, but assume one exists.
- Use filtered lead time to facilitate scheduling and selection (encourages earlier start).

- Trade off an earlier start against the economic cost of detecting and actively managing the dependency. If dependency detection is cheap and easy, why not do it, and defer commitment until later? Notice the relationship to option pricing and Real Options thinking.
- Capacity must be available on the called system when it is needed to provide prompt, trustworthy, predictable, reliable service delivery for the dependency.
- Use capacity allocation and demand shaping on the called service.
- Introduce a reservation system for the called system.
- Book a *Standby* slot on the called system. No reservation on the calling system is needed because the filtered calling system lead time distribution accounts for the effect of the dependency.

Class 4 Dependency Management: Fixed Date

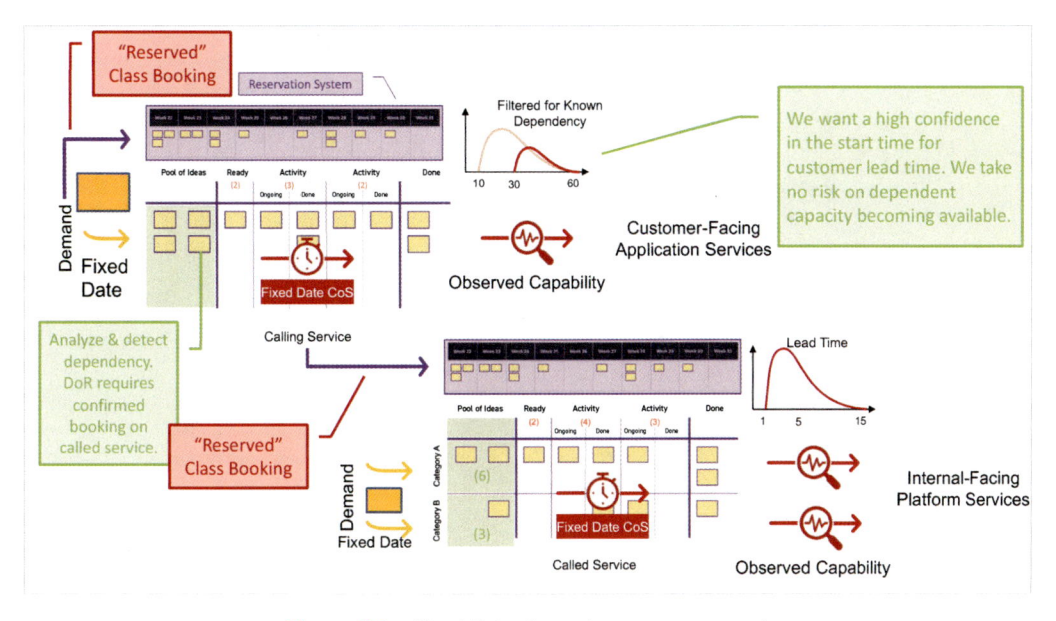

Figure F.6 Fixed Date dependency management

For Class 4, Fixed Date dependency management (see Figure F.6), there is a significant cost of delay. There is a need to deliver on or before a deadline associated with an external event. It is now necessary to determine in advance whether or not a dependency exists. Any dependency is actively managed using a filtered lead time distribution and a reservation on the called system. Class 4 Dependency Management works as follows:

- Implement a reservation system on the calling (customer-facing) service.
- Make a Reserved class booking for the customer's work item.

- Cost of delay is significant or critical, or deferred commitment is valuable (as arrival of additional information to mitigate other risks is required to facilitate [in/out] selection decisions), or it was simply not possible to start early enough to mitigate tail risk.
- Treat as Class 3 and, in addition:
    - Anticipate approximately when the dependency will occur.
    - Forecast time from commitment to when the dependency will occur.
    - Book a Reserved class kanban in the dynamic reservation system for the calling service.
    - Book a Reserved class kanban in the dynamic reservation system for the called service.
- The calling service's definition of ready requires a booking on the called service. A confirmed booking for the dependency is necessary as an initial pull criterion at replenishment.

Class 5 Dependency Management: Guaranteed On-Time

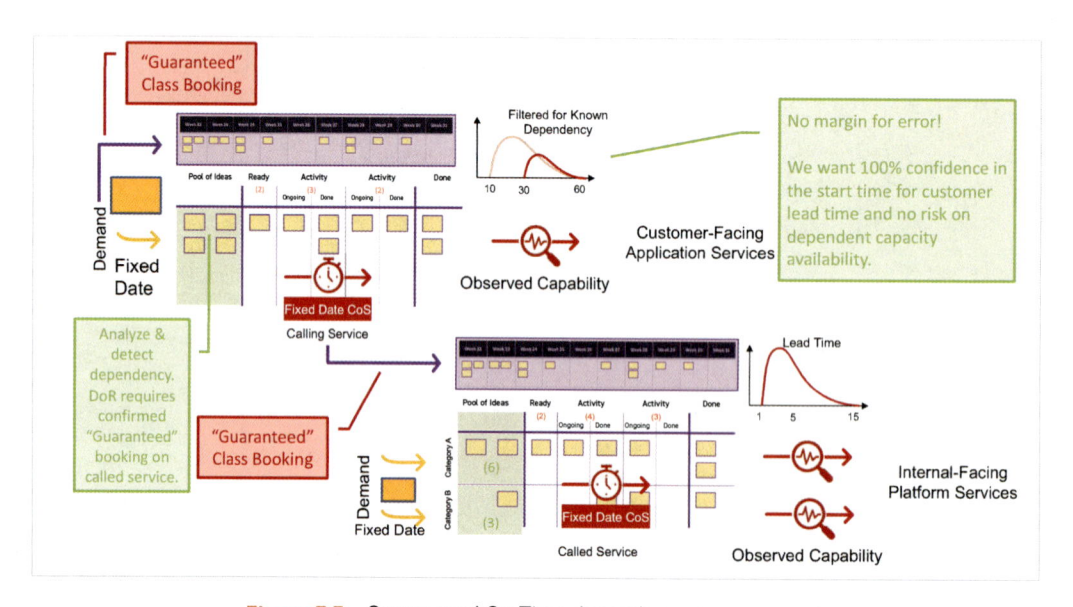

Figure F.7 Guaranteed On-Time dependency management

Class 5 dependency management, depicted in Figure F.7, is the most expensive and should be used when there is zero tolerance for late delivery: the cost of delay is significant and occurs dramatically on a known date in the future. Use Class 5 dependency management when there is no margin for error with the delivery schedule. Class 5 dependency management works as Class 4 does, but with the following addition:

- Definition of ready is tightened to Guaranteed class booking in the reservation system for the work items on both the calling and the called services.

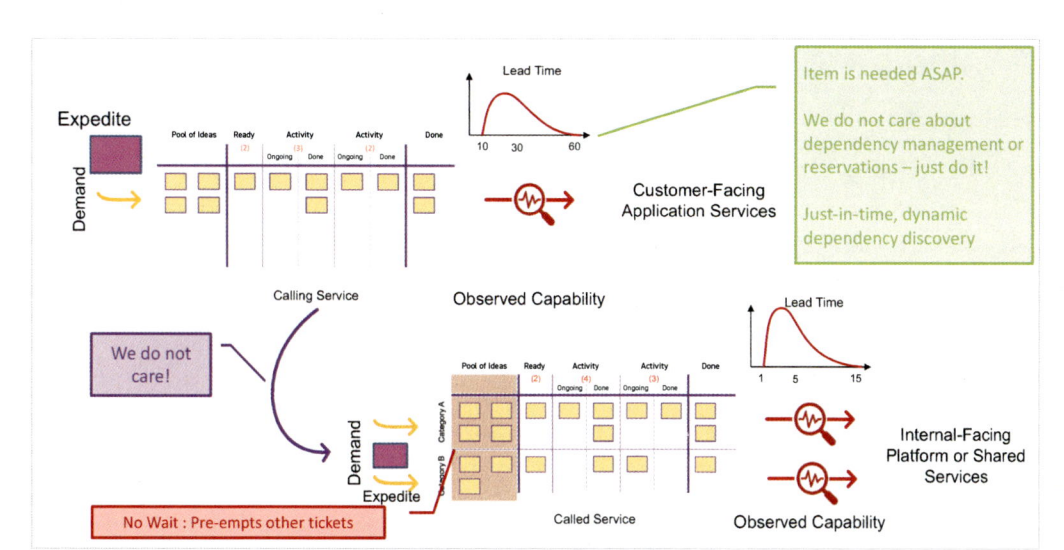

Class 6 Dependency Management: Expedite

Figure F.8 Expedite dependency management

For Class 6 (modeled in Figure F.8), the work is urgent and critical and must be delivered as soon as possible. We need to expedite the customer-requested tickets and all the dependent tickets that they spawn. Class 6 dependency management works as follows:

- We do not care about dependency management: Just do it!
- Just-in-time dynamic dependency discovery is done.
- All dependent requests receive Expedite class of service.
- Reservation systems are not used.
- No upfront dependency detection is done.

General Dependency Management with Kanban

There are many specific practices in the Kanban Method that contribute to an effective approach to dependency management, for example:

1. Checkboxes on kanban ticket design (VZ 2.9)
2. Rows on kanban boards (VZ 2.2, 2.10, 2.11, 3.7)
3. Sequential dependencies shown from left to right in the design of workflow kanban boards (MF 2.3)
4. Parent-child dependencies in the design of two-tiered kanban boards (VZ 3.8)
5. Parking lots used to hold items blocked due to dependent work external to the immediate board (VZ 3.9)

6. Mapping shared services to an existing board using a column with a WIP limit (VZ 3.17), or avatars for individuals (VZ 2.6)
7. Marking blocked tickets with different colors to indicate the type of dependency (VZ 2.5 and MF 2.6)
8. Blocker clustering (FL 2.3)
9. Risk Review (FL 3.6, 4.1)
10. Operations Review (FL 4.2)
11. Capacity allocation for types of work or sources of demand (MF 4.9)
12. Decorating tickets to show peer-to-peer dependency (VZ 3.8)
13. Split-merge board design to show integration dependencies (VZ 4.4)
14. Use of date fields on tickets to show integration dependency dates (VZ 3.8)
15. Dynamic reservation systems (MF 4.6)
16. Classes of booking (MF 4.6)
17. Classes of dependency management (MF 4.5)
18. Classes of service (VZ 3.7, VZ 4.9, LW 4.3, MF 3.10, MF 4.10)
19. Triage Tables (based on probable cost of delay in starting) (MF 3.12)
20. Delivery Planning Meeting (FL 3.3)

The Kanban Method gives us a rich palette of techniques with which to manage dependencies, and these specific practices occur at almost every level in the maturity model. Capability at managing dependencies is a spectrum covering ML2 to ML5.

G | The KMM in a Nutshell

The KMM Architecture

KANBAN MATURITY MODEL

CULTURE			PRACTICES									OUTCOMES	
Leadership	Values	Focus	Scope	Organizational Maturity Level	GP / SP	Visualize	Limit WIP	Manage Flow	Make Policies Explicit	Feedback Loops	Improve & Evolve	Actions	F4P
SELF		Who I am	Tasks	0. Oblivious	Consolidation							CHAOTIC REACTIONARY UNALIGNED	UNFIT
IDENTITY DRIVEN / HEROIC	HOLISTIC THINKING | ALIGNMENT | UNITY | SHARED PURPOSE	Who we are	Deliverables	1. Team-Focused	Transition								
					Consolidation								
			Products/Services	2. Customer-Driven	Transition								
					Consolidation								
ALTRUISTIC / PURPOSE-DRIVEN		Why we exist	Product Lines and Services in a Business Unit	3. Fit-for-Purpose	Transition							EXPLAINABLE ANTICIPATORY CONGRUENT	UNSUSTAINABLE
					Consolidation								
		What we do		4. Risk-Hedged	Transition								
					Consolidation								
HUMBLE		How we do it	Multiple Business Units	5. Market Leader	Transition								SUSTAINABLE
					Consolidation								
DUTY-DRIVEN		Challenge How, What, Why, & Who		6. Built for Survival	Transition								
					Consolidation								

447

The KMM Cultural Values

Organizational Maturity	VALUES
0 Oblivious	• Achievement
1 Team-Focused	• Collaboration • Taking Initiative • Transparency
2 Customer-Driven	• Acts of Leadership • Customer Awareness • Evolutionary Change • Flow • Narrative • Respect • Understanding (internal)
3 Fit-for-Purpose	• Agreement • Balance • Customer Service • Fitness for Purpose • Leadership at All Levels • Short-term Results • Understanding (external) • Unity & Alignment
4 Risk-Hedged	• Business Focus • Competition • Customer Intimacy • Data-driven Decision Making • Deeper Balance • Fairness • Leadership Development • Regulatory Compliance
5 Market Leader	• Equality of Opportunity • Experimentation • Perfectionism • Social Mobility
6 Built for Survival	• Congruence • Long-term Survival • Tolerance & Diversity

The KMM Outcomes and Benefits

Level	Maturity	Outcomes	Benefits
0	**Oblivious** — Every customer has their "pet"	• Failure to understand the need for a process • Faith in the individual to deliver	**Relief from Overburdening:** • Get things done • Improved transparency • Less overburdened people
1	**Team-Focused** — Individual heroics	• Emerging process • Very inconsistent delivery	
2	**Customer-Driven** — Managerial heroics	• Consistent process • Inconsistent delivery	**Customer Awareness** • Basic understanding of workflow • Improved collaboration • Greater empathy • Improved quality of work • Basic understanding of demand and capability • Managerial coordination
3	**Fit-for-Purpose** — No more heroes any more; Trustworthy	• Consistent process • Consistent delivery	**Meeting customer expectations** • Shorter lead time • Fast and balanced workflow • Predictability • Meet SLAs • Actionable metrics • Satisfied customers
4	**Risk-Hedged** — Secure, valued	• Consistent process • Predictable delivery • Consistent economics	**Risk Management** • Risk Hedging • Quantitative analysis • Dynamic scheduling • Economically robust
5	**Market Leader** — Highly secure, highly valued, Admired	• Optimized processes • Best-in-class delivery • Market-leading economics	**Organizational Agility** • Reconfigurable shared services • Workforce flexibility • Perfectionism
6	**Built for Survival** — A history of dramatic and surprising reinvention	• Old business lines retired • New business lines begun • Economically sustainable reinvention	**Long-term Survival** • Congruent decision making • Robust to external changes • Capability for reinvention • Long-term security

450 The KMM in a Nutshell

The KMM Evolutionary Change Model

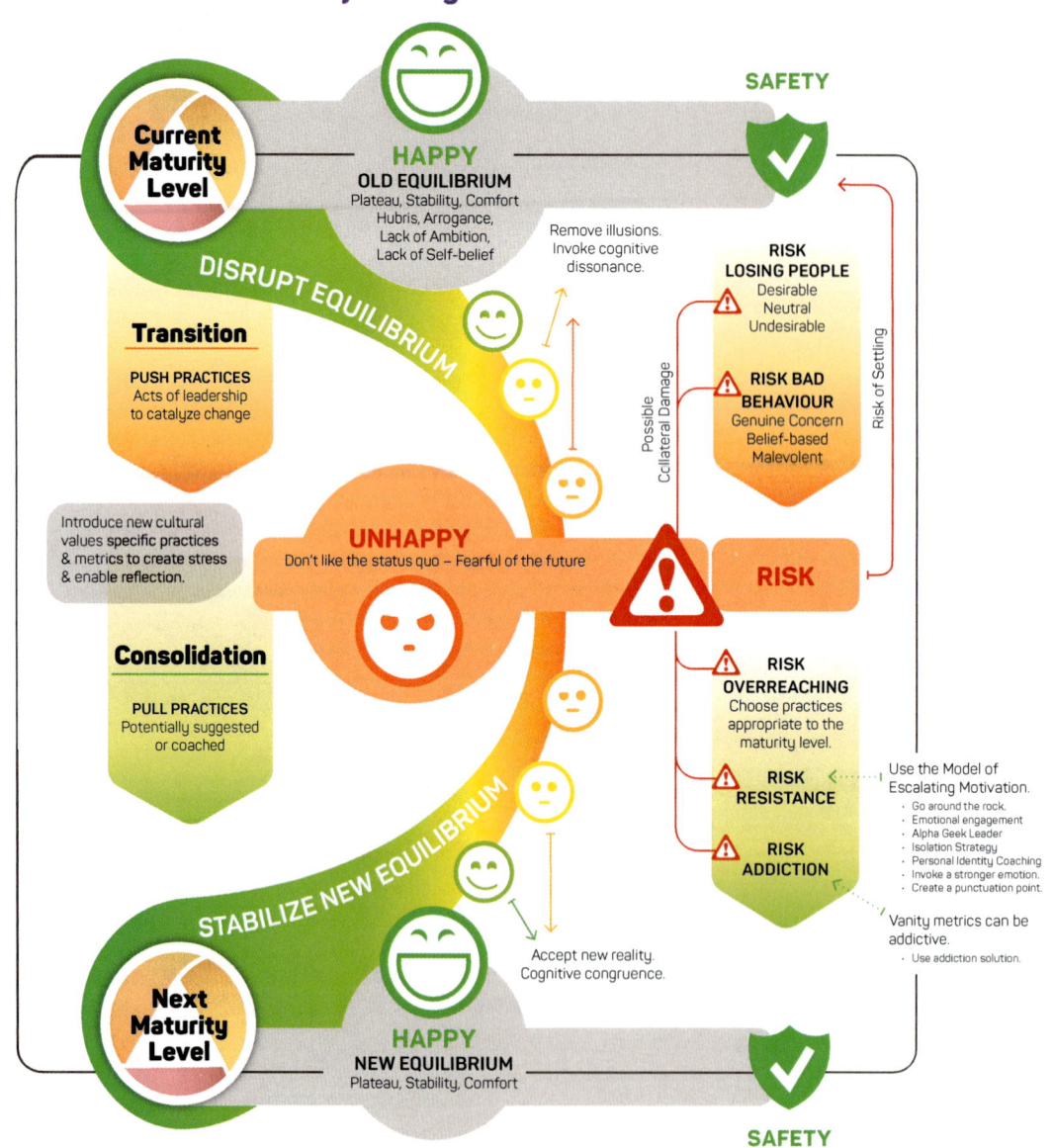

The KMM Practices
Visualize

Maturity Level		Visualize (VZ) Practices	Page
ML0 Oblivious	Consolidation	VZ 0.1 Visualize a person's work by means of a individual kanban board.	120
		VZ 0.2 Visualize basic work item related information on a ticket.	121
ML1 Team-Focused	Transition	VZ 1.1 Visualize work for several people by means of an aggregated individual kanban board.	122
		VZ 1.2 Visualize discovered initial policies.	122
		VZ 1.3 Use avatars to visualize an individual's workload.	123
	Consolidation	VZ 1.4 Visualize the work carried out by a team by means of a team kanban board.	124
		VZ 1.5 Visualize basic policies.	125
ML2 Customer-Driven	Transition	VZ 2.1 Visualize progress using a horizontal position on an emergent workflow kanban board.	125
		VZ 2.2 Visualize work types by means of card colors or board rows.	126
		VZ 2.3 Visualize blocked work items, defects, and rework.	128
		VZ 2.4 Visualize work item aging.	129
		VZ 2.5 Visualize dependencies on another service or system.	130
		VZ 2.6 Visualize dependencies on shared services using avatars.	131
		VZ 2.7 Visualize basic service policies.	132
	Consolidation	VZ 2.8 Visualize constant WIP (CONWIP) on an emergent workflow delivery kanban board.	133
		VZ 2.9 Visualize concurrent or unordered activities with checkboxes on the ticket.	134
		VZ 2.10 Visualize optional, unordered, potentially concurrent activities using two columns of checkboxes on the ticket.	134
		VZ 2.11 Visualize optional multiple unordered, nonconcurrent activities performed by specialist teams using partial rows within a column on the board.	135
		VZ 2.12 Visualize defined workflow using a kanban board.	136
		VZ 2.13 Visualize multiple services by means of an aggregated service delivery overview board.	138
ML3 Fit-for-Purpose	Transition	VZ 3.1 Visualize Ready to Commit status, also known as Ready to Pull.	138
		VZ 3.2 Visualize request acceptance criteria, also known as entry criteria.	139
		VZ 3.3 Visualize workflow and team's work items by means of an aggregated teams kanban board.	140
		VZ 3.4 Visualize Ideas development by means of an upstream (discovery) kanban board.	141
		VZ 3.5 Visualize discarded options on an upstream (discovery) kanban board.	143
		VZ 3.6 Visualize aborted work.	143
		VZ 3.7 Visualize class of service using ticket colors, board rows, or ticket decorators.	144
		VZ 3.8 Visualize parent-child and peer-to-peer dependencies.	145
		VZ 3.9 Use a parking lot to visualize currently waiting or blocked work requests dependent on another service or system.	146
		VZ 3.10 Visualize pull signals.	147

Maturity Level		Visualize (VZ) Practices (continued)	Page
ML3 Fit-for-Purpose	Consolidation	**VZ 3.11** Visualize replenishment signals.	148
		VZ 3.12 Visualize pull criteria (also known as pull policies, definition of done, or exit criteria).	149
		VZ 3.13 Visualize what is pullable.	150
		VZ 3.14 Visualize available capacity.	150
		VZ 3.15 Visualize failure demand versus value demand.	151
		VZ 3.16 Visualize target date or SLA.	151
		VZ 3.17 Visualize dependencies on shared services using a column with a WIP limit.	152
ML4 Risk-Hedged	Transition	**VZ 4.1** Visualize local cycle time.	153
		VZ 4.2 Use ticket decorators to indicate risk.	154
		VZ 4.3 Visualize risk classes with different swim lanes.	155
		VZ 4.4 Visualize split-and-merge workflows.	156
		VZ 4.5 Visualize waiting time in a dependencies parking lot.	157
		VZ 4.6 Visualize SLA exceeded in a dependencies parking lot.	158
	Consolidation	**VZ 4.7** Visualize WIP limits in a dependencies parking lot.	158
		VZ 4.8 Visualize capacity allocation by work type.	159
		VZ 4.9 Visualize capacity allocation by class of service.	160
ML5 Market Leader	Transition		
	Consolidation	**VZ 5.1** Visualize fixed teams and floating workers (shared resources) across aggregated services.	161

Limit Work-in-Progress

Maturity Level		Limit Work-in-Progress (LW) Practices	Page
ML0 Oblivious	Consolidation	**LW 0.1** Establish personal WIP limits.	165
ML1 Team-Focused	Transition	**LW 1.1** Establish per-person WIP limits.	166
	Consolidation	**LW 1.2** Establish team WIP limits.	166
ML2 Customer-Driven	Transition		
	Consolidation	**LW 2.1** Establish constant WIP (CONWIP) limits on an emergent workflow.	167
		LW 2.2 Establish WIP limits on an aggregated service delivery overview board.	168
ML3 Fit-for-Purpose	Transition	**LW 3.1** Establish activity-based WIP limits.	168
	Consolidation	**LW 3.2** Use an order point (minimum limit) for upstream replenishment.	169
		LW 3.3 Use a maximum (max) limit to constrain upstream capacity.	170
		LW 3.4 Bracket WIP limits across sub-states.	170
		LW 3.5 Bracket WIP limits across activities.	171
		LW 3.6 Create a full kanban system.	172
ML4 Risk-Hedged	Transition		
	Consolidation	**LW 4.1** Limit WIP for a dependency parking lot.	173
		LW 4.2 Limit WIP by type of work.	174
		LW 4.3 Limit WIP by class of service.	174

Manage Flow

Maturity Level		Manage Flow (MF) Practice	Page
ML0 Oblivious	Consolidation	**MF 0.1** Categorize tasks based on the nature of the work and its urgency, importance, and impact.	177
ML1 Team-Focused	Transition	No specific practices at ML1; same as ML0, but at a team level.	
	Consolidation		
ML2 Customer-Driven	Transition	**MF 2.1** Define work types based on customer requests. **MF 2.2** Define basic services. **MF 2.3** Map upstream and downstream flow. **MF 2.4** Collect flow-related data (e.g., lead time). **MF 2.5** Capture the desired delivery date.	178 178 179 180 180
	Consolidation	**MF 2.6** Manage blocking issues. **MF 2.7** Manage defects and other rework types. **MF 2.8** Manage aging WIP. **MF 2.9** Implement Flow Manager role.	181 181 182 182
ML3 Fit-for-Purpose	Transition	**MF 3.1** Organize around the knowledge discovery process. **MF 3.2** Defer commitment (decide before the last responsible moment). **MF 3.3** Measure and analyze the service's fitness-for-purpose. **MF 3.4** Use cumulative flow diagrams to monitor queues. **MF 3.5** Use Little's Law. **MF 3.6** Report rudimentary flow efficiency. **MF 3.7** Gradually eliminate infinite buffers. **MF 3.8** Actively close upstream requests that meet the discard criteria. **MF 3.9** Analyze and report on aborted work. **MF 3.10** Use classes of service to affect selection. **MF 3.11** Analyze and report on failure demand.	183 185 187 188 189 191 192 193 193 194 195
	Consolidation	**MF 3.12** Develop triage discipline. **MF 3.13** Manage peer-to-peer and parent-child dependencies. **MF 3.14** Use two-phase commit. **MF 3.15** Establish a service level agreement (SLA). **MF 3.16** Determine the due date. **MF 3.17** Forecast delivery. **MF 3.18** Apply qualitative Real Options Thinking. **MF 3.19** Implement Service Delivery Manager role. **MF 3.20** Implement Service Request Manager role.	195 196 196 198 199 200 201 203 204
ML4 Risk-Hedged	Transition	**MF 4.1** Collect and report detailed flow efficiency analysis. **MF 4.2** Use explicit buffers to smooth flow. **MF 4.3** Analyze to anticipate dependencies. **MF 4.4** Establish refutable versus irrefutable demand. **MF 4.5** Use classes of dependency management according to cost of delay. **MF 4.6** Use classes of booking in a dynamic reservation system.	205 207 208 209 211 217

Maturity Level		Manage Flow (MF) Practice (continued)	Page
ML4 Risk-Hedged	Consolidation	**MF 4.7** Determine a reference class data set. **MF 4.8** Forecast using reference classes, Monte Carlo simulations, and other models. **MF 4.9** Allocate capacity by work type. **MF 4.10** Allocate capacity by class of service. **MF 4.11** Assess forecasting models for robustness. **MF 4.12** Make appropriate use of forecasting. **MF 4.13** Use statistical methods for decision making.	219 219 220 221 222 224 225
ML5 Market Leader	Transition		
	Consolidation	**MF 5.1** Use hybrid fixed service teams together with a flexible labor pool.	226

Make Policies Explicit

Maturity Level		Make Policies Explicit (XP) Practice	Page
ML0 Oblivious	Consolidation	**XP 0.1** Make the rules for the individual kanban explicit.	230
ML1 Team-Focused	Transition	**XP 1.1** Discover initial policies.	231
	Consolidation	**XP 1.2** Define basic policies.	232
ML2 Customer-Driven	Transition	**XP 2.1** Define flow-related metrics (e.g., lead time). **XP 2.2** Define basic service policies.	232 233
	Consolidation	**XP 2.3** Define policies for managing aging WIP. **XP 2.4** Define policies for managing blocking issues. **XP 2.5** Define policies for managing defects and other rework types. **XP 2.6** Define basic policies for dependency management.	234 234 235 236
ML3 Fit-for-Purpose	Transition	**XP 3.1** Define Fit-for-Purpose–related metrics. **XP 3.2** Explicitly define request acceptance criteria. **XP 3.3** Define policies for discarding requests upstream. **XP 3.4** Define criteria for aborted work. **XP 3.5** Define basic classes of service based on qualitative cost of delay.	237 238 238 239 240
	Consolidation	**XP 3.6** Establish a commitment point. **XP 3.7** Explicitly define pull criteria. **XP 3.8** Establish a delivery point and a delivery buffer. **XP 3.9** Establish customer expectations for each work item or class of work items. **XP 3.10** Explicitly define fitness-for-purpose and manage it based on metrics.	242 244 244 245 246
ML4 Risk-Hedged	Transition		
	Consolidation	**XP 4.1** Establish demand-shaping policies. **XP 4.2** Establish SLA on dependent services.	247 248

Implement Feedback Loops

Maturity Level		Implement Feedback Loops (FL) Practice		Page
ML0 Oblivious	Consolidation	FL 0.1	Engage in personal reflection.	252
ML1 Team-Focused	Transition	FL 1.1	Conduct Team Kanban Meeting.	252
	Consolidation	FL 1.2	Conduct Team Retrospective.	254
		FL 1.3	Conduct Team Replenishment Meeting.	254
ML2 Customer-Driven	Transition	FL 2.1	Conduct Workflow Replenishment Meeting.	255
	Consolidation	FL 2.2	Conduct Workflow Kanban Meeting.	256
		FL 2.3	Conduct Blocker Clustering.	256
		FL 2.4	Conduct Flow Review.	257
ML3 Fit-for-Purpose	Transition	FL 3.1	Conduct Improvement Suggestions Review.	259
	Consolidation	FL 3.2	Conduct Replenishment Meeting.	260
		FL 3.3	Conduct Delivery Planning Meeting.	261
		FL 3.4	Conduct Service Delivery Review (downstream).	262
		FL 3.5	Conduct Service Request Review (upstream).	262
		FL 3.6	Conduct Service Risk Review.	263
ML4 Risk-Hedged	Transition	FL 4.1	Conduct Organizational Risk Review.	265
		FL 4.2	Conduct Operations Review.	266
		FL 4.3	Conduct Marketing Strategy Review.	268
	Consolidation	FL 5.1	Conduct Organizational Strategy Review.	269

Improve Collaboratively, Evolve Experimentally

Maturity Level		Improve Collaboratively, Evolve Experimentally (IE) Practice		Page
ML2 Customer-Driven	Transition	IE 2.1	Identify sources of dissatisfaction.	273
	Consolidation	IE 2.2	Identify sources of delay.	273
		IE 2.3	Revise problematic policies.	274
		IE 2.4	Define actions to develop basic understanding of the process and improve flow.	275
ML3 Fit-for-Purpose	Transition	IE 3.1	Solicit change and improvement suggestions.	275
		IE 3.2	Identify transaction and coordination costs.	276
	Consolidation	IE 3.3	Analyze blocker likelihood and impact.	278
		IE 3.4	Analyze lead time tail risk.	279
		IE 3.5	After meetings: Discuss a problem spontaneously; then bring it to the Service Delivery Review.	280
ML4 Risk-Hedged	Transition	IE 4.1	Develop qualitative understanding of chance versus assignable cause for process performance variation.	280
	Consolidation			

Maturity Level		Improve Collaboratively, Evolve Experimentally (IE) Practice (continued)		Page
ML5 Market Leader	Transition	**IE 5.1**	Identify bottlenecks.	283
		IE 5.2	Identify impact of shared resources.	285
		IE 5.3	Develop quantitative understanding of chance versus assignable cause for process performance variation.	285
	Consolidation	**IE 5.4**	Exploit, subordinate to, and elevate bottlenecks.	288
		IE 5.5	Exploit, subordinate to, and elevate shared resources.	289
		IE 5.6	After meetings: Discuss – Suggest – Take actions – Seek forgiveness.	290
ML6 Built for Survival	Transition			
	Consolidation	**IE 6.1**	After meetings: Take congruent actions with confidence.	290

References

13th Annual State of Agile Report. https://stateofagile.com/#ufh-i-613553418-13th-annual-state-of-agile-report/7027494

Achouiantz, Christophe. *The Kanban Kick-start Field Guide*. http://bit.ly/KanbanFieldGuide

Anderson, David J. *Agile Management for Software Engineering: Applying the Theory of Constraints for Business Results*. Upper Saddle River, NJ: Prentice Hall, 2003.

———. Blog post, "Is Agile Costing You Too Much?" https://djaa.com/is-agile-costing-you-too-much/

———. *Kanban: Successful Evolutionary Change for Your Technology Business*. Seattle, WA: Blue Hole Press, 2010.

Anderson, David J., and Alexi Zheglov. *Fit for Purpose: How Modern Businesses Find, Satisfy, & Keep Customers*. Seattle, WA: Blue Hole Press, 2018.

Birkinshaw, Julian. "The New Boardroom Imperative: From Agility to Resilience." *Forbes*, March 28, 2020. https://www.forbes.com/sites/lbsbusinessstrategyreview/2020/03/28/the-new-boardroomimperative-from-agility-to-resilience/#2164fe386711

Bozheva, Teodora, and Juan José Gil Bilbao. "BBVA: Developing Agility with KMM." *Enterprise Agility Everywhere 2020*. Speech, n.d.

Branson, Richard. *Screw Business as Usual*. New York: Portfolio/Penguin, 2017.

Bungay, Stephen. "The New Model Organisation: A Visit to Jimdo." https://www.stephenbungay.com/news/97785/The-New-Model-Organisation/

Butler, Anthony. *Cyril Ramaphosa: The Road to Presidential Power*. Martlesham: James Currey, 2019.

Diamond, Jared M. *Upheaval: Turning Points for Nations in Crisis*. New York, NY: Back Bay Books, Little Brown and Company, 2020.

Fukuyama, Francis. *Identity: The Demand for Dignity and the Politics of Resentment*. New York: Picador, 2019.

Genîzî, Ûrî, and John A. List. *The Why Axis: Hidden Motives and the Undiscovered Economics of Everyday Life.* London: Random House Business Books, 2013.

Gerstner, Louis V. *Who Says Elephants Can't Dance?: Leading a Great Enterprise through Dramatic Change.* New York: HarperBusiness, 2004.

Geus, Arie de. *The Living Company:* Boston, MA: Harvard Business School Press, 2002.

Gladwell, Malcolm. *Blink!: The Power of Thinking without Thinking.* New York: Back Bay Books, 2019.

Glen, Paul. *Leading Geeks: How to Manage and Lead People Who Deliver Technology.* San Francisco, CA: Jossey-Bass, 2003.

Goldratt, Eliyahu M. *What Is This Thing Called Theory of Constraints and How Should It Be Implemented?* Croton-on-Hudson, NY: North River Press, 1990.

Honkonen, Sami. "Scheduling Work in Kanban." https://www.slideshare.net/AGILEMinds/sami-honkonen-scheduling-work-in-kanban

Immelman, Ray. *Great Boss, Dead Boss.* Gurnee, IL: Stewart Philip International, 2003.

Kay, J. A. *Obliquity: Why Our Goals Are Best Achieved Indirectly.* New York: Penguin, 2012.

Lee, Bruce, and John R. Little. *Striking Thoughts: Bruce Lee's Wisdom for Daily Living.* North Clarendon, VT: Tuttle, 2002.

Maassen, Olav, Chris Matts, and Chris Geary. *Commitment: Novel about Managing Project Risk.* Amsterdam: Hathaway te Brake Publications, 2016.

Mehta, Merwan, David J Anderson, and David Raffo. "Providing Value to Customers in Software Development through Lean Principles." *Software Process: Improvement and Practice* 13, no. 1 (2008): 101–9. https://doi.org/10.1002/spip.367.

Plato, and D. J. Allan, ed. *Republic.* London: Bristol Classical Press, 1993.

Project Management Institute. "Organizational Change Management." https://www.pmi.org/-/media/pmi/documents/public/pdf/learning/thought-leadership/pulse/organizational-change-management.pdf?sc_lang_temp=en

Putnam, Robert. *Making Democracy Work: Civic Traditions in Modern Italy.* New York: Princeton Univ. Press, 1992.

de la Sablonnière, Roxane. "Toward a Psychology of Social Change: A Typology of Social Change." *Frontiers*, March 2, 2017. https://doi.org/10.3389/fpsyg.2017.00397.

Schwaber, Ken. "Scrum is Hard and Disruptive." http://static1.1.sqspcdn.com/static/f/447037/6486484/1270930467650/Scrum+Is+Hard+and+Disruptive.pdf

Senge, Peter M. *The Fifth Discipline: The Art and Practice of the Learning Organization.* New York: Doubleday, 1990.

Solomon, Robert C., and Fernando Flores. *Building Trust in Business, Politics, Relationships, and Life.* New York: Oxford University Press, 2003.

Steele, Claude M., Steven J. Spencer, and Joshua Aaronson. "Contending with Group Image: The Psychology of Stereotype and Social Identity Threat." (https://www.sciencedirect.com/science/article/pii/S0065260102800090)

Taleb, Nassim Nicholas. *Antifragile: Things That Gain from Disorder.* New York: Random House, 2016.

———. *The Black Swan: The Impact of the Highly Improbable.* New York: Random House, 2012.

———. *Fooled by Randomness: the Hidden Role of Chance in Life and in the Markets.* New York: Random House, 2005.

———. *Skin in the Game: Hidden Asymmetries in Daily Life.* New York: Random House, 2018.

Weinberg, Gerald M. *Quality Software Management, Vol. 1: Systems Thinking.* New York: Dorset House, 1991.

———. *Quality Software Management, Vol.4: Anticipating Change.* New York: Dorset House, 1997.

Womack, James P., and Daniel T. Jones. *Lean Thinking: Banish Waste and Create Wealth in Your Corporation.* New York: Free Press, 2003.

Index

A
A3 Thinking, 27
aborted work, 143–144, 193–194
 criteria for, 239–240
Achouiantz, Christophe, 359
Age of Reason, 323–324
Agendashift, integration with Kanban, 378–379
Agile Decision Filter, 103–105
Agile Management for Software Engineering (Anderson), 359
Agile methods, 39, 305, 346
agility of organizations, 35, 37, 41, 42, 51, 52, 75, 90, 97, 160, 183, 261, 298, 352, 382
agreement
 Maturity Level 3 (fit-for-purpose), 73–74
 trust, respect, and explicit policies, 343
Akers, John, 91
alignment
 Maturity Level 3 (fit-for-purpose), 76–77
 strategy and values, 355
altruistic behavior, 60
anticipation and Maturity Level 4 (risk-hedged), 77–78
anticipatory rather than merely reactionary, 363
antifragile/antifragility, xii, 95, 270, 302, 376, 377
Antifragile (Taleb), 362, 376
Apple iPhone/iOS, 354, 406, 407
architectural extensions, 114–115
Atlassian, 347
Auftragstaktik (Mission Command), xv, 75, 379
avatars
 using, for visualizing dependencies on shared services, 131–132
 to visualize individual's workload, 123–124

B
Balance, 9, 14, 19, 22, 164, 188, 252, 330, 363, 372, 378
 Maturity Level 3 (fit-for-purpose), 19, 73, 74, 138–139, 140–141, 168, 187, 189, 194, 236,
 Maturity Level 4 (risk-hedged), 23, 24, 77, 78, 81, 247
Balmer, Steve, 336–337
barriers to adoption
 breadth of adoption as mitigation to inertia, 340–341
 customer intimacy, lack of, 355
 generally observed barriers, 339–340
 individual maturity, lack of, 341–342
 legacy tooling, 347, 353
 managers not trained in Kanban, 346–347
 mathematical literacy, lack of, 352, 356
 common, at Maturity Level 2 (customer-driven), 344–347
 common, at Maturity Level 3 (fit-for-purpose), 347–354
 common, at Maturity Level 4 (risk-hedged), 354–356
 negotiation skills, lack of, 352–353
 organizational blueprint, 346
 qualitative risk management, lack of, 351–352
 quantitative understanding of business risks, lack of, 355
 risk-management literacy, lack of 356
 service orientation or customer focus, lack of, 345–346
 values as mitigation to inertia, 342–343
basic service policies, 233–234
 define, 230, 233
 visualizing, 132

BBBEE. *See* Broad-Based Black Economic Empowerment
BBVA case study, 39–52, 360
Beane, Billy, 337
Beckham, David, 337
behavior, abusive and bullying, 350
bell curve value acquisition lifecycle functions, 423
benchmark, 84
benefits of the Kanban Maturity Model (KMM), 33–38
Birkinshaw, Julian, 361–362, 368
The Black Swan (Taleb), 376
Blink! (Gladwell), 325
Blizzard Sport, 409
blocked work items, 128–129, 181
blocker clustering, 68, 256–257, 278–279
blocker-related metrics, 233
blockers
 analyzing likelihood and impact, 278–279
 management policies, 234–235
 visualizing, 68
blocker tickets, 128–129
blocking issues, 127–129, 181, 234–235, 274, 382
bottlenecks, 136, 192, 283–284, 287–288
 elevating and subordinating to, 288–289
 identifying, 283–285
 smoothing flow, 207–208
Branson, Richard, 56, 103, 363
Broad-Based Black Economic Empowerment (BBBEE), 85
buffers
 bottlenecks, 284
 infinite buffers, 192–193
 purposes, 192
 reducing size, 34
building resilience, 361–368
Built for Survival (Maturity Level 6), 88–91, 95

C
called service, 211–217, 438–445
capability
 acquire, 4
 comparing with strategy, 30
 kanban systems, 266–267
 demand and, 19, 22, 39, 42, 45–47, 50, 68, 78, 138–139, 183, 187–189, 232, 233, 236, 262, 266, 381
Capability Maturity Model Integration (CMMI) integration with Kanban, 379–382
capability-related metrics, 232–233
capacity allocation, 24
 by class of service, 160–161, 221–222
 by work type, 159–160, 220–221
capacity-constrained resources, managing, 287–288
Central Limit Theorem, 222, 327
chance versus assignable cause for process performance variation, 280–283

change
 acts of leadership, 315–316
 anxiety, stress, and fear of, 320
 context change, 304–305
 emergent structural change, 299, 300
 emotionally affecting people, 325–326
 evolutionary, 67, 295–309
 fitness criteria, 312
 high-maturity organizations, 309
 improvement and, 27
 incremental, 298–299
 initially normative, 298
 J-curve effect, 303–309
 leaders signaling changes, 37
 leading in periods of equilibrium, 315
 low-maturity organizations, 309
 motivation for, 105–107, 321, 328–337
 normative, 295–296, 299, 316–317, 329
 overwhelming, 320
 red squirrel, grey squirrel, 330–333
 reflection mechanisms, 315–316
 resistance to, 321, 325–329, 329
 risks associated with, 320–321
 social, 296
 soliciting suggestions, 275–276
 stressors, 315–316, 326
 structural, 295–296
 why do people resist, 323–337
 workers resisting, in workplace, 298–299
 workforce empowered to suggest and implement, 26
change management principles, 373
classes of dependency management
 cost of delay, 211–216
 Don't Care class, 212–213, 438, 440
 Expedite class, 216, 438, 445
 Fixed Date class, 215, 438, 443–444
 Guaranteed On-Time class, 216, 438, 444–445
 Tail-Risk Mitigation class, 214, 442–443
 Trusted Availability class, 212–213, 438, 441–442
classes of reservation, 436–438
classes of service, 144–145, 289
 affecting selection, 194–195
 allocating capacity by, 221–222
 based on start date, 433–434
 default, 409
 distribution of lead time, 279–280
 Expedite class, 240, 242, 409
 Fixed Date class, 241, 409
 Intangible class, 242, 411
 qualitative cost of delay, 240–242
 relating to cost of delay, 409–411
 Standard class, 241, 411
 work-in-progress (WIP) limits, 174, 221
Clinton, Bill, 87
CMMI. *See* Capability Maturity Model Integration

Cockburn, Alistair, 305
COD. *See* cost of delay
collaboration, 19, 23, 43, 333
    building trust, 60
    Maturity Level 1 (team-focused), 59–60
    positive and negative evidence, 60
    social capital, 98
    teams, 59, 76
Collapse (Diamond), 364
commitment, deferring, 185–187
Commitment (Matts and Maassen), 202
commitment point, 133, 143, 147–148, 185–187, 204, 233, 239, 242–243, 260, 284, 288, 383
competition
    fitter-for-purpose than, 23
    market leader key objective for, 84
    Maturity Level 4 (risk-hedged), 79
    stress, 79
concurrent activities, 135
confidence, 99, 356
congruence
    lack of, with strategy and values, 355
    Maturity Level 6 (built for survival), 89
congruent actions, 29, 290–291
congruent organizations, 29–30
conservative cultures, 95
Constant Rate Value function, 407, 423
constant WIP (CONWIP), 16
    delivery kanban board, 133
    emergent workflow, 167–168
Constraints, Theory of, 27, 335
context, 4
    change, 304–305
continuous improvement, 26, 35, 232, 236, 266, 375
    Maturity Level 5 (market leader), 35
convolution, 425
CONWIP. *See* constant WIP
coordination costs, identifying, 276–277
coping with crisis, 364–368
copying organizational blueprint, 346
Corbis, 299, 358, 427
cost of delay (COD), 154–155, 331–332, 420, 428, 430
    classes of dependency management, 211–216
    class of service based on start date, 433–434
    class of service relating to, 409–411
    delivery delay cost calculations, 420–424
    Extremistan range, 419–420
    Mediocristan range, 419–420
    Probable Cost of Delay in Starting (PCoDS) function, 425–430
    shelf-life ratio, 431–432
    Triage Table configuration, 432
    urgency, 426
crisis management, 295, 364–367
cultural mantra, 103–104

culture, 3, 4, 111
    achievement, 43, 56–57
    acts of leadership, 64–66
    agreement, 73–74
    alignment, 76–77
    anticipation, 77–78
    anticipatory rather than reactionary, 73
    ask permission culture, 61
    balance, 74
    business focus, 78–79
    collaboration, 19, 23, 43, 59–60
    collective behavior, 73
    congruence, 89
    conservative, 95
    continuous improvement, 26
    customer intimacy, 23, 66, 79–80
    customer service, 43, 74
    data-driven decision making, 80–81
    defining and actively managing, 30
    defining what people value, 4
    development of, 33
    diversity, 90–91
    equality of opportunity, 84–86
    evolutionary change, 67
    experimentation, 86–87
    fairness, 23, 77, 81
    flow, 67–68
    focus on employees, 55
    focus on self, 56
    frameworks for decision making, 23, 100
    heroic individual contributor, 9, 59
    high-maturity organizations, 83–91
    initiative, 61
    integrity, 89
    leadership, 75, 81
    liberal, 362
    long-term survival, 89–90
    low-maturity organizations, 55–70
    making it stick, 108
    Maturity Level 0 (oblivious), 5–6, 56–57
    Maturity Level 1 (team-focused), 9, 57–63
    Maturity Level 2 (customer-driven), 13, 63–70
    Maturity Level 3 (fit-for-purpose), 18–19, 71–82
    Maturity Level 4 (risk-hedged), 23, 35, 77–82
    Maturity Level 5 (market leader), 27, 84–88
    Maturity Level 6 (built for survival), 30, 88–91
    regulatory compliance, 81–82
    short-term results, 75–76
    social capital, 56
    social mobility, 87–88
    three social dimensions of, 94
    tolerance, 90–91, 362
    transparency, 19, 23, 43, 61–63
    trust, 19, 23, 95
    unity, 76–77

culture hacking
    changing IBM culture, 93–94
    decision filters, 103–105
    making culture stick, 108
    motivating change, 105–107
    social capital, 97–101
    social cohesion, 101–103
    tribal culture, 105–107
cumulative flow diagrams (CFDs), 181, 188–189, 284
customer awareness, 66
customer-driven, 12–16
customer expectations, 4, 21, 23
    additional, 237
    determining due date, 199
    understanding motivation for, 66
    work items or class of work items, 245–246
customer-facing service, 26, 345
customer intimacy
    lack of, 342, 345–346, 355
    Maturity Level 4 (risk-hedged), 79–80
customer lead time, 237, 243, 258, 384
customer's order, 8, 185, 226, 350
customer-requested work orders, 5, 137
customer request, 9, 10, 13, 14, 19, 26, 51, 60, 63, 66, 76, 108, 137, 178, 183–184, 211, 214–216, 238, 240, 345, 347, 348, 351, 438, 442, 445
customers
    anxious about dependencies, 435
    change representing improvement in eyes of, 34
    as collaborators, 73
    committing outcomes and delivery date to, 261–262
    delay and dissatisfaction, 68
    explicit role of, 34–35
    fitness criteria metrics, 18
    fulfilling needs of, 72
    identifying sources of dissatisfaction, 273
    improvement opportunities aligned with fitness criteria metrics, 26
    insights about, 76
    loyalty, 79
    service classes aligned with fitness criteria, 24
    trust, 11, 13, 18, 23, 73
    unreliable service delivery, 10
    variable experience, 12
customer satisfaction, 68, 84, 160, 176, 181, 196, 240–241, 269, 371, 375–376, 385, 387, 396
    Maturity Level 5 (market leader), 27
customer service, 19, 34–35, 61, 66, 379
    Maturity Level 3 (fit-for-purpose), 72–75, 79
customer-valued deliverables, 13

D

data-driven decision making, 23, 78
    Maturity Level 4 (risk-hedged), 80–81, 86

DDD. *See* desired delivery date
deadline, 199
decision filters, 103–105
decision frameworks, 4, 9, 12–13, 18, 23, 35, 62, 98, 100, 291, 341, 362
decision making
    data-driven, 23, 80–81
    institutionalized understanding of who we are, 30
    prioritization, 330
    statistical methods for, 225–226
    survival, 30
default class of service, 409
defects
    managing, 181–182, 235
    metrics, 233
    visualizing, 128–129
defined workflow, 125, 136–137
defining what people value, 4
definition of done, 149–150
de Geus, Arie, 362
deliveries
    anticipated date, 200
    consistency, 22
    delay cost calculations, 420–424
    fit-for-purpose service, 203–204
    fixed date, 200
    item ready for, 383–384
    replenishing queue for, 254–255
    scheduling, 21
    service level agreements (SLAs), 198
    timely and/or predictable, 68
delivery, two-phase commit for, 196–197
delivery point, 244–245
delivery date, 199
    capture desired, 180–181
    committing to customer, 261–262
Delivery Delay Cost function, 421–426, 432
delivery commitment, 196–197, 201, 261–262
delivery forecasts, 200–201
delivery kanban boards, 14, 133
Delivery Meetings, 132
Delivery Planning Meetings, 19–21, 149–150, 204, 250, 261–262, 264, 316
delivery rate, 60
demand
    analyze and report, 232–233
    and capability, balancing, 19, 22, 39, 42, 45–47, 50, 68, 78, 138–139, 183, 187–189, 232, 233, 236, 262, 266, 381
    customer
    failure, 151, 195
    patterns of, 187, 189, 232
    refutable versus irrefutable, 209–210
    review of, 266–267
    shaping, 213

source of, 156–157, 178
types of, 175
understand the, 178
demand-related metrics, 232–233
demand shaping, 213
demand-shaping policies, 247
Deming, W. Edwards, 91, 107, 283
Depeche Mode, 407
dependencies
    anticipating, 208–209
    customers anxious about, 435
    deterministic approach, 209
    kanban systems, 266–267
    manage, 24, 236, 435–46
    not managing homogeneously, 435
    peer-to-peer and parent-child, 196
    probabilistic approach, 208–209
    on shared services, visualizing using avatars, 131–132
    on shared services, visualizing using column with WIP limit, 131–132
    visualize, 130
    work items, 130
dependencies parking lot, 157–159
    limiting work-in-progress (WIP), 173–174
dependency discovery, 211–216
dependency management, 24, 236, 435–466
    classes, 211–216, 438–445
    reservation systems, 436–438
design
    assessing against expectations, 30
    fitness-for-purpose, 22, 245–246
desired delivery date (DDD), 185, 186, 411–412
Diamond, Jared, 364, 368
discretionary work, 209
dissatisfaction, identifying sources of, 273
diversity
    Maturity Level 6 (built for survival), 90–91
Don't Care class of dependency, 212–213, 438, 440
Douady, Raphael, 399
double-loop learning, 35–36
due date
    performance metrics, 233
    service level agreements (SLAs), 199
    service level expectation (SLEs), 199
Dumitriu, Dragos, xxi, 330–331, 358
dynamic reservation system, 213, 217–218

E

economic performance, 27
economic value flow, 105
efficiency to reliability, 362–363
ego strength (resilience), 367
Einheit, 37, 75, 342, 379
emergent social behavior, 299

emergent structural change, 299, 300
emergent workflow and constant WIP (CONWIP), 167–168
emergent workflow kanban board, 125–126
emotions, 323–325
    countering emotional resistance with stronger emotions, 335–337
    negative, 336–337
    positive, 336–337
empathy
    forming, 334–335
    transparency, 340
    visualization, 340
employees
    commitment to development, 23
    pigeonholing, 88
    suggestions, 259
empowerment
    explicitly defined boundaries, 100
    explicit policies, 340
end-to-end (E2E) processes, 360
end-to-end workflow
    defined workflow, 125, 136–137
    managing, 136–137
    relieved of overburdening, 34
    upstream and downstream flow, 49, 137, 141–142, 169–170, 173, 179, 185, 203–204, 207, 284
engaging people emotionally
    coached identity change, 335
    countering emotional resistance with stronger emotions, 335–337
    experiential immersion, 334
    flipping the alpha, 335
    forming empathy, 334–335
    punctuation point creation, 337
    social and collaboration, 333
    visualize, 333
The Enlightenment, 323
Enterprise Services Planning (ESP), 30, 114–115, 353, 365, 368, 377, 418
    Maturity Level 5 (market leader), 27
entry criteria, 20, 139–140, 186
equality of opportunity
    good ideas, innovations, or epiphanies, 85
    Maturity Level 5 (market leader), 84–86
    not discriminating, 84–85
    resilience, robustness, and antifragility, 84
    social mobility, 87
    South Africa, 85–86
equilibrium, 200, 296–297
    chaos followed by stabilization, 311–313
    leading change in periods of, 315
    punctuated equilibrium, 311–313
    stability, 311–313
    variation, 311–313

escalating motivation for change, 328
  better version of yourself, not new identity, 329–330
  engaging people emotionally, 333–335
  go around the rock, 329–333
  red squirrel, grey squirrel, 330–333
ESP. *See* Enterprise Services Planning
evolutionary change, 4, 67
  emergent structural change, 299
  evolutionary relics, 301–303
  fit-for-purpose processes, 67
  identifying opportunities for improvement, 67
  J-curve effect, 303–309
  Kanban Maturity Model (KMM), 309
  punctuated equilibrium, 311
  why pursue, 295–309
Evolutionary Change Model (EVM), 326, 367
  addiction to bad behaviors, 321
  fostering willingness to improve, 318–320
  ineffective or problematic people, 318–320
  losing people vital to business, 319
  mapping to Kanban Maturity Model (KMM), 317
  objections and bad behavior, 319–320
  overreaching, 321
  pulling further changes, 320–321
  resistance, 319
  risk of settling, 320
  risks and challenges to consolidating changes, 321
  transition sub-level practices, 318–320
evolutionary relics, 301–303
exceptional circumstances, 22
exit criteria, 149–150
Expedite class of service, 206, 216, 240, 242, 409, 428–429, 438, 445
experiential immersion, 334
explicit buffers, 207–208
explicit decision frameworks, 100
explicitly defined boundaries of responsibility and empowerment, 100
explicit policies, 100, 341, 343, 382
  aborted work criteria, 239–240
  aging work-in-progress (WIP) management policies, 234
  basic classes of service based on qualitative cost of delay, 240–242
  basic service policies, 233–234
  benefits from applying general practice, 229
  blocking issues management policies, 234–235
  commitment point, 244–245
  customer expectations, 245–246
  defects and rework types management policies, 235
  defining basic policies, 231–232
  demand-shaping policies, 247
  dependency management policies, 236
  discarding requests upstream policies, 238–239
  empowerment, 340
  explicit rules for individual kanban, 230–231
  Fit-For-Practice (F4P)-related metrics, 237–238
  fitness-for purpose, managing it with metrics, 246
  flow-related metrics, 232–233
  general practice goal, 229
  initial policies, 231
  Maturity Level 0 (oblivious), 230–231
  Maturity Level 1 (team-focused), 231–232
  Maturity Level 2 (customer-driven), 232–236
  Maturity Level 3 (fit-for-purpose), 236–246
  Maturity Level 4 (risk-hedged), 247–248
  pull criteria, 244
  replenishment commitment point, 242–244
  request acceptance criteria, 238
  service level agreements (SLAs) on dependent services, 248
  social capital, 340
  specific practices summary, 230
  trust, 340
explicit values, 99, 368
Exponential probability distribution, 225
Extended Life delivery delay cost function, 424
Extreme Programming (XP), 103–104
Extremistan probability distribution function range, 225, 396, 400, 419–420

F
failure, 100
failure demand
  analyzing and reporting on, 195
  versus value demand, 151
fairness
  balance, 78
  Maturity Level 4 (risk-hedged), 81
feedback loops, 43, 342
  benefits from applying general practice, 249
  blocker clustering, 256–257
  Delivery Planning Meeting, 261–262
  enabling organization's evolution, 250
  Flow Review (FR), 257–258
  forecasting, 225
  general practice goal, 249
  Improvement Suggestion Review, 194, 259, 276
  implementing, 112, 249–270
  Marketing Strategy Review, 268–269
  Maturity Level 0 (oblivious), 252
  Maturity Level 1 (team-focused), 252–255
  Maturity Level 2 (customer-driven), 255–258
  Maturity Level 3 (fit-for-purpose), 258–262
  Maturity Level 4 (risk-hedged), 24, 264–270
  Maturity Level 5 (market leader), 27, 269–270
  Operations Review, 266–267
  Organizational Risk Review, 265–266
  Organizational Strategy Review, 269–270
  overview, 250

personal reflection, 252
Replenishment Meeting, 260
Service Delivery Review (SDR), 262
Service Request Review, 262–263
Service Risk Review, 263–264
specific practices summary, 251
Team Kanban Meeting, 252–253
Team Replenishment Meeting, 254–255
Team Retrospective, 254
Workflow Kanban Meeting, 256
Workflow Replenishment Meeting, 255–256
feedback mechanisms, 18, 20, 27, 35, 282, 342, 349, 355, 362, 365, 367
Ferguson, Alex, 337
The Fifth Discipline (Senge), 298, 325
filtered lead time, 214
fit-for-purpose, 4
  business, 26
  design, 22
  implementation, 22
  metrics, 237–238
  organizations, culture in, 71–82
  processes, 67
  products, 10, 18, 30
  service delivery, 22, 34–35, 203–204
  services, 10, 18, 30
Fit for Purpose (Anderson and Zheglov), 79–80, 106
Fit-for-Purpose Framework, 24, 30, 246, 349, 362, 366–368
  anticipating customer needs, 363
  customer intimacy, 355
  improvement in eyes of customer, 34
  Marketing Strategy Review and, 268
  Maturity Level 3, 17–21
  Maturity Level 4 (risk-hedged), 24
  Maturity Level 5 (market leader), 27
fitness criteria
  change, 312
  customer improvement opportunities aligned with metrics, 26
  metrics, 18
  See also fit-for-purpose, metrics
fitness-for-purpose
  defining, 246
  design, 245–246
  efficiency, 363
  implementation, 245–246
  managing with metrics, 246
  service delivery, 245–246
fittest-for-purpose, 87
Fixed Date class of service, 199–200, 241, 409, 429, 438, 443–444
Fixed Date class of dependency management, 215
fixed teams across aggregated services, 161–162
Fleck, Alexander, 88

flexibility and Kanban Maturity Model (KMM), 367
  See also agility of organizations
  See also resilience
floating workers across aggregated services, 161–162
flow
  blockers, 43
  collecting flow-related data, 180
  decisions for improving, 68
  economic value, 105
  efficiency, 150, 205–207
  failure to be fit-for-purpose, 68
  failure to value, 342–343
  improving, 275
  flow-related metrics, 232–233
  Little's Law, 168–169, 173, 189–191, 194, 201, 213, 224–225, 248, 382, 387, 389, 394, 398
  managing, 175–227
  mapping upstream and downstream, 179–180
  Maturity Level 2 (customer-driven), 67–68
  risk management, 105
  rudimentary efficiency, 191–192
  trust, 105
  unevenness, 342–343
  WIP aging, 68, 182, 233–234
  See also defects and other types of rework; aging WIP; Little's Law; Manage Flow
Flow Decision Filter, 105
Flow Manager, 360, 396
  facilitating Flow Review, 258
  lack of, 347
  role of, 16, 182–183, 204, 356, 357
flow-related metrics, 232–233
Flow Review, 67, 187, 257–258
Fooled by Randomness (Taleb), 376
forcing use of organization's standard process, 346
forecast
  by means of predictive models, 26, 205
  delivery, 200–201
  how much, 200
  future outcomes, 219, 223
  Monte Carlo, 223
  when, 200
forecasting, 224–225
  delivery, 200–201
  deterministic, 208, 209, 303
  estimation,
  feedback loop, 225
  probabilistic, 200, 208, 212, 213, 214, 326, 327, 440, 441, 442
  range of probable outcomes, 200
  using Little's Law for, 168–169, 173, 189–191, 194, 201, 213, 224–225, 248, 382, 387, 389, 394, 398
forecasting models
  Gaussian-distributed data sets, 222–223
  Monte Carlo simulations, 223

forecasting models (*cont.*)
    Pareto-distributed data sets, 223
    predictive models, 205
    for robustness, 222–224
    simulation algorithms, 222–224
F4P. *See* Fit-for-Purpose
fragile organizations, 377
framework for appraising organizational maturity, 33
Fukuyama, Francis, 57–58, 63
full kanban system, 172–173

G
Gates, Bill, 106, 107, 427
Gaussian range of bell curve–like functions, 225, 389, 391–393, 396–397
Gerstner, Lou, 90–91, 93–94, 106
Gladwell, Malcolm, 325
global warming problem, 297–298
go around the rock, 329–333
Goldratt, Eli, 335–336
go-to-market strategies, 268–269
Grand Budapest Hotel, 87
Grove, Andy, 106

H
hedging risk classes of reservation, 436
heroic individual contributor, 59
high-maturity organizations
    change management, 309
    culture, 83–91
holistic thinking, 23, 249, 315, 328, 339, 342, 379
homogenous groups, 90
house of resilience, 368
human condition
    brain, 323–325
    cognitive agility, 325
    emotion, 323–325
    engaging people emotionally, 333–335
    Maslow's Hierarchy of Needs, 324
    psyche, 325
    resistance to change, 323–326
    stubbornness, 325
hybrid fixed service teams together with flexible labor pool, 226–227

I
IBM, 31, 90–91, 93–94, 106, 408–409
ICI, 88
ideas, process of elaborating, 141–143
identity
    broad sense of, 365
    coached identity change, 335
    individual focus on, 37
    managing, 57–58
    organizations, 30
    role of, 63

Identity (Fukuyama), 57–58
Immelman, Ray, 105–107
implementation
    assessing against expectations, 30
    fit-for-purpose, 22
    fitness-for-purpose, 245–246
implementing roles
    barriers to adoption, 356–360
    group shared responsibility, 358
    individual additional responsibility, 358
    new position and organizational structure, 358–360
    See also Flow Manager; Service Delivery Manager; Service Request Manager
Improve Collaboratively, Evolve Experimentally
    after-meetings, 289–290
    analyzing blocker likelihood and impact, 278–279
    basic understanding of process and improving flow, 275
    benefits from applying general practice, 272
    bottlenecks, 283–284, 287–288
    chance versus assignable cause for process performance variation, 280–283, 285–287
    general practice goal, 271
    lead time tail risk, 279
    at Maturity Level 2 (customer-driven), 273–275
    at Maturity Level 3 (fit-for-purpose), 275–280
    at Maturity Level 4 (risk-hedged), 280–283
    at Maturity Level 5 (market leader), 283–290
    at Maturity Level 6 (built for survival), 290–291
    problematic policies, 274
    Service Delivery Review, 280
    shared resources, 284–285, 288–289
    change and improvement suggestions, 275–276
    sources of delay, 273–274
    sources of dissatisfaction, 273
    transaction and coordination costs, 276–277
improvement, 30
    change and, 27
    employees' suggestions, 259
    fostering willingness to improve, 318–320
    identifying opportunities for, 67
    job satisfaction, 26–27
    solicit suggestions, 275–276
improvement drivers, 26
Improvement Suggestions Review, 187, 259
Impulse delivery delay cost function, 423
Impulse Value Acquisition Lifecycle function, 429
The Incerto (Taleb), 376
incremental change, 298–299
individual kanban board, 10
    at Maturity Level 0 (oblivious), 6
    relief from too much work-in-progress, 33
    tickets, 121
    visualize individual's work with, 120–121

visualize work for several individuals by means of aggregated, 122
individual kanban explicit rules, 230–231
infinite buffers, 192–193
Infosys, 103
initial policies
    discover, 231
    visualizing, 122–123
    See also define basic policies; define basic service policies
Intangible class of service, 242, 411, 430
integration with other models and methods
    Agendashift, 378–379
    Capability Maturity Model Integration (CMMI), 379–382
    Lean, 375–376
    Mission Command, 379
    Real World Risk Model, 376–378
    Toyota Production System (TPS), 375–376
integrity, 344
    Maturity Level 6 (built for survival), 89
Intel, 106
irrefutable demand versus refutable, 209–210
irrefutable work, 209–210
ISACA, xv

J

J-curve effect, 359
    patience, 307–308
    safety, 307–308
    transitioning organization to new, desired process, 303
Jimdo, 103
Jira, 347
Jones, Daniel, 104
justice system, 100–101

K

Kahneman, Daniel, 323, 325
kaizen, 266
kaizen events, 27
Kanban
    agendas, 371
    anti-fragility, 302
    barriers to adoption, 339–360
    breadth of adoption, 340–341
    case studies, 366–367
    change management principles, 373
    delivery rate, 60
    dependency management, 445–446
    evolutionary change, 308, 346–347
    full kanban system, 172–173
    general practices, 373
    global community, 366
    Implement Feedback Loops, 249
    Improve Collaboratively, Evolve Experimentally, 271
    lead time, 60, 189–192
    Limit Work-in-Progress, 163
    Make Policies Explicit, 229
    Manage Flow, 175
    misconception: appropriate for services but not product development, 48
    scaling principles, 372
    Service Delivery Principles, 48, 49, 371–372
    Service Orientation agenda, 371
    Service-Oriented Organization (SOO), 362
    simulation games in training, 334
    Survivability agenda, 371
    Sustainability agenda, 371
    Systems Thinking Approach to Introducing Kanban (STATIK), 373
    values, 448
    Visualize, 117
kanban boards
    aggregated service delivery overview board, 137
    aggregated individual kanban board, 10–11
    aggregated teams kanban board, 19, 140–141
    class of service, 144–145, 160–161
    commitment point, 133, 142, 147–148, 185–187, 204, 233, 239, 242–243, 260, 284, 288, 383
    customer-facing service, 183
    customer focus, 14
    defined workflow, 136–137
    downstream (delivery) kanban board, 14, 133
    dependencies parking lot, 157–158
    delivery point, 244–245
    emergent workflow kanban board, 125–126
    Expedite lane, 145–146
    floating worker, 161–162
    individual kanban board, 10
    kanban patterns, 6–7, 10–11, 14–15, 19–20, 24–25, 27, 361
    mapping workflow, 19, 137
    parking lot, 130, 146–147
    physical slot kanban board, 150–151
    policies, 132
    risks, 155–156
    team kanban board, 14, 124, 125
    ticket design, 121, 126–130, 133-137
    upstream (discovery) kanban board, 141–142
    visualize, 117
Kanban Cadences, 24, 67, 250, 316, 347, 372, 381
Kanbanize, 366
Kanban Maturity Model eXtension (KMMX), 114–115
Kanban Maturity Model (KMM), 3, 366–367
    adaptable organization, xii, 29, 33, 35, 99
    appraising organizational maturity, 33
    architecture, 111–116
    architectural extensions, 114–115
    BBVA, 39–52

Kanban Maturity Model (*cont.*)
    benefits, 33–38
    case studies, 366–367
    change in periods of equilibrium, 315
    cultural mantra, 103–104
    culture, 3–4, 33, 43, 362
    culture pillar, 55, 71, 83
    economic improvements, 362–363
    evolutionary change, 309
    Evolutionary Change Model (ECM), 311, 317, 326, 450
    explicit policies, 382
    feedback loops, 43, 249–270, 342
    feedback mechanisms, 35, 362
    flexibility, 367
    fragile organizations, 377
    institutional memory through narrative, 367
    leadership at all levels, 362
    limiting work-in progress (WIP), 42, 163–174
    low-maturity organizations culture, 55–70
    loyalty, 367
    Managed Evolution, 112, 295
    managing flow, 42–43, 175–228
    Maturity Level 0 (oblivious), 5–8
    Maturity Level 1 (team-focused), 8–12
    Maturity Level 2 (customer-driven), 12–16
    Maturity Level 3 (fit-for-purpose), 17–20
    Maturity Level 4 (risk-hedged), 22–26
    Maturity Level 5 (market leader), 26–28
    Maturity Level 6 (built for survival), 29–31
    normative change, 329
    Outcomes pillar, 3
    Practices pillar, 111
    reinvention, 31, 33, 35, 55, 84, 97, 270, 362, 364, 367, 375
    resilient organization, xii, 18, 33, 35, 52, 60, 67, 81, 95, 270, 343, 362, 363, 368, 376, 377
    robust organization, xii, 22, 23, 26, 29, 36, 77, 82, 95, 303, 344, 377
    sports coaching model, 317
    three pillars, 3–16
Kanban Meetings
    Delivery Planning, 19, 21, 150, 197, 203, 261–262
    reflection mechanism, 14, 64, 316
    social and collaboration, 333
    Team, 9, 64, 149–150, 183, 250, 253, 316, 381
    Team Replenishment, 234, 254–255, 260
    Team Retrospective, 9, 254
    Workflow, 256
    Workflow Replenishment, 255–256
Kanban Method, 369–374
    Agendashift and, 378–379
    BBVA, 39
    Capability Maturity Model Integration (CMMI) and, 379–382
    change management principles, 67, 311–321, 373
    Corbis implementation, 409
    general practices, 373,
    Implement Feedback Loops, 249–270
    Improve Collaboratively, Evolve Experimentally, 271–191
    integration with other models and methods, 375–382
    Kanban Cadences, 316
    Lean and, 375–376
    Limit Work-in-Progress, 163–174
    Make Policies Explicit, 229–248
    Manage Flow, 175–277
    Mission Command and, 379
    Real World Risk Model and, 376–378
    service delivery principles, 10, 49, 182, 232, 371
    Toyota Production System (TPS) and, 375–376
    Visualize, 117–162
kanban patterns
    individual kanban, 6
    Maturity Level 0 (oblivious), 6–7
    Maturity Level 1 (team-focused), 10
    Maturity Level 2 (customer-driven), 14–16
    Maturity Level 3 (fit-for-purpose), 19–21
    Maturity Level 4 (risk-hedged), 24–25
    Maturity Level 5 (market leader), 27–28
    metrics, 24
    See also kanban boards
Kanban Reviews
    Marketing Strategy Review, 268–269
    Service Delivery Review, 262
    Service Request Review, 262–263
    Service Risk Review, 263–264
    Operations Review, 266–267
    Organizational Risk Review, 265–266
    Organizational Strategy Review, 269–270
Kanban scaling principles, 372
Kanban Service Delivery Principles, 10, 49, 182, 232, 371
Kanban: Successful Evolutionary Change for Your Technology Business (Anderson), 64, 74, 299, 315, 330–331, 356, 409, 430
kanban systems, 266–267
Kanban University, 365–366, 385, 413, 418
Kay, John, 88
key performance indicators (KPIs), 43, 187, 237, 268–269
Kiviat charts, 154
Klipp, Paul, 301, 302
KMMX. *See* Kanban Maturity Model eXtension
knowledge discovery process, 183–185
KPIs. *See* key performance indicators

L
labor pool liquidity, 226–227
Last Responsible Moment (LRM), 185–187, 412

leadership
    acts of, 64–66, 315–316
    at all levels, 75, 362
    by command, 65–66
    commitment to development, 23
    development, 342
    by example, 61
    expressing, 65
    focus on purpose and identity, 30
    by inspiration, 65–66
    lack of, 342
    leading by example, 65–66, 95
    overcoming addiction to bad behaviors, 321
    personal risk, 65
    role of, 64
    by signaling, 65–66
    signaling change, 37
    signaling liberal leanings, 95
    valuing, 64
Leading Geeks (Glen), 352
lead time, 60, 68, 180, 232–233
    cumulative flow diagrams (CFDs), 181, 188–189, 284
    definition of, 383
    fat-tailed distributions, 387, 389, 413
    Gaussian range of bell curve-like functions, 389, 391–393
    interpreting curve, 386–401
    Little's Law, 387, 389
    mathematical properties of lead time curves, 389–401
    mean, 386–388
    median, 386
    mode, 386
    multi-modal data, 388–389
    nature of, 384–386
    Pareto range of power-law functions, 389, 400–401
    planning, 387
    probability distribution function, 384–386
    sub-exponential range, 398–400
    super-exponential range, 393–396
    track, 213
    thin-tailed distributions, 413
    Weibull function, 389, 390–391
Lead Time Distribution function, 425
lead time tail risk, 279–280
Lean Decision Filter, 105
Lean integration with Kanban, 375–376
Lean Startup, 27
Lean Thinking (Womack and Jones), 104
lean value stream mapping, 305–306
learning from failure, 100
Lee, Bruce, 329
legacy tooling, 347, 353
liberal cultures, 95, 362
    Enlightenment, 95
    high-trust, tight-knit organizations, 102–103
    mapping to deeper levels of organizational maturity, 95
    Maturity Level 5 (market leader), 95
    Maturity Level 6 (built for survival), 95
limiting work-in-progress (WIP)
    activity-based WIP limits, 168–169
    benefits from applying general practice, 164
    bracket WIP limits across activities, 171–172
    bracket WIP limits across sub-states, 170–171
    by class of service, 174
    constant WIP (CONWIP) on emergent workflow, 167–168
    dependency parking lot, 173–174
    full kanban system, 172–173
    general practice goals, 163–164
    individual limits, 165–166
    Maturity Level 0 (oblivious), 165–166
    Maturity Level 1 (team-focused), 166–167
    Maturity Level 2 (customer-driven), 167–168
    Maturity Level 3 (fit-for-purpose), 168–173
    Maturity Level 4 (risk-hedged), 173–174
    maximum (max) limit to constrain upstream capacity, 170
    order point (minimum limit) for upstream replenishment, 169–170
    per-person limits, 166
    saying no to customer, 327
    team work-in-progress (WIP) limits, 166–167
    by type of work, 174
    underutilizing resources, 327
    visualize, 163–174
    work-in-progress (WIP) limits on aggregated service delivery board, 168
Linden-Reed Janice, 321
Lindy Effect, 225
Linear function, 424, 426, 429
List, John, 100
Little's Law, 168–169, 173, 189–191, 194, 201, 213, 224–225, 248, 382, 387, 389, 394, 398
London Taxi Drivers Association (LTDA), 80
long-term survivability, 35–36, 343
    Maturity Level 6 (built for survival), 89–90
low-maturity organizations, 37
    conformance to social norms and established tribal behaviors, 37
    culture, 55–70
    focus on employees, 55
    highly socially cohesive, 37
    inertia against change, 37
    lack of respect, 343
    low-maturity leaders, 308
    Maturity Level 0 (oblivious), 6–7, 56–57
    Maturity Level 1 (team-focused), 8–12
    Maturity Level 2 (customer-driven), 12–16

low-maturity organizations (*cont.*)
   nascent or emerging markets, 37
   stress, 367
LRM. *See* Last Responsible Moment
Lydon, John (Johnnie Rotten), 96

M

Maassen, Olav, 202
Magennis, Troy, xx, 389, 394
Major, John, 87
Make Policies Explicit practice, 100, 132
Making Democracy Work (Putnam), 94
Managed Evolution, 3, 112
Manage Flow
   aborted work, 143–144, 193–194, 239–240
   actively close upstream requests that meet discard criteria, 193
   aging work-in-progress (WIP), 182
   allocating capacity by class of service, 221–222
   allocating capacity by work type, 220–221
   analyzing and reporting on aborted work, 193–194
   analyzing and reporting on failure demand, 195
   appropriate use of forecasting, 224–225
   basic services definition, 178–179
   benefits from applying general practice, 175–176
   blockers, 68, 234–235, 278–279
   blocking issues, 181
   capture desired delivery date, 180–181
   categorizing tasks based on nature of work and urgency, importance, and impact, 177
   classes of booking in dynamic reservation system, 217–218
   classes of dependency management according to cost of delay, 211–216
   classes of service to affect selection, 194–195
   cumulative flow diagrams (CFDs), 188–189
   defects and other rework types, 181–182
   defer commitment (decide before last responsible moment), 185–187
   defining work types based on customer requests, 178
   delivery forecasts, 200–201
   dependencies, 24, 130, 196, 208–209, 236, 266–267, 435–446
   desired delivery date, 180–181, 185–186, 199, 211–219
   due date, 199
   dynamic reservation system, 213, 217–218
   explicit buffers, 207–208
   failure demand, 151, 195
   flow efficiency, 191–192, 205–207
   Flow Manager role, 182–183
   flow-related data, 180
   forecasting models for robustness, 222–224
   forecast using reference classes, Monte Carlo simulations and other models, 219–220
   general practice goal, 175
   gradually eliminating infinite buffers, 192–193
   hybrid fixed service teams together with flexible labor pool, 226–227
   knowledge discovery process, 183–185
   Little's Law, 189–191
   mapping upstream and downstream flow, 179–180
   Maturity Level 0 (oblivious), 177
   Maturity Level 2 (customer-driven), 178–183
   Maturity Level 3 (fit-for-purpose), 183–205
   Maturity Level 4 (risk-hedged), 205–226
   Maturity Level 5 (market leader), 226–227
   peer-to-peer and parent-child dependencies, 196
   Real Options Theory, 201–203
   reference class data set, 219
   refutable versus irrefutable demand, 209–210
   rudimentary flow efficiency, 191–192
   Service Delivery Manager (SDM) role, 203–204
   service level agreements (SLAs), 198
   service level expectations (SLEs), 147, 158, 199, 212–213
   Service Request Manager (SRM) role, 204–205
   service's fitness-for-purpose, 187
   specific practices summary, 176–177
   statistical methods for decision making, 225–226
   triage discipline, 195–196
   two-phase commit, 196–198
management
   leadership development, 365
   Marketing Strategy Review, 268–269
   Operations Review, 67, 79, 143–144, 151, 158, 173, 250, 262, 266, 316–317, 358, 362, 378
   Organizational Risk Review, 265–266
   Organizational Strategy Review, 269–270
   practices improving satisfaction, business reliance, and reinvention, 33
   Service Delivery Review, 67, 121, 144–145, 151, 173, 204, 250, 262, 264, 267, 316
   Service Request Review, 250, 262–264, 267
   Service Risk Review, 261, 263
   training, 365
managers
   customers trusting, 13
   Flow Manager, 16, 182–183, 204, 258, 356, 357, 360, 396,
   good understanding of workflow, 20
   heroic to expedite important customer requests, 13
   not trained in Kanban, 346–347
   Service Delivery Manager (SDM), 16, 20, 185, 203–204, 226–227, 267, 356–357
   Service Request Manager (SRM), 20, 185, 203–205, 263, 265, 267, 356, 357
   taking care of customers' needs, 63
Manchester United, 337
Mandela, Nelson, 85

marketing
    current markets, 268–269
    go-to-market strategies, 268–269
    key performance indicators (KPIs), 268–269
Marketing Strategy Review, 268–269
Market Leader (Maturity Level 5), 26–28, 84
markets, 30, 328
Maslow's Hierarchy of Needs, 105, 324
mathematical literacy, 352, 356
Matts, Chris, 202
Maturity Level 0 (Oblivious), 5–8
Maturity Level 1 (Team-Focused), 8–12
Maturity Level 2 (Customer-Driven), 12–16
Maturity Level 3 (Fit-for-Purpose), 17–20
Maturity Level 4 (Risk-Hedged), 22–26
Maturity Level 5 (Market Leader), 26–28
Maturity Level 6 (Built for Survival), 29–31
Mauvisoft Menta Triage DS, 412
Mauvius Group, 365–366
Mbeki, Thabo, 85
McKinsey, James, 303, 305
McLaren, Malcolm, 96, 97
McNabb, Stephen, 408
Mediocristan probability distribution function range, 225, 396, 400, 419–420
Mehta, Merwan, 104
metrics
    blocker-related, 233
    capability-related, 232–233
    defects, 233
    due-date performance, 233
    Fit-for-Purpose (F4P)-related metrics, 237–238
    fitness criteria, 18
    fitness-for-purpose, 246
    flow efficiency, 205–207
    flow-related, 232–233
    improvement driver metrics, 26
    Maturity Level 2 (customer-driven), 14
    Maturity Level 3 (fit-for-purpose), 19
    Maturity Level 4 (risk-hedged), 24
    quantitative analysis of, 22
    rework-type related, 233
    time stamps, 233
    understanding, 340
    vanity metrics, 237
    WIP aging-related, 233
Microsoft, 106–107, 337, 352
Microsoft Windows, 407
Microsoft XIT, 358
Mission Command, 75
    integration with Kanban, 379
mobile.de, 103
Moneyball moment, 337
Monte Carlo simulation, 201, 220, 223, 327, 397–398
muda (non-value adding activity or waste), 68, 164

mura (unevenness), 68, 164
muri (overburdening), 68, 164

N
Nabisco, 91, 93
narratives, 334
Nave, 347, 366
negative emotions, 336–337
negotiation skills, 352–353
non-instant availability resources, 208, 284–285
normative change, 295–296, 299, 316–317, 329
norms, 4

O
Oakland Athletics, 337
Obliquity (Kay), 88
Oblivious (Maturity Level 0), 5–8
observable results, 4
Operations Review, 67, 79, 143–144, 151, 158, 173, 250, 262, 266, 316–317, 358, 362, 378
    Maturity Level 4 (risk-hedged), 24
opportunities
    equality of, 84–86
    for improvement, 67
options, 141–143, 201–203
    Real Options Thinking, 201–203, 214, 443
Oracle, 352
organizational agility and adaptability, 34–36
Organizational Maturity, 111–112, 368
Organizational Risk Review, 265–266
    See also Service Risk Review
Organizational Strategy Review, 269–270
    See also Marketing Strategy Review
outcomes, 3, 111
    business fit-for-purpose, 4
    KMM Outcomes and Benefits, 449
    Managed Evolution, 3
    Maturity Level 0 (oblivious), 8
    Maturity Level 1 (team-focused), 10–12
    Maturity Level 2 (customer-driven), 16
    Maturity Level 3 (fit-for-purpose), 21
    Maturity Level 4 (risk-hedged), 24
    Maturity Level 5 (market leader), 28
    Maturity Level 6 (built for survival), 31
    observable results, 4
    practice and an outcome, 327–328
    what our business looks like, 4
overburdening
    relief from, xii, xiii, 6, 14, 33–34, 68, 74, 167, 371, 376
    steady arrival of work relieving, 68
    triage discipline, 195–196

P
parent-child dependencies, 145–146, 196
Pareto distribution, 225, 396
Pareto range of power-law functions, 400–401

patience when coping with crisis, 367
PCoDS. *See* Probable Cost of Delay in Starting
PDFs. *See* probability density functions; probability distribution functions
peer-to-peer dependencies, 145–146, 196
perfection
    Maturity Level 5 (market leader), 87
    relentless pursuit of, 27, 84
performance
    chance versus assignable cause for process variation, 280–283, 285–287
    kanban systems, 266–267
    work-in-progress (WIP), 14
personalization, 362
personal maturity, 6
personal reflection, 252
physical slot kanban board, 150–151
pigeonholing, 88
planning
    lack of, 356
    lead time, 387
Plato, 323–325
PMI. *See* Project Management Institute
policies
    agreement, 73
    basic, 125, 231–232
    class of service, 144–145
    consistent usage, 18
    discarding requests upstream policies, 238–239
    explicit, 100, 229–248
    initial, 122–123, 231
    managing aging WIP, 182, 183, 234
    managing blocking issues, 127–129, 181, 234–235, 274, 382
    managing defects and other rework types, 12, 182, 235
    per-person work-in-progress (WIP) limits, 123
    revising problematic, 274
    visualizing, 122–123, 125, 132, 140–141, 145–146, 150–152
    See also explicit policies
Porno (Welsh), 321
portfolio kanban boards, 16
positive emotions, 336–337
Posit Science, 319, 321, 430
PPPM. *See* Project, Program, and Portfolio Management
practices, 3, 4, 111, 451–456
    consolidation, 114
    Implement feedback loops, 249-270
    Improve collaboratively, evolve experimentally, 271-294
    Limit work in progress, 163-174
    Manage flow, 175-228

    Make policies explicit, 229-248
    Maturity Level 0 (oblivious), 6
    Maturity Level 1 (team-focused), 9–10
    Maturity Level 2 (customer-driven), 13–14
    Maturity Level 3 (fit-for-purpose), 19
    Maturity Level 4 (risk-hedged), 24
    Maturity Level 5 (market leader), 27
    Maturity Level 6 (built for survival), 30
    resistance to adoption, 326–328
    transition, 114
    visualize, 117–162
predictability, 99
probabilistic scheduling, 214
probability density functions (PDFs), 198, 383–384
probability distribution functions (PDFs), 225–226, 384–386
Probable Cost of Delay in Starting (PCoDS) functions, 425–430
processes
    bottlenecks, 283–284
    chance versus assignable cause for process performance variation, 280–283, 285–287
    consistency of, 12, 18, 22
    fit-for-purpose processes, 67
    improvement, 27
    insights and feedback about, 275–276
    leading versus lagging indicators, 286–287
    organization's context changed to fit, 303–304
    repeatable, 19
    turbulence, 285–287
    understanding of, 21, 118, 275
    understood, defined, and repeatable, 12–13
product development, 48
productivity, 26, 66, 163, 166, 211, 307, 392, 438
products
    effective delivery of, 263–264
    fit-for-purpose, 10, 18, 30, 72–77
    market-leading, 83
    risk, 265–266
professional services, 68
Project Management Institute (PMI), xvii, 308
project-management organization (PMO), 62
projects
    end-to-end workflow, 256
    managing larger and riskier, 20
pull
    pullable, 150
    pull criteria, 149–150, 244
    pull policies, 149
    pull signals, 147–148
punctuated equilibrium, 311–312
punctuation points, 313–315, 337
punk, 96
Putnam, Robert, 94

Q

qualitative
    Real Options Thinking, 201–203, 214, 443
    risk management, 352
    understanding of process performance, 280–283, 285–287
Quality Software Management (J. Weinberg), 59, 89
Quant, Mary, 96
quantitative
    analysis, 22, 27, 354, 223, 225, 287, 356, 377
    data, 23
    decision making, 23
    Maturity Level 5 (market leader), 27
    risk management, 355
    understanding of process performance, 280–283, 285–287
queues
    cumulative flow diagrams (CFDs), 188–189
queuing discipline, 34

R

Ramaphosa, Cyril, 86
Rangaswami, JP, 103–104
reactionary, 363
Ready to Commit status, 138–139
Real Options Thinking, 201–203, 214
Real World Risk Model integration with Kanban, 376–378
Reason, Age of, 323
recruitment, repeatable system for, 23
red squirrel, grey squirrel, 330–333
reference class data set, 219
reference classes, 220
reflection mechanisms, 315–317
refutable versus irrefutable demand, 219–210
refutable work, 209
regime change, 350
regulatory compliance
    Maturity Level 4 (risk-hedged), 81–82
reinvention, 35–36, 362
reliability, 362–363
repeatable processes, 19
replenishment
    commitment, 196, 242–244
    indicating need for, 148–149
    questions, 331
    signals, 148–149
Replenishment Meetings, 19, 132, 138–139, 143–144, 149, 170, 185, 196–197, 242, 244, 250, 260, 316, 329, 331
    reservation system board for each time period, 436
    triage, 404
The Republic (Plato), 323, 324
reputation, 99
request acceptance criteria, 139–140, 238
reservation systems
    classes of reservation, 436–438
    dynamic booking, 213, 217–218, 436
resilience, 362, 367
    anticipatory rather than merely reactionary, 363
    building, 361–368
    from bureaucracy to emergence, 361–362
    coping with crisis, 364–366
    efficiency to reliability, 362–363
    formalization to personalization, 362
    four principles of, 361
    house of, 368
    profit to meaning, 363
    social mobility, 87
resistance to change
    resistance to practice adoption, 326–328
    why people resist change, 323–327
    See also escalating motivation for change
resources, impact of shared, 284–285
respect, 64, 67, 69, 73, 74, 77, 78, 82, 106–107, 295, 297–298, 318, 324, 329, 339, 343, 358, 373, 378
    balance, 74, 78
    Maturity Level 2 (customer-driven), 69
responsibility, 362
    abdication of, 366
    accepting in crisis, 366
    explicitly defined boundaries, 100
return on investment (ROI), 331–332
rework, 13
    management policies, 235
    managing, 181–182
    visualizing, 128–129
risk-assessment framework, 24
Risk-Hedged (Maturity Level 4), 22–26, 77–82
Risk Reviews, 20–21, 67–68, 143–144, 151, 225, 250, 262, 267, 316, 362
    Organizational, 265–266
    Service, 263–264
risk(s)
    classes, different swim lanes for, 155–156
    cost of delay (COD), 154
    flow, 105
    insurance against unforeseen events, 23
    lack of understanding, 355
    literacy, 356
    management, 35, 73, 105, 112, 155–156, 176, 202–203, 225, 240, 247, 269–270, 272, 282–283, 363, 376–377, 384–385, 389–400, 412, 422
    poor asymmetrical, 350
    product lines, 265–266
    profile, 265–266
    qualitative management, 351–352
    service classes directly linked to, 22
    services, 265–266

risk(s) (*cont.*)
    ticket decorators to indicate, 154–155
    visualization, 154–155
    work classified by, 22
robustness, 362
    forecasting models for, 222–224
    organization, xii, 22, 23, 26, 29, 36, 77, 82, 95, 303, 344, 377
Rodgers, Everett, 404
ROI. *See* return on investment
Rudolph the Red-Nosed Reindeer, 312

S

Sandvik, 359
scheduling
    classes of service and, 351
    dynamic scheduling (or reservation system), 377
    lack of scheduling at scale, 356
    lead time to facilitate, 214
    Maturity Level 4 (risk-hedged), 22
    probabilistic scheduling, 212, 214, 440, 441, 442
    start of work, 436–438
    triage tables guidance, 418
Schmidt, Eric, 337
Schwaber, Ken, 304
Scientific Revolution, 323–324
Scrum, 304
    dramatic change, 304
    Planning Poker, 326
    social status, 330
SDM. *See* Service Delivery Manager
SDR. *See* Service Delivery Review
Service Delivery, 34–35, 346
    assessing against expectations, 30
    customer expectations, 18
    fit-for-purpose, 22, 34–35, 208, 363
    fitness-for-purpose, 245–246
    insights and feedback about, 275–276
    unfit-for-purpose, 33
Service Delivery Manager (SDM), 20, 185, 226–227, 267
    Delivery Planning Meeting, 261
    Organizational Risk Review, 265
    role, 16, 203–204, 356, 357
    Service Delivery Review (SDR), 67, 121, 144, 151, 173, 204, 250, 262, 264, 267, 316
    Service Risk Review, 261, 263
Service delivery principles, Kanban, 48, 49, 371–372
Service Delivery Review (SDR), 67, 121, 144, 151–152, 173, 204, 250, 262, 264, 267, 316
service level agreements (SLAs), 147, 198
    dependencies parking lot, 158
    dependent services, 248
    due date, 199
    trusted delivery, 212–213
    visualizing, 151–152

service level expectations (SLEs), 147, 158, 199, 212–213
    dependencies parking lot, 158
    due date, 199
    trusted delivery, 212–213
service orientation, 23, 43, 45–48, 51, 1254, 183, 273, 339, 349, 371
    agenda, 371
    lack of, 345–346
    product development, 48
Service Orientation agenda, 371
service oriented organizational (SOO) design, 26, 35, 114
service oriented organizations, 60, 346, 361–362, 368
service policies, 132
Service Request Manager (SRM), 20, 185, 203, 267
    Organizational Risk Review, 265
    role of, 204–205, 356, 357
    Service Risk Review, 263
Service Request Review, 250, 262–264, 267
Service Risk Review, 261, 263
services
    basic, 178–179
    capacity allocation by class of, 160–161
    classes of, 22, 24, 144–145
    customer-facing service, 345
    delivered service, 257–258
    effective delivery of, 263–264
    end-to-end workflow, 256
    examining and improving, 262
    fit-for-purpose, 10, 18, 30, 72–77
    interdependent network, 342
    managing and improving work process, 250
    metrics and indicators, 237
    performance of network of services, 250
    reservation system, 215
    risk, 265–266
    service level agreements (SLA) on dependent services, 248
    shared, 18
    as systems, 342
    viewing work as, 13
    visualizing and successfully managing, 24
    workflows, 13
shared resources, 284–285, 288–289
shared services
    delay, 284–285
    impact, 284–285
    smoothing flow, 208
shelf-life ratio, 408–409, 431–432
short-term results
skin in the game, 343
Skin in the Game (Taleb), 362, 376
SLAs. *See* service level agreements
SLEs. *See* service level expectations
social behavior, 299, 333

Index   475

social capital, 62, 94, 98–100
    developing, 57–58
    explicit decision frameworks, 100
    explicit policies, 100, 340
    explicit values, 99
    justice system, 100–101
    lack of, 340
    transparency, 98
    trust, 95, 101
    vulnerability, 98
social change, 296, 313
social cohesion, 94, 101–103, 335, 358–359
    lack of, 340
    narratives, 68
social engineers' role, 30
social groups, 94–95, 101–103
social innovation, 94
    conservatives, 95–97
    liberals, 95–97
social mobility, 87–88
social norms, 69
social status, 343–344
SOO. *See* Service-oriented Organizational Design
South Africa, 85–86
SPC. *See* statistical process control
split-and-merge workflows, 156–157
sports coaching model, 317
Spotify model, 304, 346
SRM. *See* Service Request Manager
stability, 296–297
Standard class of service, 206, 241, 411, 429
Standby class of reservations, 436–438
STATIK. *See* Systems Thinking Approach to Introducing Kanban
statistical methods for decision making, 225–226
statistical process control (SPC), 287
strategic concerns, 29
strategic direction, 355
strategic planning, 29
strategy
    comparing observed capability with, 30
    focus on purpose and identity, 30
    lack of alignment and congruence with, 355
Strategy Reviews, 27, 30, 250, 267, 316, 362, 377–378
stress, 315–317
    change, 326
    competition, 79
    low-maturity organizations, 367
    Maturity Level 3 (fit-for-purpose), 73
    Maturity Level 4 (risk-hedged), 22
    Maturity Level 5 (market leader), 27
Striking Thoughts (Lee), 329
structural change, 295–301
sub-exponential range of probability distribution functions, 225, 398–400

super-exponential range of probability distribution functions, 225, 393–396
Survivability agenda, 371
Sustainability agenda, 371
Swift Kanban, 366
Systems Thinking Approach to Introducing Kanban (STATIK), 213, 352, 373, 441

T
tail risk, 213
tail-risk mitigation class of dependency management, 214, 442–443
taking initiative, 61
Taleb, Nassim Nicholas, 225, 302, 362, 368, 376, 394, 419
Taoism, 329
tasks, categorizing, 177
team kanban board, 9, 13–14, 124–126
Team Kanban Meeting, 252–253
Team Replenishment Meeting, 254–255
Team Retrospective, 9, 254, 274, 276
teams, 9, 58, 340
    alignment among, 13
    collaboration, 10, 18–19, 34, 59–60, 72, 76, 340
    cooperation, 9, 13, 59, 63, 66, 76
    customer expectations, 66
    decision making, 10
    feel-good metrics, 9–10
    identity and markers, 59
    kanban boards, 9, 13–14
    managing dependencies between, 41
    overburdening, 34
    social groups, 57–58
    status and recognition, 58
    subordinating needs to greater good, 72
    Team Retrospectives, 9
    transparency, 61–63
    tribal behavior, 59
    trust, 9, 13, 63
    values and expected behaviors, 58
    vanity metrics, 9
    as victims, 37
    work-in-progress (WIP), 34, 166–167
Theory of Constraints, 27, 335
Thinking Fast and Slow (Kahneman), 323
three social dimensions of culture, 94–97
tickets
    blocker tickets, 128–129
    decorators, 154–155
    design, 122, 134, 445
Time-to-Market objective, 44
tolerance, 90–91
tolerance of failure, 100
Toyota, 27, 169
Toyota Kata, 27

Toyota Production System (TPS) integration with Kanban, 375–376
Toyota Way, 68
TPS. *See* Toyota Production System
Trainspotting (Welsh), 321
transaction costs, 276–277
transitions, 316–317
transparency, 23, 43
triage, 202, 209, 403–418
    deciding when to use, 403–404
    developing discipline, 195–196
    Improvement Suggestions Review, 187, 259
    policies, 172–173, 266
    options, 209, 351, 403–404
    Upstream Kanban, 404
Triage Tables, 195, 385
    classes of service related to cost of delay, 409–411
    configuration, 432
    cost of delay, 431–432
    default class of service, 409
    determining modifier, 313–414
    Fixed Date zone, 432
    four dimensions of priority, 417
    Intangible cost of delay zone, 432
    modified class of service, 414
    modifiers for fat-tailed lead time, 416
    modifiers for thin-tailed lead time, 415
    Replenishment Meeting, 404
    shelf-life ratio, 408–409
    Standard class of service zone, 432
    start date range, 409–410
    value-acquisition lifecycle (VAL), 404–408
tribal culture, 105–107
trust, 23, 60, 343–344
    acts of, 101
    balance, 78
    culture, 95
    customers, 11, 23, 73
    explicit policies, 340
    extensive, 19
    flow, 105
    low, 350
    Maturity Level 1 (team-focused), 9, 57–58
    Maturity Level 4 (risk-hedged), 77
    more frequent is more trustworthy, 99
    narratives, 68
    short-term results, 75–76
    social group, 95
    society, 95
    teams, 9, 63
    transparency, 340
    visualization, 340
    work is done consistently, 18
Trusted Availability class of dependency management, 212–212, 438, 441–442
turbulence, 285–287
two-phase commit, 196–197

U

ultra-short shelf-life ratio (SLR), 408
unbounded queues. *See* infinite buffers
unexpected events
    developing robustness against, 22
    learning from, 23
    recovering from, 4
unordered activities, 134–136
Upheaval (Diamond), 364
upstream
    (discovery) kanban board, 141–143
    flow, 207–208
    maximum (max) limit, 170
    minimum (min) limit, 169–170
    requests, discarding, 193
    Service Request Manager, 20, 185, 203, 267
    Service Request Review, 250, 262–264, 267

V

value acquisition lifecycle (VAL), 404–408, 420, 424, 429
    functions, 422–423, 426, 432
value demand versus failure demand, 151
values
    explicit, 99
    lack of alignment and congruence with, 355
    as mitigation to inertia, 342–343
value stream, 305–306
vanity metrics, 237, 321
Very Front-loaded delivery delay cost function, 429
Very Late Decay delivery delay cost function, 423
Virgin Group, 56, 103
visualize
    aborted work, 143–144
    applying practice benefits, 118
    available capacity, 150–151
    avatars for individual's workload, 123–124
    basic policies, 125, 132
    blocked work items, defects, and rework, 128–129
    capacity allocation by class of service, 160–161
    capacity allocation by work type, 159–160
    class of service, 144–145
    concurrent or unordered activities, 134–135
    constant WIP (CONWIP), 133
    defined workflow, 136–137
    dependencies on shared services using avatars, 131–132
    dependencies on shared services using column with WIP limit, 131–132
    discarded options, 143
    failure demand versus value demand, 151
    fixed teams and floating workers (shared resources) across aggregated services, 161–162
    general practice goals, 117–118

ideas development, 142–143
individual's work, 120–121
initial policies, 122–123
local cycle time, 153–154
Maturity Level 0 (oblivious), 120–121
Maturity Level 1 (team-focused), 122–125
Maturity Level 2 (customer-driven), 125–138
Maturity Level 3 (fit-for-purpose), 138–153
Maturity Level 4 (risk-hedged), 153–161
Maturity Level 5 (market leader), 161–162
multiple services, 137
optional, unordered concurrent activities, 134–135
optional multiple unordered, nonconcurrent activities performed by specialists, 135–136
parent-child and peer-to-peer dependencies, 145–146
practices summary, 118–120
progress, 125–126
pullable, 149–150
pull criteria, 149–150
pull signals, 147–148
Ready to Commit status, 138–139
replenishment signals, 148–149
request acceptance criteria, 139–140
risk classes, 156–157
service level agreements (SLAs), 151–152, 158
service level expectations (SLEs), 158
specific practice descriptions, 120–161
split-and-merge workflows, 156–157
target date, 151–152
ticket decorators to indicate risk, 154–155
waiting or blocked work requests dependent on another service or system, 146–147
waiting time, 157–158
work carried out by team, 124
workflow and teams' work, 141–142
work for several individuals, 122
work-in-progress (WIP), 163–174
work-in-progress (WIP) limits, 124, 158
work item, 121
work item aging, 129–130
volatility regimes, 285
von Moltke, Helmut, 379
vulnerability and social capital, 98

W

wait state, 205
waste elimination, 105
Watson AI technology, 31
Watson family, 31, 91
Weibull, Waloddi, 390
Weibull function, 224–225, 386, 389–391, 396, 398
Weinberg, Jerry, xv, 59, 89
Welsh, Irvine, 321
Westwood, Vivienne, 96–97

What Is This Thing Called Theory of Constraints and How Should It Be Implemented? (Goldratt), 335–336
Who Says Elephants Can't Dance (Gerstner), 93
The Why Axis (Gneezy and List), 100
why people resist change
　escalating motivation for change, 328–337
　human condition, 323–326
　resistance to practice adoption, 326–328
why pursue evolutionary change, 295–309
WIP. *See* work-in-progress
Womack, Jim, 104
work
　aborted work, 143–144, 193–194
　capacity limitations, 22
　consistency, 13, 23
　cost of delay, 331–332
　criteria for aborted, 239–240
　customer requests, 178
　customer risks, 22
　demand shaping, 22
　discarded, 143–144, 193–194, 238–239
　discretionary, 209
　flow, 67–68
　irrefutable, 209–210
　managing, 10, 250
　parent-child dependencies, 145–146
　peer-to-peer dependencies, 145–146
　predictability, 35, 257–258
　prioritizing, 14, 331
　refutable, 209
　risks associated with, 13
　scheduling, 436–438
　smooth, steady arrival of, 68
　types, 126–127
　viewing as service, 13
　work-in-progress (WIP) limits, 174
workers
　autonomy, 26
　customer expectations, 66
　individual tasks, 6
　job satisfaction, 26–27
　ownership over processes, 26
　personal maturity, 6
　position of power, 6
　pride in capabilities and outcomes, 26
　process, roles, and responsibilities, 18
　resisting change, 298–299
　selfishness, 37
　self-management, 6
　team-focused, 8–12
Workflow Kanban Meeting, 256
Workflow Replenishment Meeting, 255–256
workflow, 63
　analyzing design or implementation of, 282

workflow (*cont.*)
    charts, 20–21
    defined, 18, 136–137
    downstream, 20, 126, 137, 141–142, 157–158, 170, 179, 185, 193, 203–205, 239, 262, 283–285, 288, 384
    effective management of, 347
    end-to-end, 256
    smoothing, 14, 207–208
    split-and-merge workflows, 156–157
    stabilizing, 19
    uneven, 14
    upstream, 141–142
    visualizing, 19, 140–141
    See also Manage Flow
workforce
    drive out fear, 107
    ready to embrace change, 106
    suggesting and implementing change, 26
work-in-progress (WIP), 6, 60
    aging, 68, 182, 233–234
    bracket, 170–172, 192
    CONWIP, 133, 167–168
    dependencies parking lot, 158–159
    Gaussian distribution, 174
    individual limits, 165–166
    limiting, 19, 42, 68, 163–174
    performance depending on, 14
    per-person limits, 14, 166
    team limits, 166–167
    visualizing blockers, 68
    visualizing limits, 124
work items
    aborted, 239–240
    blocked, 146–147, 234–235
    customer expectations for, 245–246
    dependencies, 130, 145–146
    desired delivery date (DDD), 411–412
    input buffer, 148–149
    last responsible moment (LRM), 412
    local cycle time, 153–154
    pullable, 149–150
    Reserved class of booking, 215
    reviewing, 148–149
    service delivery, 245–246
    start date range, 411–412
    tickets, 121, 126–130, 133–137
    visualizing aging, 129–130
work types
    allocating capacity by, 159–160, 220–221

X–Z

XP. *See* Extreme Programming
Zheglov, Alexei, xx, 28, 79–80, 106, 394, 396, 398, 399
Zuma, Jacob, 85

About the Authors

David J Anderson is an innovator in management thinking for 21st Century professional services businesses. He is the CEO of Mauvius Group Inc., a group of companies that offers management training, events, publications, and decision support software tools with offices in Seattle, USA, and Bilbao, Spain. During a long career in the technology industry, he has worked with IBM, Sprint, Motorola, and Microsoft before founding his own firm in 2008. He is the pioneer of the Kanban Method, the Fit-for-Purpose Framework, and Enterprise Services Planning.

Teodora Bozheva is a management consultant dedicated to improving the performance and business outcomes of organizations from small to large ones. She uses her extensive experience in software engineering, project management, Kanban, Lean Six Sigma and CMMI to create appropriate, effective solutions for companies in different sectors: banking, insurance, industry, IT. She is a lecturer in various Spanish universities. She is the CEO of Berriprocess Agility, a company located in Bilbao, Spain, which offers training, coaching, and management tools integration services to companies seeking greater business agility.

Made in the USA
Middletown, DE
04 November 2020